Library of
Davidson College

THE MIDDLE LENGTH SAYINGS
MAJJHIMA-NIKĀYA
VOLUME III

Pali Text Society

TRANSLATION SERIES, NO. 31

THE COLLECTION OF
THE MIDDLE LENGTH SAYINGS
(MAJJHIMA-NIKĀYA)

VOL. III
THE FINAL FIFTY DISCOURSES
(UPARIPAṆṆĀSA)

TRANSLATED FROM THE PALI BY
I. B. HORNER, M.A.
Associate of Newnham College, Cambridge
Translator of "The Book of the Discipline," volumes I-V

Published by
THE PALI TEXT SOCIETY, LONDON

Distributed by
ROUTLEDGE & KEGAN PAUL LTD.
LONDON, HENLEY AND BOSTON
1977

First published 1959
Reprinted 1977

ISBN 0 7100 8748 9

© PALI TEXT SOCIETY

PRINTED IN GREAT BRITAIN BY
UNWIN BROTHERS LIMITED
THE GRESHAM PRESS, OLD WOKING, SURREY, ENGLAND
A MEMBER OF THE STAPLES PRINTING GROUP

CONTENTS

	PAGE
Translator's Introduction	ix
Abbreviations	xxxiii

THE FINAL FIFTY DISCOURSES (UPARIPAṆṆĀSA)

I. THE DEVADAHA DIVISION (DEVADAHAVAGGA)

101.	Discourse at Devadaha (Devadahasutta)	3
102.	Discourse on the Threefold Five (Pañcattayasutta)	15
103.	Discourse on "What then?" (Kintisutta)	24
104.	Discourse at Sāmagāma (Sāmagāmasutta)	29
105.	Discourse to Sunakkhatta (Sunakkhattasutta)	37
106.	Discourse on Beneficial Imperturbability (Āṇañjasappāyasutta)	46
107.	Discourse to Gaṇaka-Moggallāna (Gaṇakamoggallānasutta)	52
108.	Discourse to Gopaka-Moggallāna (Gopakamoggallānasutta)	58
109.	Greater Discourse (at the time) of a Full Moon (Mahāpuṇṇamasutta)	65
110.	Lesser Discourse (at the time) of a Full Moon (Cūḷapuṇṇamasutta)	70

II. THE DIVISION OF THE UNINTERRUPTED (ANUPADAVAGGA)

111.	Discourse on the Uninterrupted (Anupadasutta)	77

		PAGE
112.	Discourse on the Sixfold Cleansing (Chabbisodhanasutta)	81
113.	Discourse on the Good Man (Sappurisasutta)	89
114.	Discourse on what is to be Followed and what is not to be Followed (Sevitabba-asevitabbasutta)	94
115.	Discourse on the Manifold Elements (Bahudhātukasutta)	104
116.	Discourse at Isigili (Isigilisutta)	110
117.	Discourse pertaining to the Great Forty (Mahācattārīsakasutta)	113
118.	Discourse on Mindfulness when Breathing In and Out (Ānāpānasatisutta)	121
119.	Discourse on Mindfulness of Body (Kāyagatāsatisutta)	129
120.	Discourse on Uprising by means of Aspiration (Saṁkhāruppattisutta)	139

III. THE DIVISION ON EMPTINESS
(SUÑÑATAVAGGA)

121.	Lesser Discourse on Emptiness (Cūḷasuññatasutta)	147
122.	Greater Discourse on Emptiness (Mahāsuññatasutta)	152
123.	Discourse on Wonderful and Marvellous Qualities (Acchariyabbhutadhammasutta)	163
124.	Discourse by Bakkula (Bakkulasutta)	170
125.	Discourse on the "Tamed Stage" (Dantabhūmisutta)	175
126.	Discourse to Bhūmija (Bhūmijasutta)	183

Contents

		PAGE
127.	Discourse with Anuruddha (Anuruddhasutta)	190
128.	Discourse on Defilements (Upakkilesasutta)	197
129.	Discourse on Fools and the Wise (Bālapaṇḍitasutta)	209
130.	Discourse on the Deva-Messengers (Devadūtasutta)	223

IV. THE DIVISION ON ANALYSIS (VIBHAṄGAVAGGA)

131.	Discourse on the Auspicious (Bhaddekarattasutta)	233
132.	Ānanda's Discourse on the Auspicious (Ānandabhaddekarattasutta)	235
133.	Mahākaccāna's Discourse on the Auspicious (Mahākaccānabhaddekarattasutta)	237
134.	Lomasakaṅgiya's Discourse on the Auspicious (Lomasakaṅgiyabhaddekarattasutta)	245
135.	Discourse on the Lesser Analysis of Deeds (Cūḷakammavibhaṅgasutta)	248
136.	Discourse on the Greater Analysis of Deeds (Mahākammavibhaṅgasutta)	254
137.	Discourse on the Analysis of the Sixfold (Sense-)Field (Saḷāyatanavibhaṅgasutta)	263
138.	Discourse on an Exposition and Analysis (Uddesavibhaṅgasutta)	271
139.	Discourse on the Analysis of the Undefiled (Araṇavibhaṅgasutta)	277
140.	Discourse on the Analysis of the Elements (Dhātuvibhaṅgasutta)	285
141.	Discourse on the Analysis of the Truths (Saccavibhaṅgasutta)	295
142.	Discourse on the Analysis of Offerings (Dakkhiṇavibhaṅgasutta)	300

V. THE DIVISION OF THE SIXFOLD SENSE(-FIELD) (SALĀYATANAVAGGA)

PAGE

143. Discourse on an Exhortation to Anāthapiṇḍika - - 309
(Anāthapiṇḍikovādasutta)
144. Discourse on an Exhortation to Channa - - - 315
(Channovādasutta)
145. Discourse on an Exhortation to Puṇṇa - - - - 319
(Puṇṇovādasutta)
146. Discourse on an Exhortation from Nandaka - - - 322
(Nandakovādasutta)
147. Lesser Discourse on an Exhortation to Rāhula - - 328
(Cūḷarāhulovādasutta)
148. Discourse on the Six Sixes - - - - - - 331
(Chachakkasutta)
149. Discourse pertaining to the Great Sixfold (Sense-)Field - 336
(Mahāsaḷāyatanikasutta)
150. Discourse to the People of Nagaravinda - - - 339
(Nagaravindeyyasutta)
151. Discourse on Complete Purity for Alms-Gathering - 342
(Piṇḍapātapārisuddhisutta)
152. Discourse on the Development of the Sense-Organs - 346
(Indriyabhāvanasutta)

INDEXES

I. Topics - - - - - - - - - - 351
II. Similes - - - - - - - - - - 360
III. Names - - - - - - - - - - 360
IV. Some Pali Words in the Notes - - - - - 363

TRANSLATOR'S INTRODUCTION

The Final Fifty-two Discourses of the *Majjhima* occupy this volume and with them the translation is completed. As the First Fifty and the Middle Fifty Discourses are each arranged in five Divisions of ten Discourses each, so are the Final Fifty-two, the only difference being that there are here these two extra Discourses.

The " rich variety " of the *M.* is still so conspicuous in this third volume that it is impossible in the space of a merely general Introduction to do it even a fragment of the justice it deserves; but I can give some indications perhaps of the variety by taking the work more or less Sutta by Sutta and mentioning various points that seem of outstanding interest to me, although I am aware that this probably means omitting others the interest of which is equally outstanding. Each *Majjhima* Sutta merits long and intensive study not only for itself but for the relation it may bear to others. There are, besides, several passages in this volume of great difficulty for a translator. Some are discussed in the notes and a few are discussed in this Introduction.

Internal evidence found in the *Mahācattārīsaka* (No. 117), the *Mahākammavibhaṅga* (No. 136) and the *Mahāsaḷāyatanika* (No. 149) suggests that in none of these Discourses does the prefix *Mahā-* refer to the Discourse as such but rather to the nature of its subject-matter: the Great Forty, the Great Analysis of Deeds, the Great Sixfold Sense-field. It would therefore follow that the title of Sta. 135, the *Cūḷakammavibhaṅga*, should be translated as the Discourse on the Lesser Analysis of Deeds (and not the Lesser Discourse on the Analysis of Deeds) and that this Discourse and the *Mahā-kammavibhaṅga* do not form a pair in the sense indicated in the Introduction to *M.L.S.* vol. i. It would also follow that since the prefix *Mahā-* of the *Mahācattārīsaka* and the *Mahāsaḷāyatanika Suttas* refers to the contents of the Discourses, it would be vain to search the Pali Canon for *Cūḷa-* Discourses bearing these titles. For there is no lesser " forty," and nothing less, equally nothing more than the " six fields of sense," therefore Discourses dealing with such matters could not exist. The " forty " are great because they are associated with the Way; the six fields of sense are great because the practice of Buddhism is, broadly speaking, for the man who has all his six senses intact. And this is where the main emphasis lies in these Final Fifty-two Suttas. They have none of the talk on asceticism found among the First Fifty, or of the threefold knowledge which is so recurrent a theme among the Second Fifty; the senses, their control and the right attitude towards them, are here the chief thing.

The name of the first of these five Divisions is that of a place, Devadaha, where the Discourse placed first in it is recorded to have been given. The second Division likewise takes its name from that of the Discourse placed first in it, the *Anupadasutta*. The third Division is again named after the first, or the first and second Discourses it contains. These form a pair of *Cūḷa-* and *Mahā-*Suttas, and are disquisitions on the concept of emptiness, *suññatā*. The fourth Division is the one with twelve Discourses. Each contains a detailed analysis, *vibhaṅga*, of various matters briefly stated in it. Though the word *vibhaṅga* occurs only in the titles of the last eight Discourses in this Division and not in the first four, these four all the same follow the scheme of analysing in some detail concisely made statements. One cannot say that this scheme is peculiar to this Division or even to the *M.*; only that this fourth Division contains nothing but such analyses and that the word *vibhaṅga* is not part of the title of any other *M.* Discourse. A neat classification of material has been made here and the Division is well named the *Vibhaṅgavagga*, the Division of Analysis. Every Discourse in the fifth Division is concerned with the six fields of sense-experience. Exhortations, *ovāda*, on this subject were given on five separate occasions (Stas. 143-147), and sense-experience also forms the main topic of Discourse 148, addressed to monks, and of Nos. 150, 151 and 152. Moreover, Sta. 149, the *Mahāsaḷāyatanika-sutta*, is devoted to the same theme. This Division is therefore suitably named the *Saḷāyatana*, that on the Sixfold Sense-field. Yet the question arises of why the *Saḷāyatanavibhaṅga-sutta* (No. 137, in the preceding Division) was not included in a Division that deals so consistently with sense-data and sense-awareness (*cf. Saḷāya-tanasaṁyutta, S.* iv. 1-204) as does the *Saḷāyatanavagga*. One might reply, in answer to this question, that so great is the number of Discourses treating of the sense-fields, not only in *M.* but in many parts of the Pali Canon besides, that one having the word *vibhaṅga* in its title would fall more naturally into place and be more easily found in the Division on Analysis than anywhere else. On the other hand, there appears to be some confusion over the name of Sta. 149, for though it is here called the *Mahāsaḷāyatanika*, some MSS. call it the *Saḷāyatanavibhaṅga* which, however, seems to be the usual title of Sta. 137.

In the First Division, the *Devadahavagga* (Sta. 101-110), there is still pre-occupation with the Jains (Stas. 101, 104) and with the speculative views of members of other sects (*e.g.* Sta. 102),[1] such as are also to be found set forth, either in groups or severally, in other parts of the *M*. After this there is little or no further reference to them. The *Pañcattayasutta* (No. 102) is the only *M*. Discourse to present the whole corpus of tenets of the 62 heretical sects. In this it resembles the *Brahmajāla* of the *D*. but is not identical with it. For, to take one example of the differences between the two, in addition to the difference in arrangement the *Pañcattaya*, as is noticed at *MA*. iv. 25, speaks of "own body," *sakkāya*, but the *Brahmajāla* does not. Why is this? *MA*. replies that it is because when the *Brahmajāla* was first spoken the *Pañcattaya* had not yet been spoken. If this statement can be trusted it provides a valuable clue to the relative age of the two Discourses.

Sta. 101 contains two passages noteworthy for their combination of singularly difficult terms and grammar. At *M*. ii. 223 there is the sudden introduction of the word *attā*, around which controversy has grown with the centuries. Here it appears to be used in no more than the ordinary way in which we all speak of "self." It is unmastered, *an-addha-bhūta*, which suggests that the monk still has to make an effort and strive so as to prevent this self from being mastered by anguish, *dukkha*. And there is too that term of many meanings, *saṁkhāra*,[2] here in the singular. The monk then is said to comprehend: *imassa kho me dukkhanidānassa saṁkhāraṁ padahato saṁkhārappadhānā virāgo hoti*. I could have translated this as: "while I am exerting (*me padahato*) activity (*saṁkhāraṁ*) against this source of anguish, from the exertion of activity there is detachment (for me)," that is, according to *MA*. iv. 11, if he has really attained arahantship, with the implication that he is not merely pretending to have done so. That *padahati* takes the accusative is of course normal (*cf. padhānaṁ padahitvāna, Budv*. IV. 13 *et seq*.); but *nidānassa* would have to be taken not as a genitive but as a dative

---

[1] See *M.L.S*. ii. Intr., p. xii, xiv *ff*., xxi *f*.
[2] See *M.L.S*. i. Intr., p. xxiv.

of purpose: with the purpose of mastering this source of *dukkha*, his foe, hence he exerts activity *against* it.

We then come, in the same Sta., to the equally difficult passage (*M*. ii. 225) when the monk says of himself *dukkhāya pana me attānaṁ padahato*. This seems to mean " while exerting my self (*me attānaṁ*) against anguish." Here *dukkhāya* is the regular neuter dative, as it is also in the two following expressions: *so dukkhāya attānaṁ padahati* . . . ; *bhikkhu dukkhāya attānaṁ padaheyya* (*M*. ii. 225). The Comy. fails to explain why the forceful word *attā* figures in these passages. From another angle its appearance must give those who like to say that the Buddha "denied" *attā* pause to think. *Attā* is not denied here, or anywhere else in the Pali Canon; it is accepted.

Suttas 103 and 104 both have in mind dispute and contention, not over " mere trifles," but over things that matter: the Way and the Course. There might be argument about these, stirred up by monks of unamiable character, especially after the Lord's *parinibbāna*. Recourse to the *Vinaya* is then necessary, and Sutta 104, in recapitulating the four legal questions, *adhikaraṇa*, under which such disputes should be classified and the seven ways of settling them, is consequently characterised by strong *Vinaya* features.

Again, Suttas 103 and 104 both speak of the Lord teaching from his super-knowledge the 37 things belonging to enlightenment, *bodhipakkhiyadhammā*, though this compendious word is not itself used. In Sta. 104 the seven groups of things that together constitute the 37 *bodhipakkhiyadhammā* are enumerated instead; and in Sta. 103 there appears to be a reference to them in the word *abhidhamma* (*M*. ii. 239), for this is the meaning *MA*. iv. 29 ascribes to the *abhidhamma* about which two monks might speak differently. This Sta. speaks of nibbāna as an aim, though not one to be realised so long as monk quarrelled with monk, for contention would preclude the winning of imperturbability (*āṇañja* according to *M*. spelling), a topic and an ideal with which Stas. 105 and 106 are largely concerned.

These two Suttas and No. 107 all take up, as does No. 103, the subject of nibbāna. Sta. 105 has the unusual expression *sammānibbāna*, right or perfect nibbāna, presumably to distinguish the nibbāna of the followers of the Buddha's *sāsana* from that of those who were " outside " this.[1] *Sammānibbāna*, a goal not to be won by those who had become proud and puffed up as a result of their

---

[1] *Cf. M*. i. 4 (*M.L.S*. i. 5 and *n*. 11) and Māgandiya's statement at *M*. i. 509 that health is nibbāna and body is nibbāna (*M.L.S*. ii. 188).

being intent on it, was accessible solely to those who refused to indulge in wrong enjoyment of the senses, recognising that herein lay a deterrent to their achievement of the goal.

Sta. 106 asks why some monk may attain final or complete nibbāna, *parinibbāyeyya*, but another fail to do so. The attainment or the failure depends on whether there is grasping or whether there is not, even grasping after equanimity, *upekhā*; for deathlessness or the undying, *amata*, is deliverance of thought without grasping, *anupādā cittassa vimokho* (*M*. ii. 265).

In Sta. 107 nibbāna is spoken of as the unchanging goal, *niṭṭhā*, to be won, if won at all, by a gradual training (*cf. Sekhasutta*). It is again driven home that it all depends on the person himself whether he attains it or not, for the Teaching is the same for all,[1] and to all who want to listen the Way is pointed out by the Tathāgata, the Shower of the Way (*M*. iii. 6).

This aspect of the Tathāgata as Way-Shower[2] recurs in Sta. 108, a Discourse recording a conversation said to have been held between Ānanda and the brahman Gopaka-Moggallāna after the Lord's *parinibbāna*.[3] Here the Lord is spoken of not only as one who showed a Way not shown before, but also as a Knower and Understander of the Way.[4] In these respects not a single monk resembles him; his disciples are not Way-showers but Way-followers, not one of whom was designated either by the Lord or by the Order to be the mainstay, arbiter or support, *paṭisaraṇa*, for the others after his passing. The place of a human successor was taken by Dhamma, the cause of unity, the reason for it, *hetu sāmaggiyā*. So, instead of any one monk, instead of any one disciple, "Dhamma is our support" (*M*. iii. 9), that is after the Lord's *parinibbāna*, a statement fully according with the injunction: "The Dhamma I have taught and the Vinaya I have laid down—*that*[5] after my passing is (to be) your Teacher" (*D*. ii. 154). The Lord and his Dhamma are one: "Who sees Dhamma sees me" (*S*. iii. 120, *Iti*. p. 91, etc.). And the epithet *dhammakāya* (D. iii. 84), applicable only to the Lord, and not to arahants, points in this same direction. So *Miln*. can say (p. 75) *dhammakāyena . . . sakkā Bhagavā nidassetuṁ*, "The Lord is able to point out by means of the Dhamma-body" even

---

[1] *Cf. S*. iv. 315-316.
[2] *Cf. Dhp*. 276, *akkhātāro tathāgatā*, Tathāgatas are showers (*i.e.* of the Way).
[3] See *M.L.S*. ii. Intr., p. xxii.   [4] As at *S*. i. 191.
[5] "That," *so*, meaning I think *satthusāsana*, the Teacher's instruction, of which Dhamma and Vinaya are the two component parts.

though he himself has " set " like the sun, has " gone home," and cannot be said to be either here or there. In this sense the Lord exists while Dhamma exists and cannot be called extinct—a tenet developed and made much of in some Mahāyāna Buddhist Sūtras.

Stas. 109 and 110 form a pair of *Mahā* and *Cūḷa-* Discourses as far as their titles are concerned, for both (as also Sta. 118) were given at the time[1] of a full moon and hence are called the *Mahāpuṇṇamā* and *Cūḷapuṇṇamā* Suttas respectively. But this is all they have in common. The *Mahāpuṇṇamā* is occupied with the five groups of grasping, with what is a wrong view and what a right view of these groups, with the satisfaction and peril they contain, and with the escape from them. On the other hand the *Cūḷapuṇṇamā* has nothing to say about grasping. It concentrates on various outstanding characteristics of a good man and a bad man, *sappurisa* and *asappurisa*. Its affinities are therefore more with Sta. 113, the title of which is *Sappurisasutta*. But though Stas. 110 and 113 have not a single passage in common, yet since the main topic of both is the good man, *sappurisa*, their material is in consequence more cognate than is that of Stas. 109 and 110.

The first Discourse in the Second Division, the *Anupadavagga* (Stas. 111-120), is marked by an inspiring eulogy of Sāriputta who symbolises the perfect disciple, and to this is added his unique capacity for rolling on the Wheel of Dhamma set rolling by the Tathāgata. This Discourse contains a number of psychological terms that are more fully expounded in the *Dhs.*; and for others reference may be made to the *Pṭs.* Since " Sāriputta's special proficiency was in Abhidhamma,"[2] what could be more apt than to eulogise him in words of a markedly Abhidhamma stamp ?

Sta. 112 sets forth six ways in which a monk's claim to be an arahant can be scrutinised by other monks: they may ask him about things he has seen, heard, sensed or cognised; about the five groups of grasping; about the six elements; about the six sense-fields; and about this consciousness-informed body and the phenomena external to it. In answer to each group of questions the monk who claims arahantship for himself relates the process by which he reached this height. It is of course the usual process, found for example in the *Cūḷahatthapadopamasutta*, the *Kandarakasutta* and elsewhere,[3] and

---

[1] *M.L.S.* i. Intr., p. xii.
[2] *D.P.P.N.*, p. 1116, which gives a short account of how this came about.
[3] See *M.L.S.* i. 224, *n.* 3, for some further references.

could hardly be otherwise for the fruits of the Way are only for the man or woman who closely follows the Way, " the one sole Way for the purification of beings " (*M*. i. 55), and there is very little latitude.

Sta. 113, as it has been already remarked, should be studied in conjunction with Sta. 110. Both deal with the good man who, in effect, is the man-of-naught, *na kiñci na kuhiñci na kenaci*, " he is not aught or anywhere or in anything " (*M*. iii. 45). Even if he lack this or that possession, quality or habit he realises all the same that it is not those possessions, qualities or habits that turn a man into a good man; and so he makes the Course itself the main thing, *so paṭipadaṁ yeva antaraṁ karitvā*, an expression the latter part of which also occurs at *M*. iii. 14 in Sta. 108. And if he have not the desire for the meditative planes he may comfort himself by thinking: " Lack of desire, *atammayatā*, (for any of these planes) has been spoken of by the Lord, for whatever people imagine them to be they are otherwise." So he makes lack of desire itself the main thing, and he is then able to attain one meditative plane after another until he enters on and abides in the stopping of perceiving and feeling, the highest and culminating stage in meditation.

In Sta. 114 a brief utterance attributed to the Lord[1] is expounded at great length by Sāriputta in his presence. There then follow two other sets of brief statements which, though to some extent expanded by Sāriputta, yet lack the detail he lavished on his exposition of the first statement. The Lord, however, corroborates them all, and we may therefore conclude that they become *Buddhavacana*, the authentic Teaching of the Dhamma as taught by the Buddha. That a disciple should teach this too merely shows that he has well remembered, well understood and well pondered in his mind what he has heard.

Sta. 115 contains six different lists of the elements, *dhātu*: eighteen, six, another six, a third six, three, and then two; an enumeration of the six sense-fields; a statement of conditioned genesis or dependent origination, *paṭiccasamuppāda*, prefaced by " If this is, that comes to be " etc.; and then there follows a long list of situations the occurrence of which is either possible or impossible according to (karmic) circumstances (*cf. A*. i. 26 *ff.*). At the end Ānanda was given five titles, as he was at the end of the *Brahmajāla-suttanta*, by which he might remember this disquisition on Dhamma. The

---

[1] See below, p. 94.

Discourse is more generally known under the first of these alternative titles, as is the *Brahmajāla*.

Sta. 116 is curiously unlike any other *M.* Discourse. After telling how the mountain Isigili came to be so called (and, as is said, it has always had this name though the names of other mountains round Rājagaha have changed with the passage of time), this Discourse proceeds to give, partly in prose and partly in verse, the names of many paccekabuddhas, in several cases adding some outstanding attribute. Although short, the Discourse does justice to the names of these Buddhas who have won enlightenment for themselves but are unable to teach Dhamma to others. From its very nature this Discourse, little more than a catalogue, is neither homiletic nor hortative.

Sta. 117 has the character of an expanded analysis of the short statement: " I will teach you the ariyan right concentration with the causal associations and the accompaniments." As on other occasions also, both the statement and its analysis are attributed to the Bhagavan. But nowhere in this Sutta does he say he will give an analysis nor is he asked to do so; he simply explains this " heading " in greater amplitude. If it be held that Buddhas teach Dhamma in brief and not in full (*MA.* v. 60), then the whole of this Discourse must be regarded as one among the many expansions of the eightfold Way and its components. This Way was the chief substance of the first Discourse which the Lord delivered, the *Dhammacakkappavattanasutta* (*Vin.* i. 10). This covers so much of the Teaching, stated in brief, that many passages in the Nikāyas have the appearance, not of breaking new ground but of extracting every shade of meaning the *Dhammacakkappavattana's* short statements may hold, and of elaborating every aspect of them and every circumstance in which they may bear on a monk's life, thought and behaviour. All through Sta. 117 it is insisted that right view comes first, or is the forerunner: *sammādiṭṭhi pubbaṅgamā hoti*. Because right view is of the mind and mental in character, this statement is no contradiction of the opening words of the *Dhp.*: " mental states have mind as forerunner," *manopubbaṅgamā dhammā*, or of the passage at *A.* i. 11 which reads *ye keci dhammā kusalā . . . sabbe te manopubbaṅgamā*, " all those mental states that are skilled have mind as forerunner." *Pubbaṅgama* therefore appears to refer to something without which another thing could not be. So, unless there is right view, there cannot be right concentration; without mind or thought, *manas*, there can be no mental states, *dhammā*. Other difficult words in this Discourse are *upanisa* (*sa-upanisa*), a word the history of which "has yet to be written" (*PED.*), and *sa-parikkhāra*. The Commentaries tend to equate the former with *kāraṇa* and *paccaya*; and the latter seems to mean the seven remaining components of the Way all of which necessarily and inevitably go with right concentration as its "requisite" (*parikkhāra*) companions. This Discourse, called a disquisition on Dhamma at *M*. iii. 77, is given by means of defining the eight components of a learner's course and showing their relation to one another (the eightfold Way). But for an arahant the Way has ten components: the regular eight with the addition of right knowledge and right freedom.[1] All the more does this show the Way to be but a means to an end, not an end in itself, and therefore to be discarded (*cf.* Parable of the Raft[2]) when the Way-follower has ultimately achieved his goal.

Stas. 118 and 119 are but partial presentations of the *Satipaṭṭhānasutta* as given in *M*. Sta. 10 and *D*. Sta. 22, although both contain material not found there. The *Satipaṭṭhāna*, itself a basic Discourse, can also be regarded as an expansion of the "brief statement" of the one word *sammāsati* which occurs in the *Dhammacakkappavattanasutta*.

Sta. 120 is interesting for its unusual use of *saṁkhāra* as purpose or intellectual wish. The word *saṁkhāra* occurs a number of times in the *M*., as a glance at the Indexes to either the text or the translations will show, but never again with this sense of forging a determination for the type of rebirth desired by deliberately fixing one's mind on it. If a man have five other qualities besides this determination of his: faith, moral habit, learning, renunciation and wisdom, and abides longing to arise among the wealthy of the earth or among this class of *devas* or that, then this is the way and this is the course that tend to guarantee such an uprising for him. This Discourse may be compared with *M*. Sta. 6, the *Ākankheyya*, where too it is held that a monk's wishes may be fulfilled if he observe certain practices. Obviously the best kind of arising is the one mentioned last: the abiding in the freedom of mind and the freedom through intuitive wisdom that are cankerless. For when the meditating monk, who is now an arahant, has achieved this freedom he does not arise anywhere, he arises nowhere, *na katthaci uppajjati na kuhiñci uppajjati*—a phrase which may be set beside that found

---

[1] *Cf.* below, p. 119.   [2] *M*. i. 134 *f*.

in Sta. No. 113 (*M*. iii. 45): the good man *na kiñci na kuhiñci na kenaci*. Birth is at an end for him.

The third Division is called that on the concept of Emptiness, the *Suññatavagga* (Stas. 121-130). The first two Discourses, a *Cūḷa-* and *Mahā-* pair, give an excellent picture of what this concept means in the Pali Canon; and though it may be possible to fill it out from other passages, never elsewhere, I think, do the Nikāyas treat the subject at such length. The conclusion of Sta. 121 is important: though one may empty the mind of all disturbing factors, including the three cankers,[1] yet the six sensory fields remain tied to the body for as long as there is life in it. So that the final act of comprehension during the long discipline in mastering the concept of emptiness is to understand that " while that (*i.e.* the living body) is, this (*i.e.* the sensory apparatus) is," *taṁ santaṁ idam atthi*, and in regard to this concept of emptiness this is incomparably the highest realisation of it.

Sta. 122 describes how a monk can enter on an inward concept of emptiness in which there are no signs of the phenomenal world, *animitta*. Perhaps this should therefore be regarded as a development of the concept of emptiness mentioned in Sta. 121 in which the sensory fields are regarded as still being in full play. But in Sta. 122 the meditator's mind and senses are so closed to external events that, until he emerges from his meditation, they present no sign to him that can call forth any reaction.

If the *Isigili Sutta* (No. 116) is unique in one way among the *M*. Discourses, so in another is Sta. 123. This enumerates the wonderful and marvellous qualities of the Bodhisatta, mainly in respect of his nativity. Its affinities are with the *Mahāvastu*[2] and the character of its material is legendary.

Sta. 124 is likewise taken up with wonderful and marvellous qualities; but with those evinced by Bakkula during the eighty years he had been a monk. His answers to many of the questions put to him by Acela Kassapa, an ascetic, contain *Vinaya* elements and portray a monk of austere and extremely disciplined life, although lived at a lower level than that envisaged by Sāriputta when he addressed the monks concerning the uncouth Gulissāni who usually stayed in a forest (*M*. Sta. 69). According to *MA*. iv.

---

[1] See *M.L.S.* i. Intr., p. xxiii.
[2] See vol. i, p. 35 of J. J. Jones's translation (*S.B.B.*, vol. 16).

193 all Bakkula's answers were endorsed by the recensionists[1] who, in a kind of chorus appended to the end of each, applaud each of his achievements, which mostly amount to a scrupulous observance of *Vinaya* rules, as a wonderful and marvellous quality in him. At the conclusion of the Discourse it is stated that he entered on *parinibbāna* which, as other Suttas show (*e.g.* Nos. 106, 145), was a prerogative of others besides the Tathāgata.

Sta. 125 puts forward the customary method of taming oneself: by morality, guarding the sense-organs, moderation in eating, vigilance, being mindful and clearly conscious, frequenting remote lodgings and overcoming the five hindrances, after which a monk may devote himself to developing the four applications of mindfulness and the *jhānā*, etc. It is suggestive of possible methods used in arranging the *M*. Suttas that the title of No. 125 is *Dantabhūmi*, the Tamed Stage, and that of No. 126 is *Bhūmija*, which is a personal name. That is to say, they may have been placed next to one another merely on the score of the chance occurrence of a common element in their titles. Besides this similarity, they are both recorded to have been prompted by the questions Prince Jayasena asked; and both contain striking similes, all different however, which the Lord tells Jayasena's two interlocutors they should have produced for his benefit and then he would have had trust in them. But each objects that this was not possible (*M*. iii. 131, 144) as these similes had never been heard before, *assutapubba*. As one of the six occurs at *M*. ii. 129 and two others may well be compared with similar similes at *M*. i. 240, 242, it may be supposed, without prejudging the relative age of these Discourses, that it was owing to " chance " or to *kamma* that neither of Jayasena's interlocutors had himself heard them before. So much was spoken during the forty years of the Buddha's ministry, so many similes used,[2] that it would not have been possible for any one member of the Order to know everything, as is witnessed to by the special repeaters, *bhāṇakas*, for the various Nikāyas.

As Prince Jayasena appears in Stas. 125, 126, but apparently nowhere else in the Pali Canon, so does the venerable Anuruddha

---

[1] *Cf. ThagA.* iii. 58, which, in referring to ver. 869, 870, says *ime dve gāthā saṅgītikārakā ṭhapesuṁ*, " the recensionists established these two verses." This Comy. contains other similar statements.

[2] See, for example, Indexes to Similes in the 3 vols. of *M.L.S.*, the 5 vols. of *G.S.*, and the 5 of *K.S.*; and also " Similes in the Nikāyas," compiled by Mrs. Rhys Davids, *J.P.T.S.* 1907.

appear in Stas. 127 and 128, though he, it is true, appears in many
another context as well. Sta. 127 is concerned with the freedom of
mind that is widespread, *mahaggatā cetovimutti*. It first defines the
freedom of mind that is boundless, *appamāṇā cetovimutti*, by the
usual statement of the *brahmavihāra* formula which includes, besides
the term *pharitvā*, the terms *appamāṇa* and *mahaggata* also. I have
consistently translated *pharitvā* by " having suffused " or " suffusing," especially the four quarters, etc., in all occurrences of the
brahmavihāra formula in these three volumes. When Sta. 127 goes
on to describe what is meant by *mahaggatā cetovimutti*, its first
statement, setting the pattern for those that follow, is: *bhikkhu
yāvatā ekaṁ rukkhamūlaṁ mahaggatan ti pharitvā adhimuccitvā
viharati*. One of the chief difficulties for the translator, met with
also in the similar phrase *pharitvā adhimuccitvā viharati* in *M*.
Sta. 120 (*M*. iii. 101), is with *adhimuccitvā* and what it refers to.
Another difficulty in Sta. 127 is with the *ti* in the sentence quoted
above and with the question of what it qualifies. Does it qualify
the whole clause *yāvatā . . . mahaggataṁ*, or only the one word
mahaggataṁ ?

Adhimuccati, a verb with a number of meanings (see *PED* and
CPD), is perhaps best rendered in the present context, where it
takes the accusative and not the locative case, as to be intent on,
to adhere to, to apply oneself to, to settle or fix one's thoughts on
something and so to pervade this thing with one's thoughts. At
M. iii. 99 *ff.* I have rendered the expression *cittaṁ dahati* as " fixes
the mind on," thus following the translation of *A*. iv. 239 at
G.S. iv. 163. Here, too, an identical sequence of expressions occurs,
and in addition there is to be found the phrase *hīne 'dhimuttaṁ*,
" set on low things." On the principle that all different Pali
technical and semi-technical terms should be translated as far as
possible by different English words in an attempt to preserve and
convey the shades of Pali thought, I had to find a translation other
than " set the thoughts or mind on " for *adhimuccati*, since this
appears to be quite a good and literal translation of *cittaṁ dahati*.
At *Vbh*. 273 *ff. pharitvā* is explained by *adhimuccitvā*. This not
only has the merit of simplicity and brevity, but justifies the
translation of " pervading," for *adhimuccitvā* as being nearly
equivalent to " suffusing " for *pharitvā*. After much hesitation I
decided to use this word. It will be found to suit the passages at
M. iii. 101 *ff.* also: " he abides suffusing and pervading " the various
world-systems and the beings that have uprisen there. The whole

process is of course a meditative one as the Commentaries make abundantly clear.

Thus, *MA*. iv. 200 on *M*. iii. 146 explains the phrase *bhikkhu yāvatā . . . adhimuccitvā viharati* as " the monk, having covered (*ottharitvā*) a place the size (*pamāṇa*) of a single root of a tree with the mental reflex (or image) of a meditational device (*kasiṇanimittena*), (then) dwells suffusing and pervading a widespread meditation (*jhāna*) on that mental reflex of the meditational device. ' Widespread ' means (*mahaggatan ti*, or: thinking ' widespread ') there is no ideation (*ābhoga*) for him (*i.e.* the monk); it only refers to the incidence (*pavatti*) of widespread meditation . . . ' Widespread ' means that the mental reflex of the meditations on the meditational devices grows, (its) removal comes to be, there is (or follows, *hoti*) (its) transcending." Although this Commentarial passage gives no clear indication whether the *ti* refers only to *mahaggataṁ* or to the preceding words as well, yet judging by the arrangement of the terms here for exegetical purposes, I incline to the opinion that *ti* refers to the whole phrase *yāvatā ekaṁ rukkhamūlaṁ mahaggataṁ*. In view of the considerations here put forward and with the help of some valuable and suggestive remarks Mr. J. J. Jones kindly sent me, I would rather tentatively propose to translate this perplexing passage as: " a monk, thinking (*ti*) it (*i.e.* meditation, *jhāna*, in which there is freedom of mind) is widespread (*mahaggataṁ*) like as (*yāvatā*) a single root of a tree (and so on), dwells suffusing and pervading it (*i.e.* that size, being the object of his meditation, *jhāna*, which is made possible by the mental reflex or image he has obtained from the *kasiṇa* device he used to induce this meditation)." This is an example of the allusiveness of the Pali texts. It does not detract from their precision, but only shows it is we who must find the key to what at one time was probably obvious and well understood.

Sta. 128 also has a number of difficulties. I have a note on the word *obhāsa* on p. 202 below. I was not satisfied with " aura " which has been used as a translation. For this word is either used in a narrowly theosophical sense of the colour of the light people are supposed to emit, invisible however to all but the initiated, or it is taken to mean some such subtle emanation as an odour, a light breeze, a current of air electrically discharged, or a sensation (pathological). But *obhāsa* has none of these meanings here. It is connected with the appearance of light produced in meditation by which objects can be seen by the non-physical *deva*-vision operating as it does super- or extra-sensibly. I think light-manifestation or light-radiation is better. The connotation has also to be differentiated from that of *dassana*, the appearance, also in meditation, of objects otherwise perceptible by the senses. These are now " seen " by and become visible to the meditator, though no longer through the medium of his physical eye, whereas the light, *obhāsa*, does no more than indicate that this more final occurrence may be about to take place. For as a rule *obhāsa* and *dassana* do not occur simultaneously.

The Comy. says nothing about the change at *M*. iii. 161 from the hitherto usual *obhāsañ c'eva sañjānāmi dassanañ ca rūpānaṁ* to the new *obhāsaṁ hi kho sañjānāmi (na) ca rūpāni passāmi*. No doubt these material shapes are also " seen " by *deva*-vision. Yet this unheralded change is curious and its significance further confused by the introduction into the context of the term *rūpanimitta*, " reflex-image of material shapes " (*M*. iii. 161). It is as well to remember however that this Discourse is not only dealing with a meditational theme but also with one that is mostly " autobiographical." It refers to an episode in the Bodhisatta's life and hence to his struggles to win unshakable freedom of mind (see *M*. iii. 162). The reflex-image of material shapes he saw though failing to perceive their light-radiation spurred him on to overcome this defect. After investigating the possible causes of such a contingency, he came to the conclusion that it was due to the presence in him of eleven defilements of the mind. To recognise them as defilements was to eliminate them and to set up in their place a threefold concentration, or a concentration by a threefold method, *tividhena samādhi*,[1] by developing which the Bodhisatta established himself in arahantship. This alone is sufficient to show that this " autobiographical " fragment of the Bodhisatta's life refers not to an anterior birth but to this last one in which he attained Buddhahood. An arahant, one of unshakable freedom of mind who has done what was to be done and brought the Brahma-faring to a close, comprehends that there is no longer again-becoming, *punabbhava*, or rebirth for him: " This is my last birth." In a word it had not been possible for the Bodhisatta as such to gain arahantship before as the Buddha he had taught the Way to it. So that the question arises whether the three words repeatedly recurring in sequence in

---

[1] See notes at p. 207 below; also *cf. pañcangika samādhi*, *Thag*. 916, and for this see *ThagA*. iii. 72, *Pss. Breth.*, p. 330, *n*. 4, and *Vbh*. 334.

this Discourse (as elsewhere in the *M*.; see Indexes to the 3 vols. of *M.L.S.* under "diligent"): "diligent, ardent, self-resolute," *appamatta ātāpi pahitattā*, constitute one of the four main formulae of arahantship, even when they are cut off from the two words that often precede them, *eko vūpakaṭṭha*, "alone, secluded." Or are the five words of the full formula necessary to express such a state ? And, if so, do the three when truncated from the full formula, as here, merely indicate some of the conditions necessary for attaining arahantship ?

In passing it may be interesting to remark that while Buddhaghosa usually paraphrases *pahitatta* by *pesitatta, e.g.* at *MA*. i. 126, ii. 80 (with the variant reading *pesitacitta*), iii. 107, *DA*. 363, 684, *SA*. i. 110, etc., his friend Dhammapāla, *e.g.* at *UdA*. 174, *ThagA*. iii. 90, says *pahitattā ti nibbānaṁ paṭipesitacittā*, which appears to mean "*pahitatta* means the mind is sent out towards nibbāna." Dhammapāla, like Buddhaghosa, wrongly derives *pahita* from *pahiṇati*, to send, instead of from *padahati*, to be resolute, strive, exert oneself. If, as Dhammapāla suggests, the object is to win nibbāna, this is not only in general accordance with the whole Teaching, but may also contain an allusion both to a striking phrase: *padhānaṁ padahitvāna*, " striving the striving," of frequent recurrence in the *Buddhavaṁsa* with which the *prahāṇaṁ prahitaṁ mayā* of *Mhvu*. ii. 238 may be compared,[1] and to the striving that the Bodhisatta realised he would have to undertake once he had determined to seek for nibbāna: *alaṁ vat' idaṁ kulaputtassa padhānatthikaṁ padhānāya . . . so kho ahaṁ . . . nibbānaṁ pariyesamāno*: " Indeed this does well for the striving of a young man set on striving . . . so I . . . seeking nibbāna " (*M*. i. 167). It is therefore not easy to find justification for the " purged of self " used in *Fur. Dial.* as a rendering of *pahitatta*. To see and realise nibbāna is the object and aim of all these strenuous endeavours; and while it is still the object and aim, not yet fulfilled, it cannot be said that arahantship has been won. Endeavour, resolution is still necessary, and it must be self-resolution because no one can purify another (*Dhp*. 165) and no one can tread the Way for another (see *M*. Stas. 106, 107, 108 and elsewhere).

As there is a point, or points, in common between Stas. 123 and 124, between Stas. 125 and 126 and between Stas. 127 and 128, so also is there between Stas. 129 and 130. For both of these narrate the horrors of Niraya Hell, the former saying it is not easy to

---

[1] See *Mhvu. Translation*, J. J. Jones, vol. ii, p. 225.

describe this Hell in full, so many are its anguishes; nor, so many are the anguishes of animal birth, is it easy to describe this in full. On the other hand, the seven Treasures of a wheel-rolling monarch are adduced to indicate how many are the happinesses of heaven beside which even these Treasures pale and wane. Sta. 129 also has the curious simile of the blind (marine) turtle, a most impressive fantasy also occurring, with slight differences, at *S.* iv. 453. It is a simile used to stress the difficulties that, though almost insuperable, do not quite hopelessly debar the fool who has been reborn in a sorrowful way from regaining human status. The props and stays and guides for walking on the Way taught by the Tathāgata do not exist there. But even so, as recorded in *M.*, but not in *S.*, the fool, after the passage of an enormously long time, may one day be born as a man again, though in the most miserable conditions. Nor would he fare by Dhamma, but in fact against it and so would pass to a sorrowful state once more when he died. This is a vicious circle, and it is not suggested that there is any method by which the fool can break the wheel to which he is so firmly bound. It is however assumed that he can; but the reason why he can, "if at all" (in the words of Sta. 129) must be regarded as analogous to the reason why Devadatta's time in Niraya Hell will eventually come to an end as the karmic result of some good deed done by him in a long distant previous birth.

The difficulty of being reborn as a human being finds expression in other parts of the Pali Canon, for example at *A.* i. 35: "So few are the beings reborn among men; more numerous are those beings born among others than men"; and the Therī Sumedhā, in giving full rein to her eloquence so as to convince her parents and suitor that it is better to leave the world for the homeless state than live in it enslaved by sense-desires, adduces the Simile of the Blind Turtle:

> "Remember how the parable was told
> Of purblind turtle in the Eastern seas,
> Or other oceans, once as time goes by
> Thrusting his head thro' hole of drifting yoke—
> So rare as this the chance of human birth"
> (*Thīg.* ver. 500,
> translated by Mrs. Rhys Davids, *Pss. Sist.*)

"The difficulty of being a man, as told in the Simile of the Blind Turtle" is remarked upon at *Asl.* p. 60. Further, Nāgasena referred to this simile when he was trying to make King Milinda understand how vast a span of time had separated all the births in which the Bodhisatta and Devadatta had met: " And when, sire, you say that Devadatta and the Bodhisatta kept moving on together (in *saṁsāra*), that meeting was not after the lapse of a hundred or a thousand or a hundred thousand births; it was from time to time at the end of an immeasurable period. And, sire, the Simile of the Blind Turtle was delivered by the Lord in order to show the difficulty of acquiring human status—you should consider the meetings of these two (the Bodhisatta and Devadatta) in the light of this simile " (*Miln.* p. 204). This simile certainly caught the imagination of the compilers of old. Its " moral " of course is that it is vitally important for the man or woman who has acquired human status to make every possible endeavour to fare by Dhamma if he wants to go on being reborn as a human being. For only then does he have the opportunity eventually to win the stage where he can make an end of birth and dying, of coming to be and passing away.

Sta. 130, with its five *deva*-messengers, is another Discourse without parallel in the *M.*, though there is a similar passage in *A.*, but with only three *deva*-messengers. The man who ignores their warnings is brought before King Yama and tossed into Niraya Hell with no hope of escape until he has undergone all its tortures for eons. He does not die. He cannot die, or do his karmic time, until his evil deed wears to its (karmic) end: *na tāva kālaṁ karoti yāva na taṁ pāpakammaṁ byantihoti*, a phrase which occurs in both Sta. 129 and 130 (and *cf. M.* i. 428). King Yama, realising the fearfulness of the punishments such a man has to meet, expresses a great longing for human status so as to hear Dhamma from whatever Lord and Tathāgata would be arisen in the world at that time. For, as Sta. 129 has already made plain, it is only a human being that can make an end of being born and dying. In addition, the assumption, here put into words by King Yama, that the Buddha Gotama is not the last Buddha who will arise, has an interest of its own.

The Fourth Division, that on Analysis, the *Vibhaṅgavagga* (Stas. 131-142) is markedly consistent in that all its twelve Discourses, except the last, are expansions of statements the Buddha is said to have made in brief. The last Discourse, No. 142, though it contains an analysis or enlargement of its topic, has neither a short statement nor an expansion of this in the style characterising the others where, at the request of monks and various people who had failed to grasp properly the full import of the concise statements, these were expanded either by the Buddha himself or by his disciples, twice for example by Mahā-Kaccāna, the most eminent expounder in full of what had been stated in brief (*A*. i. 23). These short statements are constantly referred to by Buddhaghosa as *mātikā*, headings, summaries, and are in fact a type of compendium. It is not improbable that he is right in saying that the whole of the teaching of Dhamma by Buddhas is in brief and that there is no extended teaching (see above on Stas. 117, 118, 119). That this is very likely true of the *Dhammacakkappavattanasutta* is again borne out by the analysis of the Middle Course, *majjhimā paṭipadā*, in Sta. 139, and of the four ariyan truths in the *Saccavibhaṅgasutta*, No. 141. Nor should Bu's remark at *AA*. ii. 101 pass unnoticed: *sakalaṁ pi hi tepiṭakaṁ saṁkhepadesanā-vitthāradesanā ti etth' eva saṁkhaṁ gacchati*, " the whole of the three Piṭakas is reckoned as an extended teaching of a brief teaching " (not, I think: a teaching in brief and a teaching in full).

If the internal connection between the brief statements contained in some of these Discourses (*e.g.* Nos. 137, 139) is not immediately obvious, it usually becomes clearer as the Discourse in question develops its analysis of these short utterances. One cannot suppose and need not suppose these to have been collected together, Discourse by Discourse, in a haphazard way; on the contrary, it would seem that they were placed together because they belong together, and if rightly appreciated will be seen as parts of a whole. They are indeed a valuable contribution to the Teaching of a gradual approach to the goal and a gradual development in self-taming so characteristic of Pali Buddhism. By attending to one thing at a time and mastering it the aspirant has prepared himself to proceed to the next. Thus (Sta. 139) the existence of the Middle Course enables a man or a monk to advance step by step until he himself becomes a teacher of Dhamma. There is then given what appears to be a basic theme for the teaching he could give; and finally the circumstances (not vexatiously), the manner (slowly) and the language (dialect if necessary) he could give it in.

Stas. 131-134 all have the term Bhaddekaratta as part of their title; and this presents something of a puzzle. *MA*. v. 1 attempts an explanation of this word by saying: *vipassanānuyogasamannāgattā bhaddakassa* (*v.l.* *bhaddassa*) *ekarattassa*, " of one who is happy (?auspicious) for one night because he is possessed of intentness of insight." Neumann renders the term by " Glücksäligeinsam," lonely blissfulness. But *ekatta* is loneliness; *ekaratta* usually means "for one night." But the *Bhaddekaratta Suttas* do not appear to envisage withdrawal from thoughts of the past, future and present for so little as one night. On the contrary, the verses that form the *mātikā* say that the person to be called *bhaddekaratta* is he who abides ardently and unweariedly day and night, that is, surely, for some consecutive time lasting longer than "one night." I thought it best to translate only the first part of the baffling compound, and have rendered *bhadda* by "auspicious," not in its sense of betokening success but in that of prosperous, prospering. For the sage who comes to be at peace has prospered by not following after the past, by not desiring the future to be such or so, and by cultivating a right attitude to present things. His position is not due to luck, a happy chance or fortune's favours; it is due to his own successful efforts, determined resolution and shunning of indolence.

Sta. 137 speaks of three *satipaṭṭhānā*. These have nothing at all to do with the four usual ones (see *M*. Sta. 10) and seem to contain a hidden reference to the eighteen special qualities of a Buddha that are better known to the later literature than to the Pali Canon (*cf.* references to *Divy.* and *Mhvu.* in the note at p. 263 below). One would have expected them to allude to the Buddha's indifference to praise and blame, but the wording of the passage hardly bears this out. These three *satipaṭṭhānā* are the attitudes a teacher may adopt, or should adopt, to the reactions of his disciples when they hear a teaching from him: they may not listen; some may not listen and some may; or all may listen. In the first case the Tathāgata, the type of supreme teacher, is represented as being neither delighted nor as experiencing delight, where we would have expected to find it said of him that he was neither depressed nor experiencing depression. But depression appears to assail him in the second alternative of the second case where some disciples listen, although this cannot be assumed for certain and perhaps would be too strange to be assumed at all, in which case textual errors would almost have to be posited. In the third clause where all the disciples listen, the Tathāgata is said to be delighted. Nevertheless, the main result is that however the disciples respond the Tathāgata remains unmoved, mindful and clearly conscious. He teaches Dhamma and points out the Way; it is for his hearers to choose to become Way-followers or to seek something different.

The last Division, the *Saḷāyatanavagga* (Sta. 143-152), that on the Sixfold Sense-field, appears to take its name from the Discourse placed seventh in it, the *Mahāsaḷāyatanika-sutta* (No. 149). Preceding this are five *ovāda*-discourses and one other, the *Chachakka* (No. 148). The exhortations, *ovāda*, are individually addressed to various persons. In Sta. 143 it is recorded that Sāriputta went to exhort the dying Anāthapiṇḍika as he is also recorded to have gone to exhort the brahman Dhānañjāni shortly before he died (*M*. Sta. 97). Anāthapiṇḍika became a *deva*, or *devaputta*, after his death, and Dhānañjāni gained the Brahma-world.[1] Sta. 144 was an exhortation given by Sāriputta to the monk Channa who was in such pain that, in spite of Sāriputta's protests and offers of help, he committed suicide. But he incurred no blame for his action for he did not grasp after another body.[2] He therefore had no bourn or going, *gati*, and no future state, *abhisamparāya*, and was in fact to be regarded as an arahant.[3] In Sta. 145 the monk Puṇṇa asked the Lord for an exhortation in brief. Though this was given to him it was not expounded in full as Puṇṇa was advanced enough in the Teaching to work out the details for himself in the solitude he wished to seek for that very purpose. In the first rainy season he attained arahantship and later final nibbāna, *parinibbāyi*. So, as he had overpassed rebirth, he was another for whom there was no bourn or future state. Sta. 146 contains an exhortation to nuns by the monk Nandaka, who was ordered by the Buddha to instruct them since it was his turn to do so; but this was in despite of Mahāpajāpatī's plea to the Lord that he himself should instruct them. Sta. 142 records that the Lord refused to accept the gift she offered him and entreated him to accept. She too, like Ānanda, knew or suspected that a gift given to the Buddha was of the greatest merit; there was not another like it, not even a gift to the Saṃgha. Nandaka's exhortation took the form of a dialogue in which he put questions to the nuns about the impermanence of the six sense-fields, and they answered in a fully informed manner. Sta. 147 records an exhortation given to Rāhula by the Lord, also on impermanence, at the conclusion of which Rāhula's mind was freed from the cankers without any grasping remaining.

These five *ovāda*-Discourses are followed by the Discourse on the Six Sixes, *Chachakka* (No. 148): six internal sense-fields, six external, six classes of consciousness and so on. These are the brief state-

---

[1] See *M.L.S.* ii. Intr., p. xxix.   [2] See above, p. xiii.
[3] *Cf.* the monk Godhika, *S*. i. 120 *ff*., who committed suicide but for whom there was no more again-becoming for, having rooted out *taṇhā*, craving, he attained final nibbāna, *parinibbuto*.

ments or headings; they are followed by fuller explanations of the meanings.

Sta. 149, the *Mahāsaḷāyatanika*, also continues to analyse grasping after the six sense-fields until the zealous disciple eradicates all craving for them and obtains instead a right view of what really is, *yathābhūtaṁ*, together with aspiration and endeavour for it, mindfulness of it, and concentration on it. While he is cultivating these five factors of the Eightfold Way he can explore other aspects of the Teaching, such as the 37 things helpful to enlightenment, get rid of craving for becomings, develop meditational calm and insight and realise the arahant's two extra factors of the Way: knowledge and freedom. Thus once more in the space of a short Discourse we find it was normally expected for a man that his progress in self-control and self-development would be gradual, and if he were resolute then this method of progress would " lead on gradually up to the Highest " (*A*. v. 2). Once he had attained a right and unshakable attitude to the unavoidable impact of sense-data on their appropriate sense-organs he was well set on the way to win two distinguishing and transcendental marks of an arahant, that is, knowledge and freedom: knowledge of these sense-data as they really are and freedom from reaction to them, because to like them or dislike them has no further meaning for the sage at peace.

Sta. 150 is on the whole a plea for the recognition of the lofty nature of those who attempt to secure for themselves detachment from mental stimuli. Even though they may sometimes lapse and fare along unevenly, nevertheless their efforts for detachment are more worthy of esteem than are their backslidings of disapprobation.

Sta. 151, while returning to the concept of emptiness (see Stas. 121, 122), again emphasises that even right things or states of mind such as the 37 things helpful to enlightenment or knowledge and freedom should be forsaken and relinquished (see Parable of the Raft, *M*. i. 134). A monk should be indeed a man-of-naught; only then is he sufficiently purified to walk for alms. If this appears to be something of an anti-climax, a whole essay, so abundant is the material, could easily be devoted to showing that it is not. For example, one may adduce the answer to the first of the ten Great Questions (*Mahāpañhā, A*. v. 54), also called the Questions for a Boy (or, Boys, *Kumārapañhā, Khp*. IV.): " All beings are subsisters by food." If a monk thinks of food he should turn his systematic attention to the first of the applications of mindfulness; he should realise that it is food that is the cause of the arising of attachment not yet arisen (*K.S.* v. 52); and when he has understood that food is the source of impermanence he should feel disgust for it and turn away from it—in thought, of course, is to be understood. For all beings must subsist by food. But a man who has entered on the Way should keep a proper sense of proportion about this as about other matters: moderation in eating and grasping after nothing in the world are part of the well-learnt learner's course designed to culminate in arahantship.

All this is set out, albeit in other words, in this Discourse. In addition, the value of giving to the giver of alms is recognised as it is throughout the Pali Canon (see *e.g. M.* Sta. 142). And again, *dāna*, giving, liberality, came at some time to be ranked as the first of the ten *pāramitā*, a word that is usually associated with the later literature. Nowhere, I think, in the four main Nikāyas are the *pāramitā* themselves enumerated so as to form a category.[1] The taking of sufficient food to support the body, and through it the mind, which is the Brahma-farer's essential tool in his quest, is not only accepted as unavoidable by a Teaching that detests self-mortification whether practised through starvation or any other means; but also the thought of food, if viewed in the right way, will help both donor and recipient to realise the impermanence of all conditioned or constructed things.

Sta. 152 might be regarded as a kind of summing up of all that has been said of the six senses (including naturally that of taste, so referring to food) during the course of this Division, and in many other parts of *M.* and in the remaining Nikāyas as well. A monk learns to have such control over his sense-organs, *indriya*, which is equivalent to bringing them to proper development, *bhāvanā*, that, whether he likes, dislikes or both likes and dislikes the sense-impressions that impinge upon his mind, he can stop these with the utmost rapidity so that there remain only the real and the excellent, which is here *upekhā*, even-mindedness or equanimity.

The senses indeed are of prime importance. While the difficulty is to restrain the enjoyment of them, the discipline is to regard them aright as not mine, not I, not my self, and to turn away from them with an indifference and even-mindedness that has come to be well

---

[1] *pāramippatta* at *M.* ii. 11, 211, iii. 28 is not used in a sense involving any of the ten *pāramitā*.

established and immovable, in the conviction and the experience that there is a happiness excelling that derived from the senses (*M*. i. 398). The senses are of the here and now; but the real and the excellent are to be found by means of the unhampered mind well liberated from reaction to sense-impingement. The external world and the disciple's interest in it must shrink in proportion as his internal world and mastery of it grow and come to maturity. One cannot help feeling that the *M*. ends on a fitting note.

If the Teaching is that of an idealist it is also that of a realist, and it is meant for realists. There is to be no atrophy of the senses, no atrophy of the mind, no derangement of it by seeking the goal through such excessive physical hardships as must inevitably lead to psychopathological states. Victory in the struggle is to be won by the human being who refuses to be moved or affected by the passing show, however faint or shadowy it may become as the level of meditation gradually recedes from its influence. While there is any trace of sense-reaction remaining, Māra will be there with all his lures and wiles. The activity of the senses can only be stopped entirely by transcending it in the deepest meditative stage where "all is still" (*Sn*. 902) and where a man's senses are so completely withdrawn from the external world as to be totally irresponsive to it. This is true self-conquest, the fruit of self-training and self-taming. The stopping of perception and feeling indicates that a man, Sāriputta for example, has attained to mastery and to going beyond, *pāramipatta*, in the ariyan moral habit, the ariyan concentration, the ariyan wisdom and the ariyan freedom (*M*. iii. 29). "Though one should conquer a thousand thousand men in battle, he indeed is the greatest of conquerors who could conquer one self" (*Dhp*. 103). Of him it may truly be said *kataṁ karaṇiyaṁ*, done is what was to be done. For now he is endowed with that "highest ariyan wisdom which is the knowledge of the complete destruction of anguish. And that freedom of his, founded on truth, is unshakable. For that highest ariyan truth . . . is nibbāna, beyond all suppositions, where there is no more coming to birth and ageing and dying" (*M*. iii. 245 *f*.), and hence completely opposed to *saṁsara* in which life is led under the thrall of sense-desires for sense-experience.

While this volume was still in typescript I had the inestimable advantage of receiving valuable and stimulating suggestions for its improvement from my colleague, the late Mr. J. J. Jones, the scholarly translator of *Mahāvastu*,[1] a work that contains several passages similar to ones found in the Nikāyas. As my notes by no means show the extent of my indebtedness to him, it is all the more my pleasure, and duty, to acknowledge here my gratitude for the great help he so unstintingly gave me.

I. B. HORNER.

London, 1957.

---

[1] *S.B.B.*, vols. 16, 18, 19, published in 1949, 1952, 1956.

ABBREVIATIONS

A.	= Anguttara-Nikāya.
AA.	= Commentary on A.
Asl.	= Atthasālinī.
B.D.	= Book of the Discipline.
B.H.S.D.	= Buddhist Hybrid Sanskrit Dictionary (Franklin Edgerton).
BudvA.	= Commentary on Buddhavaṁsa.
C.P.D.	= Critical Pali Dictionary (Dines Andersen and Helmer Smith).
Comy.	= Commentary.
D.	= Dīgha-Nikāya.
DA.	= Commentary on D.
DhA.	= Commentary on Dhp.
Dhp.	= Dhammapada.
Dhs.	= Dhammasangaṇi.
Dial.	= Dialogues of the Buddha.
Divy.	= Divyāvadāna.
D.P.P.N.	= Dictionary of Pali Proper Names (G. P. Malalasekera).
Expos.	= Expositor.
G.S.	= Gradual Sayings.
Iti.	= Itivuttaka.
Jā.	= Jātaka.
J.P.T.S.	= Journal of the Pali Text Society.
J.R.A.S.	= Journal of the Royal Asiatic Society.
KhpA.	= Commentary on Khuddakapāṭha.
K.S.	= Kindred Sayings.
Kvu.	= Kathāvatthu.
M.	= Majjhima-Nikāya.
MA.	= Commentary on M.
Mhvs.	= Mahāvaṁsa.
Mhvu.	= Mahāvastu.
Miln.	= Milindapañha.
M.L.S.	= Middle Length Sayings.
Nd.	= Niddesa.

Abbreviations

Netti.	= Nettipakaraṇa.
Pāc.	= Pācittiya.
P.E.D.	= Pali-English Dictionary
	(T. W. Rhys Davids and W. Stede).
Pss. Breth.	= Psalms of the Brethren.
Pss. Sist.	= Psalms of the Sisters.
P.T.C.	= Pali Tipiṭakaṁ Concordance
	(F. L. Woodward, E. M. Hare, etc.).
Pts.	= Paṭisambhidāmagga.
Pts. Contr.	= Points of Controversy.
Pug.	= Puggalapaññatti.
S.	= Saṁyutta-Nikāya.
SA.	= Commentary on S.
S.B.B.	= Sacred Books of the Buddhists.
Sn.	= Suttanipāta.
SnA.	= Commentary on Sn.
Sta.	= Sutta.
Thag.	= Theragāthā.
ThagA.	= Commentary on Thag.
Thīg.	= Therigāthā.
ThīgA.	= Commentary on Thīg.
Ud.	= Udāna.
UdA.	= Commentary on Ud.
Up.	= Upanishad.
Vbh.	= Vibhanga.
VbhA.	= Commentary on Vbh.
Vin.	= Vinaya-piṭaka.
VinA.	= Commentary on Vin.
Vism.	= Visuddhimagga.
VvA.	= Commentary on Vimānavatthu.

1. THE DEVADAHA DIVISION

(Devadahavagga)

101. DISCOURSE AT DEVADAHA
(Devadahasutta)

[214] Thus have I heard: At one time the Lord was staying among the Sakyans. A market town of the Sakyans was called Devadaha.[1] While he was there the Lord addressed the monks, saying: "Monks." "Revered One," these monks answered the Lord in assent. The Lord spoke thus:

"There are, monks, some recluses and brahmans who speak thus and are of these views: 'Whatever this individual experiences, whether pleasant or painful or neither painful nor pleasant, all is due to what was previously done. Thus by burning up,[2] by making and end of ancient deeds, by the non-doing of new deeds, there is no overflowing into the future. From there being no overflowing into the future comes the destruction of deeds; from the destruction of deeds comes the destruction of anguish; from the destruction of anguish comes the destruction of feeling; from the destruction of feeling all anguish will become worn away.' Jains speak thus, monks. I, monks, speak thus—having approached Jains, I speak thus:

'Is it true, as is said, reverend Jains, that you speak thus and are of these views: Whatever this individual experiences . . . (as above) . . . all anguish will become worn away'? If, monks, these Jains on being asked this by me acknowledge it, saying Yes, then I speak thus: 'But do you, reverend Jains, know[2] that you yourselves were in the past, that you were not not?'

'Not this, your reverence.'

'But do you, reverend Jains, know that you yourselves did this evil deed in the past, that you did not not do it?'

'Not this, your reverence.'

'But do you, reverend Jains, know that you did not do an evil deed like this or like that?'

'Not this, your reverence.'

'But do you, reverend Jains, know that so much anguish is worn

---

[1] Mentioned at S. iii. 5, iv. 124; Jā. i. 52; BudvA. 274. It was near the Lumbini Grove, and here the Lord was staying, MA. iv. 1.

[2] As at M. i. 93; see M.L.S. i. 122.

away, or that so much anguish is to be worn away, or that when so much anguish is worn away, all anguish will become worn away ?'

[215] 'Not this, your reverence.'

'But do you, reverend Jains, know the getting rid of unskilled states of mind here and now, the arising of skilled states ?'

'Not this, your reverence.'

'From what you say, reverend Jains, you do not know whether you yourselves were in the past, or whether you were not not; you do not know whether in the past you yourselves did this evil deed, or whether you did not not do it; you do not know whether you did an evil deed like this or like that; you do not know that so much anguish is worn away, or that so much anguish is to be worn away, or that when so much anguish is worn away, all anguish will become worn away; you do not know the getting rid of unskilled states of mind here and now, or the arising of skilled states. This being so, it would not be suitable that the reverend Jains should explain, saying: " Whatever this individual experiences . . . (*as above*) . . . all anguish will become worn away." But if you, reverend Jains, were to know: " We ourselves were in the past, we were not not "; if you were to know: " We ourselves did this evil deed in the past, we did not not do it "; if you were to know: " We did not do an evil deed like this or like that "; if you were to know: " So much anguish is worn away, or so much anguish is to be worn away, or when so much anguish is worn away, all anguish will become worn away "; if you were to know the getting rid of unskilled states of mind here and now, or the arising of skilled ones—this being so, it would be suitable that the reverend Jains should explain, saying: " Whatever this individual experiences, whether pleasant or painful or neither painful nor pleasant, all that is due to what was previously done. Thus [216] by burning up, by making an end of ancient deeds, by the non-doing of new deeds, there is no overflowing into the future. From there being no overflowing into the future comes the destruction of deeds; from the destruction of deeds comes the destruction of anguish; from the destruction of anguish comes the destruction of feeling; from the destruction of feeling all anguish will become worn away."

Reverend Jains, it is as if a man were pierced by an arrow that was thickly smeared with poison.[1] And because he has felt the arrow he might experience a feeling that was painful, severe, sharp. His

---

[1] As at *M*. ii. 256; *cf.* also *M*. i. 429.

friends and acquaintances, kith and kin might procure a physician and surgeon. That physician and surgeon might cut round the opening of his wound with a knife, but on account of cutting round the opening of the wound with the knife the man might experience a feeling that was painful, severe, sharp. That physician and surgeon might probe him for the arrow with a (surgeon's) probe,[1] but on account of his being probed for the arrow with the (surgeon's) probe he might also experience a feeling that was painful, severe, sharp. That physician and surgeon might extract the arrow from him, but on account of having the arrow extracted he might also experience a feeling that was painful, severe, sharp. The physician and surgeon might dress the opening of his wound with medicated powder,[2] but on account of having the opening of the wound dressed with medicated powder he might also experience a feeling that was painful, severe, sharp. After a time when the skin had healed on the wound he would be well, at ease, independent, his own master, going wherever he liked.[3] This might occur to him: " Once upon a time I was pierced by an arrow that was thickly smeared with poison. And because I felt the arrow I experienced a feeling that was painful, severe, sharp. My friends and acquaintances, kith and kin procured a physician and surgeon. That physician and surgeon cut round the opening of my wound . . . on account of having the opening of the wound dressed with medicated powder I also experienced a feeling that was painful, severe, sharp. [217] But now that the skin has healed on the wound I am well, at ease, independent, my own master, going wherever I like." Even so, reverend Jains, if you were to know: " We ourselves were in the past, we were not not " . . . if you were to know the getting rid of unskilled states of mind here and now or the arising of skilled states—this being so, it would be suitable that the reverend Jains should explain, saying: " Whatever this individual experiences . . . is due to what was previously done . . . from the destruction of feeling all anguish will become worn away."

' But as you, reverend Jains, do not know: " We ourselves were in the past, we were not not "; nor know: " We ourselves did this evil deed in the past, we did not not do it "; nor know: " We did not do

---

[1] *esani*. *MA*. iv. 2: with a probe that is a small stick, *salāka* (*cf. Miln.* 112, 149, perhaps a stick of caustic) or even with a shred of cloth, *nantakavaṭṭī*.

[2] *agadaṅgāra*. *MA*. iv. 2 says a powder, *cuṇṇa*, of myrobalans that was *jhāma*, hot, burning. Perhaps a hot compress.

[3] As at *M*. i. 506.

an evil deed like this or like that "; nor know: " So much anguish is worn away, or so much anguish is to be worn away, or when so much anguish is worn away all anguish will become worn away "; nor know the getting rid of unskilled states of mind here and now, nor the arising of skilled ones—therefore it would not be suitable that the reverend Jains should explain, saying: " Whatever this individual experiences, whether pleasant or painful or neither painful nor pleasant, all that is due to what was previously done. Thus by burning up, by making an end of ancient deeds, by the non-doing of new deeds, there is no overflowing into the future. From there being no overflowing into the future comes the destruction of deeds; from the destruction of deeds comes the destruction of anguish; from the destruction of anguish comes the destruction of feeling; from the destruction of feeling all anguish will become worn away." '

When this had been said, monks, these Jains spoke to me thus: [218] ' Your reverence, Nāṭaputta the Jain is all-knowing, all-seeing[1]; he claims all-embracing knowledge-and-vision, saying: " Whether I am walking or standing still or asleep or awake, knowledge-and-vision is permanently and continuously before me." He speaks thus: " If there is, reverend Jains, an evil deed that was formerly done by you, wear it away by this severe austerity. That which is the non-doing of an evil deed in the future is from control of body, control of speech, control of thought here, now. Thus by burning up, by making an end of ancient deeds, by the non-doing of new deeds, there is no overflowing into the future. From there being no overflowing into the future comes the destruction of deeds; from the destruction of deeds comes the destruction of anguish; from the destruction of anguish comes the destruction of feeling; from the destruction of feeling all anguish will become worn away." And because that is approved of by us as well as being pleasing to us, therefore we are delighted.'

When this had been said I, monks, spoke thus to those Jains: ' These five conditions here-now, reverend Jains, have a twofold result. What five ? Faith, inclination, tradition, consideration of reasons, reflection on and approval of some view.[2] These, reverend Jains, are five conditions here-now that have a twofold result. As to this, what was the faith that in the past the reverend Jains had in a teacher, what was their inclination, what the tradition, what the

---

[1] This paragraph also occurs at *M*. i. 92-93 (*M.L.S.* i. 122).
[2] *Cf. S.* ii. 115, iv. 138; *A*. i. 189, ii. 191.

consideration of reasons, what the reflection on and approval of some view?' I, monks, speaking thus, beheld no reasoned response[1] among the Jains. And again, monks, I spoke to these Jains thus: 'What do you think about this, reverend Jains? At a time when there is severe effort for you, severe striving, do you at that time experience a feeling that is severe, acute, painful, severe, sharp? But at a time when there is no severe effort for you, no severe striving, do you at that time experience a feeling that is not severe, acute, painful, severe, sharp?'

'Reverend Gotama, at a time when there is severe effort for us, severe striving, at that time we experience a feeling that is severe, acute, painful, severe, sharp. But at [219] a time when there is no severe effort for us, no severe striving, at that time we do not experience a feeling that is severe ... sharp.'

'So really it is, reverend Jains: At a time when there is severe effort for you, severe striving, at that time you experience a feeling that is severe ... sharp. But at a time when there is no severe effort for you, no severe striving, at that time you do not experience a feeling that is severe ... sharp. This being so, it would be suitable that the reverend Jains should explain, saying: "Whatever this individual experiences, whether pleasant or painful ... from the destruction of feeling all anguish will become worn away." If, reverend Jains, at a time when there is severe effort for you, severe striving, at that very time there might be a feeling that is acute, painful, severe, sharp; but at the time when there is no severe effort for you, no severe striving, at that very time there might (also) be a feeling that is acute ... sharp—this being so, it would be suitable that the reverend Jains should explain, saying: "Whatever this individual experiences, whether pleasant or painful ... from the destruction of feeling all anguish will become worn away." But inasmuch, reverend Jains, as at a time when there is severe effort for you, severe striving, at that time you experience a feeling that is severe, acute, painful, severe, sharp; but at a time when there is no severe effort for you, no severe striving, at that time you do not experience a feeling that is severe, acute, painful, severe, sharp—then it is precisely you yourselves who, while experiencing a feeling that is acute, painful, severe, sharp, are deceived by ignorance, nescience, confusion, [220] saying: "Whatever this individual experiences,

---

[1] *sahadhammikaṁ vādaparihāraṁ*; on p. 220 (text) *vādapaṭihāraṁ*, also at *MA.* iv. 4.

whether pleasant or painful or neither painful nor pleasant, all that is due to what was previously done. Thus by burning up, by making an end of ancient deeds, by the non-doing of new deeds, there is no overflowing into the future. From there being no overflowing into the future comes the destruction of deeds; from the destruction of deeds comes the destruction of anguish; from the destruction of anguish comes the destruction of feeling; from the destruction of feeling all anguish will become worn away." ' Again, monks, I, speaking thus, beheld no reasoned response among the Jains.

And again, monks, I spoke to these Jains thus: ' What do you think about this, reverend Jains ? Is it possible to say: " Let that deed[1] which is to be experienced here and now be, through effort or striving, one to be experienced in a future state (instead)[2] " ?'

' Not this, your reverence.'

' Is it possible to say: " Let that deed which is to be experienced in a future state be, through effort or striving, one to be experienced here and now (instead)" ?'

' Not this, your reverence.'

' What do you think about this, reverend Jains ? Is it possible to say: " Let that deed which is to be experienced as pleasant be, through effort or striving, one to be experienced as painful ? " '

' Not this, your reverence.'

' But is it possible to say: " Let that deed which is to be experienced as painful be, through effort or striving, one to be experienced as pleasant ?" '

' Not this, your reverence.'

' What do you think about this, reverend Jains ? Is it possible to say: " Let that deed which is to be experienced as thoroughly ripened[3] be, through effort or striving, one to be experienced as not thoroughly ripened ?[4]" '

---

[1] *M*. ii. 220 reads *kamma*, deed, throughout. *MA*. iv. 4 supplies *vipākadāyaka*, whose fruits are produced: in this very existence.

[2] *I.e.* in a future birth, such as the second or third from this one. For the following pairs of questions, see *A*. iv. 382.

[3] *I.e.* in this birth (*attabhāva*, individuality). *MA*. iv. 5 says: whatever is done in youth gives its fruit, *vipāka*, in youth, middle or old age; if done in middle age, the fruit is in middle or old age; if done in old age it gives its fruit then—this is called what is to be experienced here and now, *diṭṭhadhammavedanīya*. But whatever gives its fruit within seven days is called " to be experienced as thoroughly ripened," *paripakkavedanīya* (or, to be experienced complete). *Cf. AA*. iv. 175: *laddhavipākavāra*.

[4] *I.e.* some of the effects or fruits overflowing into future births.

'Not this, your reverence.'

'But is it possible to say: "Let that deed which is to be experienced as not thoroughly ripened be, through striving or effort, one to be experienced as thoroughly ripened " ?'

'Not this, your reverence.'

'What do you think about this, reverend Jains ? [221] Is it possible to say: " Let that deed which is to be much experienced be, through effort or striving, one to be little experienced " ?'

'Not this, your reverence.'

'But is it possible to say: "Let that deed which is to be little experienced be, through effort or striving, one to be much experienced " ?'

'Not this, your reverence.'

'What do you think about this, reverend Jains ? Is it possible to say: " Let that deed which is to be experienced[1] be, through effort or striving, one not to be experienced " ?'

'Not this, your reverence.'

'But is it possible to say: " Let that deed which is not to be experienced be, through effort or striving, one to be experienced " ?'

'Not this, your reverence.'

'So really it is, reverend Jains: It is not possible to say: " Let that deed which is to be experienced here and now be, through effort or striving, one to be experienced in a future state . . . Let that deed which is to be experienced in a future state be, through effort or striving, one to be experienced here and now . . . Let that deed which is to be experienced as pleasant be . . . experienced as painful. Let that deed which is to be experienced as painful be . . . experienced as pleasant. Let that deed which is to be experienced as thoroughly ripened be . . . experienced as not thoroughly ripened. Let that deed which is to be experienced as not thoroughly ripened be . . . experienced as thoroughly ripened. Let that deed which is to be much experienced be . . . one to be little experienced. Let that deed which is to be little experienced be . . . one to be much experienced. Let that deed which is to be experienced be . . . one not to be experienced. Let that deed which is not to be experienced be . . . one to be experienced." This being so, the effort of the reverend Jains [222] is fruitless, their striving fruitless.' Monks, Jains speak thus; monks, the ten reasoned theses of the Jains who speak thus give occasion for contempt.[2]

---

[1] *vedanīya*, explained at *MA*. iv. 9 as *savipākakamma*, a deed with a result or fruit. *Cf. AA*. iv. 175.

[2] See *M*. i. 368 (and *M.L.S*. ii. 33 for further references).

If, monks, the pleasure and pain which creatures undergo are due to what was previously done,[1] certainly, monks, the Jains were formerly doers of deeds that were badly done in that they now experience such painful, severe, sharp feelings. If, monks, the pleasure and pain which creatures undergo are due to creation by an overlord,[1] certainly, monks, the Jains were created by an evil overlord in that they now experience such painful, severe, sharp feelings. If, monks, the pleasure and pain which creatures undergo are due to necessary conditions,[2] certainly, monks, the Jains are evil of necessity in that they now experience such painful, severe, sharp feelings. If, monks, the pleasure and pain which creatures undergo are due to the species[3] (to which they belong), certainly, monks, the Jains are of an evil species in that they now experience such painful, severe, sharp feelings. If, monks, the pleasure and pain which creatures undergo are due to effort here and now, certainly, monks, the Jains are of evil effort here and now in that they now experience such painful, severe, sharp feelings. If, monks, the pleasure and pain which creatures undergo are due to what was previously done, the Jains are contemptible; and if the pleasure and pain which creatures undergo is not due to what was previously done the Jains are contemptible. If, monks, the pleasure and pain which creatures undergo are due to ... not due to creation by an overlord, the Jains are contemptible. If, monks, the pleasure and pain which creatures undergo are due to ... not due to necessary conditions, the Jains are contemptible. If monks, the pleasure and pain which creatures undergo are due to ... not due to necessary conditions, the Jains are contemptible. If, monks, the pleasure and pain which creatures undergo are due to ... not due to the species (to which they belong), the Jains are contemptible. If, monks, the pleasure and pain which creatures undergo are due to ... not due to effort here and now, [**223**] the Jains are contemptible. Monks, Jains speak thus; monks, these ten reasoned theses of the Jains who speak thus give occasion for contempt. Even so, monks, is fruitless effort, fruitless striving.

And how, monks, is effort fruitful, striving fruitful ? Herein, monks, a monk does not let his unmastered self be mastered by anguish, and he does not cast out rightful happiness and is undefiled

---

[1] *Cf. A.* i. 173.
[2] *Cf. D.* i. 53 for *saṅgatibhāva*, destiny or fate.
[3] *abhijāti. MA.* iv. 10 interprets as the six species or classes into which certain heretical teachers divided mankind. See *M.* i. 517, *D.* i. 53, *A.* iii. 383. But apparently used in a Buddhist sense above and at *D.* iii. 250, *Netti.* 158.

by[1] that happiness. He comprehends thus: ' While I am striving against the aggregate[2] of this source of anguish,[3] from striving against the aggregate there is detachment for me. But while I am indifferent to that source of anguish, through (my) developing equanimity there is detachment for me.' While (a monk) is striving against the aggregate of this source of anguish, from striving against the aggregate there is detachment for him—accordingly[4] he strives against the aggregate; but while he is indifferent to that source of anguish, through (his) developing equanimity there is detachment for him—accordingly he develops equanimity. While he is striving against the aggregate of that source of anguish, from striving against the aggregate there is detachment (for him). Even so is that anguish worn away for him. While he is indifferent to that[5] source of anguish, through (his) developing equanimity there is detachment for him. Even so is that anguish also worn away for him.

Monks, it is like a man, passionately in love with a woman, his desire acute, his longing acute. He might see that woman standing and talking, joking and laughing with another man. What do you think about this, monks ? Would it not be that grief, sorrow, suffering, lamentation and despair did not rise up in that man when he saw that woman standing and talking, joking and laughing with another man ? "

" Yes, revered sir. What is the reason for this ? It is that that man is passionately in love with that woman, his desire acute, his longing acute. [224] Therefore, seeing that woman standing and ... laughing with another man, grief, sorrow, suffering, lamentation and despair rise up (in him)."

" But then, monks, that man might think thus: ' I am passionately in love with this woman, my desire acute, my longing acute; grief, sorrow, suffering, lamentation and despair rise up in me when I see this woman standing and ... laughing with another man. Suppose I were to get rid of my desire and attachment for that woman ? ' So he may get rid of his desire and attachment for that woman. After a time he may see that woman standing and ... laughing with another

---

[1] *anadhimucchito hoti*, with loc. " undefiled " because he does not cling to the happiness.
[2] *saṁkhāraṁ padahato ti sampayogaṁ viriyaṁ karontassa*, MA. iv. 11.
[3] MA. iv. 11 says the source of the anguish of the five *khandhā* is in thirst or craving, *taṇhā*.
[4] *tattha*, " he strives with the striving of the Way," MA. iv. 12.
[5] *tassa tassa*. But I think the duplication is an error.

man. What do you think about this, monks ? Would it not be that grief, sorrow, suffering, lamentation and despair did not rise up in that man on seeing that woman standing and talking, joking and laughing with that other man ? "

" No, revered sir. What is the reason for this ? It is, revered sir, that this man is (now) without passion for that woman. Therefore on seeing that woman standing and talking, joking and laughing with another man, grief, sorrow, suffering, lamentation and despair do not rise up (in him)."

" Even so, monks, one does not let his unmastered self be mastered by anguish . . . (as above) . . . Even so is that anguish worn away for him; [225] while he is indifferent to that source of anguish, through (his) developing equanimity there is detachment for him. Even so is that anguish also worn away for him. Thus, monks, is effort fruitful, is striving fruitful.

And again, monks, a monk reflects thus: ' Dwelling as I please, unskilled states grow much, skilled states decline, but while striving against my self through anguish[1] unskilled states decline, skilled states grow much. Suppose I were to strive against self through anguish ? ' He strives against self through anguish; striving against self through anguish his unskilled states decline, skilled states grow much. After a time he does not strive against self through anguish. What is the reason for this ? Monks, the purpose[2] of that monk who might strive against self through anguish is accomplished, therefore after a time he does not strive against self through anguish. Monks, it is like a fletcher who heats and scorches a shaft between two fire-brands to make it straight and serviceable. But when, monks, the fletcher's shaft has been heated and scorched between the two fire-brands and made straight and serviceable, he no longer heats and scorches the shaft between the two fire-brands to make it straight and serviceable. What is the reason for this ? Monks, the purpose for which the fletcher might heat and scorch the shaft between the two fire-brands to make it straight and serviceable is accomplished; therefore he no longer heats and scorches it between the two fire-brands to make it straight and serviceable. Even so, monks, a monk reflects thus: ' Dwelling as I please, unskilled states grow much, skilled states decline . . .' After a time he does not strive against self through anguish. [226] What is the reason for this ? It is, monks, that that purpose for which the monk might

---

[1] dukkhāya pana me attānaṁ padahato.   [2] attha, aim, goal, purpose.

strive against self through anguish is accomplished, therefore he no longer strives against self through anguish. So too, monks, is effort fruitful, is striving fruitful.

And again, monks, a Tathāgata arises here in the world, perfected one, fully Self-awakened One, endowed with right knowledge and conduct, well-farer, knower of the worlds ... (*as at M.L.S.* i. 223-227) ... he purifies his mind of doubt.

He, by getting rid of these five hindrances, which are defilements of the mind and deleterious to intuitive wisdom, aloof from pleasures of the senses, aloof from unskilled states of mind, enters and abides in the first meditation, which is accompanied by initial thought and discursive thought, is born of aloofness and is rapturous and joyful. Thus too, monks, is effort fruitful, striving fruitful.

And again, monks, a monk, by allaying initial thought and discursive thought, his mind subjectively tranquillised and fixed on one point, enters and abides in the second meditation, which is devoid of initial thought and discursive thought, is born of concentration and is rapturous and joyful. Thus too, monks, is effort fruitful, striving fruitful.

And again, monks, a monk, by the fading out of rapture, dwells with equanimity, attentive and clearly conscious, and he experiences in his person that joy of which the ariyans say: 'Joyful lives he who has equanimity and is mindful,' and he enters and abides in the third meditation. Thus too, monks, is effort fruitful, striving fruitful.

And again, monks, a monk, by getting rid of joy, by getting rid of anguish, by the going down of his former pleasures and sorrows, enters and abides in the fourth meditation, which has neither anguish nor joy, and which is entirely purified by equanimity and mindfulness. Thus too, monks, is effort fruitful, striving fruitful.

Thus with mind composed, quite purified ... (*as at M.L.S.* i. 228-229) ... Thus he recollects divers former habitations in all their mode and detail. Thus too, monks, is effort fruitful, striving fruitful.

Thus with the mind composed, quite purified ... (*as at M.L.S.* i. 229) ... he comprehends that beings are mean, excellent, foul, fair, in a good bourn, in a bad bourn, according to the consequences of deeds. Thus too, monks, is effort fruitful, striving fruitful.

[227] Thus with the mind composed, quite purified ... (*as at M.L.S.* i. 229) ... he comprehends: 'Destroyed is birth, brought to a close the Brahma-faring, done is what was to be done, there is no

more of being such or so.' Thus too, monks, is effort fruitful, striving fruitful.

The Tathāgata speaks thus, monks; ten reasoned theses of a Tathāgata who speaks thus, monks, give occasion for praise:[1] if, monks, the pleasure and pain which creatures undergo are due to what was previously done, certainly, monks, the Tathāgata was formerly a doer of deeds that were well done in that he now experiences such cankerless pleasant feelings. If, monks, the pleasure and pain which creatures undergo are due to creation by an overlord, certainly, monks, the Tathāgata was created by an auspicious overlord in that he now experiences such cankerless pleasant feelings. If, monks, the pleasure and pain which creatures undergo are due to necessary conditions, certainly, monks, the Tathāgata is lovely of necessity in that he now experiences such cankerless pleasant feelings. If, monks, the pleasure and pain which creatures undergo are due to the species (to which they belong), certainly, monks, the Tathāgata is of a lovely species in that he now experiences such cankerless pleasant feelings. If, monks, the pleasure and pain which creatures undergo are due to effort here and now, certainly, monks, the Tathāgata is of lovely effort here and now in that he now experiences such cankerless pleasant feelings. If, monks, the pleasure and pain which creatures undergo are due to what was previously done, the Tathāgata is praiseworthy; and if the pleasure and pain which creatures undergo is not due to what was previously done, the Tathāgata is praiseworthy. If, monks, the pleasure and pain which creatures undergo are due to ... not due to creation by an overlord, the Tathāgata is praiseworthy. If, monks, the pleasure and pain which creatures undergo are due to ... not due to necessary conditions, the Tathāgata is praiseworthy. If, monks, the pleasure and pain which creatures undergo are due to ... not due to the species (to which they belong), the Tathāgata is praiseworthy. If, monks, the pleasure and pain which creatures undergo are due to ... not due to effort here and now, [228] the Tathāgata is praiseworthy. Monks, the Tathāgata speaks thus; monks, these ten reasoned theses of the Tathāgata who speaks thus give occasion for praise."

Thus spoke the Lord. Delighted, these monks rejoiced in what the Lord had said.

Discourse at Devadaha:
The First

---

[1] At *A.* v. 129 a different ten are given.

102. DISCOURSE ON THE THREEFOLD FIVE[1]
(Pañcattayasutta)

THUS have I heard: At one time the Lord was staying near Sāvatthī in the Jeta Grove in Anāthapiṇḍika's monastery. While he was there the Lord addressed the monks, saying: "Monks." "Revered One," these monks answered the Lord in assent. The Lord spoke thus: "There are, monks, some recluses and brahmans[2] who, conjecturing about the future,[3] speculating about the future, in many a figure maintain assertions concerning the future.[4] Some maintain[5] that after dying the self, unimpaired,[6] perceives.[7] Some maintain[8] that after dying the self, unimpaired, does not perceive. Some maintain[9] that after dying the self, unimpaired, neither perceives nor does not perceive. They lay down[10] the cutting off, the destruction, the

---

[1] This Discourse, an exposition of heretical views, should be read in conjunction with the *Brahmajāla-suttanta* (to which the Comy. refers) and also with the *Mahānidāna-suttanta* §23 *et seq.* (*D.* Stas. Nos. 1 and 15.)

[2] *MA.* iv. 5: recluses because they have gone forth, brahmans by birth; or, they are called "recluses" and "brahmans" by the world. So *samaṇabrāhmaṇā* should be translated either "recluses and brahmans" or "brahman recluses." But since the phrase *samaṇo vā brāhmaṇo vā* is found later in the Sta., I have chosen the former rendering.

[3] *aparantakappika*, or, "supposing there is a future." On the two *kappas* of craving, *taṇhā*, and views, *diṭṭhi*, see *Nd.* I. 112-113. The former is associated with thoughts of "mine," the latter with false views about one's own body (see below, p. 19), other false views and with taking up extreme views. Cf. *D.* i. 30 *f.*

[4] As at *D.* i. 30, which adds "on forty-four grounds."

[5] In sixteen ways, *MA.* iv. 16. For these see *D.* i. 31.

[6] *aroga*, not ill, hale, healthy; but *MA.* iv. 16, *DA.* 119 give *nicca*, enduring, permanent. Rhys Davids, at *Dial.* i. 44 *ff.*, translated as "not subject to decay."

[7] *saññin*, is perceptive, perceiving. I keep to this rather than to "consciousness" which Rhys Davids uses, because I use "perception" for *saññā* (as one of the *khandha*) and "consciousness" for *viññāṇa* (also a *khandha*, etc.).

[8] In eight ways, *MA.* iv. 16. For these see *D.* i. 32.

[9] Also in eight ways, *MA.* iv. 16. For these see *D.* i. 33.

[10] On seven grounds, see *D.* i. 34-35. *Bṛhad. Up.* II. 4. 12-14 states the problem of consciousness, *vijñāna*, and the lack of it, in a clear manner. *Cf.* also *Kaṭha Up.* I. 1. 20: "there is doubt about a man who has 'departed,' *prete*, some saying he is and others that he is not," and see Radhakrishnan, *The Principal Upanishads*, p. 603.

disappearance[1] of the essential being.[2] Or some maintain there is nibbāna here and now.[3] Thus they lay down that after dying the self, unimpaired, is existent.[4] Or they lay down the cutting off, the destruction, the disappearance of the essential being. Or some maintain that there is nibbāna here and now. Thus these (theories), having been five become three, having been three become five. This is the exposition of the three fives.

As to this, monks, those recluses and brahmans who [**229**] lay down that after dying the self, unimpaired, perceives—these worthy recluses and brahmans lay down that after dying the self, perceiving and unimpaired, has form;[5] or these worthy recluses and brahmans lay down that after dying the self, perceiving and unimpaired, has not form ... both has and has not form ... neither has nor has not form. Or these worthy recluses and brahmans lay down that after dying the self, perceiving and unimpaired, perceives unity[6] ... diversity ... the limited[7] ... the immeasurable. But some of these maintain that this consciousness-device[8] when gone beyond is immeasurable, imperturbable. As to this, monks, the Tathāgata comprehends that there are those recluses and brahmans who lay down that after dying the self, unimpaired, perceives; and that these recluses and brahmans either lay down that after dying the self, perceiving and unimpaired, has form; or these recluses and brahmans lay down that after dying the self, perceiving and unimpaired, has not form; or ... both has and has not form; or ... neither has nor has not form; or ... perceives unity; or ... perceives diversity; or ... perceives the limited; or ... perceives the immeasurable. Or (he comprehends) which of these (forms of) perception is pointed out

---

[1] As at *D.* i. 34; on seven grounds. *MA.* iv. 16, *DA.* 120 say that these three terms are synonymous, but they gloss *vināsa* by *adassana* and *vibhava* by *bhavavigama*.

[2] As at *M.* i. 140, where this thesis was wrongly ascribed to Gotama.

[3] On five grounds. See *D.* i. 36. *MA.* iv. 17, *DA.* 121 say that this is the allaying of anguish in this very existence.

[4] *santaṁ*, *i.e.* in reference to the three modes of consciousness.

[5] See *D.* i. 31.

[6] See *D.* i. 31. *MA.* iv. 18, *DA.* 119 appear to refer this to the *samāpatti*, the nine meditative attainments, while "diversity" or multiformity is incomplete attainment.

[7] *DA.* 119 refers "limited," the small, *paritta*, and "the immeasurable" to the *kasiṇa*-devices.

[8] *viññāṇakasiṇa*. See *M.* ii. 14-15, *A.* v. 60, where each of the ten "devices" is to be understood in five ways, the fifth way being as "immeasurable."

as absolutely pure, the highest, the best, the pre-eminent: [**230**] whether perception of fine-materiality,[1] perception of immateriality,[2] perception of unity or perception of diversity. Saying, 'There is no-thing,'[3] some maintain that the plane of no-thing-ness is immeasurable, imperturbable. Knowing that what is constructed[4] is gross-material,[5] but that there is this that is the stopping of the constructions,[6] the Tathāgata, seeing the escape from it,[7] has gone beyond it.

As to this, monks, those recluses and brahmans who lay down that after dying the self, unimpaired, does not perceive—these worthy recluses and brahmans lay down that after dying the self, not perceiving and unimpaired, has form . . . has not form . . . both has and has not form . . . neither has nor has not form. As to this, monks, some revile those recluses and brahmans who lay down that after dying the self perceives and is unimpaired. What is the reason for this ? They say, ' Perception is an ill, perception is an imposthume, perception is a barb; this is the real, this the excellent, that is to say non-perception.' As to this, monks, the Tathāgata comprehends that there are those recluses and brahmans who lay down that after dying the self, unimpaired, does not perceive; and that these recluses and brahmans either lay down that after dying the self, not perceiving and unimpaired, has form; or these recluses and brahmans lay down that after dying the self, not perceiving and unimpaired, has not form; or . . both has and has not form; or . . . neither has nor has not form. Monks, this situation does not occur that any recluse or brahman could say: 'Apart from material shape, apart from feeling, apart from perception, apart from the habitual tendencies, apart from consciousness, I will lay

---

[1] This refers to the fourth *jhāna*. *Cf. Expos.* i. 216 *ff.*
[2] This refers to the planes of infinite *ākāsa* and infinite consciousness, *MA.* iv. 18. *Cf. Expos.* i. 269 *ff.*
[3] At *A.* v. 63, according to the perception of some beings this is the topmost perception.
[4] *MA.* iv. 19 says that all this—perception together with views—is constructed and formed by the coming together of conditions, *paccaya*.
[5] *oḷārika*, material, gross, coarse.
[6] *saṁkhārā*, or activities. This is nibbāna, according to *MA.* iv. 19. At *S.* iv. 217 the stopping of the *saṁkhārā* is spoken of as gradual. See *M.L.S.* i. Intr., p. xxiv.
[7] *I.e.* from the compounded. On the stopping of whatever is the compounded being the escape from it, see *D.* iii. 275, *Iti.* p. 61, and *cf. Iti.* p. 37, *Ud.* 80.

down a coming or a going or a deceasing or an uprising or expansion or maturity.'[1] Knowing that what is constructed is gross-material, [231] but that there is this that is the stopping of the constructions, the Tathāgata, seeing the escape from it, has gone beyond it.

As to this, monks, those recluses and brahmans who lay down that after dying the self, unimpaired, neither perceives nor does not perceive—these worthy recluses and brahmans lay down that after dying the self, neither perceiving nor not perceiving and unimpaired, has form . . . has not form . . . both has and has not form . . . neither has nor has not form. As to this, monks, some revile those recluses and brahmans who lay down that after dying the self perceives and is unimpaired, and some also revile those worthy recluses and brahmans who lay down that after dying the self, unimpaired, does not perceive. What is the reason for this ? They say, ' Perception is an ill, an imposthume, a barb; lack of perception is confusion; this is the real, this the excellent, that is to say neither-perception-nor-not-perception.' As to this, monks, the Tathāgata comprehends that there are those recluses and brahmans who lay down that after dying the self, unimpaired, neither perceives nor does not perceive; and that these recluses and brahmans lay down that after dying the self, unimpaired, neither perceiving nor not perceiving, either has form; or . . . has not form; or . . . both has and has not form; or . . . neither has nor has not form. Yet whoever are the recluses and brahmans who lay down the acquiring of this plane merely through the activities[2] of what is to be seen, heard, experienced, cognised—this is shown, monks, as destructive to acquiring that plane. [232] For it is not this plane, monks, that is shown to be attainable by attainments which have the constructions present; this plane is shown, monks, to be attainable by attainments where no constructions remain.[3] Knowing that what is constructed[4] is gross-material, but that there is this that is the stopping of the constructions, the Tathāgata, seeing the escape from it, has gone beyond it.

As to this, monks, those recluses and brahmans who lay down the cutting off, the destruction, the disappearance of the essential being— as to this, monks, some revile those recluses and brahmans who lay down that after dying the self, unimpaired, perceives; and some also

---

[1] A statement ascribed at *MA.* iv. 20 to sophists, *vitaṇḍavādī*.

[2] *saṁkhāramattena*, referring to *oḷārika*, the gross or material *saṁkhārā*, *MA.* iv. 20. " This plane " is of course that of neither-perception-nor-not-perception.

[3] This plane is subtle, *sukhuma*.   [4] *saṅkhata*.

revile those worthy recluses and brahmans who lay down that after dying the self, unimpaired, does not perceive; and some also revile those worthy recluses and brahmans who lay down that after dying the self, unimpaired, neither perceives nor does not perceive. What is the reason for this ? It is that all these worthy recluses and brahmans loftily maintain attachment[1] itself, saying: ' We will be such hereafter, we will be such hereafter.'[2] It is as though a merchant who has gone out trading should think, ' I will have this from there, I will get this from that '—even so methinks these worthy recluses and brahmans are like the merchant when they say, ' We will be such hereafter, we will be such hereafter.' As to this, monks, the Tathāgata comprehends: Those worthy recluses and brahmans who lay down the cutting off, the destruction, the disappearance of the essential being, these, afraid of their own body, loathing their own body, simply keep running and circling round their own body. Just as a dog[3] that is tied by a leash to a strong post or stake [233] keeps running and circling round that post or stake, so do these worthy recluses and brahmans, afraid of their own body, loathing their own body, simply keep running and circling round their own body. Knowing that what is constructed is gross-material, but that there is this that is the stopping of the constructions, the Tathāgata, seeing the escape from it, has gone beyond it.

Whatever recluses and brahmans, monks, conjecturing about the future, speculating about the future, in many a figure maintain assertions concerning the future, all maintain precisely these five positions,[4] or one of them.

There are, monks, some recluses and brahmans who, conjecturing about the past, speculating about the past, in many a figure maintain assertions concerning the past. Some maintain, ' Eternal is self and the world,[5] this is indeed the truth, all else is falsehood.' Some maintain, ' Not eternal is self and the world,[6] this is indeed the truth, all else is falsehood.' Some maintain, ' Both eternal and not eternal is self and the world[7] . . . falsehood.' Some maintain,

---

[1] *āsatti*, sticking to, craving.
[2] A noble warrior or a brahman, *MA*. iv. 21.
[3] *Cf. S.* iii. 150.
[4] *āyatana*, here glossed at *MA*. iv. 22 by *kāraṇāni*. Now, after having spoken of the 44 assertions concerning the future, the 18 concerning the past will be spoken of (beginning with the next paragraph).
[5] *Cf. D.* i. 13, 43; the views of the Eternalists.
[6] The views of the Annihilationists.
[7] The views of the partial-eternalists, see *D.* i. 17.

' Neither eternal nor not eternal is self and the world[1] . . . falsehood.'
Some maintain, ' Having an end is self and the world[2] . . . falsehood.'
Some maintain, ' Not having an end is self and the world . . . falsehood.' Some maintain, ' Both having an end and not having an end is self and the world . . . falsehood.' Some maintain, ' Neither having an end nor not having an end is self and the world, this is indeed the truth, all else is falsehood.' Some maintain, ' Perceptive of unity is self and the world . . . falsehood.' Some maintain, ' Perceptive of diversity is self and the world . . . falsehood.' Some maintain, ' Perceptive of the limited is self and the world . . . falsehood.' Some maintain, ' Perceptive of the immeasurable is self and the world, this is indeed the truth, all else is falsehood.' Some maintain, ' Exclusively happy is self and the world[3] . . . falsehood.' Some maintain, ' Exclusively sorrowful is self and the world . . . [234] . . . falsehood.' Some maintain, ' Happy and sorrowful is self and the world . . . falsehood.' Some maintain, ' Not sorrowful nor happy is self and the world, this is indeed the truth, all else is falsehood.' Monks, as for those recluses and brahmans who speak thus and are of this view: ' Eternal is self and the world, this is indeed the truth, all else is falsehood '—this situation cannot occur that, apart from faith, apart from inclination, apart from tradition, apart from consideration of reasons, apart from reflection on and approval of some view, knowledge will become thoroughly pure for each one, thoroughly cleansed.[4] If, monks, knowledge is not thoroughly pure for each one, not thoroughly cleansed, even that mere fraction of knowledge that these worthy recluses and brahmans thoroughly cleanse, even that is pointed out as grasping on the part of these worthy recluses and brahmans. Knowing that what is constructed is gross-material, but that there is this that is the stopping of the constructions, the Tathāgata, seeing the escape from it, has gone beyond it.

Monks, as for those recluses and brahmans who speak thus and are of this view: ' Not eternal is self and the world . . . Both eternal and not eternal . . . world . . . Neither eternal nor not eternal is self and the world . . . Having an end is self and the world . . . Not having an end . . . Both having and not having an end . . . Neither having an end nor not having an end is self and the world . . . Conscious of

---

[1] The views of the " eel-wrigglers," see *D.* i. 24-27, *Pts.* i. 155.
[2] See *D.* i. 31. [3] *Cf. M.* ii. 35 *f.*
[4] *Cf. S.* ii. 115 where the monk Musīla knew, apart from faith, etc., that " the stopping of becoming is nibbāna," and was classed among the arahants.

unity is self and the world ... Conscious of diversity ... Conscious of the limited ... Conscious of the immeasurable is self and the world ... Exclusively happy is self and the world ... Exclusively sorrowful ... Happy and sorrowful ... Not sorrowful nor happy is self and the world, this is indeed the truth, all else is falsehood '—this situation cannot occur that, apart from faith, apart from ... reflection on and approval of some view, knowledge will become thoroughly pure for each one, thoroughly cleansed. [**235**] If, monks, knowledge is not thoroughly pure for each one, not thoroughly cleansed, even that mere fraction of knowledge that these worthy recluses and brahmans thoroughly cleanse, even that is pointed out as a grasping on the part of these worthy recluses and brahmans. Knowing that what is constructed is gross-material, but that there is this that is the stopping of the constructions, the Tathāgata, seeing the escape from it, has gone beyond it.

In this case,[1] monks, some recluse or brahman by casting out speculation concerning the past and by casting out speculation concerning the future, by not throughout fixing his mind on the fetters of the senses, entering on the rapture of aloofness,[2] abides therein. He thinks, 'This is the real, this the excellent, that is to say, entering on the rapture of aloofness I am abiding therein.' But if that rapture of aloofness of his is stopped,[3] from the stopping of the rapture of aloofness sorrow arises; from the stopping of sorrow, the rapture of aloofness arises. As, monks, the heat of the sun suffuses whatever the shade quits, as the shade suffuses whatever the heat of the sun quits, even so, monks, from the stopping of the rapture of aloofness, sorrow arises; from the stopping of sorrow, the rapture of aloofness arises. As to this, monks, the Tathāgata comprehends: 'This worthy recluse or brahman, by casting out speculation concerning the past, by casting out speculation concerning the future, by not throughout fixing his mind on the fetters of the senses ...

---

[1] *MA.* iv. 25 says that up to here the 62 views have been handed down in the *Brahmajāla*: the four eternalist views, the four partial-eternalist, the four about " end " and " no end," the four eel-wrigglings, the two concerned with " attainment," the sixteen views on the " perceiving " person, the eight on the non-perceiving person, the eight on the person who neither perceives nor does not perceive, the seven annihilationist views, and the five views of nibbāna here and now. But in this Discourse (*i.e.* M. Sta. 102) views of " own body " are also spoken of (see above, p. 19).

[2] *pavivekaṁ pītiṁ.* The rapture, *pīti*, of the first two *jhāna* in which it is an element.

[3] With the stopping of these two *jhāna*.

from the stopping of sorrow, the rapture of aloofness arises.' Knowing that what is constructed is gross-material, but that there is this that is the stopping of the constructions, the Tathāgata, seeing the escape from it, has gone beyond it.

But in this case, monks, some recluse or brahman by casting out speculation concerning the past and by casting out speculation concerning the future, by not throughout fixing his mind on the fetters of the senses, by passing beyond the rapture of aloofness, entering on spiritual happiness,[1] abides therein. He thinks, ' This is the real, this the excellent, that is to say, entering on spiritual happiness I am abiding therein.' But if that spiritual happiness of his is stopped, from the stopping of spiritual happiness there arises the rapture of aloofness; from the stopping of the rapture of aloofness spiritual [**236**] happiness arises. As, monks, the heat of the sun suffuses whatever the shade quits, as the shade suffuses whatever the heat of the sun quits, even so, monks, from the stopping of spiritual happiness there arises the rapture of aloofness; from the stopping of the rapture of aloofness spiritual happiness arises. As to this, monks, the Tathāgata comprehends: ' This worthy recluse or brahman, by casting out speculation . . . from the stopping of the rapture of aloofness spiritual happiness arises.' Knowing that what is constructed is gross-material, but that there is this that is the stopping of the constructions, the Tathāgata, seeing the escape from it, has gone beyond it.

In this case, monks, some recluse or brahman by casting out speculation concerning the past and by casting out speculation concerning the future, by not fixing his mind throughout on the fetters of the senses, by passing beyond the rapture of aloofness, by passing beyond spiritual happiness, entering on feeling that is neither painful nor pleasant,[2] abides therein. He thinks, ' This is the real, this the excellent, that is to say, entering on feeling that is neither painful nor pleasant I am abiding therein.' But if that feeling of his that is neither painful nor pleasant is stopped, from the stopping of the feeling that is neither painful nor pleasant there arises spiritual happiness; from the stopping of spiritual happiness there arises a feeling that is neither painful nor pleasant. As,

---

[1] *I.e.* the third *jhāna*. The word *nirāmisa*, as the opposite of the " physical," is hard to translate here. In some contexts " ghostly " is not too far away from the meaning. Chalmers gives " bliss immaterial "; but I have used " immaterial " for *arūpa*.

[2] The fourth *jhāna*.

monks, the heat of the sun suffuses whatever the shade quits, as the shade suffuses whatever the heat of the sun quits, even so, monks, from the stopping of feeling that is neither painful nor pleasant there arises spiritual happiness; from the stopping of spiritual happiness feeling that is neither painful nor pleasant arises. As to this, monks, the Tathāgata comprehends: This worthy recluse or brahman, by casting out speculation concerning the past and by casting out speculation concerning the future, by not throughout attending to the fetters of the senses, by passing beyond the rapture of aloofness, by passing beyond spiritual happiness, entering on feeling that is neither painful nor pleasant, abides therein. He thinks, ' This is the real, this the excellent, that is to say, [237] entering on feeling that is neither painful nor pleasant I am abiding therein.' If that feeling of his that is neither painful nor pleasant is stopped, from the stopping of the feeling that is neither painful nor pleasant there arises spiritual happiness; from the stopping of spiritual happiness feeling that is neither painful nor pleasant arises. Knowing that what is constructed is gross-material, but that there is this that is the stopping of the constructions, the Tathāgata, seeing the escape from it, has gone beyond it.

But in this case, monks, some recluse or brahman, by casting out speculation concerning the past and by casting out speculation concerning the future, by not throughout fixing his mind on the fetters of the senses, by passing beyond the rapture of aloofness, by passing beyond spiritual happiness, by passing beyond feeling that is neither painful nor pleasant, beholds, ' Tranquil am I, allayed am I, without grasping am I.' As to this, monks, the Tathāgata comprehends: This worthy recluse or brahman . . . beholds, ' Tranquil am I, allayed am I, without grasping am I '—certainly this venerable one maintains the very course that is suitable for nibbāna.[1] On the other hand, *that* worthy recluse or brahman, grasping, either grasps after speculation concerning the past[2] or, grasping, grasps after speculation concerning the future[3] or, grasping, grasps after a fetter of the senses or, grasping, grasps after the rapture of aloofness or, grasping, grasps after spiritual happiness or, grasping, grasps after feeling that is neither painful nor pleasant. And inasmuch as this venerable one beholds, ' Tranquil am I, allayed am I, without grasping am I,' this too is shown as a grasping on the part of that

---

[1] *Cf. S.* iv. 133. [2] Eighteen views.
[3] Forty-four views which, with the above eighteen, together constitute the sixty-two heretical views.

worthy recluse or brahman. Knowing that what is constructed is gross-material, but that there is this that is the stopping of the constructions, the Tathāgata, seeing the escape from it, has gone beyond it.

But now, monks, this incomparable matchless path to peace[1] was awakened to by the Tathāgata, that is to say, having known the arising and the setting and the satisfaction and the peril of the six fields of sensory impingement and the escape as it really is, there is deliverance without grasping.[2] And as, monks, this incomparable matchless path to peace was awakened to by the Tathāgata, [**238**] that is to say, having known the arising and the setting and the satisfaction and the peril of the six fields of sensory impingement and the escape as it really is, there is deliverance without grasping."

Thus spoke the Lord. Delighted, these monks rejoiced in what the Lord had said.

Discourse on the Threefold Five:
The Second

103. DISCOURSE ON "WHAT THEN?"
(Kintisutta)

THUS have I heard: At one time the Lord was staying near Kusinārā in the Wood of the Offerings.[3] While he was there, the Lord addressed the monks, saying: "Monks." "Revered One," these monks answered the Lord in assent. The Lord spoke thus: "What then is there for you, monks, in me ? Is it that the recluse Gotama teaches *dhamma* for the sake of robe-material or that the recluse Gotama teaches *dhamma* for the sake of almsfood or that the recluse Gotama teaches *dhamma* for the sake of lodgings or that the

---

[1] *Cf. M.* i. 163.
[2] *Cf. A.* v. 64; also *D.* i. 17. *Anupāda* is "without clinging" or grasping, and therefore without further "fuel" for *saṁsāra*. *MA.* iv. 28 says that this elsewhere is nibbāna, but here it is the attainment of the fruit of arahantship.
[3] Baliharaṇa, so called because they bring oblations here for creatures. Mentioned also at *A.* i. 174, v. 79. See *G.S.* i. 251, v. 55 for notes.

recluse Gotama teaches *dhamma* for the sake of success or decline[1] in this or that ?"

" No, Lord; we do not think, The recluse Gotama teaches *dhamma* for the sake of almsfood . . . for the sake of success or decline in this or that."

" Certainly, monks, there is not this for you in me that the recluse Gotama teaches *dhamma* for the sake of . . . success or decline in this or that. So what then is there, monks, for you in me ?"

" It is thus, Lord, in the Lord for us: The Lord, compassionate, seeking welfare, teaches *dhamma* out of compassion."

" Certainly, monks, it is thus for you in me: The Lord, compassionate, seeking welfare, teaches *dhamma* out of compassion.

Wherefore, monks, those things taught to you by me out of super-knowledge,[2] that is to say the four applications of mindfulness, the four right efforts, the four bases of psychic power, the five controlling faculties, the five powers, the seven [**239**] links in awakening, the ariyan eightfold Way—all together, in harmony and without contention you should train yourselves in each and all of these. But when you, monks, all together, in harmony and without contention have trained yourselves in these, there might be two monks speaking differently about Further-*dhamma*.[3] If it should occur to you concerning this: ' Between these venerable ones there is a difference as to denotation and a difference as to connotation,' then, approaching that monk whose speech you deem the more pleasing, you should speak thus to him: ' Between the venerable ones there is a difference as to denotation and a difference as to connotation, on account of which these venerable ones should know that there is a difference as to denotation and a difference as to connotation. Do not let the venerable ones fall into contention.' After this, having approached whatever monk on the other side of the factious monks whose speech you deem the more pleasing, you should speak thus to him: ' Between the venerable ones there is a difference as to denotation and a

---

[1] *iti bhavābhava*. *MA*. iv. 28 says " depending on the working of good, *puñña*, according to this teaching, I will experience happiness in this or that becoming." *DA*. iii. 1021, *AA*. iii. 12 give *bhavābhava* as oil, honey, ghee, etc.; these would thus take the place of the fourth requisite, medicines for the sick, which normally would have been expected here; see *Dial*. iii. 220, *n*. 3 and *G.S.* ii. 11, *n*. 1. But at *ItA*. ii. 256, and other Comys., *bhava* is given as growth or success, and *abhava* as failure or decline. At *D*. iii. 228, *A*. ii. 10, 248 and *Iti*. p. 109 these four items are called the production of craving.

[2] *M*. ii. 245. *Cf*. *M*. ii. 9.

[3] *abhidhamma*, here meaning the 37 things helpful to awakening, *MA*. iv. 29.

difference as to connotation, on account of which these venerable ones should know that there is a difference as to denotation and a difference as to connotation. Do not let the venerable ones fall into contention.' In this way what is hard to grasp should be remembered as hard to grasp; having remembered what is hard to grasp as hard to grasp, that which is *dhamma*, that which is discipline should be spoken.

If it should occur to you concerning this,[1] ' Although there is a difference between these venerable ones as to denotation, there is agreement as to connotation,' then having approached that monk whose speech you deem to be the more pleasing, you should speak to him thus: ' Although these venerable ones differ as to denotation, there is agreement as to connotation, therefore these venerable ones should know that although they differ as to denotation, there is agreement as to connotation. Do not let the venerable ones fall into contention.' After this, having approached whatever monk on the other side of the factious monks whose speech you deem the more pleasing, you should speak thus to him: ' Although these venerable ones differ as to denotation . . . Do not let these venerable ones fall into contention.' [**240**] In this way what is hard to grasp should be remembered as hard to grasp; what is easy to grasp should be remembered as easy to grasp; having remembered what is hard to grasp as hard to grasp, having remembered what is easy to grasp as easy to grasp, that which is *dhamma*, that which is discipline should be spoken.

If it should occur to you concerning this, ' Although there is agreement between these venerable ones as to denotation, there is difference as to connotation,' then having approached that monk whose speech you deem to be the more pleasing, you should speak thus to him: ' Between the venerable ones there is agreement as to denotation, there is difference as to connotation, on account of which these venerable ones should know that there is agreement as to denotation, difference as to connotation. But this is a mere trifle, that is to say connotation. Do not let the venerable ones fall into contention over a mere trifle.' After this, having approached whatever monk on the other side of the factious monks whose speech you deem the more pleasing, you should speak thus to him: ' Between these venerable ones there is agreement as to denotation, there is difference as to connotation . . . Do not let these venerable ones fall

---

[1] *tatra*, this too refers to the 37 things helpful to awakening, *MA*. iv. 29.

into contention over a mere trifle.' In this way what is easy to grasp should be remembered as easy to grasp; what is hard to grasp snould be remembered as hard to grasp; having remembered what is easy to grasp as easy to grasp, having remembered what is hard to grasp as hard to grasp, that which is *dhamma*, that which is discipline should be spoken.

If it should occur to you concerning this: ' Between these venerable ones there is agreement as to denotation and there is agreement as to connotation,' then having approached that monk whose speech you deem the more pleasing, you should speak thus to him: ' Between the venerable ones there is agreement as to denotation and there is agreement as to connotation, on account of which these venerable ones should know that there is agreement as to denotation and agreement as to connotation. Do not let the venerable ones fall into contention.' After this, having approached whatever monk on the other side of the factious monks whose speech you deem the more pleasing, you should speak thus to him: ' Between the venerable ones there is agreement . . . [**241**] Do not let the venerable ones fall into contention.' In this way what is easy to grasp should be remembered as easy to grasp; having remembered what is easy to grasp as easy to grasp, that which is *dhamma*, that which is discipline should be spoken.

And when you, monks, all together, in harmony and without contention are trained in these, a certain monk might have an offence, might have a transgression. As to this, monks, one should not hasten with reproof—the individual must be examined. (You may think): ' There will be no vexation for me nor annoyance for the other individual; for if the other individual is without wrath, without rancour, is of quick view and easy to convince, I have the power to raise this individual from unskill and establish him in what is skill.' If it occurs to you thus, monks, it is right to speak. But if you think, monks, ' There will be no vexation for me but (there will be) annoyance for the other individual; for though the other individual is wrathful, rancorous, of slow view (but) easy to convince, I have the power to raise this individual from unskill and establish him in what is skill. For this is a mere trifle, that is to say the other individual's annoyance. And this is of the greater moment, that I have the power to raise this individual from unskill and establish him in what is skill.' If it occurs to you thus, monks, it is right to speak. But if you think, monks: ' There will be vexation for me but no annoyance for the other individual; for if the other individual is without wrath, without rancour, is of quick view though hard to convince, I have the power to raise this individual from unskill and establish him in what is skill. For this is a mere trifle, that is to say my vexation. And this is of the greater moment, that I have the power to raise this individual from unskill and establish him in what is skill.' If it occurs to you thus, monks, it is right to speak. But if you think, monks: ' There will be vexation for me and annoyance for the other individual; yet though the other [**242**] individual is wrathful, rancorous, of slow view and hard to convince, I have the power to raise this individual from unskill and establish him in what is skill. For this is a mere trifle, that is to say my vexation and the other individual's annoyance. And this is of the greater moment, that I have the power to raise this individual from unskill and establish him in what is skill.' If it occurs to you thus, monks, it is right to speak. But if you think, monks: ' There will be vexation for me and annoyance for the other individual; for the other individual is wrathful, rancorous, of slow view and hard to convince, and I have not the power to raise this individual from unskill and establish him in what is skill '—equanimity, monks, should not be disdained for such an individual.

And when you, monks, all together, in harmony and without contention have trained yourselves in these there might arise between you an activity of speech,[1] an offensive view, malice in thought, discontent, dissatisfaction. In that case, having approached that monk whom you deem the more easy of the factious monks to speak to, you should speak to him thus: ' Although, your reverence, we were trained all together, in harmony and without contention, there has arisen between us an activity of speech, an offensive view, malice in thought, discontent, dissatisfaction for which the Recluse,[2] knowing of it, would blame us.' Answering aright, monks, the monk would answer thus: ' Although, your reverence, we were trained all together ... the Recluse, knowing of it, would blame us. But without getting rid of this condition,[3] your reverence, could nibbāna be realised ?' Answering aright, monks, the monk would answer thus: ' Without getting rid of this condition, your reverence, nibbāna could not be realised.' After this, having approached whatever monk on the other side of the factious monks whose speech you deem the more pleasing, you should speak thus

---

[1] *vacīsaṁkhāra*, speech activity, see *Vism.* 531, and also *cf. A.* iii. 350.
[2] The Teacher, so *MA.* iv. 31.   [3] *I.e.* of quarrelling.

to him: 'Although, your reverence, we were trained all together ... the Recluse, knowing of it, would blame us.' Answering aright, monks, the monk would answer thus: 'Although, your reverence, we were trained all together ... the Recluse, knowing of it, would blame us. But without getting rid of this condition, your reverence, could nibbāna[1] be realised?' Answering aright, monks, the monk in answering[2] **[243]** would answer thus: 'Without getting rid of this condition, your reverence, nibbāna could not be realised.'

If, monks, others should ask that monk, saying: 'Were these monks raised up from unskill and established in skill by the venerable one?' answering aright, monks, the monk would answer thus: 'I, your reverences, approached the Lord; the Lord taught me his *dhamma*; when I had heard that *dhamma*, I spoke it to those monks; when those monks had heard that *dhamma* they rose up from unskill and established themselves in what is skill.' Answering thus, monks, the monk neither exalts himself nor disparages another, he is explaining in accordance with *dhamma*, and no one of his fellow *dhamma*-men, of his way of speaking, gives grounds for reproach."

Thus spoke the Lord. Delighted, these monks rejoiced in what the Lord had said.

Discourse on "What then?"
The Third

104. DISCOURSE AT SĀMAGĀMA

(Sāmagāmasutta)

THUS have I heard: At one time the Lord was staying among the Sakyans at Sāmagāma.[3] At that time Nātaputta the Jain had

---

[1] Here however two MSS. include *na*, reading *na nibbānaṁ sacchikareyya*, while above in the same passage only one MS. adds *na*. Taking it that *na* should not be there, it seems necessary to turn the sentence into a question; by so doing it is shown that the monks were still seeking harmony and obtaining it.

[2] *vyākaramāno*, added here, is absent above.

[3] The introductory part of this Sta. is the same as *D.* iii. 117-118 (*Pāsādika-suttanta*). The strifes following Nātaputta's death are also repeated at *D.* iii. 210. Another Discourse given by Gotama while he was staying by the lotus-pool near Sāmagāma is recorded at *A.* iii. 309.

recently died at Pāvā. On his death the Jains broke up; splitting into two, striving, quarrelling, disputing, they lived wounding one another with the weapons of the tongue, saying: ' You[1] do not understand this *dhamma* and discipline, *I* understand this *dhamma* and discipline. How can you understand this *dhamma* and discipline ? You are one who fares wrongly, I am one who fares aright. There is sense in what I say, no sense in what you say; you say at the end what should be said at the beginning [**244**] and say at the beginning what should be said at the end. What you pondered[2] so long[3] is reversed; your words are refuted;[4] you are shown up. Get away, think out the argument,[5] or unravel it if you can.'[6] It seems that death verily stalked among the Jains who were Nātaputta's pupils.[7] Even the white-clad householders who were followers of Nātaputta the Jain were disgusted, disaffected, put off[8] by the Jains who were Nātaputta's pupils in that the *dhamma* and discipline were badly set forth, badly expounded, not leading onwards, not conducing to peace, expounded by one who was not fully self-awakened, the foundations wrecked, without an arbiter.

Then Cunda the novice,[9] having kept the rains at Pāvā, approached the venerable Ānanda at Sāmagāma; having approached and greeted the vernable Ānanda, he sat down at a respectful distance. As he was sitting down at a respectful distance, Cunda the novice spoke thus to the venerable Ānanda: " Revered sir, Nātaputta the Jain has recently died at Pāvā. On his death the Jains broke up, splitting into two . . . (*as above*) the foundations wrecked, without an arbiter." When this had been said, the venerable Ānanda spoke

---

[1] *Cf. M.* ii. 3, *D.* i. 8, and see notes at *Dial.* i. 14-15.
[2] *avicinṇa*. Most contexts have *v.l. adhicinṇa*.
[3] *MA*. iv. 33 gives *cirakālasevanavasena*.
[4] *Cf. Vin.* i. 60, *M.* ii. 122, *S.* i. 160.
[5] *cara vādappamokkhāya*. *MA*. iv. 33 says, " Taking a bag with food, and approaching this (person) and that, go along seeking further for thinking out the argument," *vādappamokkhatthāya*. But *DA*. i. 91 says, " Go away so as to free yourself from anger, train yourself having gone here and there." *Cf. cara* at *Vin*. iv. 139, and also see *Dial.* i. 15, *n.* 3.
[6] " Free yourself from the speech that has been refuted by me," *MA*. iv. 33.
[7] *Nātaputtiyesu*, among Nāta's sons, explained at *MA*. iv. 33 as Nātaputta's *antevāsika*, his (resident) pupils.
[8] *paṭivāṇarūpa*, no longer respectful.
[9] *samaṇuddesa* defined by *sāmaṇera* at *Vin*. iv. 139. Cunda was, according to *MA*. iv. 36, Sāriputta's younger brother, called " the novice " before he was ordained. *Thag*. 141-142 ascribes verses to Mahā-Cunda, also said to be Sāriputta's younger brother; see *Pss. Breth.* p. 119, *n.* 1.

thus to Cunda the novice: " Certainly this, reverend Cunda, is a subject on which to see the Lord. Come, reverend Cunda, we will approach the Lord; having approached, we will tell this matter to the Lord."

" Yes, revered sir," Cunda the novice answered the venerable Ānanda in assent. Then the venerable Ānanda and Cunda the novice approached the Lord; having approached and greeted the Lord, they sat down at a respectful distance. As he was sitting down at a respectful distance [**245**] the venerable Ānanda spoke thus to the Lord: " This novice Cunda, revered sir, speaks thus: ' Revered sir, Nātaputta the Jain has recently died at Pāvā . . . the foundations wrecked, without an arbiter.' It occurs to me, revered sir, that we should take care lest, after the Lord's passing, dispute arises in the Order—dispute for the woe of the manyfolk, for the grief of the manyfolk, for the misfortune of the populace, for the woe, the sorrow of *devas* and mankind."[1]

" What do you think about this, Ānanda ? Those things taught by me to you out of super-knowledge,[2] that is to say the four applications of mindfulness, the four right efforts, the four bases of psychic power, the five controlling faculties, the five powers, the seven links in. awakening, the ariyan eightfold Way—do you, Ānanda, see even two monks professing differently about these things ?"[3]

" Revered sir, those things taught to me by the Lord out of his super-knowledge, that is to say the four applications of mindfulness . . . the ariyan eightfold Way—I do not see even two monks professing differently about these things. Yet, revered sir, those people who dwell dependent on the Lord might, after the Lord's passing, stir up dispute in the Order concerning either the mode of living or the Obligations[4]—this dispute would be for the woe of the manyfolk, for the grief of the manyfolk, for the misfortune of the populace, for the sorrow of *devas* and mankind."

---

[1] Last phrase also at *Vin.* ii. 89, *D.* iii. 246, *S.* ii. 255, *A.* i. 19.

[2] As above, p. 25.

[3] *MA.* iv. 37 honourably points out that the dispute between two monks (recorded in the Kosambakkhandhaka, *Vin.* i. 352 *ff.*) grew to such great proportions that the people split into two factions.

[4] *adhipātimokkha*. *MA.* iv. 38 gives rather an elaborate explanation: a monk who claims a state of further-men falls into a Pārājika offence (No. IV); beginning with this, six rules of training are laid down in the Parivāra; with the exception of these, all the remaining rules of training are called *adhipātimokkha*.

"That dispute which concerns either the mode of living or the Obligations is a trifle, Ānanda. But, Ānanda, if there should arise in the Order a dispute either concerning the Way or concerning the course, this dispute would be for the woe of the manyfolk, the grief of the manyfolk, the misfortune of the populace, the sorrow of *devas* and mankind.

These six are the sources of dispute,[1] Ānanda. What six ? As to this, Ānanda, a monk is angry and bears ill-will. Ānanda, whatever monk is angry and bears ill-will, he lives without deference and respect towards the Teacher, he lives without deference and respect towards *dhamma*, he lives without deference and respect towards the Order, and he does not complete the training. Ānanda, whatever monk lives without deference and respect towards the Teacher, *dhamma* and the Order [**246**] and does not complete the training, he stirs up dispute in the Order, and that dispute is for the woe of the manyfolk, the grief of the manyfolk, the misfortune of the populace, the sorrow of *devas* and mankind. If you, Ānanda, should perceive a source of dispute like this among yourselves or among others, you, Ānanda, should strive therein to get rid of precisely that evil source of disputes. If you, Ānanda, should perceive no source of dispute like this among yourselves or among others, you, Ānanda, should therein follow a course so that there be no overflowing into the future of precisely that evil source of disputes. There is thus the getting rid of that evil source of disputes, there is thus no overflowing into the future of that evil source of disputes.

And again, Ānanda, a monk is harsh, unmerciful . . . he is envious and grudging . . . he is crafty and deceitful . . . he is of evil desires and wrong views . . . he is infected with worldliness, is obstinate and stubborn. Whatever monk, Ānanda, is infected with worldliness, is obstinate and stubborn, he lives without deference and respect towards the Teacher, he lives without deference and respect towards *dhamma*, he lives without deference and respect towards the Order, and he does not complete the training. Whatever monk, Ānanda, lives without deference and respect towards the Teacher, *dhamma* and the Order and does not complete the training, he stirs up dispute in the Order, and that dispute is for the woe of the manyfolk, the grief of the manyfolk, the misfortune of the populace, the sorrow of *devas* and mankind. If you, Ānanda, should perceive a source of dispute like this . . . There is thus the getting rid of that evil source

---

[1] *Cf. Vin.* ii. 89 with the following, and see *B.D.* v. 118; also *D.* iii. 246.

of disputes, [**247**] there is thus no overflowing into the future of that evil source of disputes. These, Ānanda, are the six sources of dispute.

These four, Ānanda, are the legal questions.[1] What four ? A legal question arising out of disputes, a legal question arising out of censure, a legal question arising out of offences, a legal question arising out of obligations. These, Ānanda, are the four legal questions. But these seven (rules[2]) which are for deciding legal questions are for the deciding and the settlement of legal questions arising from time to time: a verdict in the presence of[3] may be given, a verdict of innocence may be given, a verdict of past insanity may be given, it may be carried out on (his) acknowledgement, (there is) the decision of the majority, the decision for specific depravity, the covering up (as) with grass.

And what, Ānanda, is the 'verdict in the presence of'?[4] As to this, Ānanda, monks dispute, saying: 'It is *dhamma*' or 'It is not *dhamma*' or 'It is discipline' or 'It is not discipline.'[5] Ānanda, one and all of these monks should assemble in a complete Order; having assembled, what belongs to *dhamma*[6] should be threshed out; having threshed out what belongs to *dhamma* according to how it corresponds here, so should that legal question be settled. Thus, Ānanda, is the 'verdict in the presence of'; but here there is the settlement of a particular type of legal question, namely by the verdict in the presence of.

And what, Ānanda, is the 'decision of the majority'?[7] If these monks, Ānanda, are not able to settle that legal question in this residence, then, Ānanda, these monks must go to a residence where there are more monks,[8] and there one and all must assemble in a complete Order; having assembled, what belongs to *dhamma* must be threshed out . . . so should that legal question be settled. Thus, Ānanda, is 'the decision of the majority'; but here there is the settlement of a particular type of legal question, namely by the decision of the majority.

---

[1] *adhikaraṇa*, or adjudication. The four *adhikaraṇā* are explained at *Vin.* ii. 88. See also *Vin.* iii. 164, iv. 126, 238.

[2] *dhammā* at *Vin.* iv. 207, but *dhamma* as "rule" is more or less Vinaya in usage. *Cf.* also *D.* iii. 254, *A.* iv. 144.

[3] On these ways of settling legal questions, see *Vin.* iv. 207 and *B.D.* iii. 153 *f.* for notes and further references.

[4] See *Vin.* ii. 93.   [5] *Cf. Vin.* ii. 88.

[6] *dhammanetti*. *PED* says *netti=niyāma*.

[7] Here the usual order is altered. On *yebhuyyasikā* see *Vin.* ii. 93 *ff.*

[8] Even two or three more, *MA.* iv. 48.

And what, Ānanda, is the 'verdict of innocence'?[1] As to this, Ānanda, monks reprove a monk for a serious offence like this: one involving defeat[2] or one bordering on defeat, saying: 'Does the venerable one remember having fallen into a serious offence like this: one involving defeat or one bordering on defeat?' If he says: 'I, your reverences, do not remember having fallen into a serious offence like this, either one involving defeat or one bordering on defeat,' [248] to that monk, Ānanda, a verdict of innocence should be given. Thus, Ānanda, is the 'verdict of innocence'; but here there is the settlement of a particular type of legal question, namely by the verdict of innocence.

And what, Ānanda, is the 'verdict of past insanity'?[3] As to this, Ānanda, monks reprove a monk for a serious offence like this ... (*as above*) ... If he says: 'I, your reverences, do not remember having fallen into a serious offence like this, either one involving defeat or one bordering on defeat,' then, denying this, he is pressed (by the monks), saying: 'Please, venerable one, do find out properly whether you remember having fallen into a serious offence like this, either one involving defeat or one bordering on defeat.' If he says: 'I, your reverences, had become crazy and had lost my mental balance;[4] while I was crazy, much was perpetrated and said by me that was not worthy of a recluse. I do not remember that. That was done by me while I was insane,' to that monk, Ānanda, a verdict of past insanity should be given. Thus, Ānanda, is the 'verdict of past insanity'; but here there is the settlement of a particular type of legal question, namely by the verdict of past insanity.

And what, Ānanda, is the 'carrying out (of a formal act) on the acknowledgement of (a monk)'?[5] As to this, Ānanda, a monk whether reproved or not reproved remembers an offence, reveals it, discloses it. That monk, Ānanda, having approached an older monk, having arranged his upper robe over one shoulder, having saluted the older monk's feet, having sat down on his haunches, raising his joined palms, should speak thus to him: 'I, revered sir, have fallen into such and such an offence which I confess.' He speaks thus: 'Do you see it?' 'I see it.' 'Will you be restrained in the future?' 'I will be restrained.' Thus, Ānanda, is the 'carrying out

---

[1] *sativinaya*. See *Vin*. i. 325, ii. 79 *f*., 99 *f*.; and *G.S.* i. 85, *n*. 7.
[2] A *pārājika* offence.
[3] *amūḷhavinaya*. See *Vin*. ii. 80 *f*., 100, and *cf*. *Vin*. i. 123.
[4] The words here are slightly different from those at *Vin*. ii. 81. *Cf*. *S*. i. 126.
[5] *patiññātakaraṇa*. See *Vin*. i. 325, ii. 83.

(of a formal act) on the acknowledgement of a monk'; but here there is the settlement of a particular type of legal question, namely by the carrying out (of a formal act) on the acknowledgement (of a monk).

[249] And what, Ānanda, is the 'decision for specific depravity'?[1] As to this, Ānanda, monks reprove a monk for a serious offence like this, either one involving defeat or one bordering on defeat, saying: 'Does the venerable one remember having fallen into a serious offence like this, either one involving defeat or one bordering on defeat?' If he says: 'I, your reverences, do not remember having fallen into a serious offence like this, either one involving defeat or one bordering or defeat,' then, denying it, he is pressed (by the monks) who say: 'Please, venerable one, do find out properly whether you remember having fallen into a serious offence like this, either one involving defeat or one bordering on defeat.' If he says: 'I, your reverences, do not remember having fallen into a serious offence like this, either one involving defeat or one bordering on defeat; but I remember, your reverences, having fallen into such and such a slight offence,' then, denying this, he is pressed (by the monks) who say: 'Please, venerable one, do find out properly if you remember having fallen into a serious offence like this, either one involving defeat or one bordering on defeat.' If he speaks thus: 'Certainly, your reverences, although I have not been asked, I will acknowledge having fallen into this slight offence; then how could I, since I have been asked, not acknowledge having fallen into a serious offence like this, either one involving defeat or one bordering on defeat?' Someone[2] says to him: 'If you, your reverence, when not asked, will not acknowledge having fallen into this slight offence, how will you, when asked whether you have fallen into a serious offence like this, either one involving defeat or one bordering on defeat, acknowledge it? Please, venerable one, do find out properly whether you remember having fallen into a serious offence like this, either one involving defeat or one bordering on defeat.' He then says: 'I do remember, your reverence, having fallen into a serious offence like this, either one involving defeat or one bordering on defeat. When I said: I do not remember having fallen into a serious offence like this, either one involving defeat or one bordering on defeat—I was speaking thus for fun, I spoke in jest.' Thus, Ānanda, is the 'decision for specific depravity'; but here there is the settle-

---

[1] *tassapāpiyyasikā.* See *Vin.* ii. 85 *f.*, *A.* iv. 347.
[2] *so.* Chalmers: "the spokesman," Neumann: "jener."

ment of a particular type of legal question, namely by the decision for specific depravity.

[**250**] And what, Ānanda, is the 'covering up (as) with grass'?[1] As to this, Ānanda, while monks live striving, quarrelling, disputing, much is perpetrated and spoken that is not worthy of a recluse. Ānanda, one and all of these monks should gather together in a complete Order; having gathered together, an experienced monk from one of the factions of monks, rising from his seat, having arranged his upper robe over one shoulder, having joined his palms in salutation, should inform the Order, saying: 'Revered sirs, let the Order listen to me. While we were striving, quarrelling, disputing, much was perpetrated and spoken that was not worthy of a recluse. If it seems right to the Order, I would confess whatever is the offence of the venerable ones as well as whatever is my own offence, both for the sake of the venerable ones and for my own sake, unless it is a heavy sin,[2] unless it is connected with the laity,[3] (so as to obtain) a covering up (as) with grass.' After that, an experienced monk from the other faction of monks, rising from his seat . . . saying: 'Revered sirs, let the Order listen to me . . . unless it is connected with the laity, (so as to obtain) a covering up (as) with grass.' Thus, Ānanda, is the 'covering up (as) with grass'; but here there is the settlement of a particular type of legal question, namely by the covering up (as) with grass.

Ānanda, these six things are to be remembered;[4] making for affection, making for respect, they conduce to concord, to lack of contention, to harmony and unity. What six? Herein, Ānanda, a monk should offer his fellow Brahma-farers a friendly act of body both in public and in private. This is a thing to be remembered, making for affection, making for respect, which conduces to concord, to lack of contention, to harmony and unity. And again, Ānanda, a monk should offer a friendly act of speech . . . a friendly act of thought . . . both in public and in private. This too is a thing to be remembered, making for affection, [**251**] making for respect . . . to harmony and unity. And again, Ānanda, whatever are those lawful acquisitions, lawfully acquired, if they be even but what is put into the begging bowl—a monk should be one to enjoy sharing such acquisitions, to enjoy them in common with his virtuous fellow

---

[1] *tiṇavatthāraka. Cf. Vin.* ii. 86 *f.*
[2] *MA.* iv. 50, a *pārājika* or *saṅghādisesa* offence.
[3] *MA.* iv. 50 says that this refers to a monk reviling or insulting householders.
[4] As at *M.* i. 322.

Brahma-farers. This too is a thing to be remembered ... And again, Ānanda, whatever are those moral habits that are faultless, without flaw, spotless, without blemish, freeing, praised by wise men, untarnished, conducive to concentration—a monk should dwell united in moral habits such as these with his fellow Brahma-farers, both in public and in private. This too is a thing to be remembered ... And again, Ānanda, whatever view is ariyan, leading onwards, leading him who acts according to it to the complete destruction of anguish—a monk should dwell united in such a view as this with his fellow Brahma-farers, both in public and in private. This too is a thing to be remembered; making for affection, making for respect, it conduces to concord, to lack of contention, to harmony and unity. Ānanda, these are the six things to be remembered, making for affection, making for respect, which conduce to concord, to lack of contention, to harmony and unity. If you, Ānanda, undertaking these six things to be remembered should practise them, would you, Ānanda, see any way of speech, subtle or gross, that you could not endure ?"[1]

" No, revered sir."

" Wherefore, Ānanda, undertaking these six things to be remembered, practise them; for a long time it will be for your welfare and happiness."

Thus spoke the Lord. Delighted, the venerable Ānanda rejoiced in what the Lord had said.

Discourse at Sāmagāma:
The Fourth

105. DISCOURSE TO SUNAKKHATTA
(Sunakkhattasutta)

[252] THUS have I heard: At one time the Lord was staying near Vesālī in the Great Grove in the hall of the Gabled House. Now at that time a number of monks declared in the Lord's presence that they had profound knowledge, saying: " We comprehend that destroyed is birth, brought to a close the Brahma-faring, done is

---
[1] For the last sentence, cf. M. i. 129.

what was to be done, there is no more of being such or so." Sunakkhatta the son of a Licchavi[1] heard that a number of monks had declared . . . saying: " . . . there is no more of being such or so." Then Sunakkhatta the son of a Licchavi approached the Lord; having approached and greeted the Lord, he sat down at a respectful distance. As he was sitting down at a respectful distance, Sunakkhatta the son of a Licchavi spoke thus to the Lord:

"I have heard, revered sir, that a number of monks declared . . . saying: ' . . . there is no more of being such or so.' Revered sir, did those monks who declared in the Lord's presence that they had profound knowledge, saying: 'We comprehend that destroyed is birth, brought to a close the Brahma-faring, done is what was to be done, there is no more of being such or so '—did they declare properly that they had profound knowledge, or were there perhaps some monks there who, out of over-conceit,[2] declared that they had profound knowledge ?"

"Sunakkhatta, among the monks who in my presence declared that they had profound knowledge, saying: 'We comprehend that . . . there is no more of being such or so,' there were some monks there who declared properly that they had profound knowledge, but there were also some monks there who, out of over-conceit, declared that they had profound knowledge. As to this, Sunakkhatta, those monks who declared properly that they had profound knowledge, for them it is so. But as to those monks, Sunakkhatta, who, out of over-conceit, declared that they had profound knowledge, it occurs to the Tathāgata: 'I should teach these *dhamma.*' And so it is in this case, Sunakkhatta, that it occurs to the Tathāgata: 'I should teach these *dhamma.*' But there are moreover some foolish persons here who, having constructed a question, approach the Tathāgata and ask (him). In this case, Sunakkhatta, [253] this too occurs to the Tathāgata: 'I should teach these *dhamma,*' and it does not occur to him (to think) otherwise."

"It is the right time for this, Lord, it is the right time for this, Well-farer. The monks, having heard from the Lord whatever *dhamma* the Lord may teach, will remember it."

"Well then, Sunakkhatta, listen, attend carefully and I will speak."

"Yes, revered sir," Sunakkhatta the son of a Licchavi answered the Lord in assent. The Lord spoke thus:

---

[1] See *M.* Sta. 12. [2] *Cf. A.* v. 162 *ff.*

"These five, Sunakkhatta, are the strands of sense-pleasure.[1] What five? Material shapes cognisable by the eye, agreeable, pleasant, liked, enticing, connected with sensual pleasures, alluring; sounds cognisable by the ear . . . smells cognisable by the nose . . . tastes cognisable by the tongue . . . touches cognisable by the body, agreeable, pleasant, liked, enticing, connected with sensual pleasures, alluring. These, Sunakkhatta, are the five strands of sense-pleasures.

But this situation exists, Sunakkhatta, when some individual here may be set on the material things of the world,[2] and the talk of the individual who is set on the material things of the world follows a pattern in accordance with which he reflects and ponders, and he associates with that man under whom he finds felicity; but when there is talk[3] connected with imperturbability he does not listen, does not lend ear, does not arouse his mind to profound knowledge,[4] and he does not associate with that man under whom he does not find felicity. Sunakkhatta, it is like a man who may have been absent a long time from his own village or market town and may see a man recently come from that village or market town; he would ask him about the safety of that village or market town and about the plentifulness of the food and absence of sickness; that man might speak to him about the safety of that village . . . [**254**] and the absence of sickness. What do you think about this, Sunakkhatta? Would not that man listen, lend ear, arouse his mind to profound knowledge, and would he not associate with that man under whom he found felicity?"

"Yes, revered sir."

"Even so, Sunakkhatta, the situation exists when some individual here may be set on the material things of the world, and the talk of the individual who is set on the material things of the world follows a pattern in accordance with which he reflects and ponders, and he associates with that man under whom he finds felicity; but when there is talk connected with imperturbability he does not listen, does not lend ear, does not arouse his mind to profound knowledge, and he does not associate with that man under whom he does not find felicity. He should be spoken of as an individual who is set on the material things of the world.

---

[1] As at *M*. i. 85, etc.   [2] *lokāmisa*; *cf. M*. i. 12, 155 *f*.
[3] *kathāya kacchamānāya*, lit. when talk is being talked. *Kacchamāna*, pass. pres. part. of *katheti*, also at *A*. iii. 181.
[4] *Cf. Vin*. i. 10; *D*. i. 230-231.

But this situation exists, Sunakkhatta, when some individual here may be set on imperturbability, and the talk of the individual, Sunakkhatta, who is set on imperturbability follows a pattern in accordance with which he reflects and ponders, and he associates with that man under whom he finds felicity; but when there is talk connected with the material things of the world he does not listen, does not lend ear, does not arouse his mind to profound knowledge, and he does not associate with that man under whom he does not find felicity. Sunakkhatta, as a sere leaf, loosened from its stalk, cannot become green again,[1] even so, Sunakkhatta, when the fetter of the material things of the world is loosened by that individual who is set on imperturbability he should be spoken of as an individual who is set on imperturbability for he is released from the material things of the world.

But this situation exists, Sunakkhatta, when some individual here may be set on no-thing, and the talk of the individual, Sunakkhatta, who is set on the plane of no-thing follows a pattern in accordance with which he reflects and ponders, and he associates with that man under whom [255] he finds felicity; but when there is talk connected with imperturbability he does not listen, does not lend ear, does not arouse his mind to profound knowledge, and he does not associate with that man under whom he does not find felicity. Sunakkhatta, as a rock that is broken in two cannot become whole again,[2] even so, Sunakkhatta, when the fetter of imperturbability is broken by that individual who is set on the plane of no-thing, he should be spoken of as an individual who is set on the plane of no-thing for he is released from the fetter of imperturbability.

But this situation exists, Sunakkhatta, when some individual here may be set on the plane of neither-perception-nor-non-perception, and the talk of the individual, Sunakkhatta, who is set on the plane of neither-perception-nor-non-perception follows a pattern in accordance with which he reflects and ponders, and he associates with that man under whom he finds felicity; but when there is talk connected with the plane of no-thing he does not listen, does not lend ear, does not arouse his mind to profound knowledge, and he does not associate with that man under whom he does not find felicity. It is like a man, Sunakkhatta, who after eating a meal of dainties might throw away (the remains). What do you think about this, Sunakkhatta? Would that man have any further desire for that meal?"

---

[1] Cf. *Vin.* i. 96, iii. 47. [2] Cf. *Vin.* i. 97.

"No, revered sir. What is the reason for this? That meal, revered sir, is considered to be objectionable."

"Even so Sunakkhatta, when that fetter of the plane of no-thing is laid aside by the individual who is set on the plane of neither-perception-nor-non-perception, he should be spoken of as an individual who is set on the plane of neither-perception-nor-non-perception for he is released from the fetter of the plane of no-thing.

But this situation exists, Sunakkhatta, when some individual here may be set on perfect nibbāna,[1] and the talk of the individual, Sunakkhatta, who is set on perfect nibbāna follows a pattern in accordance with which he reflects and ponders; and he associates with that man under whom he finds felicity; but when there is talk connected with the plane of neither-perception-nor-non-perception [256] he does not listen, does not lend ear, does not arouse his mind to profound knowledge, and he does not associate with that man under whom he does not find felicity. Sunakkhatta, as a palm-tree whose crown has been cut off cannot grow again, even so, Sunakkhatta, when the plane of neither-perception-nor-non-perception is cut off for an individual who is set on perfect nibbāna, cut off at the root, made like a palm-tree that, eradicated, is not liable to rise up again in the future, he should be spoken of as an individual who is set on perfect nibbāna for he is released from the fetter of the plane of neither-perception-nor-non-perception.

But this situation exists, Sunakkhatta, when it occurs to some monk here that: 'Craving has been called a dart[2] by the Recluse;[3] the virus of ignorance wracks (a man) with desire, attachment and ill will. The dart of craving has been got rid of by me, drained off is the virus of ignorance, *I* am set on perfect nibbāna '—he may be thus proud of his existing goal. He may give himself up to such things as are deleterious to one who is set on perfect nibbāna: he may give himself up to deleterious vision of material shapes through the eye, he may give himself up to deleterious sounds through the ear ... to deleterious smells through the nose ... to deleterious tastes through the tongue ... to deleterious touches through the body ...

---

[1] *sammānibbāna*, an unusual expression on which *MA*. iv. on the above passage makes no comment. It is by no means a foregone conclusion that the individual who is intent on it will win it, see below. It is possibly comparable to the final meditative stage: that where perceiving and feeling are stopped.

[2] *Cf. S.* i. 140. [3] *MA*. iv. 55, Buddhasamaṇa.

to deleterious mental states through the mind. While he is given up to deleterious vision of material shapes through the eye . . . to deleterious mental states through the mind, attachment may assail his thought; with his thought assailed by attachment he may come to death or to pain like unto death. It is as if, Sunakkhatta, a man were pierced by an arrow[1] that was thickly smeared with poison; his friends and acquaintances, kith and kin, might procure a physician and surgeon; that physician and surgeon might cut round the opening of his wound with a knife; having cut round the opening of the wound with the knife, he might probe for the arrow with a (surgeon's) probe; having probed for the arrow with the (surgeon's) probe, [257] he might extract the arrow, he might drain off the virus leaving some behind but thinking none remained, and he might speak thus: ' My good man, the arrow has been extracted from you, the virus drained off so that none is left, there is no[2] danger for you, but you should eat only beneficial foods and take care lest, eating deleterious foods, your wound discharges. And from time to time you should bathe the wound, from time to time you should anoint the opening of the wound, but take care lest, bathing the wound from time to time, anointing the opening of the wound from time to time, the old blood cakes on the wound. And take care if you are anxious to go out into the wind and the heat of the sun, for unless you are careful when you go out into the wind and the heat of the sun, dust and dirt[3] may assail the opening of the wound. But if you, my good man, take care of the wound, the wound will heal.'

It may occur to him: ' The arrow has been extracted, the virus drained off so that none remains, and there is no danger for me,' and so he may eat only deleterious foods, and while doing so his wound may discharge; and he may not bathe the wound from time to time nor anoint the opening of the wound from time to time; not bathing the wound from time to time nor anointing the opening of the wound from time to time, the old blood may cake on the opening of the wound; and if he is anxious to go out into the wind and the heat of the sun, dust and dirt may assail the opening of the wound; and if he should not take care of the opening of the wound the wound does not heal. Both because he does precisely the deleterious things

---

[1] *salla* is arrow as well as dart. For this simile, cf. *M*. ii. 216.

[2] Text reads *alañ ca*, but *MA*. iv. 55 reads *analañ ca* as does *M*. text nine lines lower down.

[3] *rajosuka*. *MA*. iv. 55 says *rajo ca vīhisukādi ca sukaṁ*. Has *suka* any connection with awns of barley or paddy ?

and because, although when the noisome virus was drained off
some remained, the wound may increase in size.[1] With the wound
increased in size he may come to death or to pain like unto death—
even so, Sunakkhatta, the situation exists when it might occur to
some monk here that ' Craving has been called a dart by the Recluse;
the virus of ignorance wracks (a man) with desire, attachment and ill-
will. That dart of craving has been got rid of by me, [258] drained
off is the virus of ignorance, *I* am set on perfect nibbāna ' . . .
(*as above*) . . . while his thought is assailed by attachment he may
come to death or pain like unto death. For this, Sunakkhatta, is
death in the discipline for an ariyan: when, disavowing the training,
he returns to the secular life; and this, Sunakkhatta, is pain like
unto death: when he falls into a grievous[2] offence.

But this situation exists, Sunakkhatta, when it may occur to
some monk here: ' Craving has been called a dart by the Recluse;
the virus of ignorance wracks (a man) with desire, attachment and
ill-will. That dart of craving has been got rid of by me, drained off
is the virus of ignorance, *I* am set on perfect nibbāna.' Precisely
because he is set on perfect nibbāna he may not give himself up to
those things which are deleterious to one set on perfect nibbāna:
he may not give himself up to deleterious vision of material shapes
through the eye, he may not give himself up to . . . deleterious
mental states through the mind. Attachment may not assail the
thought of one not given up to deleterious vision of material shapes
through the eye . . . not given up to deleterious mental states through
the mind; while his [259] thought is not assailed by attachment,
he may not come to death or to pain like unto death. It is as if,
Sunakkhatta, a man were pierced by an arrow that was thickly
smeared with poison; his friends and acquaintances, his kith and
kin might procure a physician and surgeon; that physician and
surgeon might cut round the opening of the wound . . . and he might
speak thus: ' My good man, the arrow has been extracted from you
. . . (*as above*) . . . but if you, my good man, take care of the wound,
the wound will heal.' It may occur to him: ' The arrow has been
extracted, the virus drained off so that none remains, and there is
no danger for me,' but he may eat only beneficial foods, and while
doing so his wound may not discharge; and he may bathe the wound
from time to time (and anoint the opening of the wound from time

---

[1] *puthuttaṁ.* *MA.* iv. 55 explains by *mahantabhāvaṁ*, greatness.
[2] *saṅkiliṭṭha* usually means tarnished, soiled, corrupt. *MA.* iv. 55 gives *garuka*, serious, weighty.

to time[1]); since he bathes the wound from time to time and anoints the opening of the wound from time to time, the old blood will not cake on the opening of the wound; and if he is not anxious to go out into the wind and the heat of the sun, dust and dirt will not assail the opening of the wound; and if he should take care of the opening of the wound, the wound heals. Both because he does only the beneficial things and because the noisome virus is drained off with none remaining, the wound will close up; when the wound is closed by the skin he will not come to death or to pain like unto death—even so, Sunakkhatta, the situation exists when it might occur to some monk here: ' Craving has been called a dart by the Recluse; [260] . . . (*as above*) . . . He may not give himself up to such things as are deleterious to one set on perfect nibbāna: having seen a deleterious material shape with the eye, he may not give himself up to it; having heard a deleterious sound with the ear, he may not give himself up to it; he may not give himself up to a deleterious smell through the nose; he may not give himself up to a deleterious taste through the tongue; he may not give himself up to a deleterious touch through the body; he may not give himself up to a deleterious mental state through the mind. While he is not given up to deleterious vision of material shapes through the eye . . . while he is not given up to deleterious mental states through the mind, attachment may not assail his thought; with his thought not assailed by attachment he will come neither to death nor to pain like unto death. I have made this simile, Sunakkhatta, for the sake of clarifying the meaning.

Just this is the meaning here: ' The wound,' Sunakkhatta, is a synonym for the six inner (sense-) fields. ' The virus,' Sunakkhatta, is a synonym for ignorance. ' The arrow,' Sunakkhatta, is a synonym for craving. ' The (surgeon's) probe,' Sunakkhatta, is a synonym for mindfulness. ' The knife,' Sunakkhatta, is a synonym for the ariyan wisdom. ' The physician and surgeon,' Sunakkhatta, is a synonym for the Tathāgata, perfected one, fully Self-Awakened One. Indeed, Sunakkhatta, a monk who restrains himself among the six fields of (sensory) impingement, thinking: ' Clinging is the root of anguish,' and having understood it so, is without clinging, freed by the destruction of clinging.[2] That he should focus his body on clinging or devote his thought to it, this situation does not exist. It is as if, Sunakkhatta, there were a bronze goblet, fair and

---

[1] This phrase is omitted in the text, probably in error.
[2] *Cf. M.* i. 454, *A.* ii. 24.

fragrant, but charged with poison; then a man might come along, anxious to live, anxious not to die, anxious for happiness, recoiling from pain. What do you think about this, Sunakkhatta? Would that man drink out of this bronze goblet if he knew: ' Having drunk from this, I will come to death or to pain like unto death ' ?"

"No, revered sir."

[**261**] "Even so, Sunakkhatta, that monk who restrains himself among the six fields of (sensory) impingement, thinking: ' Clinging is the root of anguish,' having understood it so is without clinging, freed by the destruction of clinging. That he should focus his body on clinging or devote his thought to it—this situation does not exist. Sunakkhatta, it is like a deadly poisonous snake; and a man might come along anxious to live,[1] anxious not to die, anxious for happiness, recoiling from pain. What do you think about this, Sunakkhatta? Would that man proffer[2] his hand or toe[3] to that deadly poisonous snake if he knew: ' If I am bitten by this, I will come to death or pain like unto death ' ?"

"No, revered sir."

"Even so, Sunakkhatta, that monk who restrains himself among the six fields of (sensory) impingement, thinking: ' Clinging is the root of anguish,' having understood it so is without clinging, freed by the destruction of clinging. That he should focus his body on clinging or devote his thought to it—this situation does not exist."

Thus spoke the Lord. Delighted, Sunakkhatta the son of a Licchavi rejoiced in what the Lord had said.

Discourse to Sunakkhatta:
The Fifth

---

[1] *Cf. M.* i. 315.   [2] *dajjā*.
[3] *aṅguṭṭha* is more correctly "thumb," but this is included under *hattha*, hand.

106. DISCOURSE ON BENEFICIAL IMPERTURBABILITY
(Āṇañjasappāyasutta[1])

THUS have I heard: At one time the Lord was staying among the Kurus. A market town of the Kurus was called Kammassadhamma. While he was there the Lord addressed the monks, saying: " Monks." " Revered One," these monks answered the Lord in assent. The Lord spoke thus:
" Impermanent,[2] monks, are pleasures of the senses, hollow,[3] lying,[4] of the nature of falsehood;[5] this chatter of fools, monks, is made of illusion. Those pleasures of the senses that are here and now[6] and those pleasures of the senses that are hereafter,[7] and those [262] perceptions of pleasures of the senses that are here and now and those perceptions of pleasures of the senses that are hereafter— both[8] are of Māra's realm; this is Māra's sphere, this is Māra's crop,[9] this is Māra's pasturage.[10] Here these evil unskilled intentions[11] conduce to covetousness and ill-will and destruction, and these create a stumbling-block here in the training of an ariyan disciple. As to this, monks, an ariyan disciple reflects thus: 'Those pleasures of the senses that are here and now . . . create a stumbling-block here in the training of an ariyan disciple. Suppose I were to abide with thought that is far-reaching, wide-spread, with a determined[12] mind, having overcome the world.[13] For if I abide with my thought far-reaching, wide-spread, with my mind determined, having over-

---

[1] This " peculiarity of . . . spelling " (āṇañja) with v.ll. is noticed in PED, s.v. ānejja; cf. M. ii. 229, 253.
[2] As at A. v. 84.
[3] tuccha, empty of the essence of permanence, of stability, of self, MA. iv. 56.
[4] musa, which MA. iv. 56 explains by nassanaka, perishable.
[5] moghadhamma, v.l. mosadhamma, which is also the reading at A. v. 84 and MA. iv. 56.
[6] The five strands of human sense-pleasures, MA. iv. 57.
[7] Referring to those that are not " here and now."
[8] The sense-pleasures and the perceptions of them, MA. iv. 57.
[9] nivāpa; cf. Nivāpa-sutta, M. Sta. No. 25.
[10] Cf. S. v. 218 and v. 148-149.   [11] mānasā; see PED.
[12] Having determined on jhāna.
[13] The world of the five senses, MA. iv. 58.

come the world, these that are unskilled evil intentions: covetousness, ill-will and destruction, will not come to be; and by my getting rid of these my thought[1] will not be limited[2] (but) immeasurable,[3] well-developed.'[4] While he is faring along thus, abiding given over to this, his thought is peaceful in its sphere;[5] if he is serene either he comes to imperturbability now or he is intent on wisdom.[6] At the breaking up of the body after dying this situation exists, that that evolving consciousness[7] may accordingly[8] reach imperturbability. This, monks, is pointed to as the first course in beneficial imperturbability.

And again, monks, an ariyan disciple reflects thus:[9] 'There are those pleasures of the senses that are here and now and those pleasures of the senses that are hereafter, and there are those perceptions of pleasures of the senses that are here and now and those perceptions of pleasures of the senses that are hereafter, and whatever is material shape is material shape (consisting of) the four great elementals and derived from them.' While he is faring along thus, abiding given over to this, his thought is peaceful in its sphere; if he is serene either he comes to imperturbability now[10] or he is intent on wisdom. At the breaking up of the body after dying this situation exists, that that evolving consciousness may accordingly reach imperturbability. This, monks, is pointed to as the second course in beneficial imperturbability.

[263] And again, monks, an ariyan disciple reflects thus:[11] 'There

---

[1] In *jhāna*.

[2] *aparitta*. The mind that is small, limited, *pamāṇa* or *paritta*, has to do with pleasures of the senses. *Cf. A.* i. 249, *paritto appātumo appadukkhavihāri . . . aparitto mahattā appamāṇavihāri*.

[3] Having to do with the spheres of form (or fine-materiality) and formlessness (or immateriality).

[4] *subhāvita*, having to do with what is transcendental, supermundane.

[5] *āyatana*, which is arahantship or the vision of arahantship or the fourth *jhāna* or access to it, *MA*. iv. 59. *Āyatana* can also mean performance, doing, *kāraṇa*.

[6] This may lead to arahantship or cultivating the way to it or to the fourth or third *jhāna*. If he fails to win arahantship, then the next sentence applies.

[7] *saṁvattanika viññāṇa*, or conducive consciousness. *MA*. iv. 61 says "that monk tends, arises, because of that consciousness of (good) result."

[8] *yaṁ*. *MA*. iv. 61 gives *yena kāraṇena*, for this reason.

[9] *I.e.* when he has attained the fourth *jhāna*, *MA*. iv. 62.

[10] The imperturbability of the plane of infinite *ākāsa*, *MA*. iv. 62.

[11] *I.e.* when he has attained the plane of infinite *ākāsa*, *MA*. iv. 63. He has greater wisdom than have the two former monks.

are those pleasures of the senses that are here and now and those pleasures of the senses that are hereafter, and there are those perceptions of pleasures of the senses that are here and now and those perception of pleasures of the senses that are hereafter, and there are those material shapes that are here and now and those material shapes that are hereafter, and there are those perceptions of material shapes that are here and now [and those material shapes that are hereafter and those perceptions of material shapes that are here and now[1]] and those perceptions of material shapes that are hereafter—both are impermanent. What is impermanent is not worth rejoicing over nor worth approval nor worth cleaving to.' While he is faring along thus, abiding given over to this, his thought is peaceful in its sphere; if he is serene either he comes to imperturbability now[2] or he is intent on wisdom. At the breaking up of the body after dying this situation exists, that that evolving consciousness may accordingly reach imperturbability. This, monks, is pointed to as the third course in beneficial imperturbability.

And again, monks, an ariyan disciple reflects thus:[3] ' There are those pleasures of the senses that are here and now . . . and those perceptions of material shapes that are hereafter, and there are those perceptions of imperturbability—where all those perceptions are stopped without remainder, that is the real, that the excellent,[4] that is to say the plane of no-thing.' While he is faring along thus, abiding given over to this, his thought is peaceful in its sphere; if he is serene either he comes to the plane of no-thing now or he is intent on wisdom. At the breaking up of the body after dying this situation exists, that that evolving consciousness may accordingly reach the plane of no-thing. This, monks, is pointed to as the first course for the beneficial plane of no-thing.

And again, monks, an ariyan disciple, forest-gone or gone to the root of a tree, reflects thus:[5] ' Empty[6] is this of self or of what belongs to self.'[7] While he is faring along thus, abiding given over to this, his thought is peaceful in its sphere; if he is serene either he comes to the plane of no-thing now or he is intent on wisdom. At the break-

---

[1] These two clauses are in Chalmers's text.
[2] In the plane of infinite consciousness.
[3] *I.e.* when he has attained the plane of infinite consciousness, *MA*. iv. 63.
[4] As at *M*. i. 436, ii. 235, *A*. iv. 423, v. 8, 110, 320, etc.
[5] While he is still at the plane of infinite consciousness.
[6] The text's *saññaṁ* should be corrected to *suññaṁ*.
[7] Of thoughts of " I " and " mine," thus the emptiness is twofold, *MA*. iv. 64.

ing up of the body after dying this situation exists, that that evolving consciousness may accordingly reach the plane of no-thing. This, monks, is pointed to as the second course for the beneficial plane of no-thing.

And again, monks, an ariyan disciple reflects thus:[1] ' I am naught of anyone anywhere [264] nor is there anywhere aught of mine.'[2] While he is faring along thus, abiding given over to this, his thought is peaceful in its sphere; if he is serene either he comes to the plane of no-thing now or he is intent on wisdom. At the breaking up of the body after dying this situation exists, that that evolving consciousness may accordingly reach the plane of no-thing. This, monks, is pointed to as the third course for the beneficial plane of no-thing.

And again, monks, an ariyan disciple reflects thus:[3] ' There are those pleasures of the senses that are here and now . . . and those perceptions of material shapes that are hereafter, and there are those perceptions of imperturbability, and there are those perceptions of the plane of no-thing—where all those perceptions are stopped without remainder, that is the real, that the excellent, that is to say the plane of neither-perception-nor-non-perception.' While he is faring along thus, abiding given over to this, his thought is peaceful in its sphere; if he is serene either he comes to the plane of neither-perception-nor-non-perception now or he is intent on wisdom. At the breaking up of the body after dying this situation exists, that that evolving consciousness may accordingly reach the plane of neither-perception-nor-non-perception. This, monks, is pointed to as the course for the beneficial plane of neither-perception-nor-non-perception."

When this had been said the venerable Ānanda spoke thus to the Lord: " Revered sir, if a monk is here faring along thus and thinks: ' Had it not been it would not be mine; if it be not it will not be mine;[4] I am getting rid of what is, of what has come to be '—he is

---

[1] While he is still at the plane of infinite consciousness. But he is wiser than the five monks already referred to.

[2] This is the fourth " brahman truth " made known by Gotama at *A*. ii. 177. See also *A*. i. 206 and *cf*. *Ud*. 79, *Dhp*. 421. The emptiness is here fourfold, *MA*. iv. 64-65.

[3] *I.e.* when he has attained the plane of no-thing.

[4] As at *S*. iii. 55, 99, 183. *MA*. iv. 65 explains: had it not been for my past fivefold circle of deeds (referring to the *khandhā*) this present fivefold circle of results would not be for me; if this present fivefold circle of effects did not come to be, there would therefore be no fivefold circle of results for me in the future.

thus acquiring equanimity.[1] Has not this monk, revered sir, attained final nibbāna?"

"It may be, Ānanda, that some monk here attains final nibbāna. It may be that another monk here does not attain final nibbāna."

"What is the cause, revered sir, what the reason that some monk here may attain final nibbāna, but that some other monk here may not attain final nibbāna?"[2]

"As to this, Ānanda, if a monk is here faring along thus and thinks: 'Had it not been it would not be mine; if it be not it will not be mine; I am getting rid of what is, [265] of what has come to be'—he is thus acquiring equanimity. He rejoices in this equanimity, approves of it and cleaves to it. While he rejoices in this equanimity, approves of it and cleaves to it, consciousness is dependent on it, grasping after it. A monk who has grasping, Ānanda, does not attain final nibbāna."[3]

"But where,[4] revered sir, does a monk grasp who is grasping?"[5]

"The plane of neither-perception-nor-non-perception, Ānanda."

"Indeed, revered sir, the monk who is grasping grasps after the best of graspings."[6]

"That monk who is grasping grasps after the best of graspings, Ānanda. For this is the best of graspings, Ānanda, that is to say the plane of neither-perception-nor-non-perception. Ānanda, if a monk is here faring along thus[7] and thinks: 'Had it not been it would not be mine; if it be not it will not be mine; I am getting rid of what is, of what has come to be'—he is thus acquiring equanimity. He does not rejoice in that equanimity, does not approve of it or cleave to it. Not rejoicing in that equanimity, not approving of it or cleaving to it, consciousness is not dependent on it, not grasping after it. A monk who is without grasping, Ānanda, attains final nibbāna."

"It is wonderful, revered sir, it is marvellous, revered sir. Indeed it is by means of this and that,[8] revered sir, that the crossing of the

---

[1] Due to insight, *vipassanā*.   [2] *Cf. M.* iii. 4-6.
[3] *Cf. S.* iv. 168, *anupādiyaṁ ... parinibbāyati*.
[4] *kahaṁ*, explained by *kattha* at *MA.* iv. 66, both meaning where, where to, where unto, whither.
[5] Grasping after *paṭisandhi*, re-linking, re-instatement, *MA.* iv. 67.
[6] He tries for re-instatement in the best state.
[7] Now speaking of a monk's arahantship.
[8] *nissāya nissāya*, on account of this attainment and that, *MA.* iv. 67.

flood has been pointed out to us by the Lord.[1] But which, revered sir, is the ariyan Deliverance ?"

"As to this, Ānanda, an ariyan disciple[2] reflects thus: 'There are those pleasures of the senses that are here and now and those pleasures of the senses that are hereafter, and there are those perceptions of pleasures of the senses that are here and now and those perceptions of pleasures of the senses that are hereafter, and there are those material shapes that are here and now and those material shapes that are hereafter, and there are those perceptions of material shapes that are here and now and those perceptions of material shapes that are hereafter, and there are those perceptions of imperturbability, and there are those perceptions of the plane of no-thing, and there are those perceptions of the plane of neither-perception-nor-non-perception—whatever is 'own body' this is 'own-body.'[3] But this is deathlessness,[4] that is to say the deliverance of thought without grasping.[5] So, Ānanda, taught by me has been the course for beneficial imperturbability, taught the course for the beneficial plane of no-thing, taught the course for the beneficial plane of neither-perception-nor-non-perception, taught by means of this and that has been the crossing of the flood, taught the ariyan Deliverance. Whatever, Ānanda, is to be done from compassion by a Teacher seeking the welfare of disciples, [**266**] this has been done by me out of compassion for you. These, Ānanda, are the roots of trees, these are empty places. Meditate, Ānanda, be not slothful, be not remorseful later. This is our instruction to you."[6]

Thus spoke the Lord. Delighted, the venerable Ānanda rejoiced in what the Lord had said.

Discourse on Beneficial Imperturbability:
The Sixth[7]

---

[1] *MA.* iv. 67, 68 makes the point that in this Sta. "dry-visioned arahantship" is being spoken of.

[2] Again, a "dry-visioned" ariyan disciple.

[3] In the three spheres of *kāma, rūpa, arūpa*; beyond these there is no "own-body," *MA.* iv. 67.

[4] *MA.* iv. 67, "this is the real, this the excellent."

[5] Elsewhere called nibbāna (*e.g. Vin.* v. 164, *Pts.* ii. 45; *cf. A.* v. 64). But here the arahantship of the "dry-visioned" one is meant, *MA.* iv. 68.

[6] As at *M.* i. 46, etc.

[7] Here ends Chalmers's *Majjhima-Nikāya,* vol. II.

107. DISCOURSE TO GAṆAKA-MOGGALLĀNA
(Gaṇakamoggallānasutta)

THUS have I heard: At one time the Lord was staying near Sāvatthī in the palace of Migāra's mother[1] in the Eastern Monastery. Then the brahman Gaṇaka-Moggallāna approached the Lord; having approached he exchanged greetings with the Lord; having conversed in a friendly and courteous way, he sat down at a respectful distance. As he was sitting down at a respectful distance, Gaṇaka-Moggallāna the brahman spoke thus to the Lord: " Just as, good Gotama, in this palace of Migāra's mother there can be seen a gradual training, a gradual doing, a gradual practice,[2] that is to say as far as the last flight of stairs;[3] so too, good Gotama, for these brahmans there can be seen a gradual training, a gradual doing, a gradual practice, that is to say in the study (of the Vedas[4]); so too, good Gotama, for these archers there can be seen a gradual . . . practice, that is to say in archery; to too, good Gotama, for us whose livelihood is calculation[5] there can be seen a gradual training, a gradual doing, a gradual practice, that is to say in accountancy. For when we get a pupil, good Gotama, we first of all make him calculate: ' One one, two twos, three threes, four fours, five fives, six sixes, seven sevens, eight eights, nine nines, ten tens,' and we, good Gotama, also make him calculate a hundred. Is it not possible, good Gotama, to lay down a similar gradual training, gradual doing, gradual practice in respect of this *dhamma* and discipline ?"

[2] " It is possible, brahman, to lay down a gradual training, a gradual doing, a gradual practice in respect of this *dhamma* and discipline. Brahman, even as a skilled trainer of horses,[6] having taken on a beautiful thoroughbred, first of all gets it used to the training in respect of wearing the bit, then gets it used to further training—even so, brahman, the Tathāgata, having taken on a man

---

[1] A seven-storied palace is not to be built in one day, *MA*. iv. 69.
[2] *Cf. M.* i. 479.
[3] *yāva pacchimā sopānakalebarā; cf. M.* ii. 92, *Vin.* ii. 128.
[4] *ajjhena; cf. M.* ii. 199. "It is not possible to learn the three Vedas by heart in one day," *MA*. iv. 69; *cf. Jā.* v. 10.
[5] *gaṇanā*, see *B.D.* ii. 176, *n.* 5. Above spelt *gaṇānā*.   [6] *Cf. M.* i. 446.

to be tamed, first of all disciplines him thus: 'Come you, monk, be of moral habit, live controlled by the control of the Obligations, endowed with (right) behaviour and pasture, seeing peril in the slightest faults and, undertaking them, train yourself in the rules of training.' As soon, brahman, as the monk is of moral habit, controlled by the control of the Obligations, endowed with (right) behaviour and pasture, seeing peril in the slightest faults and, undertaking them, trains himself in the rules of training, the Tathāgata disciplines him further, saying: 'Come you, monk, be guarded as to the doors of the sense-organs;[1] having seen a material shape with the eye do not be entranced with the general appearance, do not be entranced with the detail. For if one dwells with the organ of sight uncontrolled, covetousness and dejection, evil unskilled states of mind, may flow in. So fare along controlling it, guard the organ of sight, achieve control over the organ of sight. Having heard a sound with the ear . . . Having smelt a smell with the nose . . . Having savoured a taste with the tongue . . . Having felt a touch with the body . . . Having cognised a mental state with the mind, do not be entranced with the general appearance, do not be entranced with the detail. For if one dwell with the organ of mind uncontrolled, covetousness and dejection, evil unskilled states of mind, may flow in. So fare along controlling it, guard the organ of mind, achieve control over the organ of mind.'

As soon, brahman, as a monk is guarded as to the doors of the sense-organs, the Tathāgata disciplines him further, saying: 'Come you, monk, be moderate in eating; you should take food reflecting carefully, not for fun or indulgence or personal charm or beautification, but taking just enough for maintaining this body and keeping it going, for keeping it unharmed, for furthering the Brahma-faring, with the thought: Thus will I crush out an old feeling, and I will not allow a new feeling to arise, and then there will be for me subsistence and blamelessness and abiding in comfort.'

As soon, [3] brahman, as a monk is moderate in eating, the Tathāgata disciplines him further, saying: 'Come you, monk, dwell intent on vigilance; during the day while pacing up and down, while sitting down, cleanse the mind of obstructive mental states; during the first watch of the night, pacing up and down, sitting down, cleanse the mind of obstructive mental states; during the middle watch of the night, lie down on the right side in the lion posture,

---

[1] *Cf. M.* i. 355 *ff.* for the following.

foot resting on foot, mindful, clearly conscious, reflecting on the thought of getting up again; during the last watch of the night, when you have risen, while pacing up and down, while sitting down, cleanse the mind of obstructive mental states.'

As soon, brahman, as a monk is intent on vigilance, the Tathāgata disciplines him further, saying:[1] 'Come you, monk, be possessed of mindfulness and clear consciousness,[2] acting with clear consciousness whether you are approaching or departing, acting with clear consciousness whether you are looking ahead or looking round, acting with clear consciousness whether you are bending in or stretching out (the arms), acting with clear consciousness whether you are carrying the outer cloak, the bowl or robe, acting with clear consciousness whether you are eating, drinking, munching, savouring, acting with clear consciousness whether you are obeying the calls of nature, acting with clear consciousness whether you are walking, standing, sitting, asleep, awake, talking or being silent.'

As soon, brahman, as he is possessed of mindfulness and clear consciousness, the Tathāgata disciplines him further, saying: 'Come you, monk, choose a remote lodging in a forest,[3] at the root of a tree, on a mountain slope, in a glen, a hill cave, a cemetery, a woodland grove, in the open, or on a heap of straw.' On returning from alms-gathering after the meal, the monk sits down cross-legged, holding the back erect, having made mindfulness rise up in front of him. He, getting rid of covetousness for the world, dwells with a mind devoid of covetousness, he cleanses the mind of covetousness. Getting rid of the taint of ill-will, he dwells benevolent in mind; compassionate and merciful towards all creatures and beings, he cleanses the mind of the taint of ill-will. Getting rid of sloth and torpor, he dwells without sloth or torpor; perceiving the light, mindful and clearly conscious he cleanses the mind of sloth and torpor. Getting rid of restlessness and worry, he dwells calmly; the mind inwardly tranquil, he cleanses the mind of restlessness and worry. Getting rid of doubt, he dwells doubt-crossed; unperplexed as to the states that are skilled, he cleanses his mind of doubt. [4] He, by getting rid of these five hindrances, which are defilements of the mind and deleterious to intuitive wisdom, aloof from pleasures of the senses, aloof from unskilled states of mind, enters and abides in the first meditation which is accompanied by initial

---

[1] *M.* iii. 3 now goes on differently from *M.* i. 355-356.
[2] *Cf. M.* iii. 90, 135; *D.* i. 70; *A.* ii. 210.
[3] *Cf. M.* i. 181, etc.

thought and discursive thought, is born of aloofness and is rapturous and joyful. By allaying initial thought and discursive thought, his mind subjectively tranquillised and fixed on one point, he enters and abides in the second meditation which is devoid of initial thought and discursive thought, is born of concentration and is rapturous and joyful. By the fading out of rapture, he dwells with equanimity, attentive and clearly conscious, and experiences in his person that joy of which the ariyans say: 'Joyful lives he who has equanimity and is mindful,' and he enters and abides in the third meditation. By getting rid of joy, by getting rid of anguish, by the going down of his former pleasures and sorrows, he enters and abides in the fourth meditation which has neither anguish nor joy, and which is entirely purified by equanimity and mindfulness. Brahman, such is my instruction for those monks who are learners who, perfection being not yet attained,[1] dwell longing for the incomparable security from the bonds. But as for those monks who are perfected ones, the cankers destroyed, who have lived the life, done what was to be done, shed the burden, attained their own goal, the fetters of becoming utterly destroyed, and who are freed by perfect profound knowledge—these things conduce both to their abiding in ease here and now as well as to their mindfulness and clear consciousness."

When this had been said, the brahman Gaṇaka-Moggallāna spoke thus to the Lord:

"Now, on being exhorted thus and instructed thus by the good Gotama, do all the good Gotama's disciples attain the unchanging goal[2]—nibbāna, or do some not attain it?"

"Some of my disciples, brahman, on being exhorted and instructed thus by me, attain the unchanging goal—nibbāna; some do not attain it."

"What is the cause, good Gotama, what the reason that, since nibbāna does exist,[3] since the way leading to nibbāna exists, since the good Gotama exists as adviser, some of the good Gotama's disciples on being exhorted thus and instructed thus by the good Gotama, attain the unchanging goal—nibbāna, but some do not attain it?"

---

[1] *appattamānasā*, as at *S.* i. 121. "Those who have not attained the fruits," *MA.* iv. 70; who "have not attained arahantship," *SA.* i. 183. Referring to the *sekhā*, learners, or those still undergoing training.

[2] *accantaniṭṭhā*. *Accanta* can also mean utmost, culminating, supreme.

[3] *tiṭṭhat' eva nibbānaṁ;* but it possibly means "granted that there is indeed nibbāna." This however is unnecessary since the brahman already assumes there is nibbāna, and is here only emphasising (*eva*) his belief.

"Well then, brahman, I will question you on this point in reply. As it is pleasing to you, so you may answer me. What do [5] you think about this, brahman? Are you skilled in the way leading to Rājagaha?"

"Yes, sir; skilled am I in the way leading to Rājagaha."

"What do you think about this, brahman? A man might come along here wanting to go to Rājagaha; having approached you, he might speak thus: 'I want to go to Rājagaha, sir; show me the way to this Rājagaha.' You might speak thus to him: 'Yes, my good man, this road goes to Rājagaha; go along it for a while. When you have gone along it for a while you will see a village; go along for a while; when you have gone along for a while you will see a market town; go along for a while. When you have gone along for a while you will see Rājagaha with its delightful parks, delightful forests, delightful fields, delightful ponds.' But although he has been exhorted and instructed thus by you, he might take the wrong road and go westwards. Then a second man might come along wanting to go to Rājagaha ...(as above)... '... you will see Rājagaha with its delightful ... ponds.' Exhorted and instructed thus by you he might get to Rājagaha safely. What is the cause, brahman, what the reason that, since Rājagaha does exist, since the way leading to Rājagaha exists, since you exist as adviser, the one man, although being exhorted and instructed thus by you, may take the wrong road and go westwards while the other may get to Rājagaha safely?"

[6] "What can I, good Gotama, do in this matter? A shower of the way, good Gotama, am I."

"Even so, brahman, nibbāna does exist, the way leading to nibbāna exists and I exist as adviser. But while some of my disciples, on being exhorted and instructed thus by me attain the unchanging goal—nibbāna, some do not attain it. What can I, brahman, do in this matter? A shower of the Way, brahman, is a Tathāgata."

When this had been said, the brahman Gaṇaka-Moggallāna spoke thus to the Lord:

"Good Gotama, as for those persons[1] who, in want of a way of living, have gone forth from home into homelessness without faith, who are crafty, fraudulent, deceitful, who are unbalanced and puffed up, who are shifty, scurrilous and of loose talk, the doors of whose sense-organs are not guarded, who do not know moderation in eating, who are not intent on vigilance, indifferent to recluseship, not of

---

[1] From here as far as the beginning of the simile, cf. M. i. 32.

keen respect for the training, who are ones for abundance, lax, taking the lead in backsliding, shirking the burden of seclusion, who are indolent, of feeble energy, of confused mindfulness, not clearly conscious, not concentrated but of wandering minds, who are weak in wisdom, drivellers—the good Gotama is not in communion with *them*. But as for those young men of respectable families who have gone forth from home into homelessness from faith, who are not crafty, fraudulent or deceitful, who are not unbalanced or puffed up, who are not shifty, scurrilous or of loose talk, the doors of whose sense-organs are guarded, who know moderation in eating, who are intent on vigilance, longing for recluseship, of keen respect for the training, who are not ones for abundance, not lax, shirking backsliding, taking the lead in seclusion, who are of stirred up energy, self-resolute, with mindfulness aroused, clearly conscious, concentrated, their minds one-pointed, who have wisdom, are not drivellers—the good Gotama is in communion with *them*. As, good Gotama, black gum is pointed to as chief of root-scents,[1] as red sandal-wood is pointed to as chief of pith-scents, as [7] jasmine is pointed to as chief of flower-scents—even so is the exhortation of the good Gotama highest among the teachings of today.[2] Excellent, good Gotama, excellent, good Gotama. As, good Gotama, one might set upright what had been upset, or disclose what was covered, or show the way to one who had gone astray, or bring an oil-lamp into the darkness so that those with vision might see material shapes—even so in many a figure is *dhamma* made clear by the good Gotama. I am going to the revered Gotama for refuge and to *dhamma* and to the Order of monks. May the good Gotama accept me as a lay-follower going for refuge from today forth for as long as life lasts."

Discourse to Gaṇaka-Moggallāna:
The Seventh

---

[1] *Cf. S.* iii. 156, v. 44, *A.* v. 22 and see *G.S.* v. 17, *n.* 1.

[2] *paramajjadhammesu*. *Dhammā* are things taught (among other meanings). *MA.* iv. 70 says: the teachings of today, *ajjadhammā*, mean the teachings of the six (heretical ?) teachers; among these the word of Gotama is the supreme, the utmost.

108. DISCOURSE TO GOPAKA-MOGGALLĀNA
(Gopakamoggallānasutta)

THUS have I heard: At one time, not long after the Lord's *parinibbāna*, the venerable Ānanda[1] was staying near Rājagaha in the Bamboo Grove at the squirrels' feeding place. Now at that time King Ajātasattu of Magadha, the son of the lady of Videha, distrusting King Pajjota,[2] was having Rājagaha strengthened. Then the venerable Ānanda, dressing early in the morning, taking his bowl and robe, entered Rājagaha for almsfood. Then it occurred to the venerable Ānanda: " It is still too early to walk for alms in Rājagaha. Suppose that I were to approach the brahman Gopaka-Moggallāna and his place of work ?"[3] Then the venerable Ānanda approached the brahman Gopaka-Moggallāna and his place of work. The brahman Gopaka-Moggallāna saw the venerable Ānanda coming in the distance; seeing him he spoke thus to him: " Let the good Ānanda come, there is a welcome for the good Ānanda. It is long since the good Ānanda made this opportunity, that is for coming here. Let the good Ānanda sit down, this seat is made ready." And the venerable Ānanda sat down on the appointed seat. [8] The brahman Gopaka-Moggallāna, taking a low seat, sat down at a respectful distance. As he was sitting down at a respectful distance the brahman Gopaka-Moggallāna spoke thus to the venerable Ānanda:

" Is there even one monk, Ānanda, who is possessed in every way and in every part of all those things of which the good Gotama, perfected one, fully Self-Awakened One, was possessed ?"

" There is not even one monk, brahman, who is possessed in every way and in every part of all those things of which the Lord was possessed, perfected one, fully Self-Awakened One. For, brahman, this Lord was one to make arise a Way that had not arisen (before),

---

[1] *āyasmā*, venerable, omitted in the text, no doubt in error. After the distribution of the relics Ānanda was at Rājagaha to go through the recital of *dhamma*, *MA*. iv. 70.

[2] This king was a friend of Bimbisāra who was killed by his son Ajātasattu. At *Vin*. i. 276 *ff.* (referred to at *MA*. iv. 71) Bimbisāra sent his physician, Jīvaka, to tend Pajjota once when he was ill.

[3] Outside the city, *MA*. iv. 71.

to bring about a Way not brought about (before), to show a Way not shown (before); he was a knower of the Way, an understander of the Way, skilled in the Way. But the disciples are now Way-followers following after him."[1]

But this conversation between the venerable Ānanda and the brahman Gopaka-Moggallāna was interrupted, for the brahman Vassakāra,[2] the chief minister in Magadha, while inspecting the works near Rājagaha, approached the venerable Ānanda at the brahman Gopaka-Moggallāna's place of work; having approached, he exchanged greetings with the venerable Ānanda; having conversed in a friendly and courteous way, he sat down at a respectful distance. As he was sitting down at a respectful distance the brahman Vassakāra, the chief minister in Magadha, spoke thus to the venerable Ānanda: " What now, Ānanda, was the talk for which you were sitting here ? And what was that talk of yours that was interrupted ?"

" As to this, brahman, the brahman Gopaka-Moggallāna said this to me: ' Is there even one monk, Ānanda, who is possessed in every way and in every part of all those things of which the good Gotama, perfected one, fully Self-Awakened One, was possessed ?' When this had been said, I, brahman, spoke thus to the brahman Gopaka-Moggallāna: ' There is not even one monk . . . [9] . . . But the disciples are now Way-followers following after him.' This, brahman, was the conversation that was interrupted between the brahman Gopaka-Moggallāna and myself. For then you arrived."

" Is there, good Ānanda, even one monk who was designated by the good Gotama saying: ' After my passing this one will be your support,'[3] and to whom you might have recourse now ?"

" There is not even one monk, brahman, who was designated by the Lord who knew and saw, perfected one, fully Self-Awakened One, saying: ' After my passing this one will be your support,' and to whom we might have recourse now."

---

[1] *Cf. S.* i. 191, iii. 66. The words *pacchā samannāgatā* are not commented on by *MA.* here. *SA.* i. 277 however explains: *paṭhama-gatassa Bhagavato pacchā samanugatā*, they are following after (*sam-anugatā* from *sam-anugacchati*) the Lord who has gone first. *Samannāgata* is therefore here in its sense of " followed " or " following " rather than in its more usual sense of " possessed of, endowed with." Both these meanings of the word are noted by *P.E.D.*

[2] *Cf. Vin.* iii. 43, and see *B.D.* i. 68, *n.* 1.

[3] *paṭisaraṇa*, called *avassaya* at *MA.* iv. 72. I also recommend the word " mainstay " which J. J. Jones uses in his translation of the *Mhvu.*, vol. iii.

"But is there even one monk, Ānanda, who is agreed upon by the Order and designated by a number of monks who are elders, saying: 'After the Lord's passing this one will be our support,' and to whom you might have recourse now?"

"There is not even one monk, brahman, who is agreed upon by the Order ... and to whom we might have recourse now."

"But as you are thus without a support, good Ānanda, what is the cause of your unity?"

"We, brahman, are not without support; we have a support, brahman. *Dhamma* is the support."[1]

"When you were asked: 'Is there even one monk, good Ānanda, who was designated by the good Gotama, saying: After my passing this one will be your support, and to whom you might have recourse now?' you said: 'There is not even one monk ... to whom we might have recourse now.' When you were asked: 'Is there even one monk, good Ānanda, agreed upon by the Order and designated by a number of monks who are elders, saying: After the Lord's passing this one will be our support,' and to whom you might have recourse now?' you said: 'There is not even one monk ... [10] to whom we might have recourse now.' When you were asked: 'But as you are thus without support, good Ānanda, what is the cause of your unity?' you said: 'We, brahman, are not without a support; we have a support, brahman. *Dhamma* is the support.' Good Ānanda, what meaning is to be ascribed to what has been said?"

"There is, brahman, a rule of training laid down, an Obligation appointed for monks by that Lord who knows and sees, perfected one, fully Self-Awakened One. On every Observance Day we who live depending on the same field and village each and all gather together on the same day, and when we have gathered together we inquire what has happened to each one. While this is being told if there was an offence, a transgression on the part of a monk, we have him dealt with according to the rule,[2] according to the instruction. Indeed the revered ones do not deal with us, it is the rule[3] that deals with us."

"Now is there, good Ānanda, even one monk whom you revere,

---

[1] *Cf. D.* ii. 154.

[2] *yathādhamma.* For examples see s.v. "Rule, according to the" in Indexes to *B.D.* iv, v.

[3] *dhamma.* The context here seems to require "rule" in translation, which only shows the close inner bond of *dhamma* as teaching and *dhamma* as rule.

reverence, esteem and honour and on whom, revering and reverencing him, you live in dependence ?"

"There is, brahman, even one monk whom we revere . . . and honour and on whom, revering and reverencing him, we live in dependence."[1]

"When you were asked: 'Is there even one monk, good Ānanda, who was designated by the good Gotama . . . (*as above*) [11] . . . ' you said: 'There is not even one monk, brahman, who is agreed upon by the Order and designated by a number of monks who are Elders, saying: After the Lord's passing this one will be our arbiter, and to whom we might have recourse now.' When you were asked: 'Now is there, good Ānanda, even one monk whom you revere, reverence, esteem, honour and on whom, revering and reverencing him, you live in dependence ?' you said: 'There is, brahman, even one monk whom we revere . . . and honour and on whom, revering and reverencing him, we live in dependence.' Good Ānanda, what meaning is to be ascribed to what has been said ?"

"There are, brahman, ten satisfying things[2] that have been pointed out by the Lord who knows and sees, perfected one, fully Self-Awakened One. In whomsoever of us these things exist, him do we revere, reverence, esteem and honour and on him, revering and reverencing him, do we live in dependence. What are the ten ? Herein, brahman, a monk is moral,[3] he lives controlled by the control of the Obligations, endowed with (right) behaviour and pasture, seeing peril in the slightest faults and, undertaking them, he trains himself in the rules of training. He is one who has heard much, remembers what he has heard, stores up what he has heard; those things which are lovely at the beginning, lovely in the middle and lovely at the ending and which, with the meaning and the spirit, declare the Brahma-faring wholly fulfilled, perfectly purified, such things are much heard by him, borne in mind, familiarised by speech, pondered over in the mind, well penetrated by right view. He is content with the requisites of robe-material, almsfood, lodgings and medicines for the sick. He is one who acquires at will, without trouble, without difficulty the four meditations which are of the purest mentality, abidings in ease here and now. He experiences the various forms of psychic power; having been one he becomes manifold, having been manifold he becomes one; manifest or in-

---

[1] *Cf. M.* ii. 5.
[2] *Cf. A.* ii. 22-23 for four things which make an Elder, *thera*.
[3] *Cf. M.* i. 355.

visible he goes unhindered through a wall, a rampart or a mountain as if through air; he plunges into the ground and shoots up again as if in water; he walks upon the water without parting it as if on the ground; [12] sitting cross-legged he travels through the air like a bird on the wing; with his hand he rubs and strokes this moon and sun although they are of such mighty power and majesty; and even as far as the Brahma-world he has power in respect of his person. With the purified *deva*-like hearing surpassing that of men he hears both (kinds of) sounds—*deva*-like ones and human ones, whether they be far or near. He knows intuitively by mind the minds of other beings, of other individuals so that he comprehends of a mind that is full of attachment . . . aversion . . . confusion that it is full of attachment . . . aversion . . . confusion; or of a mind that is without attachment . . . without aversion . . . without confusion that it is without attachment . . . aversion . . . confusion; or he comprehends of a mind that is contracted that it is contracted; or he comprehends of a mind that is distracted that it is distracted; or he comprehends of a mind that has become great that it has become great; or he comprehends of a mind that has not become great that it has not become great; or he comprehends of a mind that has (some other mental state) superior to it that it has (some other mental state) superior to it; or he comprehends of a mind that has no (other mental state) superior to it that it has no (other mental state) superior to it; or he comprehends of a mind that is composed that it is composed; or he comprehends of a mind that is not composed that it is not composed; or he comprehends of a mind that is freed that it is freed; or he comprehends of a mind that is not freed that it is not freed. He recollects a variety of former habitations, that is to say one birth, two births . . . he recollects a variety of former habitations. With the purified *deva*-vision surpassing that of men he sees beings as they pass hence and come to be and he comprehends that the beings are mean, excellent, fair, foul, in a good bourn, in a bad bourn according to the consequences of deeds. By the destruction of the cankers, having realised by his own super-knowledge here and now the freedom of mind and the freedom through intuitive wisdom that are cankerless, entering thereon he abides therein.

These, brahman, are the ten satisfying things that have been pointed out by the Lord who knows and sees, perfected one, fully Self-Awakened One. In whomsoever of us these things exist, him do we revere, reverence, esteem and honour and on him, revering and reverencing him, do we live in dependence."

[13] When this had been said, the brahman Vassakāra, the chief minister in Magadha, spoke thus to General Upananda:[1] "What do you think about this? If it is thus, General, that these good sirs revere what should be revered, reverence what should be reverenced, esteem what should be esteemed, honour what should be honoured, then these good sirs most certainly revere what should be revered ... honour what should be honoured. For if these good sirs were not to revere, reverence, esteem or honour this (monk), then who on earth could these good sirs revere ... and honour and on whom, revering and reverencing him, could they live in dependence?"

Then Vassakāra, the chief minister in Magadha, spoke thus to the venerable Ānanda: "But where is the good Ānanda staying at present?"

"I, brahman, am at present staying in the Bamboo Grove."

"I hope, good Ānanda, that the Bamboo Grove is pleasant, with little sound, little noise, sheltered from the winds, secluded from the haunts of men and suitable for solitary meditation?"

"Most certainly, brahman, the Bamboo Grove is pleasant, with little sound, little noise, sheltered from the winds, secluded from the haunts of men, suitable for solitary meditation as befits a guardian and warden like yourself."

"Most certainly, good Ānanda, the Bamboo Grove is pleasant, with little sound, little noise, sheltered from the winds, secluded from the haunts of men, suitable for solitary meditation as befits meditators and those disposed to meditation like the revered ones. The revered ones are both meditators and disposed to meditation. At one time, good Ānanda, the revered Gotama was staying near Vesālī in the Great Wood in the hall of the Gabled House. Then I, good Ānanda, approached the revered Gotama in the Great Wood in the hall of the Gabled House. While he was there the revered Gotama in many a figure talked a talk on meditation. A meditator was the revered Gotama and he was disposed to meditation; and the revered Gotama praised every (form of) meditation."

"No, brahman, the Lord did not praise every (form of) meditation, nor did the Lord not praise every (form of) meditation. What kind [14] of meditation, brahman, did the Lord not praise? As to this, brahman, someone dwells with his thought obsessed by attachment to pleasures of the senses, overcome by attachment to pleasures

---

[1] This may be the sole reference to him in the Pali Canon. He was "commander-in-chief of the Magadha kingdom," *D.P.P.N.*

of the senses, and he does not comprehend as it really is the
escape from the attachment to the pleasures of the senses that
has arisen; he, having made attachment to the pleasures of the
senses the main thing,[1] meditates on it, meditates absorbed, meditates more absorbed, meditates quite absorbed.[2] He dwells with
his thought obsessed by ill-will, overcome by ill-will, and he does not
comprehend as it really is the escape from the ill-will that has arisen;
he, having made ill-will the main thing, meditates on it, meditates
absorbed, meditates more absorbed, meditates quite absorbed. He
dwells with his thought obsessed by sloth and torpor . . . by restlessness and worry . . . by doubt, overcome by doubt, and he does not
comprehend as it really is the escape from the doubt that has arisen;
he, having made doubt the main thing, meditates on it, meditates
absorbed, meditates more absorbed, meditates quite absorbed. The
Lord does not praise this kind of meditation, brahman.

And what kind of meditation, brahman, does the Lord praise?
As to this, brahman, a monk, aloof from pleasures of the senses,
aloof from unskilled states of mind, enters and abides in the first
meditation which is accompanied by initial thought and discursive
thought, is born of aloofness, and is rapturous and joyful. By
allaying initial and discursive thought, with the mind subjectively
tranquillised and fixed on one point, he enters and abides in the
second meditation which is devoid of initial and discursive thought,
is born of concentration, and is rapturous and joyful . . . he enters
and abides in the third meditation and the fourth meditation. The
Lord praises this kind of meditation, brahman."

"Indeed, good Ānanda, the good Gotama contemned the meditation that is contemptible, commended that which is commendable.
But now, if you please, good Ānanda, we must be going. We are
very busy, there is much to be done."

"You, brahman, do that for which you deem it is now the right
time."

[15] Then Vassakāra, the chief minister in Magadha, rejoicing
in what the venerable Ānanda had said, giving thanks, rising from
his seat departed. Then soon after the brahman Vassakāra, the
chief minister in Magadha, had departed, the brahman Gopaka-
Moggallāna spoke thus to the venerable Ānanda: "The good
Ānanda has explained to us what we asked him."

---

[1] *antaraṁ karitvā*; *MA.* iv. 73: *abbhantaraṁ karitvā*. See *C.P.D.*, and
cf. M. iii. 38.
[2] As at *M.* i. 334.

"Did we not say to you, brahman: 'There is not even one monk, brahman, who is possessed in every way and in every part of all those things of which the Lord was possessed, perfected one, fully Self-Awakened One.' For, brahman, this Lord was one to make arise a Way that had not arisen (before), to bring about a Way not brought about (before), to show a Way not shown (before); he was a knower of the Way, an understander of the Way, skilled in the Way. But the disciples are now Way-followers following after him'?"

Discourse to Gopaka-Moggallāna:
The Eighth

109. GREATER DISCOURSE (AT THE TIME) OF A FULL MOON[1]

(Mahāpuṇṇamasutta)

THUS have I heard: At one time the Lord was staying near Sāvatthī in the palace of Migāra's mother in the Eastern Monastery. Now at that time the Lord was sitting down in the open air on the night of a full moon on an Observance day, the fifteenth,[2] surrounded by an Order of monks. Then a certain monk, rising from his seat, arranging his upper robe over one shoulder, having saluted the Lord with joined palms, spoke thus to the Lord: "I, revered sir, would ask the Lord about a particular matter if the Lord grants me the opportunity[3] to set forth a question."

"Well then, monk, you, having sat down on your own seat,[4] ask what you desire." Then that monk, having sat down on his own seat, spoke thus to the Lord:

---

[1] As at *S*. iii. 100 *ff*.
[2] The fifteenth day of the lunar month. *Cf. S*. iii. 100, *Vin*. i. 104.
[3] *okāsaṁ karoti*; *cf. Vin*. i. 114, iv. 344.
[4] *MA*. iv. 75 *f*. explains that this monk was the Elder in an Order of sixty who were staying in a forest. If he stood, they would stand, thereby showing disrespect to the Tathāgata; but if they sat while their teacher was speaking they would be showing disrespect to him. But if the teacher sat they too would sit and so, all being tranquil, they would be able to receive the teaching on *dhamma*.

"Are there not, revered sir, these five groups of grasping, [16] that is to say, the group of grasping after material shape, the group of grasping after feeling, the group of grasping after perception, the group of grasping after the habitual tendencies, the group of grasping after consciousness ?"

"These, monk, are the five groups of grasping, that is to say the group of grasping after material shape . . . the group of grasping after consciousness."

"It is good, revered sir," and this monk, having rejoiced in what the Lord had said, having given thanks, asked the Lord a further question: "But what, revered sir, is the root of these five groups of grasping ?"

"These five groups of grasping, monk, have desire for root."

"Are just these five groups of grasping the whole of grasping, revered sir ? Or is there grasping apart from these five groups of grasping ?"

"Indeed, monk, these five groups of grasping are not the whole of grasping, and yet there is no grasping apart from the five groups of grasping. Whatever, monks, is attachment to and desire for the five groups of grasping, then that is grasping."

"Might it be, revered sir, that there is diversity in the attachment to and desire for the five groups of grasping ?"

"It might be, monk," the Lord said. "It occurs to someone here, monk: 'May material shape be thus in the distant future, may feeling . . . perception . . . the habitual tendencies . . . may consciousness be such in the distant future.' Even so, monk, is there diversity in the attachment to and desire for the five groups of grasping."

"But to what extent, revered sir, is there a group-designation for the groups ?"

"Whatever, monk, is material shape, past, future or present, internal or external, gross or subtle, mean or excellent, or whatever is far or near, this is the group of material shape. [17] Whatever is feeling, past, future or present . . . Whatever is perception . . . Whatever are the habitual tendencies . . . Whatever is consciousness, past, future or present . . . far or near, this is the group of consciousness. To this extent, monk, is there a group-designation for the groups."

"What is the cause, revered sir, what the reason enabling a definition to be made of a group of material shape? What is the cause, what the reason enabling a definition to be made of the group of feeling . . . the group of perception . . . the group of the habitual tendencies . . . the group of consciousness ?"

"The four great elementals, monk, are the cause, the four great elementals are the reason enabling a definition to be made of the group of material shape. (Sensory) impingement[1] is the cause, (sensory) impingement is the reason enabling a definition to be made of the group of feeling . . . the group of perception . . . the group of the habitual tendencies. Name-and-shape is the cause, name-and-shape is the reason enabling a definition to be made of the group of consciousness."[2]

"But how, revered sir, is there (wrong) view as to 'own body'[3] ?"

"As to this, monk, an uninstructed average person, taking no count of the pure ones, unskilled in the *dhamma* of the pure ones, untrained in the *dhamma* of the pure ones, taking no count of the true men, unskilled in the *dhamma* of the true men, untrained in the *dhamma* of the true men, regards material shape as self, or self as having material shape, or material shape as in self, or self as in material shape. He regards feeling as self . . . perception as self . . . the habitual tendencies as self . . . He regards consciousness as self, or self as having consciousness, [**18**] or consciousness as in self, or self as in consciousness. Thus, monk, is there (wrong) view as to ' own body.' "

"But how, revered sir, is there not (wrong) view as to 'own body ' ?"

"As to this, monk, an instructed disciple of the pure ones, taking count of the pure ones, skilled in the *dhamma* of the pure ones, well trained in the *dhamma* of the pure ones, taking count of the true men, skilled in the *dhamma* of the true men, well trained in the *dhamma* of the true men, does not regard material shape as self. . . . He does not regard consciousness as self, nor self as having consciousness, nor consciousness as in self, nor self as in consciousness. Thus, monk, is there not (wrong) view as to ' own body.' "

"And what, revered sir, is the satisfaction in material shape, what the peril, what is the escape from it ? What is the satisfaction in feeling . . . in perception . . . in the habitual tendencies . . . in consciousness, what the peril, what is the escape from it ?"

---

[1] *phassa*. *MA*. iv. 78 says that if one is impinged upon then one feels, perceives, wills.

[2] *Cf. D.* ii. 62-63 where name-and-shape and consciousness are mutually dependent. Here re-linking consciousness is meant, *MA*. iv. 78.

[3] *Cf. M.* i. 300.

"Monk, whatever happiness and bliss arise on account of material shape, this constitutes the satisfaction in material shape. Whatever impermanence, suffering, liability to change are in material shape, this constitutes the peril in material shape. Whatever the control of attachment to and desire for material shape, the getting rid of the attachment and desire, this constitutes the escape from material shape. Monk, whatever happiness and bliss arise on account of feeling... perception... the habitual tendencies... consciousness, this constitutes the satisfaction in consciousness. Whatever impermanence, suffering, liability to change are in consciousness, this constitutes the peril in consciousness. Whatever the control of attachment to and desire for consciousness, the getting rid of the attachment and desire, this constitutes the escape from consciousness."

"But, revered sir, (for a man) knowing what, seeing what, are there no latent conceits that 'I am the doer, mine is the doer' in regard to this consciousness-informed body and all the phenomena external to it?"

"Whatever, monk, is material shape, past, future or present, internal or external, gross or subtle, mean [19] or excellent, or whatever is far or near, he, thinking of all this material shape as 'This is not mine, this am I not, this is not my self,' sees it thus as it really is by means of perfect wisdom. Whatever is feeling[1]... perception ... the habitual tendencies... whatever is consciousness, past, future or present ... he, thinking of all this consciousness as 'This is not mine, this am I not, this is not my self,' sees it thus as it really is by means of perfect wisdom. Monk, (for a man) knowing thus, seeing thus, there are no latent conceits that 'I am the doer, mine is the doer' in regard to this consciousness-informed body."

Then a reasoning arose in the mind of a certain monk thus: "It is said, sir,[2] that material shape is not self, feeling is not self, perception is not self, the habitual tendencies are not self, consciousness is not self. Then what self do deeds affect that are done by not-self?"[3]

Then the Lord, knowing by mind the reasoning in the mind of this monk, addressed the monks, saying: "This situation exists, monks,

---

[1] *vedanā*, feeling, is omitted in the text, no doubt in error.

[2] *iti kira bho*. This looks like a case where a monk, in thought, applies *bho* to himself. Or else he is thinking (as translated at *KS*. iii. 88) " so then you say."

[3] "In what self do these results appear? Speaking thus, he fell into the view of eternalism," *MA*. iv. 79.

when some foolish man here, not knowing, ignorant, with his mind in the grip of craving, may deem to go beyond[1] the Teacher's instruction thus: ' It is said, sir, that material shape is not self . . . consciousness is not self. Then what self do deeds affect that are done by not-self ?' You, monks, have been trained by me (to look for) conditions[2] now here, now there, in these things and in those. What do you think about this, monks ? Is material shape permanent or impermanent ?"

" Impermanent, revered sir."

" But is what is impermanent painful or is it pleasant ?"

" Painful, revered sir."

" And is it right to regard that which is impermanent, suffering, liable to change, as, ' This is mine, this am I, this is my self ' ?"

" No, revered sir."

" What do you think about this, monks ? Is feeling . . . perception . . . are the habitual tendencies . . . is consciousness permanent or impermanent ?"

" Impermanent, revered sir."

[20] " But is what is impermanent painful or is it pleasant ?"

" Painful, revered sir."

" And is it right to regard that which is impermanent, suffering, liable to change, as ' This is mine, this am I, this is my self ' ?"

" No, revered sir."

" Wherefore, monks, whatever is material shape, past, future or present, internal . . . thinking of all this material shape as ' This is not mine, this am I not, this is not my self,' he should see it thus as it really is by means of perfect wisdom. Whatever is feeling . . . whatever is perception . . . whatever are the habitual tendencies . . . whatever is consciousness, past, future or present, internal . . . thinking of all this consciousness as ' This is not mine, this am I not, this is not my self,' he should see it thus as it really is by means of perfect wisdom. Seeing it thus, monks, the instructed disciple of the pure ones turns away from material shape, he turns away from feeling, turns away from perception, turns away from the habitual tendencies, turns away from consciousness; turning away he is detached; by his detachment he is freed; in freedom there is the knowledge that he is freed and he comprehends: Destroyed is birth, brought to a close

---

[1] *atidhāvati*; cf. *M*. iii. 230, *S*. iii. 103, iv. 230, *Iti*. p. 43, *Ud*. 64. Explained at *UdA*. 352. It means to by-pass, deviate from, outstrip, run ahead of, " go one better than," " improve upon."

[2] *paṭicca-vinītā*, trained in conditions. *S*. iii. 104 reads *paṭipucchā vinītā*.

the Brahma-faring, done is what was to be done, there is no more of being such or so."

Thus spoke the Lord. Delighted, these monks rejoiced in what the Lord had said.

And while this exposition was being spoken the minds of as many as sixty monks[1] were freed from the cankers with no grasping (remaining).

Greater Discourse (at the Time) of a Full Moon:
The Ninth

110. LESSER DISCOURSE (AT THE TIME) OF A FULL MOON
(Cūḷapuṇṇamasutta)

THUS have I heard: At one time the Lord was staying near Sāvatthī in the palace of Migāra's mother in the Eastern Monastery. Now at that time the Lord [21] was sitting down in the open air on the night of a full moon on an Observance day, the fifteenth, surrounded by an Order of monks. Then the Lord, having looked round the Order of monks which, as he did so, became quite silent, addressed the monks, saying:

"Now, monks, could a bad man[2] know of a bad man: 'This worthy is a bad man'?"

"No, revered sir."

"It is good, monks. This is impossible, monks, it cannot come to pass that a bad man could know of a bad man: 'This worthy is a bad

---

[1] Those referred to in *MA.* on this Sta. as having lived in the forest learning meditation under a teacher who, not satisfied with their progress, brought them to the Lord and himself questioned Him. *MA.* iv. 79 says that they had meditated on the usual subjects of meditation but now, mastering a new one and not moving from their cross-legged positions, they attained arahantship on the very seats on which they were sitting.

[2] *asappurisa*, called *pāpapurisa* at *MA.* iv. 79; not a "true" man, not following "our" *dhamma* and discipline. See *A.* ii. 179 where the brahman Vassakāra (mentioned in *M.* Sta. 108) put some of these same questions to the Lord.

man.' But, monks, could a bad man know of a good man: 'This worthy is a good man' ?"

"No, revered sir."

"It is good, monks. This too is impossible, monks, it cannot come to pass that a bad man could know of a good man: 'This worthy is a good man.' A bad man, monks, is possessed of bad states of mind, he consorts with bad men, he thinks as do bad men, he advises as do bad men, he speaks as do bad men, he acts as do bad men, he has the views of bad men, he gives a gift as do bad men. And how, monks, is a bad man possessed of bad states of mind ? As to this, monks, a bad man is lacking in faith, he has no shame, no fear of blame, he has heard little, he is lazy, he is of muddled mindfulness, he is weak in wisdom—it is thus, monks, that a bad man is possessed of bad states of mind.

And how, monks, does a bad man consort with bad men ? As to this, monks, those recluses and brahmans who are lacking in faith, have no shame, no fear of blame, who have heard little, who are lazy, of muddled mindfulness, weak in wisdom—these are the friends and companions of that bad man. It is thus, monks, that a bad man consorts with bad men.

And how, monks, does a bad man think as do bad men ? As to this, monks, a bad man is set on self-torment, he is set on the torment of others, he is set on the torment of both—it is thus, monks, that a bad man thinks as do bad men.

And how, monks, does a bad man advise as do bad men ? As to this, monks, a bad man advises the torment of self and he advises the torment of others [22] and he advises the torment of both—it is thus, monks, that a bad man advises as do bad men.

And how, monks, does a bad man speak as do bad men ? As to this, monks, a bad man is of lying speech, slanderous speech, harsh speech, a gossip—it is thus, monks, that a bad man speaks as do bad men.

And how, monks, does a bad man act as do bad men ? As to this, monks, a bad man is one to make onslaught on creatures, to take what has not been given, to enjoy himself wrongly among the sense-pleasures—it is thus, monks that a bad man acts as do bad men.

And how, monks, does a bad man have the views of bad men ? As to this, monks, a bad man is of these views: 'There is no (result of) gift, there is no (result of) offering, there is no (result of) sacrifice; there is no fruit or ripening of deeds well done or ill done; there is not this world, there is not a world beyond; there is no (benefit from serving) mother, no (benefit from serving) father; there are no spontaneously arising beings; there are not in the world recluses and brahmans who are faring rightly, proceeding rightly, and who proclaim this world and the world beyond, having realised them by their own super-knowledge.' It is thus, monks, that a bad man has the views of bad men.

And how, monks, does a bad man give a gift as do bad men ? As to this, monks, a bad man gives a gift disrespectfully,[1] he gives a gift not with his own hand, he gives a gift without due consideration,[2] he gives a gift of what is not wanted,[3] he gives a gift regardless of the future.[4] It is thus, monks, that a bad man gives a gift as do bad men.

Monks, that bad man, thus possessed of bad states of mind, who thus consorts with bad men, thinks thus as do bad men, advises thus as do bad men, speaks thus as do bad men, acts thus as do bad men, who thus has the views of bad men, who thus gives a gift as do bad men, on the breaking up of the body after dying arises in some bourn of bad men. And what, monks, is a bourn of bad men ? It is Niraya hell or animal birth.

Now, monks, could a good man know of a good man: ' This worthy is a good man ' ?"

[23] " Yes, revered sir."

" It is good, monks. This situation occurs, monks, that a good man could know of a good man: ' This worthy is a good man.' But, monks, could a good man know of a bad man: ' This worthy is a bad man ' ?"

" Yes, revered sir."

" It is good, monks. This situation also occurs, monks, that a good man could know of a bad man: ' This worthy is a bad man.' A good man, monks, is possessed of good states of mind, he consorts with good men, he thinks as do good men, he advises as do good men, he speaks as do good men, he acts as do good men, he has the views of good men, he gives a gift as do good men. And how, monks, is a

---

[1] *Cf. D.* ii. 356, *A.* iii. 171 for these improper ways of giving a gift. Disrespectfully means both towards the gift and the recipient.

[2] *I.e.* either of the gift or the recipient; *acittikatvā dānaṁ deti.*

[3] *apaviddha,* not wanted, neglected, rejected (as useless). *MA.* iv. 81 says that wanting to throw it away, he gives it as though he were flinging a snake on to an ant-hill.

[4] *anāgamanadiṭṭhika, i.e.* not thinking to whom will the fruit of the gift return (*AA.* iii. 291); or, hoping it will return to himself (*MA.* iv. 81).

good man possessed of good states of mind ? As to this, monks, a good man has faith, he has shame and fear of blame, he has heard much, he is of stirred up energy, he has mindfulness aroused, he has wisdom—it is thus, monks, that a good man is possessed of good states of mind.

And how, monks, does a good man consort with good men ? As to this, monks, those recluses and brahmans who have faith, shame, fear of blame, who have heard much, are of stirred up energy, whose mindfulness is aroused, who have wisdom—these are the friends and companions of that good man. It is thus, monks, that a good man consorts with good men.

And how, monks, does a good man think as do good men ? As to this, monks, a good man is neither set on self-torment, nor on the torment of others nor on the torment of both—it is thus, monks, that a good man thinks as do good men.

And how, monks, does a good man advise as do good men ? As to this, monks, a good man advises neither self-torment nor the torment of others nor the torment of both—it is thus, monks, that a good man advises as do good men.

And how, monks, does a good man speak as do good men ? As to this, monks, a good man refrains from lying speech, from slanderous speech, from harsh speech, he refrains from gossiping—it is thus, monks, that a good man speaks as do good men.

And how, monks, does a good man act as do good men ? As to this, monks, a good man refrains from onslaught on creatures, from taking what has not been given, [**24**] from enjoying himself wrongly among the sense-pleasures—it is thus, monks, that a good man acts as do good men.

And how, monks, does a good man have the views of good men ? As to this, monks, a good man is of these views: ' There is (result of) gift, there is (result of) offering, there is (result of) sacrifice; there is fruit and ripening of deeds well done or ill done; there is this world, there is a world beyond; there is (benefit from serving) mother, there is (benefit from serving) father; there are spontaneously arising beings; there are in the world recluses and brahmans who are faring rightly, proceeding rightly and who proclaim this world and the world beyond having realised them by their own super-knowledge. It is thus, monks, that a good man has the views of good men.

And how, monks, does a good man give a gift as do good men ? As to this, monks, a good man gives a gift respectfully, he gives a gift with his own hand,¹ he gives a gift with due consideration, he gives a gift that is pure, he gives a gift with regard to the future.² It is thus, monks, that a good man gives a gift as do good men.

Monks, that good man, thus possessed of good states of mind, who thus consorts with good men, thinks thus as do good men, advises thus as do good men, speaks thus as do good men, acts thus as do good men, who thus has the views of good men, who thus gives a gift as do good men, on the breaking up of the body after dying arises in some bourn of good men. And what, monks, is a bourn of good men ? It is *deva*-greatness³ or human greatness."⁴

Thus spoke the Lord. Delighted, these monks rejoiced in what the Lord had said.

Lesser Discourse (at the time) of a Full Moon:
The Tenth

Devadaha Division:
The First

---

¹ This clause is omitted in the text, probably in error.

² He gives having faith in the deed and its ripening, *AA*. iii. 291.

³ *mahattatā*; *MA*. iv. 81 says that this means the devas of the six sensuous realms (for these *cf. Vbh.* 417).

⁴ *MA*. iv. 81, success in (or, attainment of), *sampatti*, the three skills, *kusalāni*, perhaps referring to skill in the three ways of body, speech and thought; or to skill due to the absence of attachment, hatred and confusion (?).

II. THE DIVISION OF THE UNINTERRUPTED
(Anupadavagga)

111. DISCOURSE ON THE UNINTERRUPTED

(Anupadasutta[1])

[25] THUS have I heard: At one time the Lord was staying near Sāvatthī in the Jeta Grove in Anāthapiṇḍika's monastery. While he was there the Lord addressed the monks, saying: "Monks." "Revered One," these monks answered the Lord in assent. The Lord spoke thus:

"Proficient,[2] monks, is Sāriputta; of great wisdom,[3] monks, is Sāriputta; of wide wisdom,[4] monks, is Sāriputta; of bright wisdom,[5] monks, is Sāriputta; of swift wisdom,[6] monks, is Sāriputta; of acute wisdom,[7] monks, is Sāriputta; of piercing wisdom,[8] monks, is Sāriputta. For half a month, monks, Sāriputta had uninterrupted

---

[1] *anupada* is continuous, or uninterrupted, "the next step following."

[2] *paṇḍita*, clever or wise. For this and the following words for wisdom (spoken to Sāriputta) see *S*. i. 191. *MA*. iv. 82 says he was skilled in the *dhātu*, the *āyatana*, dependent origination and in causal occasion and what is not causal occasion (*ṭhānāṭhāna*, or, the possible and the impossible), with which cf. *M*. iii. 62.

[3] *mahāpañña*. Cf. *Pts*. ii. 190, *MA*. iv. 83 which enumerate various kinds of "great wisdom," such as in the moral habits, concentration, freedom, the knowledge and vision of freedom, the causal occasion and what is not, attainments in the great abidings, the ariyan truths, the 37 things helpful to enlightenment, the fruits of recluseship, the super-knowledges and the great incomparable nibbāna. See also *A*. ii. 67.

[4] *puthupañña*. Cf. *Pts*. ii. 191, *MA*. iv. 83, the same as *mahāpañña* but with some additions. See also *A*. i. 131, ii. 67.

[5] *hāsupañña*. Cf. *S*. v. 376, *Pts*. ii. 199. The word *hāsu* would appear from *MA*. iv. 84 and *Pts*. to be connected with contentment and rapture in fulfilling the *sīla*, the control of the sense-organs, moderation in eating, vigilance, and the body of moral habits, concentration, wisdom and freedom. Cf. *hasati*, to be glad. *Hāsa* also found in *Dhs*., e.g. §9, 86, etc., in definition of *pīti*, rapture.

[6] *javanapañña*. Cf. *S*. v. 376-377, *Pts*. ii. 200. *MA*. iv. 84: he hastens quickly (in knowing) that all the *khandhā* are impermanent, suffering, not-self.

[7] *tikkhapañña*. Cf. *M*. i. 11, *D*. iii. 126 and also see *A*. i. 45. *MA*. iv. 85: he quickly cuts through the defilements, and gets rid of evil unskilled states of mind, attachment, aversion and confusion, etc., that have arisen.

[8] *nibbedhikapañña*; cf. *Pts*. ii. 201 ff., and for references see *P.E.D.* All these forms of wisdom are mentioned at *S*. i. 63 (again of Sāriputta) and at *Jā*. iv. 136. See *K.S.* i. 88, *n*. 1.

insight into things.[1] This, monks, is due to Sāriputta's uninterrupted insight into things: as to this, monks, Sāriputta, aloof from pleasures of the senses, aloof from unskilled states of mind, enters on and abides in the first meditation which is accompanied by initial thought and discursive thought, is born of aloofness, and is rapturous and joyful. And those things which belong to the first meditation: initial thought[2] and sustained thought[2] and rapture[2] and joy[2] and one-pointedness of mind,[2] impingement,[3] feeling,[3] perception,[3] will,[3] thought,[3] desire, determination, energy,[4] mindfulness,[5] equanimity,[6] attention,[7] are uninterruptedly set up[8] by him; known to him these things arise, known they persist, known they disappear. He comprehends thus: 'Thus indeed things that have not been in me come to be; having been they pass away.' He, not feeling attracted[9] by these things, not feeling repelled,[10] independent,[11] not infatuated,[12] freed,[13] released,[14] dwells with a mind that is unconfined.[15] He comprehends: 'There is a further escape.'[16] There is zealous practice for him concerning that.

And again, monks, Sāriputta, by allaying initial and discursive thought, with his mind subjectively tranquillised and fixed on one point, [26] enters on and abides in the second meditation which is devoid of initial thought and discursive thought, is born of concentration, and is rapturous and joyful. And those things which belong to the second meditation: inward tranquillity and rapture and joy and one-pointedness of mind, impingement, feeling . . . equanimity, attention, are uninterruptedly set up by him; known to him these

---

[1] Sāriputta then gained arahantship in a fortnight, *MA*. iv. 86; also *MA*. iii. 203, *DA*. 418, *DhA*. i. 97.
[2] See *Dhs*. 7-11, 84-88, 283-287, 371-375. For an extremely valuable discussion of these and many of the following terms see *Bud. Psych. Ethics*, especially the notes on p. 5-18.
[3] See *Dhs*. 2-6, 278-282, 366-370. [4] See *Dhs*. 13.
[5] *Dhs*. 332. [6] *Dhs*. 153.
[7] *Dhs*. 1334. [8] *anupadavavatthitā*.
[9] *anupāya*. The following sequence of terms occurs also at *M*. iii. 30.
[10] *anapāya*.
[11] *anissita*, i.e. of craving and wrong views, *MA*. iv. 89.
[12] *apaṭibaddha*, i.e. by attachment and desire.
[13] *vippamutta*, i.e. from attachment to sense-pleasures.
[14] *visaṁyutta*, i.e. from the four yokes or all the defilements, *MA*. iv. 89.
[15] *vimariyādikatena cetasā*; cf. *S*. iii. 31. Unconfined because of what it has eliminated.
[16] *Cf. M*. i. 38, and see *M.L.S*. i. 48, *n*. 7. But here it means, not nibbāna, but the next excellent attainment.

things . . . disappear. He comprehends . . . 'There is a further escape.' There is zealous practice for him concerning that.

And again, monks, Sāriputta, by the fading out of rapture, dwells with equanimity, is mindful and clearly conscious, and he experiences in his person that joy of which the ariyans say: ' Joyful lives he who has equanimity and is mindful,' and he enters on and abides in the third meditation. And those things which belong to the third meditation: equanimity and joy and mindfulness and clear consciousness . . . equanimity, attention, are uninterruptedly set up by him; known to him these things . . . disappear. He comprehends . . . ' There is a further escape.' There is zealous practice for him concerning that.

And again, monks, Sāriputta, by getting rid of joy, by getting rid of anguish, by the going down of his former pleasures and sorrows, enters on and abides in the fourth meditation which has neither anguish nor joy, and which is entirely purified by equanimity and mindfulness. And those things which belong to the fourth meditation: equanimity, feeling that is neither painful nor pleasant . . .[1] impassivity of mind,[2] purification by mindfulness, one-pointedness of mind, and impingement, feeling, perception, will, thought, desire, determination, energy, mindfulness, equanimity, attention, are uninterruptedly set up by him; known to him these things arise, known they persist, [27] known they disappear. He comprehends . . . ' There is a further escape.' There is zealous practice for him concerning that.

And again, monks, Sāriputta, by passing quite beyond perceptions of material shapes, by the going down of perceptions of sensory reactions, by not attending to perceptions of variety, thinking: ' Ether is unending,' enters on and abides in the plane of infinite ether. And those things which belong to the plane of infinite ether: perception in the plane of infinite ether and one-pointedness of mind and impingement, feeling . . . equanimity, attention, are uninterruptedly set up by him; known to him these things . . . disappear.

---

[1] The textual reading, *passi vedanā*, is unintelligible to me. Neumann appears to give " Reinheit." The Comy. is silent.

[2] *cetaso anābhogo*, impassivity of thought, lack of mental interest, lack of ideation, lack of inclination. See *Pts. Contr.*, p. 221, n. 4 on *ābhoga*; and see *Vism.* 164, quoted at *MA.* iv. 90 to show that *cetaso ābhogo*, which was present in the third *jhāna*, is absent in the fourth. *Cf.* also *Vbh.* 307, quoted *Kvu.* 425, *pañca viññāṇā anābhogā*; and *MA.* ii. 63 *anāvaṭṭano anābhogo*. *B.H.S.D.* under *anābhoga* suggests " effortless " (adj.) and " Non-effort, impassivity " (subst.); see also s.v. *ābhoga*.

He comprehends ... 'There is a further escape.' There is zealous practice for him concerning that.

And again, monks, Sāriputta, by passing quite beyond the plane of infinite ether, thinking, 'Consciousness is unending,' enters on and abides in the plane of infinite consciousness. And those things which belong to the plane of infinite consciousness: perception in the plane of infinite consciousness and one-pointedness of mind and impingement, feeling ... equanimity, attention, are uninterruptedly set up by him; known to him these things ... disappear. He comprehends ... 'There is a further escape.' There is zealous practice for him concerning that.

[28] And again, monks, Sāriputta, by passing quite beyond the plane of infinite consciousness, thinking: 'There is not anything,' enters on and abides in the plane of no-thing. And those things which belong to the plane of no-thing: perception in the plane of no-thing and one-pointedness of mind and impingement, feeling ... equanimity, attention, are uninterruptedly set up by him; known to him these things ... disappear. He comprehends ... 'There is a further escape.' There is zealous practice for him concerning that.

And again, monks, Sāriputta, by passing quite beyond the plane of no-thing, enters on and abides in the plane of neither-perception-nor-non-perception. Mindful, he emerges from that attainment. When he has emerged, mindful, from that attainment he regards those things that are past, stopped, changed as: 'Thus indeed things that have not been in me come to be; having been they pass away.' He, not feeling attracted by these things, not feeling repelled, independent, not infatuated, freed, released, dwells with a mind that is unconfined. He comprehends: 'There is a further escape.' There is zealous practice for him concerning that.

And again, monks, Sāriputta, by passing quite beyond the plane of neither-perception-nor-non-perception, enters on and abides in the stopping of perception and feeling. And having seen by means of intuitive wisdom, his cankers are utterly destroyed. Mindful, he emerges from that attainment. When he has emerged, mindful, from that attainment he regards those things that are past, stopped, changed as: 'Thus indeed things that have not been in me come to be; having been they pass away.' He, not feeling attracted by these things, not feeling repelled, independent, not infatuated, freed, released, dwells with a mind that is unconfined. He comprehends: 'There is no further escape.' There is no zealous practice for him concerning that.

Monks, if anyone speaking rightly could say of a man: ' He has attained to mastery, he has attained to going beyond[1] in the ariyan moral habit; he has attained to mastery, [29] he has attained to going beyond in the ariyan concentration; he has attained to mastery, he has attained to going beyond in the ariyan wisdom; he has attained to mastery, he has attained to going beyond in the ariyan freedom ' —speaking rightly he could say of Sāriputta: ' He has attained to mastery, he has attained to going beyond in the ariyan moral habit; he has attained to mastery, he has attained to going beyond in . . . the ariyan freedom.'

Monks, if anyone speaking rightly could say of a man: ' He is the Lord's own son, born of his mouth, born of *dhamma*, formed by *dhamma*, an heir to *dhamma*, not an heir to material things '— speaking rightly he could say of Sāriputta: ' He is the Lord's own son, born of his mouth, born of *dhamma*, formed by *dhamma*, an heir to *dhamma*, not an heir to material things.'

Sāriputta, monks, rolls on rightly the incomparable wheel of *dhamma* set rolling by the Tathāgata."

Thus spoke the Lord. Delighted, these monks rejoiced in what the Lord had said.

Discourse on the Uninterrupted:
The First

112. DISCOURSE ON THE SIXFOLD CLEANSING
(Chabbisodhanasutta)

THUS have I heard: At one time the Lord was staying near Sāvatthī in the Jeta Grove in Anāthapiṇḍika's monastery. While he was there the Lord addressed the monks, saying: "Monks." "Revered One," these monks answered the Lord in assent. The Lord spoke thus:

"Monks, a monk here declares profound knowledge, saying: ' Destroyed is birth, brought to a close the Brahma-faring, done is

---

[1] *pāramippatta*. *Pāramī*, excellence, perfection, accomplishment, going beyond. *MA*. iv. 91 gives *nipphattipatta*, attained accomplishment, completion, perfection.

what was to be done, there is no more of being such or so.' Monks, the words of this monk are to be neither rejoiced in nor protested against.[1] Without (your) rejoicing or protesting, the question might be asked: " Your reverence, these four modes of statement[2] have been rightly pointed out by that Lord who knows and sees, perfected one, fully Self-Awakened One. What four ? That which when seen is spoken of as seen, that which when heard is spoken of as heard, that which when sensed is spoken of as sensed, [30] that which when cognised is spoken of as cognised.[3] Your reverence, these four modes of statement have been rightly pointed out by that Lord who knows and sees, perfected one, fully Self-Awakened One. But knowing what, seeing what in respect of these four modes of statement can your reverence say that his mind is freed from the cankers with no grasping (remaining) ?' Monks, the explanation of the monk in whom the cankers are destroyed, who has lived the life, done what was to be done, laid down the burden, attained his own welfare, in whom the fetters of becoming are utterly destroyed and who is freed by right profound knowledge, would be in accordance with *dhamma* were he to say: ' I, your reverences, not feeling attracted[4] to things seen . . . heard . . . sensed . . . cognised, not feeling repelled by them, independent, not infatuated, freed, released, dwell with a mind that is unconfined. So, your reverences, as I know thus, see thus in respect of these four modes of statement, I can say that my mind is freed from the cankers with no grasping (remaining).' Monks, that monk's words should be rejoiced in and approved of by the monks, saying: ' It is good.' When they have rejoiced in and approved of his words, saying, ' It is good,' a further question might be asked:[5]

' Your reverence, these five groups of grasping have been rightly pointed out by that Lord who knows and sees, perfected one, fully Self-Awakened One. What five ? That is to say, the group of grasping after material shape, the group of grasping after feeling, the group of grasping after perception, the group of grasping after the habitual tendencies, the group of grasping after consciousness. Your reverence, these five groups of grasping have been rightly

---

[1] Or, " neither approved of nor scorned." *Cf. M.* iii. 207, *D.* ii. 124.
[2] *vohāra*.
[3] On *diṭṭha suta muta viññāta* see *B.D.* ii. 166, *n.* 3; and *cf. Vin.* iv. 2, *A.* ii. 246, iv. 307, *D.* iii. 232, *Vbh.* 376.
[4] " Attracted, repelled, independent," etc., as at *M.* iii. 25.
[5] That is, if the monks are not satisfied with his explanation.

pointed out by that Lord who knows and sees, perfected one, fully Self-Awakened One. But knowing what, seeing what in respect of these five groups of grasping can your reverence say that his mind is freed from the cankers with no grasping (remaining) ?' Monks, the explanation of the monk in whom the cankers are destroyed, who has lived the life . . . and who is freed by right profound knowledge, would be in accordance with *dhamma* were he to say: ' I, your reverences, having known that material shape . . . feeling . . . perception . . . the habitual tendencies . . . consciousness is of little strength, fading away,[1] comfortless; [**31**] by the destruction, fading away, stopping, giving up and casting out of grasping after and hankering after[2] material shape . . . feeling . . . perception . . . the habitual tendencies . . . consciousness which are mental dogmas, biases and tendencies,[3] I comprehend that my mind is freed. So, your reverences, as I know thus, see thus in respect of these five groups of grasping, I can say that my mind is freed from the cankers with no grasping (remaining).' Monks, that monk's words should be rejoiced in and approved of by the monks, saying: ' It is good.' When they have rejoiced in and approved of his words, saying: ' It is good,' a further question might be asked:

' Your reverence, these six elements have been rightly pointed out by that Lord who knows and sees, perfected one, fully Self-Awakened One. What six ? The element of extension, the element of cohesion, the element of radiation, the element of motion,[4] the element of space,[5] the element of consciousness.[6] Your reverence, these six

---

[1] *virāga*, explained at *MA*. iv. 92 as *vigacchanasabhāva*, " of the nature to disappear."

[2] *upāyupādāna*, a synonym for wrong views and craving, *MA*. iv. 92.

[3] *Cf. S*. ii. 17, iii. 10.

[4] The first four as in *M*. Sta. 1. On the five see *M*. i. 423 *f*.; and on the six see *M*. iii. 62, 240, *D*. iii. 247, *S*. ii. 248, *A*. i. 176, *Vbh*. 82 *ff*., and *cf. VbhA*. 55.

[5] *ākāsadhātu*, or possibly the element of the intangible. *Ākāsa* is explained as *asamphuṭṭha*, not filled with, not contacted (or untouched). *C.P.D*., s.v. *a-samphuṭa*, gives " not filled (with: instr.) "; *cf. Asl*. 325-326 which says it is impossible to plough, cut or break *ākāsa*, sky, space, ether. See *Dhs*. 638: *ākāso . . . asamphuṭṭhaṁ catūhi mahābhūtehi*, not filled with the four great elementals. *Bud. Psych. Ethics*, p. 194, notes 1, 2, refers to *M*. i. 423 and points out that *ākāsadhātu* appears to occur as a fifth element there. See *Miln*. 271 where of *ākāsa* and *nibbāna* it is said that neither is born of deeds, cause or the creative power of nature. The question of " space " is discussed by A. B. Keith in *Bud. Philosophy*, pp. 168-169.

[6] *viññāṇadhātu*, called at *MA*. iv. 93=*VbhA*. 55 *vijānadhātu*, element of discrimination.

elements have been rightly pointed out by that Lord who knows and sees, perfected one, fully Self-Awakened One. But knowing what, seeing what in respect of these six elements can your reverence say that his mind is freed from the cankers with no grasping (remaining)?' Monks, the explanation of that monk in whom the cankers are destroyed, who has lived the life . . . and who is freed by right profound knowledge would be in accordance with *dhamma* were he to say: 'I, your reverences, went to the element of extension as not-self and to self as not dependent on the element of extension . . . went to the element of cohesion . . . radiation . . . motion . . . space . . . consciousness as not-self and to self as not dependent on the element of consciousness; by the destruction, fading away, stopping, giving up and casting out of grasping after and hankering after these things which are dependent on the element of extension . . . cohesion . . . radiation . . . motion . . . space . . . consciousness which are mental dogmas, biases and tendencies, I comprehend that my mind is freed. So, your reverences, as I know thus, see thus in respect of these six elements, I can say that my mind is freed from the cankers with no grasping (remaining).' Monks, that monk's words [**32**] should be rejoiced in and approved of by the monks, saying: 'It is good.' When they have rejoiced in and approved of his words, saying: 'It is good,' a further question might be asked:

'Your reverence, these six internal and external (sense-)fields have been rightly pointed out by that Lord who knows and sees, perfected one, fully Self-Awakened One. What six ? The eye as well as material shapes, the ear as well as sounds, the nose as well as smells, the tongue as well as tastes, the body as well as tactile objects, the mind as well as mental states. Your reverence, these six internal and external (sense-)fields have been rightly pointed out by that Lord who knows and sees, perfected one, fully Self-Awakened One. But knowing what, seeing what in respect of these six internal and external (sense-)fields can your reverence say that his mind is freed from the cankers with no grasping (remaining) ?' Monks, the explanation of that monk in whom the cankers are destroyed, who has lived the life, done what was to be done, laid down the burden, attained his own welfare, in whom the fetters of becoming are utterly destroyed and who is freed by right profound knowledge, would be in accordance with *dhamma* were he to say: 'Your reverences, whatever is desire, whatever is attachment, whatever is delight, whatever is craving for eye, material shape, visual consciousness and for things cognisable through visual consciousness,[1] by the destruction, fading away, stopping, giving up and casting out of grasping after and hankering after these things which are mental dogmas, biases and tendencies, I comprehend that my mind is freed. Your reverences, so it is with the ear, sounds, auditory consciousness ... the nose, smells, olfactory consciousness ... the tongue, tastes, gustatory consciousness ... the body, tactile objects, bodily consciousness ... the mind, mental states, mental consciousness, with mental states cognisable through mental consciousness. So, your reverences, as I know thus, see thus in respect of these six internal-external (sense-)fields, I can say that my mind is freed from the cankers with no grasping (remaining).' Monks, that monk's words should be rejoiced in and approved of by the monks, saying: ' It is good.' When they have rejoiced in and approved of his words, saying: ' It is good,' a further question might be asked:

' But knowing what, seeing what in respect of this consciousness-informed body and all external phenomena can your reverence say that his tendency to pride that " I am the doer, mine is the doer " is properly extirpated ?' [33] Monks, the explanation of that monk in whom the cankers are destroyed, who has lived the life, done what was to be done, laid down the burden, attained his own welfare, in whom the fetters of becoming are utterly destroyed and who is freed by right profound knowledge, would be in accordance with *dhamma* were he to say: ' Formerly, your reverences, when I was a householder, I was ignorant. The Tathāgata or a disciple of the Tathāgata taught me *dhamma*. When I had heard that *dhamma* I gained faith in the Tathāgata; being possessed of that faith I had gained in him, I reflected thus: " The household life is confined and dusty,[2] going forth is in the open; it is not easy for one who lives in a house to fare the Brahma-faring wholly fulfilled, wholly pure, polished like a conch-shell. Suppose now that I, having cut off my hair and beard, having put on saffron robes, should go forth from home into homelessness ?" So I, your reverences, after a time, getting rid of my wealth, whether small or great, getting rid of my circle of relations, whether small or great, having cut off my hair and beard, having put on saffron robes, went forth from home into homelessness. I, being gone forth thus, endowed with the training and the way of living of monks, abandoning onslaught on creatures,

---

[1] Whether past, future or present, *MA.* iv. 93 *ff.* where reference is also made to the *Channovādasutta* (*M.* Sta. 144).
[2] For the following passage *cf. M.* i. 179 *ff.* (*M.L.S.* i. 224 *ff.*).

abstained from onslaught on creatures; the stick laid aside, the sword laid aside, I lived scrupulous, kindly, friendly and compassionate towards all living things and creatures. Abandoning the taking of what had not been given, I abstained from taking what had not been given; taking (only) what was given, waiting for what was given, without stealing I lived with self become pure. Abandoning unchastity, I was one that was chaste, keeping remote (from unchastity), refraining from dealings with women. Abandoning lying speech, I was one who abstained from lying speech, I was a truth-speaker, a bondsman to truth, trustworthy, dependable, no deceiver of the world. Abandoning slanderous speech, I abstained from slanderous speech; having heard something here I was not one to repeat it elsewhere for causing variance among these (people); or, having heard something elsewhere I was not one to repeat it here for causing variance among these (people). In this way I was a reconciler of those who were at variance and one who combined those who were friends. Concord was my pleasure, concord my delight, concord my joy, concord the motive of my speech. Abandoning harsh speech, I abstained from harsh speech. Whatever speech was gentle, pleasing to the ear, **[34]** affectionate, going to the heart, urbane, pleasant to the manyfolk, agreeable to the many folk —I was one who uttered speech like that. Abandoning frivolous chatter, I abstained from frivolous chatter. I was a speaker at the right time, a speaker of fact, a speaker on the goal, a speaker on *dhamma*, a speaker on discipline, I spoke words that were worth treasuring, with opportune similes, purposeful, connected with the goal. I abstained from destruction to seed-growth and vegetable-growth. I was one who ate one meal a day, desisting at night, refraining from eating at a wrong time. I abstained from watching shows of dancing, singing and music. I abstained from using garlands, scents, unguents, adornments, finery. I abstained from using high beds, large beds . . . from accepting gold and silver . . . from accepting raw grain . . . raw meat . . . women and girls . . . women slaves and men slaves . . . goats and sheep . . . fowl and swine . . . elephants, cows, horses, mares . . . fields and sites . . . I was one that abstained from the practice of sending or going on messages. I abstained from buying and selling . . . from cheating with weights, bronzes and measures. I abstained from the crooked ways of bribery, fraud and deceit . . . from maiming, murdering, manacling, highway robbery. I was contented with the robes for protecting my body, with the almsfood for sustaining my stomach. Wherever

I went I took these things with me as I went. As a bird on the wing takes its wings with it wherever it flies, even so did I, your reverences, contented with the robes for protecting my body and with the alms-food for sustaining my stomach, take these things with me wherever I went. I, possessed of this body of ariyan moral habit, inwardly experienced the bliss of blamelessness.

If I saw a material shape with the eye I was not entranced by the general appearance, I was not entranced by the detail. If I dwelt with this organ of sight uncontrolled, covetousness and dejection, evil unskilled states, might flow in. So I fared along controlling it, [35] I guarded the organ of sight, I achieved control over the organ of sight. If I heard a sound with the ear . . . If I smelt a smell with the nose . . . If I savoured a taste with the tongue . . . If I felt a touch with the body . . . If I cognised a mental state with the mind I was not entranced by the general appearance, I was not entranced by the detail . . . I achieved control over the organ of mind. I, possessed of this ariyan control over the sense-organs, inwardly experienced the bliss of being " unaffected."[1]

Whether I was setting out or returning, I was one who comported myself properly; whether I was looking down or looking round . . . bending back or stretching out (my arm) . . . carrying my outer cloak, bowl or robe . . . munching, drinking, eating, savouring . . . obeying the calls of nature . . . walking, standing, sitting, asleep, awake, talking or silent, I was one who comported myself properly.

Possessed of this ariyan body of moral habit and possessed of this ariyan control over the sense-organs and possessed of this ariyan mindfulness and clear consciousness, I chose a remote lodging in a forest, at the root of a tree, on a mountain slope, in a wilderness, a hill-cave, a cemetery, a forest haunt, in the open or on a heap of straw. Returning from alms-gathering after the meal, I sat down cross-legged, holding the back erect, having made mindfulness rise up in front of me. By getting rid of covetousness for the world, I dwelt with a mind devoid of coveting, I purified the mind of coveting. By getting rid of the taint of ill-will, I dwelt benevolent in mind; and compassionate for the welfare of all creatures and beings, I purified the mind of the taint of ill-will. By getting rid of sloth and torpor, I dwelt devoid of sloth and torpor; perceiving the light, mindful and clearly conscious, I purified the mind of sloth and torpor. By getting rid of restlessness and worry, I dwelt calmly,

---

[1] See note at *M.L.S.* ii. 11 (on *M.* i. 346).

the mind subjectively tranquillised, I purified the mind of restlessness and worry. By getting rid of doubt, I dwelt doubt-crossed, unperplexed as to the states that are skilled, I purified the mind of doubt.

[36] By getting rid of these five hindrances—defilements of the mind and weakening to intuitive wisdom—aloof from pleasures of the senses, aloof from unskilled states of mind, I entered on and abided in the first meditation which is . . . joyful. By allaying initial thought and discursive thought . . . I entered on and abided in the second meditation which is . . . joyful. By the fading out of rapture, I dwelt with equanimity . . . and I entered on and abided in the third meditation. By getting rid of joy and by getting rid of anguish . . . I entered on and abided in the fourth meditation which . . . is entirely purified by equanimity and mindfulness.

Thus with the mind composed, quite purified, quite clarified, without blemish, without defilement, grown soft and workable, stable, immovable, I directed my mind to the knowledge of the destruction of the cankers.[1] I understood as it really is: This is anguish . . . this the arising of anguish . . . this the stopping of anguish . . . this the course leading to the stopping of anguish. I understood as it really is: These are the cankers . . . this is the arising of the cankers . . . this the stopping of the cankers . . . this the course leading to the stopping of the cankers. When I knew and saw this thus, my mind was freed from the canker of the sense-pleasures and my mind was freed from the canker of becoming and my mind was freed from the canker of ignorance. In freedom the knowledge came to be that I was freed and I comprehended: Destroyed is birth, brought to a close the Brahma-faring, done is what was to be done, there is no more of being such or so. So, your reverences, as I know

---

[1] Bu. at *MA.* iv. 94 is rather hard put to it to explain the six ways of cleansing, and says the name of this Discourse is also *Ekavisajjakasutta*, the Discourse on Adhering to one (thing). Here the six to be purified are the four statements, the five groups, the six elements, the six internal-external sense-fields, one's own consciousness-informed body, and that of others. But *Theras* living overseas reduce the consciousness-informed body of oneself and of others to one (category) and speak of the six parts together with the four kinds of nutriment. But these six parts: Of what, how then, when, where have you possession, which defilements have you destroyed, how many things have you acquired ?—should be corrected by the *Vinaya* exegesis.

Bu. also says, *loc. cit.*, that former habitations and *deva*-like vision were not spoken of because monks do not ask about a mundane state but only about a supermundane one.

thus, see thus, in respect of this consciousness-informed body and all external phenomena, I can say that my tendency to pride that " I am the doer, mine is the doer " has been properly extirpated.' Monks, that monk's words should be rejoiced in and approved of by the monks, saying: ' It is good,' When they have rejoiced in and approved of his words, saying: ' It is good,' he should be informed thus: ' It is a gain for you, your reverence, [**37**] it is well gotten by you, your reverence, that we see a Brahma-farer in one such as is the venerable one.' "

Thus spoke the Lord. Delighted, these monks rejoiced in what the Lord had said.

Discourse on the Sixfold Cleansing:
The Second

113. DISCOURSE ON THE GOOD MAN
(Sappurisasutta)

THUS have I heard: At one time the Lord was staying near Sāvatthī in the Jeta Grove in Anāthapiṇḍika's monastery. While he was there the Lord addressed the monks, saying: " Monks." " Revered One," these monks answered the Lord in assent. The Lord spoke thus: " I will teach you, monks, *dhamma* of good men and *dhamma* of bad men. Listen to it, pay careful attention and I will speak." " Yes, revered sir," these monks answered the Lord in assent. The Lord spoke thus:

" And what, monks, is *dhamma* of good men ? As to this, monks, a bad man has gone forth from a high family.[1] He reflects thus: ' I have gone forth from this high family; but these other monks have not gone forth from a high family.' Because he belongs to a high family he exalts himself, disparages the others. This, monks, is *dhamma* of a bad man. But a good man, monks, reflects thus: ' It is not because of one's belonging to a high family that things of

---

[1] *MA.* iv. 98, a khattiya (noble warrior) family or a brahman family. *Cf. Vin.* iv. 6 where distinguished birth, *ukkaṭṭhā jāti*, is assigned to these two.

greed, things of aversion, things of confusion go to destruction. For even if one be not gone forth from a high family, one may still fare along in complete accordance with *dhamma*, may fare along correctly, [38] may be a farer according to *dhamma*, and therefore be one to be honoured and commended.' He, having made the course itself the main thing,[1] neither exalts himself for belonging to a high family nor disparages others. This, monks, is *dhamma* of a good man.

And again, monks, a bad man has gone forth from a great family[2] ... (to be set out at length in the way given below[3]) ... has gone forth from a very rich family ... has gone forth from an eminent family. He reflects thus: 'I have gone forth from an eminent family; but these other monks have not gone forth from an eminent family.' Because of his eminence he exalts himself, disparages the others. This too, monks, is *dhamma* of a bad man. But a good man, monks, reflects thus: 'It is not because of one's eminence that things of greed, things of aversion, things of confusion go to destruction. For even if one be not gone forth from an eminent family, one may still fare along in complete accordance with *dhamma*, may fare along correctly, may be a farer according to *dhamma*, and therefore be one to be honoured and commended.' He, having made the course itself the main thing, neither exalts himself for his eminence nor disparages others. This too, monks, is *dhamma* of a good man.

And again, monks, a bad man is well-known, famous. He reflects thus: 'I am well-known, famous, but these other monks are little known, of no esteem.'[4] Because of his being well-known he exalts himself, disparages the others. This too, monks, is *dhamma* of a bad man. But a good man reflects thus: 'It is not because of one's being well-known that things of greed, aversion, confusion go to destruction. For even if one be not well-known, famous, one may still fare along in complete accordance with *dhamma* ... honoured and commended.' He, having made the course itself the main thing, neither exalts himself for being well-known nor disparages others. This too, monks, is *dhamma* of a good man.

[39] And again, monks, a bad man acquires the requisites of robe-material, almsfood, lodgings and medicines for the sick. He reflects

---

[1] *so paṭipadaṁ yeva antaraṁ karitvā, cf. M*. iii. 14.
[2] A noble, brahman or merchant family, *MA*. iv. 98.
[3] *I.e.* "above" to us who use a printed book instead of a palm-leaf MS.
[4] *Cf. M*. i. 192.

thus: 'I am an acquirer of the requisites of . . . medicines for the sick, but these other monks are not acquirers of the requisites of . . . medicines for the sick.' Because of these acquisitions he exalts himself, disparages the others. This too, monks, is *dhamma* of a bad man. But a good man reflects thus: 'It is not through one's acquisition that things of greed, aversion, confusion go to destruction. For even if one be not an acquirer of the requisites of . . . medicines for the sick, one may still fare along in complete accordance with *dhamma* . . . honoured and commended.' . . . This too, monks, is *dhamma* of a good man.

And again, monks, a bad man is one who has heard much. He reflects thus: 'I am one who has heard much, but these other monks have not heard much.' Because of his having heard much he exalts himself and disparages the others. This too monks, is *dhamma* of a bad man. But a good man reflects thus: 'It is not through one's hearing much that things of greed . . . go to destruction. For even if one has not heard much, one may still fare along . . . commended.' . . . This too, monks, is *dhamma* of a good man.

And again monks a bad man is expert in Vinaya. He reflects thus: 'I am expert in Vinaya, but these other monks are not expert in Vinaya.' Because of his being expert in Vinaya he exalts himself, disparages the others. This too, monks, is *dhamma* of a bad man. But a good man reflects thus: 'It is not through one's being expert in Vinaya that things of greed . . . [40] . . . go to destruction. For even if one be not expert in Vinaya, one may still fare along . . . commended.' . . . This too, monks, is *dhamma* of a good man.

And again, monks, a bad man is a speaker on *dhamma* . . . he exalts himself, disparages the others. This too, monks, is *dhamma* of a bad man. But a good man reflects thus: 'It is not through one's being a speaker on *dhamma* . . . even if one is not a speaker on *dhamma*, one may still fare along . . . commended.' . . . This too, monks is *dhamma* of a good man.

And again, monks, a bad man is a forest-dweller[1] . . . a wearer of robes taken from the dust-heap [41] . . . a beggar for alms . . . one who stays at the root of a tree . . . [42] . . . in a cemetery . . . in the open air . . . one who remains in a sitting posture . . . who sits on the seat offered . . . who eats once (a day). He reflects thus: 'I eat once (a day only), but these other monks eat not once (a day only).'

---

[1] Here are mentioned nine out of the thirteen *dhūtaṅga*, or ascetic practices, for which see *Vism.* 61 *ff*.

Because of his eating once (a day only) he exalts himself, disparages the others. This too, monks, is *dhamma* of a bad man. But a good man reflects thus: ' It is not through one's eating once (a day only) that things of greed go to destruction, that things of aversion go to destruction, that things of confusion go to destruction. For even if one be not one that eats once (a day only), one may still fare along in complete accordance with *dhamma*, may fare along correctly, may be a farer according to *dhamma*, and therefore be one to be honoured and commended.' He, having made the course itself the main thing, neither exalts himself for eating once (a day only) nor disparages others. This too, monks, is *dhamma* of a good man.

And again, monks, a bad man, aloof from pleasures of the senses, aloof from unskilled states of mind, enters on and abides in the first meditation which is accompanied by initial thought and discursive thought, is born of aloofness, and is rapturous and joyful. He reflects thus: ' I am an acquirer of the attainment of the first meditation, but these other monks are not acquirers of the attainment of the first meditation.' He exalts himself for that attainment of the first meditation, disparages the others. This too, monks, is *dhamma* of a bad man. But a good man, monks, reflects thus: ' Lack of desire[1] even for the attainment of the first meditation has been spoken of by the Lord; for whatever they imagine it to be, it is otherwise.' He, [43] having made lack of desire itself the main thing, neither exalts himself on account of that attainment of the first meditation nor disparages others. This too, monks, is *dhamma* of a good man.

And again, monks, a bad man, by allaying initial thought and discursive thought, with the mind subjectively tranquillised and fixed on one point, enters on and abides in the second meditation which is devoid of initial thought and discursive thought, is born of concentration, and is rapturous and joyful . . . enters on and abides in the third meditation . . . the fourth meditation. He reflects thus . . . He exalts himself for that attainment of the fourth meditation, disparages the others. This too, monks, is *dhamma* of a bad man. But a good man reflects thus: ' Lack of desire even for the attainment of the fourth meditation has been spoken of by the Lord; for whatever they imagine it to be, it is otherwise.' He, having

---

[1] *atammayatā*. This is *nittaṇhatā*, while *tammayatā* is *taṇhā*, *MA*. iv. 99. *Cf. M*. i. 319, iii. 220, *A*. i. 150, iii. 444.

made lack of desire itself the main thing, neither exalts himself on account of that attainment of the fourth meditation nor disparages others. This too, monks, is *dhamma* of a good man.

And again, monks, a bad man, by passing quite beyond perceptions of material shape, by the going down of perceptions of sensory reactions, by not paying attention to perceptions of variety, thinking: 'Ether is unending,' enters on and abides in the plane of infinite ether . . . He exalts himself for this attainment of the plane of infinite ether, disparages the others. This too, monks, is *dhamma* of a bad man. But a good man reflects thus: 'Lack of desire even for the plane of infinite ether has been spoken of by the Lord; for whatever they imagine it to be, it is otherwise.' He, having made lack of desire itself the main thing, neither exalts himself on account of that attainment of the plane of infinite ether nor disparages others. This too, monks, is *dhamma* of a good man.

And again, monks, a bad man, by passing quite beyond the plane of infinite ether, thinking: 'Consciousness is unending,' enters on and abides in the plane of infinite consciousness . . . [**44**] . . . by passing quite beyond the plane of infinite consciousness, thinking: 'There is not anything,' enters on and abides in the plane of no-thing . . . by passing quite beyond the plane of no-thing, enters on and abides in the plane of neither-perception-nor-non-perception. He reflects thus: 'I am an acquirer of the plane of neither-perception-nor-non-perception, but these other monks are not acquirers of the plane of neither-perception-nor-non-perception.' Because of this attainment of the plane of neither-perception-nor-non-perception he exalts himself, disparages the others. This too, monks, is *dhamma* of a bad man. But a good man reflects thus, monks: 'Lack of desire even for the plane of neither-perception-nor-non-perception has been spoken of by the Lord; for whatever they imagine it to be, it is otherwise.' He, having made lack of desire itself the main thing, neither exalts himself on account of that attainment of the plane of neither-perception-nor-non-perception nor disparages others. This too, monks, is *dhamma* of a good man.

[**45**] And again, monks, a good man, by passing quite beyond the plane of neither-perception-nor-non-perception, enters on and abides in the stopping of perception and feeling; and when he has seen by means of wisdom his cankers are caused to be destroyed.[1] And,

---

[1] *parikkhayāpenti* instead of the more usual *parikkhīṇā honti*. *MA.* iv. 99 speaks of this person as a non-returner. This attainment of stopping is not for the ordinary person, *puthujjanassa sā n'atthi*.

monks, this monk does not imagine he[1] is aught or anywhere or in anything."[2]

Thus spoke the Lord. Delighted, these monks rejoiced in what the Lord had said.

Discourse on the Good Man:
The Third

114. DISCOURSE ON WHAT IS TO BE FOLLOWED AND WHAT IS NOT TO BE FOLLOWED

(Sevitabba-asevitabbasutta)

THUS have I heard: At one time the Lord was staying near Sāvatthī in the Jeta Grove in Anāthapiṇḍika's monastery. While he was there, the Lord addressed the monks, saying: " Monks." " Revered One," these monks answered the Lord in assent. The Lord spoke thus: " I will teach you a disquisition on *dhamma* regarding what is to be followed and what is not to be followed. Listen to it, pay careful attention, and I will speak." " Yes, revered sir," these monks answered the Lord in assent. The Lord spoke thus:

" I, monks, say that bodily conduct is of two kinds, one of which is to be followed and the other which is not to be followed; and there is this disparity in bodily conduct. And I, monks, say that vocal conduct . . . mental conduct is of two kinds, one of which is to be followed and the other which is not to be followed; and there is this disparity in vocal conduct . . . mental conduct. And I, monks, say that the arising of thought is of two kinds, one of which is to be followed and the other which is not to be followed; and there is this disparity [**46**] in the arising of thought. And I, monks, say that the assumption of perception . . . the assumption of views . . . the assumption of individuality[3] is of two kinds, one of which is to be

---

[1] *puggala* supplied by *MA*. iv. 99-100.
[2] *na kiñci na kuhiñci na kenaci maññati*. *Cf. M*. iii. 103, *na katthaci na kuhiñci*.
[3] *attabhāvapaṭilābha*, as at *S*. ii. 256, iii. 144; *A*. ii. 159; *Vin*. ii. 185; see *P.T.C.* for further references.

followed and the other which is not to be followed; and there is this disparity in the assumption of perception . . . the assumption of views . . . the assumption of individuality."

When this had been said, the venerable Sāriputta spoke thus to the Lord: " I, revered sir, thus understand this to be the meaning in full of what was spoken of by the Lord in brief, but of which the meaning was not explained in full: ' I, monks, say that bodily conduct is of two kinds, one of which is to be followed and the other which is not to be followed; and there is this disparity in bodily conduct.' This was said by the Lord. In reference to what was it said ? Revered sir, if a certain kind of bodily conduct is followed and unskilled states of mind grow much, skilled states of mind decrease, this kind of bodily conduct is not to be followed. Revered sir, if a certain kind of bodily conduct is followed and unskilled states of mind decrease, skilled states of mind grow much, this kind of bodily conduct is to be followed.

And what kind of bodily conduct, revered sir, does a man follow that unskilled states of mind grow much in him, skilled states of mind decrease ? As to this,[1] revered sir, someone makes onslaught on creatures, he is cruel, bloody-handed, intent on injuring and killing, without mercy to living creatures. He is a taker of what is not given; whatever property of another in village or jungle is not given to him he takes by theft. He is a wrong-goer in regard to pleasures of the senses; he has intercourse with (girls) protected by the mother, protected by the father . . . the parents . . . a brother . . . a sister . . . relations, (girls) who have a husband, and whose use involves punishments, and even with those adorned with the garlands of betrothal. If this kind of [47] bodily conduct is followed, revered sir, unskilled states of mind grow much, skilled states of mind decrease.

And what kind of bodily conduct, revered sir, does a man follow that unskilled states of mind decrease in him, skilled states of mind grow much ? As to this, revered sir, someone, abandoning onslaught on creatures, is restrained from onslaught on creatures; the stick laid aside, the sword laid aside, he lives scrupulous, merciful, kindly and compassionate to all living creatures. Abandoning taking what is not given, he is restrained from taking what is not given; he does not take by theft any property of another in village or jungle that is not given to him. Abandoning wrong-going in

---

[1] For a great deal of the following cf. M. i. 286 ff.

regard to pleasures of the senses, he is restrained from wrong-doing in regard to pleasures of the senses; he does not have intercourse with (girls) who are protected by the mother . . . nor even with those adorned with the garlands of betrothal. If this kind of bodily conduct is followed, revered sir, unskilled states of mind decrease, skilled states of mind grow much. When the Lord said: ' I, monks, say that bodily conduct is of two kinds, one of which is to be followed and the other which is not to be followed; and there is this disparity in bodily conduct,' it was said in reference to this.

' I, monks, say that vocal conduct is of two kinds, one of which is to be followed and the other which is not to be followed; and there is this disparity in vocal conduct.' This was said by the Lord. In reference to what was it said ? Revered sir, if a certain kind of vocal conduct is followed and unskilled states of mind grow much, skilled states of mind decrease, this kind of vocal conduct is not to be followed. Revered sir, if a certain kind of vocal conduct is followed and unskilled states of mind decrease, skilled states of mind grow much, this kind of vocal conduct is to be followed.

And what kind of vocal conduct, revered sir, does a man follow that unskilled states of mind grow much in him, skilled states of mind decrease ? As to this, revered sir, someone is of lying speech; [**48**] when he is cited and questioned as a witness before a council or a company or amid his relations or amid a guild or a royal family, and is told: ' Now, my good man, say what you know,' although he does not know, he says, ' I know,' and although he knows, he says, ' I do not know'; although he has not seen, he says, ' I saw,' and although he has seen, he says, ' I did not see.' Thus his speech becomes intentional lying either for his own sake or for that of another or for the sake of some material gain or other. And he is a slanderer; having heard something at one place, he makes it known elsewhere for causing variance among those people; or having heard something elsewhere he makes it known among these people for causing variance among them. In this way he sows discord among those who were in harmony or foments those who are at variance. Discord is his pleasure, his delight, his joy, the motive of his speech. And he is one of harsh speech. Whatever speech is rough, hard, severe on others, abusive of others, bordering on wrath, not conducive to concentration, such speech does he utter. And he is a frivolous chatterer, one who speaks at a wrong time, not in accordance with fact, one who speaks about what is not the goal, about non-*dhamma*, about non-discipline. He utters speech that is not worth treasuring; owing to its being at the wrong time it is incongruous, has no purpose, is not connected with the goal. If this kind of vocal conduct is followed, revered sir, unskilled states of mind grow much, skilled states of mind decrease.

And what kind of vocal conduct, revered sir, does a man follow that unskilled states of mind decrease in him, skilled states of mind grow much ? As to this, revered sir, someone, abandoning lying speech is restrained from lying speech. When he is cited and questioned as a witness before a council or company or amid his relations or amid a guild or a royal family, and is told: ' Now, my good man, say what you know,' if he does not know he says, ' I do not know,' and if he knows he says, ' I know '; if he has not seen, he says, ' I did not see,' and if he has seen, he says, [**49**] ' I saw.' Thus his speech is not intentional lying either for his own sake or for that of another or for the sake of some material gain or other. Abandoning slanderous speech, he is restrained from slanderous speech. Having heard something at one place, he is not one to repeat it elsewhere for causing variance among those people; or having heard something elsewhere he is not one to repeat it among these people for causing variance among them. In this way he is a reconciler of those who are at variance and one who combines those who are friends. Concord is his pleasure, his delight, his joy, the motive of his speech. Abandoning harsh speech, he is restrained from harsh speech. Whatever speech is gentle, pleasing to the ear, affectionate, going to the heart, urbane, pleasant to the manyfolk, agreeable to the manyfolk—such speech does he utter. Abandoning frivolous chatter, he is restrained from frivolous chatter. He is one that speaks at a right time, in accordance with fact, about the goal, about *dhamma*, about discipline. He utters speech that is worth treasuring, with opportune similes, purposeful, connected with the goal. If this kind of vocal conduct is followed, revered sir, unskilled states of mind decrease, skilled states of mind grow much. When the Lord said: ' I, monks, say that vocal conduct is of two kinds, one of which is to be followed and the other which is not to be followed; and there is this disparity in vocal conduct,' it was said in reference to this.

' I, monks, say that mental conduct is of two kinds, one of which is to be followed and the other which is not to be followed; and there is this disparity in mental conduct.' This was said by the Lord. In reference to what was it said ? Revered sir, if a certain kind of mental conduct is followed and unskilled states of mind grow much, skilled states of mind decrease, this kind of mental conduct is not to be followed. Revered sir, if a certain kind of mental conduct is followed and unskilled states of mind decrease, skilled states of mind grow much, this kind of mental conduct is to be followed.

And what kind of mental conduct, revered sir, does a man follow that unskilled states of mind grow much in him, skilled states of mind decrease ? As to this, revered sir, someone is covetous; he covets that which is the property of another, thinking: ' O might that which is the other's be mine '; he is malevolent in thought, corrupt [50] in mind and purpose, and thinks: ' Let these beings be killed or slaughtered or annihilated or destroyed, or may they not exist at all.' If this kind of mental conduct is followed, revered sir, unskilled states of mind grow much, skilled states of mind decrease.

And what kind of mental conduct, revered sir, does a man follow that unskilled states of mind decrease in him, skilled states of mind grow much ? As to this, revered sir, someone is not covetous; he does not covet that which is the property of another, thinking: ' O might that which is the other's be mine '; he is not malevolent in thought, not corrupt in mind and purpose, but thinks: ' Let these beings, free from enmity, peaceable, secure and happy, look after self.' If this kind of mental conduct is followed, revered sir, unskilled states of mind decrease, skilled states of mind grow much. When the Lord said: ' I, monks, say that mental conduct is of two kinds, one of which is to be followed and the other which is not to be followed; and there is this disparity in mental conduct,' it was said in reference to this.

' I, monks, say that the arising of thought is of two kinds, one of which is to be followed and the other which is not to be followed; and there is this disparity in the arising of thought.' This was said by the Lord. In reference to what was it said ? Revered sir, if a certain kind of arising of thought is followed and ... unskilled states of mind decrease, skilled states of mind grow much, this kind of arising of thought is to be followed.

And what kind of arising of thought, revered sir, does a man follow that unskilled states of mind grow much in him, skilled states of mind decrease ? As to this, revered sir, someone is covetous and lives with his thought given over to covetousness; he is malevolent and lives with his thought given over to malevolence; he is harmful and lives with his thought given over to harmfulness. If this kind of arising of thought is followed, revered sir, unskilled states of mind grow much, skilled states of mind decrease.

And what kind of arising of thought, revered sir, does a man follow that unskilled states of mind decrease in him, [51] skilled states of mind grow much ? As to this, revered sir, someone is not covetous and does not live with his thought given over to covetousness; he is not malevolent ... he is not harmful and does not live with his thought given over to harmfulness. If this kind of arising of thought is followed, revered sir, unskilled states of mind decrease, skilled states of mind grow much. When the Lord said: ' I, monks, say that the arising of thought is of two kinds, one of which is to be followed and the other which is not to be followed; and there is this disparity in the arising of thought,' it was said in reference to this.

' I, monks, say that the assumption of perception is of two kinds, one of which is to be followed and the other which is not to be followed; and there is this disparity in the assumption of perception.' This was said by the Lord. In reference to what was it said ? Revered sir, if a certain kind of assumption of perception is followed and ... unskilled states of mind decrease, skilled states of mind grow much, this kind of assumption of perception is to be followed.

And what kind of assumption of perception, revered sir, does a man follow that unskilled states of mind grow much in him, skilled states of mind decrease ? As to this, revered sir, someone is covetous and lives with his perception given over to covetousness; he is malevolent and lives with his perception given over to malevolence; he is harmful and lives with his perception given over to harmfulness. If this kind of assumption of perception is followed, revered sir, unskilled states of mind grow much, skilled states of mind decrease.

And what kind of assumption of perception, revered sir, does a man follow that unskilled states of mind decrease in him, skilled stated of mind grow much ? As to this, revered sir, someone is not covetous and does not live with his perception given over to covetousness; he is not malevolent ... he is not harmful and does not live with his perception given over to harmfulness. If this kind of assumption of perception is followed, revered sir, unskilled states of mind decrease, skilled states of mind grow much. When the Lord said: ' I, monks, say that the assumption of perception is of two kinds, one of which is to be followed and the other which is not to be followed; and there is this disparity in the assumption of perception,' it was said in reference to this.

[52] ' I, monks, say that the assumption of views is of two kinds, one of which is to be followed and the other which is not to be followed; and there is this disparity in the assumption of views.'

This was said by the Lord. In reference to what was it said ? Revered sir, if a certain kind of assumption of views is followed and . . . unskilled states of mind decrease, skilled states of mind grow much, this kind of assumption of views is to be followed.

And what kind of assumption of views, revered sir, does a man follow that unskilled states of mind grow much in him, skilled states of mind decrease ? As to this, revered sir, someone is of this view: ' There is no (result of) gift,[1] there is no (result of) offering, there is no (result of) sacrifice; there is no fruit or ripening of deeds well done or ill done; there is not this world, there is not a world beyond; there is no (benefit from serving) mother, no (benefit from serving) father; there are no spontaneously arising beings; there are not in the world recluses and brahmans who are faring rightly, proceeding rightly, and who proclaim this world and the world beyond, having realised them by their own super-knowledge.' If this kind of assumption of views is followed, revered sir, unskilled states of mind grow much, skilled states of mind decrease.

And what kind of assumption of views, revered sir, does a man follow that unskilled states of mind decrease in him, skilled states of mind grow much ? As to this, revered sir, someone is of this view: ' There is (result of) gift . . . there are in the world recluses and brahmans . . . who proclaim this world and the world beyond, having realised them by their own super-knowledge.' If this kind of assumption of views is followed, revered sir, unskilled states of mind decrease, skilled states of mind grow much. When the Lord said: ' I, monks, say that the assumption of views is of two kinds . . . and there is this disparity in the assumption of views,' it was said in reference to this.

' I, monks, say that the assumption of individuality is of two kinds, one of which is to be followed and the other which is not to be followed; and there is this disparity in the assumption of individuality.' This was said by the Lord. In reference to what was it said ? Revered sir, if a certain kind of [53] assumption of individuality is followed and . . . unskilled states of mind decrease, skilled states of mind grow much, this kind of assumption of individuality is to be followed.

And what kind of assumption of individuality, revered sir, does a man follow that unskilled states of mind grow much in him, skilled states of mind decrease ? If there is assumption of an individuality

---

[1] As at *M.* iii. 22, etc.

that is harmful,[1] revered sir, because of the uncompleted state of production,[2] unskilled states of mind grow much, skilled states of mind decrease.

And what kind of assumption of individuality, revered sir, does a man follow that unskilled states of mind decrease in him, skilled states of mind grow much ? If there is assumption of an individuality that is harmless,[3] revered sir, because of the completed state of production, unskilled states of mind decrease, skilled states of mind grow much. When the Lord said: ' I, monks, say that the assumption of individuality is of two kinds, one of which is to be followed and the other which is not to be followed; and there is this disparity in the assumption of individuality,' it was said in reference to this. I, revered sir, thus understand this to be the meaning in full of what was spoken of by the Lord in brief, but of which the meaning was not explained in full."

" It is good, Sāriputta, it is good. It is good that you, Sāriputta, thus understand this to be the meaning in full of what was spoken of by me in brief, but of which the meaning was not explained in full.

' I, monks, say that bodily conduct is of two kinds, one of which is to be followed and the other which is not to be followed; and there is this disparity in bodily conduct.' This was said by me. In reference to what was it said ? Sāriputta, if a certain kind of bodily conduct is followed and unskilled states of mind grow much, skilled states of mind decrease, this kind of bodily conduct is not to be followed . . . (*as above, from* bodily conduct *to* assumption of individuality, *with the necessary changes of* Sāriputta *for* revered one *and* said by me *for* said by the Lord . . . [54] . . . [55] . . . When I said: ' I, monks, say that the assumption of individuality is of two kinds, one of which is to be followed and the other which is not to be followed; and there is this disparity in the assumption of individuality,' it was said in reference to this. Thus, Sāriputta, should be understood in full the meaning of what was spoken of by me in brief.

---

[1] *MA.* iv. 100 equates *savyāpajjha* with *sadukkha*, and *avyāpajjha* with *adukkha*.
[2] *abhinibbattayato* (*v.l. abhinibbattassa yato*) *aparinitthitabhāvāya*. *MA.* iv. 100 says that in this individuality an average man is unable to bring becoming to completion; so, from the time of his re-linking, *patisandhi*, unskilled states grow, skilled ones decline, and he produces, *abhinibbatteti*, an individuality attended by *dukkha*.
[3] Said of the four types of persons: stream-attainers and so on.

And I, Sāriputta, say that material shape cognisable through the eye is of two kinds, one of which is to be followed and the other which is not to be followed. And I, Sāriputta, say that sound cognisable through the ear . . . smell cognisable through the nose . . . taste cognisable through the tongue . . . tactile objects cognisable through the body . . . mental states cognisable through the mind are of two kinds, one of which is to be followed and the other which is not to be followed."

When this had been said, the venerable Sāriputta spoke thus to the Lord: " I, revered sir, thus understand this to be the meaning in full of what was spoken of by the Lord in brief, but of which the meaning was not explained in full: ' I, Sāriputta, say that material shape cognisable through the eye is of two kinds, [56] one of which is to be followed and the other which is not to be followed.' This was said by the Lord. In reference to what was it said ? Revered sir, if a certain material shape cognisable through the eye is followed and unskilled states of mind grow much, skilled states of mind decrease, this kind of material shape cognisable through the eye is not to be followed. But if, revered sir, a certain kind of material shape cognisable through the eye is followed and unskilled states of mind decrease, skilled states of mind grow much, this kind of material shape cognisable through the eye is to be followed. When the Lord said: ' I, Sāriputta, say that material shape cognisable through the eye is of two kinds, one of which is to be followed and the other which is not to be followed,' it was said in reference to this.

(*Repeat for* sound . . . smell . . . [57] . . . taste . . . tactile objects states of mind) . . . [58] . . . When the Lord said: ' And I, Sāriputta, say that mental states cognisable through the mind are of two kinds, one of which is to be followed and the other which is not to be followed,' it was said in reference to this. I, revered sir, thus understand this to be the meaning in full of what was spoken of by the Lord in brief, but of which the meaning was not explained in full."

" It is good, Sāriputta, it is good. It is good that you, Sāriputta, thus understand this to be the meaning in full of what was spoken of by me in brief, but of which the meaning was not explained in full . . . (*Repeat the above from* material shape *to* mental states cognisable through the mind) . . . When I said: ' I, Sāriputta, say that mental states cognisable through the mind are of two kinds, one of which is to be followed and the other which is not to be followed,' it was said in reference to this. Thus, Sāriputta, should be understood in full the meaning of what was spoken of by me in brief.

And I, Sāriputta, say that robe-material is of two kinds, one of which is to be followed and the other which is not to be followed. And I, Sāriputta, say that almsfood . . . lodgings . . . a village . . . a market town . . . a town . . . a country district . . . a person is of two kinds, one of which is to be followed and the other which is not to be followed."

[**59**] When this had been said, the venerable Sāriputta spoke thus to the Lord: " I, revered sir, thus understand this to be the meaning in full of what was spoken of by the Lord in brief, but of which the meaning was not explained in full: ' And I, Sāriputta, say that robe-material . . . almsfood . . . lodgings . . . a village . . . a market town . . . a town . . . a country district . . . a person is of two kinds, one of which is to be followed and the other which is not to be followed.' This was said by the Lord. In reference to what was it said ? Revered sir, if a certain kind of robe-material . . . almsfood . . . lodgings . . . village . . . market town . . . town . . . country district . . . person is followed and unskilled states of mind grow much, skilled states of mind decrease, that almsfood . . . person is not to be followed. But if, revered sir, a certain kind of robe-material . . . person is followed and unskilled states of mind decrease, skilled states of mind grow much, that almsfood . . . person is to be followed. When the Lord said: ' And I, Sāriputta, say that robe-material . . . a person is of two kinds, one of which is to be followed and the other which is not to be followed,' it was said in reference to this. I, revered sir, thus understand this to be the meaning in full of what was spoken of by the Lord in brief, but of which the meaning was not explained in full."

" It is good, Sāriputta, it is good. It is good that you, Sāriputta, thus understand this to be the meaning in full of what was spoken of by me in brief, but of which the meaning was not explained in full.

' And I, Sāriputta say that robe-material . . . [**60**] . . . almsfood . . . lodgings . . . a village . . . market town . . . town . . . country district . . . a person is of two kinds, one of which is to be followed and the other which is not to be followed.' This was said by me. In reference to what was it said ? Sāriputta, if a certain kind of robe-material . . . person is followed and unskilled states of mind grow much, skilled states of mind decrease, that kind of robe-material . . . person is not to be followed. But if, Sāriputta, a certain kind of robe-material . . . person is followed and unskilled states of mind decrease, skilled states of mind grow much, that robe-material ... person is to be followed. This that was said by me, Sāriputta, was said in reference to this. Thus, Sāriputta, should be understood in full the meaning of what was spoken of by me in brief.

And, Sāriputta, if all nobles ... all brahmans ... all merchants ... all workers could thus understand the meaning in full of this that was spoken of by me in brief, for a long time it would be for their welfare and happiness. And, Sāriputta, if the world with the *devas*, with the Māras and Brahmās, and if the generations of recluses and brahmans, *devas* and men could thus understand the meaning in full of this that was spoken of by me in brief, for a long time it would be for their welfare and happiness."

[61] Thus spoke the Lord. Delighted, the venerable Sāriputta rejoiced in what the Lord had said.

Discourse on What is To Be Followed
and What is Not To Be Followed:
The Fourth

115. DISCOURSE ON THE MANIFOLD ELEMENTS
(Bahudhātukasutta)

THUS have I heard:[1] At one time the Lord was staying near Sāvatthī in the Jeta Grove in Anāthapiṇḍika's monastery. While he was there the Lord addressed the monks, saying, " Monks." " Revered One," those monks answered the Lord in assent. The Lord spoke thus:

" Whatever fears arise, monks, all arise for the fool, not the wise man. Whatever troubles[2] arise, all arise for the fool, not the wise man. Whatever misfortunes arise, all arise for the fool, not the wise man. Monks, as a spark of fire[3] from a house thatched with rushes or a house thatched with grass sets fire to gabled houses that

---

[1] As at *A.* i. 101 to " Wherefore " at end of next paragraph.

[2] *upaddavā*, distresses; " states of absent-mindedness," *C.P.D.*; *MA.* iv. 102, *anekaggatākāra*.

[3] *aggimukka* above and at *A.* i. 101; *v.l.* -*mutta*.

are smeared inside and out, protected from the wind, with bolts that are fastened, windows that are closed,[1] even so, monks, whatever fears ... troubles ... misfortunes arise, all arise for the fool, not the wise man. Thus, monks, it is the fool who is beset by fear, the wise man is not beset by fear; the fool has trouble, the wise man does not have trouble; the fool has misfortune, the wise man does not have misfortune. Monks, there is not fear, trouble, misfortune for the wise man. Wherefore, monks, thinking, ' Investigating, we will become wise,' this is how you must train yourselves, monks."

[62] When this had been said, the venerable Ānanda spoke thus to the Lord: " What is the stage at which it suffices to say, revered sir: ' Investigating, the monk is wise ' ?"

" Ānanda, as soon as a monk is skilled in the elements and skilled in the (sense-)fields and skilled in conditioned genesis and skilled in the possible and the impossible,[2] it is at this stage, Ānanda, that it suffices to say, ' Investigating, the monk is wise.' "

" But, revered sir, at what stage does it suffice to say, ' The monk is skilled in the elements ' ?"

" There are these eighteen elements,[3] Ānanda: the element of eye, the element of material shape, the element of visual consciousness; the element of ear, the element of sound, the element of auditory consciousness; the element of nose, the element of smell, the element of olfactory consciousness; the element of tongue, the element of taste, the element of gustatory consciousness; the element of body, the element of touch, the element of bodily consciousness; the element of mind, the element of mental states, the element of mental consciousness. When, Ānanda, he knows and sees these eighteen elements, it is at this stage that it suffices to say, ' The monk is skilled in the elements.' "

" Might there be another way also, revered sir, according to which it suffices to say, ' The monk is skilled in the elements ' ?"

" There might be, Ānanda. There are these six elements, Ānanda: the element of extension, the element of cohesion, the element of radiation, the element of mobility,[4] the element of space, the element of consciousness.[5] When, Ānanda, he knows and sees

---

[1] See *M*. i. 76, ii. 8 for this description.
[2] *ṭhānāṭṭhāna*, the causally possible and causally impossible.
[3] *Vbh*. 90. On the elements, *dhātu*, see *Vism*. 484 *ff*.
[4] In the text *vāyodhatu* stands before *tejodhātu*. I have transposed them above so as to secure the usual sequence.
[5] As at *M*. iii. 31.

these six elements, it is at this stage that it suffices to say, 'The monk is skilled in the elements.'"

"Might there be another way also, revered sir, according to which it suffices to say, 'The monk is skilled in the elements'?"

"There might be, Ānanda. There are these six elements, Ānanda: the element of happiness, the element of anguish, the element of gladness, the element of sorrowing, the element of equanimity, the element of ignorance.[1] When, Ānanda, he knows and sees these six elements, it is at this stage that it suffices to say, 'The monk is skilled in the elements.'"

"Might there be another way also, revered sir, according to which it suffices to say, 'The monk is skilled in the elements'?"

"There might be, Ānanda. There are these six elements, Ānanda: the element of sensuous pleasures, the element of renunciation, the element of malice, the element of non-malice, [63] the element of harming, the element of non-harming.[2] When, Ānanda, he knows and sees these six elements, it is at this stage that it suffices to say, 'The monk is skilled in the elements.'"

"Might there be another way also, revered sir, according to which it suffices to say, 'The monk is skilled in the elements'?"

"There might be, Ānanda. There are these three elements, Ānanda: the element of sensuous pleasures, the element of fine-materiality, the element of non-materiality.[3] When, Ānanda, he knows and sees these three elements, it is at this stage that it suffices to say, 'The monk is skilled in the elements.'"

"Might there be another way, revered sir, according to which it suffices to say, 'The monk is skilled in the elements'?"

"There might be, Ānanda. There are these two elements, Ānanda: the element that is constructed[4] and the element that is unconstructed. When, Ānanda, he knows and sees these two elements, it is at this stage that it suffices to say, 'The monk is skilled in the elements.'"

"At what stage, revered sir, does it suffice to say, 'The monk is skilled in the (sense-)fields'?"

"These six (sense-)fields, Ānanda, are internal-external: the eye

---

[1] *Vbh.* 85.
[2] *Cf.* these six at *D.* iii. 215, *A.* iii. 447, *S.* ii. 151, *Vbh.* 86.
[3] As at *D.* iii. 215, *Iti.* 45.
[4] This pair also at *D.* iii. 274. The "constructed," *saṁkhata*, is a synonym for the five *khandhā*; the "unconstructed" is a synonym for nibbāna, *MA.* iv. 106. See also *Vbh.* 72-73, 89, 421.

as well as material shape; the ear as well as sound; the nose as well as smell; the tongue as well as taste; the body as well as touch; the mind as well as mental states. When, Ānanda, he knows and sees these six internal-external (sense-)fields, it is at this stage that it suffices to say, ' The monk is skilled in the (sense-)fields.' "

" And at what stage, revered sir, does it suffice to say, ' The monk is skilled in conditioned genesis ' ?"

" As to this, Ānanda, a monk knows thus: ' If this is, that comes to be; from the arising of this, that arises; if this is not, that does not come to be; from the stopping of this, that is stopped. That is to say: Conditioned by ignorance are the (karma-)formations;[1] conditioned by the (karma-)formations is consciousness; conditioned by consciousness is name-and-shape; conditioned by name-and-shape is the field of the six (senses); conditioned by the field of the six (senses) is (sensory) impingement; conditioned by (sensory) impingement is feeling; conditioned by feeling is craving; conditioned by craving is grasping; conditioned by grasping [64] is becoming; conditioned by becoming is birth; conditioned by birth there come into being old age and dying, grief, sorrow, suffering, lamentation and despair. Thus is the origin of this whole mass of anguish. But from the utter fading away and stopping of this very ignorance is the stopping of the (karma-)formations; from the stopping of the (karma-)formations is the stopping of consciousness; from the stopping of consciousness is the stopping of name-and-shape; from the stopping of name-and-shape is the stopping of the field of the six (senses); from the stopping of the field of the six (senses) is the stopping of (sensory) impingement; from the stopping of (sensory) impingement is the stopping of feeling; from the stopping of feeling is the stopping of craving; from the stopping of craving is the stopping of grasping; from the stopping of grasping is the stopping of becoming; from the stopping of becoming is the stopping of birth; from the stopping of birth, old age and dying, grief, sorrow, suffering, lamentation and despair are stopped. Thus is the stopping of this whole mass of anguish.' It is at that stage, Ānanda, that it suffices to say, ' The monk is skilled in conditioned genesis.' "

" And at what stage, revered sir, does it suffice to say, ' The monk is skilled in the possible and the impossible ' ?"

" As to this, Ānanda, a monk comprehends: ' It is impossible, it cannot come to pass[2] that a man possessed of (right) view should

---

[1] See *M.L.S.* i. xxiv; and *cf. M.* i. 262-264. [2] As at *A.* i. 26 *ff.*

go to any construction[1] as permanent—this situation does not
occur.' He comprehends: 'But this situation occurs when an
average man might go to some construction as permanent—this
situation occurs.' He comprehends: 'It is impossible, it cannot
come to pass that a man possessed of (right) view should go to any
construction as happy—this situation does not occur. He comprehends: 'But this situation occurs when an average man might
go to some construction as happy—this situation occurs.' He
comprehends: 'It is impossible, it cannot come to pass that a man
possessed of (right) view should go to any *dhamma* as self—this
situation does not occur.' He comprehends: 'But this situation
occurs when an average man might go to some *dhamma* as self—this
situation occurs.' He comprehends: 'It is impossible, it cannot
come to pass that a man possessed of (right) view should deprive
his mother of life—this situation does not occur.' He comprehends:
'But this situation occurs when an average man might deprive his
mother of life—this situation occurs.' He comprehends: 'It is
impossible, it cannot come to pass that [65] a man possessed of
(right) view should deprive his father of life . . . should deprive one
perfected of life . . . but this situation occurs when an average man
might deprive his father . . . one perfected of life—this situation
occurs.' He comprehends: 'It is impossible, it cannot come to
pass that a man possessed of (right) view should, with murderous
intent, draw a Tathāgata's blood—this situation does not occur.'
He comprehends: 'But this situation occurs when an average man
might, with murderous intent, draw a Tāthāgata's blood—this
situation occurs.' He comprehends: 'It is impossible, it cannot
come to pass that a man possessed of (right) view should cause a
schism in the Order . . . should proclaim another Teacher—this
situation does not occur.' He comprehends: 'But this situation
occurs when an average man might cause a schism in the Order . . .
might proclaim another Teacher—this situation occurs.' He com-

---

[1] Perhaps meaning here a " construction," a " compounded thing " or a
" conditioned thing." See above, p. 106; also *M.L.S.* i. Intr., p. xxiv *f.*
Saṅkhāra and *dhamma* just below go together at *Dhp.* 277-279, the former with
anicca and *dukkha* (*sabbe saṅkhārā aniccā* . . . *dukkhā*) and the latter with
anatta (*sabbe dhammā anattā*). As a category, *dhamma* is wider than *saṅkhāra*,
for it includes the uncompounded nibbāna. This is *anatta*, but it is neither
impermanent nor painful; on the contrary it is permanent and blissful.
Everything else is impermanent and painful as well as being *anatta*. The
force of *dhamma* in this context and this sense is therefore to imply and include
nibbāna.

prehends: 'It is impossible, it cannot come to pass that in one world-system two perfected ones who are Fully Self-Awakened Ones should arise simultaneously—this situation does not occur.' He comprehends: 'But this situation occurs when in one world-system one perfected one who is a Fully Self-Awakened One might arise—this situation occurs.' He comprehends: 'It is impossible, it cannot come to pass that in one world-system two wheel-turning kings should arise simultaneously . . . but this situation occurs when in one world-system one wheel-turning king might arise—this situation occurs.' He comprehends: 'It is impossible, it cannot come to pass that a woman who is a perfected one could be a Fully Self-Awakened One . . . but the situation occurs when a man who is a perfected one could be a Fully Self-Awakened One—this situation occurs.' He comprehends: 'It is impossible, it cannot come to pass that a woman should be a wheel-turning king . . . but a man could be a wheel-turning king—this situation occurs.' He comprehends: 'It is impossible, it cannot come to pass that a woman could be a Sakka [66] . . . a Māra . . . a Brahmā . . . but this situation occurs when a man might be a Sakka . . . a Māra . . . a Brahmā—this situation occurs.' He comprehends: 'It is impossible, it cannot come to pass that from wrong conduct in body . . . speech . . . thought there could result a fruit that was agreeable, pleasant, liked . . . but the situation occurs when from wrong conduct in body . . . speech . . . thought there might result a fruit that was disagreeable, unpleasant, not liked—this situation occurs.' He comprehends: 'It is impossible, it cannot come to pass that from right conduct in body . . . speech . . . thought there might result a fruit that was disagreeable, unpleasant, not liked . . . but the situation occurs when from right conduct in body . . . speech . . . thought there might result a fruit that was agreeable, pleasant, liked—this situation occurs.' He comprehends: 'It is impossible, it cannot come to pass that one who is addicted to wrong conduct in body . . . [67] . . . speech . . . thought should, from that source, from that condition arise, on the breaking up of the body after dying, in a good bourn, a heaven world . . . but this situation occurs when one who is addicted to wrong conduct in body . . . speech . . . thought might, from that source, from that condition arise, on the breaking up of the body after dying, in the sorrowful ways, a bad bourn, the downfall, Niraya Hell—this situation occurs.' He comprehends: 'It is impossible, it cannot come to pass that one who is addicted to right conduct in body . . . speech . . . thought should, from that source, from that condition arise, on the breaking up of the body after dying, in the sorrowful ways, a bad bourn, the downfall, Niraya Hell—this situation does not occur.' He comprehends: ' But this situation occurs when one who is addicted to right conduct in body ... speech ... thought might, from that source, from that condition arise, on the breaking up of the body after dying, in a good bourn, a heaven world—this situation occurs.' It is at this stage, Ānanda, that it suffices to say: ' The monk is skilled in the possible and the impossible.' "

When this had been said the venerable Ānanda spoke thus to the Lord: " It is wonderful, revered sir, it is marvellous, revered sir. What, revered sir, is the name of this disquisition on *dhamma* ?"

" Wherefore do you, Ānanda, remember this disquisition on *dhamma* as the Manifold Elements, and remember it as the Fourfold Circle,[1] and remember it as the Mirror of Dhamma, and remember it as the Drum of Deathlessness, and remember it as the Incomparable Victory in the Battle."[2]

Thus spoke the Lord. Delighted, the venerable Ānanda rejoiced in what the Lord had said.

Discourse on the Manifold Elements:
The Fifth

116. DISCOURSE AT ISIGILI

(Isigilisutta)

[68] THUS have I heard: At one time the Lord was staying near Rājagaha on Isigili mountain. While he was there the Lord addressed the monks, saying: " Monks." " Revered One," these monks answered the Lord in assent. The Lord spoke thus:
" Do not you, monks, see this Vebhāra[3] mountain ?"
" Yes, revered sir."

---

[1] Referring to the elements, (sense-)fields, conditioned genesis, and the possible and impossible, *MA*. iv. 126.

[2] *Cf. D.* i. 46 where Ānanda is also given five titles by which he might remember the disquisition on *dhamma* (the *Brahmajālasuttanta*), and where the fifth title is the same as the fifth given above: Anuttaro Saṁgāmavijayo.

[3] This and the four following names of mountains are the names of those surrounding Rājagaha; *cf. SnA.* 382.

"There was another designation, monks, of this Vebhāra mountain, another name. Do not you, monks, see this Paṇḍava mountain ?"

"Yes, revered sir."

"There was another designation, monks, of this Paṇḍava mountain, another name. Do not you, monks, see this Vepulla mountain ?"

"Yes, revered sir."

"There was another designation, monks, of this Vepulla mountain,[1] another name. Do not you, monks, see this Gijjhakūṭa mountain ?"[2]

"Yes, revered sir."

"There was another designation, monks, of this Gijjhakūṭa mountain, another name. Do not you, monks, see this Isigili mountain ?"

"Yes, revered sir."

"This has always been the designation, monks, this always the name of this Isigili mountain. Once upon a time, monks, five hundred paccekabuddhas[3] dwelt for a long time on this Isigili mountain. They were seen as they were entering this mountain, but once they had entered they were not seen. People seeing this, spoke thus: 'This mountain swallows these seers" (*isī gilati*);[4] so did Isigili receive the very designation Isigili. I will point out to you, monks, the names of the paccekabuddhas; I will relate, monks, the names of the paccekabuddhas; I will tell, [69] monks, the names of the paccekabuddhas. Listen, attend carefully and I will speak."

"Yes, revered sir," these monks answered the Lord in assent. The Lord spoke thus:

"Ariṭṭha,[5] monks, was a paccekabuddha who lived in this Isigili mountain for a long time. Upariṭṭha[6] . . . Tagarasikhin[7] . . . Yasassin[8] . . . Sudassana[9] . . . Piyadassin . . . Gandhāra . . . Piṇḍola . . .

---

[1] See *S.* ii. 190-193.   [2] This is "Mount Vulture-Peak."

[3] Those who win enlightenment by themselves without the aid of a teacher; but they cannot preach *dhamma* to others.

[4] *MA.* iv. 127 says that when these sages returned from their almsround the mountain would open like a huge pair of doors, and when they had entered it they stayed there and were to be seen no more.

[5] These thirteen names are to be found in *D.P.P.N.*, with legends when they exist. I therefore give only a few references.

[6] *Thag.* 910.   [7] *Ud.* 50; *UdA.* 291; *S.* i. 92; *Jā.* iii. 299.
[8] *Thag.* 910.   [9] *ThagA.* i. 93; *Ap.* ii. 451.

Upāsabha ... Nītha ... Tatha ... Sutavā ... Bhāvitatta, monks, was a paccekabuddha who lived in this Isigili mountain for a long time.

> Those essences of beings,[1] unafflicted,[2] without longing, who individually have come to right enlightenment—
> Listen to me as I am relating the names of these barbless[3] incomparable men:
> Ariṭṭha, Upariṭṭha, Tagarasikhin, Yasassin and Sudassana, Piyadassin the enlightened,
> Gandhāra, Piṇḍola and Upāsabha, Nītha, Tatha, Sutavā, Bhāvitatta,
> [70] Sumbha, Subha, Methula and Aṭṭhama, Athassumegha, Anigha, Sudāṭha
> Are paccekabuddhas whose conduits for becoming are destroyed; Hiṅgū and Hiṅga of great majesty,
> The two sages Jālin,[4] and Aṭṭhaka, then Kosala the awakened one, then Subāhu,
> Upanemi, this Nemi, this Santacitta, truthful, real, stainless and wise;
> Kāḷa, Upakāḷa, Vijita and Jita and Aṅga and Paṅga and Gutijjita;
> Passin renounced cleaving to the root of anguish, Aparājita defeated Māra's might;
> Satthā, Pavattā, Sarabhaṅga, Lomahaṁsa, Uccaṅgamāya, Asita, Ānāsava,
> Manomaya, and Bandhumā the cutter away of pride, Tadādhimutta, and Ketumā the stainless;
> Ketumbarāga and Mātaṅga, Ariya, then Accuta, Accutagāma, Byāmaka,
> Sumaṅgala, Dabbila, Supatiṭṭhito, Asayha, Khemābhirata and Sorata,
> Durannaya, Saṁgha, and then Ujjaya, and then the sage Sayha of sublime courage;[5]

---

[1] *MA*. iv. 129, " having spoken the names of the thirteen paccekabuddhas, now pointing out the names of those others who are the essences of beings ... " *Sattasārā*, essences of beings, means: who have become the essences of beings, *sattānaṁ sārabhūtā*.
[2] *anigha=niddukkha*, *MA*. iv. 129.
[3] *visalla*; cf. *S*. i. 180; *Sn*. 17, 86, 367.
[4] Cūḷa- and Mahā-Jālin, *MA*. iv. 129.
[5] *anomanikkhama*; *D*. iii. 156, *MA*. iv. 129 read *-nikkama*, called *viriyattā* at *MA*.

Ānanda, Nanda, Upananda (making) twelve,[1] Bhāradvāja
bearing his last body,
Bodhi, Mahānāma, then too the other Bhāradvāja, hair-crested,
beautiful,
Tissa, Upatissa, Upasīdarin, the cutters away of the bonds of
becoming, and Sīdarin, the cutter away of craving;
The buddha[2] called Maṅgala, attachment-gone, Usabha who cut
away the ensnaring root of ill;
Upaṇīta who attained the peaceful path, Uposatha, Sundara,
Saccanāma,
Jeta, Jayanta, Paduma, Uppala and Padumuttara, Rakkhita
and Pabbata;
[71] Mānatthaddha, Sobhita, Vītarāga and the buddha[2] Kaṇha,
well freed in mind—
These and others[3] are paccekabuddhas of great majesty, their
conduits for becoming destroyed.
Praise all these immeasurable great seers who have attained
final nibbāna."

Discourse at Isigili:
The Sixth

117. DISCOURSE PERTAINING TO THE
GREAT FORTY
(Mahācattārīsakasutta)

THUS have I heard: At one time the Lord was staying near Sāvatthī
in the Jeta Grove in Anāthapiṇḍika's monastery. While he was
there the Lord addressed the monks, saying: " Monks." " Revered
One," these monks answered the Lord in assent. The Lord spoke
thus: " I will teach you, monks, the ariyan[4] right concentra-

---

[1] Four Ānandas, four Nandas and four Upanandas, *MA*. iv. 129.
[2] *I.e.* paccekabuddha.
[3] Among the five hundred paccekabuddhas, two and three and ten and twelve have the same name such as Ānanda, etc.; these and others are not spoken of separately here, *MA*. iv. 130.
[4] *MA*. iv. 130 says that the meaning of ariyan is flawless, supermundane.

tion¹ with the causal associations,² with the accompaniments.³ Listen to it, attend carefully and I will speak."

"Yes, revered sir," these monks answered the Lord in assent. The Lord spoke thus:

"And what, monks, is the ariyan right concentration with the causal associations, with the accompaniments ? It is right view, right purpose, right speech, right action, right mode of livelihood, right endeavour, right mindfulness. Whatever one-pointedness of mind, monks, is accompanied by these seven components, this, monks, is called the ariyan right concentration with the causal associations and the accompaniments.

As to this, monks, right view comes first.⁴ And how, monks, does right view come first ? If one comprehends that wrong view is wrong view and comprehends that right view is right view, that is his right view.⁵ And what, monks, is wrong view ? 'There is no (result of) gift,⁶ no (result of) offering, no (result of) sacrifice; there is no fruit or ripening of deeds well done or ill done; there is not this world, there is not a world beyond; there is no (benefit from serving) mother or father; there are no beings of spontaneous uprising; [72] there are not in the world recluses and brahmans who are faring rightly, proceeding rightly, and who proclaim this world and the world beyond having realised them by their own super-knowledge.' This, monks, is a wrong view.

And what, monks, is right view ? Now, I, monks, say that right view is twofold. There is, monks, the right view that has cankers, that is on the side of merit, that ripens unto cleaving (to new

---

¹ *Cf. D.* ii. 216 *f.* for the following. Right concentration is concentration on the Way, *MA.* iv. 130.

² *sa-upanisā. Cf. S.* ii. 29 *ff.* "The history of this word has yet to be written," *P.E.D.* s.v. *upanisā. MA.* iv. 130 gives it the meaning of *paccaya*, condition.

³ *saparikkhāra*, with the requisites, called *sa-parivāra* at *MA.* iv. 130, " with the surroundings," concomitants.

⁴ *pubbaṅgama*, it is the fore-goer, *purecārika, MA.* iv. 131. Right view is twofold: that of insight, *vipassanā*, and that of the Way. The former examines the three kinds of activities (*saṅkhāra*: of body, speech and thought) in respect of impermanence, etc. But the latter arises at the end of the examination while rooting out and allaying the stage that has been attained, *MA.* iv. 130. At *MA.* iv. 135 it is said, " In this Discourse there are five kinds of right view: through insight, of specific kamma (*cf. Dhs.* 1366, *Vbh.* 328, *MA.* v. 10), of the Way, of the fruits, through reflection on."

⁵ This is right view through insight, *MA.* iv. 135.

⁶ As at *M.* i. 287, etc.

birth).¹ There is, monks, the right view that is ariyan, cankerless, supermundane, a component of the Way. And what, monks, is the right view that has cankers, that is on the side of merit, that ripens unto cleaving (to new birth) ? 'There is (result of) gift . . . offering . . . sacrifice; there is fruit and ripening of deeds well done or ill done; there is this world, there is a world beyond; there is (benefit from serving) mother and father; there are spontaneously arising beings; there are in the world recluses and brahmans . . . who proclaim this world and the world beyond having realised them by their own super-knowledge.'² This, monks, is a right view that has cankers, is on the side of merit, that ripens unto cleaving (to new birth).

And what, monks is the right view that is ariyan, cankerless, supermundane, a component of the Way ? Whatever, monks, is wisdom, the cardinal faculty of wisdom,³ the power of wisdom,⁴ the component of enlightenment that is investigation into things,⁵ the right view that is a component of the Way in one who, by developing the ariyan Way, is of ariyan thought, cankerless thought, conversant with the ariyan Way⁶—this, monks, is a right view that is ariyan, cankerless, supermundane, a component of the Way.

Whoever makes endeavour for the riddance of wrong view, for the attainment of right view, that is his right endeavour. Mindful, he gets rid of wrong view; mindful, entering on right view, he abides in it. This is his right mindfulness. Thus these three things circle round and follow after right view, that is to say: right view, right endeavour, right mindfulness.

As to this, monks, right view comes first. And how, monks, does right view come first ? If one comprehends that wrong purpose is wrong purpose and comprehends that right purpose is right purpose, that is his [**73**] right view. And what, monks, is wrong purpose ? Purpose for sense-pleasures, purpose for ill-will, purpose for harming. This, monks, is wrong purpose. And what, monks, is right purpose ? Now I, monks, say that right purpose is twofold.

---

¹ *upadhivepakka.*
² This is the right view of specific kamma (see p. 114, *n.* 4 above), *MA.* iv. 135, *Vbh.* 328, *VbhA.* 415.
³ *paññindriya,* see *S.* v. 200.
⁴ *Cf. MA.* iv. 131: one does not tremble on account of ignorance.
⁵ *MA.* iv. 132 says that having attained the factor of enlightenment one investigates the four truths.
⁶ *ariyamaggassa samaṅgino,* also at *M.* iii. 73. *C.P.D.* says this is a wrong reading. A variant here and the reading at *M.* iii. 74, 75 is *ariyamaggasamaṅgino. Cf. Pug.* p. 10, 73: *maggasamaṅgino:* those on the four Ways.

There is, monks, the right purpose that has cankers, is on the side of merit, and ripens unto cleaving (to new birth). There is, monks, the right purpose that is ariyan, cankerless, supermundane, a factor of the Way. And what, monks, is the right purpose that has cankers, is on the side of merit, and ripens unto cleaving ? Purpose for renunciation, purpose for non-ill-will, purpose for non-harming. This, monks, is right purpose that . . . ripens unto cleaving.

And what, monks, is the right purpose that is ariyan, cankerless, supermundane, a component of the Way ? Whatever, monks, is reasoning,[1] initial thought,[2] purpose, an activity of speech through the complete focussing[3] and application of the mind in one who, by developing the ariyan Way, is of ariyan thought, of cankerless thought, and is conversant with the ariyan Way—this, monks, is right purpose that is ariyan, cankerless, supermundane, a component of the Way.

Whoever makes endeavour for the riddance of wrong purpose, for the attainment of right purpose, that is his right endeavour. Mindful, he gets rid of wrong purpose; mindful, entering on right purpose he abides in it. That is his right mindfulness. Thus these three things circle round and follow after right purpose, that is to say: right view, right endeavour, right mindfulness.

As to this, monks, right view comes first. And how, monks, does right view come first ? If one comprehends that wrong speech is wrong speech and comprehends that right speech is right speech, that is his right view. And what, monks, is wrong speech ? Lying, slanderous speech, harsh speech, gossiping. This, monks, is wrong speech. And what, monks, is right speech ? Now, I, monks, say that right speech is twofold. There is, monks, the right speech that has cankers, is on the side of merit, that ripens unto cleaving (to new birth). There is, [**74**] monks, the right speech that is ariyan, cankerless, supermundane, a component of the Way. And what, monks, is the right speech that . . . ripens unto cleaving (to new birth) ? Abstaining from lying, abstaining from slanderous speech . . . harsh speech . . . gossiping. This, monks, is the right speech that has cankers, is on the side of merit, that ripens unto cleaving (to new birth).

And what, monks, is the right speech that is ariyan, cankerless, supermundane, a component of the Way ? Whatever, monks, is

---

[1] *takka.*   [2] *vitakka. Cf. M.* i. 301, *vitakkavicārā vacīsaṁkhāro.*
[3] *Cf. Dhs.* 7.

abstention from, refraining from, avoidance of, restraint from[1] the four ways of bad conduct in speech[2] in one who, by developing the ariyan Way is of ariyan thought, of cankerless thought, and is conversant with the Way—this, monks, is right speech that is ariyan, cankerless, supermundane, a component of the Way.

Whoever makes endeavour for the riddance of wrong speech, for the attainment of right speech, that is his right endeavour. Mindful, he gets rid of wrong speech; mindful, entering on right speech, he abides in it. That is his right mindfulness. Thus these three things circle round and follow after right speech, that is to say: right view, right endeavour, right mindfulness.

As to this, monks, right view comes first. And how, monks, does right view come first ? If one comprehends that wrong action is wrong action and comprehends that right action is right action, that is his right view. And what, monks, is wrong action ? Onslaught on creatures, taking what has not been given, wrong enjoyment among the sense-pleasures.[2] This, monks, is wrong action. And what, monks, is right action ? Now, I, monks, say that right action is twofold. There is, monks, the right action that has cankers, is on the side of merit, that ripens unto cleaving (to new birth). There is, monks, the right action that is ariyan, cankerless, supermundane, a component of the Way. And what, monks, is the right action that . . . ripens unto cleaving (to new birth) ? It is, monks, abstaining from onslaught on creatures, abstaining from taking what has not been given, abstaining from wrong enjoyment among the sense-pleasures. This, monks, is the right action that has cankers, is on the side of merit, and ripens unto cleaving.

And what, monks, is the right action that is ariyan, cankerless, supermundane, a component of the way ? Whatever, monks, is abstention from, refraining from, avoidance of, restraint from the three ways of bad conduct in body[2] in one who, by developing the ariyan Way is of ariyan thought, of cankerless thought, and is conversant with the Way—this, monks, is right action [**75**] that is ariyan, cankerless, supermundane, a component of the Way.

Whoever makes endeavour for the riddance of wrong action, for the attainment of right action, that is his right endeavour. Mindful, he gets rid of wrong action; mindful, entering on right action, he abides in it. That is his right mindfulness. Thus these three things

---

[1] The four words of this sequence occur also at *Dhs.* 299, *Nd.* II. 462 in connection with right speech.

[2] See *M*. i. 286.

circle round and follow after right action, that is to say: right view, right endeavour, right mindfulness.

As to this, monks, right view comes first. And how, monks, does right view come first ? If one comprehends that wrong mode of livelihood is wrong mode of livelihood and comprehends that right mode of livelihood is right mode of livelihood, that is his right view. And what, monks, is wrong mode of livelihood ? Trickery,[1] cajolery,[2] insinuating,[3] dissembling,[4] rapacity for gain upon gain.[5] This, monks, is wrong mode of livelihood. And what, monks, is right mode of livelihood ? Now, I, monks, say that right mode of livelihood is twofold. There is, monks, the right mode of livelihood that has cankers, is on the side of merit, that ripens unto cleaving (to new birth). There is, monks, the right mode of livelihood that is ariyan, cankerless, supermundane, a component of the Way. And what, monks, is the right mode of livelihood that . . . ripens unto cleaving (to new birth) ? Herein, monks, an ariyan disciple, by getting rid of wrong mode of livelihood, earns his living by right mode of livelihood. This, monks, is right mode of livelihood that has cankers, is on the side of merit, and ripens unto cleaving.

And what, monks, is the right mode of livelihood that is ariyan,

---

[1] Cf. D. i. 8, Vism. 6 ff. for these five words. The first, kuhanā, means according to MA. iv. 134, DA. 91, that these people trick (deceive or delude, kuhayanti) the world and astonish it with three kinds of tricks. These are referred to at Jā. iv. 297. These five words also occur at A. iii. 111, and the actions (trickery, etc.) are explained at Vbh. 352 f., Vism. 23; cf. VbhA. 471. On kuhanā and lapanā cf. the phrases janakuhanattha janalapanattha at M. i. 465, A. ii. 26, Iti. pp. 28, 29.

[2] lapanā. Cf. Vism. 26 f.; also Iti. §99=A. i. 165, 168. Lapakā, translated at Dial. i. 15 " droners out (of holy words for pay) "; at G.S. iii. 88 " ranter "; at Min.Anth. ii. 186 (lapita-lāpa) " mere mutterings "; at Path Purity i. 27 " boasters." I follow G.S. ii. 28 and Min.Anth. ii. 136. MA. iv. 134: " they cajole for the sake of gains and honour."

[3] nemittakatā; cf. nimittikatā at Vin. i. 254 where, if a monk hints or insinuates that he wants kaṭhina cloth, then it cannot be said to be properly made. Dial. i. 16 translates nemittikā as diviners with note that these are interpreters of signs and omens. This it may easily mean. But in the above context the whole stress is on deceitful ways, unspecified, of obtaining gains and honours.

[4] nippesikatā. I follow translation at G.S. iii. 88. For nippesika Dial. i. 16 gives exorcists, and P.E.D. juggler. But I see no need to be so definite. MA. iv. 134 says: nippeso sīlam etesan ti nippesikā, tesaṁ bhāvo nippesikatā. AA. iii. 273 says: nippesiko ti nippiṁsanakathāya samannāgato.

[5] Cf. definition of lābha at Vin. iii. 266, iv. 154, 156: the requisites, even a lump of chunam, a toothpick and unwoven thread.

cankerless, supermundane, a component of the Way ? Whatever, monks, is abstention from, refraining from, avoidance of, restraint from wrong mode of livelihood in one who, by developing the ariyan Way is of ariyan thought, of cankerless thought, and is conversant with the Way[1]—this, monks, is right mode of livelihood that is ariyan, cankerless, supermundane, a component of the Way.

Whoever makes endeavour for the riddance of wrong mode of livelihood, for the attainment of right mode of livelihood, that is his right endeavour. Mindful, he gets rid of wrong mode of livelihood; mindful, entering on right mode of livelihood, he abides in it. This is his right mindfulness. Thus these three things circle round and follow after right mode of livelihood, that is to say: right view, right endeavour, right mindfulness.

As to this, monks, right view comes first. And how, monks, does right view come first ? [**76**] Right purpose, monks, proceeds[2] from right view;[3] right speech proceeds from right purpose; right action proceeds from right speech; right mode of livelihood proceeds from right action; right endeavour proceeds from right mode of livelihood; right mindfulness proceeds from right endeavour; right concentration proceeds from right mindfulness; right knowledge proceeds[4] from right concentration; right freedom proceeds from right knowledge. In this way, monks, the learner's course is possessed of eight components, the perfected one's of ten components.

As to this, monks, right view comes first. And how, monks, does right view come first ? Wrong view, monks, is worn away in one of right view;[5] and those various evil unskilled things that arise conditioned by wrong view are worn away in him; and various skilled things conditioned by right view come to development and fulfilment. Wrong purpose, monks, is worn away in one of right purpose; and those various evil unskilled things that arise conditioned

---

[1] *Cf. Dhs.* 301.   [2] *pahoti, cf. D.* ii. 217.

[3] *sammādiṭṭhissa; MA.* iv. 134 explains this as meaning "of the man, *puggalassa*, who is established in the right view of the Way." So the meaning may be more literally: "proceeds for one of right view," etc. *MA.* iv. 135 says that here "right view of the Way and right view of the fruits" are both being spoken of; see above, p. 114, *n.* 4.

[4] *MA.* iv. 135 says here "right view through reflection on" is being spoken of.

[5] *MA.* iv. 135 says that the repeaters of the remaining Nikāyas say the "fruit" is being spoken of, but the *M.* repeaters say the "Way" is being spoken of in the ten items to be worn away.

by wrong purpose are worn away in him; and various skilled things conditioned by right purpose come to development and fulfilment. Wrong speech, monks, is worn away in one of right speech . . . Wrong action, monks, is worn away in one of right action . . . Wrong mode of livelihood, monks, is worn away in one of right mode of livelihood . . . [77] . . . Wrong endeavour, monks, is worn away in one of right endeavour . . . Wrong mindfulness, monks, is worn away in one of right mindfulness . . . Wrong concentration, monks, is worn away in one of right concentration . . . Wrong knowledge, monks, is worn away in one of right knowledge . . . Wrong freedom, monks, is worn away in one of right freedom; and those various evil unskilled things that arise conditioned by wrong freedom are worn away in him; and various skilled things conditioned by right freedom come to development and fulfilment. So, monks, there are twenty (components) on the side of skill,[1] twenty on the side of unskill. The disquisition on *dhamma* pertaining to the Great Forty that has been rolled on is not to be rolled back by a recluse or brahman or a *deva* or a Māra or a Brahmā or by anyone in the world. Monks, whatever recluse or brahman should think that this disquisition on *dhamma* pertaining to the Great Forty should be censured, should be scorned, ten ways of speaking from the standpoint of *dhamma*[2] give grounds for censuring him here and now:[3] if the worthy one censures right view then those recluses and brahmans who are of wrong view are the worthies to be honoured, the worthies to be extolled; if the worthy one censures right thought [78] then those recluses and brahmans who are of wrong thought are the worthies to be honoured, to be extolled; if the worthy one censures right speech . . . right action . . . right mode of livelihood . . . right endeavour . . . right mindfulness . . . right concentration . . . right knowledge . . . right freedom, then those recluses and brahmans who are of wrong speech . . . freedom are the worthies to be honoured, to be extolled. Monks, whatever recluse or brahman should think that this disquisition on *dhamma* pertaining to the Great Forty should be censured, should be scorned, these ten ways of speaking from the standpoint of *dhamma* give grounds for censuring him here and now. Monks, even those who were the people of Ukkala[4] and the Vassas

---

[1] *MA.* iv. 135: ten beginning with right view and ten come under " various skilled things conditioned by right view."

[2] *vādānuvādā*; *cf. A.* iii. 4. Reading at *M.* ii. 127 is *vādānupātā*.

[3] *Cf. A.* iii. 4; also *A.* i. 161, *S.* ii. 33, 36, iii. 6, etc.

[4] *MA.* iv. 136, " dwellers in the country of Okkala." *Ukkala* at *Vin.* i. 4.

and Bhaññas,[1] deniers of cause, deniers of the effecting (by cause), affirmers of ' There is not '[2]—even these would think that the disquisition on *dhamma* pertaining to the Great Forty should not be censured, should not be scorned. What is the reason for this ? The fear of blame, of attack and reproach."

Thus spoke the Lord. Delighted, these monks rejoiced in what the Lord had said.

Discourse pertaining to the Great Forty:
The Seventh

118. DISCOURSE ON MINDFULNESS WHEN BREATHING IN AND OUT
(Ānāpānasatisutta)

THUS have I heard: At one time the Lord was staying near Sāvatthī in the Eastern Monastery in the palace of Migāra's mother, together with a number of well known elders and disciples: the venerable Sāriputta,[3] the venerable Moggallāna the Great, the venerable Kassapa the Great, the venerable Kaccāyana the Great, the venerable Koṭṭhita the Great, the venerable Kappina the Great,[4] the venerable Cunda the Great, the vernable [79] Anuruddha, the venerable Revata, the venerable Ānanda and with other well known elders and disciples. At that time the monks who were elders exhorted and instructed newly ordained monks. Some monks who were elders exhorted and instructed ten monks, and some monks who were elders exhorted and instructed twenty . . . thirty . . . forty monks. And these newly ordained monks, while being exhorted

---

[1] *MA.* iv. 136, " two peoples."

[2] For these same three types of views attributed to these same three peoples, see *A.* ii. 31, *S.* iii. 73, *Kvu.* 141; also *K.S.* iii. 63, *n.* 3; *G.S.* ii. 10; *Pts. Contr.* p. 95, *n.* 2.

[3] *Cf.* other lists of theras at *Vin.* i. 354 *f.*, ii. 15 *f.*, iv. 66, and see *B.D.* ii. 245 for references.

[4] Mentioned also at *Vin.* i. 105.

and instructed by the monks who were elders, were aware of excellent successive attainment.[1]

Now at that time on an Observance day, the fifteenth, on the night of the full moon after the " Invitation "[2] the Lord was sitting down in the open air surrounded by an Order of monks. Then the Lord, having looked round at the Order of monks which had become quite silent, addressed the monks, saying: " I am satisfied,[3] monks, with this course, I am satisfied in mind, monks, with this course. Wherefore do you, monks, stir up energy to a still greater degree for attaining the unattained, for winning what is not yet won, for realising the unrealised. Now I will wait[4] here in Sāvatthī itself for Komudī, (the festival in) the fourth month."[5] Monks who lived in the country heard that the Lord had said that he would wait there in Sāvatthī itself for Komudī, (the festival in) the fourth month. And these monks who lived in the country resorted to Sāvatthī to see the Lord.[6] And those monks who were elders were exhorting and instructing the newly ordained monks still more. Some monks who were elders were exhorting and instructing ten newly ordained monks and some monks who were elders were exhorting and instructing twenty ... thirty ... forty newly ordained monks. And these newly ordained monks, while being exhorted and instructed by the monks who were elders, [80] were aware of excellent successive attainment.

Now at that time on an Observance day, the fifteenth, on the night of the full moon at (the time of) Komudī, (a festival in) the fourth month, the Lord was sitting down in the open air surrounded by an Order of monks. Then the Lord, having looked round at the Order of monks which had become quite silent, addressed the monks, saying:

" This assembly,[7] monks, is without idle words, this assembly, monks, has no idle words, it is established on the pure pith. Monks, an Order of monks such as this company is a company worthy of veneration, of honour, of gifts, of salutation with joined palms,

---

[1] During meditation on the "devices," *MA.* iv. 137. *Cf. D.* i. 233, *A.* iv. 47, *S.* v. 154.

[2] A monastic ceremony held at the end of the rains. See *Vin.* i. 160, ii. 32; *B.D.* i. 283, 292, ii. 153, *n.* 2.

[3] *āraddha,* explained by *tuṭṭha* at *MA.* iv. 137.

[4] *MA.* iv. 137 reads *āgamessāmi;* text *āgamissāmi.*

[5] *Komudiṁ cātumāsiniṁ, cf. B.D.* ii. 157, *n.* 3. *MA.* iv. 137 says it is called *komudī* because of the existence of white lotuses, and *cātumāsinī* because it is at the conclusion of the four months of the rains.

[6] After the full moon of Kattika.   [7] *Cf. A.* ii. 183.

(with the thought): 'It is an incomparable field of merit for the world.' Monks, an Order of monks such as this company is a company to which if a little is given it becomes much, if much is given it becomes more. Monks, an Order of monks such as this company is a company that is hard to see in the world. Monks, in order to see an Order of monks such as is this company, it is fitting to go many a *yojana* with one's foodbag on one's shoulder.[1] Such, monks, is this Order of monks; such, monks, is this company.

Monks, there are monks in this Order of monks who are perfected ones, their cankers destroyed, who have lived the life, done what was to be done, laid down the burden, attained their own goal, whose fetters of becoming are utterly destroyed, and who are freed by right profound knowledge. There are, monks, such monks in this Order of monks. Monks, there are monks in this Order of monks in whom the five fetters binding to the lower (shore) are utterly destroyed, who are of spontaneous uprising, attainers of nibbāna there, not liable to return from that world. There are, monks, such monks in this Order of monks. Monks, there are monks in this Order of monks in whom the three fetters are utterly destroyed, in whom attachment, aversion and confusion are reduced; they are once-returners who, having come back once to this world, [81] will make an end of anguish. There are, monks, such monks in this Order of monks. Monks, there are monks in this Order of monks in whom the three fetters are utterly destroyed; they are stream-attainers, not liable to the downfall, but assured, bound for awakening. There are, monks, such monks in this Order of monks. Monks, there are monks in this Order of monks who live intent on the practice of the (mind-)development of the four applications of mindfulness. There are, monks, such monks in this Order of monks. Monks, there are monks in this Order of monks who live intent on the practice of the (mind-)development of the four right efforts . . . of the four bases of psychic power . . . of the five controlling faculties . . . of the five powers . . . of the seven links in awakening. There are, monks, such monks in this Order of monks. Monks, there are monks in this Order of monks who live intent on the practice of the (mind-)development of the ariyan eightfold Way. There are, monks, such monks in this Order of monks. Monks, there are monks in this Order of monks who live intent on the

---

[1] *putosenāpi*. *MA*. iv. 139 also gives another reading, *putaṅsena*. See *G.S.* ii. 192, *n*. 1.

practice of the (mind-)development that is friendliness[1] . . . [82] . . . compassion . . . sympathetic joy . . . equanimity. There are, monks, such monks in this Order of monks. Monks, there are monks in this Order of monks who live intent on the practice of the (mind-)development that is on the foul[2] . . . intent on the practice of the (mind-)development that is perception of impermanence. There are, monks, such monks in this Order of monks. Monks, there are monks in this Order of monks who live intent on the practice of the (mind-)development that is mindfulness on in-breathing and out-breathing.

Mindfulness of in-breathing and out-breathing, monks, if developed and made much of, is of great fruit, of great advantage. Mindfulness of in-breathing and out-breathing, monks, if developed and made much of, brings to fulfilment the four applications of mindfulness; the four applications of mindfulness, if developed and made much of, bring to fulfilment the seven links in awakening; the seven links in awakening, if developed and made much of, bring to fulfilment freedom through knowledge.[3]

And how, monks, is mindfulness of in-breathing and out-breathing developed ? How is it made much of ? How is it of great fruit, of great advantage ? Herein, monks, a monk[4] who is forest-gone or gone to the root of a tree or gone to an empty place, sits down cross-legged, holding his back erect, arousing mindfulness in front of him. Mindful he breathes in, mindful he breathes out. Whether he is breathing in a long (breath) he comprehends, ' I am breathing in a long (breath) '; or whether he is breathing out a long (breath) he comprehends, ' I am breathing out a long (breath) '; or whether he is breathing in a short (breath) he comprehends, ' I am breathing in a short (breath) '; or whether he is breathing out a short (breath) he comprehends, ' I am breathing out a short (breath).' He trains himself, thinking, ' I will breathe in experiencing the whole body.'[5] He trains himself, thinking, ' I will breathe out experiencing the whole body.' He trains himself, thinking, ' I will breathe in tranquillising the activity of body.' He trains himself, thinking, ' I will breathe out tranquillising the activity of body.' He trains

---

[1] For this and the following cf. M. i. 424 f.

[2] The reference is probably to the cemetery meditations.

[3] *vijjāvimutti*, as at S. v. 28, 335. See also *Pts.* ii. 243, *SA.* iii. 275.

[4] For the following see M. Sta. 10; also M. i. 425, A. v. 111, and *Ānāpānasaṁyutta* (S. v. 311).

[5] *I.e.* the breath-body.

himself, thinking, 'I will breathe in . . . breathe out experiencing rapture.' He trains himself, thinking, 'I will breathe in . . . breathe out experiencing joy.' [83] He trains himself, thinking, 'I will breathe in . . . breathe out experiencing the activity of thought . . . tranquillising the activity of thought . . . experiencing thought . . . rejoicing in thought . . . concentrating thought . . . freeing thought.' He trains himself, thinking, 'I will breathe in . . . breathe out beholding impermanence . . . beholding detachment . . . beholding stopping . . . beholding casting away.' Monks, mindfulness of in-breathing and out-breathing when developed thus, made much of thus, is of great fruit, of great advantage.

And how, monks, when mindfulness of in-breathing and out-breathing is developed, how when it is made much of, does it bring the four applications of mindfulness to fulfilment ? At the time, monks, when a monk breathing in . . . breathing out a long (breath) . . . a short (breath) comprehends, 'I am breathing in . . . breathing out a long (breath) . . . a short (breath)'; when he trains himself, thinking, 'I will breathe in . . . breathe out experiencing the whole body . . . tranquillising the activity of body,' at that time, monks, the monk is faring along contemplating the body in the body, ardent, clearly conscious (of it), mindful (of it) so as to control the covetousness and dejection in the world. I say, monks, that of bodies[1] this is one, that is to say breathing-in and breathing-out.[2] Wherefore,[3] monks, at the time when a monk is faring along contemplating the body in the body, ardent, clearly conscious (of it), mindful (of it) so as to control the covetousness and dejection in the world, at that time, monks, [84] the monk trains himself, thinking, 'I will breathe in experiencing rapture[4] . . . I will breathe out experiencing rapture . . . I will breathe in . . . breathe out experiencing joy . . . I will breathe in . . . breathe out experiencing the activity of thought . . . I will breathe in . . . breathe out tranquillising the activity of thought '; at that time, monks, the monk is faring along contemplating the feelings in the feelings, ardent, clearly conscious

---

[1] *kāyesu*. *MA*. iv. 140, among the four bodies of extension and so on, this is one (*aññatara*), I say it is the body of mobility (*vāyokāya*). Or, the body that is material shape consists of twenty-five classes of *rūpa* (mentioned at *Dhs.* §585): *rūpāyatanaṁ . . . pe . . . kabiḷiṅkāro āhāro*. Of these, breathing is a body because it is included in the field of touch.

[2] *assāsapassāsa* here.

[3] He either beholds that the body of mobility is one of the four bodies, or that breathing is one of the twenty-five classes of material shape.

[4] On the experience of rapture being two-fold see *Vism.* 287, and *Pts.* i. 187.

(of them), mindful (of them) so as to control the covetousness and dejection in the world. I say, monks, that of feelings this is one,[1] that is to say proper attention to breathing-in and breathing-out. Wherefore, monks, at the time when a monk is faring along contemplating the feelings in the feelings, ardent, clearly conscious (of them), mindful (of them) so as to control the covetousness and dejection in the world, at that time, monks, the monk trains himself, thinking, ' I will breathe in . . . breathe out experiencing thought . . . breathe in . . . breathe out rejoicing in thought . . . breathe in . . . breathe out concentrating thought . . . breathe in . . . breathe out freeing thought '; at that time, monks, the monk is faring along contemplating the mind in the mind, ardent, clearly conscious (of it), mindful (of it) so as to control the covetousness and dejection in the world. I, monks, say that the (mind-)development that is mindfulness of in-breathing and out-breathing is not for one of muddled mindfulness, not for one not clearly conscious. Wherefore, monks, when a monk is faring along contemplating the mind in the mind, ardent, clearly conscious (of it), mindful (of it) so as to control the covetousness and dejection in the world, at that time, monks, the monk trains himself, thinking, ' I will breathe in . . . breathe out beholding impermanence . . . beholding detachment . . . beholding stopping . . . beholding casting away '; at that time, monks, the monk is faring along contemplating mental states in mental states, ardent, clearly conscious (of them), mindful (of them) so as to control the covetousness and dejection in the world. He, by getting rid of[2] that which is covetousness and dejection,[3] [85] having seen it by means of wisdom,[4] is one who looks on with proper care.[5] Wherefore, monks, at this time a monk is faring along contemplating the mental states in the mental states, ardent, clearly conscious (of them), mindful (of them) so as to control the covetousness and dejection in the world.

---

[1] It is a certain feeling of pleasantness among the three kinds of feeling, *MA.* iv. 140.

[2] By contemplating impermanence, he gets rid of the perception of permanence; getting rid of is a form of knowledge, *ñāṇa*.

[3] The hindrance of sensual desire is covetousness; the hindrance of ill-will is shown by dejection.

[4] After the knowledge of getting rid of, there is insight into what constitutes impermanence, detachment, stopping and casting away.

[5] *ajjhupekkhitar*, perhaps meaning with mastery, so that he looks at the objects of thought or meditation, *ārammaṇa*, or at sense-impressions unmoved by them and indifferent to them, *MA.* iv. 142. *Cf. S.* v. 69, etc.

Monks, mindfulness of in-breathing and out-breathing when developed thus, made much of thus, brings to fulfilment the four applications of mindfulness.

And how, monks, when the four applications of mindfulness have been developed, how when they have been made much of, do they bring to fulfilment the seven links in awakening? At the time, monks, when a monk is faring along contemplating the body in the body, ardent, clearly conscious (of it), mindful (of it) so as to control the covetousness and dejection in the world, at that time unmuddled mindfulness is aroused in him. At the time, monks, when unmuddled mindfulness is aroused in the monk, at that time the link in awakening that is mindfulness is stirred up in the monk; at that time the monk develops the link in awakening that is mindfulness; at that time the link in awakening that is mindfulness comes to fulfilment of development in the monk. He, faring along mindful thus, examines, inquires into, brings this thing forward for investigation by means of wisdom. At the time, monks, when a monk, faring along mindful thus, examines, inquires into, brings this thing forward for investigation by means of wisdom, at that time the link in awakening that is investigation into things is stirred up in the monk; at that time the monk develops the link in awakening that is investigation into things; at that time the link in awakening that is investigation into things comes to fulfilment of development in the monk. While he is examining, inquiring into, bringing this thing forward for investigation by means of wisdom, unsluggish energy is stirred up in him. At the time, monks, when unsluggish energy is stirred up in a monk who is examining, inquiring into, bringing this thing forward for investigation by means of wisdom, at that time the link in awakening that is energy is stirred up in the monk; at that time the monk develops the link in awakening that is energy; at that time the link in awakening that is energy comes to fulfilment of development in that monk. When he has stirred up energy unsullied rapture arises. At the time, monks, when unsullied rapture arises in the monk of stirred up energy, [**86**] at that time the link in awakening that is rapture is stirred up in the monk; at that time the monk develops the link in awakening that is rapture; at that time the link in awakening that is rapture comes to fulfilment of development in the monk. The body of one whose mind is rapturous is tranquillised and thought is tranquillised. At the time, monks, when both the body of a monk whose mind is rapturous is tranquillised and thought is tranquillised, at that time the link in awakening

that is tranquillity is stirred up in the monk; at that time the
monk develops the link in awakening that is tranquillity; at that
time the link in awakening that is tranquillity comes to fulfilment
of development in the monk. The thought of one whose body is
tranquil and at ease is concentrated. At the time, monks, when
thought is concentrated in a monk whose body is tranquil and at
ease, at that time the link in awakening that is concentration is
stirred up in the monk; at that time the monk develops the link in
awakening that is concentration; at that time the link in awakening
that is concentration comes to fulfilment of development in the
monk. He is one who looks on with proper care at the thought
concentrated thus. At the time, monks, when a monk looks on
with proper care at the thought concentrated thus, at that time the
link in awakening that is equanimity is stirred up in the monk;
at that time the monk develops the link in awakening that is
equanimity; at that time the link in awakening that is equanimity
comes to fulfilment of development in the monk.

At the time, monks, when a monk is faring along contemplating
the feelings in the feelings . . . the mind in the mind . . . mental
states in mental states, ardent, clearly conscious (of them), mindful
(of them) so as to control the covetousness and dejection in the world,
at that time unmuddled mindfulness is aroused in him . . . (*as above*)
. . . [87] . . . at that time the link in awakening that is equanimity
comes to fulfilment of development in the monk.

Monks, the four applications of mindfulness, when developed thus,
made much of thus, bring to fulfilment the seven links in awakening.

[88] And how, monks, when the seven links in awakening are
developed, how when they are made much of, do they bring to
fulfilment freedom through knowledge ? Herein,[1] monks, a monk
develops the link in awakening that is mindfulness and is dependent
on aloofness,[2] dependent on detachment, dependent on cessation,
ending in abandoning;[3] he develops the link in awakening that is
investigation into things . . . the link in awakening that is energy

---

[1] *Cf. M.* iii. 275.

[2] *MA.* iv. 144 says that in this Discourse mindfulness on breathing, which is worldy, brings to fulfilment the applications of mindfulness which are worldly; these bring to fulfilment the seven links in awakening which are worldly; and these bring to fulfilment the supermundane nibbāna and fruit of freedom through knowledge.

[3] *vossaggapariṇāmi*, maturing (or, mature) (*pariṇāmin*) in relinquishing, letting go of, abandoning, ejecting (*vossagga*). This abandonment is two-fold: of the defilements and to the mind's leap into nibbāna, see *SA*. i. 159, *Pts*. i. 194.

... the link in awakening that is rapture ... the link in awakening that is tranquillity ... the link in awakening that is concentration ... the link in awakening that is equanimity and is dependent on aloofness, dependent on detachment, dependent on cessation, ending in abandoning. Monks, when the seven links in awakening are developed thus, are made much of thus, they bring to fulfilment freedom through knowledge."

Thus spoke the Lord. Delighted, these monks rejoiced in what the Lord had said.

Discourse on Mindfulness when Breathing In and Out:
The Eighth

119. DISCOURSE ON MINDFULNESS OF BODY[1]
(Kāyagatāsatisutta)

THUS have I heard: At one time the Lord was staying near Sāvatthī in the Jeta Grove in Anāthapiṇḍika's monastery. Then when a number of monks had returned from the alms-gathering after the meal and were sitting down gathered together in an assembly hall, there arose this conversation: " It is marvellous, revered sirs, it is wonderful, revered sirs, that mindfulness of body[2] when developed and made much of is of great fruit, of great advantage, as was said by the Lord who knows, who sees, the perfected one, the fully Self-Awakened One." But this conversation between these monks was interrupted. For the Lord, emerging from solitary meditation towards evening, approached the assembly hall; having approached, he sat down on the seat made ready. As he was sitting down, the Lord addressed the monks, saying: " What were you talking about here, monks, as you were sitting down ? And what was your conversation that was interrupted ?"

[**89**] " As to this, revered sir, when we had returned from the alms-gathering after our meal and were sitting down gathered together

---
[1] Like Discourse No. 118, No. 119 is again only a sectional presentation of the *Satipaṭṭhāna Sutta* (*M.* Sta. 10). See also *A.* i. 43 and *Vbh.* 226.
[2] This includes both *samatha* and *vipassanā*, *MA.* iv. 144.

in the assembly hall this conversation arose: 'It is marvellous, revered sirs, it is wonderful, revered sirs, that mindfulness of body when developed and made much of is of great fruit, of great advantage, as was said by the Lord . . . fully Self-Awakened One.' This, revered sir, was our conversation that was interrupted, for then the Lord arrived."

"And how, monks, when mindfulness of body has been developed, how when it has been made much of, is it of great fruit, of great advantage ? As to this, monks, a monk[1] who is forest-gone or gone to the root of a tree or gone to an empty place, sits down cross-legged, holding his back erect, arousing mindfulness in front of him. Mindful he breathes in, mindful he breathes out. Whether he is breathing in . . . breathing out a long (breath) . . . a short (breath), he comprehends, 'I am breathing in . . . out a long (breath) . . . a short (breath).' He trains himself thinking, 'I will breathe in . . . out experiencing the whole body.' He trains himself, thinking, 'I will breathe in . . . out tranquillising the activity of body.' While he is thus diligent, ardent, self-resolute, those memories and aspirations[2] that are worldly[3] are got rid of; by getting rid of them the mind itself is inwardly settled, calmed, focussed, concentrated. Thus, monks, does a monk develop mindfulness of body.

And again, monks, when a monk is walking[4] he comprehends, 'I am walking'; or when he is standing still he comprehends, 'I am standing still'; or when he is sitting down he comprehends, 'I am sitting down'; or when he is lying down he comprehends, 'I am lying down.' So that however his body is disposed he comprehends that it is like that. While he is thus diligent, ardent, self-resolute . . . the mind itself is inwardly settled, calmed, focussed, concentrated. Thus too, monks, does a monk develop mindfulness of body.

[90] And again, monks, a monk, when he is setting out or returning is one acting in a clearly conscious way; when he is looking in front or looking around . . . when he has bent in or stretched out (his arm) . . . when he is carrying his outer cloak, bowl and robe . . . when he is eating, drinking, chewing, tasting . . . when he is obeying the calls of nature . . . when he is walking, standing, sitting, asleep, awake, talking, silent, he is one acting in a clearly conscious way. While he

---

[1] *Cf.* the following with *M.* i. 56 *ff.*

[2] *sarasaṁkappā*, as at *M.* i. 453, iii. 132, *S.* iv. 76, 190.

[3] *gehasitā*, belonging to a householder, thus thoughts, etc., belonging to the five kinds of sensual pleasures.

[4] *Cf. M.* i. 56.

is thus diligent, ardent, self-resolute . . . Thus too, monks, does a monk develop mindfulness of body.

And again, monks, a monk reflects precisely on this body itself, encased as it is in skin and full of various impurities, from the soles of the feet up and from the crown of the head down, that: 'There is connected with this body hair of the head, hair of the body, nails, teeth, skin, flesh, sinews, bones, marrow, kidneys, heart, liver, membranes, spleen, lungs, intestines, mesentery, stomach, excrement, bile, phlegm, pus, blood, sweat, fat, tears, serum, saliva, mucus, synovic fluid, urine.'

Monks, it is as if there were a double mouthed provision bag that was full of various kinds of grain such as hill-paddy, paddy, kidney beans, peas, sesamum, rice; and a keen-eyed man, pouring them out, might reflect: 'That's hill-paddy, that's paddy, that's kidney beans, that's peas, that's sesamum, that's rice.' Even so, monks, does a monk reflect precisely on this body itself, encased as it is in skin and full of various impurities, from the soles of the feet up and from the crown of the head down, that: 'There is connected with this body hair of the head . . . urine.' While he is thus diligent, ardent, self-resolute . . . Thus too, monks, does a monk develop mindfulness of body.

[91] And again, monks, a monk reflects on this body itself according to how it is placed or disposed in respect of the elements, thinking: 'In this body there is the element of extension . . . of cohesion . . . of radiation . . . of motion.' Monks, it is as if a skilled cattle-butcher or his apprentice, having slaughtered a cow, might sit at the cross-roads displaying its carcase. Even so, monks, does a monk reflect on this body itself according to how it is placed or disposed in respect of the elements, thinking: 'In this body there is the element of extension . . . of cohesion . . . of radiation . . . of motion.' While he is thus diligent, ardent, self-resolute . . . Thus too, monks, does a monk develop mindfulness of body.

And again, monks, it is as if a monk might see, thrown aside in a cemetery a body that had been dead for one day or for two days or for three days, swollen, discoloured, decomposing; so he focuses on this body itself, thinking: 'This body too is of a similar nature, a similar constitution, it has not got past that (state of things).' While he is thus diligent, ardent, self-resolute . . . Thus too, monks, does a monk develop mindfulness of body.

And again, monks, it is as if a monk might see thrown aside in a cemetery a body which was being devoured by crows or ravens or vultures or wild dogs or jackals or by various small creatures; so he focusses on this body itself, thinking: 'This body too is of a similar nature, a similar constitution, it has not got past that (state of things).' While he is thus diligent, ardent, self-resolute ... Thus too, monks, does a monk develop mindfulness of body.

[92] And again, monks, it is as if a monk might see thrown aside in a cemetery a body which was a skeleton but with (some) flesh and blood, sinew-bound ... a skeleton, which was fleshless but blood-bespattered, sinew-bound ... a skeleton which was without flesh or blood, sinew-bound; or the bones scattered here and there, no longer held together: here a bone of the hand, there a foot-bone, here a leg-bone, there a rib, here a hip-bone, there a back-bone, here the skull; so he focusses on this body itself, thinking: 'This body too is of a similar nature, a similar constitution, it has not got past this (state of things).' While he is thus diligent, ardent, self-resolute ... Thus too, monks, does a monk develop mindfulness of body.

And again, monks, it is as if a monk might see thrown aside in a cemetery a body the bones of which were white and something like sea-shells ... a heap of dried up bones more than a year old ... the bones gone rotten and reduced to powder; so he focusses on this body itself, thinking: 'This body too is of a similar nature, a similar constitution, it has not got past this (state of things).' While he is thus diligent, ardent, self-resolute, those memories and aspirations that are worldly are got rid of; by getting rid of them the mind is inwardly settled, calmed, focussed, concentrated. Thus too, monks, does a monk develop mindfulness of body.

And again, monks, a monk, aloof from pleasures of the senses,[1] aloof from unskilled states of mind, enters on and abides in the first meditation which is accompanied by initial thought and discursive thought, is born of aloofness, and is rapturous and joyful. He drenches, saturates, permeates, suffuses this very body with the rapture and joy that are born of aloofness; there is no part of his whole body that is not suffused with the rapture and joy that are born of aloofness. Monks, as a skilled bath-attendant or his apprentice, having sprinkled bath-powder into a bronze vessel, might knead it while repeatedly sprinkling[2] it with water until the ball of lather had taken up moisture, was drenched with moisture, suffused with moisture inside and out, but without any oozing.

---

[1] As at *M.* i. 276-278.

[2] *paripphosakaṁ paripphosakaṁ*, as at *M.* i. 276, ii. 15, iii. 140, *D.* i. 74 See *P.E.D.*

Even so, monks, does a monk drench, saturate, permeate, suffuse this very body with the rapture and joy that are born of aloofness; [**93**] there is no part of his whole body that is not suffused with the rapture and joy that are born of aloofness. While he is thus diligent, ardent, self-resolute . . . Thus too does a monk develop mindfulness of body.

And again, monks, a monk, by allaying initial thought and discursive thought, with the mind subjectively tranquillised and fixed on one point, enters on and abides in the second meditation which is devoid of initial thought and discursive thought, is born of concentration and is rapturous and joyful. He drenches, saturates, permeates, suffuses this very body with the rapture and joy that are born of concentration; there is no part of his whole body that is not suffused with the rapture and joy that are born of concentration. Monks, it is like a pool of water with water welling up within it, but which has no inlet for water from the eastern . . . western . . . northern . . . or southern side, and even if the god does not send down showers upon it from time to time, yet the current of cool water having welled up from that pool will drench, saturate, permeate, suffuse that pool with cool water. Even so, monks, does a monk drench, saturate, permeate, suffuse this very body with the rapture and joy that are born of concentration; there is no part of his whole body that is not suffused with the rapture and joy that are born of concentration. While he is thus diligent, ardent, self-resolute . . . Thus too does a monk develop mindfulness of body.

And again, monks, a monk, by the fading out of rapture, dwells with equanimity, attentive and clearly conscious and experiences in his person that joy of which the ariyans say: 'Joyful lives he who has equanimity and is mindful,' and he enters on and abides in the third meditation. He drenches, saturates, permeates, suffuses this very body with the joy that has no rapture; there is no part of his whole body that is not suffused with the joy that has no rapture. As in a pond of white . . . or red . . . or blue lotuses, some white . . . or red . . . or blue lotuses are born in the water, grow up in the water, never rising above the surface but flourishing beneath it [**94**] and from their roots to their tips are drenched, saturated, permeated, suffused by cool water; even so, monks, does a monk drench, saturate, permeate, suffuse this very body with the joy that has no rapture; there is no part of his whole body that is not suffused with the joy that has no rapture. While he is thus diligent, ardent, self-resolute . . . Thus too does a monk develop mindfulness of body.

And again, monks, a monk, by getting rid of joy and by getting rid of anguish, by the going down of his former pleasures and sorrows, enters on and abides in the fourth meditation which has neither anguish nor joy, and which is entirely purified by equanimity and mindfulness. He, having suffused this very body with a mind that is utterly pure, utterly clean, comes to be sitting down; there is no part of his whole body that is not suffused by a mind that is utterly pure, utterly clean. Monks, it is as if a man might be sitting down who had clothed himself including his head with a white cloth; there would be no part of his whole body not covered by the white cloth. Even so, monks, a monk, having suffused this very body with a mind that is utterly pure, utterly clean, comes to be sitting down; there is no part of this whole body that is not suffused by a mind that is utterly pure, utterly clean. While he is thus diligent, ardent, self-resolute, those memories and aspirations that are worldly are got rid of; by getting rid of them the mind itself is inwardly settled, calmed, focussed, concentrated. Thus too, monks, does a monk develop mindfulness of body.[1]

Monks, those skilled states that are connected with knowledge[2] are in anyone in whom mindfulness of body has been developed and made much of. As, monks, those streams that flow down to the ocean are in anyone in whom the great ocean has been suffused by thought,[3] even so, monks, those skilled states that are connected with knowledge are in anyone in whom mindfulness of body has been developed and made much of. Monks, Māra gains access to whatever monk there is in whom mindfulness of body has not been developed, not been made much of. Monks, it is as though a man were to throw a heavy round stone into a mound of moist clay. What do you think, monks ? Would that heavy round stone gain access to[4] that mound of moist clay ?"

---

[1] The parallel passage at *M.* i. 276-278 ends here.

[2] For this passage *cf. A.* i. 43. The " skilled states that are connected with knowledge," *dhammā vijjābhāgiyā*, are given as six at *A.* iii. 334: perception of impermanence, perception of the anguish in impermanence, perception of non-self in anguish, perception of getting rid of, perception of detachment, perception of stopping. But *MA.* iv. 145 says that here the knowledge of insight, psychic power made by mind, the six super-knowledges are connected with knowledge.

[3] By *deva*-vision, *MA.* iv. 145.

[4] Although the English may suffer from the use of this strange expression, and although some such phrase as " makes an impression on " would sound more natural here, it yet seems that by translating *labhati otāraṁ* all through this passage by " gains access to " (and this is precisely what is meant in the

"Yes, revered sir."

[95] "Even so, monks, Māra gains access to, Māra gets a chance over anyone in whom mindfulness of body has not been developed, not made much of. Monks, it is as though there were a dry sapless stick,[1] and a man were to come along bringing an upper piece of fire-stick, thinking: 'I will light a fire, I will get heat.' What do you think, monks ? Could that man, bringing an upper piece of fire-stick and rubbing that dry sapless stick (with it), light a fire, could he get heat ?"

"Yes, revered sir."

"Even so, monks, Māra gains access to, Māra gets a chance over anyone in whom mindfulness of body has not been developed, not been made much of. Monks, it is as though a water-pot were standing void and empty on its support, and a man were to come along bringing a load of water. What do you think, monks ? Would that man get a chance to unload the water ?"

"Yes, revered sir."

"Even so, monks, Māra gains access to, Māra gets a chance over anyone in whom mindfulness of body has not been developed, not been made much of. (But), monks, Māra does not gain access to, Māra does not get a chance over anyone in whom mindfulness of body has been developed and made much of. Monks, it is as though a man were to throw a light ball of thread against a door-panel[2] made entirely from heartwood. What do you think, monks ? Would that light ball of thread gain access to a door-panel made entirely from heartwood ?"

"No, revered sir."

"Even so, monks, Māra does not gain access to, Māra does not get a chance over anyone in whom mindfulness of body has been developed and made much of. It is as though, monks, there were a wet sappy stick,[3] and a man were to come along bringing an upper piece of fire-stick, thinking: 'I will light a fire, I will get heat.' What [96] do you think, monks ? Could that man, bringing an upper piece of fire-stick and rubbing that wet sappy stick (with it), light a fire, could he get heat ?"

---

case of Māra), the Pali sequence of thought and argument is better preserved and conveyed.

[1] *Cf. M.* i. 242.
[2] *aggaḷaphalaka*, the board and bolt. *MA.* iv. 145 says *kavāṭa*, the panel of a door.
[3] *Cf. M.* i. 240.

"No, revered sir."

"Even so, monks, Māra does not gain access to, Māra does not get a chance over anyone in whom mindfulness of body has been developed and made much of. Monks, it is as though[1] a full water-pot, brimming with water so that a crow could drink from it, were placed in a support, and a man were to come along bringing a load of water. What do you think, monks? Would that man get a chance to unload the water?"

"No, revered sir."

"Even so, monks, Māra does not gain access to, Māra does not get a chance over anyone in whom mindfulness of body has been developed and made much of. Anyone, monks, in whom mindfulness of body has been developed and made much of, turns his mind to this or that realisation through super-knowledge of a thing that may be realised through super-knowledge and achieves ability as a witness now here, now there, whatever may be the plane.[2] Monks, it is as though a full water-pot, brimming with water so that a crow could drink from it, were placed in a support and a strong man were to rock it from side to side—would the water spill?"

"Yes, revered sir."

"Even so, monks, anyone in whom mindfulness of body has been developed and made much of, turns his mind to this or that realisation through super-knowledge of a thing that may be realised through super-knowledge and achieves ability as a witness now here, now there, whatever may be the plane. Monks, it is as though[3] there were a tank on a level stretch of ground, its four sides strengthened with dykes, full and brimming with water so that a crow could drink from it, and a strong man were to loosen a dyke at this side or that—would the water spill?"

"Yes, revered sir."

"Even so, monks, anyone in whom mindfulness of body has been developed and made much of, turns his mind to this or that realisation through super-knowledge of a thing that may be realised through super-knowledge and achieves ability as a witness now here, now there, whatever may be the plane. Monks, it is as though[4]

---

[1] *Cf. A.* iii. 27.

[2] *tatra tatr' eva sakkhibhavyataṁ pāpuṇāti sati sati āyatane. Cf. M.* i. 494, *A.* i. 255-258, iii. 17-19, 27; quoted at *Asl.* 141. At *MA.* iv. 146 *āyatana* is explained by *kāraṇa*, in its turn explained by *abhiññā*. Therefore now one, now another of the high meditative planes, *āyatana*, is suggested.

[3] As at *A.* iii. 28. [4] As at *M.* i. 124, *A.* iii. 28, *S.* iv. 176.

at a cross-roads on level ground a chariot were standing harnessed with thoroughbreds, the goad hanging ready; and a skilled groom, a charioteer of horses to be tamed, having mounted it, having taken the reins in his left hand, the goad in his right, were to drive up and down as he liked; even so, monks, anyone whomsoever in whom mindfulness of body has been developed and made much of, turns his mind to this and that realisation through super-knowledge of a thing that may be realised through super-knowledge and achieves ability as a witness now here, now there, whatever may be the plane.

Monks, these ten advantages are to be expected from pursuing mindfulness of body, developing it, making much of it, making it a vehicle, making it a foundation, practising it, increasing it, and fully undertaking it.[1] What ten ? He is one who overcomes dislike and liking,[2] and dislike (and liking) do not overcome him; he fares along constantly conquering any dislike (and liking) that have arisen. He is one who overcomes fear and dread,[3] and fear and dread do not overcome him; and he fares along constantly conquering any fear and dread that have arisen. He is one who bears[4] cold, heat, hunger, thirst, the touch of gadfly, mosquito, wind and sun, creeping things, ways of speech that are irksome, unwelcome; he is of a character to bear bodily feelings which, arising, are painful, acute, sharp, shooting, disagreeable, miserable, deadly. [98] He is one who at will,[5] without trouble, without difficulty, acquires the four meditations that are of the purest mentality, abidings in ease here and now. He experiences the various forms of psychic power: having been one he is manifold; having been manifold he is one; manifest or invisible he goes unhindered through a wall, a rampart, a mountain as if through air; he plunges into the ground and shoots up again as if in water; he walks upon the water without parting it as if on the ground; sitting cross-legged he travels through the air like a bird on the wing; with his hand he rubs and strokes this moon and sun

---

[1] *Cf. S.* iv. 200; also *D.* ii. 103, *A.* iv. 290, *Ud.* 62.

[2] As at *M*. i. 33, *A*. v. 132. *Aratiratisaho*: Neumann, vol. iii, p. 214 proposes to read here *arati-r-atisaho*, because *M*. text proceeds: *na ca taṁ aratiṁ sahati, uppannaṁ aratim abhibhuyya*. But it would seem better to follow *A*. v. 132 which reads: *aratiratisaho assaṁ na ca mam aratirati saheyya uppannam aratiratim abhibhuyya*. Here " dislike and liking " are kept throughout, and moreover this pair balances the next: " fear and dread."

[3] As at *M*. i. 33, *A*. v. 132.

[4] *Cf. M*. i. 10 where these are cankers to be got rid of by endurance; *cf.* also *A*. iii. 389, v. 132.

[5] As at *M*. i. 33, which see also for the remainder of the above passage.

although they are of such mighty power and majesty; and even as far as the Brahma-world he has power in respect of his person. By the purified *deva*-like hearing which surpasses that of men he hears both (kinds of) sounds—*deva*-like ones and human ones, whether they be far or near. He comprehends by mind the minds of other beings, of other individuals, so that he comprehends of a mind that is full of attachment . . . aversion . . . confusion, that it is full of attachment . . . aversion . . . confusion; or of a mind that is without attachment . . . aversion . . . confusion, that it is without attachment . . . aversion . . . confusion; or he comprehends of a mind that is contracted that it is contracted, or of a mind that is distracted that it is distracted; or of a mind that has become great that it has become great, or of a mind that has not become great that it has not become great; or of a mind with (some other mental state) superior to it that it has (some other mental state) superior to it, or of a mind that has no (other mental state) superior to it that it has no (other mental state) superior to it; or of a mind that is composed that it is composed, or of a mind that is not composed that it is not composed; or of a mind that is freed that it is freed, or of a mind that is not freed that it is not freed. He recollects manifold former habitations, that is to say one [**99**] birth and two births and . . . Thus he recollects (his) former habitations in all their modes and detail. With the purified *deva*-vision surpassing that of men he beholds beings as they pass hence and come to be; he comprehends that beings are mean, excellent, fair, foul, in a good bourn, in a bad bourn according to the consequences of deeds. By the destruction of the cankers, having realised here and now by his own super-knowledge the freedom of mind and the freedom through intuitive wisdom that are cankerless, entering thereon, he abides therein. Monks, these ten advantages are to be expected from pursuing mindfulness of body, developing it, making much of it, making it a vehicle, making it a foundation, practising it, increasing it and fully undertaking it."

Thus spoke the Lord. Delighted, these monks rejoiced in what the Lord had said.

Discourse on Mindfulness of Body:
The Ninth

120. DISCOURSE ON UPRISING BY MEANS OF ASPIRATION[1]

(Saṁkhāruppattisutta)

THUS have I heard: At one time the Lord was staying near Sāvatthī in the Jeta Grove in Anāthapiṇḍika's monastery. While he was there the Lord addressed the monks, saying: "Monks." "Revered One," these monks answered the Lord in assent. The Lord spoke thus:

"I will teach you, monks, uprising through aspiration. Listen to it, pay careful attention and I will speak."

"Yes, revered sir," these monks answered the Lord in assent. The Lord spoke thus:

"Herein, monks, a monk is endowed with faith, he is endowed with moral habit, he is endowed with learning, he is endowed with relinquishment, he is endowed with wisdom. It occurs to him: 'O that at the breaking up of the body after dying I might arise in companionship with rich nobles.' He fixes his mind on this, he resolves his mind on this, he develops his mind for this.[2] [100] These aspirations and abidings[3] of his, developed thus, made much of thus, conduce to uprising there. This, monks, is the way, this the course that conduces to uprising there.

And again, monks, a monk is endowed with faith . . . with wisdom. It occurs to him: 'O that at the breaking up of the body after dying I might arise in companionship with rich brahmans . . . with rich householders.' He fixes his mind on this . . . This, monks, is the way, this the course that conduces to uprising there.

And again, monks, a monk is endowed with faith . . . with wisdom. He hears that the Four Great Regent Devas are long-lived, beautiful,

---

[1] *Saṅkhāra* is not here carrying any of its more usual senses, but has the meaning of purposeful intellection; see *P.E.D.* s.v. *saṅkhāra*. This is recognised at *MA.* iv. 146 which explains by *patthanā*, aiming at, wishing, aspiration. This is one thing while "the five things beginning with faith" are another. Both are necessary to assure the bourn, *gati*.

[2] *Cf. A.* iv. 239 for this sequence and for the following passage; but it enumerates fewer classes of *devas* than does this Discourse.

[3] Reading *vihārā* with *MA.* iv. 146 and one textual *v.l.*, as against text's *vihāro*.

abounding in happiness. It occurs to him: ' O that . . . I might arise in companionship with the Four Great Regent Devas.' He fixes his mind on this . . . This, monks, is the way, this the course that conduces to uprising there.

And again, monks, a monk is endowed with faith . . . with wisdom. He hears that the Devas of the Thirty-Three . . . the Yāma Devas . . . the Devas of Delight . . . the Devas who delight in creating . . . the Devas who have power over the creations of others are long-lived, beautiful, abounding in happiness. It occurs to him: ' O that . . . I might arise in companionship with the Devas who have power over the creations of others.' He fixes his mind on this . . . This, monks, is the way, this the course that conduces to uprising there.

And again, monks, a monk is endowed with faith [**101**] . . . with wisdom. He hears that the Brahmā of a thousand-world-system is long-lived, beautiful, abounding in happiness. Monks, a Brahmā of a thousand-world-system dwells suffusing and pervading (in meditation)[1] the system of the thousand worlds;[2] and he dwells too suffusing and pervading (in meditation) those beings that have uprisen there. It is as though, monks, a man with vision had taken some emblic myrobalan[3] in his hand and were to gaze at it; even so, monks, does a Brahmā of a thousand-world-system dwell suffusing and pervading (in meditation) the system of the thousand worlds; and he dwells too suffusing and pervading (in meditation) those beings that have uprisen there. It occurs to him:[4] ' O that . . . I might arise in companionship with a Brahmā of a thousand-world-system.' He fixes his mind on this . . . This, monks, is the way, this the course that conduces to uprising there.

And again, monks, a monk is endowed with faith . . . with wisdom. He hears that the Brahmā of a two-thousand . . . three-thousand . . . four-thousand . . . five-thousand-world-system is long-lived, beautiful, abounding in happiness. Monks, a Brahmā of a five-thousand-world-system dwells suffusing and pervading (in meditation) the

---

[1] On *pharitvā adhimuccitvā* see Intr., p. xx.
[2] *Cf. A.* i. 228; *D.* i. 46; *DA.* i. 301.
[3] *āmaṇḍa* (not in *P.E.D.*) explained by *āmalaka*, the usual word for emblic myrobalan, at *MA.* iv. 147. Childers and Monier-Williams give the castor-oil plant however for *āmaṇḍa*. In either case it seems likely that the seeds are being referred to rather than the plants themselves. Pali knows *eraṇḍa* (Skrt. also *eraṇḍa*) for castor-oil plant, *Ricinus communis*. Among the Indian vernacular names for this are *amanakkam* and *amadam*, George Watt, *Commercial Products of India*, London, 1908, p. 915.
[4] *I.e.* the monk.

system of the five-thousand worlds. And he dwells too suffusing and pervading (in meditation) those beings that have uprisen there. It is as though, monks, a man with vision had taken five emblic myrobalans in his hand and were to gaze at them; even so, monks, does a Brahmā of a five-thousand-world-system dwell suffusing and pervading (in meditation) the system of the five-thousand worlds; and he dwells too suffusing and pervading (in meditation) those beings that have uprisen there. It occurs to him: 'O that . . . I might arise in companionship with a Brahmā of a five-thousand-world-system.' He fixes his mind on that . . . This, monks, is the way, this the course that conduces to uprising there.

And again, monks, a monk is endowed with faith . . . with wisdom. He hears that the Brahmā of a ten-thousand-world-system is long-lived, beautiful, abounding in happiness. Monks, a Brahmā of a ten-thousand-world-system [**102**] dwells suffusing and pervading (in meditation) the system of the ten-thousand worlds; and he dwells too suffusing and pervading (in meditation) those beings that have uprisen there. Monks, it is like a lovely beryl gem[1] of the finest water, superbly cut with eight facets, which shines and gleams when laid on a pale cloth; even so, monks, does a Brahmā of a ten-thousand-world-system dwell suffusing and pervading (in meditation) the system of the ten-thousand worlds; and he dwells too suffusing and pervading (in meditation) those beings that have uprisen there. It occurs to him: 'O that . . . I might arise in companionship with a Brahmā of a ten-thousand-world-system.' He fixes his mind on that . . . This, monks, is the way, this the course that conduces to uprising there.

And again, monks, a monk is endowed with faith . . . with wisdom. He hears that the Brahmā of a hundred-thousand-world-system is long-lived, beautiful, abounding in happiness. Monks, a Brahmā of a hundred-thousand-world-system dwells suffusing and pervading (in meditation) the system of the hundred-thousand worlds; and he dwells too suffusing and pervading (in meditation) the beings that have uprisen there. Monks, as an ornament[2] of river-gold,[3] most

---

[1] As at *M*. ii. 17; *D*. i. 76, ii. 13; *S*. i. 65, etc.

[2] *nekkha*; with *v.l. nikkha*. *Cf. S.* i. 65; *A.* i. 181, ii. 8, 29; *Dhp.* 230; *DhA.* 239 and see *G.S.* ii. 8, *n*. 2. At *MA*. iv. 147 a *nikkha* is spoken of as worth five *suvaṇṇas*, and at *VvA*. 104 as fifteen *suvaṇṇas*. The value may have changed according to the locality.

[3] *jambonada*. According to *MA*. iv. 147 and *SA*. i. 125 this is produced by the leaves of great *jambu*-trees; they fall into the rivers on whose banks the trees grow and gradually reach the sea.

skilfully wrought in the crucible of a clever goldsmith, shines and glows and gleams when laid on a pale cloth; even so, monks, does a Brahmā of a hundred-thousand-world-system dwell suffusing and pervading (in meditation) the system of the hundred-thousand worlds; and he dwells too suffusing and pervading (in meditation) the beings that have uprisen there. It occurs to him: ' O that ... I might arise in companionship with a Brahmā of a hundred-thousand-world-system.' He fixes his mind on that ... This, monks, is the way, this the course that conduces to uprising there.

And again, monks, a monk is endowed with faith ... with wisdom. He hears that the Devas of Splendour ... of limited Splendour ... of boundless Splendour ... of Light ... of limited Light ... of boundless Light ... the Radiant Devas are long-lived, beautiful, abounding in happiness. It occurs to him ... that conduces to uprising there.

And again, monks, a monk is endowed with faith ... with wisdom. He hears that the Devas of Lustre ... of limited Lustre ... of boundless Lustre ... the Lustrous Devas are long-lived, beautiful, abounding in happiness. It occurs to him ... that conduces to uprising there.

And again, monks, a monk is endowed with faith ... [103] ... with wisdom. He hears that the Vehapphala Devas ... the Aviha Devas ... the Atappa Devas ... the Sudassi Devas ... the Akaniṭṭha Devas are long-lived, beautiful, abounding in happiness. It occurs to him ... that conduces to uprising there.

And again, monks, a monk is endowed with faith ... with wisdom. He hears that the Devas that have reached the plane of infinite ākāsa are long-lived, beautiful, abounding in happiness. It occurs to him ... that conduces to uprising there.

And again, monks, a monk is endowed with faith, he is endowed with moral habit, he is endowed with learning, he is endowed with relinquishment, he is endowed with wisdom. He hears that the Devas that have reached the plane of infinite consciousness ... the Devas that have reached the plane of no-thing ... the Devas that have reached the plane of neither-perception-nor-non-perception are long-lived, beautiful, abounding in happiness. It occurs to him: ' O that at the breaking up of the body after dying I might arise in companionship with the Devas that have reached the plane of neither-perception-nor-non-perception.' He fixes his mind on this, he resolves his mind on this, he develops his mind for this. These aspirations and abidings of his, developed thus, made much of thus, conduce to uprising there. This, monks, is the way, this the course that conduces to uprising there.

And again, monks, a monk is endowed with faith, moral habit, learning, relinquishment and wisdom. It occurs to him: ' O that by the destruction of the cankers, having realised here and now by my own super-knowledge the freedom of mind and the freedom through intuitive wisdom that are cankerless, entering thereon, I might abide therein.' He, by the destruction of the cankers, having here and now realised through his own super-knowledge the freedom of mind and the freedom through intuitive wisdom that are cankerless, entering thereon, abides therein. This monk uprises not anywhere, monks, he uprises nowhere."[1]

Thus spoke the Lord. Delighted, these monks rejoiced in what the Lord had said.

Discourse on Uprising by means of Aspiration:
The Tenth

Division of the Uninterrupted:
The Second

---

[1] *na katthaci uppajjati na kuhiñci uppajjati.* *Cf. M.* iii. 45 where it is also said of an arahant *na kiñci na kuhiñci na kenaci maññati.*

III. THE DIVISION ON EMPTINESS
(Suññatavagga)

121. LESSER DISCOURSE ON EMPTINESS
(Cūḷasuññatasutta)

[104] THUS have I heard: At one time the Lord was staying near Sāvatthī in the Eastern monastery in the palace of Migāra's mother. Then the venerable Ānanda, emerging from solitary meditation towards evening, approached the Lord; having approached and greeted the Lord, he sat down at a respectful distance. As he was sitting down at a respectful distance, the venerable Ānanda spoke thus to the Lord:

"At one time, revered sir, the Lord was staying among the Sakyans. Nagaraka is the name of a market town of the Sakyans. And while I was there, revered sir, face to face with the Lord I heard, face to face I learnt: 'I, Ānanda, through abiding in (the concept of) emptiness, am now abiding in the fulness thereof.'[1] I hope that I heard this properly, revered sir, learnt it properly, attended to it properly and understood it properly?"

"Certainly, Ānanda, you heard this properly, learnt it properly, attended to it properly and understood it properly. Formerly I, Ānanda, as well as now, through abiding in (the concept of) emptiness, abide in the fulness thereof. As this palace of Migāra's mother is empty of elephants, cows, horses and mares, empty of gold and silver, empty of assemblages of men and women, and there is only this that is not emptiness, that is to say the solitude[2] grounded on the Order of monks;[3] even so, Ānanda, a monk, not attending to the perception of village, not attending to the perception of human beings, attends to solitude grounded on the perception of forest.[4] His mind is satisfied with,[5] pleased with, set on and freed in[6] the

---

[1] *Cf. M.* iii. 294, *Vin.* ii. 304. See *Pts. Contr.*, p. 142, *n.* 4 and *Bud. Psych. Ethics*, p. 91, *n.* 2.

[2] *ekatta* is also unity, oneness. *MA.* iv. 151 explains by *ekabhāva*.

[3] *bhikkhusaṁghaṁ paṭicca ekattaṁ*.

[4] He attends to one (particular) forest, thinking, " this is the forest, this a tree, this an incline, this a thicket," *MA.* iv. 151. *Cf. A.* iii. 343, *araññasaññaṁ yeva manasikarissati ekattaṁ*; and *Thag.* 110, *araññasaññiṁ*.

[5] *pakkhandati*, perhaps " leaps forward," glossed at *MA.* iv. 151 by *otarati*, goes down into. *Cf. M.* i. 186 for this sequence of terms, also *Miln.* 326.

[6] *vimuccati* throughout the text, *adhimuccati* in the Comy.

perception of forest. He comprehends thus: 'The disturbances there might be resulting from the perception of village do not exist here; the disturbances there might be resulting from the perception of human beings do not exist here. There is only this degree of disturbance, that is to say solitude grounded on the perception of forest.' He comprehends, 'This perceiving is empty of the perception of village.' He comprehends, 'This perceiving is empty of the perception of human beings. And there is only this that is not emptiness, that is to say solitude grounded on the perception of forest.' He regards that which is not there as empty of it. [105] But in regard to what remains there he comprehends, 'That being, this is.' Thus, Ānanda, this comes to be for him a true, not a mistaken, utterly purified realisation of (the concept of) emptiness.[1]

And again, Ānanda, a monk, not attending to the perception of human beings, not attending to the perception of forest, attends to solitude grounded on the perception of earth. Ānanda, it is like a bull's hide well stretched on a hundred pegs, its virtue gone. Even so, Ānanda, a monk, not attending to anything on this earth: dry land and swamps,[2] rivers and marshes,[3] (plants) bearing stakes and thorns, hills and plains, attends to solitude grounded on the perception of earth. His mind is satisfied with, pleased with, set on and freed in the perception of earth. He comprehends thus: 'The disturbances there might be resulting from the perception of human beings do not exist here; the disturbances there might be resulting from the perception of forest do not exist here. There is only this degree of disturbance, that is to say solitude grounded on the perception of earth.' He comprehends, 'This perceiving is empty of the perception of human beings; this perceiving is empty of the perception of forest. And there is only this that is not emptiness, that is to say solitude grounded on the perception of earth.' He regards that which is not there as empty of it. But in regard to what remains there he comprehends, 'That being, this is.' Thus, Ānanda, this too comes to be for him a true, not mistaken, and utterly purified realisation of (the concept of) emptiness.

And again, Ānanda, a monk, not attending to the perception of forest, not attending to the perception of earth, attends to solitude grounded on the perception of the plane of infinite *ākāsa*. His mind is satisfied with, pleased with, set on and freed in the perception

---

[1] *suññatāvakkanti*.
[2] *ukkūlavikūla* as at *A*. i. 35; *MA*. iv. 153 says the dry parts and the swamps.
[3] As at *A*. i. 35.

of the plane of infinite *ākāsa*. He comprehends thus: 'The disturbances there might be resulting from the perception of forest do not exist here; the disturbances there might be [**106**] resulting from the perception of earth do not exist here. There is only this degree of disturbance, that is to say solitude grounded on (the perception of[1]) the plane of infinite *ākāsa*.' He comprehends, 'This perceiving is empty of the perception of forest.' He comprehends, 'This perceiving is empty of the perception of earth. And there is only this that is not emptiness, that is to say the solitude grounded on the perception of the plane of infinite *ākāsa*.' He regards that which is not there as empty of it. But in regard to what remains there he comprehends, 'That being, this is.' Thus, Ānanda, this too comes to be for him a true . . . realisation of (the concept of) emptiness.

And again, Ānanda, a monk, not attending to the perception of earth, not attending to the perception of the plane of infinite *ākāsa*, attends to solitude grounded on (the perception of[1]) the plane of infinite consciousness. His mind is satisfied with . . . and freed in the perception of the plane of infinite consciousness. He comprehends thus: 'The disturbances there might be resulting from the perception of earth . . . from the perception of the plane of infinite *ākāsa* do not exist here. There is only this degree of disturbance, that is to say solitude grounded on the perception of the plane of infinite consciousness.' He comprehends, 'This perceiving is empty of the perception of earth . . . empty of the perception of the plane of infinite *ākāsa*. And there is only this that is not emptiness, that is to say solitude grounded on the perception of the plane of infinite consciousness.' He regards that which is not there as empty of it. But in regard to what remains he comprehends, 'That being, this is.' Thus, Ānanda, this too comes to be for him a true . . . realisation of (the concept of) emptiness.

And again, Ānanda, a monk, not attending to the perception of the plane of infinite *ākāsa*, not attending to the perception of the plane of infinite consciousness, attends to solitude grounded on the perception of the plane of no-thing. His mind is satisfied with . . . and freed in the perception of the plane of no-thing. He comprehends thus: 'The disturbances there might be resulting from the perception of the plane of infinite *ākāsa* . . . from the perception of the plane of infinite consciousness do not exist here. There is only this degree of disturbance, that is to say solitude grounded on

---

[1] Omitted in the text, but needed for the sake of consistency.

the perception of the plane of no-thing.' He comprehends, ' This perceiving is empty of the perception of the plane of infinite ākāsa.' [107] He comprehends, ' This perceiving is empty of the perception of the plane of infinite consciousness. And there is only this that is not emptiness, that is to say solitude grounded on the perception of the plane of no-thing.' He regards that which is not there as empty of it. But in regard to what remains there he comprehends, ' That being, this is.' Thus, Ānanda, this too comes to be for him a true . . . realisation of (the concept of) emptiness.

And again, Ānanda, a monk, not attending to the perception of the plane of infinite consciousness, not attending to the perception of the plane of no-thing, attends to solitude grounded on the perception of the plane of neither-perception-nor-non-perception. His mind is pleased with . . . and freed in the perception of the plane of neither-perception-nor-non-perception. He comprehends thus: ' The disturbances there might be resulting from the perception of the plane of infinite consciousness . . . resulting from the perception of the plane of no-thing do not exist here. There is only this degree of disturbance, that is to say solitude grounded on the perception of the plane of neither-perception-nor-non-perception.' He comprehends, ' This perceiving is empty of the perception of the plane of infinite consciousness . . . of the perception of the plane of no-thing. And there is only this that is emptiness, that is to say solitude grounded on the perception of the plane of neither-perception-nor-non-perception.' He regards that which is not there as empty of it. But in regard to what remains there he comprehends, ' That being, this is.' Thus, Ānanda, this too comes to be for him a true . . . realisation of (the concept of) emptiness.

And again, Ānanda, a monk, not attending to the perception of the plane of no-thing, not attending to the perception of the plane of neither-perception-nor-non-perception, attends to solitude grounded on the concentration of mind that is signless.[1] His mind is satisfied with . . . and freed in the concentration of mind that is signless. He comprehends thus: ' The disturbances there might be resulting from the perception of the plane of no-thing . . . from the perception of the plane of neither-perception-nor-non-perception do not exist here. There is only this degree of disturbance, that is to say the six sensory fields that, conditioned by life, are grounded on this

---

[1] The concentration of mind in insight, *vipassanācittasamādhi, MA*. iv. 153, which also says that as it is without a permanent sign it is called " signless," *animitta*.

body itself. [**108**] He comprehends: 'This perceiving is empty of the plane of no-thing ... empty of the perception of the plane of neither-perception-nor-non-perception. And there is only this that is not emptiness, that is to say the six sensory fields that, conditioned by life, are grounded on this body itself.' He regards that which is not there as empty of it. But in regard to what remains there he comprehends, 'That being, this is.' Thus, Ānanda, this too comes to be for him a true, not mistaken, utterly purified realisation of (the concept of) emptiness.

And again, Ānanda, a monk, not attending to the perception of the plane of no-thing, not attending to the perception of the plane of neither-perception-nor-non-perception, attends to solitude grounded on the concentration of mind that is signless.[1] His mind is satisfied with, pleased with, set on and freed in the concentration of mind that is signless. He comprehends thus, 'This concentration of mind that is signless is effected and thought out.[2] But whatever is effected and thought out, that is impermanent, it is liable to stopping.' When he knows this thus, sees this thus, his mind is freed from the canker of sense-pleasures and his mind is freed from the canker of becoming and his mind is freed from the canker of ignorance. In freedom is the knowledge that he is freed and he comprehends: 'Destroyed is birth, brought to a close the Brahma-faring, done is what was to be done, there is no more of being such or so.' He comprehends thus: 'The disturbances there might be resulting from the canker of sense-pleasures do not exist here; the disturbances there might be resulting from the canker of becoming do not exist here; the disturbances there might be resulting from the canker of ignorance do not exist here. And there is only this degree of disturbance, that is to say the six sensory fields that, conditioned by life, are grounded on this body itself.' He comprehends: 'This perceiving is empty of the canker of sense-pleasures.' He comprehends: 'This perceiving is empty of the canker of becoming.' He comprehends: 'This perceiving is empty of the canker of ignorance. And there is only this that is not emptiness, that is to say the six sensory fields that, conditioned by life, are grounded on this body itself.' He regards that which is not there as empty of it. But in regard to what remains he comprehends: 'That being,

---

[1] *MA*. iv. 154 says that *animitta* is spoken of again in order to show *vipassanāya paṭivipassanaṁ*, the insight that is complementary to (? *paṭi-*) insight, or a reflex of it.

[2] *Cf. M.* i. 350, iii. 244, *S.* ii. 65, *A.* v. 343.

this is.' Thus, Ānanda, this [109] comes to be for him a true, not mistaken, utterly purified and incomparably highest realisation of (the concept of) emptiness.

And those recluses or brahmans, Ānanda, who in the distant past, entering on the utterly purified and incomparably highest (concept of) emptiness, abided therein—all these, entering on precisely this utterly purified and incomparably highest (concept of) emptiness, abided therein. And those recluses or brahmans, Ānanda, who in the distant future, entering on the utterly purified and incomparably highest (concept of) emptiness, will abide therein—all these, entering on precisely this utterly purified and incomparably highest (concept of) emptiness, will abide therein. And those recluses or brahmans, Ānanda, who at present, entering on the utterly purified and incomparably highest (concept of) emptiness, are abiding in it— all these, entering on precisely this utterly purified and incomparably highest (concept of) emptiness, are abiding therein. Wherefore, Ānanda, thinking: ' Entering on the utterly purified and incomparably highest (concept of) emptiness, I will abide therein '—this is how you must train yourself, Ānanda."

Thus spoke the Lord. Delighted, the venerable Ānanda rejoiced in what the Lord had said.

Lesser Discourse on Emptiness:
The First

122. GREATER DISCOURSE ON EMPTINESS

(Mahāsuññatasutta)

THUS have I heard: At one time the Lord was staying among the Sakyans near Kapilavatthu in Nigrodha's park.[1] Then the Lord, having dressed early in the morning, taking his bowl and robe entered Kapilavatthu for almsfood. When he had walked in Kapilavatthu for almsfood and was returning from the almsgathering after the meal, he approached the dwelling-place of the Sakyan Kāḷakhe-

---

[1] See *M.L.S.* i. 119.

maka[1] for the day-sojourn. Now at that time many lodgings[2] were prepared in the dwelling-place of Kāḷakhemaka the Sakyan. The Lord saw these many [110] lodgings prepared in the dwelling-place of Kāḷakhemaka the Sakyan, and when the Lord had seen them it occurred to him: " Many lodgings are prepared in the dwelling-place of Kāḷakhemaka the Sakyan. Are many monks staying here ?"

Now at that time the venerable Ānanda together with many monks was making up robe-material in the dwelling-place of Ghaṭāya the Sakyan.[3] Then the Lord, emerging from solitary meditation towards evening, approached the dwelling-place of Ghaṭāya the Sakyan; having approached, he sat down on a seat that was ready. While he was sitting down the Lord addressed the venerable Ānanda, saying: " Many lodgings, Ānanda, are prepared in the dwelling-place of Kāḷakhemaka the Sakyan. Are many monks staying there ?"

"Many lodgings, revered sir, are prepared in the dwelling-place of Kāḷakhemaka the Sakyan; many monks are staying there. It is our time, revered sir, for making up robe-material."

"Ānanda, a monk does not shine[4] who delights in his own group,[5] is delighted by his own group, is intent on delight in his own group,[6] who delights in some other group, is delighted by some other group, is rejoiced by some other group. Indeed, Ānanda, the situation does not exist when a monk, delighting in his own group, delighted by his own group, intent on delight in his own group, delighting in some other group, delighted by some other group, rejoicing in some other group, can be one who acquires at will, without trouble, without difficulty, that which is the happiness of renunciation,[7] the happiness of aloofness,[8] the happiness of calm,[9] the happiness of self-awakening.[10] But, Ānanda, the situation exists when it is

---

[1] Khemaka was his name; his complexion was dark, kāḷa, MA. iv. 155.

[2] Of various kinds: beds, seats, mattresses, squatting mats, straw mats, strips of hide, grass, leaves, branches, all placed touching one another, for this is where groups of monks were staying, MA. iv. 155.

[3] Like the dwelling-place of Kāḷakhemaka, Ghaṭāya's was also built in Nigrodha's park (or, monastery), MA. iv. 157.

[4] In the Buddha's teaching, MA. iv. 158.

[5] saṁgaṇika is explained as a coming together of one's own company, while a group, gaṇa, is a coming together of various persons, MA. iv. 158. It is only the monk who delights in solitude who " shines."

[6] As at D. ii. 78.   [7] Of the sense-pleasures, MA. iv. 158.

[8] From the sense-pleasures.

[9] This conduces to allaying attachment, aversion and confusion.

[10] This conduces to the goal of awakening to the way(s).

expected of a monk who dwells alone, remote from a group, that he will be one who acquires at will, without trouble, without difficulty, that which is the happiness of renunciation, the happiness of aloofness, the happiness of calm, the happiness of self-awakening.

Indeed, Ānanda, the situation does not exist when a monk, delighting in his own group ... rejoicing in some other group, entering on the freedom of mind that is temporal and pleasing[1] or on that which is not temporal and is unshakable,[2] will abide in it. But, Ānanda, the situation exists when it is expected of a monk who dwells alone, remote from a group, that, entering on the freedom of mind that is temporal and pleasing [111] or on that which is not temporal and is unshakable, he will abide in it. I, Ānanda, do not behold one material shape[3] wherein is delight, wherein is content, but that from its changing and becoming otherwise there will not arise grief, sorrow, suffering, lamentation and despair.

But this abiding, Ānanda, has been fully awakened to by the Tathāgata, that is to say, by not attending to any signs,[4] the entering on and abiding[5] in an inward (concept of) emptiness.[6] And if, Ānanda, while the Tathāgata is abiding in this abiding there are monks, nuns, men and women lay followers, kings and kings' ministers, leaders and disciples of other sects who approach him, then, Ānanda, the Tathāgata with his whole mind tending to aloofness, leaning to aloofness, inclining to aloofness, remote, delighting in renunciation, bringing to an end all the things on which the cankers are founded, speaks there[7] as one intent only on inspiring them.[8] Wherefore, Ānanda, if a monk should desire: 'Entering on

---

[1] *sāmāyikā kantā cetovimutti*. At the time the mind is concentrated there is freedom from the defilements. *MA.* iv. 158, quoting *Pts.* ii. 40 says that this temporal (or temporary) deliverance consists in the attainments of the four *jhāna* and the four planes of immateriality. See *M.* i. 196 *f.*, and *M.L.S.* i. 243.

[2] *asāmāyikā akuppā cetovimutti*. This is freedom from the defilements and has not to do with things of time. So it is freedom that is immovable, supermundane. It consists of the four ariyan Ways and the four fruits of recluseship, *MA.* iv. 159, quoting *Pts.* ii. 40 which adds *nibbāna*.

[3] *rūpa*, called *sarīra*, body, at *MA.* iv. 159.

[4] *nimitta*, signs of the phenomenal world.

[5] *viharitum*, with *v.ll. viharatam, viharati*.

[6] As though alone, even though sitting in the midst of a company.

[7] In the midst of that company, *MA.* iv. 160.

[8] *aññadatthu uyyojaniyapaṭisamyuttam yeva katham kattā hoti*; also at *A.* iv. 233. This is a passage of great difficulty, partly because of the two meanings of *uyyojeti*: (1) to incite, instigate, (2) to dismiss. *MA.* iv. 160, reading *uyyojanikapaṭisamyuttam*, says that, in saying, "Go away, you," the

an inward (concept of) emptiness, may I dwell therein,' that monk, Ānanda, should steady, calm, make one-pointed and concentrate[1] his mind precisely on what is inward.

And how, Ānanda, does a monk steady, calm, make one-pointed and concentrate his mind precisely on what is inward ? As to this, Ānanda, a monk, aloof from pleasures of the senses, aloof from unskilled states of kind, entering on it abides in the first mediation . . . the second . . . the third . . . the fourth meditation. Even so, Ānanda, does a monk steady, calm, make one-pointed and concentrate his mind precisely on what is inward.

[112] He attends to an inward (concept of) emptiness. While he is attending to the inward (concept of) emptiness, his mind is not satisfied with, not pleased with, not set on, not freed in the inward (concept of) emptiness. This being so, Ānanda, the monk comprehends thus: 'While I was attending to an inward (concept of) emptiness my mind was not satisfied with . . . not freed in the inward (concept of) emptiness.' So he is clearly conscious in regard to it. He attends to an external (concept of) emptiness.[2] He attends to an inward and to an external (concept of) emptiness.[3] He attends to imperturbability.[4] While he is attending to imperturbability his

---

expression is thus connected with words of dismissal, *uyyojanikena vacanena*. And it proceeds: When the Lord had arisen after lying down after a meal . . . he attained the attainment of the fruit(s). At that time the company assembled to hear *dhamma*. The Lord . . . taught *dhamma*, and without letting pass the right time (to hear it), he *vivekaninnena cittena parisaṁ uyyojeti*. This could mean either: with his mind tending to aloofness he dismissed the company; or: with his mind tending to aloofness he inspired the company. E. M. Hare at *G.S.* iv. 158 renders the phrase as: " entirely confines his talk to the subject of going apart." It is possible that *uyyojeti* should be understood in both its meanings: that the Lord incited the company to seek aloofness for themselves and also dismissed them in order that they might do so. If we were to take *uyyojeti* only as " to dismiss," this would imply a certain selfishness on the Lord's part, and the *AA*. (iv. 122) is apparently against this: *tesaṁ upaṭṭhānagamanakaṁ yevā ti attho*, the meaning is going to their service (*i.e.* helping them).

[1] *Cf. M.* i. 116, *A.* ii. 94.
[2] To the five *khandhā* of another (person), *MA.* iv. 161.
[3] Sometimes to the one and sometimes to the other, *MA*. iv. 161. *Cf*. the internal and external contemplation of the body at *M*. i. 56 (*M.L.S.* i. 72 and see there *n.* 4).
[4] *ānañja*. *Cf. M*. ii. 229, *Vin*. iii. 4. " Thinking, I will become freed both ways," he attends to the attainment of immateriality and imperturbability, *āñaja-arūpasamāpatti*, *MA*. iv. 161. *VinA*. 157 glosses by *acala*, unshaking, steady.

mind is not satisfied with . . . not freed in imperturbability. This being so, Ānanda, the monk comprehends thus: 'While I was attending to imperturbability my mind was not satisfied with . . . not freed in imperturbability.' So he is clearly conscious in regard to it. Ānanda, that monk should steady, calm, make one-pointed and concentrate his mind precisely on what is inward in that earlier[1] sign of concentration itself. He attends to the inward (concept of) emptiness. While he is attending to the inward (concept of) emptiness, his mind is satisfied with, pleased with, set on and freed in the inward (concept of) emptiness. This being so, Ānanda, the monk comprehends thus: 'While I was attending to an inward (concept of) emptiness my mind was not satisfied with . . . not freed in the inward (concept of) emptiness.' So he is clearly conscious in regard to it. He attends to an external (concept of) emptiness. He attends to an inward and to an external (concept of) emptiness. He attends to imperturbability. While he is attending to imperturbability his mind is satisfied with, pleased with, set on and freed in imperturbability. This being so, Ānanda, the monk comprehends thus: 'While I was attending to imperturbability my mind was satisfied with, pleased with, set on and freed in imperturbability.' So he is clearly conscious in regard to it.

If, Ānanda, while this monk is abiding in this abiding,[2] he turns his mind to pacing up and down, then he paces up and down, thinking: 'While I am pacing up and down thus, no covetousness or dejection—evil unskilled states—[113] will flow in.' So he is clearly conscious in regard to it.[3] If, Ānanda, while this monk is abiding in this abiding, he turns his mind to standing . . . to sitting down . . . to lying down, then he lies down, thinking: 'While I am lying down, no covetousness or dejection—evil unskilled states—will flow in.' So he is clearly conscious in regard to it. If, Ānanda, while this monk is abiding in this abiding, he turns his mind to speaking, then he thinks: 'I will not talk that kind of talk which is low, of the village, of the ordinary folk, unariyan, not connected with the goal, which does not conduce to turning away from nor to detachment nor to stopping nor to calm nor to super-knowledge

---

[1] The text reads *parimasmiṁ*. *P.E.D.* and Geiger, *Pali Lit. u. Sprache* §19, say that *parima* is equivalent to *parama*. But *MA*. iv. 161 reads *purimasmiṁ*, and I follow this. I think the meaning is that the monk should make another attempt to enter and abide in the inward concept of emptiness.

[2] An abiding in calm and insight, *MA*. iv. 162.

[3] That is, to this *kammaṭṭhāna*, or exercise in meditation, *MA*. iv. 162.

nor to self-awakening nor to nibbāna—that is to say talk of kings, talk of thieves, talk of great ministers, talk of armies, talk of fears, talk of battles, talk of food, talk of drink, talk of clothes, talk of beds, talk of garlands, talk of scents, talk of relations, talk of vehicles, talk of villages, talk of market towns, talk of towns, talk of the country, talk of women, talk of valiant men,[1] talk of streets, talk of wells, talk of those departed before, talk of diversity, speculation about the world, speculation about the sea, talk on becoming or not becoming such or so.' So he is clearly conscious in regard to it. But, Ānanda, in regard to that talk which is austere,[2] a help to opening up the mind and which conduces to complete turning away from, to detachment, stopping, calm, super-knowledge, self-awakening and nibbāna, that is to say talk about wanting little, talk about contentment, talk about aloofness, talk about ungregariousness, talk about putting forth energy, talk about moral habit, talk about concentration, talk about intuitive wisdom, talk about freedom, talk about the knowledge and vision of freedom—he thinks: ' I will talk talk like this.' So he is clearly conscious in regard to it.

If, Ānanda, while this monk is abiding in this abiding [**114**] he turns his mind to thought,[3] he thinks: ' I will not think those kinds of thought which are low, of the village, of the ordinary folk, unariyan, not connected with the goal and which do not conduce to turning away from nor to detachment nor to stopping nor to calm nor to super-knowledge nor to self-awakening nor to nibbāna, that is to say thoughts of sense-pleasures, thoughts of malevolence, thoughts of harming.' So he is clearly conscious in regard to it. But, Ānanda, in regard to those thoughts which are ariyan, leading forward, which lead forward the thinker (of them) to the complete destruction of anguish,[4] that is to say thoughts of renunciation, thoughts of non-malevolence, thoughts of harmlessness—he thinks: 'I will think thoughts like these.' So he is clearly conscious in regard to them.

---

[1] Here reading *sūrakathā*. See notes on these kinds of talk at *B.D.* iii. 82.

[2] As at *Ud.* 36, *A.* iii. 117, iv. 352, v. 67; quoted at *MA.* i. 97

[3] *vitakka*.

[4] *niyyanti* (*niyyāti*) *takkarassa sammādukkhakkhayāya* is stock, *e.g.* at *M.* i. 68, 81, 322. It is suggested that in the above passage *kara*, normally " doing " (*i.e.* in *takkarassa*, of one doing thus), would be better rendered as " thinker."

Ānanda, there are these five strands of sense-pleasures.[1] What five ? Material shapes cognisable by the eye, agreeable, pleasant, liked, enticing, connected with sensual pleasure, alluring. Sounds cognisable by the ear . . . Smells cognisable by the nose . . . Tastes cognisable by the tongue . . . Touches cognisable by the body, agreeable, pleasant, liked, enticing, connected with sensual pleasure, alluring. These, Ānanda, are the five strands of sense-pleasures. Wherefore a monk should constantly reflect in his own mind: ' Does there arise in my mind any dealing with this or that field of the five strands of sense-pleasures ?' If, Ānanda, while the monk is reflecting he comprehends thus: ' There does arise in my mind some dealing with this or that field of the five strands of sense-pleasures '—this being so, Ānanda, the monk comprehends thus: ' That which is my desire and attachment to the five strands of sense-pleasures has not been got rid of.' So he is clearly conscious in regard to it. But if, Ānanda, while the monk is reflecting he comprehends thus: ' No dealing arises in my mind with this or that field of the five strands of sense-pleasures '—this being so, Ānanda, the monk comprehends thus: ' That which was my desire and attachment to the five strands of sense-pleasures has been got rid of by me.'[2] So he is clearly conscious in regard to it.

And, Ānanda, there are these five groups of grasping. Wherefore they should be forsaken by a monk who realises (their) rise and fall, with the thought: ' This is material shape, this the arising of material shape, this the setting of material shape; this is feeling, this [115] the arising of feeling, this the setting of feeling; this is perception . . . these are the habitual tendencies . . . this is consciousness, this the arising of consciousness, this the setting of consciousness.' While he is abiding realising the rise and fall of these five groups of grasping, whatever among these five groups of grasping was his bias towards " I am," that is got rid of. This being so, Ānanda, the monk comprehends thus: ' Whatever among these five groups of grasping was my bias towards " I am," that has been got rid of by me.' So he is clearly conscious in regard to it. These states, Ānanda, concerned solely with what is skilled,[3] are ariyan, supermundane, beyond the range of the Malign One.

---

[1] As at *M.* i. 85, etc.

[2] *me* is not in the text at the corresponding passage above.

[3] *kusalāyatikā*; *MA.* iv. 163 says *kusalato āgatā*, derived from what is skilled; but the sense of the exegesis and of the *v.ll.* seems to be " leading on (step by step) to what is skilled."

What do you think about this, Ānanda ? From his beholding what reason does a disciple regard it as fit that, even though he is being repulsed,[1] he should follow after a teacher ?"

"Things for us,[2] revered sir, are rooted in the Lord, have the Lord for conduit, the Lord for arbiter. It were good indeed, revered sir, if this speech of the Lord's were explained; having heard it from the Lord, the monks would remember it."

"Ānanda, it is not fit that a disciple should follow after a teacher if it is for the sake of an exposition of the Discourses that are in prose and in prose and verse.[3] What is the reason for this ? It is that for a long time, Ānanda, these things have been heard, borne in mind, repeated out loud, pondered over in the mind, well comprehended by (right) understanding.[4] But, Ānanda, that talk which is austere, a help to opening up the mind and which conduces to complete turning away from, to detachment, stopping, calm, superknowledge, self-awakening and nibbāna, that is to say talk about wanting little, talk about contentment, talk about aloofness, talk about ungregariousness, talk about putting forth energy, talk about moral habit, talk about concentration, talk about intuitive wisdom, talk about freedom, talk about the knowledge and vision of freedom—it is fit, Ānanda, that a disciple, even though being repulsed, should follow after a teacher for the sake of talk like this.

This being so,[5] Ānanda, there is affliction for teachers; this being so, there is affliction for pupils; this being so, there is affliction for Brahma-farers.

And how, Ānanda, is there affliction for teachers ? As to this, Ānanda, some teacher[6] chooses a secluded lodging in a forest, at the

---

[1] The reading above, and again below, is *payujjamāno*, passive present participle of *payuñjati*, to harness, yoke, employ. I have taken it however as *panujjamāno* as at *M*. i. 108.

[2] *Cf. M*. i. 310.

[3] Of the nine divisions into which the Teaching was classified only the first two are mentioned here, *sutta* and *geyya*. The word *veyyākaraṇa*, "exposition," which also occurs in the above passage, is not being used there with the special sense of the third division of the Teaching, "the Expositions," but in a general and untechnical sense.

[4] As at *M*. i. 213.

[5] *evaṁ sante*. While some disciples are living alone, the matter (connected with the ten topics of talk) does not prosper; therefore, to show the peril, *ādīnava*, besetting solitude, he said *evaṁ sante*, which means: being in solitude thus, *evaṁ ekībhāve sante*, *MA*. iv. 164-165.

[6] *MA*. iv. 165, an outside teacher who is a ford-maker, *i.e.* the leader of an "heretical" sect.

root of a tree, on a mountain slope, in a wilderness, a hill-cave, a cemetery, [116] a forest-haunt, in the open air or on a heap of straw. While he is living remote like this brahman householders crowd in on him and townsfolk as well as countryfolk. When the brahman householders, the townsfolk and the countryfolk crowd in on him he becomes infatuated,[1] he falls in love,[1] he becomes envious, he reverts to abundance. This, Ānanda, is called the afflicted teacher. Because of the teacher's affliction evil unskilled states that are connected with the defilements, with again-becoming, that are fearful, and the results of which are anguish, leading to birth, ageing and dying in the future,[2] strike at him. In this way, Ānanda, is there affliction for teachers.

And how, Ānanda, is there affliction for pupils ? As to this, Ānanda, a teacher's pupil, imitating[3] the teacher's aloofness, chooses a secluded lodging in a forest, at the root of a tree ... in the open air or on a heap of straw. While he is living remote like this brahman householders crowd in on him ... he reverts to abundance. This, Ānanda, is called the afflicted pupil. Because of the pupil's affliction evil unskilled states ... leading to birth, ageing and dying in the future, strike at him. In this way, Ānanda, is there affliction for pupils.

And how, Ānanda, is there affliction for Brahma-farers ? As to this, Ānanda, a Tathāgata arises in the world, perfected one, fully Self-Awakened One, endowed with knowledge and right conduct, well-farer, knower of the world(s), incomparable charioteer of men to be tamed, teacher of *devas* and men, an Awakened One, a Lord. He chooses a secluded lodging in a forest, at the root of a tree, on a mountain slope, in a wilderness, a hill-cave, a cemetery, a forest-haunt, in the open air or on a heap of straw. While he is living remote like this brahman householders crowd in on him and townsfolk as well as countryfolk. When the brahman householders, the townsfolk and the countryfolk crowd in on him he does not become infatuated, he does not fall in love, he does not become envious, he does not revert to abundance. [117] But a disciple of this Teacher, applying himself to this Teacher's aloofness, cultivating[4] it, chooses

---

[1] Text reads *mucchati kāmayati*; but Siam. version and *MA*. iv. 165 read *muccham nikāmayati*. The latter explains: *mucchanataṇham pattheti pavatteti*, which seems to mean: he longs for and sets going the craving for infatuation, i.e. for falling in love, a meaning which *kāmeti (kāmayati)* bears at e.g. *M*. ii. 40.

[2] *Cf. M*. i. 280.   [3] *anubrūhayamāno*.

[4] *vivekam anuyutto brūhayamāno*. *Cf. M*. Sta. 6, "the cultivator of empty places."

a remote lodging in a forest ... in the open air or on a heap of straw. While he is living remote like this brahman householders crowd in on him and townsfolk as well as countryfolk. When the brahman householders, the townsfolk and the countryfolk crowd in on him he becomes infatuated, falls in love, becomes envious and reverts to abundance. This, Ānanda, is called the afflicted Brahma-farer. Because of the Brahma-farer's affliction evil unskilled states connected with the defilements, with again-becoming, that are fearful and the results of which are anguish, leading to birth, ageing and dying in the future, strike at him. In this way, Ānanda, is there affliction for Brahma-farers. But, Ānanda, this affliction of Brahma-farers is more ill in result,[1] more terrible in result that either the affliction of teachers or the affliction of pupils; and moreover it conduces to the Downfall.[2]

Wherefore, Ānanda, conduct yourselves towards me with friendliness, not with hostility; and for a long time that will be for your welfare and happiness. And how, Ānanda, do disciples conduct themselves towards a teacher with hostility, not with friendliness ? As to this, Ānanda, the teacher, compassionate, teaches *dhamma* to disciples, seeking their welfare, out of compassion, saying: ' This is for your welfare, this is for your happiness.' But his disciples do not listen, do not lend ear, do not prepare their minds for profound knowledge but, turning aside, they move away from the teacher's instruction. Even so, Ānanda, do a teacher's disciples conduct themselves towards him with hostility, not with friendliness.

And how, Ānanda, do disciples conduct themselves towards a teacher with friendliness, not with hostility ? As to this, Ānanda, the teacher, compassionate, teaches *dhamma* to disciples, seeking their welfare, out of compassion, saying: ' This is for your welfare, this is for your happiness.' And his disciples listen, lend ear,[3] prepare their minds for profound knowledge and, not turning aside, they do not[4] move away from the teacher's instruction. Even so, Ānanda, do a teacher's disciples conduct themselves towards him with friendliness, not with hostility. Wherefore, [118] Ānanda, conduct yourselves towards me with friendliness, not with hostility;

---

[1] Those who have gone forth in this Dispensation, *sāsana*, should be able to attain the four ways, the four fruits and nibbāna but, failing of the instruction, *sāsana*, they fail of these nine strands of the supermundane.
[2] *Cf. S.* ii. 128.
[3] The *na* of the text should be omitted as it is in some MSS.
[4] The *ca* should read *na ca* as in one MS. version.

for a long time that will be for your welfare and happiness. And I, Ānanda, will not proceed with you as does a potter with an unbaked (vessel), not fully dry.[1] I will speak, Ānanda, constantly reproving,[2] constantly cleansing.[3] That which is the pith will stand fast."[4]

Thus spoke the Lord. Delighted, the venerable Ānanda rejoiced in what the Lord had said.

Greater Discourse on Emptiness:
The Second

---

[1] *āmake āmakamatte. MA.* iv. 166 says *āmake* is *apakkhe,* and *āmakamatte ti āmake nātisukkhe bhājane,* " an unbaked vessel, not quite dry." " The potter gently takes these vessels in both hands, saying: ' Do not break '; but I will not proceed with you as the potter proceeds." I do not see the full force of this simile; therefore my translation must remain very tentative. But I believe it means that whereas the potter gives, and can give, his vessels one chance only, the Teacher is undefeated by any initial failure there may be, and proceeds undeterred with the expectation of final success on the part of his pupil.

[2] *niggayha niggayha. MA.* iv. 166 says, " having exhorted once, I will not be silent; constantly reproving (*niggahetvā niggahetvā*) again and again I will exhort, I will instruct." *Cf. niggayhavādin* at *Dhp.* 76; and see *DhA.* ii. 108 which quotes the above passage.

[3] *pavayha pavayha* as at *M.* i. 442, 443. From *pavāhati,* to cause to be carried away, to remove (stains), hence to cleanse: of faults or taints, *dosa,* as at *MA.* iv. 166 which also says: as a potter, having removed, *pavāhetvā* (*v.l. pajahitvā*) the cracked and broken vessels (reading with Siam. edn. *bhinnachinnabhājanāni*) from among those that have been baked, takes the well baked ones, tapping (*i.e.* testing) them again and again. So too I, having repeatedly removed (stains from you), will again and again exhort and instruct (you).

[4] *yo sāro so ṭhassati*: " while you are being exhorted thus by me that which is the pith of the ways and the fruits will persist," *MA.* iv. 167. *Sāra* is the heartwood, pith, core. It is no doubt meant that this will persist and endure (like well baked vessels) when all the mistakes and errors that dog a learner's path have been cleared away and removed (like the cracked and broken vessels from among those that have been well baked).

123. DISCOURSE ON WONDERFUL AND MARVELLOUS QUALITIES
(Acchariyabbhutadhammasutta)

THUS have I heard: At one time the Lord was staying near Sāvatthī in the Jeta Grove in Anāthapiṇḍika's monastery. Then this conversation arose among a number of monks who, having returned from the alms-gathering after the meal, were seated gathered together in an assembly hall: " Wonderful,[1] your reverences, marvellous, your reverences, are the great psychic power and the great majesty of the Tathāgata inasmuch as he should know[2] of former Awakened Ones[3] who have attained nibbāna with the impediments[4] cut off, the whirligig cut through,[5] the rolling on finished[6] and all anguish spent,[7] that these Lords were of such a family and that these Lords were of such a name and . . . such a clan and . . . such moral habit and . . . such mental habits[8] and . . . such intuitive wisdom and . . . such an abiding[9] and that these Lords were of such freedom."[10]

---

[1] Cf. the whole of this Discourse with D. Sta. 14; and see Dial. ii. 8 ff. for notes.

[2] jānissati. D. ii. 8 reads anussarissati, (will), should recollect.

[3] Cf. S. iv. 52.

[4] papañca, i.e. to progress along the Way. Given at MA. iv. 167, DA. ii. 425 as " craving, pride, false views: these three defilements (kilesa)."

[5] chinnavaṭuma. Vaṭuma, from root vṛt, to revolve, turn round, referring to the cycle, circle, revolution (on, or of, the wheel of saṁsāra). MA. iv. 167, DA. ii. 425 say, " here the whirligig is called the rolling on of skilled and unskilled deeds."

[6] A synonym for the former phrase, DA. ii. 425 adding that the rolling on of all deeds is finished.

[7] As to results or effects in the future.

[8] Here dhamma is the middle term of the triad usually appearing as sīla samādhi paññā. MA. iv. 167-168 says that here evaṁ-dhammā means the mental states, dhammā, that are allied to samādhi, concentration, a concentration concerned (both) with what is worldly and what is supermundane. DA. ii. 426 adds that the meaning is concentration on the Way(s) and concentration on the fruits.

[9] MA. iv. 168 and DA. ii. 426 say that these Lords were abiders in the attainment of stopping, i.e. the stopping of knowing and feeling. This is the ninth and culminating plane of the meditative process.

[10] Five kinds of freedom given at MA. iv. 168, DA. ii. 426: freed by eliminat-

When this had been said, the venerable Ānanda spoke thus to these monks: " Indeed, your reverences, Tathāgatas are wonderful and possessed of wonderful qualities; indeed, your reverences, Tathāgatas are marvellous and possessed of marvellous qualities."

[119] And this was the conversation of these monks that was interrupted. Then the Lord, emerging from solitary meditation towards evening, approached the assembly hall; having approached, he sat down on the appointed seat. As he was sitting down, the Lord addressed the monks, saying: " What, monks, were you talking about just now ? What was your conversation that was interrupted ?"

" Revered sir, when we had returned from the alms-gathering after the meal and were seated gathered together in the assembly hall, this conversation arose among us: ' Wonderful, your reverences, marvellous, your reverences . . . and that these Lords were of such freedom.' When this had been said, revered sir, the venerable Ānanda spoke thus to us: ' Indeed, your reverences, Tathāgatas are wonderful . . . and possessed of marvellous qualities.' This was our conversation, revered sir, that was interrupted. And then the Lord arrived."

Then the Lord addressed the venerable Ānanda, saying: " Wherefore, Ānanda, deliver[1] at greater length the Tathāgata's wonderful and marvellous qualities."

" Face to face with the Lord, revered sir, have I heard this, face to face have I learnt: ' The Bodhisatta arose in the Tusita group[2] mindful and clearly conscious, Ānanda.' And inasmuch, revered sir, as the Bodhisatta arose in the Tusita group mindful and clearly conscious, I regard this as a wonder, a marvellous quality of the Lord's.

Face to face with the Lord, revered sir, have I heard this, face to face have I learnt: ' The Bodhisatta remained in the Tusita group mindful and clearly conscious, Ānanda.' And inasmuch, revered sir, as the Bodhisatta remained in the Tusita group mindful and clearly conscious, I regard this too as a wonder, a marvellous quality of the Lord's.

---

ing (the hindrances); freed for certain; freed by cutting off (the defilements); freed by the subsiding of the defilements; the freedom of escape (which is nibbāna). They are freed in respect of these five freedoms.

[1] *MA.* iv. 168, " Since you say that Tathāgatas are wonderful, so let there occur to you," *paṭibhantu, i.e.* deliver, speak forth, speak out.

[2] *I.e.* of *devas.*

Face to face with the Lord, revered sir, have I heard this, face to face have I learnt: ' The Bodhisatta remained in the Tusita group for as long as his life-span lasted,[1] Ānanda.' And inasmuch, revered sir, as the Bodhisatta remained in the Tusita group for as long as his life-span lasted, I regard this too as a wonder, a marvellous quality of the Lord's.

Face to face with the Lord, revered sir, have I heard this, face to face have I learnt: ' The Bodhisatta, deceasing from the Tusita group mindful and clearly conscious, entered his mother's womb, Ānanda.' And inasmuch, [**120**] revered sir, as the Bodhisatta, deceasing from the Tusita group mindful and clearly conscious, entered his mother's womb, I regard this too as a wonder, a marvellous quality of the Lord's.

Face to face with the Lord, revered sir, have I heard this, face to face have I heard: ' When, Ānanda, the Bodhisatta, having deceased from the Tusita group, entered his mother's womb, then an illimitable glorious radiance, surpassing even the *deva*-majesty of *devas*, appeared in the world with its *devas*, its Māras, its Brahmās, among the generations with recluses and brahmans, *devas* and men. And even in those spaces between the worlds,[2] gloomy,[3] baseless,[4] regions of blackness plunged in blackness, where the moon and the sun, powerful and majestic though they are, cannot make their light prevail[5]—even there there appeared the illimitable glorious radiance, surpassing even the *deva*-majesty of *devas*. And those beings who had uprisen there[6] recognised one another by means of this radiance, and they thought: " Indeed there are other beings who are uprising here." And this ten-thousand-world-system quaked, trembled and shook, and there appeared there the illimitable glorious radiance

---

[1] Owing to his having fulfilled all the *pārami*, excellences or " goings beyond," there being no gift he had not given, no *sīla* he had not observed, *MA*. iv. 170.

[2] *lokantarikā*, which appear to be Niraya Hells, see *MA*. iv. 177, *Jā*. i. 76, *VbhA*. 4. With this passage *cf. A*. ii. 130, *D*. ii. 12, *S*. v. 454, and *Mhvu*. i. 35, and see notes at *Mhvu*. Transln. (J. J. Jones), vol. i. p. 35 which I have largely followed.

[3] *aghā*, meaning dark. *MA*. iv. 177 explains by *niccavivaṭā*: perpetually concealed (*i.e.* from the light).

[4] *asaṁvutā*, explained at *MA*. iv. 177 as *heṭṭhāpi appatiṭṭhā*, " not supported from below."

[5] *ābhāya nānubhonti*. *MA*. iv. 178 says: *attano pabhāya nappahonti*, they are unable with their own light.

[6] In a great Niraya Hell, *MA*. iv. 178.

surpassing even the *deva*-majesty of *devas*.' And inasmuch, revered sir, . . . I regard this too as a wonder, a marvellous quality of the Lord's.

Face to face with the Lord, revered sir, have I heard, face to face have I learnt: 'When, Ānanda, the Bodhisatta is entering his mother's womb, four *devas*[1] approach so as to guard the four quarters, saying: " Do not let a human being or a non-human being or anyone whatever annoy the Bodhisatta or the Bodhisatta's mother." ' And inasmuch, revered sir, . . . I regard this too as a wonder, a marvellous quality of the Lord's.

Face to face with the Lord, revered sir, have I heard, face to face have I learnt: 'When, Ānanda, the Bodhisatta is entering his mother's womb, the Bodhisatta's mother is virtuous through her own nature, restrained from onslaught on creatures, restrained from taking what has not been given, restrained from wrong enjoyment of pleasures of the senses, restrained from lying speech, restrained from the occasions of slothfulness resulting from (drinking) strong intoxicants.'[2] And inasmuch, revered sir, . . . I regard this too as a wonder, a marvellous quality of the Lord's.

[121] Face to face with the Lord, revered sir, have I heard, face to face have I learnt: ' When, Ānanda, the Bodhisatta is entering his mother's womb, no desire connected with the strands of sensual pleasures arises in the Bodhisatta's mother towards men, and the Bodhisatta's mother is not to be transgressed against by any man of infatuated thoughts.' And inasmuch, revered sir, . . . I regard this too as a wonder, a marvellous quality of the Lord's.

Face to face with the Lord, revered sir, have I heard, face to face have I learnt: ' When, Ānanda, the Bodhisatta is entering his mother's womb, the Bodhisatta's mother is enjoying the five strands of sensual pleasures and she diverts herself, endowed with and possessed of the five strands of sensual pleasures.' And inasmuch, revered sir, . . . I regard this too as a wonder, a marvellous quality of the Lord's.

Face to face with the Lord, revered sir, have I heard, face to face have I learnt: ' When the Bodhisatta is entering his mother's womb, no ailment whatever arises in the Bodhisatta's mother; the Bodhisatta's mother is at ease, her body not tired; and within her

---

[1] *devaputta*: the four Great Kings (of the quarters), *MA*. iv. 179. They wanted to ward off pisācas and yakkhas and terrifying non-human beings in case they frightened the mother.

[2] *Cf. Mhvu*. i. 145.

womb the Bodhisatta's mother sees the Bodhisatta, complete in all his limbs, his sense-organs perfect.[1] As, Ānanda, an emerald jewel[2] of lovely water and well cut into eight facets might be strung on a thread—a deep green or yellow or red or white or an orange-coloured thread, and as a man with vision, having taken it in his hand, might reflect: " This is an emerald jewel of lovely water, it is well cut into eight facets and strung on a thread—a deep green ... or an orange-coloured thread "; even so, Ānanda, when the Bodhisatta is entering his mother's womb ... the Bodhisatta's mother sees the Bodhisatta, complete in all his limbs, his sense-organs perfect.' And inasmuch, revered sir, ... I regard this too as a wonder, a marvellous quality of the Lord's.

[122] Face to face with the Lord, revered sir, have I heard, face to face have I learnt: ' Ānanda, the Bodhisatta's mother dies seven days after the Bodhisatta is born and arises in the Tusita group.' And inasmuch, revered sir, ... I regard this too as a wonder, a marvellous quality of the Lord's.

Face to face with the Lord, revered sir, have I heard, face to face have I learnt: ' While, Ānanda, other women carry the child in their womb for nine or ten months[3] before they give birth, the Bodhisatta's mother does not give birth to the Bodhisatta in this way. The Bodhisatta's mother carries the Bodhisatta in her womb for exactly ten months before she gives birth.' And inasmuch, revered sir, ... I regard this too as a wonder, a marvellous quality of the Lord's.

Face to face with the Lord, revered sir, have I heard, face to face have I learnt: ' While, Ānanda, other women give birth sitting or lying down, the Bodhisatta's mother does not give birth to the Bodhisatta in this way: the Bodhisatta's mother gives birth to the Bodhisatta while she is standing.'[4] And inasmuch, revered sir, ... I regard this too as a wonder, a marvellous quality of the Lord's.

Face to face with the Lord, revered sir, have I heard, face to face

---

[1] *abhinindriya*, see *P.E.D.* He was sitting cross-legged, facing East, like a teacher of *dhamma* on a *dhamma*-seat, *MA.* iv. 181. But *cf. Mhvu.* i. 144 where Bodhisattas are said to stand in their mothers' womb. It is interesting to find the following simile occurring there too, but in rather a different form.

[2] See also *D.* ii. 13, *M.* ii. 17.

[3] *MA.* iv. 182 says this is to be understood as meaning children born after seven or eight or eleven or twelve months. All live except the eight months' child (reading at *MA.* iv. 182 should be *atthamāsajāto na jīvati* as at *DA.* ii. 437), but the seven months' child cannot stand heat or cold.

[4] *Cf. Mhvu.* i. 217.

have I learnt: 'When, Ānanda, the Bodhisatta is issuing from his mother's womb, *devas* receive him first, men afterwards.' And inasmuch, revered sir, . . . I regard this too as a wonder, a marvellous quality of the Lord's.

Face to face with the Lord, revered sir, have I heard, face to face have I learnt: 'When, Ānanda, the Bodhisatta is issuing from his mother's womb, the Bodhisatta does not at once touch the earth; the four *devas*, having received him, place him in front of his mother, saying: "Rejoice, lady, mighty is the son that is born to you."'[1] And inasmuch, revered sir, . . . I regard this too as a wonder, a marvellous quality of the Lord's.

Face to face with the Lord, revered sir, have I heard, face to face have I learnt: 'When, Ānanda, the Bodhisatta is issuing from his mother's womb, he issues quite stainless, undefiled by watery matter, undefiled by mucus, undefiled by blood, undefiled [123] by any impurity, pure and unstained. Ānanda, it is as when a jewel is laid on Benares muslin, neither does the jewel stain the Benares muslin nor does the Benares muslin stain the jewel. What is the reason for this? It is due to the purity of both. Even so, Ānanda, when the Bodhisatta is issuing from his mother's womb, he issues quite stainless . . . pure and unstained.' And inasmuch, revered sir, . . . I regard this too as a wonder, a marvellous quality of the Lord's.

Face to face with the Lord, revered sir, have I heard, face to face have I learnt: 'When, Ānanda, the Bodhisatta is issuing from his mother's womb, two streams of water appear from the sky,[2] the one cool, the other warm, wherewith they perform a water-libation for the Bodhisatta and his mother.' And inasmuch, revered sir, . . . I regard this too as a wonder, a marvellous quality of the Lord's.

Face to face with the Lord, revered sir, have I heard, face to face have I learnt: 'The moment, Ānanda, the Bodhisatta has come to birth, standing on even feet and facing north, he takes seven strides,[3] and while a white sunshade is being held over him, he scans all the quarters[4] and utters as with the voice of a bull:[5] "I am chief in the world, I am best in the world, I am eldest in the world. This is the last birth, there is not now again-becoming."' And inasmuch,

---

[1] *Cf. Mhvu.* i. 149-150.
[2] *Cf. Mhvu.* i. 220-222. According to *MA.* iv. 184=*DA.* ii. 438, as these streams of water were not needed to wash away any defilements, the warm one was for playing in and the cool one for drinking.
[3] *Cf. Mhvu.* i. 221.   [4] See *Jā.* i. 53.
[5] *MA.* iv. 185, *DA.* ii. 439 say *āsabhin ti uttamaṁ*.

revered sir, ... I regard this too as a wonder, a marvellous quality of the Lord's.

Face to face with the Lord, revered sir, have I heard, face to face have I learnt: 'When, Ānanda, the Bodhisatta was issuing from his mother's womb, then an illimitable glorious radiance, surpassing even the *deva*-majesty of *devas*, appeared in the world with its *devas*, its Māras, its Brahmās, among the generations with recluses and brahmans, *devas* and men. And even in those spaces between the worlds, gloomy, baseless, regions of blackness plunged in blackness, where the moon and the sun, powerful and majestic though they be, cannot make their light prevail—[124] even there there appeared the illimitable glorious radiance, surpassing even the *deva*-majesty of *devas*. And those beings who had uprisen there recognised one another by means of this radiance, and they thought: " Indeed there are other beings who are uprising here." And this ten-thousand-world-system quaked, trembled and shook, and there appeared there the illimitable glorious radiance surpassing even the *deva*-majesty of *devas*.' And inasmuch, revered sir, ... I regard this too as a wonder, a marvellous quality of the Lord's."

" Wherefore do you, Ānanda, regard this too as a wonder, a marvellous quality of the Tathāgata's: As to this, Ānanda, the feelings that arise in the Tathāgata are known; known they persist; known they go to destruction; perceptions are known; the thoughts that arise are known; known they persist; known they go to destruction. So do you, Ānanda, regard this too as a wonder, a marvellous quality of the Tathāgata's."

" Inasmuch, revered sir, as the feelings that arise in the Lord are known; known they persist; known they go to destruction;[1] perceptions are known; thoughts that arise are known; known they persist; known they go to destruction—I regard this too, revered sir, as a wonder, a marvellous quality of the Lord's."

Thus spoke the venerable Ānanda. The Teacher approved. Delighted, these monks rejoiced in what the venerable Ānanda had said.

Discourse on Wonderful and Marvellous Qualities:
The Third

---

[1] Buddhas have nothing not capable of (being known by) insight, therefore knowing the three marks, *tilakkhaṇa*, they get rid of them, *MA*. iv. 190.

124. DISCOURSE BY BAKKULA
(Bakkulasutta)

THUS have I heard: At one time the venerable Bakkula[1] was staying near Rājagaha in the Bamboo Grove at the squirrels' feeding place. Then Kassapa the Unclothed[2] (wanderer)[3] who had formerly been a friend of the venerable Bakkula when he was a householder, [**125**] approached the venerable Bakkula; having approached and exchanged greetings of courtesy and friendliness with the venerable Bakkula he sat down at a respectful distance. As Kassapa the Unclothed was sitting down at a respectful distance, he spoke thus to the venerable Bakkula:

"How long is it since you, reverend Bakkula, went forth?"

"It must be eighty years, friend, since I went forth."

"And how many times during these eighty years have you, reverend Bakkula, indulged in sexual intercourse?"

"Friend Kassapa, you should not question me thus: 'And how many times during these eighty years have you, reverend Bakkula, indulged in sexual intercourse?' But you could question me thus, friend Kassapa: 'And how many times during these eighty years, reverend Bakkula, did perceptions of sensual pleasure rise in you?'"

"And how many times during these eighty years, reverend Bakkula, did perceptions of sensual pleasure rise in you?"

"During the eighty years that I have gone forth, friend Kassapa,

---

[1] Bakkula means "two families," *dvakkula, dvikkula*, for according to *MA*. iv. 190 *ff.* the king judged him to belong to his own mother and to the councillor's wife who had cherished him after he had been found, unhurt, inside a fish that was caught in a river; *cf. ThagA*. ii. 87 *ff.*, *AA*. i. 304 *ff.* See the explanation of *bakkula* (as a word, not a proper name) at *J.P.T.S.* 1886, pp. 94 *ff.* At *A*. i. 25 Bakkula is called the monk foremost in good health. This gives rise to a dilemma at *Miln*. 215 *f*. Verses are ascribed to him at *Thag*. 225-227.

[2] Acela-Kassapa, an ascetic. At the end of the *Kassapa-Sīhanāda-suttanta*, *D*. i. 161 *ff.*, he is said to have undergone a four months' probation (usual for members of other sects joining the Buddhist Order of monks) and then to have gained arahantship.

[3] *DA*. ii. 349 calls him a *paribbājaka*.

I am not aware of (any) perception of sensual pleasure rising in me."

(" Inasmuch as for eighty years the venerable Bakkula is not aware of (any) perception of sensual pleasure rising in him—we regard this as a wonder, a marvellous quality in the venerable Bakkula."[1])

" During the eighty years that I have gone forth, your reverence,[2] I am not aware of (any) perception of malevolence or (any) perception of harming rising in me."

(" Inasmuch as for eighty years the venerable Bakkula is not aware of (any) perception of malevolence or (any) perception of harming rising in him—we regard this too as a wonder, a marvellous quality in the venerable Bakkula.")

" During the eighty years that I have gone forth, your reverence, I am not aware of (any) thought of sensual pleasure, (any) thought of malevolence or (any) thought of harming rising in me."

(" Inasmuch as for eighty years . . . a marvellous quality in the venerable Bakkula.")

[126] " During the eighty years that I have gone forth, your reverence, I am not aware of having accepted householder's robe-material."[3]

(" Inasmuch as that for eighty years . . .")

" During the eighty years that I have gone forth, your reverence, I am not aware of having cut out robe-material with a knife."[4]

(" Inasmuch as for eighty years . . .")

" During the eighty years that I have gone forth, your reverence, I am not aware of having sewn robe-material with a needle."[5]

(" Inasmuch as that for eighty years . . .")

" During the eighty years that I have gone forth, your reverence, I am not aware of having dyed robe-material with dye."[6]

(" Inasmuch as for eighty years . . .")

---

[1] According to *MA*. iv. 193 all these portions, beginning here were spoken by the Elders who made the recension of Dhamma.

[2] *āvuso*, whereas formerly (with one exception) he had said āvuso Kassapa.

[3] This layman's gift (of robe-material) is the easy way to obtain it, the difficult or ascetic way, *dhutaṅga*, being to collect rags from the refuse-heaps. *Cf. M.* i. 31, *A.* iii. 391 *f., Vin.* iii. 172. At *MA*. iv. 193 this kind of robe-material is said to be for the rains-residence.

[4] *MA*. iv. 193 explains *satthena* by *pipphalikena*, with scissors (?). *Cf. pipphalaka* at *DA*. i. 70.

[5] Needles allowed to be used by monks at *Vin*. ii. 115.

[6] Rules for dyeing by monks are given at *Vin*. i. 286.

" During the eighty years ... I am not aware of having sewn robe-material on a *kaṭhina*-frame."[1]

(" Inasmuch as that for eighty years ... ")

" During the eighty years ... I am not aware of having been occupied with making up the robe-material of fellow Brahma-farers ... of having accepted an invitation[2] ... I am not aware of a thought having ever arisen such as this: ' O that someone might invite me.' "

(" Inasmuch as that for eighty years ... ")

" During the eighty years ... I am not aware of having sat down amid the houses[3] ... of having eaten amid the houses ... of having observed in detail the characteristics of women-kind ... of having taught *dhamma* to women, even a verse of four feet[4] ... of having approached nuns' quarters[5] ... I am not aware of having taught *dhamma* to nuns ... to probationers[6] ... to female novices."

(" Inasmuch as that for eighty years ... ")

" During the eighty years ... I am not aware of having let (anyone) go forth ... of having ordained (anyone) ... of having given guidance[7] ... of having had a novice to attend me[8] ... of having bathed in a bathroom[9] ... of having bathed with chunam[9] ... of having had fellow Brahma-farers massage my limbs ... I am not

---

[1] Allowed at *Vin.* ii. 116 where regulations for the use of this *kaṭhina* are given. See *B.D.* v. 158 *ff*. *MA.* iv. 193 here asks how the thera got his robes if he did not accept material from householders and did not cut out or sew robe-material; and it answers that he was well known in two towns and that the people made and dyed the robe-material for him and then hung it out while he was bathing. He then clothed himself. So he got things as easily as did the thera Nigrodha from Asoka.

[2] *I.e.* to a meal.

[3] *MA.* iv. 194-195 says that in the *Mahāsakuludāyisutta* (*M.* Sta. 77, *MA.* iii. 240) " amid the houses " means from the village post, but here it means from the *nimbodakapatanaṭṭhāna*. The thera simply went up to the doors of the houses with his almsbowl and the people filled this with foods of various flavours.

[4] At *Vin.* iv. 21 monks are prohibited to teach *dhamma* to women in more than five or six sentences. *MA.* iv. 195 says that the thera did not do this even though it was allowable, and although practically all the theras who depended on families did so.

[5] Although it was allowable to go if asked by an ill nun (*Vin.* iv. 57, *Pāc.* 23), the thera did not do this.

[6] Always women; defined at *Vin.* iv. 332.

[7] *nissayaṁ detā*; rules for giving guidance are laid down at *Vin.* i. 60 *ff*.

[8] See *Vin.* i. 62 *ff*.

[9] Procedure for bathing in a bathroom and using chunam is laid down at *Vin.* i. 47.

aware that (any) [**127**] illness has ever arisen even for an instant[1] ... of having carried medicine, even bits from the yellow myrobalan tree[2] ... of having reclined against a reclining board[3] ... of having lain down to sleep ... of having gone for the rains to a lodging near a village."[4]

("Inasmuch as that for eighty years the venerable Bakkula is not aware of having gone for the rains to a lodging near a village—we regard this too as a wonder, a marvellous quality in the venerable Bakkula.")

"For exactly seven days[5] I, your reverence, (still) having defilements,[6] ate the country's almsfood;[7] then on the eighth day profound knowledge arose."[8]

("Inasmuch as that for exactly seven days the venerable Bakkula, (still) having defilements, ate the country's almsfood and then on the eighth day profound knowledge arose (in him)—we regard this too as a wonder, a marvellous quality in the venerable Bakkula.")

"May I, reverend Bakkula, receive the going forth in this *dhamma* and discipline, may I receive ordination."

And Kassapa the Unclothed received the going forth in this *dhamma* and discipline, he received ordination.[9] Not long after he had been ordained, living alone, aloof, diligent, ardent, self-resolute, the venerable Kassapa having soon attained here and now

---

[1] *gaddūhanamattaṁ*, explained at *MA*. iv. 195 and *SA*. ii. 224 as the time it would take to get one drop of milk by pulling a cow's teat. The word occurs at *S*. ii. 264 but in another connection. That the thera was free from illness is said to be due to the deeds of healing done by him under the former Buddhas, Padumuttara and Kassapa.

[2] *harītakikhaṇḍa*. Monks allowed to eat the fruits of this tree when they were ill, *Vin*. i. 201. *Cf*. also *Vin*. i. 206.

[3] When he was sleeping he therefore maintained the sitting posture (one of the *dhutaṅga* and called *nesajjika*), as the next also shows. Reclining boards allowed at *Vin*. ii. 175.

[4] *Cf. M*. i. 31.   [5] As at *S*. ii. 221.

[6] *sāṇa*. *MA*. iv. 196, reading *saraṇa* (=*sa+raṇa*, desire or fault), explains by *sa-kilesa*. *SA*. ii. 199 reads *sāṇo ti sakileso, sa-iṇo* (with a debt) *hutvā*. I think Bakkula means to point to the suddenness with which *aññā*, profound knowledge or gnosis, arises and thus wipes out the debt, to the past and to past *kamma*. He is now free of this, being an arahant. See *a-raṇa* in *M*. Sta. 139.

[7] The gifts of those with faith; *cf. Dhp*. 308.

[8] He was therefore no longer just a thera; he was also an arahant: *na thero ahaṁ arahā ti āha, MA*. iv. 196.

[9] *MA*. iv. 196 explains that though the thera (Bakkula) did not himself let go forth or ordain, he got this done by other monks.

through his own super-knowledge that incomparable goal of the Brahma-faring for the sake of which young men of family rightly go forth from home into homelessness, entering on it, abided in it. And he knew: " Destroyed is birth, brought to a close the Brahma-faring, done is what was to be done, there is no more of being such or so." And the venerable Kassapa was one of the perfected ones.

Then after a time the venerable Bakkula took his key and going from dwelling-place to dwelling-place, spoke thus: " Let the venerable ones come forward, let the venerable ones come forward, today I will attain final nibbāna."[1]

(" Inasmuch as the venerable Bakkula took his key and going from dwelling-place to dwelling-place, spoke thus: ' Let the venerable ones come forward, let the venerable ones come forward, today I will attain final nibbāna '—we regard this too as a wonder, a marvellous quality in the venerable Bakkula.")

[128] Then the venerable Bakkula, as he was sitting in the midst of the Order of monks,[2] attained final nibbāna.

(" Inasmuch as that the venerable Bakkula, as he was sitting in the midst of the Order of monks, attained final nibbāna—we regard this too as a wonder, a marvellous quality in the venerable Bakkula.")

Discourse by Bakkula[3]
The Fourth

---

[1] *ajja me parinibbānaṁ bhavissati.*

[2] He did not want his body to be a burden to any other monk after his *parinibbāna* so he entered into the condition of heat, *tejodhātu*; a flame sprang from his body, and his skin, flesh and blood burnt like ghee and were destroyed, MA. iv. 196.

[3] Also called *Bakkulatheracchariyabbhutasutta* and *Bakkulassa acchariyabbhutasuttanta.* MA. iv. 197 says *idaṁ pana suttaṁ dutiyasaṅgahe saṅgahītaṁ,* " this Discourse was included in the second collection (or recension)." It will be noted that there is no mention of the Buddha in this Discourse.

125. DISCOURSE ON THE "TAMED STAGE"
(Dantabhūmisutta)

THUS have I heard: At one time the Lord was staying near Rājagaha in the Bamboo Grove at the squirrels' feeding place. Now at that time the novice[1] Aciravata was staying in the Forest Hut.[2] Then Prince Jayasena,[3] who was always pacing up and down, always roaming about on foot,[4] approached the novice Aciravata; having approached he exchanged greetings with the novice Aciravata; having exchanged greetings of friendliness and courtesy, he sat down at a respectful distance. While he was sitting down at a respectful distance, Prince Jayasena spoke thus to the novice Aciravata:

"I have heard, good Aggivessana,[5] that if a monk is abiding here diligent, ardent, self-resolute, he may attain one-pointedness of mind."

"That is so, prince; that is so, prince. A monk, abiding here diligent, ardent, self-resolute, may attain one-pointedness of mind."[6]

"It were good if the reverend Aggivessana were to teach me *dhamma* as he has heard it, as he has mastered it."

"I, prince, am not able to teach you *dhamma* as I have heard it, as I have mastered it. Now, if I were to teach you *dhamma* as I have heard it, as I have mastered it, and if you could not understand the meaning of what I said, that would be a weariness to me, that would be a vexation to me."[7]

[129] "Let the reverend Aggivessana teach me *dhamma* as he has heard it, as he has mastered it. Perhaps I could understand the meaning of what the good Aggivessana says."

"If I were to teach you *dhamma*, prince, as I have heard it, as I have mastered it, and if you were to understand the meaning of

---

[1] *samanuddesa*, defined at *Vin*. iv. 139, 140 by *sāmaṇera*.
[2] A hut in a secluded part of the Bamboo Grove for the use of monks who wanted to practise striving, *padhāna*; *MA*. iv. 197.
[3] A son of Bimbisāra.   [4] Stock phrase, as *e.g.* at *M*. i. 108.
[5] For note on this name, see *M.L.S*. i. 280, *n*. 6.
[6] "Faring along thus, he attains an attainment, *samāpatti*, he attains *jhāna*; I have heard this," *MA*. iv. 197.
[7] Aciravata here uses the words ascribed to Gotama when he was first hesitating whether to teach *dhamma*, *Vin*. i. 5.

what I say, that would be good; if you should not understand the meaning of what I say, you must remain as you are;[1] you must not question me further on the matter."

" Let the reverend Aggivessana teach me *dhamma* as he has heard it, as he has mastered it. If I understand the meaning of what the good Aggivessana says, that will be good; if I do not understand the meaning of what the good Aggivessana says, I will remain as I am; I will not question the revered[2] Aggivessana further on the matter."

Then the novice Aciravata taught *dhamma* to Prince Jayasena as he had heard it, as he had mastered it. When this had been said, Prince Jayasena spoke thus to the novice Aciravata:

" This is impossible, good Aggivessana, it cannot come to pass that a monk, abiding diligent, ardent, self-resolute should attain one-pointedness of mind." Then Prince Jayasena, having declared to the novice Aciravata that this was impossible and could not come to pass, rising from his seat, departed.

And soon after Prince Jayasena had departed, the novice Aciravata approached the Lord; having approached and greeted the Lord, he sat down at a respectful distance. As he was sitting down at a respectful distance, the novice Aciravata told the Lord the whole of the conversation he had had with Prince Jayasena as far as it had gone. When this had been said, the Lord spoke thus to the novice Aciravata:

" What is the good of that,[3] Aggivessana ? That Prince Jayasena, living as he does in the midst of sense-pleasures, enjoying sense-pleasures, being consumed by thoughts of sense-pleasures, burning with the fever of sense-pleasures, eager in the search for sense-pleasures, [130] should know or see[4] or attain or realise that which can be known by renunciation, seen by renunciation, attained by renunciation, realised by renunciation—such a situation does not exist. It is as if,[5] Aggivessana, among elephants or horses or oxen to be tamed, two elephants, two horses or two oxen are well tamed, well trained, and two are not tamed, not trained. What do you

---

[1] " You must simply remain in your own state of not understanding," *MA*. iv. 197.

[2] Jayasena in addressing Aciravata uses the epithets *bho, bhavaṁ* and now *bhavantaṁ*.

[3] *Taṁ kut' ettha labbhā.*

[4] I suggest emending the Pali reading at *M*. iii. 130 from *dakkhati vā karissati* to *dakkhati vā pāpuṇissati vā sacchikarissati vā*, thus balancing the modes by which renunciation can be apprehended, given in the same sentence.

[5] As at *M*. ii. 129.

think about this, Aggivessana ? Would those two elephants or horses or oxen that were to be tamed and that were well tamed, well trained—would these on being tamed reach tamed capacity, would they, being tamed, attain a tamed stage ?"

"Yes, revered sir."

"But those two elephants or horses or oxen that were to be tamed but that were neither tamed nor trained—would these, not being tamed, reach tamed capacity, and would they, not being tamed, attain a tamed stage as do the two elephants or horses or oxen to be tamed that were well tamed, well trained ?"

"No, revered sir."

"Even so, Aggivessana, that Prince Jayasena, living as he does in the midst of sense-pleasures . . . should know or see or attain or realise that which can be known . . . realised by renunciation—such a situation does not exist. It is as if, Aggivessana, there were a great mountain slope near a village or a market-town which two friends, coming hand in hand from that village or market-town might approach; having approached the mountain slope one friend might remain at the foot while the other might climb to the top. Then the friend standing at the foot of the mountain slope might speak thus to the one standing on the top: ' My dear, what do you see as you stand on the top of the mountain-slope ?' He might reply: ' As I stand on the top of the mountain-slope I, my dear, see delightful parks, delightful woods, delightful stretches of level ground, delightful ponds.' But the other might speak thus: ' This is impossible, it [131] cannot come to pass, my dear, that, as you stand on the top of the mountain slope, you should see delightful . . . ponds.' Then the friend who had been standing on the top of the mountain slope, having come down to the foot and taken his friend by the arm, making his climb to the top of the mountain slope and giving him a moment in which to regain his breath, might speak to him thus: ' Now, my dear, what is it that you see as you stand on the top of the mountain slope ?' He might speak thus: ' I, my dear, as I stand on the top of the mountain slope see delightful parks . . . delightful ponds.' He might speak thus: ' Just now, my dear, we understood you to say: This is impossible, it cannot come to pass that, as you stand on the top of the mountain slope, you should see delightful . . . ponds. But now we understand you to say: ' I, my dear, as I stand on the top of the mountain slope see delightful parks . . . delightful ponds.' He might speak thus: ' That was because I, my dear, hemmed in by this great mountain slope, could not see what was to be seen.'

Even so but to a still greater degree, Aggivessana, is Prince Jayasena hemmed in, blocked, obstructed, enveloped by this mass of ignorance. Indeed, that Prince Jayasena, living as he does in the midst of sense-pleasures, enjoying sense-pleasures, being consumed by thoughts of sense-pleasures, burning with the fever of sense-pleasures, eager in the search for sense-pleasures, should know or see or attain or realise that which can be known . . . seen . . . attained . . . realised by renunciation—such a situation does not exist. Had these two similes[1] occurred to you, Aggivessana, for Prince Jayasena, Prince Jayasena naturally[2] would have trusted you and, having trust, would have acted in the manner of one having trust in you."

"But how could these two similes for Prince Jayasena have occurred to me, revered sir, seeing that they are spontaneous, that is to say to the Lord, and had never been heard before ?"[3]

[132] "As, Aggivessana, a noble anointed king addresses an elephant hunter saying: ' You, good elephant hunter, mount the king's elephant and go into an elephant forest. When you see a forest elephant, tie him to the neck of the king's elephant.' And, Aggivessana, the elephant hunter, having answered, ' Yes, sire,' in assent to the noble anointed king, mounts the king's elephant . . . ties him to the neck of the king's elephant. So the king's elephant brings him out into the open; and to this extent, Aggivessana, the forest elephant gets out into the open. But, Aggivessana, the forest elephant has this longing, that is to say for the elephant forest. But in regard to him the elephant hunter tells the noble anointed king that the forest elephant has got out into the open. The noble anointed king then addresses an elephant tamer, saying: ' Come you, good elephant tamer, tame the forest elephant by subduing his forest ways, by subduing his forest memories and aspirations and by subduing his distress, his fretting and fever for the forest, by making him pleased with the villages and by accustoming him to human ways.'

And, Aggivessana, the elephant tamer, having answered ' Yes, sire,' in assent to the noble anointed king, driving a great post into the ground ties the forest elephant to it by his neck so as to subdue his forest ways . . . and accustom him to human ways. Then the elephant tamer addresses him with such words as are gentle, pleasing

---

[1] *Cf.* the four similes for Jayasena at *M*. iii. 144.
[2] *anacchariyaṁ*, not wonderful, appearing naturally or spontaneously.
[3] On *anacchariyā pubbe assutapubbā seyyathāpi Bhagavantaṁ* see *C.P.D.*, s.v. *anacchariya*.

to the ear, affectionate, going to the heart, urbane, pleasant to the manyfolk, liked by the manyfolk. And, Aggivessana, the forest elephant, on being addressed with words that are gentle . . . liked by the manyfolk, [**133**] listens, lends ear and bends his mind to learning. Next the elephant tamer supplies him with grass-fodder and water. When, Aggivessana, the forest elephant has accepted the grass-fodder and water from the elephant tamer, it occurs to the elephant tamer: ' The king's elephant will now live.' Then the elephant tamer makes him do[1] a further task, saying: ' Take up,[2] put down.' When, Aggivessana, the king's elephant is obedient to the elephant tamer and acts on his instructions to take up and put down, then the elephant tamer makes him do a further task, saying: ' Advance, retreat ' . . . a further task, saying: ' Get up, sit down.' When, Aggivessana, the king's elephant is obedient to the elephant tamer and acts on his instructions to get up and sit down, then the elephant tamer makes him do a further task, known as ' standing your ground '[3]: he ties a shield to the great beast's trunk; a man holding a lance is sitting on his neck, and men holding lances are standing surrounding him on all sides; and the elephant tamer, holding a lance with a long shaft, is standing in front. While he is doing the task of ' standing your ground ' he does not move a fore-leg nor does he move a hind-leg, nor does he move the forepart of his body, nor does he move the hindpart of his body, nor does he move his head, nor does he move an ear, nor does he move a tusk, nor does he move his tail, nor does he move his trunk. A king's elephant is one who endures[4] blows of sword, axe, arrow, hatchet,[5] and the resounding din of drum and kettle-drum, conch and tam-tam, he is (like) purified gold purged of all its dross and impurities,[6] fit for a king,[7] a royal possession and reckoned as a kingly attribute.

[**134**] Even so, Aggivessana, does a Tathāgata arise here in the

---

[1] Reading with one MS. version *kāreti* instead of text's *karoti*.

[2] *ādissa*. See *P.E.D.* s.v. It is an imperative in some correspondence with *ādāna* of next line but one. Under *ādiyati P.E.D.* says " imper. *ādiya* M. iii. 133 (so read for *ādissa* ?)."

[3] *ānejja-kāraṇa*. *P.E.D.* says " trick of immovability, *i.e.* pretending to be dead (done by an elephant, but see differently Morris, *J.P.T.S.* 1886, p. 154)."

[4] See also definition of *rañño nāgo khamo* at *A.* ii. 117.

[5] *parasattuppahārānaṁ*, possibly a misreading for *parasuppahāra*; but *pharasu-* at *A.* ii. 117, and elsewhere, but *parasu* also at *S.* v. 441, *Jā.* iii. 179.

[6] *nihitaninnītakasāva*; *cf. A.* i. 254.

[7] *Cf. A.* i. 244, 284, ii. 113, 170.

world, perfected one, fully Self-Awakened One . . . (*as in vol. i. p.* 179, *ll.* 2-20=*M.L.S. vol. i, pp.* 223-224) . . . goes forth from home into homelessness. To this extent, Aggivessana, the ariyan disciple gets out into the open. But, Aggivessana, *devas* and mankind have this longing, that is to say for the five strands of sense-pleasures. The Tathāgata disciplines him further, saying: ' Come you, monk, be moral,[1] live controlled by the control of the Obligations, possessed of (right) behaviour and pasture, seeing danger in the slightest faults; undertaking them, train yourself in the rules of training.'

And when, Aggivessana, the ariyan disciple is moral, lives controlled by the control . . . undertaking them, trains himself in the rules of training, then the Tathāgata disciplines him further, saying: ' Come you, monk, be guarded as to the doors of the sense-organs. Having seen a material shape with the eye be not entranced by the general appearance, be not entranced by the detail. For if you dwell with the organ of sight uncontrolled, covetousness and dejection, evil unskilled states of mind, might flow in. So fare along for its control, guard the organ of sight, achieve control over the organ of sight. Having heard a sound with the ear . . . Having smelt a smell with the nose . . . Having savoured a taste with the tongue . . . Having felt a touch with the body . . . Having cognised a mental state with the mind, be not entranced by the general appearance, be not entranced by the detail. For if you dwell with the organ of mind uncontrolled, covetousness and dejection, evil unskilled states of mind, might flow in. So fare along for its control, guard the organ of mind, achieve control over the organ of mind.'

And when, Aggivessana, the ariyan disciple is guarded as to the doors of the sense-organs, then the Tathāgata disciplines him further, saying: ' Come you, monk, be moderate in eating. You should take food reflecting carefully, not for fun or indulgence or personal charm or beautification, but just enough for maintaining this body and keeping it going, for keeping it unharmed, for furthering the Brahma-faring, with the thought: Thus am I crushing out an old feeling, and I will not allow a new feeling to arise, and then there will be for me subsistence and blamelessness and abiding in comfort.'

When, [**135**] Aggivessana, the ariyan disciple is moderate in eating, then the Tathāgata disciplines him further, saying: ' Come you, monk, abide intent on vigilance. During the day, while pacing up and down, while sitting down, cleanse the mind of obstructive

---

[1] For following passage see also *M.* i. 354-355 (*M.L.S.* ii. 20 *f.*).

mental states; during the first watch of the night while pacing up and down, while sitting down, cleanse the mind of obstructive mental states; during the middle watch of the night you should lie down on your right side in the lion-posture, foot resting on foot, mindful, clearly conscious, reflecting on the thought of getting up again; during the last watch of the night when you have risen and are pacing up and down or sitting down, you should cleanse the mind of obstructive mental states.'

And when, Aggivessana, the ariyan disciple is intent on vigilance, then the Tathāgata disciplines him further, saying: ' Come you, monk, be possessed of mindfulness and clear consciousness. Be one who acts with clear consciousness whether you are setting out or returning[1] . . . looking down or looking around . . . bending back or stretching out (the arm) . . . carrying the outer cloak, the bowl, the robe . . . munching, drinking, eating, savouring . . . obeying the calls of nature . . . walking, standing, sitting, asleep, awake, talking, silent.'

And when, Aggivessana, the ariyan disciple is possessed of mindfulness and clear consciousness, then the Tathāgata disciplines him further, saying: ' Come you, monk, choose a remote lodging in a forest, at the root of a tree, on a mountain slope, in a wilderness, a hill-cave, a cemetery, a forest haunt, in the open or on a heap of straw.' He chooses a remote lodging in a forest . . . or on a heap of straw. Returning from alms-gathering after the meal, he sits down cross-legged, holding the back erect, having made mindfulness rise up in front of him. He, by getting rid of coveting for the world, dwells with a mind devoid of coveting, he purifies the mind of coveting. By getting rid of the taint of ill-will he dwells benevolent in mind, compassionate for the welfare of all creatures and beings, he purifies the mind of the taint of ill-will. By getting rid of sloth and torpor, he dwells devoid of sloth and torpor; perceiving the light, mindful, clearly conscious, he purifies the mind of sloth and torpor. By getting rid of restlessness and worry, he dwells calmly; the mind subjectively tranquillised, he purifies the mind of restlessness and worry. [136] By getting rid of doubt, he dwells doubt-crossed, unperplexed as to the states that are skilled, he purifies the mind of doubt. He, by getting rid of these five hindrances which are defilements of the mind and weakening to intuitive wisdom, dwells contemplating the body in the body, ardent, clearly

---

[1] As far as the simile *cf*. *M*. i. 274-275 (*M.L.S.* i. 328-329).

conscious (of it), mindful (of it) so as to control the covetousness and dejection in the world. He fares along contemplating the feelings ... the mind ... the mental states in mental states, ardent, clearly conscious (of them), mindful (of them) so as to control the covetousness and dejection in the world.

As, Aggivessana, an elephant tamer, driving a great post into the ground, ties a forest elephant to it by his neck so as to subdue his forest ways, so as to subdue his forest aspirations, and so as to subdue his distress, his fretting and fever for the forest, so as to make him pleased with villages and accustom him to human ways—even so, Aggivessana, these four applications of mindfulness are ties of the mind so as to subdue the ways of householders and to subdue the aspirations of householders and to subdue the distress, the fretting and fever of householders; they are for leading to the right path, for realising nibbāna.[1]

The Tathāgata then disciplines him further, saying: 'Come you, monk, fare along contemplating the body in the body, but do not apply yourself to a train of thought connected with the body; fare along contemplating the feelings in the feelings ... the mind in the mind ... mental states in mental states, but do not apply yourself to a train of thought connected with mental states.' He, by allaying initial thought and discursive thought, with the mind subjectively tranquillised and fixed on one point, enters on and abides in the second meditation which is devoid of initial and discursive thought, is born of concentration and is rapturous and joyful; he enters on and abides in the third meditation.

Then with the mind composed thus ... (*as in vol. i.* 22-23=*M.L.S.* i. 28-29. *Also vol. i.* 347-348=*M.L.S. ii.* 12 *ff.*) ... done is what was to be done, there is no more or being such or so.

That monk is able to endure heat, cold, hunger, thirst, the touch of mosquitoes, gadflies, wind, sun and creeping things, abusive language and unwelcome modes of speech; he has grown to bear bodily feelings which as they arise [137] are painful, acute, sharp, severe, wretched, miserable, deadly. Purged of all the dross and impurities of attachment, aversion and confusion, he is worthy of oblations, offerings, respect and homage, an unsurpassed field for merit in the world.

If, Aggivessana, a king's elephant dies in old age, untamed, untrained, the king's old elephant that has died is reckoned as one

---

[1] *Cf. M.* i. 56, and see notes at *M.L.S.* i. 71.

that has died untamed. And so, Aggivessana, of a king's elephant that is middle aged. And too, Aggivessana, if a king's elephant dies young, untamed, untrained, the king's young elephant that has died is reckoned as one that has died untamed. Even so, Aggivessana, if a monk who is an elder dies with the cankers not destroyed, the monk who is an elder that has died is reckoned as one that has died untamed. And so, Aggivessana, of a monk of middle standing. And too, Aggivessana, if a newly ordained monk dies with the cankers not destroyed, the newly ordained monk that has died is reckoned as one that has died untamed. If, Aggivessana, a king's elephant dies in old age, well tamed, well trained, the king's old elephant that has died is reckoned as one that has died tamed. And so, Aggivessana, of a king's elephant that is middle aged. And too, Aggivessana, if a king's elephant dies young, well tamed, well trained, the king's young elephant that has died is reckoned as one that has died tamed. Even so, Aggivessana, if a monk who is an elder dies with the cankers destroyed, the monk who is an elder that has died is reckoned as one that has died tamed. And so, Aggivessana, of a monk of middle standing. And too, Aggivessana, if a newly ordained monk dies with the cankers destroyed, the newly ordained monk that has died is reckoned as one that has died tamed."

Thus spoke the Lord. Delighted, the novice Aciravata rejoiced in what the Lord had said.

Discourse on the " Tamed Stage ":
The Fifth

126. DISCOURSE TO BHŪMIJA
(Bhūmijasutta)

[138] THUS have I heard: At one time the Lord was staying near Rājagaha in the Bamboo Grove at the squirrels' feeding place. Then the venerable Bhūmija,[1] having dressed early in the morning, taking his bowl and robe, approached Prince Jayasena's abode;

---

[1] Uncle of Jayasena, *MA.* iv. 199. He entered the Order with his friends Sambhūta (Sītavaniya), Jeyyasena and Abhirādhana, *ThagA.* i. 47.

having approached, he sat down on the appointed seat. And Prince Jayasena approached the venerable Bhūmija; having approached, he exchanged greetings with the venerable Bhūmija; having conversed in a friendly and courteous way, he sat down at a respectful distance. As he was sitting down at a respectful distance, Prince Jayasena spoke thus to the venerable Bhūmija:

"There are, good Bhūmija, some recluses and brahmans who speak thus and are of these views: ' If one fares the Brahma-faring with an expectation,[1] one is incapable of obtaining the fruit. And if one fares the Brahma-faring without an expectation, one is incapable of obtaining the fruit. And if one fares the Brahma-faring both with an expectation and without,[2] one is incapable of obtaining the fruit. And if one fares the Brahma-faring neither with an expectation nor without, one is incapable of obtaining the fruit.' What does the good Bhūmija's teacher say about this, what does he point out?"

"I have not heard this face to face with the Lord, Prince, nor have I learnt it face to face. But the situation exists that the Lord might explain it thus: If, with an expectation, one fares the Brahma-faring inattentively, one is incapable of obtaining the fruit. And if, without an expectation . . . both with an expectation and without . . . neither with an expectation nor without, one fares the Brahma-faring inattentively, one is incapable of obtaining the fruit. But if, with an expectation, one fares the Brahma-faring attentively . . . [**139**] . . . without an expectation . . . both with an expectation and without . . . neither with an expectation nor without, one fares the Brahma-faring attentively, one is capable of obtaining the fruit. I have not heard this face to face with the Lord, Prince, I have not learnt it face to face. But the situation exists that the Lord might explain it thus."

"If the good Bhūmija's teacher speaks thus, points out thus, it seems to me that the good Bhūmija's teacher stands head and shoulders above[3] all ordinary recluses and brahmans." Then Prince Jayasena offered the venerable Bhūmija his own (dish of) rice cooked in milk.

Then the venerable Bhūmija, returning from alms-gathering after

---

[1] *āsañ ce pi karitvā*, having made a longing, hope or expectation. The word *āsā* occurs at e.g. *Vin.* i. 260.

[2] At times the one, at times the other, *MA.* iv. 199.

[3] *muddhānam āhacca tiṭṭhati*, stands striking the head, or pressing it down, therefore above it.

the meal, approached the Lord; having approached and greeted the Lord, he sat down at a respectful distance. As he was sitting down at a respectful distance, the venerable Bhūmija spoke thus to the Lord:

" Now, revered sir, I, having dressed early in the morning[1] . . . '. . . stands head and shoulders above all ordinary recluses and brahmans.' I hope, revered sir, that when questioned thus and answering thus, I was asserting (fairly) what the Lord affirms, that I was not misrepresenting the Lord with what is not fact, but was explaining a *dhamma* that conforms to *dhamma* and that no fellow *dhamma*-man, a holder of (my) views, comes to a position incurring blame ?"[2]

[**140**] " Indeed, Bhūmija, when questioned thus and answering thus, you were asserting (fairly) what I[3] affirm, you were not misrepresenting me with what is not fact, you were explaining a *dhamma* that conforms to *dhamma* and no fellow *dhamma*-man, a holder of (your) views, comes to a position incurring blame.

If, Bhūmija, those recluses or brahmans who are of wrong view, wrong aspiration, wrong speech, wrong action, wrong mode of livelihood, wrong endeavour, wrong mindfulness, wrong concentration, fare the Brahma-faring with an expectation, they are incapable of obtaining the fruit. And if they fare the Brahma-faring without an expectation they are incapable of obtaining the fruit. And if they fare the Brahma-faring both with an expectation and without . . . neither with an expectation nor without, they are incapable of obtaining the fruit. What is the reason for this ? This is not the method,[4] Bhūmija, for obtaining the fruit.

Bhūmija, it is like a man walking about in need of oil, seeking for oil, looking about for oil who, having heaped sand into a trough, should press it while sprinkling it continuously with water. Even though he had an expectation, he would be incapable of obtaining oil by heaping sand into a trough and pressing it while sprinkling it continuously with water. And even though he were without an expectation . . . were both with an expectation and without . . . were neither with an expectation nor without, he would be incapable of obtaining oil by heaping sand into a trough and pressing it while sprinkling it continuously with water. What is the reason for this ?

---

[1] Bhūmija repeats the whole of his conversation with Jayasena.
[2] As at *Vin.* i. 234.
[3] I follow the *v.l. me* instead of text's *Bhagavato*.
[4] *ayoni h'esā. Cf. S.* i. 203, *ayoniṁ paṭinissajja.*

This is not the method, Bhūmija, for obtaining oil. In the same way, Bhūmija, if those recluses or brahmans who are of wrong view ... wrong concentration, fare the Brahma-faring with an expectation ... without an expectation ... both with an expectation and without ... neither with an expectation nor without, they are incapable of obtaining the fruit. [141] What is the reason for this ? This is not the method, Bhūmija, for obtaining the fruit.

Bhūmija, it is like a man walking about in need of milk, seeking for milk, looking about for milk, who should pull a young cow by the horn. Even though he had an expectation, he would be incapable of obtaining milk by pulling the young cow by the horn. And even though he were without an expectation ... were both with an expectation and without ... were neither with an expectation nor without, he would be incapable of obtaining milk by pulling a young cow by the horn. What is the reason for this ? This is not the method, Bhūmija, for obtaining milk. In the same way, Bhūmija, if those recluses or brahmans who are of wrong view ... they are incapable of obtaining the fruit. What is the reason for this ? This is not the method, Bhūmija, for obtaining the fruit.

Bhūmija, it is like a man walking about in need of butter, seeking for butter, looking about for butter who, having sprinkled water into a jar, should swirl it round with a churning-stick.[1] Even though he had an expectation, he would be incapable of obtaining butter by sprinkling water into a jar and swirling it round with a churning-stick. And even though he were without an expectation ... were both with an expectation and without, were neither with an expectation nor without, he would be incapable of obtaining butter by sprinkling water into a jar and swirling it round with a churning-stick. What is the reason for this ? This is not the method, Bhūmija, for obtaining butter. In the same way, Bhūmija, if those recluses or brahmans who are of wrong view ... they are incapable of obtaining the fruit. What is the reason for this ? This is not the method, Bhūmija, for obtaining the fruit.

---

[1] *matthena āviñjeyya.* In the simile of pulling the young cow by the horn we get *visāṇato āviñjeyya.* But the precise meaning of *āviñjati* in these similes is obscure. In this one it seems to mean to twirl, to churn. *Matthena* should perhaps read *matthakena,* top, summit. Or has some confusion with the verb *mathati,* to stir, crept in (*cf. abhimattheyya* in the next simile) ? Or should the reading be *manthena,* with a churning-stick? I have adopted tentatively this last alternative as it makes here, and in the " favourable " simile below, the greater amount of sense.

Bhūmija, it is like a man walking about in need of fire, seeking for fire, looking about for fire who, bringing an upper piece of fire-stick, should rub a wet sappy stick (with it).[1] [**142**] Even though he had an expectation, he would be incapable of obtaining fire by bringing an upper piece of fire-stick and rubbing a wet sappy stick (with it). And even though he were without an expectation . . . were both with an expectation and without . . . were neither with an expectation nor without, he would be incapable of obtaining a fire by bringing an upper piece of fire-stick and rubbing a wet sappy stick (with it). What is the reason for this ? This is not the method, Bhūmija, for obtaining fire. In the same way, Bhūmija, if those recluses or brahmans who are of wrong view . . . are incapable of obtaining the fruit. What is the reason for this ? This is not the method, Bhūmija, for obtaining the fruit.

But if, Bhūmija, those recluses or brahmans who are of right view, right aspiration, right speech, right action, right mode of livelihood, right endeavour, right mindfulness, right concentration, fare the Brahma-faring with an expectation, they are capable of obtaining the fruit. And if they fare the Brahma-faring without an expectation, they are capable of obtaining the fruit. And if they fare the Brahma-faring both with an expectation and without . . . neither with an expectation nor without, they are capable of obtaining the fruit. What is the reason for this ? This is the method, Bhūmija, for obtaining the fruit.

Bhūmija, it is like a man walking about in need of oil, seeking for oil, looking about for oil who, having heaped oil-seeds into a trough, should press them while sprinkling them continuously with water. If he had an expectation, he would be capable of obtaining oil by heaping oil-seeds into a trough and pressing them while sprinkling them continuously with water. What is the reason for this ? This is the method, Bhūmija, for obtaining oil. And if he were without an expectation . . . were both with an expectation and without . . . were neither with an expectation nor without, he would be capable of obtaining oil by heaping oil-seeds into a trough and pressing them while sprinkling them continuously with water. What is the reason for this ? This is the method, Bhūmija, for obtaining oil. In the same way, Bhūmjia, if those recluses or brahmans who are of right view . . . right concentration, fare the Brahma-faring with an expectation, [**143**] they are capable of

---

[1] *Cf. M.* i. 240.

obtaining the fruit. And if they fare the Brahma-faring without an expectation . . . both with an expectation and without . . . neither with an expectation nor without, they are capable of obtaining the fruit. What is the reason for this ? This is the method, Bhūmija, for obtaining the fruit.

Bhūmija, it is like a man walking about in need of milk, seeking for milk, looking about for milk, who should pull a young cow by the teat. If he had an expectation he would be capable of obtaining milk by pulling the young cow by the teat. And if he were without an expectation . . . were both with an expectation and without . . . were neither with an expectation nor without he would be capable of obtaining milk by pulling the young cow by the teat. What is the reason for this ? This is the method, Bhūmija, for obtaining milk. In the same way, Bhūmija, if those recluses or brahmans who are of right view . . . fare the Brahma-faring with an expectation . . . without an expectation . . . both with an expectation and without . . . neither with an expectation nor without, they are capable of obtaining the fruit. What is the reason for this ? This is the method, Bhūmija, for obtaining the fruit.

Bhūmija, it is like a man walking about in need of butter, seeking for butter, looking about for butter who, having sprinkled curds into a jar, should swirl them around with a churning-stick. If he had an expectation he would be capable of obtaining butter by sprinkling curds into a jar and swirling them around with a churning-stick. And if he were without an expectation . . . were both with an expectation and without . . . were neither with an expectation nor without, he would be capable of obtaining butter by sprinkling curds into a jar and swirling them around with a churning-stick. What is the reason for this ? This is the method, Bhūmija, for obtaining butter. In the same way, Bhūmija, if those recluses or brahmans who are of right view . . . fare the Brahma-faring without an expectation . . . both with an expectation and without . . . neither with an expectation nor without, they are capable of obtaining the fruit. What is the reason for this ? This is the method, Bhūmija, for obtaining the fruit.

Bhūmija, it is like a man walking about in need of fire, seeking for fire, looking about for fire who, bringing an upper piece of fire-stick, should rub a dry sapless stick (with it).[1] And if he had an expectation he would be capable of obtaining fire by bringing an upper piece

---

[1] *Cf. M.* i. 242.

of fire-stick and rubbing a dry sapless stick (with it).[1] And if he were without an expectation, he would be capable of obtaining fire by bringing an upper piece of fire-stick and rubbing a dry sapless stick (with it). [144] And if he were both with an expectation and without . . . were neither with an expectation nor without, he would be capable of obtaining fire by bringing an upper piece of fire-stick and rubbing a dry sapless stick (with it). What is the reason for this? This is the method, Bhūmija, for obtaining fire. In the same way, Bhūmija, if those recluses or brahmans who are of right view . . . right concentration fare the Brahma-faring with an expectation, they are capable of obtaining the fruit. And if they fare the Brahma-faring without an expectation, they are capable of obtaining the fruit. And if they fare the Brahma-faring both with an expectation and without, they are capable of obtaining the fruit. And if they fare the Brahma-faring neither with an expectation nor without, they are capable of obtaining the fruit. What is the reason for this ? This is the method, Bhūmija, for obtaining the fruit.

If, Bhūmija, these four similes[2] had occurred to you for Prince Jayasena, Prince Jayasena would naturally have trusted you and, having trust, would have acted in the manner of one having trust in you."

"But how could these four similes for Prince Jayasena have occurred to me, revered sir, seeing that they are spontaneous, that is to say to the Lord, and had never been heard before ?"[3]

Thus spoke the Lord. Delighted, the venerable Bhūmija rejoiced in what the Lord had said.

Discourse to Bhūmija:
The Sixth

---

[1] This phrase, from " And if," missed out in the text, is needed both for the balance of these expectation clauses and for that of this favourable fire-simile with the unfavourable one, no less than for that of the construction of all the simile-paragraphs.

[2] *Cf. M.* iii. 131 (two similes).

[3] This is a very curious ending to a Discourse, and seems little more than an absent-minded repetition of *M.* iii. 131.

127. DISCOURSE WITH ANURUDDHA
(Anuruddhasutta)

THUS have I heard: At one time the Lord was staying near Sāvatthī in the Jeta Grove in Anāthapiṇḍika's monastery. Then the carpenter Fivetools[1] addressed a certain man, saying: " Come you, my good man, approach the venerable Anuruddha; having approached him, in my name [145] salute the venerable Anuruddha's feet with your head and speak thus: ' Fivetools the carpenter, revered sir, salutes the venerable Anuruddha's feet with his head and speaks thus: Revered sir, may the venerable Anuruddha and three others[2] consent to a meal with Fivetools the carpenter on the morrow; and, revered sir, may the venerable Anuruddha arrive punctually as Fivetools the carpenter is very busy and has much to do that is to be done for the king.' "

And the man, having answered " Yes, sir," in assent to Fivetools the carpenter, approached the venerable Anuruddha; having approached and greeted the venerable Anuruddha, he sat down at a respectful distance. As he was sitting down at a respectful distance this man spoke thus to the venerable Anuruddha:

" Fivetools the carpenter salutes the venerable Anuruddha's feet with his head and speaks thus:

' Revered sir, may the venerable Anuruddha and three others consent to a meal with Fivetools the carpenter on the morrow; and, revered sir, may the venerable Anuruddha arrive punctually as Fivetools the carpenter is very busy and has much to do that is to be done for the king.' " The venerable Anuruddha consented by becoming silent.

Then the venerable Anuruddha, towards the end of that night, having dressed in the early morning, taking his bowl and robe approached the abode of Fivetools the carpenter; having approached, he sat down on the appointed seat. Then Fivetools the carpenter with his own hand served and satisfied the venerable Anuruddha with sumptuous food, solid and soft. And when the venerable Anuruddha had eaten and had withdrawn his hand from the bowl,

---

[1] *Pañcakaṅga.* See *M.* i. 386.   [2] *attacatuttho* as at *M.* i. 383.

Fivetools the carpenter, taking a low seat, sat down at a respectful distance. As Fivetools the carpenter was sitting down at a respectful distance, he spoke thus to the venerable Anuruddha:

" Now, revered sir, monks who are elders, have approached me and spoken thus: ' Householder, develop boundless[1] freedom of mind.' Some elders spoke thus: ' Householder, develop widespread[2] freedom of mind.' Revered sir, as to boundless freedom of mind and widespread freedom of mind—are these states different in connotation as well as [146] different in denotation, or are they identical in connotation and different only in denotation ?"[3]

" Well then, householder, speak forth what occurs to you about this; from doing so it will become clear to you."

" Revered sir, it occurs to me thus: That which is boundless freedom of mind and that which is widespread freedom of mind— these states are identical in connotation, differing only in denotation."

" Householder, as to that which is boundless freedom of mind and that which is wisespread freedom of mind—these states are different in connotation as well as different in denotation. Wherefore, householder, this should be understood according to the method whereby these states are different in connotation as well as different in denotation.

And what, householder, is boundless freedom of mind ? As to this, householder, a monk abides, having suffused the first quarter with a mind of friendliness, likewise the second, likewise the third, likewise the fourth; just so above, below, across; he abides, having suffused the whole world everywhere and in every way with a mind of friendliness that is far-reaching, widespread, immeasurable, without enmity, without malevolence. He abides, having suffused the first quarter with a mind of compassion . . . with a mind of sympathetic joy . . . with a mind of equanimity . . . far-reaching, widespread, immeasurable, without enmity, without malevolence. This, householder, is called boundless freedom of mind.

And what, householder, is widespread freedom of mind ? As to this, householder, a monk, thinking (meditation) is widespread like as a single root of a tree, dwells suffusing and pervading (that size in meditation).[4] This, householder, is called the freedom of mind

---

[1] Defined at *M*. i. 297. *Appamāṇa* is " boundless " or " immeasurable."
[2] *Mahaggata*. This and *appamāṇa* are two words regularly connected with the *brahmavihāra*.
[3] *Cf. M.* i. 297.   [4] On *pharitvā adhimuccitvā* see Intr., p. xx.

that is widespread. As to this, householder, a monk, thinking (meditation) is widespread like as two or three roots of a tree ... like as one village-field ... [147] ... like as two or three village-fields ... like as one kingdom ... like as two or three kingdoms, dwells suffusing and pervading (that size in meditation). This, householder, is called the freedom of mind that is widespread. As to this, householder, a monk, thinking (meditation) is widespread like as the sea-girt earth, abides suffusing and pervading (that size in meditation). This, householder, is called the freedom of mind that is widespread. Wherefore, householder, this should be understood according to the method whereby these states are different in connotation as well as different in denotation.

These, householder, are four uprisings into a (new) becoming. What four ? As to this, householder, someone, thinking of limited light, abides suffusing and pervading (it in meditation); at the breaking up of the body after dying he arises in companionship with the Devas of limited Light. As to this, householder, someone, thinking of boundless light,[1] abides suffusing and pervading (it in meditation); at the breaking up of the body after dying he arises in companionship with the Devas of boundless Light. As to this, householder, someone, thinking of tarnished Light, abides suffusing and pervading (it in meditation); at the breaking up of the body after dying he arises in companionship with the Devas of tarnished Light. As to this, householder, someone, thinking of pure light, abides suffusing and pervading (it in meditation); at the breaking up of the body after dying he arises in companionship with the Devas of pure Light. These, householder, are four uprisings into a (new) becoming.

There is a time, householder, when those that are *devatās* gather together; when they are gathered together a difference in colour[2] can be seen but not a difference in light. It is as though, householder, a man should take several oil-lamps into a house; when they are being taken into the house a difference in flame would be discernible but not a difference in light. Even so, householder, at the time when those that are *devatās* gather together, [148] when they are gathering together a difference in colour can be seen but not a difference in light. There is a time, householder, when those that are

---

[1] Text's reading *appamāṇā ti* should be *appamāṇābhā ti*, for which there is commentarial support as well as the gaining of the necessary textual consistency.

[2] Of their bodies, *sarīra, MA.* iv. 201.

devatās go away from there; when they are going away from there not only can a difference in colour be seen but also a difference in light. It is as though, householder, a man should take out those several oil-lamps from that house; when these are being taken out from there not only would a difference in flame be discernible but also a difference in light. Even so, householder, there is a time when those that are *devatās* go away from there; when they are going away from there not only can a difference in colour be seen but also a difference in light. Householder, this does not occur to those *devatās*: ' This is permanent or steadfast or eternal for us.' Moreover, wherever it may be that these *devatās* are dwelling it is there that these *devatās* enjoy themselves. As, householder, it does not occur to flies as they are being borne along on a pingo[1] or basket: ' This is permanent or steadfast or eternal for us,' and as, moreover, wherever it may be that those flies are living it is there that these flies enjoy themselves; in the same way, householder, it does not occur to those *devatās*: ' This is permanent or steadfast or eternal for us,' and, moreover, wherever it may be that those *devatās* are dwelling it is there that these *devatās* enjoy themselves."

When this had been said, the venerable Abhiya Kaccāna[2] spoke thus to the venerable Anuruddha: " It is good, revered Anuruddha, but I have something further to ask on this matter. Are those that are Devas of Light, revered sir, all of limited Light or are there some *devatās* of boundless Light ?"

" According to circumstances,[3] reverend Kaccāna, some *devatās* there are of limited Light but other *devatās* there are of boundless Light."

" What is the cause, revered Anuruddha, what the reason that, although these *devatās* have uprisen into a single class of *devatās*, there are **[149]** some *devatās* there of limited Light and other *devatās* there of boundless Light ?"

" Well then, reverend Kaccāna, on this matter I will ask you a question in return. As it pleases you so you may answer it. What do you think about this, reverend Kaccāna ? This that the monk, when thinking (meditation) is widespread like as a single root of

---

[1] For carrying conjey, rice, oil, butter, fish, meat, *MA*. iv. 202.

[2] A variant reading calls him Sabhiya Kaccāna; this is adopted by *D.P.P.N.* (s.v. Sabhiya 3). There is a Sabhiya Kaccāna at *S*. iv. 401 *f.* See also *K.S.* iv. p. 292, *n.* 3.

[3] *tadaṅgena*; explained at *MA*. iv. 202 as *tassā bhavupapattiyā aṅgena*, according to the character of their uprising in a (new) becoming.

a tree, abides suffusing and pervading (that size in meditation); and this that the monk, when thinking (meditation) is widespread like as two or three roots of a tree, abides suffusing and pervading (that size)—of these two developments of mind[1] which is the more widespread ?"

" This that the monk, revered sir, when thinking (meditation) is widespread like as two or three roots of a tree, abides suffusing and pervading (that size)—this of these two developments of mind is the more widespread."

" What do you think about this, reverend Kaccāna ? This that the monk, when thinking (meditation) is widespread like as two or three roots of a tree, abides suffusing and pervading (that size in meditation); and this that the monk, when thinking (meditation) is widespread like as a single village-field, abides suffusing and pervading (that size)—of these two developments of mind which is the more widespread ?"

" This that the monk, revered sir, when thinking (meditation) is widespread like as a single village-field, abides suffusing and pervading (that size)—this of these two developments of mind is the more widespread."

" What do you think about this, reverend Kaccāna ? This that the monk, when thinking (meditation) is widespread like as a single village-field, abides suffusing and pervading (that size in meditation); and this that the monk, when thinking (meditation) is widespread like as two or three village-fields, abides suffusing and pervading (that size)—of these two developments of mind which is the more widespread ?"

" This that the monk, revered sir, when thinking (meditation) is widespread like as two or three village-fields, abides suffusing and pervading (that size in meditation)—this of these two developments of mind is the more widespread."

" What do you think about this, reverend Kaccāna ? This that the monk, when thinking (meditation) is widespread like as two or three village-fields, [150] abides suffusing and pervading (that size in meditation); and this that the monk, when thinking (meditation) is widespread like as a single kingdom, abides suffusing and pervading (that size in meditation)—of these two developments of mind which is the more widespread ?"

" This that the monk, revered sir, when thinking (meditation) is

---

[1] *cittabhāvanānaṁ.*

widespread like as a single kingdom, abides suffusing and pervading (that size)—this of these two developments of mind is the more widespread."

"What do you think about this, reverend Kaccāna ? This that the monk, when thinking (meditation) is widespread like as a single kingdom, abides suffusing and pervading (that size in meditation); and this that the monk, when thinking (meditation) is widespread like as two or three kingdoms, abides suffusing and pervading (that size in meditation)—of these two developments of mind which is the more widespread ?"

"This that the monk, revered sir, when thinking (meditation) is widespread like as two or three kingdoms, abides suffusing and pervading (that size)—this of these two developments of mind is the more widespread."

"What do you think about this, reverend Kaccāna ? This that the monk, when thinking (meditation) is widespread like as two or three kingdoms, abides suffusing and pervading (that size in meditation); and this that the monk, when thinking (meditation) is widespread like as the sea-girt earth, abides suffusing and pervading (that size in meditation)—of these two developments of mind which is the more widespread ?"

"This that the monk, revered sir, when thinking (meditation) is widespread like as the sea-girt earth, abides suffusing and pervading (that size)—this of these two developments of mind is the more widespread."

"This is the cause, reverend Kaccāna, this is the reason that, although these *devatās* have uprisen into a single class of *devatās*, there are some *devatās* there of limited Light and other *devatās* there of boundless Light."

"It is good, revered Anuruddha, but I have something further to ask on this matter. Are those that[1] are Devas of Light, revered sir, all of tarnished Light, or are there some *devatās* there of pure Light ?"

[151] "According to circumstances, revered Kaccāna, some *devatās* there are of tarnished Light but other *devatās* there are of pure Light."

"What is the cause, revered Anuruddha, what the reason that, although these *devatās* have uprisen into a single class of *devatās*, there are some *devatās* there of tarnished Light and other *devatās* there of pure Light ?"

---

[1] The *yāvatā* of the text should read *yā tā* as on text p. 148.

"Well then, reverend Kaccāna, I will make a simile for you. For it is by a simile that some intelligent man here understands the meaning of what is said. It is as though, reverend Kaccāna, the oil of a burning oil-lamp is foul and the wick is foul. Because of the foulness of the oil and the foulness of the wick, (the lamp) burns but dimly. Even so, reverend Kaccāna, some monk here, thinking of tarnished light, abides suffusing and pervading (it in meditation); his bodily unchastity[1] is not properly suppressed, his sloth and torpor are not properly removed, and his restlessness and worry are not properly disciplined.[2] Because his bodily unchastity is not properly suppressed, and because his sloth and torpor are not properly removed, and because his restlessness and worry are not properly disciplined, he burns[3] but dimly. At the breaking up of the body after dying he arises in companionship with the Devas of tarnished Light. It is as though, reverend Kaccāna, the oil of a burning oil-lamp is pure and the wick is pure. Because of the purity of the oil and the purity of the wick, (the lamp) does not burn but dimly. Even so, reverend Kaccāna, some monk here, thinking of pure light, abides suffusing and pervading (it in meditation); his bodily unchastity is properly suppressed, and his sloth and torpor are properly removed, and his restlessness and worry are properly disciplined. Because his bodily unchastity is properly suppressed, and because his sloth and torpor are properly removed, and because his restlessness and worry are properly disciplined, he does not burn but dimly. At the breaking up of the body after dying he arises in companionship with the Devas of pure Light. [152] This, reverend Kaccāna, is the cause, this the reason that, although these *devatās* have uprisen into a single class of *devatās*, there are some *devatās* there of tarnished Light, and other *devatās* there of pure Light."

When this had been said, the venerable Abhiya Kaccāna spoke thus to the venerable Anuruddha: "It is good, revered Anuruddha.

---

[1] *kāyaduṭṭhulla*; called *kāyâlasiyābhāvo* at *MA*. iv. 202, " physical laziness."

[2] Restlessness and worry, and sloth and torpor are two of the five hindrances barring a man's attainment of the *jhāna*. I suspect that *kāyaduṭṭhulla* is here in place of the more usual *kāmacchanda*, desire for sense-pleasures, the first of these five hindrances.

[3] The verb *jhāyati* means both to burn and to meditate; but the former is from the Skrt. *kṣāyati* and the latter from *dhyāyati*. It seems however that *MA*. iv. 202 interprets *jhāyati* (the monk's "burning" or meditation) by *jalati*, to burn, to shine. This only shows that meditation, *jhāna*, is a state of mental incandescence, a burning up of what is to be got rid of, a consuming of it, so that the pure light can shine forth.

Revered sir, the venerable Anuruddha did not speak thus: ' Thus have I heard ' or ' It ought to be so.'[1] On the contrary, revered sir, the venerable Anuruddha merely said that these *devatās* are such and those *devatās* are thus. Revered sir, it occurs to me thus: The venerable Anuruddha must certainly have lived previously and talked previously and held converse previously with these *devatās*."

" This speech of yours, reverend Kaccāna, comes close and challenges me to a statement;[2] and I, moreover, will answer you. For a long time have I, reverend Kaccāna, lived previously with these *devatās* and talked previously to them and held converse previously with them."[3]

When this had been said, the venerable Abhiya Kaccāna spoke thus to Fivetools the carpenter: " It is a gain for you, householder, it is well gotten by you, householder, that you got rid of the doubt you had and also obtained a chance to hear this disquisition on *dhamma*."

Discourse with Anuruddha:
The Seventh

128. DISCOURSE ON DEFILEMENTS
(Upakkilesasutta)

THUS have I heard:[4] At one time the Lord was staying near Kosambī in Ghosita's monastery. Now at that time the monks of Kosambī, who were disputatious, quarrelsome and contentious, lived wounding one another with the weapons of the tongue.[5] Then a certain monk approached the Lord; [**153**] having approached and greeted the Lord, he stood at a respectful distance. As he was standing at a respectful

---

[1] *evaṁ arahati bhavituṁ*.

[2] *āsajja upanīyavācā bhāsitā*, as at *A*. i. 172; see note at *G.S.* i. 156.

[3] *MA*. iv. 202 says that, fulfilling the excellences (*pāramiyo*), having gone forth in the going forth of sages, having practised the attainments, after 300 existences, he attained the Brahma-world.

[4] *Cf. Vin.* i. 341, 349 *ff.*, and see notes at *B.D.* iv. 488 *f.* and 498 *ff.*

[5] This is the same as the opening of the *Kosambiyasutta* (*M*. Sta. 48).

distance, this monk spoke thus to the Lord: " Revered sir, the monks of Kosambī, who are disputatious, quarrelsome and contentious, live wounding one another with the weapons of the tongue. It would be good, revered sir, if the Lord out of compassion were to approach these monks." The Lord consented by becoming silent. Then the Lord approached those monks and having approached, he spoke thus to those monks: " Enough, monks; no disputes, no quarrels, no contention, no argument."

When this had been said, a certain monk[1] spoke thus to the Lord: " Revered sir, let the Lord, the Dhamma-master, wait; revered sir, let the Lord, untroubled, abide intent on abiding in ease here and now,[2] for it is we who will be (held) accountable for this dispute, quarrel, contention and argument." And a second time ... And a third time the Lord spoke thus to those monks: " Enough, monks; no ... argument." And a third time did that monk speak thus to the Lord: " Revered sir, let the Lord, the Dhamma-master wait ... for it is we who will be (held) accountable for this dispute, quarrel, contention and argument."

Then the Lord,[3] having dressed early in the morning, taking his bowl and robe, entered Kosambī for almsfood. Having walked in Kosambī for almsfood and returning from the alms-gathering after the meal, he packed away his lodging and, taking his bowl and robe, spoke these verses as he was standing:

[154] " When all in chorus bawl, none feels a fool,
nor though the Order is divided, thinks otherwise.

With wandering wits the wiseacres range all the field of talk;
with mouths agape to full extent, what leads them on they know not.

They who (in thought) belabour this: That man
has me abused, has hurt, has worsted me,
has me despoiled: in these wrath's not allayed.

They who do not belabour this: That man
has me abused, has hurt, has worsted me,
has me despoiled: in them is wrath allayed.

---

[1] Called at *Vin.* i. 341 " one who spoke what was not-*dhamma*."
[2] See *M.L.S.* ii. Intr., p. xxvii *ff*.
[3] As at *Vin.* i. 349 *ff*. See *B.D.* iv. 498 *ff*. for notes.

Nay, not by wrath are wrathful moods allayed here (and) at
  any time,
but by not-wrath are they allayed: this is an (ageless) endless
  rule.

Some others don't discern that here we straitened are (in life,
  in time),
but those who do discern, thereby their quarrels are allayed.

Ruffians who maim and kill, steal cattle, steeds,
and wealth, who plunder realms—for these is concord.
Why should there not be for you?

If one find friend with whom to fare
Rapt in the well-abiding, apt,
surmounting dangers one and all,
with joy fare with him mindfully.

Finding none apt with whom to fare,
none in the well-abiding rapt,
as rajah quits the conquered realm,
fare lonely as bull-elephant in elephant-jungle.

Better the faring of one alone
than companionship with the foolish;
fare lonely, unconcerned, working no evil,
as bull-elephant in elephant-jungle."

Then the Lord, having spoken these verses as he was standing, approached Bālakaloṇakāra village. Now at that [155] time the venerable Bhagu was staying in Bālakaloṇakāra village. Then the venerable Bhagu saw the Lord coming from afar; seeing him, he made ready a seat and water for the feet. The Lord sat down on the seat made ready, and as he was sitting down he bathed his feet. Then the venerable Bhagu, having greeted the Lord, sat down at a respectful distance. The Lord spoke thus to the venerable Bhagu as he was sitting down at a respectful distance: " I hope, monk, things are going well with you, I hope you are keeping going, I hope you are not short of almsfood."

" Things are going well with me, Lord, I am keeping going, Lord, and I, revered sir, am not short of almsfood." Then the Lord, having delighted, rejoiced, roused, gladdened the venerable Bhagu with talk on *dhamma*, rising from his seat, approached the Eastern Bamboo Grove.

Now at that time[1] the venerable Anuruddha and the venerable Nandiya and the venerable Kimbila were staying in the Eastern Bamboo Grove. The keeper of the grove saw the Lord coming in the distance, and seeing him he spoke thus to the Lord: " Do not, recluse, enter this grove; there are three young men of family staying here desiring Self; do not cause them discomfort." But the venerable Anuruddha heard the keeper of the grove conferring with the Lord; on hearing him, he spoke thus to the keeper of the grove: " Do not, good grove-keeper, impede the Lord. It is our Teacher, the Lord, who is arriving." Then the venerable Anuruddha approached the venerable Nandiya and the venerable Kimbila, and having approached he spoke thus to the venerable Nandiya and the venerable Kimbila: " Go forward, venerable ones, go forward, venerable ones, our Teacher, the Lord, is arriving."

Then the venerable Anuruddha and the venerable Nandiya and the venerable Kimbila, went out to meet the Lord. One received his bowl and robe, one made ready a seat, one set out water for the feet. Then the Lord sat down on the seat made ready; as he was sitting down the Lord bathed his feet. Then these venerable ones, having greeted the Lord, sat down at a respectful distance. As the venerable Anuruddha was sitting down at a respectful distance, the Lord spoke thus:

" I hope things are going well with you, Anuruddhas,[2] I hope you are keeping going, I hope you are not short of almsfood ?"

[156] " Things are going well with us, Lord, we are keeping going, Lord, and, revered sir, we are not short of almsfood."

" I hope that you, Anuruddhas, are living all together on friendly terms and harmoniously, as milk and water blend, regarding one another with the eye of affection ?"

" Yes, certainly, revered sir, we are living all together on friendly terms and harmoniously, as milk and water blend, regarding one another with the eye of affection."

" And how is it that you, Anuruddhas, are living all together . . . regarding one another with the eye of affection ?"

" As to this, revered sir, it occurred to me: ' Indeed it is a gain for

---

[1] From here also at *M*. i. 205 *ff*. See *M.L.S*. i. 257 *ff*. for notes.

[2] The plural, Anuruddhā, is used in place of the names of the three separate monks.

me, indeed it is well gotten by me, that I am living with such fellow Brahma-farers.' On account of this, revered sir, for these venerable ones friendliness as to acts of body . . . acts of speech . . . acts of thought, whether openly or in private, has risen up in me. Because of this, revered sir, it occurred to me: ' Now, suppose that I, having surrendered my own mind, should live only according to the mind of these venerable ones ?' So I, revered sir, having surrendered my own mind, am living only according to the mind of these venerable ones. Revered sir, we have divers bodies, but assuredly only one mind."

And the venerable Nandiya and the venerable Kimbila too spoke thus to the Lord: " As to this, revered sir . . . Revered sir, we have divers bodies, but assuredly only one mind."

" Thus it is that we, revered sir, are living all together on friendly terms and harmoniously, as milk and water blend, regarding one another with the eye of affection."

" Good, it is good, Anuruddhas. But I hope that you, Anuruddhas, are living diligent, ardent, self-resolute ?"

[157] " Yes, certainly, revered sir, we are living diligent, ardent, self-resolute."

" And how is it that you, Anuruddhas, are living diligent, ardent, self-resolute ?"

" As to this, revered sir, whoever of us returns first from (going to) a village for almsfood makes ready a seat, sets out water for drinking and water for washing (the feet), and sets out a refuse-bowl. Whoever returns last from (going to) a village for almsfood, if there are the remains of a meal and if he so desires, he eats them; if he does not desire to do so, he throws them out where there are no crops, or he drops them into water where there are no living creatures; he puts up the seat, he puts away the water for drinking and the water for washing, he puts away the refuse-bowl, he sweeps the refectory. Whoever sees a vessel for drinking-water or a vessel for washing-water or a vessel (for water) for rinsing after evacuation, void and empty, he sets out (water). If it is impossible for him (to do this) by a movement of his hand, having invited a companion to help us by signalling (to him) with the hand, we set out (the water); but we do not, revered sir, for such a reason, break into speech. And then we, revered sir, once in every five nights sit down together for talk on *dhamma*. It is thus, revered sir, that we are living diligent, ardent, self-resolute."[1]

---

[1] *Vin.* i. 352 goes on differently from here.

"Good, it is good, Anuruddhas. But have you, Anuruddhas, while living thus diligent, ardent, self-resolute, attained states of further-men, the excellent knowledge and insight befitting the ariyans, an abiding in comfort ?"[1]

"As to this, we, revered sir, while living diligent, ardent, self-resolute, perceive the light-manifestation[2] as well as the appearance[3] of material shapes.[4] But soon the light-manifestation vanishes for us as well as the appearance of material shapes; and we do not understand the reason."[5]

"But the reason should be understood by you, Anuruddhas. I, too, Anuruddhas, before the Self-Awakening while I was yet the Bodhisatta, not fully awakened, perceived the light-manifestation as well as the appearance of material shapes. But soon the light-manifestation [158] vanished for me as well as the appearance of material shapes. Anuruddhas, this occurred to me: 'Now what is the cause, what the reason that the light-manifestation vanishes for me as well as the appearance of material shapes ?' Anuruddhas, this occurred to me: 'Doubt has arisen in me; and because there was

---

[1] *M*. i. 207 goes on differently from here.

[2] *obhāsa*. See Intr., p. xxi; *P.T.C.* s.v. *obhāsa* for further references; and also *A*. iv. 302 where *obhāsa* occurs and is translated at *G.S.* iv. 201 by E. M. Hare as "auras," and he quotes the Comy.: "rays known to the clairvoyant." The "clairvoyant" must be understood as one who, in meditation, has won the knowledge of *deva*-vision; it is with this that he "sees," *cf*. *MA*. iv. 207: *dibbacakkhunā rūpadassanañ ca sañjānāma*. Nyanatiloka, in *Bud. Dicty.*, says, s.v. *obhāsa*, "Effulgence of light, Aura appearing at times during deep Insight (*vipassanā*) may become a 'defilement of insight,' *vipassanūpakkilesa*." *Obhāsa* is a difficult word for a translator and its meaning or meanings, for these seem to vary from context to context, need further investigation. "Effulgence of light" is perhaps rather too strong, and "aura" can hardly be accepted as the right rendering. Nor will "light" do for, though light is implied, there is the definite and important word *āloka*. This and *obhāsa* occur in the same passage at *D*. i. 220 and certainly appear to have different meanings. At *M*. iii. 120 I have translated *obhāsa* in a context that has nothing to do with meditation as "radiance," that is "effulgence of light," and for the above I tentatively suggest light-manifestation or light-radiation; see under *avabhāsa* in the Skrt. lexicons. According to *MA*. iv. 207 the *obhāsa* in this passage is preparatory, *parikammobhāsa*.

[3] *dassana*, appearance, showing.

[4] This appears to mean they are perceived extra-sensibly for *MA*. iv. 207 says "We perceive the appearance of material shapes through *deva*-vision ... seeing a variety of material shapes through *deva*-vision," and the whole passage points to processes in meditation.

[5] *nimitta*.

doubt, concentration fell away from[1] me; when concentration falls away, the light-manifestation vanishes as well as the appearance of material shapes. So I will act in such a way that doubt will not arise in me again.' So I, Anuruddhas, living diligent, ardent, self-resolute, perceived the light-manifestation as well as the appearance of material shapes. But soon the light-manifestation vanished for me as well as the appearance of material shapes. Anuruddhas, this occurred to me: ' Now, what is the cause, what the reason that the light-manifestation vanishes for me as well as the appearance of material shapes ?' Anuruddhas, this occurred to me: ' Lack of proper attention[2] has arisen in me; and because there was lack of proper attention, concentration fell away from me; when concentration falls away, the light-manifestation vanishes as well as the appearance of material shapes. So I will act in such a way that doubt will not arise in me again nor lack of proper attention.' So I, Anuruddhas ... material shapes. Anuruddhas, this occurred to me: ' Sloth and torpor has arisen in me; and because there was sloth and torpor, concentration fell away from me; when concentration falls away, the light-manifestation vanishes as well as the appearance of material shapes. So I will act in such a way that doubt will not arise in me again, nor lack or proper attention nor sloth and torpor.' So I, Anuruddhas ... material shapes. Anuruddhas, this occurred to me: ' Consternation has arisen in me; and because there was consternation, concentration fell away from me; when concentration falls away, the light-manifestation vanishes as well as the appearance of material shapes.' Anuruddhas, it is as though a man were going along a high road and murderers should jump out at him from both sides; consternation would arise in him from such a source.[3] Even so, Anuruddhas, did consternation arise in me; and because there was consternation, concentration fell away from me; when concentration falls away, the light-manifestation vanishes as well as the appearance of material shapes. So I thought: ' I will act [159] in such a way that doubt will not arise in me again, nor lack of

---

[1] According to *MA*. iv. 207 this is *parikammasamādhi*, preparatory concentration. *Cavi*, which I have here rendered as " fell away," is the aorist of *cavati*, a verb used regularly for the passing, deceasing or falling from one existence (to be reborn in another). Above however it is clearly not being used in this special sense.

[2] *amanasikāra*.

[3] I follow the v.l.'s *tato nidānaṁ* in preference to the text's *ubhatonidānaṁ*, from both sources, perhaps thinking of the two murderers.

proper attention nor sloth and torpor nor consternation.' So I, Anuruddhas... material shapes. Anuruddhas, this occurred to me: 'Elation[1] has arisen in me; and because there was elation ... the light-manifestation vanishes as well as the appearance of material shapes.' Anuruddhas, it is as though a man who was seeking for one opening to (some hidden) treasure were to come at one and the same time on five openings to the treasure;[2] from that source elation would arise in him. Even so, Anuruddhas, elation arose in me; and because there was elation, concentration fell away from me; when concentration falls away, the light-manifestation vanishes as well as the appearance of material shapes. So I thought: 'I will act in such a way that doubt will not arise in me again, nor lack of proper attention nor sloth and torpor nor consternation nor elation.' So I, Anuruddhas, . . . material shapes. Anuruddhas, this occurred to me: 'Distress has arisen in me; and because there was distress ... the light-manifestation vanishes as well as the appearance of material shapes. So I will act in such a way that doubt will not arise in me again, nor lack of proper attention nor sloth and torpor nor consternation nor elation nor distress.' So I, Anuruddhas, . . . material shapes. Anuruddhas, this occurred to me: 'Too much energy[3] has arisen in me; and because there was too much energy, concentration fell away from me; when concentration falls away, the light-manifestation vanishes as well as the appearance of material shapes.' Anuruddhas, it is as though a man were to take such a tight grip of a quail that it died then and there. Even so, Anuruddhas, did too much energy arise in me; and because there was too much energy... the light-manifestation vanishes as well as the appearance of material shapes. So I thought: 'I will act in such a way that doubt will not arise in me again, nor lack of proper attention nor sloth and torpor nor consternation nor elation nor distress nor too much energy.' So I, Anuruddhas, . . . material shapes. Anuruddhas, this occurred to me: 'Too feeble an energy [**160**] has arisen in me; and because there was too feeble an energy . . . the light-manifestation vanishes as well as the appearance of material shapes . . .' Anuruddhas, it is as though a man were to take such a loose

---

[1] *ubbilla*, pleasurable excitement. The word appears to occur only here in the Pali canon, although *ubbillāvitatta* occurs at *M.* i. 140 and a few other passages.

[2] *Cf. M.* i. 352.

[3] On too much and too little energy, see the Parable of the Lute, *Vin.* i. 182, *A.* iii. 375.

grip of a quail that it could fly up out of his hand. Even so, Anuruddhas, did too feeble an energy arise in me; and . . . the light-manifestation vanishes as well as the appearance of material shapes. So I thought: ' I will act in such a way that doubt will not arise in me again, nor . . . too much energy nor too feeble an energy.' So I, Anuruddhas, . . . material shapes. Anuruddhas, this occurred to me: ' Longing[1] has arisen in me; and because there was longing . . . the light-manifestation vanishes as well as the appearance of material shapes. So I will act in such a way that doubt will not arise in me again, nor . . . too feeble an energy nor longing.' So I, Anuruddhas . . . material shapes. Anuruddhas, this occurred to me: ' Perception of diversity has arisen in me; and because there was perception of diversity . . . the light-manifestation vanishes as well as the appearance of material shapes. So I will act in such a way that doubt will not arise in me again, nor . . . longing nor perception of diversity.' So I, Anuruddhas, living diligent, ardent, self-resolute, perceived the light-manifestation as well as the appearance of material shapes. But soon the light-manifestation vanished for me as well as the appearance of material shapes. Anuruddhas, this occurred to me: ' Now, what is the cause, what the reason that the light-manifestation vanishes for me as well as the appearance of material shapes ?' Anuruddhas, this occurred to me: ' A state of being too intent on material shapes has arisen in me; and because there was a state of being too intent on material shapes, concentration fell away from me; when concentration falls away, the light-manifestation vanishes as well as the appearance of material shapes. So I will act in such a way that doubt will not arise in me again, nor . . . perception of diversity nor the state of being too intent on material shapes.'

So I, Anuruddhas, knowing that doubt is a defilement of the mind,[2] got rid of the defilement of the mind that is doubt. Knowing that lack of proper attention is a defilement of the mind, I got rid of the defilement of the mind that is lack of proper attention. Knowing that sloth and torpor is a defilement of the mind . . . that consternation is a defilement of the mind . . . that elation is a defilement of the mind . . . that distress is a defilement of the mind . . . that too much

---

[1] *abhijappā*, explained at *MA*. iv. 208 by *taṇhā*, arising when one has made the light, *āloka*, increase as far as the confines of the *deva*-world and has seen a company of *devas*. The word also occurs at *Dhs*. 1059, *Vbh*. 361.

[2] None of these states appears as a defilement of the mind, *cittassa upakkilesa*, at *M*. i. 36.

energy is a defilement of the mind . . . that too feeble an energy is a defilement of the mind . . . that longing is a defilement of the mind . . . that perception of diversity is a defilement of the mind, I got rid of the defilement of the mind that is perception of diversity. Knowing that the state of being too intent on material shapes [**161**] is a defilement of the mind, I got rid of the defilement of the mind that is the state of being too intent on material shapes.

So I, Anuruddhas, living diligent, ardent, self-resolute, perceived the light-manifestation but did not see material shapes; then for a whole night and a whole day and a whole night and day I saw material shapes but did not perceive the light-manifestation. Concerning this, Anuruddhas, it occurred to me: ' Now, what is the cause, what the reason that I perceived the light-manifestation but did not see material shapes; and then for a whole night and a whole day and a whole night and day I saw material shapes but did not perceive the light-manifestation ?' Concerning this, Anuruddhas, it occurred to me: ' It was at the time when I, not paying proper attention to the reflex-image of material shapes,[1] was paying attention to the reflex-image of the light-manifestation that I perceived the light-manifestation but did not see material shapes. But it was at the time when I, not paying proper attention to the reflex-image of the light-manifestation, was paying attention to the reflex-image of material shapes that, for a whole night and a whole day and a whole night and day, I saw material shapes but did not perceive the light-manifestation.'

So I, Anuruddhas, living diligent, ardent, self-resolute, both perceived a limited light-manifestation[2] and saw a limited (number of) material shapes; and for a whole night and a whole day and a whole night and day I perceived a boundless light-manifestation and saw a boundless (number of) material shapes. Concerning this, it occurred to me, Anuruddhas: ' Now, what is the cause, what the reason that I both perceive a limited light-manifestation and see a limited (number of) material shapes as well as for a whole night and a whole day and a whole night and day perceive a boundless light-manifestation and see a boundless (number of) material shapes ?' Concerning this, it occurred to me, Anuruddhas: ' At the time when concentration is limited my vision is limited, so with limited vision

---

[1] *rūpanimitta.* Probably *nimitta* is here the reflex-image which, by means of certain exercises in concentration, appears as if seen by the eye.

[2] *paritta obhāsa*, explained at *MA.* iv. 209 as *parittakammaṭṭhāne obhāsaṁ*, light-manifestation in regard to a limited object of meditational exercise.

I both perceive a limited light-manifestation and see a limited (number of) material shapes. But at the time when my concentration is not limited my vision is boundless, so with boundless vision for a whole night and a whole day and a whole night and day I both perceive a boundless light-manifestation and see a boundless (number of) material shapes.'

When [**162**] I knew, Anuruddhas, that doubt was a defilement of the mind, the defilement of the mind that is doubt was got rid of. When I knew that lack of proper attention was a defilement of the mind, the defilement of the mind that is lack of proper attention was got rid of. When I knew that sloth and torpor ... consternation ... elation ... distress ... too much energy ... too feeble an energy ... longing ... perception of diversity was a defilement of the mind, the defilement of the mind that is perception of diversity was got rid of. When I knew that the state of being too intent on material shapes was a defilement of the mind, the defilement of the mind that is the state of being too intent on material shapes was got rid of. Concerning this, it occurred to me, Anuruddhas: 'Those that were defilements of my mind are got rid of by me. Truly now I am developing concentration by three modes.'[1] So I, Anuruddhas, developed the concentration that has initial thought and discursive thought; and I developed the concentration that is without initial thought and has only discursive thought;[2] and I developed the concentration that is without initial thought and without discursive thought. And I developed the concentration that has rapture;[3] and

---

[1] These are usually taken to be the first three of the following modes of concentration, *samādhi*. At *Kvu.* 413 it is agreed that these three (forms of) *samādhi* were spoken of by the Lord: *e.g.* at *D.* iii. 219, above (*M.* iii. 162), *S.* iv. 360, *A.* iv. 300 which last is identical with *M.* iii. 162 and appears to speak of seven forms of *samādhi*. At *S.* iv. 360, 362-363 the three forms, among a number of other attainments, are called the Way leading to the Uncompounded. See also *A.* iv. 440 *ff.*, *Miln.* 337, *Vism.* 95; and *Pts. Contr.* p. 239, *n.* 1, *Bud. Psych. Ethics*, p. 52, *n.* 1, *Comp.* p. 85; and also *A.* i. 299, *n.* 2.

[2] This has reference to the fivefold system of *jhāna*, obtained by successive instead of simultaneous elimination of *vitakka* and *vicāra*. This happens in the second *jhāna*, but the " three (forms of) *samādhi* in *jhāna* occur both in the (more usual) fourfold system of *jhāna* as well as in the fivefold," *MA.* iv. 209.

[3] *sappītika*. This belongs to the second and third *jhānas*, *MA.* iv. 209, but according to *AA.* ii. 153 it is the happiness, *sukha*, of the first and second *jhānas*. This, and the three succeeding forms of concentration are also mentioned at *A.* iv. 300 *f.*, while at *A.* i. 91 they form two of the various forms of happiness, *dve sukhāni*: the happiness without rapture being chief over that with rapture, and the happiness of even-mindedness or equanimity being chief over the happiness of delight, *sāta*.

I developed the concentration that is without rapture;[1] and I developed the concentration that is accompanied by delight;[2] and I developed the concentration that is accompanied by equanimity.[3] When, Anuruddhas, there was developed in me the concentration that has initial and discursive thought, when there was developed the concentration that is without initial thought and has only discursive thought, when there was developed the concentration that is without initial thought and without discursive thought, and when there was developed the concentration that has rapture, and when there was developed the concentration that is without rapture, and when there was developed the concentration that is accompanied by delight, and when there was developed the concentration that is accompanied by equanimity, then the knowledge and vision arose in me: Unshakable is freedom of mind for me, this is the last birth, there is not now again-becoming."

Thus spoke the Lord. Delighted, the venerable Anuruddha rejoiced in what the Lord had said.

Discourse on Defilements:
The Eighth

---

[1] The *samādhi* of the third and fourth *jhānas*, *MA*. iv. 209; the *sukha* of these at *AA*. ii. 153.

[2] *sāta*; again belonging to the third and fourth *jhānas*, *MA*. iv. 209; but *AA*. ii. 153 discriminates, saying *sātasukha* is happiness among the three *jhānas*, while *upekhāsukha* is the happiness of the fourth *jhāna*. At *Vism*. 85 *sukha* takes the place of *sāta*.

[3] *upekhā*. *MA*. iv. 209 says " this belongs to the fourth *jhāna* in the fourfold system, and to the fifth in the fivefold system. But when did the Lord develop this threefold *samādhi* ? During the last watch (of the night) when he was sitting at the root of the great Bo-tree. His first Way is connected with the first *jhāna*, his second, third and fourth Ways with the second, third and fourth *jhānas*. In the fivefold system there is no way of the fifth *jhāna*." Are the three modes of *samādhi* really (1) that connected with initial and discursive thought, (2) that connected with rapture, (3) that connected with delight and equanimity ? (Or are they taken to be so in this Discourse ?) On this point see the numbered classification of *samādhi* at *Vism*. 85. See also above, Intr., p. xxii.

129. DISCOURSE ON FOOLS AND THE WISE
(Bālapaṇḍitasutta)

[163] THUS have I heard: At one time the Lord was staying near Sāvatthī in the Jeta Grove in Anāthapiṇḍika's monastery. While he was there the Lord addressed the monks, saying: "Monks." "Revered One," these monks answered the Lord in assent. The Lord spoke thus:

"Monks, these are the three marks of a fool,[1] signs of a fool, stamps of a fool. What three? As to this, monks, a fool is one thinking wrong thoughts,[2] speaking wrong words,[3] a doer of deeds wrongly done.[4] If, monks, a fool were not one thinking wrong thoughts, speaking wrong words, and a doer of deeds wrongly done, how could the wise know of him: This fine fellow is a fool, not a true man? It is because, monks, a fool is one thinking wrong thoughts ... and a doer of deeds wrongly done, that the wise know of him: This fine fellow is a fool, not a true man.

Monks, he who is a fool experiences a threefold anguish and dejection here and now. If, monks, a fool is sitting down in an assembly room or by a carriage-road or at a cross-roads and if the people there held appropriate suitable talk about him and if, monks, the fool were one who made onslaught on creatures, were a taker of what had not been given, one who behaved wrongly in regard to sense-pleasures, a liar, and one given up to occasions for sloth consequent upon (drinking) arrack, toddy and strong liquor, and if, monks, it then occurs to that fool: 'These people are holding an appropriate suitable talk about me, for these states exist in me and I engage in[5] these states,' this, monks, is the first (kind of) anguish and dejection that the fool experiences here and now.

And again, monks, a fool sees kings who, having arrested a thief, an evil-doer, are meting out various punishments:[6] [164] they lash

---

[1] This description of a fool also occurs at *A.* i. 102.
[2] Thoughts connected with covetousness, malevolence and wrong views, *MA.* iv. 210.
[3] Lying words and so on.   [4] Making onslaught on creatures and so on.
[5] *sandissāmi*, or to agree to, live conformably with, connive at.
[6] As at *M.* i. 87. See *M.L.S.* i. 115 for further references.

him with whips and they lash him with canes and they lash him with (birch) rods, and they cut off his hand . . . his foot . . . his hand and foot . . . his ear . . . his nose . . . his ear and nose, and they give him the ' gruel-pot ' punishment . . . the ' shell-tonsure ' punishment . . . ' Rāhu's mouth ' . . . the ' fire-garland ' . . . the ' flaming hand ' . . . the ' hay-twist ' . . . the ' bark-dress ' . . . the ' antelope ' . . . ' flesh-hooking ' . . . the ' disc-slice ' . . . the ' pickling process ' . . . ' circling the pin ' . . . and they give him the ' straw-mattress,' and they spray him with burning oil, give him as food to the dogs, impale him alive on stakes, and they decapitate him with a sword. Thereupon, monks, it occurs to the fool: ' Because of such and such evil deeds kings, having arrested a thief, an evil-doer, mete out various punishments: they lash him with whips . . . and they decapitate him with a sword. But these states exist in me and I engage in these states. So if kings should know about me, they might have me arrested too, and mete out various punishments: they might lash me with whips and they might lash me with canes . . . and they might decapitate (me) with a sword.' This, monks, is the second (kind of) anguish and dejection that the fool experiences here and now.

And again, monks, while a fool is on a chair or bed or lying on the ground, at such a time those evil deeds that he has formerly wrongly done by body, speech and thought rest on him, lie on him, settle on him.[1] Monks, as at eventide the shadows of the great mountain peaks rest, lie and settle on the earth, so, monks, do these evil deeds that the fool has formerly wrongly done by body, speech and thought rest, lie and settle on him as he is on a chair or bed or lying on the ground. [165] Thereupon, monks, it occurs thus to the fool: ' Indeed what is lovely has not been done by me,[2] what is skilled has not been done, no refuge against fearful (consequences)[3] has been made, evil has been done, cruelty has been done, violence has been done. Insofar as there is a bourn for those who have not done what is lovely, have not done what is skilled, have not made a refuge against fearful (consequences), who have done evil, cruelty and violence, to that bourn I am going hereafter.' He grieves, mourns, laments, beats his breast, wails and falls into disillusionment. This,

---

[1] *olambanti ajjholambanti abhippalambanti.* The second of these words occurs at *S.* iii. 137 and is translated at *K.S.* iii. 116 by " overhangs " which suits the context there.

[2] With this passage *cf. A.* ii. 174, *Iti.* p. 25.

[3] *bhīruttāṇa; cf. Iti.* p. 25, *Vin.* iii. 72. See *B.D.* i. 124, *n.* 1; *VinA.* 436, *AA.* iii. 161.

monks, is the third (kind of) anguish and dejection that the fool experiences here and now.

He, monks,[1] who is a fool, having fared wrongly in body, having fared wrongly in speech, having fared wrongly in thought, at the breaking up of the body after dying arises in the sorrowful ways, the bad bourn, the Downfall, Niraya Hell. Anyone, monks, speaking rightly of him would say he is thoroughly undesirable, thoroughly disagreeable, thoroughly unpleasant, as in speaking rightly of Niraya Hell he would say it is thoroughly undesirable, thoroughly disagreeable, thoroughly unpleasant. As to this, monks, even a simile is not easy, so many are the anguishes of Niraya Hell."

When this had been said, a certain monk spoke thus to the Lord: " But is it possible to make a simile for me, revered sir ?"

" It is possible, monk," the Lord said. " It is as though, monk, men should arrest a thief, an evil-doer, and bring him before the king, with the words: ' This, sire, is a thief, an evil-doer to you. Decree for him whatever punishment you wish,' and the king should speak thus concerning him: ' Go along, good sirs, stab[2] this man early in the morning with a hundred spears.' And early in the morning they would stab him with a hundred spears. Then at midday the king would speak thus: ' My good fellows, how is that man ?' ' He is still alive, sire.' Then the king would speak thus concerning him: ' Go along, good sirs, stab this man at midday with a hundred spears.' And at midday they would stab him with a hundred spears. Then towards evening the king would speak thus: ' My good fellows, how is that man ?' ' He is still alive, sire.' Then the king would speak thus concerning him: ' Go along, good sirs, stab this man towards evening with a hundred spears.' And towards evening [166] they would stab him with a hundred spears. What do you think about this, monks, would not that man, while he was being stabbed with three hundred spears, from that source experience anguish and dejection ?"

" That man, revered sir, being stabbed with only one spear from that source would experience anguish and dejection. How much more then[3] with three hundred spears ?"

---

[1] I think *bhikkhu* here should read *bhikkhave* as on text p. 171.

[2] *hanatha* cannot mean kill or destroy here, as in what follows, although they might stab or strike, *haneyyuṁ*, the thief, they do not manage to kill him at once. The idea of to stab or to thrust at is borne out at *MA*. iv. 211 which explains as " having pierced (where the spear) comes out, so that on each occasion two blows fall."

[3] *ko pana vādo*, who (can) say ?

Then the Lord, having picked up a small stone, the size of his hand, addressed the monks, saying: "What do you think about this, monks? Now, which is the greater, this small stone, the size of my hand, that I have picked up, or the Himalaya,[1] lord of mountains?"

"This small stone, revered sir, that the Lord picked up, the size of his hand, is insignificant; compared with the Himalaya, lord of mountains, it does not count, it does not amount even to an infinitesimal fraction (of it), it cannot even be compared (with it)."[2]

"Even so, monks, that anguish and dejection that that man experiences while he is being stabbed with three hundred spears, compared with the anguish of Niraya Hell does not count, it does not amount even to an infinitesimal fraction (of it), it cannot even be compared (with it). Monks, the guardians of Niraya Hell subject him to what is called the fivefold pinion.[3] They drive a red-hot iron stake through each hand and each foot and a red-hot iron stake through the middle of his breast. Thereat he feels feelings that are painful, sharp, severe. But he does not do his time[4] until he makes an end of that evil deed.

Then the guardians of Niraya Hell lay him down and plane him with adzes. Thereat he feels feelings that are painful, sharp, severe. But he does not do his time until he makes an end of that evil deed.

Then, monks, the guardians of Niraya Hell place him feet up and head down and plane him with razors. Thereat . . .

Then, monks, the guardians of Niraya Hell bind him to a chariot and drive him up and down over ground that is burning, aflame, ablaze. [167] Thereat . . .

Then, monks, the guardians of Niraya Hell push him up and down a great mountain slope of glowing cinders, burning, aflame, ablaze. Thereat . . .

Then, monks, the guardians of Niraya Hell take him, feet up and head down, and plunge him into a glowing brazen cauldron, burning, aflame, ablaze. There he is boiled and rises to the surface with the

---

[1] Himavā.   [2] *Cf. S.* ii. 263, v. 457; *Ud.* 23.

[3] Mentioned at *Jā.* i. 174. The following description of Niraya is also found at *M.* iii. 183, *A.* i. 141-142.

[4] *na ca tāva kālaṁ karoti yāva na taṁ pāpaṁ kammaṁ byantihoti.* The meaning is that he must do enough karmic time to work off the evil effects of evil deeds. So long as *kālaṁ karoti* is translated as "dies" a wrong impression is created. One may die and die again and again (*marati*) before one finishes one's karmic time for the effects of a deed may still be active in the next or subsequent "births."

scum. Boiling there and rising to the surface with the scum, he comes up once and goes down once and once he goes across. Thereat he feels feelings that are painful, sharp, severe. But he does not do his time until he makes an end of that evil deed.

Then, monks, the guardians of Niraya Hell toss him into the Great Niraya Hell. Now, monks, this Great Niraya Hell[1] (is so described):

> Four-cornered and with four gates,[2]
> It is divided into equal portions,
> Encircled by an iron wall, with a roof of iron above;
> Its incandescent floor is made of glowing iron;
> All round it stands a hundred *yojanas* square.[3]

In many a disquisition could I, monks, talk a talk about Niraya Hell, but it is not easy to describe in full,[4] monks, so many are the anguishes of Niraya Hell.

There are, monks, animals, breathing creatures that are grass-eaters. These eat moist and dry grasses, chewing them with their teeth. And which, monks, are the animals, the breathing creatures, that are grass-eaters ? Horses, cattle, asses, sheep, deer, and whatever other animals, breathing creatures there are that are grass-eaters. Monks, that fool who formerly enjoyed tastes here, having done evil deeds here, at the breaking up of the body after dying arises in companionship with those beings that are grass-eaters.

There are, monks, animals, breathing creatures that are dung-eaters. Having smelt the smell of dung from afar they run up, thinking: ' We will eat here, we will eat here.' Monks, it is like brahmans who run up at the smell of a sacrifice, thinking: ' We will eat here, we will eat here '—even so, monks, there are animals, breathing creatures that are dung-eaters. These having smelt [**168**] the smell of dung from afar run up, thinking: ' We will eat here, we will eat here.' And which, monks are the animals, the breathing creatures that are dung-eaters ? Cocks, swine, dogs, jackals, and whatever other animals, breathing creatures there are that are dung-eaters. Monks, that fool who formerly enjoyed tastes here,

---

[1] At *MA*. iv. 234, *AA*. ii. 232 Mahāniraya is called Avīci.

[2] *Cf. Vin*. ii. 203: *avīciniraya catudvāra*.

[3] *MA*. iv. 234 says this Avīci is 100 *yojanas* in length and 100 in width. The ground and the roof are bronze, and each wall is 99 *yojanas*. *Cf. Mhvu*. i. 9. The last line is quoted at *DhA*. i. 127.

[4] Even if one talked for a hundred or a thousand years, *MA*. iv. 213.

having done evil deeds here, at the breaking up of the body after dying arises in companionship with those beings that are dung-eaters.

There are, monks, animals, breathing creatures that are born in the dark, grow old in the dark and die in the dark. And which, monks, are the animals, the breathing creatures that are born, grow old and die in the dark? Beetles, maggots, earth-worms and whatever other animals, breathing creatures there are that are born, grow old and die in the dark. Monks, that fool who formerly enjoyed tastes here ... after dying arises in companionship with those beings that are born, grow old and die in the dark.

There are, monks, animals, breathing creatures that are born in water, grow old in water, die in water. And which, monks, are the animals, the breathing creatures that are born, grow old and die in water? Fishes, turtles, crocodiles and whatever other animals, breathing creatures there are that are born, grow old and die in water. Monks, that fool who formerly enjoyed tastes here ... after dying arises in companionship with those beings that are born, grow old and die in water.

There are, monks, animals, breathing creatures that are born in filth, grow old in filth, die in filth. And which, monks, are the animals, the breathing creatures that are born, grow old and die in filth? Those beings, monks, that are born in rotting fish or that grow old in rotting fish or that die in rotting fish; or in rotting carcases; or in rotting rice; or in a pool at the entrance to a village; or that are born in a dirty pool near a village ... or that die in a dirty pool near a village. Monks, that [**169**] fool who formerly enjoyed tastes here, having done evil deeds here, at the breaking up of the body after dying arises in companionship with those beings that are born in filth, grow old in filth, die in filth.

In many a disquisition could I, monks, talk a talk about animal birth, but it is not easy to describe in full, monks, so many are the anguishes of animal birth.

Monks, it is like a man who might throw a yoke with one hole[1] into the sea. An easterly wind might take it westwards, a westerly wind might take it eastwards, a northerly wind might take it southwards, a southerly wind might take it northwards. There might be

---

[1] *ekacchigaḷa yuga.* This simile is referred to at *Thīg.* 500, where the device is called *yugacchida.* It is also to be found at *S.* v. 455 where the wording is not quite the same as above. Also referred to at *Miln.* 204, *Asl.* 60. *Chiggaḷa* is a perforated device for archers to shoot their arrows through. *Cf. tāḷachiggaḷa* at *S.* v. 453.

a blind turtle there who came to the surface once in a hundred years. What do you think about this, monks ? Could that blind turtle push his neck through that one hole in the yoke ?"

" If at all,[1] revered sir, then only once in a very long while."

" Sooner or later, monks, could the blind turtle push his neck through the one hole in the yoke; more difficult than that, do I say, monks, is human status once again for the fool who has gone to the Downfall. What is the cause of that ? Monks, there is no *dhamma*-faring there, no even-faring, no doing of what is skilled, no doing of what is good. Monks, there is devouring of one another there and feeding on the weak.[2] Monks, if some time or other once in a very long while that fool came to human status (again), he would be born into those families that are low:[3] a family of low caste or a family of hunters or a family of bamboo-plaiters or a family of cartwrights or a family of refuse-scavengers,[4] in such a family as is needy, without enough to drink or to eat, where a covering for the back is with difficulty obtained. Moreover, he would be ill-favoured, ugly, dwarfish, sickly, blind or deformed or lame or paralysed; he would be unable to get food, drink, [170] clothes, vehicles, garlands, scents and perfumes, bed, dwelling, and lights; he would fare wrongly in body, wrongly in speech, wrongly in thought. Because he had fared wrongly in body, speech and thought, at the breaking up of the body after dying he would arise in the sorrowful ways, a bad bourn, the Downfall, Niraya Hell.

Monks, it is as though a gambler at the very first losing throw (at dice) were to lose his son, his wife and all his property and, further, were to undergo imprisonment himself. Insignificant, monks, is that losing throw by which the gambler at the very first losing throw were to lose his son, his wife and all his property and, further, were to undergo imprisonment himself. Greater than this is the losing throw by which the fool, having fared wrongly in body, wrongly in speech, wrongly in thought, at the breaking up of the body after dying arises in the sorrowful ways, the bad bourn, the Downfall, Niraya Hell. This, monks, is the fool's condition, completed in its entirety.[5]

---

[1] *yadi nūna*.   [2] *dubbalamārikā*, with v.l. *dubbalakhādikā*.
[3] *Cf. A.* i. 107.
[4] These five kinds of low birth occur at *M.* ii. 152, 183, *Vin.* iv. 6, *S.* i. 93, *A.* i. 107, ii. 85, *Pug.* 51.
[5] *MA.* iv. 214: the fool, having completed the three wrong ways (of acting, speaking and thinking), is reborn in Niraya. Because of " maturing " there

These, monks, are the three marks of a wise man, signs of a wise man, stamps of a wise man. What three ? As to this, monks, a wise man is one thinking right thoughts, speaking right words, and a doer of deeds rightly done. If, monks, a wise man were not one thinking right thoughts, speaking right words, a doer of deeds rightly done, how could the wise know of him: This worthy man is a wise man, a true man ? It is because, monks, a wise man is one thinking right thoughts . . . and a doer of deeds rightly done that the wise know of him: This worthy man is a wise man, a true man.

Monks, he who is a wise man experiences a threefold happiness and joy here and now. If, monks, the wise man is sitting down in an assembly room or by a carriage road or at a cross-roads and the people there held appropriate suitable talk about him, and if, monks, the wise man abstained from onslaught on creatures, from taking what had not been given, from wrong behaviour in regard to the sense-pleasures, [**171**] from lying, from occasions for sloth consequent upon (drinking) arrack, toddy and strong liquor, and if, monks, it thereupon occurred to the wise man: ' These people are holding an appropriate suitable talk about me; these states exist in me and I engage in these states '—this, monks, is the first (kind of) happiness and joy that the wise man experiences here and now.

And again, monks, a wise man sees kings who having arrested a thief, an evil-doer, are meting out various punishments: they lash him with whips . . . (*as on p. 164 of vol. iii*) . . . and they decapitate him with a sword. Thereupon, monks, it occurs to the wise man: ' Because of such and such evil deeds kings, having arrested a thief, an evil-doer, mete out various punishments: they lash him with whips . . . they decapitate him with a sword. But these states do not exist in me and I do not engage in these states.' This, monks, is the second (kind of) happiness and joy that the wise man experiences here and now.

And again, monks, while a wise man is on a chair or bed or lying on the ground, at such a time those lovely deeds that he has formerly rightly done by body, speech and thought rest on him, lie on him, settle on him. Monks, as at eventide the shadows of the great mountain peaks rest, lie and settle on the earth, so, monks, do those lovely deeds that the wise man has formerly rightly done by body,

---

he comes to human status, being reborn in one of the five low families; then having again completed the three wrong ways of behaving he is reborn in Niraya. This is the whole complete *bālabhūmi*, stage, level, condition, position or situation of a fool.

speech and thought rest, lie and settle on him as he is on a chair or bed or lying on the ground. Thereupon, monks, it occurs to the wise man: ' Indeed what is evil has not been done by me, cruelty has not been done, violence has not been done, what is lovely has been done, what is skilled has been done, a refuge against fearful (consequences) has been found. Insofar as there is a bourn for those who have not done evil, cruelty or violence, who have done what is lovely, what is skilled, and who have found a refuge against fearful (consequences), to that bourn I am going hereafter.' He does not grieve, mourn, lament, beat his breast, wail or fall into disillusionment. This, monks, is the third (kind of) happiness and joy that the wise man experiences here and now.

He, monks, who is a wise man, having fared rightly in body, speech and thought, [172] at the breaking up of the body after dying arises in a good bourn, a heaven world. Anyone, monks, speaking rightly of him would say: ' Thoroughly desirable, thoroughly agreeable, thoroughly pleasant,' as in speaking rightly of heaven he would say: ' Thoroughly desirable, thoroughly agreeable, thoroughly pleasant.' As to this, monks, even a simile is not easy, so many are the happinesses of heaven."

When this had been said, a certain monk spoke thus to the Lord: " But is it possible, revered sir, to make a simile ?"[1]

" It is possible, monk," the Lord said. " It is as though, monk, a wheel-rolling king,[2] endowed with seven Treasures and four efficacies,[3] should experience happiness and joy from that source. From what seven ?

As to this, monk, when a noble anointed king has bathed his head on an Observance day, the fifteenth, and has gone for the Observance to an upper storey of his palace, there then appears the *deva*-like Treasure of the Wheel with its nave, its tyres and all its thousand spokes complete. On seeing it, this occurs to the noble anointed king: ' I have heard this, that if a noble anointed king has bathed his head on an Observance day, the fifteenth, and has gone for the Observance to an upper storey of his palace, and there then appears

---

[1] *me*, for me, as on text p. 165 is omitted here.

[2] From here to the top of text p. 177 occurs also at *D*. ii. 174-178. See notes at *Dial*. ii. pp. 202 *ff*.

[3] *iddhi*. As will be seen in the context below " there is nothing supernatural about these Iddhis " (*Dial*. ii. 208, *n*. 2). They are attributes or endowments, capabilities, competences or prerogatives adding to the efficacy, potency or dignity of a king.

the *deva*-like Treasure of the Wheel with its nave, its tyres, and all its thousand spokes complete, he becomes a wheel-rolling king. May I then be a wheel-rolling king.' Then, monks,[1] the noble anointed king rising from his seat, taking a ceremonial water jar in his left hand, with his right sprinkles (water) over[2] the Treasure of the Wheel, saying: ' May the honoured Treasure of the Wheel roll on, may the honoured Treasure of the Wheel be all-conquering.' Then, monks, the Treasure of the Wheel rolls on towards the eastern quarter and after it (goes) the wheel-rolling king together with a fourfold army. And wherever, monks, the Treasure of the Wheel stops, there the wheel-rolling king settles down together with the fourfold army. And, [**173**] monks, rival kings in the eastern quarter, having approached the wheel-rolling king, speak thus: ' Come, sire, you are welcome, sire, (all is) yours, sire, instruct (us), sire.' The wheel-rolling king speaks thus: ' Breathing things should not be killed, what has not been given should not be taken, wrong enjoyment of sense-pleasures should not be indulged in, lies should not be told, strong drink should not be drunk, and you should eat in moderation.'[3] And, monks, those rival kings of the eastern quarter become vassals of the wheel-rolling king. And then, monks, the Treasure of the Wheel, plunging into the eastern sea and rising out (of it again), rolls on to the southern quarter . . . plunging into the southern sea and rising out (of it again), rolls on to the western quarter . . . plunging into the western sea and rising out (of it again), rolls on to the northern quarter and after it (goes) the wheel-rolling king together with the fourfold army. And wherever, monks, the Treasure of the Wheel stops, there the wheel-rolling king settles down together with the fourfold army. And, monks, rival kings in the northern quarter, having approached the wheel-rolling king, speak thus: ' Come, sire, you are welcome, sire, (all is) yours, sire, instruct (us), sire.' The wheel-rolling king speaks thus: ' Breathing things should not be killed . . . and you should eat in moderation.' And, monks, those rival kings of the northern quarter become vassals of the wheel-rolling king. And then, monks, when the Treasure of the Wheel has conquered all the sea-girt earth, returning to that royal city itself, it stands as if fixed by the axle[4] to the gateway of the wheel-rolling king's palace, adorning the gateway of the wheel-

---

[1] Notice the change from *bhikkhu* to *bhikkhave*.
[2] *abbhukkirati*. See *P.E.D.* s.v.
[3] *yathābhuttañ ca bhuñjatha*; see *P.E.D.* s.v. *bhutta*.
[4] *Cf. A.* i. 112.

rolling king's palace. So, monks, does the Treasure of the Wheel appear to the wheel-rolling king.

And again, monks, the Treasure of the Elephant appears to the wheel-rolling king; it is all white, seven-fold firm, going through the sky by psychic potency, an elephant-king named Uposatha.[1] On seeing him the wheel-rolling king is pleased at heart and thinks: ' Glorious indeed is an elephant-vehicle, if he will submit to taming.' Then, monks, [**174**] that Treasure of an Elephant, like a fine thoroughbred elephant long since well tamed, submits to taming then and there. Once upon a time, monks, the wheel-rolling king, while testing that very Treasure of an Elephant, mounted it early one morning and it passed over the sea-girt earth and returned to that royal city itself in time for the morning meal. So, monks, does the Treasure of the Elephant appear to the wheel-rolling king.

And again, monks, the Treasure of the Horse appears to the wheel-rolling king; it is all white, with a head (as black as) a crow's, a dark mane, going through the sky by psychic potency, a king of horses named Valāha.[2] On seeing him the wheel-rolling king is pleased at heart and thinks: ' Glorious indeed is a horse-vehicle, if he will submit to taming.' Then, monks, . . . (*as above, reading* horse *for* elephant) . . . So, monks, does the Treasure of the Horse appear to the wheel-rolling king.

And again, monks, the Treasure of the Jewel[3] appears to the wheel-rolling king. It is an emerald jewel, of purest water, well cut into eight facets. And the light of that Treasure of the Jewel, monks, is shed all round for a *yojana*. Once upon a time, monks, the wheel-rolling king, in order to test that very Treasure of the Jewel, arrayed the fourfold army, raised aloft the jewel on the top of a standard and went out into the dense darkness of the night. And, monks, the villagers all around set about their daily work by its effulgence, thinking it to be day. So, monks, does the Treasure of the Jewel appear to the wheel-rolling king.

And again, monks, the Treasure of the Woman appears to the wheel-rolling king. She is lovely, good to look upon, charming, endowed with the greatest beauty of complexion; not too tall, not too short, [**175**] not too thin, not too stout, not too dark, not too

---

[1] *Cf. Jā.* iv. 232. The Comys. name two tribes of elephants from which the Elephant Treasure comes to a wheel-rolling king; if from the Uposatha tribe he is the eldest of the tribe, if from the Chaddanta the youngest. See *D.P.P.N.*

[2] See *Jā.* iv. 232.   [3] This comes from Vepulla Mountain, *Jā.* iv. 232, etc.

fair; surpassing human beauty, though she has not attained *deva*-like beauty. And the touch of the body of this Treasure of the Woman is such, monks, that it is like that of a tuft of cotton or a tuft of thistle-down. And, monks, the limbs of this Treasure of the Woman are warm when (the weather) is cool and cool when it is warm. The perfume of sandal-wood is wafted from the body of this Treasure of the Woman, monks; from her mouth is wafted the perfume of lotuses. And this Treasure of the Woman, monks, is one to get up earlier than the wheel-rolling king and retire later to rest, an obedient servant carrying out his pleasure, speaking affably.[1] And, monks, that Treasure of the Woman is never unfaithful to the wheel-rolling king even in thought, how then could she be physically ? So, monks, does the Treasure of the Woman appear to the wheel-rolling king.

And again, monks, the Treasure of the Householder[2] appears to the wheel-rolling king. As a result of *kamma* he has *deva*-like vision by which he sees treasure whether it has an owner or not. Approaching the wheel-rolling king, he speaks thus: ' Be you untroubled, sire, I will deal with your wealth as wealth should be dealt with.' Once upon a time, monks, the wheel-rolling king, in order to test this Treasure of the Householder, embarked in a boat, pushed out into the middle of the stream of the river Ganges, and spoke thus to the Treasure of the Householder: ' I have need, householder, of gold coins and gold.' ' Well then, your majesty, let the boat come in to one of the banks.' ' It is just here, householder, that I have need of gold coins and gold.' Then, monks, that Treasure of the Householder, touching the water with both his hands, drew up a jar full of gold coins and gold and spoke thus to the wheel-rolling king: ' Is this enough, your majesty, have I done enough, your majesty, is the service enough, your majesty ?' The wheel-rolling king spoke thus: ' It is enough, householder, you have done enough, householder, the service is enough, householder.' So, monks, does the Treasure of the Householder appear to the wheel-rolling king.

And again, monks, the Treasure of the Adviser[3] appears to the wheel-rolling king. [**176**] He is clever, experienced, wise; he is pro-

---

[1] As at *M*. ii. 84.
[2] *Dial.* ii. 206, *n*. 3 gives interesting reasons for translating *gahapati* here as Treasurer but, while hoping I will not " convey a wrong impression " of his functions, I incline more to the usual rendering of " householder."
[3] He is as the king's eldest son, *MA*. iv. 229.

ficient in procuring what should be procured for the wheel-rolling king, in removing what should be removed, in retaining what should be retained.[1] Having approached the wheel-rolling king, he speaks thus: 'Be you untroubled, sire, I will instruct (you).' So, monks, does the Treasure of the Adviser appear to the wheel-rolling king.

The wheel-rolling king, monks, is endowed with these seven Treasures.

And with what four efficacies?[2] As to this, monks, a wheel-rolling king is lovely, good to look upon, charming, endowed with the greatest beauty of complexion surpassing other men's. Monks, a wheel-rolling king is endowed with this first efficacy.

And again, monks, a wheel-rolling king is of long life, living long, surpassing other men. Monks, a wheel-rolling king is endowed with this second efficacy.

And again, monks, a wheel-rolling king has little illness, does not ail, is possessed of a good digestion that is neither too cold nor too hot,[3] surpassing other men's. Monks, a wheel-rolling king is endowed with this third efficacy.

And again, monks, a wheel-rolling king is dear to brahmans and householders and beloved by them. As, monks, fathers are dear to and beloved by their children, so, monks, is a wheel-rolling king dear to and beloved by brahmans and householders. And, monks, brahmans and householders are dear to and beloved by the wheel-rolling king. As, monks, children are dear to and beloved by their father, so, monks, are brahmans and householders dear to and beloved by the wheel-rolling king. Once upon a time, monks, a wheel-rolling king went out to a pleasure ground with a fourfold army. Then, monks, brahmans and householders, approaching the wheel-rolling king, spoke thus: 'Go on slowly, sire, that we may look on you for longer.' And, monks, the wheel-rolling king addressed the charioteer, saying: [177] 'Drive on slowly, charioteer, that I may look on the brahmans and householders for longer.' Monks, a wheel-rolling king is endowed with this fourth efficacy.

---

[1] The meaning of these three words in this passage: *upaṭṭhapetuṁ* (*D*. ii. 177 *upayāpetuṁ*), *apayāpetuṁ* and *ṭhapetuṁ*, is doubtful. In the absence of help from the Comys., they might also be rendered to appoint, dismiss and retain such a person as should be appointed to, dismissed from or retained in the king's service.

[2] There seems to be a sentence missing here, the equivalent of which occurs at *D*. ii. 177.

[3] Said of Raṭṭhapāla at *M*. ii. 67.

Monks, a wheel-rolling king is endowed with these four efficacies. What do you think about this, monks ? Does not a wheel-rolling king, endowed with these seven Treasures and these four efficacies, experience happiness and joy from that source ?"

" A wheel-rolling king, revered sir, if possessed of only one Treasure would experience happiness and joy from that source. How much more then from seven Treasures and four efficacies ?"

Then the Lord, having picked up a small stone the size of his hand, addressed the monks, saying: " What do you think about this, monks ? Now which is the greater, this small stone, the size of my hand, that I have picked up, or the Himalaya, lord of mountains ?"

" This small stone, revered sir, that the Lord has picked up, the size of his hand, is insignificant; compared with the Himalaya, lord of mountains, it does not count, it does not amount even to an infinitesimal fraction (of it), it cannot even be compared (with it)."

" Even so, monks, that happiness and joy that the wheel-rolling king experiences from the seven Treasures and the four efficacies, compared with *deva*-like happiness does not count, it does not amount to an infinitesimal fraction (of it), it cannot even be compared (with it). Monks, if sometime or other once in a very long while that wise man came to human status, he would be born into one of those families that are high: a family of rich nobles or a family of rich brahmans or a family of rich householders, in such a family as is well-to-do, of great possessions, of great resources, with abundant gold and silver, abundant means, abundant wealth in grains. Moreover, he would be lovely, good to look upon, charming, endowed with the greatest beauty of complexion; he would be able to get food, drink, clothes, vehicles, garlands, scents and perfumes, bed, dwelling and lights; he would fare rightly in body, rightly in speech, rightly in thought. Because [178] he had fared rightly in body, speech and thought, at the breaking up of the body after dying he would arise in a good bourn, a heaven world.

Monks, it is as though a gambler at the very first winning throw (at dice) were to win a great mass of possessions. Insignificant, monks is that winning throw by which the gambler at the very first winning throw were to win a great mass of possessions. Greater than this is the winning throw by which the wise man, having fared rightly in body, rightly in speech, rightly in thought, at the breaking up of the body after dying arises in a good bourn, the heaven world. This, monks, is the wise man's condition completed in its entirety."

Thus spoke the Lord. Delighted, these monks rejoiced in what the Lord had said.

Discourse on Fools and the Wise:
The Ninth

130. DISCOURSE ON THE DEVA-MESSENGERS[1]
(Devadūtasutta)

THUS have I heard: At one time the Lord was staying near Sāvatthī in the Jeta Grove in Anāthapiṇḍika's monastery. While he was there the Lord addressed the monks, saying: "Monks." "Revered One," these monks answered the Lord in assent. The Lord spoke thus:

"Monks, it is as if there were two houses with doors[2] and a man with vision standing there between them might see people entering a house and leaving it and going back and forth and walking across. Even so do I, monks, with the purified *deva*-vision surpassing that of men see beings as they are passing hence, as they are coming to be, and see[3] that beings are mean, excellent, comely, ugly, well-going, ill-going according to the consequences of deeds, (and I think): 'Indeed these worthy beings, who are endowed with right conduct in body, speech and thought, who are not scoffers at the ariyans, are of right view, incurring kamma consequent on right view, at the breaking up of the body after dying are arising in a good bourn, a heaven world. Or these worthy beings, who are endowed with right conduct in body, speech and thought, [179] who are not scoffers at the ariyans, are of right view, incurring kamma consequent on right view, at the breaking up of the body after dying are arising among men. Indeed these worthy beings, who are endowed with

---

[1] Referred to at *MA*. ii. 422 with special reference to the explanation of Niraya.

[2] Simile as at *M*. i. 279, ii. 21.

[3] Again *passāmi*, but other contexts mostly read *pajānāmi*.

wrong conduct in body, speech and thought, who are scoffers at the ariyans, are of false view, incurring kamma consequent on wrong view, at the breaking up of the body after dying are arising in the realm of the departed. Or these worthy beings, who are endowed with wrong conduct . . . incurring kamma consequent on wrong view, at the breaking up of the body after dying are arising in an animal womb. Or these worthy beings, endowed with wrong conduct . . . are arising in the sorrowful ways, the bad bourn, the Downfall, Niraya Hell.'

Monks,[1] the guardians of Niraya Hell, having seized that person by both arms, present him to King Yama, saying: ' This man, sire, has no respect for his mother, no respect for his father,[2] he does not honour recluses, he does not honour brahmans, he does not pay due respect to the elders of the family. Let your majesty decree a punishment for him.'

Then, monks, King Yama cross-questions him, questions him closely and speaks to him concerning the first *deva*-messenger, saying: ' My good man, did you not see the first *deva*-messenger who appeared among men ?' He speaks thus: ' I did not see him, revered sir.' So, monks, King Yama speaks to him thus: ' My good man, did you not see among men a young baby boy lying on his back, fallen prostrate among his own excrements ?' He speaks thus: ' I saw him, revered sir.' King Yama, monks, speaks thus to him: ' My good man, although you are sensible and grown up, did it not occur to you: I too am liable to birth, I have not outstripped birth; come, I (shall) do what is lovely in body, speech and thought '? He speaks thus: ' I was not able to, revered sir, I was indolent,[3] revered sir.' King Yama, monks, speaks to him thus: ' If it was because of indolence, my good man, that you did not do what was lovely in body, speech and thought, they will undoubtedly do unto you, my good man, in accordance with that indolence. For this that is an evil deed is yours; it was not done by mother, it was not done by father, [180] it was not done by brother, it was not done by sister, it was not done by friends and acquaintances, it was not done by kith and kin, it was not done by recluses and brahmans, it was not done by *devatās*. This evil deed was done by you; it is you yourself that will experience its ripening.'

---

[1] From here onwards *cf. A.* i. 138 *ff.*, where however there are only three *deva*-messengers.
[2] Omitted in Chalmers' *M.* text, but found at *A.* i. 138, *D.* iii. 72.
[3] Or, heedless.

King Yama, monks, having cross-questioned him, questioned him closely and spoken to him concerning the first *deva*-messenger, then cross-questions him, questions him closely and speaks to him concerning the second *deva*-messenger, saying: 'My good man, did you not see the second *deva*-messenger who appeared among men?' He speaks thus: 'I did not see him, revered sir.' King Yama, monks, speaks thus to him: 'My good man, did you not see among men a woman or a man eighty or ninety or a hundred years old, aged, crooked as a rafter, bent, leaning on a stick, going along palsied, miserable, youth gone, teeth broken, hair thinned, skin wrinkled, stumbling along, the limbs discoloured?' He speaks thus: 'I saw this, revered sir.' King Yama, monks, speaks thus: 'My good man, although you are sensible and grown up, did it not occur to you: I too am liable to old age, I have not outstripped old age; come, I (shall) do what is lovely in body, speech and thought'? He speaks thus: 'I was not able to, revered sir, I was indolent, revered sir.' King Yama, monks, speaks to him thus: 'If it was because of indolence, my good man, that you did not do what was lovely in body, speech and thought . . . This evil deed was done by you; it is you yourself that will experience its ripening.'

King Yama, monks, having cross-questioned him, questioned him closely and spoken to him concerning the second *deva*-messenger, then cross-questions him, questions him closely and speaks to him concerning the third *deva*-messenger, saying: [181] 'My good man, did you not see the third *deva*-messenger who appeared among men?' He speaks thus: 'I did not see him, revered sir.' King Yama, monks, speaks to him thus: 'My good man, did you not see among men a woman or a man afflicted with illness, suffering, grievously ill, fallen prostrate among his own excrements, (only) rising with (the help of) others, (only) getting to bed with (the help of) others?' He speaks thus: 'I saw this, revered sir.' King Yama, monks, speaks to him thus: 'My good man, although you are sensible and grown up, did it not occur to you: I too am liable to illness, I have not outstripped illness; come, I (shall) do what is lovely in body, speech and thought'? He speaks thus: 'I was not able to, revered sir, I·was indolent, revered sir.' King Yama, monks, speaks to thim thus: 'If it was because of indolence, my good man, that you did not do what was lovely in body, speech and thought . . . This evil deed was done by you; it is you yourself that will experience its ripening.'

King Yama, monks, having cross-questioned him, questioned him closely and spoken to him concerning the third *deva*-messenger, then cross-questions him, questions him closely and speaks to him concerning the fourth *deva*-messenger, saying: ' My good man, did you not see the fourth *deva*-messenger who appeared among men ?' He speaks thus: ' I did not see him, revered sir.' King Yama, monks, speaks to him thus: ' My good man, did you not see among men kings who, having arrested a thief, an evil-doer, were subjecting him to various punishments: they lashed him with whips and they lashed him with canes and they lashed him with (birch) rods . . . (*as at text vol. iii. p.* 164) . . . and they decapitated him with a sword ?' He speaks thus: ' I saw this, revered sir.' King Yama, monks, speaks to him thus: ' My good man, although you are sensible and grown up, did it not occur to you: Indeed those who do evil deeds are subjected to various punishments like these here and now, and what about [**182**] hereafter ? Come, I (shall) do what is lovely in body, speech and thought '? He speaks thus: ' I was not able to, revered sir, I was indolent, revered sir.' King Yama, monks, speaks to him thus: ' If it was because of indolence, my good man, that you did not do what was lovely in body, speech and thought . . . This evil deed was done by you; it is you yourself that will experience its ripening.'

King Yama, monks, having cross-questioned him, questioned him closely and spoken to him concerning the fourth *deva*-messenger, then cross-questions him, questions him closely and speaks to him concerning the fifth *deva*-messenger, saying: ' My good man, did you not see the fifth *deva*-messenger who appeared among men ?' He speaks thus: ' I did not see him, revered sir.' King Yama, monks, speaks to him thus: ' My good man, did you not see among men a woman or a man dead for one, two or three days, swollen, discoloured, decomposing ?' He speaks thus: ' I saw this, revered sir.' King Yama, monks, speaks to him thus: ' My good man, although you are sensible and grown up, did it not occur to you: I too am liable to death, I have not outstripped death; come, I (shall) do what is lovely in body, speech and thought '? He speaks thus: ' I was not able to, revered sir, I was indolent, revered sir.' King Yama, monks, speaks to him thus: ' If it was because of indolence, my good man, that you did not do what is lovely in body, speech and thought, they will undoubtedly do unto you, my good man, in accordance with that indolence. For this that is an evil deed is yours; it was not done by mother, it was not done by father, it was not done by brother, it was not done by sister, it was not done by friends and acquaintances, it was not done by kith and kin, it was not done by recluses and brahmans, it was not done by *devatās*. This evil deed was done by you; it is you yourself that will experience its ripening.'

King Yama, monks, having cross-questioned him, questioned him closely and spoken to him concerning the fifth *deva*-messenger, was silent.

Monks, the guardians of Niraya Hell [183] subject him to what is called the fivefold pinion:[1] they drive a red-hot iron stake through each hand and foot and a red-hot iron stake through the middle of his breast . . .

> Four-cornered and with four gates,
> It is divided into equal portions,
> Encircled by an iron wall, with a roof of iron above;
> Its incandescent floor is made of glowing iron;
> All round it stands a hundred *yojanas* square.

The flames that leap up by the eastern wall of this Great Niraya Hell, monks, are hurled against the western wall; the flames that leap up by the western wall [184] are hurled against the eastern wall; the flames that leap up by the northern wall are hurled against the southern wall; the flames that leap up by the southern wall are hurled against the northern wall; the flames that leap up from below are hurled above; the flames that leap up from above are hurled below. Thereat he feels feelings that are painful, sharp, severe. But he does not do his time until he makes an end of that evil deed.[2]

Monks, there comes a time once in a very long while when the eastern gateway of this Great Niraya Hell is opened. He rushes there swiftly and speedily; while he is rushing swiftly and speedily his skin burns and his hide burns and his flesh burns and his tendons burn and his eyes[3] are filled with smoke—such is his plight.[4] And though he has attained much,[5] the gateway is nevertheless closed

---

[1] This description of Niraya Hell, down to the end of the verse, occurs also at *M*. iii. 166-167.

[2] See above, p. 212, *n*. 4.

[3] I propose reading *akkhīni* instead of text's *aṭṭhīni*; cf. *DhA*. i. 425, *akkhīni me dhūmāyanti*.

[4] *ubbhataṁ tādisaṁ eva hoti*, such is his pulling out (or pulling back). But as yet he is unable to pull out quickly enough. The next time the eastern gateway is opened he goes out by it.

[5] *bahusampatta*. *MA*. iv. 235, after saying that he has attained many hundred thousand years in Avīci but that it takes him all this time to work off the ripening of his evil deed, then describes the crucifixion of Devadatta in the midst of the six fires of Avīci, a name that appears to mean there is no interval in (or suspension of) anguish.

against him. Thereat he feels feelings that are painful, sharp, severe. But he does not do his time until he makes an end of that evil deed.

Monks, there comes a time once in a very long while when the western gateway . . . the northern gateway . . . the southern gateway of this Great Niraya Hell is opened. He rushes there swiftly and speedily; while he is rushing swiftly and speedily his skin burns . . . the gateway is nevertheless closed against him. Thereat he feels feelings that are painful, sharp, severe. But he does not do his time until he makes and end of that evil deed.

Monks, there comes a time once in a very long while when the eastern gateway of this Great Niraya Hell is opened. He rushes there swiftly and speedily . . . such is his plight. He issues forth by this gateway.

But, monks, adjacent to this Great Niraya Hell [**185**] is the Great Filth Hell.[1] He falls into it. And, monks, in that Filth Hell needle-mouthed creatures cut away his skin; having cut away his skin they cut away his hide; having cut away his hide they cut away his flesh; having cut away his flesh they cut away his tendons; having cut away his tendons they cut away his bones; having cut away his bones they devour the marrow of the bones. Thereat he feels feelings that are painful, sharp, severe. But he does not do his time until he makes an end of that evil deed.

And, monks, adjacent to this Filth Hell is the great Ember Hell.[2] He falls into it. Thereat he feels feelings that are painful, sharp, severe. But he does not do his time until he makes an end of that evil deed.

And, monks, adjacent to that Ember Hell is the great Forest of Silk-Cotton Trees[3] towering a *yojana* high with prickles a finger-breadth long, burning, aflame, ablaze. They make him climb up and they make him climb down. Thereat he feels feelings . . . But he does not do his time until he makes an end of that evil deed.

And, monks, adjacent to that Forest of Silk-Cotton Trees is the great Sword-leafed Forest.[4] He enters it. Its leaves, stirred by the wind, cut off his hands and cut off his feet and cut off his hands and feet . . . ears . . . nose and cut off his ears and nose. Thereat

---

[1] Gūthaniraya, mentioned also at *VvA*. 226. See *D.P.P.N*. for all these Hells.

[2] Kukkuḷaniraya. At *Mhvu*. i. 6 it is said that the people here run about in flames.

[3] Simbalavana.   [4] Asipattavana.

he feels feelings that are painful, sharp, severe. But he does not do his time until he makes and end of that evil deed.

And, monks, adjacent to that Sword-leafed Forest is the great River of Caustic Water.[1] He falls into it. There he is carried with the steam and he is carried against the stream and he is carried with and against the stream.[2] Thereat he feels feelings that are painful, sharp, severe. But he does not do his time until he makes an end of that evil deed.

Monks, the guardians of Niraya Hell haul him out[3] with a fish-hook, [186] set him on dry ground and speak thus to him: ' My good man, what do you want ?' He speaks thus: ' I am hungry, revered sirs.' Monks, the guardians of Niraya Hell, opening his mouth with a glowing iron spike, burning, aflame, ablaze, then push into his mouth a glowing copper pellet, burning, aflame, ablaze. It burns his lips and it burns his mouth and it burns his throat and it burns his chest and it passes out below taking with it his bowels and intestines. Thereat he feels feelings . . . But he does not do his time until he makes an end of that evil deed.

Then, monks, the guardians of Niraya Hell speak thus to him: ' My good man, what do you want ?' He speaks thus: ' I am thirsty, revered sirs.' Monks, the guardians of Niraya Hell, opening his mouth with a glowing iron spike, burning, aflame, ablaze, sprinkle glowing copper and bronze into his mouth, burning, aflame, ablaze. It burns his lips and it burns his mouth and it burns his throat and it burns his chest and it passes out below taking with it his bowels and intestines. Thereat he feels feelings that are painful, sharp, severe. But he does not do his time until he makes an end of that evil deed.

Then, monks, the guardians of Niraya Hell push him back again into the Great Niraya Hell.

Once upon a time, monks, it occurred to King Yama: ' Those that do evil deeds in the world are subjected to a variety of punishments like these. O that I might acquire human status and that a

---

[1] Khārodakā nadī. Called at *MA.* iv. 237 the river Vetaraṇī. *Mhvu.* i. 7 also implies that this river, Vaitaraṇī, is near the Sword-leafed Forest, Asipatravana, which there is apparently a " secondary hell " (the meaning of which may more properly be Kumbha). For *utsada-niraya* as meaning " secondary hell " (sixteen attached to each of the eight hells), see *Mhvu. Trans.*, vol. i, p. 6, *n.* 1.

[2] He does not get across—to the safety of the Further Shore.

[3] *Cf. Mhvu.* i. 7-8.

Tathāgata might arise in the world, a perfected one, a fully Self-Awakened One, and that I might wait on that Lord, and that that Lord might teach me *dhamma*, and that I might understand that Lord's *dhamma*.'

What I am talking about, monks, I have heard from no other recluse or brahman; and moreover what I am talking about is known only by me myself, seen by myself, discerned by myself."

[187] Thus spoke the Lord. When the Well-farer had said this, the Teacher further spoke thus:

" If young men, warned by *deva*-messengers, are indolent,
For a long time they grieve—men going to lowly assemblies.
But those who here are truly men, when warned by *deva*-messengers
Are never indolent in the ariyan *dhamma*;
Seeing peril in grasping, in the origin of birth and dying,
They are freed without grasping through the destruction of birth and dying.
These, attaining security, happy, here and now perfectly allayed,[1]
Outstripping all hatred and fear, pass beyond all anguish."

Discourse on the Deva-Messengers:
The Tenth

Division on Emptiness:
The Third

---

[1] *abhinibbutā.* This verse also occurs at *A.* i. 142, and the last four lines at *A.* iii. 311.

IV. THE DIVISION ON ANALYSIS
(Vibhaṅgavagga)

131. DISCOURSE ON THE AUSPICIOUS[1]
(Bhaddekarattasutta)

THUS have I heard: At one time the Lord was staying near Sāvatthī in the Jeta Grove in Anāthapiṇḍika's monastery. While he was there the Lord addressed the monks, saying: "Monks." "Revered One," these monks answered the Lord in assent. The Lord spoke thus: "I will teach you, monks, the exposition and the analysis of the Auspicious. Listen to it, pay careful attention and I will speak." "Yes, revered sir," these monks answered the Lord in assent. The Lord spoke thus:

"The past[2] should not be followed after,[3] the future not desired.
What is past is got rid of and the future has not come.
But whoever has vision[4] now here, now there, of a present thing,[5]
Knowing that it is immovable, unshakable,[6] let him cultivate it.
Swelter at the task[7] this very day. Who knows whether he will die tomorrow?
There is no bargaining with the great hosts of Death.
Thus abiding ardently, unwearied day and night,
He indeed is 'Auspicious' called, described as a sage at peace."

[188] And how, monks, does one follow after the past? He

---

[1] This title is hard to translate. *MA.* v. 1 connects the word *bhaddekaratta* with being endowed with intentness on *vipassanā*, insight gained in meditation. See Intr., p. xxvi. This is the Vagga that has 12 Discourses. If it were thought desirable to reduce them to the normal 10, this Discourse, spoken by the Lord, would rank as one, and the next three, spoken by disciples, would have to be counted together as another single Discourse.

[2] The five *khandhas* in the past, *MA.* v. 1. These verses are also at *Netti.* 149, *Ap.* p. 506.

[3] *nānvāgameyya*, which *MA.* v. 1 explains as *nānugaccheyya*, to follow after. The meaning of *anvāgameti* appears to be to cause to come back, *i.e.* to recall, because of craving and wrong view.

[4] *vipassati*, that is, in meditation.

[5] Realising that it is impermanent and so on.

[6] By attachment and so on.

[7] *ajj' eva kiccaṁ ātappaṁ*; cf. *Dhp.* 276. This line and the next are quoted at *UdA.* 89, *DhA.* iii. 430.

thinks: 'Such was my material shape in the distant past' and finds[1] delight therein. He thinks: 'Such was my feeling ... my perception ... such were my habitual tendencies ... such was my consciousness in the distant past' and finds delight therein. Even so, monks, does one follow after the past.

And how, monks, does one not follow after the past? He thinks: 'Such was my material shape in the distant past' but does not find delight therein. He thinks: 'Such was my feeling ... my perception ... my habitual tendencies ... my consciousness in the distant past' but does not find delight therein. Even so, monks, does one not follow after the past.

And how, monks, does one desire the future? He thinks: 'May my material shape ... feeling ... perception ... habitual tendencies ... consciousness be thus in the distant future' and finds delight therein. Even so, monks, does one desire the future.

And how, monks, does one not desire the future? He thinks: 'May my material shape ... feeling ... perception ... habitual tendencies ... consciousness be thus in the distant future' but does not find delight therein. Even so, monks, does one not desire the future.

And how, monks, is one drawn away among present things?[2] As to this, monks, an uninstructed ordinary person, taking no count of the pure ones, unskilled in the *dhamma* of the pure ones, untrained in the *dhamma* of the pure ones, taking no count of the true men, unskilled in the *dhamma* of the true men, untrained in the *dhamma* of the true men, regards material shape as self or self as having material shape or material shape as in self or self as in material shape; or he regards feeling ... perception ... the habitual tendencies ... consciousness [189] as self or self as having consciousness or consciousness as in self or self as in consciousness. Even so, monks, is one drawn away among present things.

And how, monks, is one not drawn away among present things? As to this, monks, an instructed disciple of the pure ones, taking count of the pure ones, skilled in the *dhamma* of the pure ones, trained in the *dhamma* of the pure ones, taking count of the true men, skilled in the *dhamma* of the true men, trained in the *dhamma*

---

[1] *samanvāneti*, continues to take, explained by *anupavatteti*, to keep moving on after, at *MA*. v. 3.

[2] *paccuppannesu dhammesu saṁhīrati*. *Saṁhīrati* is to be drawn into or to be caught; also to be drawn away by craving and false view from developing insight or vision, *vipassanā*, *MA*. v. 2.

of the true men, does not regard material shape as self or self as having material shape or material shape as in self or self as in material shape; and he does not regard feeling... perception... the habitual tendencies... consciousness as self or self as having consciousness or consciousness as in self or self as in consciousness. Even so, monks, is one not drawn away among present things.

> The past should not be followed after, the future not desired.
> (... *as above* ...)
> He indeed is 'Auspicious' called, described as a sage at peace.

When I said: 'I will teach you, monks, the exposition and the analysis of the Auspicious,' it was said in reference to this."

Thus spoke the Lord. Delighted, these monks rejoiced in what the Lord had said.

Discourse on the Auspicious:
The First

132. ĀNANDA'S DISCOURSE ON THE AUSPICIOUS

(Ānandabhaddekarattasutta)

Thus have I heard: At one time the Lord was staying near Sāvatthī in the Jeta Grove in Anāthapiṇḍika's monastery. Now at that time the venerable Ānanda gladdened, roused, incited and delighted the monks with talk on *dhamma* in an assembly hall; [**190**] and he spoke the exposition and the analysis of the Auspicious. Then the Lord, emerging from solitary meditation towards evening, approached that assembly hall; having approached, he sat down on the seat made ready. As he was sitting down, the Lord addressed the monks, saying: "Now, who, monks, gladdened, roused, incited, and delighted the monks with talk on *dhamma* in the assembly hall ? And did he speak the exposition and the analysis of the Auspicious ?"

"The venerable Ānanda, revered sir, gladdened... delighted the monks with talk on *dhamma* in the assembly hall; and he spoke the exposition and the analysis of the Auspicious."

Then the Lord addressed the venerable Ānanda, saying: "But how is it that you, Ānanda, gladdened, roused, incited and delighted the monks with talk on *dhamma* ?[1] Did you speak the exposition and the analysis of the Auspicious ?"

"I, revered sir, gladdened . . . delighted the monks with talk on *dhamma* thus. I spoke the exposition and the analysis of the Auspicious:

'The past should not be followed after, the future not desired.
. . . (*as in the foregoing Discourse*) . . .
He indeed is "Auspicious" called, described as a sage at peace.'

And how, your reverences, does one follow after the past ? He thinks that he was of such a material shape . . . such feeling . . . such perception . . . such habitual tendencies . . . such consciousness in the distant past, and finds delight therein . . . (*as in the foregoing Discourse*) . . . Even so, your reverences, is one not drawn away among present things.

'The past should not be followed after, the future not desired.
. . . (*as in the foregoing Discourse*) . . .
He indeed is "Auspicious" called, described as a sage at peace.'

It was thus, revered sir, that I gladdened, roused, incited, delighted the monks with talk on *dhamma* and spoke the exposition and analysis of the Auspicious."

"It is good, Ānanda, it is good; it is good that you, Ānanda, gladdened . . . delighted the monks with talk on *dhamma* and spoke the exposition and analysis of the Auspicious:

'The past should not be followed after, the future not desired.[2]
. . .   .
He indeed is "Auspicious" called, described as a sage at peace.'

And how, Ānanda, does one follow after the past ? . . . Even so, Ānanda, does one follow after the past. And how, Ānanda, does one not follow after the past ? . . . Even so, Ānanda, does one not follow after the past. And how, Ānanda, does one desire the future ? . . . Even so, Ānanda, does one desire the future. And how, Ānanda, does one not desire the future ? . . . Even so, Ānanda, does one not desire the future. And how, Ānanda, is one drawn

---

[1] See p. 245, *n.* 3 below.
[2] The whole of Discourse No. 131 from the first line of the verse to the last line of its second occurrence is here supposed to be repeated.

away among present things?... Even so, Ānanda, is one drawn away among present things. And how, Ānanda, is one not drawn away among present things?... Even so, Ānanda, is one not drawn away among present things.

'The past should not be followed after, the future not desired. ... (as in the foregoing Discourse) ... He indeed is "Auspicious" called, described as a sage at peace.'"

Thus spoke the Lord. Delighted, the venerable Ānanda rejoiced in what the Lord had said.

Ānanda's Discourse on the Auspicious:
The Second

133. MAHĀKACCĀNA'S DISCOURSE ON THE AUSPICIOUS
(Mahākaccānabhaddekarattasutta)

[192] THUS have I heard: At one time the Lord was staying near Rājagaha in the Tapoda monastery.[1] Then the venerable Samiddhi,[2] getting up when the night was waning, went to the Tapoda (lake) to bathe his limbs. When he had bathed his limbs in the Tapoda (lake) and had come out (of the water), he stood in one robe drying his limbs. Then, when the night was far spent,[3] a certain *deva* illumining with his radiant beauty the whole of the Tapoda,[4] approached the venerable Samiddhi and, having approached, stood at one side. While he was standing at one side, this *deva* spoke thus to the venerable Samiddhi:

---

[1] So called because it faced the Tapoda lake. At *MA*. v. 4 this is called "hot," *tatta*. *Cf. SA*. i. 38, *VinA*. ii. 512 and see *B.D*. i. 188, *n*. 1, 274, *n*. 6, *K.S*. i. 14, *n*. 5. See also *S*. i. 8 where likewise a *devatā* spoke to Samiddhi at this place.

[2] See *M*. Sta. 136. At *Thag*. 46 a verse is ascribed to him. See *Pss. Breth.*, p. 51, *n*. 3.

[3] For notes on words in this passage see *M.L.S*. i. 183.

[4] Probably both the lake and the monastery.

"Do you, monk, remember the exposition and the analysis of the Auspicious?"

"I, friend,[1] do not remember the exposition and the analysis of the Auspicious. But do you, friend, remember the exposition and the analysis of the Auspicious?"

"I too, monk, do not remember either the exposition or the analysis of the Auspicious. But do you, monk, remember the verses of the Auspicious?"

"I, friend, do not remember the verses of the Auspicious. But do you, friend, remember the verses of the Auspicious?"

"I too, monk, do not remember the verses of the Auspicious. But do you, monk, learn the exposition and the analysis of the Auspicious; do you, monk, master the exposition and the analysis of the Auspicious; do you, monk, remember the exposition and the analysis of the Auspicious. For the exposition and the analysis of the Auspicious, monk, are connected with the goal, they are fundamental to the Brahma-faring."

Thus spoke this *deva*; having said this, he disappeared then and there. Then the venerable Samiddhi towards the end of that night approached the Lord; having approached and greeted the Lord, he sat down at a respectful distance. As he was sitting down at a respectful distance, the venerable Samiddhi spoke thus to the Lord:

"Now I, revered sir, when the night was waning went to the Tapoda (lake) to bathe my limbs. [193] When I had bathed my limbs in the Tapoda (lake) and had come out (of the water), I stood in one robe while drying my limbs. Then, revered sir, when the night was far spent a certain *deva* . . . (*as above*) ' . . . fundamental to the Brahma-faring.' Thus spoke this *deva*, revered sir. Having said this, he disappeared then and there. It were good, revered sir, if the Lord would teach me the exposition and the analysis of the Auspicious."

"Well then, monk, listen and attend carefully and I will speak."

"Yes, revered sir," the venerable Samiddhi answered the Lord in assent. The Lord spoke thus:

"The past should not be followed after, the future not desired.
   . . . (*as in Discourse No.* 131) . . .
He indeed is ' Auspicious ' called, described as a sage at peace."

Thus spoke the Lord. When he had said this,[2] the Well-farer rose

---

[1] *āvuso*.   [2] *Cf. M.* i. 110 *ff.*

from his seat and entered a dwelling-place. Soon after the Lord had gone, it occurred to those monks: "Your reverences, the Lord, having recited this exposition to us in brief, but not having explained the meaning in full, rose from his seat and entered a dwelling-place:

'The past should not be followed after, the future not desired.
. . . (*as in Discourse No.* 131) . . .
He indeed is "Auspicious" called, described as a sage at peace.'

Now, who can explain the meaning in full of this exposition that was recited in brief by the Lord but the meaning of which was not explained in full?" [**194**] Then it occurred to these monks: "Now the venerable Kaccāna the Great is both praised by the Teacher and revered by intelligent fellow-Brahma-farers; and the venerable Kaccāna the Great is able to explain in full the meaning of this exposition that was recited in brief by the Lord but the meaning of which was not explained in full. Suppose we were to approach the venerable Kaccāna the Great, and having approached, were to question him on this meaning?"

Then these monks approached the venerable Kaccāna the Great; having approached, they exchanged greetings with him, and when they had conversed in a friendly and courteous way, they sat down at a respectful distance. As they were sitting down at a respectful distance, these monks spoke thus to the venerable Kaccāna the Great:

"Reverend Kaccāna, the Lord, having recited this exposition to us in brief but not having explained its meaning in full, rose from his seat and entered a dwelling-place:

'The past should not be followed after, the future not desired.
. . . (*as in Discourse No.* 131) . . .
He indeed is "Auspicious" called, described as a sage at peace.'

Soon after the Lord had departed, it occurred to us, reverend Kaccāna: 'Your reverences, the Lord, having recited this exposition to us in brief, but not having explained the meaning in full, rose from his seat and entered a dwelling-place:

The past should not be followed after, the future not desired.
. . . (*as in Discourse No.* 131) . . .
He indeed is "Auspicious" called, described as a sage at peace.

Now, who can explain the meaning in full of this exposition that was recited in brief by the Lord but the meaning of which was not explained in full ?' Then, reverend Kaccāna, it occurred to us: ' Now the venerable Kaccāna the Great is both praised by the Teacher ... Suppose we were ... to question him on this meaning.' May the venerable Kaccāna the Great explain it."

"Your reverences, as a man walking about aiming at the pith, searching for the pith, looking about for the pith of a great, stable and pithy tree, [195] might pass by the root, pass by the trunk, thinking that the pith was to be looked for in the branches and foliage—even so is this performance of the venerable ones, for (although) you had the Teacher face to face, yet you have ignored that Lord and judge that it is I who should be questioned on this meaning. But, your reverences, the Lord knows what should be known, sees what should be seen, he has become vision, become knowledge, become *dhamma*, become Brahma, he is the propounder, the expounder, the bringer of the goal, the giver of the Deathless, *dhamma*-lord, Tathāgata. This was the time when you should have questioned the Lord on this meaning so that you might have understood what the Lord explained to you."

"Undoubtedly, reverend Kaccāna, the Lord knows what should be known ... This was the time when we should have questioned the Lord on this meaning so that we might have understood what the Lord explained to us. But the venerable Kaccāna the Great is both praised by the Teacher and revered by intelligent fellow Brahma-farers; and the venerable Kaccāna the Great is able to explain in full the meaning of this exposition that was recited in brief by the Lord but the meaning of which was not explained in full. May the venerable Kaccāna explain it, without finding it troublesome."

"Well then, your reverences, listen, pay careful attention and I will speak."

"Yes, your reverence," these monks answered the venerable Kaccāna the Great in assent. The venerable Kaccāna the Great spoke thus:

"In regard to that exposition, your reverences, that the Lord recited in brief but the meaning of which he had not explained in full when he rose from his seat and entered a dwelling-place:

' The past should not be followed after, the future not desired.
. . .   .
He indeed is "Auspicious" called, described as a sage at peace.'

Of this exposition that was recited by the Lord in brief but the meaning of which he did not explain in full, I, your reverences, understand the meaning in full thus:

And how, your reverences, does one follow after the past ? He thinks: [**196**] 'Such was my vision[1] in the distant past, such were material shapes,' and his consciousness[2] is bound fast there by desire and attachment; because his consciousness is bound fast by desire and attachment, he delights in it;[3] delighting in it he follows after the past. He thinks: 'Such was my ear in the distant past, such were sounds . . . Such was my nose in the distant past, such were smells . . . Such was my tongue in the distant past, such were flavours . . . Such was my body in the distant past, such were tactile objects . . . Such was my mind in the distant past, such were mental states,' and his consciousness is bound fast there by desire and attachment; because his consciousness is bound fast by desire and attachment, he delights in it; delighting in it, he follows after the past. It is thus, your reverences, that one follows after the past.

And how, your reverences, does one not follow after the past ? He thinks: 'Such was my vision in the distant past, such were material shapes' but without his consciousness being bound fast there by desire and attachment; because his consciousness is not bound fast by desire and attachment, he does not delight in it; not delighting in it, he does not follow after the past. He thinks: 'Such was my ear in the distant past, such were sounds . . . Such was my nose in the distant past, such were smells . . . Such was my tongue in the distant past, such were flavours . . . Such was my body in the distant past, such were tactile objects . . . Such was my mind in the distant past, such were mental states ' but without his consciousness being bound fast there by desire and attachment; because his consciousness is not bound fast by desire and attachment, he does not delight in it; not delighting in it, he does not follow after the past. It is thus, your reverences, that one does not follow after the past.

And how, your reverences, does one desire the future ? He thinks: 'May my vision be such in the distant future, material

---

[1] *MA.* v. 5-6 explains that in the two preceding Discourses and in the following one the headings (*mātikā*) and the analysis were made in respect of the five *khandhā*; but here the headings refer to the 12 (sense-)fields (*āyatana*), *i.e.* the six sensory organs and their six (appropriate) sense-data.

[2] *MA.* v. 6 reads with a Burmese edn. *nikanti viññāṇa*, consciousness that is desire, craving, longing for.

[3] *I.e.* in " vision," etc. *Cf. S.* iv. 13 *f.*, where one rejoices in the six sense-fields.

shapes such' and bends his thought to the acquisition of what is not (yet) acquired; because he so bends his thought, he delights in that; delighting in that, he desires the future. He thinks: 'May my ear ... sounds ... nose ... smells ... tongue ... flavours ... body ... tactile objects ... May my mind be such in the distant future, [197] mental states such' and bends his thought to the acquisition of what is not (yet) acquired; because he so bends his thought, he delights in that; delighting in that, he desires the future. It is thus, your reverences, that one desires the future.

And how, your reverences, does one not desire the future ? He thinks: 'May my vision be such in the distant future, material shapes such' but does not bend his thought to the acquisition of what is not (yet) acquired; because he does not so bend his thought, he does not delight in that; not delighting in that, he does not desire the future. He thinks: 'May my ear ... may my mind be such in the distant future, mental states such' but does not bend his thought to the acquisition of what is not (yet) acquired; because he does not so bend his thought, he does not delight in that; not delighting in that, he does not desire the future. It is thus, your reverences, that one does not desire the future.

And how, your reverences, is one drawn away among present things ? If, your reverences, there are at this present time[1] both vision and material shapes[2] to which his consciousness is bound fast by desire and attachment at this same present time,[3] (then) because his consciousness is bound fast by desire and attachment, he delights in them;[4] delighting in them, he is drawn away among present things. If, your reverences, there are at this present time both ear and sounds ... nose and smells ... tongue and flavours ... body and tactile objects ... mind and mental states to which his consciousness is bound fast by desire and attachment at this same present time, (then) because his consciousness is bound fast by desire and attachment, he delights in them; delighting in them, he is drawn away among present things. It is thus, your reverences, that one is drawn away among present things.

---

[1] *etaṁ paccuppannaṁ.*

[2] It would appear that " vision and material shapes " form a pair, expressed by the word *ubhayaṁ*. Attachment, etc., is to this (pair), *tasmiṁ*. So with the ear and sounds, etc.

[3] *yeva paccuppanne.*

[4] *I.e.* desire and attachment, but expressed by *taṁ*, again referring to the pair=both.

And how, your reverences, is one not drawn away among present things? If, your reverences, there are at this present time both vision and material shapes to which his consciousness is not bound fast by desire and attachment at this same present time, (then) because his consciousness is not bound fast by desire and attachment, he does not delight in them; not delighting in them he is not drawn away among present things. If, your reverences, there are at this present time both ear and sounds . . . nose and smells . . . tongue and flavours . . . body and tactile objects . . . mind and mental states[1] to which his [**198**] consciousness is not bound fast by desire and attachment at this same present time, (then) because his consciousness is not bound fast by desire and attachment, he does not delight in them; not delighting in them, he is not drawn away among present things. It is thus, your reverences, that one is not drawn away among present things.

In regard to that exposition, your reverences, that the Lord recited in brief but the meaning of which he had not explained in full when he rose from his seat and entered a dwelling-place:

'The past should not be followed after, the future not desired.
. . . .
He indeed is "Auspicious" called, described as a sage at peace.'

Of this exposition that was recited by the Lord in brief but the meaning of which he did not explain in full, I, your reverences, understand the meaning in full thus. But if you, venerable ones, so desire, having approached the Lord, you can question him as to the meaning, so that as the Lord explains it to you so you may understand it."

Then these monks, delighting and rejoicing in what the venerable Kaccāna the Great had said, rising from their seats, approached the Lord; having approached and greeted the Lord, they sat down at a respectful distance. As they were sitting down at a respectful distance, these monks spoke thus to the Lord:

"Revered sir, the Lord, having recited this exposition to us in brief, rose from his seat and entered a dwelling-place before he had explained the meaning in full:

The past should not be followed after, the future not desired.
. . . .
He indeed is 'Auspicious' called, described as a sage at peace.

---

[1] Quoted at *Asl.* 420.

And, revered sir, not long after the Lord had departed, it occurred to us: ' Your reverences, the Lord, having recited this exposition to us in brief, but not having explained the meaning in full, rose from his seat and entered a dwelling-place:

> The past should not be followed after, the future not desired.
> ... ...
> He indeed is "Auspicious" called, described as a sage at peace.

[199] Now, who can explain the meaning in full of this exposition that was recited in brief by the Lord but the meaning of which was not explained in full ?' Then it occurred to us, revered sir, ' Now, your reverences, the venerable Kaccāna the Great is both praised by the Teacher . . . Suppose we were . . . to question him on this meaning ?' Then we, revered sir, approached the venerable Kaccāna the Great, and having approached we questioned the venerable Kaccāna the Great on this meaning. The meaning of these (words), revered sir, was explained to us by the venerable Kaccāna the Great by these methods, by these sentences, by these words."

"Learned, monks, is Kaccāna the Great, of great wisdom, monks, is Kaccāna the Great. For if you, monks, had questioned me as to this meaning, I too would have explained it precisely as it was explained by Kaccāna the Great. Indeed, this is the exact meaning of that, and thus should you remember it."

Thus spoke the Lord. Delighted, these monks rejoiced in what the Lord had said.

Mahākaccāna's Discourse on the Auspicious:
The Third

134. LOMASAKAṄGIYA'S DISCOURSE ON THE AUSPICIOUS

(Lomasakaṅgiyabhaddekarattasutta)

THUS have I heard: At one time the Lord was staying near Sāvatthī in the Jeta Grove in Anāthapiṇḍika's monastery. Now at that time the venerable Lomasakaṅgiya[1] was staying among the Sakyans near Kapilavatthu in Nigrodha's park. Then, when the night was far spent, the *deva*[2] Candana, illumining with his radiant beauty the whole of Nigrodha's park, approached the venerable Lomasakaṅgiya; and having approached, he stood at one side. As he was standing at one side the deva Candana spoke thus to the venerable Lomasakaṅgiya:

"Do you, monk, remember the exposition and the analysis of the Auspicious?"

[200] "I, friend, do not remember the exposition and the analysis of the Auspicious. But do you, friend, remember the exposition and the analysis of the Auspicious?"

"I too, monk, do not remember either the exposition or the analysis of the Auspicious. But do you, monk, remember the verses of the Auspicious?"

"I, friend, do not remember the verses of the Auspicious. But do you, friend, remember the verses of the Auspicious?"

"I, monk, remember the verses of the Auspicious."

"But how is it[3] that you, friend, remember the verses of the Auspicious?"

---

[1] *MA*. v. 6 says this Elder's name was Aṅga, but as he had only a little down on his body he was known as Lomasakaṅgiya. His verse is at *Thag.* 27, and the story of how in a former life he wanted to recite the *Bhaddekaratta* occurs at *ThagA.* i. 89 *f.* See *Ap.* ii. 504 *f.*, where the story, both of the past and the present, differs in various details.

[2] *devaputta.* As such he was known by the same name, Candana, as he had had as a rich upāsaka in the time of the Buddha Kassapa, *MA*. v. 7. See *M.L.S.* i. 183.

[3] *yathākathaṁ dhāresi.* This might also be translated as "do you remember according to what had been said," *i.e.* do you remember the verses on the Auspicious according to how they were spoken ? It would, indeed, be important to know the verses exactly as they had been spoken for, as the

"At this one time, monk, the Lord was staying among the Devas of the Thirty-Three at the root of the Coral Tree on the ornamental stone.[1] While he was there the Lord spoke the exposition and the analysis of the Auspicious to the Devas of the Thirty-Three:

'The past should not be followed after, the future not desired.
What is past is got rid of and the future has not come.
But whoever has vision now here, now there, of a present thing,
Knowing that it is immovable, unshakable, let him cultivate it.
Swelter at the task this very day. Who knows whether he will die tomorrow?
There is no bargaining with the great hosts of Death.
Thus abiding ardently, unwearied day and night,
He indeed is "Auspicious" called, described as a sage at peace.'

Thus it is that I, monk, remember the verses of the Auspicious. Do you, monk, learn[2] the exposition and the analysis of the Auspicious; do you, monk, master[3] the exposition and the analysis of the Auspicious; do you, monk, remember[4] the exposition and the analysis of the Auspicious. The exposition and the analysis of the Auspicious, monk, are connected with the goal, they are fundamental to the Brahma-faring."

Thus spoke the *deva* Candana; having said this, he disappeared then and there. Then the venerable Lomasakaṅgiya towards the end of that night, having packed away his lodging, set out on tour for Sāvatthī, taking his bowl and robe. [201] Walking on tour, he gradually approached Sāvatthī, the Jeta Grove, Anāthapiṇḍika's monastery and the Lord; having approached and greeted the Lord, he sat down at a respectful distance. As he was sitting down at a

---

sequel states, they are connected with the goal. The above rendering may be justified however since the following sentences appear to be an answer to a question in such a form. *Cf. yathākathaṁ sandassesi*, etc., at *M*. iii. 190 above.

[1] *paṇḍukambalasilā*, usually the name of Sakka's throne. *Paṇḍukambala* is a light red woollen blanket, in this case the colour of a heap of *jayasumara* (Victory's joy) flowers. According to *MA*. v. 7 the Buddha went to the abode of the Thirty-Three seven years after the Enlightenment and after he had performed the twin miracle, and stayed there for a year.

[2] Sitting down in silence while hearing it means "he learns," *MA*. v. 8.

[3] Rehearsing it out loud means "he masters it."

[4] Speaking it to others means "he remembers it."

respectful distance the venerable Lomasakaṅgiya spoke thus to the Lord:

"At this one time, revered sir, I was staying among the Sakyans near Kapilavatthu in Nigrodha's park. Then, revered sir, when the night was far spent a certain *deva*, illumining with his radiant beauty the whole of Nigrodha's park, approached me and, having approached, stood at one side. As he was standing at one side, revered sir, that *deva* spoke to me thus: 'Do you, monk, remember the exposition and the analysis of the Auspicious?' When this had been said I, revered sir, spoke thus to that *deva*: 'I, friend, do not remember the exposition and the analysis of the Auspicious. But do you, friend, remember the exposition and the analysis of the Auspicious?' 'I too, monk . . . The exposition and the analysis of the Auspicious, monk, are connected with the goal, they are fundamental to the Brahma-faring.' This *deva* said this, revered sir, and having said this he disappeared then and there. It were good, revered sir, if the Lord were to teach me the exposition and the analysis of the Auspicious."

"But do you, monk, know this *deva*?"

"I, revered sir, do not know that *deva*."

"This *deva*, monk, is called Candana. The *deva* Candana, monk, having applied himself, having attended, and having concentrated all his mind, listened to *dhamma* with ready ears.[1] Well then, do you, monk, listen, attend carefully and I will speak."

"Yes, revered sir," the venerable Lomasakaṅgiya answered the Lord in assent. The Lord spoke thus:

"The past should not be followed after, the future not desired.
. . . (*as above*) . . .
He indeed is 'Auspicious' called, described as a sage at peace.

And how, monk, does one follow after the past? He thinks: 'Such was my material shape in the distant past . . . such was my feeling . . . perception . . . habitual tendencies . . . such was my consciousness in the distant past' and finds delight therein. Even so, monk, does one follow after the past.

[202] And how, monk, does one not follow after the past? . . .

And how, monk, does one desire the future? . . . (*as in Discourse No.* 131) . . . Even so, monk, is one not drawn away among present things.

---

[1] As at *M*. i. 325, which see for further references.

The past should not be followed after, the future not desired.
... ...
He indeed is ' Auspicious ' called, described as a sage at peace."

Thus spoke the Lord. Delighted the venerable Lomasakaṅgiya rejoiced in what the Lord had said.

Lomasakaṅgiya's Discourse on the Auspicious:
The Fourth

135. DISCOURSE ON THE LESSER ANALYSIS OF DEEDS

(Cūḷakammavibhaṅgasutta)[1]

THUS have I heard: At one time the Lord was staying near Sāvatthī in the Jeta Grove in Anāthapiṇḍika's monastery. Then the brahman youth Subha, Todeyya's son,[2] approached the Lord; having approached, he exchanged greetings with the Lord; having conversed in a friendly and courteous way, he sat down at a respectful distance. As he was sitting down at a respectful distance the brahman youth Subha, Todeyya's son, spoke thus to the Lord:
" Now, good Gotama, what is the cause, what the reason that

---

[1] Called at *MA.* v. 8, 15 *Subhasutta*, the latter passage saying that it is also called *Cullakammavibhaṅgasutta*. There is a *Subhasutta* at *M*. Sta. 99 and *D.* Sta. 10. See S. Levi, *Mahākarmavibhaṅga*, etc., Paris, 1932, for an interesting dissertation on the Karmavibhaṅgas, and also Mrs. Rhys Davids, *Wayfarer's Words*, vol. iii, p. 1093 (reprinted from *J.R.A.S.*, 1934). That the prefix *Cūḷa* here qualifies *kammavibhaṅga* (and not *sutta*) must be understood on the analogy of *Mahā-* in the next Discourse which, from internal evidence, is not a description of *sutta* but of *kammavibhaṅga*; see below, p. 254, *n.* 1.

[2] Todeyya was Pasenadi's brahman priest. He was very rich and very mean. Born as a dog in his own house, he barked at the Buddha when he was visiting Subha. The Buddha recognised him and identified him to the unwilling Subha by getting the dog to find some treasure he had hidden as a man.

lowness and excellence are to be seen among human beings while they are in human form ?[1] For, good Gotama, human beings of short life-span are to be seen and those of long life-span; those of many and those of few illnesses; those who are ugly, those who are beautiful; those who are of little account, those of great account; those who are poor, those who are wealthy; those who are of lowly families, those of high families;[2] those who are weak in wisdom, [203] those who are full of wisdom. Now what, good Gotama, is the cause, what the reason that lowness and excellence are to be seen among human beings while they are in human form ?"

"Deeds[3] are one's own, brahman youth, beings are heirs to deeds,[4] deeds are matrix, deeds are kin, deeds are arbiters.[5] Deed divides beings, that is to say by lowness and excellence."

"I do not understand the meaning in full of that which was spoken by the good Gotama in brief and the meaning of which was not explained in full. It were well if the good Gotama were so to teach me *dhamma* that I should understand the meaning in full of that which was spoken by the good Gotama in brief but the meaning of which was not explained in full."

"Well then, brahman youth, listen, attend carefully and I will speak."

"Yes, sir," the brahman youth Subha, Todeyya's son, answered the Lord in assent. The Lord spoke thus:

"Brahman youth, here some woman or man is one that makes onslaught on creatures, is cruel, bloody-handed, intent on injuring and killing, and without mercy to living creatures.[6] Because of that

---

[1] *manussānaṁ yeva sataṁ manussabhūtānaṁ*. This of course assumes that human beings need not always be in human form, and this appears to have been the case with Todeyya. It seems clear that some distinction between the two words is to be made although in the sequel only human beings are dealt with. Pali is precise where we perhaps cannot be. Another word to be considered in this connection is *manussaviggaha*, taking up form as a human being, see *Vin*. iii. 73 where this word is defined, and *Vin*. iv. 214 =269, where the compound *tiracchānagata-manussaviggaha* appears to be a man who has taken up animal form.

[2] Defined at *Vin*. iv. 6.

[3] *Cf. A*. iii. 72, 186, v. 288, *Miln*. 65. *Kamma*, here translated as deed or deeds, is equally the compelling force of *kamma* as inescapable recompense: one arises according to what one does, *yaṁ karoti tena upapajjati, M*. i. 390.

[4] As at *M*. i. 390.

[5] *kammapaṭisaraṇa*; *cf. dhammapaṭisaraṇa* at *M*. iii. 9.

[6] As at *M*. i. 286.

deed, accomplished thus, firmly held[1] thus, he, at the breaking up of the body after dying arises in the sorrowful ways, the bad bourn, the Downfall, Niraya Hell. But if, at the breaking up of the body after dying he does not arise in the sorrowful ways, the bad bourn, the Downfall, Niraya Hell, but comes to human status, then wherever he is born (in a new existence) he is of a short life-span. This course is conducive to shortness of life-span, brahman youth, that is to say making onslaught on creatures, being cruel, bloody-handed, intent on injuring and killing, and without mercy to living creatures.

But, brahman youth, here some woman or man, by getting rid of onslaught on creatures is one who abstains from onslaught on creatures; the stick laid aside, the sword laid aside, he lives scrupulous, merciful, kindly and compassionate to all living creatures. Because of that deed, accomplished thus, firmly held thus, at the breaking up of the body after dying he arises in a good bourn, a heaven world. But if, at the breaking up of the body after dying he does not arise in a good bourn, a heaven world, but comes to human status, then wherever he is born (in a new existence) he is of a long life-span. This course is conducive to length of life-span, brahman youth, that is to say, if one, by getting rid of onslaught on creatures, [204] abstains from onslaught on creatures, (and with) the stick laid aside, the sword laid aside, lives scrupulous, merciful, kindly and compassionate to all living creatures.

Brahman youth, here some woman or man is by nature harmful to creatures with his hand or with a clod of earth or with a stick or with a sword. Because of that deed, accomplished thus, firmly held thus, he, at the breaking up of the body after dying arises in the sorrowful ways, the bad bourn, the Downfall, Niraya Hell. But if, at the breaking up of the body after dying he does not arise in . . . Niraya Hell but comes to human status, then wherever he is born (in a new existence) he has many illnesses. This course is conducive to many illnesses, brahman youth, that is to say being by nature harmful to creatures with his hand . . . or with a sword.

But, brahman youth, here some woman or man is not by nature harmful to creatures with his hand or with a clod of earth or with a stick or with a sword. Because of that deed, accomplished thus . . . he arises in . . . a heaven world . . . he has few illnesses. This

---

[1] *samādinna*, explained at *MA*. v. 11 by *gahita* and *parāmaṭṭha*, which may mean that the deed and its effect had been taken and acquired in a previous birth. The word, together with *samatta*, "accomplished," also occurs at *M*. iii. 214.

course is conducive to few illnesses, brahman youth, that is to say not being by nature harmful to creatures with his hand . . . or with a sword.

Brahman youth, here some woman or man is wrathful; turbulent on being spoken to even about a trifle, he takes offence, gets angry, disagrees, resists, and evinces anger, hatred and resentment.[1] Because of that deed, accomplished thus . . . he arises in the sorrowful ways . . . is ugly. This course is conducive to ugliness, brahman youth, that is to say being wrathful . . . and evincing . . . resentment.

But, brahman youth, here some woman or man is not wrathful; not turbulent on being spoken to even about a large matter, he takes no offence, does not get angry, does not disagree, resist or evince anger, hatred and resentment. Because of that deed, accomplished thus . . . he arises in a good bourn . . . is lovely.[2] This course is conducive to loveliness, brahman youth, that is to say not being wrathful . . . not evincing . . . resentment.

Brahman youth, here some woman or man is jealous-minded; he is jealous, revengeful[3] and harbours jealousy on account of others' gains, honour, fame and the marks of respect and reverence paid to them. Because of that deed, accomplished thus . . . he arises in the sorrowful ways . . . is of little account. This course is conducive to being of little account, brahman youth, that is to say being jealous-minded . . . of respect and reverence paid to them.

[205] But, brahman youth, here some woman or man is not jealous-minded; he is not jealous or revengeful nor does he harbour jealousy on account of others' gains, honour, fame and the marks of respect and reverence paid to them. Because of that deed . . . he arises in a good bourn . . . is of great account. This course is conducive to being of great account, brahman youth, that is to say not being jealous-minded . . . of respect and reverence paid to them.

Brahman youth, here some woman or man is not a giver[4] to recluse or brahman of drink, food, clothing, vehicle, garlands, scents, unguents, bed, lodging, light. Because of that deed . . . he arises in the sorrowful ways . . . is poor. This course is conducive to poverty,

---

[1] As at *A.* i. 126-127. *Cf.* also *A.* ii. 203 *ff.*
[2] *pāsādika* here instead of *vaṇṇavant* as earlier.
[3] *upadussati*. So Childers. *MA.* v. 14 says that because of his jealousy, being censorious he does wrong (*dussati*, or is corrupted). It is possible that the three verbs *dussati padussati upadussati* denote a gradual intensification similar to, *e.g.*, *jhāyanti pajjhāyanti nijjhāyanti apajjhāyanti* at *M.* i. 334.
[4] Because he is stingy.

brahman youth, that is to say not being a giver . . . of bed, lodging, light.

But, brahman youth, here some woman or man is a giver to recluse or brahman of drink, food . . . bed, lodging, light. Because of that deed . . . he arises in a good bourn . . . is wealthy. This course is conducive to wealth, brahman youth, that is to say being a giver . . . of bed, lodging, light.

Brahman youth, here some woman or man is callous and proud; he does not greet one who should be greeted, does not stand up for one who should be stood up for, he does not give a seat to one meriting a seat, he does not make room[1] for one meriting room, he does not respect, revere, reverence, honour one who should be respected, revered, reverenced, honoured. Because of that deed . . . he arises in the sorrowful ways . . . is of a lowly family. This course is conducive to being in a lowly family, brahman youth, that is to say being one who . . . does not honour one who should be . . . honoured.

But, brahman youth, here some woman or man is not callous or proud; he greets one who should be greeted . . . honours one who should be . . . honoured. Because of that deed . . . he arises in the good bourn . . . in a high family. This course is conducive to being in a high family, brahman youth, that is to say being one who . . . honours one who should be honoured.

Brahman youth, here some woman or a man, having approached a recluse or a brahman, is not one that asks: ' What, revered sir, is skill ? What is unskill ? What is blameable ? What unblameable ? What should be practised ? What not practised ? What, being done by me, is for long for my woe and anguish ? Or what, being done by me, is for long for my welfare and happiness ?' Because of this deed . . . he arises in the sorrowful ways . . . is weak in wisdom. This course is conducive to being weak in wisdom, brahman youth, that is to say . . . not being one who asks: ' . . . Or what, being done by me, is for long for my welfare and happiness ?'

[206] But, brahman youth, here some woman or man, having approached a recluse or brahman, is one that asks: ' What, revered sir, is skill ? . . . Or what, being done by me, is for long for my welfare and happiness ?' Because of that deed . . . he arises in a good bourn . . . is of great wisdom. This course is conducive to great wisdom,

---

[1] *maggaṁ deti*, to make room or space for, to let pass, to give way; *cf. Vin.* ii. 221.

brahman youth, that is to say ... being one who asks: '... Or what, being done by me, is for long for my welfare and happiness?'

So, brahman youth, the course conducive to a short life-span leads to shortness of life-span; the course conducive to a long life-span leads to length of life-span; the course conducive to many illnesses leads to having many illnesses; the course conducive to few illnesses leads to having few illnesses; the course conducive to being ugly leads to ugliness; the course conducive to being lovely leads to loveliness; the course conducive to being of small account leads to smallness of account; the course conducive to being of great account leads to greatness of account; the course conducive to being poor, leads to poverty; the course conducive to being wealthy leads to wealth; the course conducive to being of lowly family leads to being in a lowly family; the course conducive to being of high family leads to being in a high family; the course conducive to being weak in wisdom leads to weakness of wisdom; the course conducive to being of great wisdom leads to greatness in wisdom.

Deeds are one's own, brahman youth, beings are heirs to deeds, deeds are the matrix, deeds the kin, deeds the arbiters. Deed divides beings, that is to say by lowness and excellence."

When this had been said, the brahman youth Subha, Todeyya's son, spoke thus to the Lord: "It is excellent, good Gotama, it is excellent, good Gotama. It is as if, good Gotama, one might set upright or ... bring an oil-lamp into the darkness so that those with vision might see material shapes; even so, in many a figure has *dhamma* been made clear by the good Gotama. I am going to the revered Gotama for refuge and to *dhamma* and to the Order of monks. May the revered Gotama accept me as a lay-follower going for refuge from this day forth for as long as life lasts."

Discourse on the Lesser Analysis of Deeds:
The Fifth

136. DISCOURSE ON THE GREATER ANALYSIS OF DEEDS[1]

(Mahākammavibhaṅgasutta)

[207] THUS have I heard: At one time the Lord was staying near Rājagaha in the Bamboo Grove at the squirrels' feeding place. Now at that time the venerable Samiddhi[2] was staying in a little forest hut. Then the wanderer Potali's son, who was always pacing up and down, always roaming about on foot, approached the venerable Samiddhi; having approached, he exchanged greetings with the venerable Samiddhi, and having conversed in a friendly and courteous way he sat down at a respectful distance. As he was sitting down at a respectful distance, the wanderer Potali's son spoke thus to the venerable Samiddhi:

"Reverend Samiddhi, from the recluse Gotama's own mouth have I heard, from his own mouth have I learnt that deed of body is foolish,[3] deed of speech is foolish, only deed of mind is truth;[4] and that there is that attainment on attaining which one experiences nothing."[5]

"Do not, friend Potali's son, speak thus; do not, friend Potali's son, speak thus. Do not misrepresent the Lord; for neither is misrepresentation of the Lord good nor would the Lord speak thus: Deed of body is foolish . . . only deed of mind is truth; (or say) there is that attainment on attaining which one experiences nothing."

"How long have you been gone forth, reverend Samiddhi?"

"Not long, friend, three years."

---

[1] Because the word *mahākammavibhaṅga* occurs in this Discourse the prefix *mahā* must be taken to qualify *kammavibhaṅga* and not *sutta*; see *M.L.S.*, vol. i, Intr. p. xiii.

[2] Mentioned in *M*. Sta. 133.

[3] *mogha*, empty, vain, useless; called at *MA*. v. 15 *tuccha aphala*, empty, fruitless; also opposed to *sacca* at *D*. i. 187, *M*. ii. 169, etc.

[4] *sacca*, explained at *MA*. v. 15 as *tatha bhūta*, real, fact; the Comy also refers to the *Upāli-sutta* (*M*. Sta. 56) where it is said that deed of mind is the more blameable . . . deed of body and deed of speech are not like it.

[5] Referred by *MA*. v. 16 to the *Poṭṭhapāda-sutta* (*D*. Sta. 9): *kathan nu kho abhisaññā-nirodho hoti*, *D*. i. 180.

"Now, why should we speak to monks who are Elders when even a newly ordained monk thinks that the Teacher should be defended thus ? Reverend Samiddhi, when one has intentionally done a deed by body, speech or thought, what does one experience ?"

"When one has intentionally done a deed by body, speech or thought, friend Potali's son, one experiences anguish."

Then the wanderer Potali's son, neither rejoicing in nor protesting against what the venerable Samiddhi had said, rose from his seat and departed without rejoicing, without protesting. Not long after the wanderer Potali's son had departed, the venerable Samiddhi approached the venerable Ānanda; [208] having approached, he exchanged greetings with the venerable Ānanda, and having conversed in a friendly and courteous way, he sat down at a respectful distance. As he was sitting down at a respectful distance, the venerable Samiddhi told the venerable Ānanda the whole of the conversation he had had with the wanderer Potali's son as far as it had gone. When this had been said, the venerable Ānanda spoke thus to the venerable Samiddhi:

"This, reverend Samiddhi, is a subject of conversation that should be told to the Lord. Wait, reverend Samiddhi, until we can approach the Lord; when we have approached the Lord we should tell him this matter; as the Lord explains it to us, so should we remember it."

"Yes, your reverence," the venerable Samiddhi answered the venerable Ānanda in assent. Then the venerable Ānanda and the venerable Samiddhi approached the Lord; having approached and greeted the Lord, they sat down at a respectful distance. As he was sitting down at a respectful distance, the venerable Ānanda told the Lord the whole of the conversation the venerable Samiddhi had had with the wanderer Potali's son as far as it had gone. When this had been said the Lord spoke thus to the venerable Ānanda:

"But I, Ānanda, do not even recognise the wanderer Potali's son's premise, how then (can I recognise) a conversation like this ? The question of the wanderer Potali's son was given a one-sided answer by the foolish man Samiddhi (although) it needed a discriminating explanation."

When this had been said the venerable Udāyin[1] spoke thus to the Lord: "But if this, revered sir, were the meaning of what the

---

[1] Lāḷ-Udāyin. *MA.* v. 16. See *D.P.P.N.*, "an elder who possessed the knack of saying the wrong thing."

venerable Samiddhi said, (then) whatever one experiences is anguish."[1]

Then the Lord addressed the venerable Ānanda, saying: " Now, do you, Ānanda, see this foolish man Udāyin's (wrong) approach ?[2] I, Ānanda, knew that this foolish man Udāyin, opening up (this question) now, would open it up to no purpose.[3] Ānanda, the wanderer Potali's son really asked about the three feelings. If,[4] Ānanda, this foolish man Samiddhi [**209**] had explained thus when he was questioned thus by the wanderer Potali's son: ' When, friend Potali's son, one has intentionally done a deed by body, speech or thought for experiencing pleasure . . . pain . . . neither pain nor pleasure, he experiences pleasure, pain, neither pain nor pleasure respectively,' explaining thus, Ānanda, the foolish man Samiddhi would have explained properly to the wanderer Potali's son. And moreover, Ānanda, there are foolish and inexperienced wanderers who are members of other sects who would find out about the Tathāgata's great analysis of deeds[5] if you, Ānanda, would listen while the Tathāgata is classifying[6] the great analysis of deeds."

" It is the time for this, Lord, it is the time for this, Well-farer, that the Lord should classify the great analysis of deeds. When the monks have heard the Lord, they will remember."

" Well then, Ānanda, listen, attend carefully, and I will speak."

---

[1] *dukkhasmiṁ*, explained at *MA*. v. 16 as *sabbaṁ dukkhaṁ*, i.e. the anguish of rolling on, of the defilements and of the *saṁkhārā*.

[2] *ummagga*, with v.l. *ummaṅga* is explained at *MA*. v. 16 as *paññā ummaggaṁ*; *cf. SnA*. 50 *ummaggo paññā pavuccati*. In the context it would seem that *ummaṅga*, emergence " of a desire for knowledge leading to questioning " is the better reading. See *G.S*. ii. 184, *n*. 5.

[3] *ummujjamāno ayoniso ummujjissati*, wanting to speak he stretches out his neck, moves his jaws and twitches his face, he is not able to sit still. The Lord saw all this and did not come to know about it either through *deva*-vision or reasoning of mind or omniscience, *MA*. v. 16-17. Again, see *G.S*. ii. 184, *n*. 5 and the connection noted there that has been made between *ummujja* and Skrt. *unmiñjita*; and for *unmiñja*, *unmiñjita* one may now consult *B.H.S.D*.: " opening, as of the mouth."

[4] This sentence is quoted at *Asl*. 88 as belonging to a Discourse in which *kamma* is thought of as volition, or intentional. The wanderer's name is given as Pātaliputta.

[5] *mahākammavibhaṅga*, the term which appears to give this Discourse its name.

[6] *bhajantassa*, apparently from *bhajati*, to follow, associate with. *Vibhajati* is to dissect, divide, classify, and is the word Ānanda uses (immediately below) in his response.

"Yes, revered sir," the venerable Ānanda answered the Lord in assent. The Lord spoke thus:

"There are these four (types of) persons, Ānanda, existing in the world.[1] What four ? Some individual here, Ānanda, is one who makes onslaught on creatures, takes what has not been given, wrongly enjoys pleasures of the senses, is a liar, of slanderous speech, of harsh speech, a gossip, covetous, malevolent in mind, and of false view. At the breaking up of the body after dying he arises in the sorrowful ways, a bad bourn, the Downfall, Niraya Hell.

Some individual here, Ānanda, is one who makes onslaught on creatures . . . (*as above*) . . . is of false view. At the breaking up of the body after dying he arises in a good bourn, a heaven world.

But some individual here, Ānanda, refrains from onslaught on creatures, refrains from taking what has not been given, refrains from wrong enjoyment of the sense-pleasures, refrains from lying, refrains from slanderous speech, [210] refrains from harsh speech, refrains from gossip, is not covetous, not malevolent in mind, and is of right view. At the breaking up of the body after dying he arises in a good bourn, a heaven world.

Some individual here, Ānanda, refrains from onslaught on creatures . . . (*as above*) . . . is of right view. At the breaking up of the body after dying he arises in the sorrowful ways, a bad bourn, the Downfall, Niraya Hell.

This is a case,[2] Ānanda, where some recluse or brahman, as a result of ardour, as a result of striving, as a result of application, as a result of diligence, as a result of right mental work,[3] attains such concentration of mind that while the mind is concentrated he sees with the purified *deva*-like vision surpassing that of men some individual here who made onslaught on creatures, took what had not been given, wrongly enjoyed sense-pleasures, was a liar, of slanderous speech, of harsh speech, a gossip, covetous, malevolent in mind, and of false view—and he sees that at the breaking up of the body after dying he has arisen in the sorrowful ways, a bad bourn, the Downfall, Niraya Hell. He speaks thus: ' Indeed there are evil deeds, there is

---

[1] *MA.* v. 18 says that these four are *mātikā* (headings, summaries) set out so as to detail the knowledge of the great analysis of deeds, but they are not themselves the classification of such knowledge.

[2] As at *D.* i. 13.

[3] *MA.* v. 18 says that these five (ardour to right mental work) are names for energy.

fruition of wrong faring. And the individual I saw here making onslaught on creatures, taking what had not been given ... who was of slanderous speech ... of false view, I now see at the breaking up of the body after dying arisen in the sorrowful ways ... Niraya Hell.' He speaks thus: 'Indeed everyone who makes onslaught on creatures ... and is of false view, at the breaking up of the body after dying arises in the sorrowful ways ... Niraya Hell. Those who know thus know rightly. False is the knowledge of those that know otherwise.' In this way he obstinately holds to and adheres to[1] that which he has known by himself, seen by himself, discerned by himself as ' This alone is the truth, all else is falsehood.'

But there is this case, Ānanda, when some recluse or brahman, [211] as a result of ardour, striving, application, diligence and right mental work ... sees ... some individual here who made onslaught on creatures ... of false view, and sees that at the breaking up of the body after dying he has arisen in a good bourn, a heaven world. He speaks thus: ' Indeed there are no evil deeds, no fruition of wrong faring. And the individual I saw here making onslaught on creatures, taking what had not been given ... of false view, I now see at the breaking up of the body after dying arisen in a good bourn, a heaven world.' He speaks thus: 'Indeed everyone who makes onslaught on creatures ... of false view, at the breaking up of the body after dying arises in a good bourn, a heaven world. Those who know thus know rightly. False is the knowledge of those that know otherwise.' In this way he obstinately holds to and adheres to that which he has known, seen and discerned by himself as ' This alone is the truth, all else is falsehood.'

This is a case, Ānanda, where some recluse or brahman, as a result of ardour, as a result of striving, as a result of application, as a result of diligence, as a result of right mental work ... sees ... some individual here who was restrained from making onslaught on creatures, restrained from taking what had not been given, from wrong enjoyment of sense-pleasures, from lying, from slanderous speech, harsh speech, gossipping, who was not covetous, who was benevolent in mind and of right view, and sees that at the breaking up of the body after dying he has arisen in a good bourn, a heaven world. He speaks thus: ' Indeed there are lovely deeds; there is fruition of right faring. And the individual that I saw here restrained from making onslaught on creatures ... of right view, I now see at

---

[1] As at *M*. i. 130, 257, 498.

the breaking up of the body after dying arisen in a good bourn, a heaven world.' He speaks thus: ' Indeed everyone who is restrained from making onslaught on creatures . . . of right view, at the breaking up of the body after dying arises in a good bourn, a heaven world. Those who know thus know rightly. False is the knowledge of those that know otherwise.' In this way he obstinately holds to and adheres to that which he has known, seen and discerned by himself as ' This alone is the truth, all else is falsehood.'

But there is this case, Ānanda, when some recluse or brahman, as a result of ardour . . . [212] sees . . . some individual here who was restrained from making onslaught on creatures . . . of right view, and sees that at the breaking up of the body after dying he has arisen in the sorrowful ways, a bad bourn, the Downfall, Niraya Hell. He speaks thus: ' Indeed there are no lovely deeds, there is no fruition of right faring. And the individual that I saw here restrained from making onslaught on creatures . . . of right view, I now see at the breaking up of the body after dying arisen in the sorrowful ways, a bad bourn, the Downfall, Niraya Hell.' He speaks thus: ' Indeed everyone who is restrained from making onslaught on creatures . . . of right view, at the breaking up of the body after dying arises in the sorrowful ways, a bad bourn, the Downfall, Niraya Hell. Those who know thus know rightly. False is the knowledge of those that know otherwise.' In this way he obstinately holds to and adheres to that which he has known, seen and discerned by himself as ' This alone is the truth, all else is falsehood.'

As to this, Ānanda, whatever recluse or brahman speaks thus: ' Indeed there are evil deeds, there is fruition of wrong faring '—this I allow to him. And if he speaks thus: ' The individual that I saw here making onslaught on creatures, taking what had not been given . . . of false view, I now see at the breaking up of the body after dying arisen in the sorrowful ways . . . Niraya Hell '—this too I allow to him. But if he speaks thus: ' Everyone who makes onslaught on creatures, takes what has not been given . . . and is of false view, at the breaking up of the body after dying arises in the sorrowful ways, a bad bourn, the Downfall, Niraya Hell ' —this I do not allow to him. And if he speaks thus: ' Those who know thus know rightly. False is the knowledge of those that know otherwise ' —neither do I allow this to him. And whoever obstinately holds to and adheres to that which he has known by himself, seen by himself, discerned by himself as ' This alone is the truth, all else is falsehood ' —neither do I allow this to him. What is the cause of this ? The

Tathāgata's knowledge of the great analysis of deeds is otherwise, Ānanda.

As to this, Ānanda, whatever recluse or brahman speaks thus: 'Indeed there are no evil deeds, there is no fruition of wrong faring'—this I do not allow to him. And if he speaks thus: 'The individual that I saw here making onslaught on creatures, taking what had not been given ... of false view, I now see at the breaking up of the body after dying arisen in a good bourn, a heaven world'—this I allow to him. But if he speaks thus: 'Everyone who makes onslaught on creatures, takes what has not been given ... is of false view, at the breaking up of the body after dying arises in a good bourn, a heaven world'—[213] this I do not allow to him. And if he speaks thus: 'Those who know thus know rightly. False is the knowledge of those that know otherwise'—neither do I allow this to him. And whoever obstinately holds to and adheres to that which he has known, seen and discerned by himself as 'This alone is the truth, all else in falsehood'—neither do I allow this to him. What is the cause of this? The Tathāgata's knowledge of the great analysis of deeds is otherwise, Ānanda.

As to this, Ānanda, whatever recluse or brahman speaks thus: 'Indeed there are lovely deeds, there is fruition of right faring'—I allow this to him. And if he speaks thus: 'The individual that I saw here restrained from making onslaught on creatures, restrained from taking what had not been given ... of right view, I now see at the breaking up of the body after dying arisen in a good bourn, a heaven world'—this too I allow to him. But if he speaks thus: 'Everyone who is restrained from making onslaught on creatures, is restrained from taking what has not been given ... is of right view, at the breaking up of the body after dying arises in a good bourn, a heaven world'—this I do not allow to him. And if he speaks thus: 'Those who know thus know rightly. False is the knowledge of those that know otherwise'—neither do I allow this to him. And whoever obstinately holds to and adheres to that which he has known, seen and discerned by himself as 'This alone is the truth, all else is falsehood'—neither do I allow this to him. What is the cause of this? The Tathāgata's knowledge of the great analysis of deeds is otherwise, Ānanda.

As to this, Ānanda, whatever recluse or brahman speaks thus: 'Indeed there are no lovely deeds, there is no fruition of right faring'—this I do not allow to him. But if he speaks thus: 'The individual that I saw here restrained from making onslaught on creatures, restrained from taking what had not been given ... of right view, I now see at the breaking up of the body after dying arisen in the sorrowful ways, a bad bourn, the Downfall, Niraya Hell '—this I allow to him. But if he speaks thus: ' Everyone who is restrained from making onslaught on creatures, restrained from taking what had not been given ... of right view, at the breaking up of the body after dying arises in the sorrowful ways ... Niraya Hell ' —this I do not allow to him. And if he speaks thus: [**214**] ' Those who know thus know rightly. False is the knowledge of those that know otherwise '—neither do I allow this to him. And whoever obstinately holds to and adheres to that which he has known, seen and discerned for himself as ' This alone is the truth, all else is falsehood '—neither do I allow this to him. What is the cause of this ? The Tathāgata's knowledge of the great analysis of deeds is otherwise, Ānanda.

As to this, Ānanda, whatever individual there is who makes onslaught on creatures, takes what has not been given ... is of false view and who, at the breaking up of the body after dying arises in the sorrowful ways ... Niraya Hell—either an evil deed to be experienced as anguish was done by him earlier, or an evil deed to be experienced as anguish was done by him later, or at the time of dying a false view was adopted and firmly held by him; because of this, at the breaking up of the body after dying he arises in the sorrowful ways, a bad bourn, the Downfall, Niraya Hell. And he who made onslaught on creatures here, took what had not been given ... was of false view undergoes its fruition which arises here and now or in another mode.

As to this, Ānanda, whatever individual there is who makes onslaught on creatures, takes what has not been given ... is of false view and who, at the breaking up of the body after dying arises in a good bourn, a heaven world—either a lovely deed to be experienced as happiness was done by him earlier, or a lovely deed to be experienced as happiness was done by him later, or at the time of dying a right view was adopted and firmly held by him; because of this, at the breaking up of the body after dying he arises in a good bourn, a heaven world. If he[1] made onslaught on creatures here, took what had not been given ... and was of false view, he undergoes its fruition which arises here and now or in another mode.

As to this, Ānanda, whatever individual there is who is restrained

---

[1] *sace kho so* here; *yañ ca kho so* in the other paragraphs.

from making onslaught on creatures, is restrained from taking what has not been given ... is of right view and who, at the breaking up of the body after dying, arises in a good bourn, a heaven world—either a lovely deed to be experienced as happiness was done by him earlier, or a lovely deed to be experienced as happiness was done by him later, or at the time of dying a right view was adopted and firmly held by him; because of this, on the breaking up of the body after dying he arises in a good bourn, a heaven world. And he who was restrained from making onslaught on creatures here, [**215**] was restrained from taking what had not been given ... and was of right view undergoes its fruition which arises either here and now or in another mode.

As to this, Ānanda, whatever individual there is who is restrained from making onslaught on creatures, is restrained from taking what has not been given ... is of right view and who, at the breaking up of the body after dying, arises in the sorrowful ways, a bad bourn, the Downfall, Niraya Hell—either an evil deed to be experienced as anguish was done by him earlier, or an evil deed to be experienced as anguish was done by him later, or at the time of dying a false view was adopted and firmly held by him; because of this, on the breaking up of the body after dying he arises in the sorrowful ways ... Niraya Hell. And he who was restrained from making onslaught on creatures here, was restrained from taking what had not been given ... and was of right view undergoes its fruition which arises either here and now or in another mode.

So, Ānanda, there is the deed that is inoperative,[1] apparently inoperative;[2] there is the deed that is inoperative, apparently operative; there is the deed that is both operative and apparently operative; there is the deed that is operative, apparently inoperative."

Thus spoke the Lord. Delighted, the venerable Ānanda rejoiced in what the Lord had said.

Discourse on the Greater Analysis of Deeds:
The Sixth

---

[1] *atthi kammaṁ abhabbaṁ* (one version reading *n'atthi*).
[2] *abhabbābhāsa*.

137. DISCOURSE ON THE ANALYSIS OF THE SIXFOLD (SENSE-)FIELD

(Saḷāyatanavibhaṅgasutta)

THUS have I heard: At one time the Lord was staying near Sāvatthī in the Jeta Grove in Anāthapiṇḍika's monastery. While he was there the Lord addressed the monks, saying: " Monks." " Revered One," these monks answered the Lord in assent. The Lord spoke thus: " I will teach you, monks, the analysis of the sixfold (sense-) field. Listen to it, attend carefully and I will speak." " Yes, revered sir," these monks answered the Lord in assent. The Lord spoke thus:

[216] " Six internal sense-fields are to be known. Six external sense-fields are to be known. Six classes of consciousness are to be known. Six classes of (sense-)impingement are to be known. Eighteen mental ranges[1] are to be known. Thirty-six modes for creatures[2] are to be known. Wherefore, because of this get rid of this.[3] There are three arousings of mindfulness[4] each of which

---

[1] *manopavicārā*. *MA*. v. 21 says *manassa upavicārā*, discriminations or applications, ranges or spheres of the mind or mental activity. See *B.H.S.D.*

[2] *sattapadā*. *MA*. v. 21 calls this the tracks, ways, lots, *padā*, of creatures rooted in *vaṭṭa*, the whirligig of becoming (eighteen modes) and *vivaṭṭa* (eighteen modes).

[3] *tatr' idaṁ nissāya idaṁ pajahatha*. All these brief expositions, statements or headings (*mātikā*) are explained during the course of this Sutta.

[4] These three *satipaṭṭhāna* have nothing to do with the four usual ones, as is clear from the analysis below, p. 269. They are, more precisely, *āveṇikā* (special, exceptional) *satipaṭṭhānā* of a Buddha, his even-mindedness, *samacittatā*, when his audience listens, does not listen, or partly both. See *B.H.S.D.* under *āveṇika* and *smṛty-upasthāna*. At *Divy*. 182, 268, we get: *tribhir āveṇikaiḥ smṛtyupasthānair*; and at *Divy*. 126 *tribhiḥ smṛtyupasthānair*. *Cf*. the eighteen special, peculiar attributes of a Buddha, *āveṇikā Buddhadharmā*, enumerated at *Mhvu*. i. 160. And *cf. e.g. Śatasāhasrikā* ix. 1449-1450 (translated at *Buddhist Texts through the Ages*, p. 145) where among the attributes is included " his mindfulness never fails " and " there is no falling off in mindfulness," *nāsti smṛtihāniḥ*, although this, from the context, almost certainly refers not to the three, but to the four arousings of mindfulness. Pali has no such list, although eighteen *Buddhadhammā* are referred to at *Miln*. 105, 285, *UdA*. 87. Apart from the above Discourse, I know of no other passage in the Pali canon that expounds these three *satipaṭṭhānā*.

an ariyan practises and, practising which, is an ariyan who is a teacher fit to instruct a group.[1] Of trainers[2] he is called the incomparable charioteer of men to be tamed.

This is the exposition[3] of the analysis of the sixfold sense-field:

When it is said, ' Six internal sense-fields[4] are to be known,' in reference to what is it said ? To the sense-field of eye, the sense-field of ear, the sense-field of nose, the sense-field of tongue, the sense-field of body, the sense-field of mind. When it is said, ' Six internal sense-fields are to be known,' it is said in reference to this.

When it is said, ' Six external sense-fields are to be known,' in reference to what is it said ? To the sense-field of material shape, the sense-field of sound, the sense-field of smell, the sense-field of taste, the sense-field of touch, the sense-field of mental states. When it is said, ' Six external sense-fields are to be known,' it is said in reference to this.

When it is said, ' Six classes of consciousness are to be known,' in reference to what is it said ? To visual consciousness, auditory consciousness, olfactory consciousness, gustatory consciousness, tactile consciousness, mental consciousness. When it is said, ' Six classes of consciousness are to be known,' it is said in reference to this.

When it is said, ' Six classes of (sense-)impingement[5] are to be known,' in reference to what is it said ? To visual impact, auditory impact, olfactory impact, gustatory impact, tactile impact, mental impact. When it is said, ' Six classes of (sense-)impingement are to be known,' it is said in reference to this.

---

[1] *tayo satipaṭṭhānā yad ariyo sevati yad ariyo sevamāno satthā gaṇaṁ anusāsituṁ arahati*. The two occurrences of *yad* in this sentence have the effect of referring not to these three *satipaṭṭhānā* as a whole or unit but to whichever one of them is called forth by the circumstances: of the disciples listening, not listening, or some listening and some not; see previous note. Also see the gloss of *yad ariyo* at *MA*. v. 27: *yad ariyo ti ye satipaṭṭhāne ariyo sammāsambuddho sevati*. *Tattha tīsu ṭhānesu ṭhapento satipaṭṭhāne sevati ti veditabbo*: " which an ariyan " means those arousings of mindfulness which an ariyan who is a fully self-awakened one practises. Here it is to be understood that, setting up mindfulness in the three (sets of) circumstances, he practises the arousings of mindfulness.

[2] *yoggācariya*, as at *M*. i. 124, iii. 97.

[3] *uddesa*, called at *MA*. v. 21 *mātikāṭhapanaṁ*, the establishment or statement of the headings.

[4] For this and the next three headings *cf. D.* iii. 243, etc.

[5] *Cf.* the " six feelings " at *S.* iv. 232.

When it is said, ' Eighteen mental ranges[1] are to be known,' in reference to what is it said ? Having seen a material shape with the eye[2] one ranges over[3] the material shape that gives rise to joy, ranges over the material shape that gives rise to sorrow, ranges over the material shape that gives rise to equanimity. Having heard a sound with the ear ... Having smelt a smell with the nose ... Having tasted a flavour with the tongue ... [217] Having felt a touch with the body ... Having cognised a mental state with the mind one ranges over the mental state that gives rise to joy, ranges over the mental state that gives rise to sorrow, ranges over the mental state that gives rise to equanimity. In this way there are six ranges for joy, six ranges for sorrow, six ranges for equanimity. When it is said, ' Eighteen mental ranges are to be known,' it is said in reference to this.

When it is said, ' Thirty-six modes for creatures[4] are to be known,' in reference to what is it said ? The six joys connected with worldly life, the six joys connected with renunciation; the six sorrows connected with worldly life, the six sorrows connected with renunciation; the six equanimities connected with worldly life, the six equanimities connected with renunciation.

Herein what are the six joys connected with worldly life ? There is the joy that arises either from attaining and from beholding the attainment of material shapes cognisable through the eye, pleasant, agreeable, liked, delightful, connected with the material things of the world; or from remembering that what was formerly attained is past, arrested, altered. Joy such as this is called joy connected with worldly life. There is the joy that arises either from attaining and from beholding the attainment of sounds cognisable through the ear ... of smells cognisable through the nose ... of flavours cognisable through the tongue ... of touches cognisable through the body ... of mental states cognisable through the mind, pleasant, agreeable, liked, delightful, connected with the material things of the world; or from remembering that what was formerly attained is past, arrested, altered. Joy such as this is called joy connected with worldly life.[5] These are the six joys connecred with worldly life.

Herein what are the six joys connected with renunciation ? When

---

[1] *Cf. M.* iii. 239 *f.* for *cha somanassūpavicārā cha domanassūpavicārā cha upekhūpavicārā*, also recorded at *D.* iii. 244 *f., Vbh.* 381. *Cf.* the " eighteen feelings " at *S.* iv. 232.

[2] With visual consciousness, *MA.* v. 22; *cf. VbhA.* 508.   [3] *upavicarati*.

[4] *Cf.* the " thirty-six feelings " at *S.* iv. 232.   [5] *Cf. Vism.* 319.

one has known the impermanency of material shapes themselves, their alteration, disappearance[1] and arrest, and thinks, 'Formerly as well as now all these material shapes are impermanent, painful, liable to alteration,' from seeing this thus as it really is by means of perfect wisdom, joy arises. Joy such as this is called joy connected with renunciation. When one has known the impermanency of sounds themselves... of smells themselves... of flavours themselves ... of touches themselves ... of mental states [**218**] themselves, their alteration, disappearance and arrest, and thinks, 'Formerly as well as now all these mental states are impermanent, painful, liable to alteration,' from seeing this thus as it really is by means of perfect wisdom, joy arises. Joy such as this is called joy connected with renunciation. These are the six joys connected with renunciation.

Herein what are the six sorrows connected with worldly life ? There is the sorrow that arises either from not attaining and from beholding the non-attainment of material shapes cognisable through the eye, pleasant, agreeable, liked, delightful, connected with the material things of the world; or from remembering that what was formerly not attained is past, arrested, altered. Sorrow such as this is called sorrow connected with worldly life. There is the sorrow that arises either from not attaining and from beholding the non-attainment of sounds cognisable through the ear . . . of smells cognisable through the nose . . . of flavours cognisable through the tongue . . . of touches cognisable through the body . . . of mental states cognisable through the mind, pleasant, agreeable, liked, delightful, connected with the material things of the world; or from remembering that what was formerly not attained is past, arrested, altered. Sorrow such as this is called sorrow connected with worldly life.[2] These are the six sorrows connected with worldly life.

Herein what are the six sorrows connected with renunciation ? When one has know the impermanency of material shapes themselves, their alteration, disappearance and arrest, and thinks, 'Formerly as well as now all these material shapes are impermanent, painful, liable to alteration,' from seeing this thus as it really is by means of perfect wisdom, he evinces a desire for the incomparable Deliverances,[3] thinking, 'When can I, entering on abide in that plane which the ariyans, now entering on, are abiding in ?' Thus, from evincing

---

[1] *virāga*, explained at *MA*. v. 22 by *vigacchanena virāgaṁ*.
[2] *Cf. Vism.* 319.
[3] *MA*. v. 23 says incomparable deliverance is called arahantship.

a desire for the incomparable Deliverances sorrow arises as a result of the desire. Sorrow such as this is called sorrow connected with renunciation. When one has known the impermanency of sounds themselves ... of smells themselves ... of flavours themselves ... of touches themselves ... of mental states themselves, their alteration, disappearance, arrest, and thinks, 'Formerly as well as now these mental states are impermanent, painful, liable to alteration,' [219] from seeing this thus as it really is by means of perfect wisdom, he evinces a desire for the incomparable Deliverances, thinking, 'When can I, entering on abide in that plane which the ariyans, now entering on, are abiding in ?' Thus from his evincing a desire for the incomparable Deliverances sorrow arises as a result of the desire. Sorrow such as this is called sorrow connected with renunciation. These are the six sorrows connected with renunciation.

Herein what are the six equanimities connected with worldly life ? When a foolish, errant, average person has seen a material shape with the eye, there arises the equanimity of an uninstructed average person who has not conquered (his defilements),[1] who has not conquered fruition,[2] who does not see the peril[3]—equanimity such as this does not go further than material shape. Therefore this is called equanimity connected with worldly life.[4] When a foolish average person has heard a sound with the ear ... smelt a smell with the nose ... tasted a flavour with the tongue ... felt a touch with the body ... cognised a mental state with the mind, there arises the equanimity of an uninstructed average person who has not conquered (his defilements), who has not conquered fruition, who does not see the peril—equanimity such as this does not go further than mental state. Therefore this is called equanimity connected with worldly life. These are the six equanimities connected with worldly life.

Herein what are the six equanimities connected with renunciation ? When one has known the impermanency of material shapes themselves ... of sounds themselves ... of smells themselves ... of

---

[1] *anodhijina*, one who has not conquered the whole extent (*odhi*, or, to the limit) of the *kilesas*, therefore one whose cankers are not destroyed, *MA.* v. 24. *Cf. Vbh.* 246.

[2] *avipākajina*. *MA.* v. 24 says, similarly one whose cankers are not destroyed. For a conqueror of fruition is called one whose cankers are destroyed because he has conquered *āyatiṁ vipākaṁ*, the fruition (of deeds done here or in former births) to their (full) stretch.

[3] *ādīnava*, which, often connected with sense pleasures, is at *MA.* v. 24 connected with misfortune or distress, *upaddava*.

[4] It is the equanimity of not knowing, *MA.* v. 24.

flavours themselves . . . of touches themselves . . . of mental states themselves, their alteration, disappearance and arrest, and thinks, ' Formerly as well as now all these mental states are impermanent, painful, liable to alteration,' from seeing this thus as it really is by means of perfect wisdom, equanimity arises. Equanimity such as this goes further than mental state. Therefore it is called equanimity connected with renunciation. These are the six equanimities connected with renunciation. When it is said, ' Thirty-six modes for creatures are to be known,' it is said in reference to this.

[220] Herein when it is said, ' Wherefore, because of this get rid of this ' in reference to what is it said ? Herein, monks, because of[1] and by means of[1] these six joys connected with renunciation, get rid of and transcend those six joys connected with worldly life. Thus is the getting rid of these, thus is their transcending.[2] Herein, monks, because of and by means of these six sorrows connected with renunciation, get rid of and transcend those six sorrows connected with worldly life. Thus is the getting rid of these, thus is their transcending. Herein, monks, because of and by means of these six equanimities connected with renunciation, get rid of and transcend those six equanimities connected with worldly life. Thus is the getting rid of these, thus is their transcending. Herein, monks, because of and by means of these six joys connected with renunciation, get rid of and transcend those six sorrows connected with renunciation. Thus is the getting rid of these, thus is their transcending. Herein, monks, because of and by means of these six equanimities connected with renunciation, get rid of and transcend those six joys connected with renunciation. Thus is the getting rid of these, thus is their transcending.

There is, monks, equanimity in face of multiformity, connected with multiformity; there is equanimity in face of uniformity, connected with uniformity.[3] And what, monks, is equanimity in face of multiformity, connected with multiformity ? It is, monks, equanimity among material shapes, among sounds, smells, flavours, touches. This, monks, is equanimity in face of multiformity, connected with multiformity. And what, monks, is equanimity in face of uniformity, connected with uniformity ? It is, monks, equanimity connected with the plane of infinite ether, connected with the plane of infinite consciousness, connected with the plane

---

[1] *tāni nissāya tāni āgamma.* Cf. *KhpA.* 229 *āgammā ti nissāya.*
[2] Cf. *M.* i. 445.   [3] Cf. *M.* i. 364-367.

of no-thing, connected with the plane of neither-perception-nor-non-perception. This, monks, is equanimity in face of uniformity, connected with uniformity. Herein, monks, because of and by means of this equanimity in face of uniformity, connected with uniformity, get rid of and transcend that equanimity in face of multiformity, connected with multiformity. Thus is the getting rid of it, thus is its transcending. Because of lack of desire,[1] monks, by means of lack of desire, get rid of and transcend that equanimity in face of uniformity, connected with uniformity. Thus is the getting rid of it, thus is its transcending. [**221**] When it is said, ' Wherefore because of this get rid of this,' it is said in reference to this.

When it is said, ' There are three arousings of mindfulness each of which an ariyan practises and, practising which, is an ariyan who is a teacher fit to instruct a group,' in reference to what is it said ? As to this,[2] monks, a teacher teaches *dhamma* to disciples, compassionate, seeking their welfare, out of compassion, saying: ' This is for your welfare, this is for your happiness.' But his disciples do not listen, do not lend ear, do not prepare their minds for profound knowledge and, turning aside, move away from the teacher's instruction. Herein, monks, the Tathāgata is neither delighted nor does he experience delight, but dwells untroubled,[3] mindful and clearly conscious. This, monks, is the first arousing of mindfulness that the ariyan practises and, practising it, is an ariyan who is a teacher fit to instruct a group.

And again, monks, a teacher teaches *dhamma* to disciples . . . saying: ' This is for your welfare, this is for your happiness.' Some of his disciples do not listen, do not lend ear, do not prepare their minds for profound knowledge and, turning aside, move away from the teacher's instruction. But some disciples listen, lend ear, prepare their minds for profound knowledge and, not turning aside, do not move away from the teacher's instruction. Herein, monks, the Tathāgata is neither delighted nor does he experience delight and neither is he depressed nor does he experience depression. Having ousted both delight and depression, he dwells with equanimity, mindful and clearly conscious. This, monks, is the second arousing of mindfulness that the ariyan practises and, practising it, is an ariyan who is a teacher fit to instruct a group.

---

[1] *atammayatā* as at *M*. iii. 42.   [2] *Cf. M*. iii. 117.
[3] *anavassuta*; here, not overflowing with repulsion, *paṭigha*, *MA*. v. 27.

And again, monks, a teacher teaches *dhamma* to disciples . . . saying; ' This is for your welfare, this is for your happiness.' His disciples listen, lend ear, prepare their minds for profound knowledge and, not turning aside, do not move from the teacher's instruction. Herein, monks, the Tathāgata is delighted and he experiences delight but he dwells untroubled,[1] mindful and clearly conscious. This, monks, is the third arousing of mindfulness that the ariyan practises and, practising it, is an ariyan who is a teacher fit to instruct a group. [222] When it is said: ' There are three arousings of mindfulness each of which an ariyan practises and, practising which, is an ariyan who is a teacher fit to instruct a group,' it is said in reference to this.

When it is said, ' Of trainers he is called the incomparable charioteer of men to be tamed,' in reference to what is it said ? When, monks, an elephant to be tamed is driven[2] by the elephant-tamer it runs in one direction only—to the east or west or north or south. When, monks, a horse to be tamed . . . a bull to be tamed is driven by the horse-tamer or the tamer of bulls it runs in one direction only—to the east or west or north or south. When, monks, a man to be tamed is driven by the Tathāgata, perfected one, fully Self-Awakened One he courses[3] to eight quarters:[4] Being in the fine-material sphere, he sees material shapes; this is the first quarter. Not perceiving material shape internally he sees external material shapes; this is the second quarter. By thinking of the Fair, he is intent on it; this is the third quarter. By passing quite beyond perceptions of material shape, by sinking perceptions of sensory reactions, by not attending to perceptions of variety, and thinking, ' Ether is unending,' entering on the plane of infinite ether he abides in it; this is the fourth quarter. By passing quite beyond the plane

---

[1] Here, not overflowing with *rāga*, attachment.

[2] *sārita*, past participle both of *sāreti*, causative of *sarati*, to go, to run, to move along, to flow; and of *sarati*, to call to mind, to remember. *Cf. sāreyya* at *M*. i. 124, explained by *MA*. ii. 98 as *ujukuṁ peseyya*, should send (him) forth straight; but *MA*. v. 27 explains *sārita* by *damita*, tamed.

[3] *vidhāvati*, to run about, to roam, to rove; *dhāvati* being to run, to run quickly. Here *vidhāvati* is used of the mind only; for the man sits down cross-legged, does not twist his body round for no matter which quarter he is facing (in the physical sense, E, W, N, S), he attains these eight attainments: the Deliverances at the same time as the " quarters," *MA*. v. 28; and naturally, since they appear to be the same as one another.

[4] These quarters or directions are the same as the eight Deliverances as given, *e.g.* at *M*. ii. 12, and which are to be (mentally) developed.

of infinite ether, thinking, ' Consciousness is unending,' entering on the plane of infinite consciousness, he abides in it; this is the fifth quarter. By passing quite beyond the plane of infinite consciousness, thinking, ' There is not anything,' entering on the plane of no-thing, he abides in it; this is the sixth quarter. By passing quite beyond the plane of no-thing, entering on the plane of neither-pereception-nor-non-perception, he abides in it; this is the seventh quarter. By passing quite beyond the plane of neither-perception-nor-non-perception, entering on the stopping of perception and feeling, he abides in it; this is the eighth quarter. When, monks, a man to be tamed is driven by the Tathāgata, perfected one, fully Self-Awakened One, he courses to these eight quarters. When it is said, ' Of trainers he is called the incomparable charioteer of men to be tamed,' it is said in reference to this."

Thus spoke the Lord. Delighted, these monks rejoiced in what the Lord had said.

Discourse on the Analysis of the Sixfold (Sense-)Field:
The Seventh

138. DISCOURSE ON AN EXPOSITION AND ANALYSIS
(Uddesavibhaṅgasutta)[1]

[223] THUS have I heard: At one time the Lord was staying near Sāvatthī in the Jeta Grove in Anāthapiṇḍika's monastery. While he was there the Lord addressed the monks, saying: " Monks." " Revered One," these monks answered the Lord in assent. The Lord spoke thus: " I will teach you, monks, an exposition and (its) analysis. Listen to it, attend carefully, and I will speak." " Yes, revered sir," these monks answered the Lord in assent. The Lord spoke thus:

---

[1] *MA*. v. 28 says *uddesañ ca vibhaṅgañ ca mātikañ ca vibhajanañ cā ti.* So *uddesa* is the statement of the headings (*mātikā*) which will be analysed in this Discourse.

"Monks, a monk should so investigate[1] (things) that, as he investigates, his consciousness of what is external be undistracted, not diffused, and of what is internal be unslackened so that it[2] may not be disturbed by grasping; monks, if consciousness of what is external be undistracted, not diffused, of what is internal be unslackened, then, for him who is (thus) undisturbed by grasping there is in the future no origin or rise of birth, old age and dying or of anguish." Thus spoke the Lord. When he had said this, the Well-farer rose from his seat and entered a dwelling-place. Soon after the Lord had gone, it occurred to these monks: "Your reverences, the Lord, recited this exposition to us in brief: 'Monks, a monk should so investigate (things) that . . . there is in the future no origin or rise of birth, old age and dying or of anguish.' But without having explained the meaning in full he rose from his seat and entered a dwelling-place. Now, who can explain the meaning in full of this exposition which was recited in brief by the Lord but the meaning of which he did not explain in full?" Then it occurred to these monks: "Now, the venerable Kaccāna the Great is both praised by the Teacher and revered by intelligent Brahma-farers . . .[3] [224, 225] . . . May the venerable Kaccāna explain it without finding it troublesome."

"Well then, your reverences, listen, pay careful attention and I will speak."

"Yes, your reverence," these monks answered the venerable Kaccāna the Great in assent. The venerable Kaccāna the Great spoke thus:

"In regard to that exposition, your reverences, which was recited in brief by the Lord but the meaning of which he had not explained in full when he rose from his seat and entered a dwelling-place: 'Monks, a monk should so investigate (things) that . . . there is in the future no origin or rise of birth, old age and dying and of anguish '—of this exposition which was recited in brief by the Lord but the meaning of which he did not explain in full, I, your reverences, understand the meaning in full thus:

And what, your reverences, is called distracted, diffused consciousness of what is external? If, your reverences, after a monk has seen a material shape with the eye, his consciousness runs after signs of material shape, is tied by satisfaction in signs of material

---

[1] *upaparikkheyya*, should weigh, measure, explore, mark out, *MA.* v. 28. *Cf. Iti.*, p. 94, where this " heading " also occurs.

[2] Consciousness, *MA.* v. 28.   [3] As at *M.* iii. 194-195.

shapes, is bound to satisfaction in signs of material shapes, is fettered by the fetter of satisfaction in the signs of material shapes, then the consciousness of what is external is said to be distracted and diffused. If, having heard a sound with the ear . . . having smelt a smell with the nose . . . having tasted a flavour with the tongue . . . having felt a touch with the body . . . having cognised a mental state with the mind, his consciousness runs after signs of mental states . . . is fettered by the fetter of satisfaction in mental states, then the consciousness of what is external is said to be distracted and diffused. It is thus, your reverences, that consciousness of what is external is called distracted and diffused.

And what, your reverences, is called undistracted, undiffused consciousness of what is external ? If, your reverences, after a monk has seen a material shape with the eye, his consciousness does not run after signs of material shape, is not tied by satisfaction in signs of material shape, is not bound to satisfaction in signs of material shapes, is not fettered by the fetter of satisfaction in the signs of material shapes, then the consciousness of what is external is said to be undistracted and undiffused. [**226**] If, having heard a sound with the ear . . . having cognised a mental state with the mind, his consciousness does not run after signs of mental states, is not tied by satisfaction in signs of mental states, is not bound to satisfaction in signs of mental states, is not fettered by the fetter of satisfaction in the signs of mental states, then the consciousness of what is external is said to be undistracted and undiffused. It is thus, your reverences, that consciousness of what is external is called undistracted and undiffused.

And what, your reverences, is called slackened thought in regard to what is internal ? As to this, your reverences, a monk, aloof from pleasures of the senses, aloof from unskilled states of mind, entering into abides in the first meditation which is accompanied by initial thought and discursive thought, is born of aloofness, and is rapturous and joyful. If his consciousness runs after the rapture and joy that are born of aloofness, if it is tied by . . . bound to . . . fettered by the fetter of satisfaction in the rapture and joy that are born of aloofness, then his thought is called slackened in regard to what is internal.

And again, your reverences, a monk, by allaying initial thought and discursive thought, with the mind subjectively tranquillised and fixed on one point, enters into and abides in the second meditation which is devoid of initial thought and discursive thought, is born of concentration, and is rapturous and joyful. If his consciousness runs after the rapture and joy that are born of concentration, if it is tied by . . . bound to . . . fettered by the fetter of satisfaction in the rapture and joy that are born of concentration, then his thought is called slackened in regard to what is internal.

And again, your reverences, a monk, by the fading out of rapture abides with equanimity, mindful and clearly conscious and experiences in his person that joy of which the ariyans say: ' Joyful lives he who has equanimity and is mindful,' entering into the third meditation, he abides in it. If his consciousness runs after the joy of equanimity,[1] if it is tied by . . . bound to . . . fettered by the fetter of satisfaction in the joy of equanimity, then his thought is called slackened in regard to what is internal.

And again, your reverences, a monk, by getting rid of joy, by getting rid of anguish, by the going down of his former pleasures and sorrows, entering into abides in the fourth meditation which has neither anguish nor joy, and which is entirely purified by equanimity and mindfulness. If his consciousness runs after what is neither-anguish-nor-joy, if it is tied by . . . bound to . . . fettered by the fetter of satisfaction in what is neither-anguish-nor-joy, then his thought is called slackened in regard to what is internal. It is thus, your reverences, that thought is called slackened in regard to what is internal.

[227] And what, your reverences, is called unslackened thought in regard to what is internal ? As to this, your reverences, a monk, aloof from pleasures of the senses . . . abides in the first meditation which is . . . rapturous and joyful. If his consciousness does not run after the rapture and joy that are born of aloofness, if it is not tied by . . . not bound to . . . not fettered by the fetter of satisfaction in the rapture and joy that are born of aloofness, then his thought is called unslackened in regard to what is internal.

And again, your reverences, a monk, by allaying initial thought and discursive thought . . . abides in the second meditation which is . . . rapturous and joyful. If his consciousness does not run after the rapture and joy that are born of concentration, if it is not tied by . . . not bound to . . . not fettered by the fetter of satisfaction in the rapture and joy that are born of concentration, then his thought is called unslackened in regard to what is internal.

---

[1] Text here reads *upekhānusārī*; but I think it necessary to insert *sukha* into this compound as in the negative clause below: *upekhāsukhānusārī*.

And again, your reverences, a monk, by the fading out of rapture
... entering into the third meditation, abides in it. If his consciousness does not run after the joy of equanimity, if it is not tied by ... not bound to ... not fettered by the fetter of satisfaction in the joy of equanimity, then his thought is called unslackened in regard to what is internal.

And again, your reverences, a monk, by getting rid of joy, by getting rid of anguish ... abides in the fourth meditation which has neither anguish nor joy, and which is entirely purified by equanimity and mindfulness. If his consciousness does not run after what is neither-anguish-nor-joy, if it is not tied by ... not bound to ... not fettered by the fetter of satisfaction in what is neither-anguish-nor-joy, then his thought is called unslackened in regard to what is internal. It is thus, your reverences, that thought is called unslackened in regard to what is internal.

And what, your reverences, is being disturbed by grasping?[1] As to this, your reverences, an uninstructed average person, taking no count of the pure ones, unskilled in the *dhamma* of the pure ones, untrained in the *dhamma* of the pure ones, taking no count of the true men, unskilled in the *dhamma* of the true men, untrained in the *dhamma* of the true men, regards material shape as self or self as having material shape or material shape as in self or self as in material shape. His material shape alters and becomes otherwise; with the alteration and otherwiseness in his material shape, his consciousness is occupied with the alteration in the material shape;[2] there is disturbance for him born of his occupation with the alteration in the material shape; mental objects, arising, persist in obsessing his thought; because of this obsession of his thought he is afraid and annoyed and full of longing[3] and he is disturbed by grasping.[4]
[228] He regards feeling ... perception ... the habitual tendencies ... consciousness as self or self as having consciousness or consciousness as in self or self as in consciousness. His consciousness alters and becomes otherwise; with the alteration and otherwiseness

---

[1] For the rest of Mahā-Kaccāna's explanation, *cf. S.* iii. 15 *ff.*

[2] In Chalmers' text a sentence is here inserted, presumably in error as it has no counterpart in the repetitions below or in the *S.* version: *tassa rūpaṁ viparināmānuparivatti viññāṇaṁ hoti* should therefore be deleted.

[3] *upekhavā* of Chalmers' text should probably read, with *S. apekhavā*. *MA.* v. 30, reading *apekkhavā*, explains by *sālayo sapiho*, with pleasure and affection.

[4] *anupādāya*. The reading at *S.* iii. 16, which I follow, is *upādāya*.

in his consciousness, his consciousness is occupied with the alteration in his consciousness; mental objects, arising, persist in obsessing his thought; because of this obsession of his thought he is afraid and annoyed and full of longing and he is disturbed by grasping. This, your reverences, is what is being disturbed by grasping.

And what, your reverences, is not being disturbed by grasping? As to this, your reverences, an instructed disciple of the ariyans, taking count of the pure ones, skilled in the *dhamma* of the pure ones, well trained in the *dhamma* of the pure ones, taking count of the true men, skilled in the *dhamma* of the true men, well trained in the *dhamma* of the true men, does not regard material shape as self or self as having material shape or material shape as in self or self as in material shape. His material shape alters and becomes otherwise; but with the alteration and otherwiseness in his material shape, his consciousness is not occupied with the alteration in his material shape; no disturbance for him is born of his occupation with the alteration in the material shape; mental objects, arising, do not persist in obsessing his thought; because of this non-obsession of his thought he is neither afraid nor annoyed or full of longing and he is not disturbed by grasping. He does not regard feeling . . . perception . . . the habitual tendencies . . . consciousness as self or self as having consciousness or consciousness as in self or self as in consciousness. His consciousness alters and becomes otherwise; with the alteration and otherwiseness in his consciousness, his consciousness is not occupied with the alteration in his consciousness; no disturbance for him is born of his occupation with the alteration in his consciousness; mental objects, arising, do not persist in obsessing his thought; because of this non-obsession of his thought he is neither afraid nor annoyed or full of longing and he is not disturbed by grasping. This ,your reverences, is what is not being disturbed by grasping.

In regard to that exposition, your reverences, which the Lord recited in brief but the meaning of which he had not explained in full when he rose from his seat and entered a dwelling-place: ' Monks, a monk should so investigate (things) that . . . there is in the future no origin or rise of birth, old age and dying and of anguish '—of this exposition which was recited by the Lord in brief but the meaning of which he did not explain in full, I, your reverences [**229**] understand the meaning in full thus. But if you, venerable ones, so desire, you can approach the Lord and question him as to the meaning so that as the Lord explains it to you so may you understand it."

Then these monks ... (*as at M. iii.* 198-199, *above, p.* 243, reading Monks, a monk should so investigate (things) that ... there is in the future no origin or rise of birth, old age and dying and of anguish *instead of* The past should not be followed after, the future not desired ... He is indeed 'Auspicious' called, described as a sage at peace) ...

"Learned, monks, is Kaccāna the Great, of great wisdom, monks, is Kaccāna the Great. For if you, monks, had questioned me as to this meaning, I too would have explained it precisely as it was explained by Kaccāna the Great. Indeed, this is the exact meaning of that, and thus should you remember it."

Thus spoke the Lord. Delighted, these monks rejoiced in what the Lord had said.

Discourse on an Exposition and Analysis:
The Eighth

139. DISCOURSE ON THE ANALYSIS OF THE UNDEFILED[1]
(Araṇavibhaṅgasutta)

[230] THUS have I heard: At one time the Lord was staying near Sāvatthī in the Jeta Grove in Anāthapiṇḍika's monastery. While he was there the Lord addressed the monks, saying: "Monks." "Revered One," these monks answered the Lord in assent. The Lord spoke thus: "I will teach you, monks, the analysis of the undefiled. Listen carefully to it, pay attention and I will speak." "Yes, revered sir," these monks answered the Lord in assent. The Lord spoke thus:

---

[1] *Araṇa* might also be translated as peace and *saraṇa* as disturbance: the peace that comes from absence of the defilements and the disturbance due to their presence. At *MA.* v. 32 it is said that *araṇa* means free from passion or the defilements, *kilesa*; *cf. AA.* i. 220, *SA.* i. 101, *nikkilesa*. At *Vbh.* 19 *f.* the *khandha* of feeling is twofold, *saraṇa* and *araṇa*. *Saraṇa = sa+raṇa*, concomitant with war, stain or defilement. See *B.H.S.D.* under *araṇa* and *raṇa*. At *A.* i. 24 Subhūti is chief of abiders in non-defilement or peace, referred to at *MA.* v. 31 *f.*

"You should not be intent on the happiness of sense-pleasures which is low, of the villager, of the average person, unariyan, not connected with the goal; nor should you be intent on the practice of self-mortification which is sorrowful, unariyan, not connected with the goal. Not approaching either of these two dead-ends, there is the Middle Course awakened to by the Tathāgata, making for vision, making for knowledge, and conducing to calm, super-knowledge, self-awakening and nibbāna. One should know approval and one should know disapproval, and having known approval, having known disapproval, one should neither approve nor disapprove—one should simply teach *dhamma*. One should know how to judge what happiness is; having known how to judge what happiness is, one should be intent on inward happiness. One should not utter a secret speech;[1] face to face (with a man) one should not tell (him) a vexatious thing.[2] One should speak quite slowly, not hurriedly. One should not affect the dialect of the countryside, one should not deviate from recognised parlance. This is the exposition of the analysis of the undefiled.

When it is said, 'You should not be intent on the happiness of sense-pleasures . . . nor should you be intent on the practice of self-mortification which is sorrowful, unariyan, not connected with the goal,' in reference to what is it said ? Whatever is happiness in association with sense-pleasures and intentness on a joy that is low, of the villager, of the average man, unariyan, not connected with the goal—this is a thing that has anguish,[3] annoyance, trouble and fret; it is a wrong course. But whatever is happiness in association with sense-pleasures but not intentness on a joy [231] that is low, of the villager . . . not connected with the goal—this is a thing without anguish, annoyance, trouble or fret; it is the right course. Whatever is intentness on self-mortification which is sorrowful, unariyan, not connected with the goal—this is a thing that has anguish, annoyance, trouble and fret; it is a wrong course. But whatever is nonintentness on self-mortification which is sorrowful, unariyan, not connected with the goal—this is a thing without anguish, annoyance, trouble or fret; it is the right course. When it is said, 'You should not be intent on the happiness of sense-pleasures . . . nor

---

[1] One should not defame, *i.e.* carry tales to another person.
[2] *khiṇa*, explained at *MA.* v. 30 as *ākiṇṇa*, confused, troubled, and as *kiliṭṭha*, soiled. It means that one should not say what is detrimental, annoying or improper.
[3] That is, as to its ripening and as to the defilements, *MA.* v. 31.

should you be intent on the practice of self-mortification which is sorrowful, unariyan, not connected with the goal,' it is said in reference to this.

When it is said, ' Not approaching either of these two dead-ends, there is the Middle Course awakened to by the Tathāgata, making for vision, making for knowledge, that conduces to calm, superknowledge, self-awakening and nibbāna,' in reference to what is it said ? It is the ariyan Eightfold Way itself, that is to say: right view, right aspiration, right speech, right action, right mode of livelihood, right endeavour, right mindfulness, right concentration. When it is said, ' Not approaching either of these two dead-ends, there is the Middle Course . . . that conduces to . . . nibbāna,' it is said in reference to this.

When it is said, ' One should know approval and one should know disapproval, and having known approval, having known disapproval, one should neither approve nor disapprove—one should simply teach *dhamma*,' in reference to what is it said ?

And what, monks, is approval and what is disapproval but not the teaching of *dhamma* ? He disapproves of some (people) here, saying: ' All those who find happiness in association with sensepleasures and are intent on a joy that is low, of the villager, of the average man, unariyan, not connected with the goal, have anguish, annoyance, trouble and fret; they are faring along wrongly.' He approves of some (people) here, saying: ' All those who find happiness in association with sense-pleasures but are not intent on a joy that is low . . . not connected with the goal, are without anguish, annoyance, trouble or fret; they are faring along rightly.' He disapproves of some (people) here, saying: ' All those who are intent on the practice of self-mortification, which is sorrowful, unaryian, not connected with the goal, [**232**] have anguish, annoyance, trouble and fret; they are faring along wrongly.' He approves of some (people) here, saying: ' All those who are not intent on the practice of selfmortification, which is sorrowful, unariyan, not connected with the goal, are without anguish, annoyance, trouble or fret; they are faring along rightly.' He disapproves of some (people) here, saying: ' All those in whom the fetter of becoming[1] is not got rid of have anguish, annoyance, troble and fret; they are faring along wrongly.' He approves of some (people) here, saying: ' All those in whom the fetter

---

[1] That is, thirst, *taṇhā*, *MA*. v. 31 which also says that when Subhūti was teaching *dhamma* he was not interested in the differences among individuals but simply laid down, " This is a wrong course, this the right one."

of becoming[1] is got rid of are without anguish, annoyance, trouble or fret; they are faring along rightly.' This, monks, is what is approval and disapproval but not the teaching of *dhamma*.

And what, monks, is neither approval nor disapproval, but the teaching of *dhamma* ? He does not speak thus: ' All those who find happiness in association with sense-pleasures and are intent on a joy that is low, of the villager, of the average man, unariyan, not connected with the goal, have anguish, annoyance, trouble and fret; they are faring along wrongly.' He simply teaches *dhamma*, saying: ' Intentness is a thing that has anguish, annoyance, trouble and fret; it is a wrong course.' He does not speak thus: ' All those who find happiness in association with sense-pleasures but are not intent on a joy that is low ... not connected with the goal, are without anguish, annoyance, trouble or fret; they are faring along rightly.' He simply teaches *dhamma*, saying: ' Non-intentness is a thing that is without anguish, annoyance, trouble or fret; it is the right course.' He does not speak thus: ' All those who are intent on the practice of self-mortification which is sorrowful, unariyan, not connected with the goal, have anguish, annoyance, trouble and fret; they are faring along wrongly.' He simply teaches *dhamma*, saying: ' Intentness is a thing that has anguish ... fret; it is a wrong course.' He does not speak thus: ' All those who are not intent on the practice of self-mortification ... are without anguish ... fret; they are faring along rightly.' He simply teaches *dhamma*, saying: ' Non-intentness is a thing that is without anguish ... fret; it is the right course.' He does not speak thus: ' All those in whom the fetter of becoming is not got rid of have anguish, annoyance, trouble and fret; they are faring along wrongly.' [233] He simply teaches *dhamma*, saying: ' While the fetter of becoming is not got rid of, becoming is not got rid of.' He does not speak thus: ' All those in whom the fetter of becoming is got rid of are without anguish ... fret; they are faring along rightly.' He simply teaches *dhamma*, saying: ' If the fetter of becoming is got rid of, becoming is got rid of.' This, monks, is what is neither approval nor disapproval, but the teaching of *dhamma*. When it is said: ' One should know approval and one should know disapproval, and having known approval, having known disapproval, one should neither approve nor disapprove— one should simply teach *dhamma*,' it is said in reference to this.

---

[1] *vibhava* here. It should perhaps read *bhava* as at the end of the next paragraph.

When it is said: ' One should know how to judge what happiness is; having known how to judge what happiness is, one should be intent on inward happiness,' in reference to what is it said ? These five, monks, are the strands of sense-pleasures. What five ? Material shapes cognisable by the eye . . . sounds cognisable by the ear . . . smells cognisable by the nose . . . tastes cognisable by the tongue . . . touches cognisable by the body, agreeable, pleasant, liked, enticing, connected with sensual pleasure, alluring. These, monks, are the five strands of sense-pleasures. Whatever happiness or joy, monks, arises in consequence of these five strands of sense-pleasures is said to be a happiness of sense-pleasures, a vile happiness, the happiness of an average person, an unariyan happiness. I say of this happiness that it is not to be pursued, developed or made much of—it is to be feared. As to this, monks, a monk, aloof from pleasures of the senses, aloof from unskilled states of mind, enters on and abides in the first meditation . . . the second . . . the third . . . the fourth meditation. This is said to be the happiness of renunciation, the happiness of aloofness, the happiness of tranquillity, the happiness of self-awakening. I say of this happiness that it is to be pursued, developed and made much of—it is not to be feared. [**234**] When it is said: ' One should know how to judge what happiness is; having known how to judge what happiness is, one should be intent on inward happiness,' it is said in reference to this.

When it is said: ' One should not utter a secret speech; face to face (with a man) one should not tell (him) a vexatious thing,' in reference to what is it said ? As to this, monks, knowing a secret speech is not fact, untrue, not connected with the goal, one should not, if possible, utter that secret speech; and if, knowing that secret speech is fact, true, but not connected with the goal, he should train himself not to speak it. But if one knows that secret speech is fact, true, and connected with the goal, then he will know the right time to speak that secret speech to that (other person). As to this, monks, knowing a vexatious speech (made) face to face (with a man) is not fact, untrue, not connected with the goal, one should not, if possible, utter that vexatious speech face to face (with a man); and if, knowing that vexatious speech (made) face to face (with a man) is fact, true, but not connected with the goal, he should train himself not to speak it. But if one knows that vexatious speech (made) face to face (with a man) is fact, true, and connected with the goal, then he will know the right time to speak that vexatious speech face to face with that (other person). When it is said: ' One should not utter a secret speech; face to face (with a man) one should not tell (him) a vexatious thing,' it is said in reference to this.

When it is said: ' One should speak quite slowly, not hurriedly,' in reference to what is it said ? As to this, monks, if one speak hurriedly the body tires and thought suffers and the sound suffers and the throat is affected; the speech of one in a hurry is not clear or comprehensible. As to this, monks, if one speak slowly the body does not tire and thought does not suffer and the sound does not suffer and the throat is not affected; the speech of one not in a hurry is clear and comprehensible. When it is said: ' One should speak quite slowly, not hurriedly,' it is said in reference to this.

When it is said: ' One should not affect the dialect of the countryside, one should not deviate from recognised parlance,' in reference to what is it said ? And what, monks, is affectation of the dialect of the countryside and what is departure from recognised parlance ? In this case, monks, in different districts they know (the different words): Pāti[1] [**235**] ... Patta ... Vittha ... Sarāva ... Dhāropa ... Poṇa ... Pisīla. Thus as they know the word as this or that in these various districts so does a person, obstinately clinging to it and adhering to it, explain: ' This indeed is the truth, all else is falsehood.'[2] Thus, monks, is affectation of the dialect of the countryside and departure from recognised parlance. And what, monks, is non-affectation of the dialect of the countryside and non-departure from recognised parlance ? In this case, monks, in different districts they know (the different words): Pāti ... Patta ... Poṇa ... Pisīla, yet although they know the word as this or that in these various districts a person does not cling to it but explains: ' These venerable ones definitely express it thus.' Thus, monks, is non-affectation of the dialect of the countryside and non-departure from recognised parlance. When it is said: ' One should not affect the dialect of the countryside, one should not deviate from recognised parlance,' it is said in reference to this.

Wherefore, monks, whatever is happiness in association with sense-pleasures and intentness on a joy that is low, of the villager, of the average man, not connected with the goal, this is a thing that has anguish, annoyance, trouble and fret; it is a wrong course. Therefore this thing is defiled. Wherefore, monks, whatever is

---

[1] This and the following six words are all words for " bowl."

[2] As this phrase is of fairly frequent occurrence in *M.* and I have throughout translated it thus, I leave it thus here. Here however it clearly means: This is the true word, every other word is false.

happiness in association with sense-pleasures but non-intentness on a joy that is low . . . this is a thing without anguish . . . fret; it is a right course. Therefore this thing is undefiled. Wherefore, monks, whatever is intentness on self-mortification which is sorrowful, unariyan, not connected with the goal, this is a thing that has anguish . . . fret; it is a wrong course. Therefore this thing is defiled. Wherefore, monks, whatever is non-intentness on the practice of self-mortification which is sorrowful, unariyan, not connected with the goal, this is a thing without anguish . . . fret; it is the right course. [236] Therefore this thing is undefiled. Wherefore, monks, that Middle Course awakened to by the Tathāgata, making for vision, making for knowledge, and conducive to calm, super-knowledge, self-awakening and nibbāna, this is a thing without anguish . . . fret; it is the right course. Therefore this thing is undefiled. Wherefore, monks, whatever is approval and disapproval and not the teaching of *dhamma*, this is a thing that has anguish . . . fret; it is a wrong course. Therefore this thing is defiled. Wherefore, monks, whatever is neither approval nor disapproval but is the teaching of *dhamma*, this is a thing without anguish . . . fret; it is the right course. Therefore this thing is undefiled. Wherefore, monks, that happiness in sense-pleasures, a vile happiness, the happiness of an average person, an unariyan happiness, this is a thing that has anguish . . . fret; it is a wrong course. Therefore this thing is defiled. Wherefore, monks, that happiness in renunciation, the happiness of aloofness, the happiness of tranquillity, the happiness of self-awakening, this is a thing without anguish . . . fret; it is the right course. Therefore this thing is undefiled. Wherefore, monks, that secret speech that is not fact, untrue, not connected with the goal, this is a thing that has anguish . . . fret; it is a wrong course. Therefore this thing is defiled. Wherefore, monks, that secret speech that is fact, true, but not connected with the goal, this is a thing that has anguish . . . fret; it is a wrong course. Therefore this thing is defiled. Wherefore, monks, that secret speech that is fact, true, and connected with the goal, this is a thing without anguish . . . fret; it is the right course. Therefore this thing is undefiled. Wherefore, monks, that vexatious speech (made) face to face (with a man) that is not fact, untrue, not connected with the goal, this is a thing that has anguish . . . fret; it is a wrong course. Therefore this thing is defiled. Wherefore, monks, that vexatious speech (made) face to face (with a man) that is fact, true, but not connected with the goal, this too is a thing that has anguish . . . fret; it is a wrong course. Therefore this thing is defiled. Wherefore, monks, that [237] vexatious speech (made) face to face (with a man) that is fact, true, and connected with the goal, this is a thing without anguish . . . fret; it is the right course. Therefore this thing is undefiled. Wherefore, monks, that which is spoken by one in a hurry, this is a thing that has anguish . . . fret; it is a wrong course. Therefore this thing is defiled. Wherefore, monks, that which is spoken by one not in a hurry, this is a thing without anguish . . . fret; it is the right course. Therefore this thing is undefiled. Wherefore, monks, affectation of the dialect of the countryside and departure from recognised parlance, this is a thing that has anguish . . . fret; it is a wrong course. Therefore this thing is defiled. Wherefore, monks, non-affectation of the dialect of the countryside and non-departure from recognised parlance, this is a thing without anguish, annoyance, trouble or fret; it is the right course. Therefore this thing is undefiled.

Wherefore, monks, this is how you must train yourselves: ' I will know the defiled thing and I will know the undefiled thing, and knowing the defiled thing and knowing the undefiled thing, I will fare along the undefiled course.' Thus, monks, must you train yourselves. But Subhūti,[1] monks, the young man of family, is (already ?) faring along the undefiled course."

Thus spoke the Lord. Delighted, these monks rejoiced in what the Lord had said.

Discourse on the Analysis of the Undefiled:
The Ninth

---

[1] *MA.* v. 32 points out that he was among the Etad Aggas on two counts; and that when he went for alms with Sāriputta, Sāriputta stood at the doors of the houses attaining *nirodha* (the final meditative stage) while Subhūti attained *mettajhāna*, the meditation on friendliness. *Cf. AA.* i. 220, *ThagA.* i. 20, *UdA.* 348. See also *B.H.S.D.* under *araṇa* where Edgerton very tentatively puts the question of whether *araṇa* was not originally an adjective with a fem. noun: *samāpatti* or *maitri*, Pali *mettā*.

140. DISCOURSE ON THE ANALYSIS OF THE ELEMENTS
(Dhātuvibhaṅgasutta)

THUS have I heard: At one time the Lord, walking on tour among the people of Magadha, arrived at Rājagaha and approached the potter Bhaggava;[1] having approached, he spoke thus to Bhaggava the potter: "If it is not inconvenient to you, Bhaggava, I would spend one night in your dwelling."

"It is not convenient to me, revered sir. For there is here one gone forth who came before you to stay. But if he allow it, do stay, revered sir, according to your pleasure."

[238] At that time there was a young man of family called Pukkusāti[2] who had gone forth from home into homelessness through faith in the Lord. He it was that had arrived first at that potter's dwelling. Then the Lord approached the venerable Pukkusāti; having approached, he spoke thus to the venerable Pukkusāti: "If it is not inconvenient to you, monk, I will spend a night in the dwelling."

"Spacious,[3] friend,[4] is the potter's dwelling; let the venerable one stay according to his pleasure."

Then the Lord, having entered the potter's dwelling and laid down a spreading of grass to one side, sat down cross-legged, keeping his back erect and arousing mindfulness in front of him. And the Lord passed much of that night sitting down. And the venerable Pukkusāti too spent much of that night sitting down. Then it occurred to the Lord: "This young man of respectable family certainly comports himself pleasantly. Suppose I were to question him?" And the Lord spoke thus to the venerable Pukkusāti:

"On account of whom have you, monk, gone forth? Who is your teacher? Whose *dhamma* do you profess?"

"There is, friend, the recluse Gotama, son of the Sakyans, gone

---

[1] Here Bhaggava seems to be the potter's personal name. See *M.L.S.* ii. 248 (=*M*. ii. 52).

[2] *MA*. v. 33 *ff.* gives a long history of this monk; see *D.P.P.N.*

[3] *ūruṇḍa*, which perhaps should be *uruddha*, giving space for (breathing). *MA*. v. 47 explains by *vivitta*, isolated, secluded, and *asambādha*, not crowded.

[4] *āvuso*.

forth from the Sakyan clan; concerning this Lord Gotama a lovely reputation has gone abroad thus: He is indeed Lord, perfected one, fully Self-Awakened One, endowed with (right) conduct and knowledge, well-farer, knower of the world(s), matchless charioteer of men to be tamed, teacher of *devas* and mankind, the Awakened One, the Lord. On account of this Lord have I gone forth, and this Lord is my teacher; I profess this Lord's *dhamma*."

" But where, monk, is this Lord, perfected one, fully Self-Awakened One, staying now ?"

" There is a town called Sāvatthī, friend, in the northern districts; this Lord, perfected one, fully Self-Awakened One is now staying there."

" Have you, monk, ever seen this Lord ? If you saw him would you know him ?"

[239] " No, friend, I have never seen this Lord, so I would not know him if I saw him."

Then it occurred to the Lord: " This young man of respectable family has gone forth on account of me. Suppose I were to teach him *dhamma* ?" And the Lord addressed the venerable Pukkusāti, saying: " I will teach you *dhamma*, monk; listen carefully, pay attention and I will speak."

" Yes, friend," the venerable Pukkusāti answered the Lord in assent. The Lord spoke thus:

" Monk, this man has six elements, six fields of (sense-)impingement, eighteen mental ranges,[1] four resolves.[2] Where there is stability, conceit and boasting do not continue in existence, and when they do not continue in existence the sage is said to be at peace. He[3] should not be slothful in wisdom, he should guard the truth, cultivate relinquishment,[4] and train himself for peace itself.[5]

This is the exposition of the analysis of the six elements:

---

[1] As at *M*. iii. 216. The first three of these headings are also stated and analysed at *A*. i. 175, but the four ariyan truths are given there in place of the four resolves.

[2] *D*. iii. 229.

[3] Perhaps referring to the " man," *purisa*, of the first heading in this paragraph.

[4] *cāga*, the giving up of, abandoning or forsaking all the defilements, *MA*. v. 52; all the clingings, *M*. iii. 245.

[5] It is, I think a question whether the order of these last two headings should not be reversed to tally with the order of the analysis below which appears to be the more logical sequence. But the commentarial exegesis, *MA*. v. 51 *f*. is against this, for it takes the headings as they stand above.

Monk, when it is said: 'This man has six elements,' in reference to what is it said? To the element of extension, the liquid element, the element of radiation, of motion, of *ākāsa*, of consciousness. Monk, when it is said, 'This man has six elements,' it is said in reference to this.

Monk, when it is said, 'This man has six fields of (sense-)impingement,' in reference to what is it said? To the field of visual impingement, of auditory ... olfactory ... gustatory ... tactile ... mental impingement. Monk, when it is said, 'This man ... ', it is said in reference to this.

Monk, when it is said, 'This man has eighteen mental ranges,' in reference to what is it said? Having seen a material shape with the eye ... [240] ... cognised a mental state with the mind, one ranges over the mental state that gives rise to joy, ranges over the mental state that gives rise to sorrow, ranges over the mental state that gives rise to equanimity. Thus there are six ranges for joy, six for sorrow, six for equanimity. Monk, when it is said, 'This man has eighteen mental ranges,' it is said in reference to this.

Monk, when it is said, 'This man has four resolves,' in reference to what is it said? To the resolve for wisdom, the resolve for truth, the resolve for relinquishment, the resolve for calm. Monk, when it is said ... it is said in reference to this.

Monk, when it is said: 'He should not be slothful in wisdom, he should guard the truth, cultivate relinquishment and train himself for peace itself,' in reference to what is it said? And how, monk, is one not slothful in wisdom?

There are these six elements: the element of extension, the liquid element, the element of radiation, of motion, of *ākāsa*, of consciousness. And what, monk, is the element of extension?[1] The element of extension may be internal, it may be external. And what, monk, is the internal element of extension? Whatever is hard, solid, is internal, referable to an individual and derived therefrom, that is to say: the hair of the head, the hair of the body, nails, teeth, skin, flesh, sinews, bones, marrow of the bones, kidneys, heart, liver, pleura, spleen, lungs, intestines, mesentery, stomach, excrement, or whatever other thing is hard, solid, is internal, referable to an individual or derived therefrom—this, monk, is called the internal element of extension. Whatever is the internal element of

---

[1] Down to the element of space, see *M*. 1. 421 *ff*. See also *M*. i. 185 *ff*. and *M.L.S*. i. 231 *ff*. for notes.

extension and whatever is the external element of extension, just these are the element of extension. By means of perfect intuitive wisdom this should be seen as it really is, thus: This is not mine, this am I not, this is not my self. Having seen this thus as it really is by means of perfect intuitive wisdom, he disregards the element of extension, he cleanses his mind of the element of extension.

And what, monk, is the liquid element? The liquid element may be internal, [**241**] it may be external. And what, monk, is the internal liquid element? Whatever is liquid, fluid, is internal, referable to an individual and derived therefrom, that is to say: bile, phlegm, pus, blood, sweat, fat, tears, serum, saliva, mucus, synovial fluid, urine or whatever other thing is liquid, fluid, is internal, referable to an individual and derived therefrom, this, monk, is called the internal liquid element. Whatever is an internal liquid element and whatever is an external liquid element, just these are the liquid element. By means of perfect intuitive wisdom . . . he cleanses his mind of the liquid element.

And what, monk, is the element of radiation? The element of radiation may be internal, it may be external. And what, monk, is the internal element of radiation? Whatever is heat, warmth, is internal, referable to an individual and derived therefrom, such as that by which one is vitalised and that by which one is consumed, and that by which one is burnt up, and that which one has munched, drunk, eaten and tasted which is properly transformed (in digestion), or whatever other thing is heat, warmth, is internal, referable to an individual or derived therefrom, this, monk, is called the internal element of radiation. Whatever is an internal . . . external element of radiation, just these are the element of radiation. By means of perfect intuitive wisdom . . . he cleanses his mind of the element of radiation.

And what, monk, is the element of motion? The element of motion may be internal, it may be external. And what, monk, is the internal element of motion? Whatever is motion, wind, is internal, referable to an individual and derived therefrom, such as winds going upwards, winds going downwards, winds in the abdomen, winds in the belly, winds that shoot across the several limbs, in-breathing, out-breathing, or whatever other thing is motion, wind, is internal, referable to an individual and derived therefrom, this, monk, is called the internal element of motion. Whatever is an internal . . . external element of motion, just these are the element of motion. By means of perfect intuitive wisdom . . . he cleanses his mind of the element of motion.

And what, monk, is the element of space ? The element of space may be internal, it may be external. And what, monk, is the internal [**242**] element of space ? Whatever is space, spacious, is internal, referable to an individual and derived therefrom, such as the auditory and nasal orifices, the door of the mouth and that by which one swallows what is munched, drunk, eaten and tasted, and where this remains, and where it passes out (of the body) lower down, or whatever other thing is space, spacious, is internal, referable to an individual and derived therefrom, this, monk, is called the internal element of space. Whatever is an internal element of space and whatever is an external element of space, just these are the element of space. By means of perfect intuitive wisdom this should be seen as it really is, thus: This is not mine, this am I not, this is not my self. Having seen this thus as it really is by means of perfect intuitive wisdom, he disregards the element of space, he cleanses his mind of the element of space.

And when the consciousness that remains is quite pure, quite clean, he knows something by means of that consciousness: he discriminates pleasure and he discriminates pain and he discriminates what is neither painful nor pleasant. If, monk, because of impingement there arises an experience of pleasure it is a pleasant feeling. He, experiencing that pleasant feeling, comprehends that he is experiencing a pleasant feeling. On the cessation of the impingement whence comes that experience of pleasure he comprehends: ' The pleasant feeling arisen on account of an impingement experienced as a complemental[1] pleasant experience is stopped, is allayed.' If, monk, because of impingement there arises an experience of pain . . . an experience of what is neither painful nor pleasant it is a feeling that is neither painful nor pleasant. He, experiencing that feeling that is neither painful nor pleasant, comprehends that he is experiencing a feeling that is neither painful nor pleasant. On the cessation of the impingement whence comes that experience of what is neither painful nor pleasant he comprehends: ' The feeling that is neither painful nor pleasant arisen on account of an impingement experienced as a complemental experience that is neither painful nor pleasant is stopped, is allayed.'

Monk, it is like the heat obtained, the light produced from the contact and friction of two sticks; when these two sticks are separated their complemental heat is stopped, is allayed. Even so, monk,

---

[1] *tajja*, as at *M*. i. 190. *S*. iv. 215, *Dhs*. 3-6.

[243] does a pleasant feeling arise on account of the impingement of an experience of pleasure . . . a painful feeling . . . a feeling that is neither painful nor pleasant. He . . . comprehends . . . 'The feeling that is neither painful nor pleasant arisen on account of an impingement experienced as a complemental experience that is neither painful nor pleasant is stopped, it is allayed.'

And further, the equanimity that remains is quite pure, quite cleansed, soft and pliable and resplendent. Monk, it is like a skilled goldsmith or a goldsmith's apprentice preparing a furnace; when he has prepared the furnace he lights the smelting-pot; when he has lit the smelting-pot he takes up the gold with tongs and places it in the smelting-pot; and then from time to time he blows on it, from time to time he sprinkles water over it, and from time to time he looks at it carefully—that gold becomes clear, pure, cleansed, (the impurities) removed, free from dross, soft and pliable and resplendent so that whatever kind of ornament one requires, a ring or earring or necklace or golden garland, it is suitable for that purpose. Even so, monk, the equanimity that then remains is quite pure, quite cleansed, soft and pliable and resplendent.

He comprehends thus: ' If I should focus this equanimity, purified thus, cleansed thus, on the plane of infinite ether and should develop my thought in accordance with that, then would this equanimity, supported by this, nourished by this, stand firm in me for a very long time. If I should focus this equanimity . . . on the plane of infinite consciousness . . . [244] . . . on the plane of no-thing . . . on the plane of neither-perception-nor-non-perception and should develop my thought in accordance with that, then would this equanimity, supported by this, nourished by this, stand firm in me for a very long time.'

He comprehends thus: ' If I should focus this equanimity, purified thus, cleansed thus, on the plane of infinite ether . . . on the plane of infinite consciousness . . . on the plane of no-thing . . . on the plane of neither-perception-nor-non-perception and should develop my thought in accordance with that, this[1] is constructed.'[2] He therefore

---

[1] " This," *etaṁ*, appears to refer to " life-span," *āyu*, so *MA.* v. 55: " however much this life-span is of 20,000 kappas . . . it is not permanent or eternal, it is temporary, liable to deceasing, falling, breaking up and shattering; it is dogged by birth, bestrewn by disease, struck down by death; it is founded on anguish, with no authority, no refuge. . . . All these perils are spoken of by the one phrase: this is constructed," *saṅkhatam etaṁ*.

[2] *saṅkhatam etaṁ*. The meaning probably is that, however much one applies

neither constructs nor thinks out[1] for becoming or for de-becoming.[2] Not constructing, not thinking out for becoming or for de-becoming, he grasps after nothing in the world; not grasping, he is not troubled, being untroubled he himself is individually attained to nibbāna, and he comprehends: 'Destroyed is birth, brought to a close the Brahma-faring, done is what was to be done, there is no more of being such or so.' If he experiences a pleasant feeling... a painful feeling... a feeling that is neither painful nor pleasant, he comprehends that it is impermanent... not to be cleaved to... not an object of enjoyment. If he experiences a pleasant... painful feeling... a feeling that is neither painful nor pleasant, then detached from it he experiences it. Experiencing a feeling that is limited by the body,[3] he comprehends that he is experiencing a feeling that is limited by the body. [245] Experiencing a feeling that is limited by the life-principle he comprehends that he is experiencing a feeling that is limited by the life-principle. He comprehends that on the breaking up of the body after the life-principle has come to an end all enjoyable experiences here will become cool.[4]

---

equanimity to the various meditative planes and develops thought according to them, *still* this life-span remains. It is therefore a construction: *saṅkhāra* (and hence impermanent, *cf. M.* i. 336, *sabbasaṅkhāresu aniccānupassino*, translated at *M.L.S.* i. 400 as: beholding the impermanence of all constructions; and *cf. Dhp.* 277 *sabbe saṅkhārā aniccā*, impermanent are all the constructions), or it is a construct, *saṅkhata*; or it is constructed, *saṅkhata*. The underlying idea is one of activity (see *M.L.S.* i., Intr., p. xxv), a karmic " effecting " or bringing about, which, in this context above, is a result of the decision the meditator has just taken to focus his equanimity and develop his thought. But, as he immediately perceives, this will only lead to the constructing of new effects in the future. So he stills his mind in order to bring no new constructs into existence. Therefore, following his realisation that *saṅkhatam etaṁ*, he seeks to go no further with such mental activity as will bear future karmic fruit and *n'eva abhisaṅkharoti nābhisañcetayati*, neither constructs nor thinks out. At *M.* i. 350 the bhikkhu comprehends of each *jhāna*, of each *brahmavihāra* and of each of the first three meditative planes that it is " effected " (or constructed or produced—by past mental activity) and thought out (or planned) and is therefore impermanent (and all that this entails). So that here again it is implied, as above, that the realisation and comprehension of such impermanence is a stepping-stone to further progress on the Way, whereas the lack of realisation is a hindrance or obstacle to such progress.

[1] Now speaking from the height of arahantship.
[2] *bhava* and *vibhava* are called growth and decline respectively; they are said to be connected with eternalism and annihilationism, again respectively.
[3] *D.* i. 46, ii. 128, *S.* ii. 83, *A.* ii. 198.
[4] *sītibhavissanti*. The term *sītibhūta*, become cool, is often combined with

Monk, as an oil-lamp burns on account of the oil and on account of the wick but goes out[1] from lack of fuel if the oil and the wick come to an end and no others are brought, even so, monk, experiencing a feeling that is limited by the body . . . limited by the life-principle, he comprehends that he is experiencing a feeling limited by the body . . . limited by the life-principle. He comprehends that on the breaking up of the body after the life-principle has come to an end all enjoyable experiences here will become cool.

Therefore a monk, endowed thus, is endowed with this highest resolve for wisdom. For this, monk, is the highest ariyan wisdom, that is to say the knowledge of the complete destruction of anguish. That freedom of his, founded on truth, is unshakable. For that which is liable to falsity, monk, is falsehood; that truth which is not liable to falsity is nibbāna. Therefore, endowed thus, a monk is endowed with this highest resolve for truth. For this, monk, is the highest ariyan truth, that is to say nibbāna that is not liable to falsity. Verily, his former[2] foolish clingings[3] are ended and done with. These are got rid of by him, cut off at the root, made like a palm-tree stump that can come to no future growth. Therefore, endowed thus, a monk is endowed with this highest resolve for relinquishment. For this, monk, is the highest ariyan relinquishment, that is to say the casting away of all clingings. His former foolish covetousness was passionate desire. This is got rid of by him, cut off at the root, made like a palm-tree stump that can come to no future growth. His former foolish hostility was malevolence and corruption. This is got rid of by him, cut off at the root, made like a palm-tree stump that can come to no future growth. His former foolish ignorance was confusion and corruption. This is got rid of by him, cut off at the root, [246] made like a palm-tree stump that can come to no future growth. Therefore, endowed thus, a monk is endowed with this highest resolve for calm. For this, monk, is the highest ariyan calm, that is to say the calm in regard to attachment, hatred and confusion. When it is said, ' One

---

nibbuta, gone out, extinguished. For *nibbuta* see *P.E.D.* The fires of *rāga dosa* and *moha* no longer burn in one who is *nibbuta sītibhūta*; it is in respect of these that a man is extinguished and cooled.

[1] *nibbāyati. Cf. Thīg.* 116 *padīpass' eva nibbānaṁ*: the going out of the lamp.

[2] Referring to the time when he was a *puthujjana*, an ordinary average person.

[3] To the *khandhā*, to the defilements, to the " activities " (*abhisaṅkhārā*) and to the five strands of sensual pleasure, *MA.* v. 60.

should not be slothful is wisdom, he should guard the truth, cultivate relinquishment and train himself for peace itself,' it is said in reference to this.

Monk, when it is said, 'Where there is stability, conceit and boasting do not continue in existence, and when they do not continue in existence the sage is said to be at peace,' in reference to what is it said? 'I am,' monk, this is a supposition. 'This am I' ... 'I will be' ... 'I will not be' ... 'I will be possessed of form' ... 'I will be incorporeal' ... 'I will be possessed of perception' ... 'I will not be possessed of perception' ... 'I will be possessed of neither perception nor non-perception,' this is a supposition. A supposition, monk, is an ill, a supposition is an imposthume, a supposition is a barb. Monk, when he has gone beyond all suppositions the sage is said to be at peace. But, monk, a sage who is at peace is not born, does not age, is not agitated, does not envy. As there is nothing by which he can be born, how, monk, not being born could he age? Not ageing, how could he die? Not dying, how could he be agitated? Not being agitated, how could he envy? When it is said: 'Where there is stability, conceit and boasting do not continue in existence, and when they do not continue in existence the sage is said to be at peace,' it is said in reference to this.

Do you, monk, remember my analysis in brief[1] of the six elements."

Then the venerable Pukkusāti thought: " Indeed it is the Teacher that has come to me; indeed it is the Well-farer that has come to me; indeed it is the Fully Self-Awakened One that has come to me," and rising from his seat, arranging his robe over one shoulder and bowing his head to the Lord's feet, he spoke thus to the Lord:

" A transgression, revered sir, has overcome me[2] in that foolish, errant and [247] unskilled as I was, I supposed the Lord could be addressed with the epithet 'friend.' Revered sir, may the Lord acknowledge my transgression as a transgression for the sake of restraint in the future."

" Indeed, monk, a transgression overcame you in that . . . you

---

[1] Bu. here says, *MA*. v. 60, that the whole teaching of Dhamma by the Buddhas is " in brief "; there is no extended teaching. Even the whole of the Paṭṭhānakathā is in brief. Among the four types of persons (reference appears to be to *A*. ii. 135, *Pug*. 41), beginning with the one who could understand Dhamma in a condensed form (*ugghāṭitaññū*), Pukkusāti was a *vipacitaññū* (i.e. a " diffuse-learner," to whom Dhamma had to be explained in detail). It was because of this that the Lord spoke the Dhātuvibhaṅgasutta.

[2] The wording is stock, only the transgression, *accaya*, varies in the different contexts. See *P.T.C*. under *accaya*.

supposed I could be addressed with the epithet 'friend.' But if you, monk, seeing this transgression as a transgression, confess it according to the rule, we acknowledge it for you. For this is growth, monk, in the discipline for an ariyan, that whoever, seeing a transgression as a transgression, confesses it according to rule, he comes to restraint in the future."

"Revered sir, may I receive ordination in the Lord's presence?"

"But are you, monk, complete as to bowl and robe?"

"Revered sir, I am not complete as to bowl and robe."

"Monk, Tathāgatas do not ordain anyone not complete as to bowl and robe."

Then the venerable Pukkusāti, having rejoiced in what the Lord had said, having given thanks for it, rising from his seat greeted the Lord and, keeping his right side towards him, departed in order to search for a bowl and robe. But while he was touring about in search of a bowl and robe a cow swerved[1] and deprived him of life.

Then a number of monks approached the Lord; having approached, having greeted the Lord, they sat down at a respectful distance. As they were sitting down at a respectful distance, these monks spoke thus to the Lord: 'That young man of family, Pukkusāti, revered sir, whom the Lord exhorted with an exhortation in brief, has died.[2] What is his bourn, what his future state?"

"Clever,[3] monk, was Pukkusāti, the young man of family; he followed after *dhamma* according to the various parts of *dhamma*, and he did not annoy me with questionings about *dhamma*. Monks, Pukkusāti, the young man of family, by the complete destruction of the five fetters binding to this lower (shore), is of spontaneous uprising, one who attains nibbāna there, not liable to return from that world."

Discourse on the Analysis of the Elements:
The Tenth

---

[1] *bhantagāvī*, a swerving or staggering cow. *MA.* v. 62 explains she was rushing after her wandering young calf.

[2] *kālam karoti*, has done his (karmic) time.

[3] *Cf. M.* ii. 146 for this paragraph.

141. DISCOURSE ON THE ANALYSIS OF THE TRUTHS
(Saccavibhaṅgasutta)

[248] THUS have I heard: At one time the Lord was staying near Benares in the deer-park at Isipatana. While he was there the Lord addressed the monks, saying: "Monks." "Revered One," these monks answered the Lord in assent. The Lord spoke thus: "The matchless Wheel of *dhamma* set rolling by the Tathāgata, the perfected one, fully Self-Awakened One in the deer-park at Isipatana near Benares cannot be rolled back by a recluse or brahman or *deva* or Māra or Brahmā or by anyone in the world. That is to say, it was a proclamation of the four ariyan truths, a teaching, laying down, establishing, opening up, analysing, and making of them plain. Of what four? It was a proclamation, a teaching, laying down, establishing, opening up, analysing and making plain of the ariyan truth of anguish . . . of the ariyan truth of the arising of anguish . . . of the ariyan truth of the stopping of anguish . . . of the ariyan truth of the course leading to the stopping of anguish. The matchless Wheel of *dhamma*, monks, set rolling by the Tathāgata . . . in the deer-park at Isipatana near Benares cannot be rolled back by a recluse . . . or anyone in the world. That is to say, it was a proclamation of the four ariyan truths . . . a making of them plain. Monks, follow Sāriputta and Moggallāna; monks, associate with Sāriputta and Moggallāna; they are wise monks who are helpers[1] to Brahma-farers. Monks, like a mother, so is Sāriputta; like a child's foster-mother, so is Moggallāna. Sāriputta, monks, trains (one) in the fruit of stream-attainment, Moggallāna in the highest

---

[1] *anuggāhakā*. At *S.* iii. 5, v. 162 Sāriputta alone is so spoken of; translated at *K.S.* as "patron." *SA.* ii. 256 instances two forms of help, *anuggaha*, help with material things and help with Dhamma. At *Vin.* iv. 325 "should neither help," *n'eva anuggaṅheyya*, is defined to mean: "should neither herself help (her pupil) with the recitation, interrogation, exhortation and instruction." This therefore must be regarded as help with Dhamma. It also appears that when *anuggaṅhāti* is used in relation to the attitude of a more experienced member of the Order to a less experienced one, it carries a technical or semi-technical sense. See *P.T.C.* under *anuggaṅhāti* for further references.

goal.[1] Sāriputta, monks, is able to proclaim, teach, lay down, establish, open up, analyse and make plain the four ariyan truths in full."[2] Thus spoke the Lord; and having said this, the Well-farer rose from his seat and entered a dwelling-place.

[249] Soon after the Lord had departed the venerable Sāriputta addressed the monks who were there, saying: " Reverend monks." " Your reverence," these monks answered the venerable Sāriputta in assent. The venerable Sāriputta spoke thus:

" Your reverences, the matchless Wheel of *dhamma* set rolling by the Tathāgata, perfected one, fully Self-Awakened One in the deer-park at Isipatana near Benares cannot be rolled back . . . It was a proclamation, a teaching, laying down, establishing, opening up, analysing and making plain of the ariyan truth of anguish . . . of the ariyan truth of the course leading to the stopping of anguish.

And what, your reverences, is the ariyan truth of anguish ?[3] Birth is anguish and ageing is anguish and dying is anguish; and grief, sorrow, suffering, misery and despair are anguish. And not getting what one desires, that too is anguish. In brief, the five groups of grasping are anguish.

And what, your reverences, is birth ? It is the conception, the production, the descent,[4] the rebirth,[5] the coming forth of various beings in the various classes of beings, the appearance of the groups (of grasping), the acquiring of the sense-bases. This, your reverences, is called birth.

And what, your reverences, is old age ? It is the old age, decrepitude, broken teeth, greying hair, wrinkly skin, the dwindling of the life-span, the collapse of the sense-organs of the various beings in the various classes of beings. This, your reverences, is called old age.

And what, your reverences, is dying ? It is the falling away, the passing away, the breaking up, the disappearance, the death and

---

[1] *uttamattha*, *i.e.* arahantship. It seems that Sāriputta expends himself on newly ordained monks rather than on those he knows to be on the higher ways.

[2] This is Sāriputta's aspect as Dhammasenāpati, Captain or General of Dhamma, next to the Buddha in power to roll on the Dhamma-wheel.

[3] The remainder of this Discourse is found in the *Mahāsatipaṭṭhānasuttanta* (*D*. Sta. 22) from *D*. ii. 305-313, *i.e.* to the end of the ariyan truth of the course leading to the stopping of anguish. The first portion of the *D's Mahāsatipaṭṭhānasuttanta* is found in *M*. Sta. 10, the *Satipaṭṭhānasutta*. See *M.L.S.* i, Intr., p. xiv. Also *cf. M*. i. 49 *f.*, *S*. ii. 3.

[4] *I.e.* into a womb.   [5] *nibbatti*, not at *M*. i. 49.

dying, the action of time, the breaking up of the groups (of grasping), the laying down of the body. This, your reverences, is called dying.

And what, your reverences, is grief? It, your reverences, is the grief, sorrow, sorrowfulness, the inward grief, the inner pain of one visited by some kind of calamity or other, smitten by some kind of ill or other. It is the crying, the wailing, [**250**] the act of crying, the act of wailing, the state of crying, the state of wailing of one visited by some calamity or other, smitten by some kind of ill or other. This, your reverences, is called sorrow.

And what, your reverences, is suffering? It, your reverences, is physical suffering, physical disagreeableness arising from an impingement on the body and experienced as suffering, as disagreeableness. This, your reverences, is called suffering.

And what, your reverences, is misery? It, your reverences, is mental suffering,[1] mental disagreeableness arising from an impingement on the mind and experienced as suffering, as disagreeableness. This, your reverences, is called misery.

And what, your reverences, is despair? It, your reverences, is despondency, despair, the state of despondency, the state of despair of one visited by some calamity or other, smitten by some kind of ill or other. This, your reverences, is called despair.

And what, your reverences is meant by 'not getting what one desires, that too is anguish'? Your reverences, a wish like this arises in creatures liable to birth: ' O might we be not liable to birth and birth not come to us.' But this is not to be had for the wishing. So 'not getting what one desires, that too is anguish.' Your reverences, a wish like this arises in creatures liable to ageing . . . to disease . . . to dying . . . in creatures liable to grief, sorrow, suffering, misery and despair: ' O might we not be liable to grief, sorrow, suffering, misery and despair, and grief, sorrow, suffering, misery and despair not come to us.' But this is not to be had for the wishing. So 'not getting what one desires, that too is anguish.'

And what, in brief, your reverences, are the five groups of grasping that are anguish? These are: the group of grasping after material shape, the group of grasping after feeling . . . after perception . . . after the habitual tendencies . . . after consciousness. Your reverences, these ase called in brief the five groups of grasping that are anguish.

---

[1] *cetasikaṁ dukkhaṁ* is omitted, probably in error, in Chalmers' text, but occurs at *D.* ii. 306.

Your reverences, this is called the ariyan truth of anguish.

And what, your reverences, is the ariyan truth of the arising of anguish ? Whatever craving is connected with again-becoming, accompanied by delight and attachment, finding delight in this and that, namely the craving for sense-pleasures, the craving for becoming, [**251**] the craving for annihilation—this, your reverences, is called the ariyan truth of the arising of anguish.

And what, your reverences, is the ariyan truth of the stopping of anguish ? Whatever is the stopping, with no attachment remaining, of that self-same craving, the relinquishment of it, casting aside of it, release from it, independence of it, this, your reverences, is called the ariyan truth of the stopping of anguish.

And what, your reverences, is the ariyan truth of the course leading to the stopping of anguish ? It is this ariyan Eightfold Way itself, that is to say: right view, right aspiration, right speech, right action, right mode of livelihood, right endeavour, right mindfulness, right concentration.

And what, your reverences, is right view ? Whatever, your reverences, is knowledge of anguish, knowledge of the arising of anguish, knowledge of the stopping of anguish, knowledge of the course leading to the stopping of anguish—this, your reverences, is called right view.

And what, your reverences, is right aspiration ? Aspiration for renunciation, aspiration for non-malevolence, aspiration for harmlessness—this, your reverences, is called right aspiration.

And what, your reverences, is right speech ? Refraining from lying speech, refraining from slanderous speech, refraining from harsh speech, refraining from gossip, this, your reverences, is called right speech.

And what, your reverences, is right action ? Refraining from onslaught on creatures, refraining from taking what has not been given, refraining from going wrongly among the sense-pleasures, this, your reverences, is called right action.

And what, your reverences, is right mode of livelihood ? As to this, your reverences, a disciple of the ariyans, getting rid of a wrong mode of livelihood, makes his living by a right mode of livelihood. This, your reverences, is called right mode of livelihood.

And what, your reverences, is right endeavour ? As to this, your reverences, a monk generates desire, endeavours, stirs up energy, exerts his mind and strives for the non-arising of evil unskilled states that have not arisen . . . for the getting rid of evil unskilled states that have arisen ... [252] for the arising of skilled states that have not arisen ... for the maintenance, preservation, increase, maturity, development and completion of skilled states that have arisen. This, your reverences, is called right endeavour.

And what, your reverences, is right mindfulness? As to this, your reverences, a monk fares along contemplating the body in the body ... the feelings in the feelings ... the mind in the mind ... the mental states in the mental states, ardent, clearly conscious (of them), mindful (of them) so as to control the covetousness and dejection in the world. This, your reverences, is called right mindfulness.

And what, your reverences, is right concentration? As to this, your reverences, a monk, aloof from pleasures of the senses, aloof from unskilled states of mind, enters on and abides in the first meditation which is accompanied by initial thought and discursive thought, is born of aloofness, and is rapturous and joyful. By allaying initial thought and discursive thought, with the mind subjectively tranquillised and fixed on one point, he enters on and abides in the second meditation which is devoid of intial thought and discursive thought, is born of concentration, and is rapturous and joyful. By the fading out of rapture ... he enters on and abides in the third meditation ... the fourth meditation. This, your reverences, is called right concentration.

This, your reverences, is called the ariyan truth of the course leading to the stopping of anguish.

Your reverences, the matchless Wheel of *dhamma* set rolling by the Tathāgata, perfected one, fully Self-Awakened One in the deer-park at Isipatana near Benares cannot be rolled back by a recluse or brahman or *deva* or Māra or Brahmā or by anyone in the world. That is to say, it was a proclamation, a teaching, laying down, establishing, opening up, analysing, and making plain of these four ariyan truths."

Thus spoke the venerable Sāriputta. Delighted, these monks rejoiced in what the venerable Sāriputta had said.

Discourse on the Analysis of the Truths:
The Eleventh

142. DISCOURSE ON THE ANALYSIS OF OFFERINGS
(Dakkhiṇavibhaṅgasutta)

[253] THUS have I heard: At one time the Lord was staying among the Sakyans in Nigrodha's monastery near Kapilavatthu. Then Mahāpajāpatī[1] the Gotamid,[2] bringing a pair of new cloths,[3] approached the Lord; having approached and greeted the Lord, she sat down at a respectful distance. As she was sitting down at a respectful distance, Mahāpajāpatī the Gotamid spoke thus to the Lord: " Revered sir, this pair of new cloths has been cut out by me and woven by me specially for the Lord; revered sir, may the Lord out of compassion accept it from me."

When this had been said, the Lord spoke thus to Mahāpajāpatī the Gotamid:

" Give it to the Order,[4] Gotami. If you give it to the Order I will be honoured and the Order too." And a second time . . . And a third time[5] did the Lord speak thus to Mahāpajāpatī the Gotamid: " Give it to the Order, Gotami. If you give it to the Order I will be honoured and the Order too."

When this had been said, the venerable Ānanda spoke thus to the Lord:

---

[1] At *A.* i. 25 called foremost of nuns of long experience. Her verses are at *Thīg.* 157-162. The younger sister of Mahāmāyā, Gotama's mother, she attained arahantship soon after her ordination, *ThīgA.* 141. The story of her ordination, with a number of Sakyan ladies, is given at *Vin.* ii. 253, *A.* iv. 274.

[2] Her family name.

[3] *MA.* v. 66 explains she thought that as she had not given Gotama anything, not even cakes or fruit, in the 29 years he had led a household life she would now give him an outer cloak and a robe, but only what was made by hand would satisfy her. But *sāmaṁ vāyitaṁ*, according to *MA.* v. 66, does not mean woven by her own hand, but that every day, surrounded by a group of foster-mothers, she went to the weaving place for women artisans and, taking the movable part of her loom, worked there.

[4] As at *Miln.* 240, though there she was giving cloths for the rains.

[5] She was much disappointed; but Gotama, according to *MA.* v. 67, was acting out of compassion, for what is given to an Order is of great fruit, and a gift given both to him and the Order will twice arouse the three thoughts connected with giving.

"Revered sir, let the Lord accept the Gotamid Mahāpajāpatī's new pair of cloths.[1] Revered sir, Mahāpajāpatī the Gotamid has been of much service to the Lord.[2] She is his maternal aunt, the one who brought him up,[3] who looked after him[4] and gave him milk, for when the Lord's own mother passed away she suckled him.[5] And, revered sir, the Lord has been of much service to Mahāpajāpatī the Gotamid. Revered sir, it is due to the Lord that Mahāpajāpatī the Gotamid has gone to the Awakened One for refuge, has gone to *dhamma* for refuge, has gone to the Order for refuge. Revered sir, it is due to the Lord, that Mahāpajāpatī the Gotamid refrains from onslaught on creatures, refrains from taking what has not been given, refrains from going wrongly among the sense-pleasures, refrains from lying speech, refrains from occasions of sloth induced by intoxicants. Revered sir, it is due to the Lord that Mahāpajāpatī the Gotamid is possessed of unwavering confidence in the Awakened One, is possessed of unwavering confidence in *dhamma*, is possessed of unwavering confidence in the Order, [**254**] is possessed of the moral habits pleasing to the ariyans. Revered sir, it is due to the Lord that Mahāpajāpatī is not doubtful about anguish, is not doubtful about the origin of anguish, is not doubtful about the stopping of anguish, is not doubtful about the course leading to the stopping of anguish. So, revered sir, the Lord has been of much service to Mahāpajāpatī the Gotamid."

"That is so, Ānanda, that is so, Ānanda. And if it is due to a person[6] that some (other) person[7] goes to the Awakened One for refuge, to *dhamma* for refuge, to the Order for refuge, I say of this person, Ānanda, that there is no proper requital in regard to that person, that is to say as regards greeting, rising up for, saluting with joined palms, doing what is suitable (to do for him), and as regards procuring him gifts of the requisites of robes, almsfood, lodgings and medicines for the sick. If it is due to a person that some (other) person refrains from onslaught on creatures, from taking what

---

[1] Ānanda knew there was no gift higher than one made to the Teacher.
[2] This description of Mahāpajāpatī (except for the word *bahūpakāra*, of much service) is also ascribed to Ānanda at *Vin.* ii. 289.
[3] Making him do things with his hands and feet.
[4] Who, two or three times a day, washed him and gave him to eat and to drink, *MA.* v. 69.
[5] In preference to her own son, Nanda, whom she gave to foster-mothers.
[6] A teacher, *ācariya*. The behaviour of pupils and teachers towards one another is given at *Vin.* i. 44 *ff.*
[7] A pupil, *antevāsika*, *MA.* v. 70.

has not been given, from going wrongly among sense-pleasures, from lying speech, from occasions of sloth induced by intoxicants, I say of this person, Ānanda, that there is no proper requital in regard to that person, that is to say as regards greeting . . . medicines for the sick. If it is due to a person that some (other) person is possessed of unwavering confidence in the Awakened One, *dhamma* and the Order and of the moral habits pleasing to the ariyans, I say of this person, Ānanda, that there is no proper requital in regard to that person, that is to say as regards greeting . . . medicines for the sick. If it is due to a person that some (other) person is not doubtful about anguish, its origin, its stopping and the course leading to its stopping, I say of this person, Ānanda, that there is no proper requital in regard to that person, that is to say as regards greeting . . . medicines for the sick.

Now, Ānanda, there are these fourteen offerings graded as to individuals.[1] One gives a gift to a Tathāgata, perfected one, fully Self-Awakened One—this is the first offering graded as to individuals. One gives a gift to one enlightened for and by himself alone[2]—this is the second offering . . . One gives a gift to a Tathāgata's disciple who is one perfected—this is the third offering . . . One gives a gift to one faring along for the realisation of the fruit of perfection—this is the fourth offering . . . One gives a gift to a non-returner—this is the fifth offering . . . [255] One gives a gift to one faring along for the realisation of the fruit of non-returning—this is the sixth offering . . . One gives a gift to a once-returner—this is the seventh offering . . . One gives a gift to one faring along for the realisation of the fruit of once-returning—this is the eighth offering . . . One gives a gift to a stream-attainer—this is the ninth offering . . . One gives a gift to one faring along for the realisation of the fruit of stream-attainment —this is the tenth offering . . . One gives a gift to one who is beyond and without attachment to sense-pleasures[3]—this is the eleventh offering . . . One gives a gift to an ordinary person of moral habit— this is the twelfth offering . . . One gives a gift to an ordinary person of poor moral habit—this is the thirteenth offering . . . One gives a gift to an animal—this is the fourteenth offering graded as to individuals.

---

[1] *pāṭipuggalikā dakkhiṇā*, the worth and merit of the offerings are reckoned according to the worth and merit of the recipient.

[2] *paccekabuddha*; he does not teach others.

[3] *bāhirake kāmesu vītarāge*, of which *MA.* v. 71 says *kammavādikiriyavādin hi lokiyapañcabhiññe*, in regard to the five mundane super-knowledges he is a speaker on the deed and on the efficacy of the deed.

As to this, Ānanda, when a gift has been given to an animal, it is expected that the offering (yields) a hundredfold;[1] when a gift has been given to an ordinary person of poor moral habit, it is to be expected that the offering (yields) a thousandfold. When a gift has been given to an ordinary person of moral habit, it is to be expected that the offering (yields) a hundred thousandfold. When a gift[2] has been given to one who is beyond and without attachment to sense-pleasures, it is to be expected that the offering (yields) a hundred thousandfold of crores. When a gift has been given to one faring along for the realisation of the fruit of stream-attainment,[3] it is to be expected that the offering (yields) what is incalculable and immeasurable. So what can be said of the stream-attainer ? What can be said of the one faring along for the realisation of the fruit of once-returning . . . of the once-returner . . . of one faring along for the realisation of the fruit of non-returning . . . of the non-returner . . . of one faring along for the realisation of the fruit of perfection . . . of one perfected . . . of a Tathāgata's disciple who is one perfected . . . of one enlightened for and by himself alone ? So what can be said of a Tathāgata, perfected one, fully Self-Awakened One ?

And there are these seven kinds of offerings to the Order, Ānanda: one gives a gift to both Orders with the Awakened One at the head[4] —this is the first offering to the Order.[5] One gives a gift to both Orders after the Awakened One has attained final nibbāna[6]—this is the second offering to the Order. One gives a gift to the Order of monks—this is the third offering to the Order. One gives a gift to the Order of nuns—this is the fourth offering to the Order. One gives a gift, saying, ' May so many monks and nuns [**256**] be specified for me by the Order '—this is the fifth offering to the Order. One

---

[1] A hundred advantages, according to *MA*. v. 71; *cf. A.* iii. 42.

[2] From here to " So what can be said of a stream-attainer ? " is quoted at *MA*. i. 187 where this Discourse is called *Dakkhiṇāvisuddhisutta*.

[3] *MA*. v. 72 says even a lay-follower gone to the three Refuges is called one faring along for the fruit of stream-attainment.

[4] Or *Buddhapamukhe* may mean with the Buddha facing them or before them. For *MA*. v. 73 says " on one side is the Order of monks, on the other the Order of nuns, and the Teacher is sitting in the middle."

[5] This explains why, if Mahāpajāpatī gives a gift to the Order, the Lord will be honoured as well as the Order. This is an offering unequalled by any other, and neither the second nor any other reaches this highest offering, *MA*. v. 73.

[6] *parinibbute*. Bu. explains that an image is placed on a chair before both Orders, and having given everything first of all to the Teacher, it is then to be given to both Orders.

gives a gift, saying: ' May so many monks be specified for me by the Order '—this is the sixth offering to the Order. One gives a gift, saying, ' May so many nuns be specified for me by the Order '—this is the seventh offering to the Order.

But, Ānanda, in the distant future there will be those of the ariyan clan,[1] the yellow robes around their necks,[2] who will be of bad morality and evil character; and a gift will be given to the Order specially for these of bad morality. But when I, Ānanda, say that an offering to the Order is incalculable and immeasurable I by no means say that a gift graded as to individuals is of greater fruit than an offering to the Order.

There are these four purifications of offerings,[3] Ānanda. What four ? There is, Ānanda, the offering purified by the giver but not by the recipient. There is, Ānanda, the offering purified by the recipient but not by the giver. There is, Ānanda, the offering purified neither by the giver nor the recipient. There is, Ānanda, the offering purified both by the giver and the recipient.

And what offering, Ānanda, is purified by the giver but not by the recipient ? As to this, Ānanda, the giver is of moral habit and lovely character, the recipients are of poor morality and of evil character. It is thus, Ānanda, that an offering is purified by the giver but not by the recipient.

And what offering, Ānanda, is purified by the recipient but not by the giver ? As to this, Ānanda, the giver is of poor morality and evil character, the recipients are of moral habit and lovely character. It is thus, Ānanda, that an offering . . .

And what offering, Ānanda, is purified neither by the giver nor the recipient ? As to this, Ānanda, the giver is of poor morality and evil character and the recipients are of poor morality and evil character. It is thus, Ānanda, that an offering . . .

And what offering, Ānanda, is purified both by the giver and the recipient ? As to this, Ānanda, the giver is of moral habit and lovely character and the recipients are of moral habit and lovely [257] character. It is thus, Ānanda, that an offering is purified both by the giver and the recipient. These, Ānanda, are the four purifications in offerings."

Thus spoke the Lord; the Well-farer having spoken thus, the Teacher further said:

---

[1] *gotrabhū*, see *G.S.* iv. 247. Defined at *Pug.* 12, 13.
[2] *kāsāvakaṇṭha*, as at *Dhp.* 307 = *Iti.* 43.   [3] *Cf. A.* ii. 80.

Whoever, moral in habit, gives to the poor in moral habit
A gift rightfully acquired, the mind well pleased,[1]
Firmly believing in the rich fruit of kamma—
This is an offering purified by the giver.

Whoever, poor in moral habit, gives to those of moral habit
A gift unrightfully acquired, the mind not pleased,
Not believing in the rich fruit of kamma—
This is an offering purified by the recipient.

Whoever, poor in moral habit, gives to the poor in moral habit
A gift unrightfully acquired, the mind not pleased,
Not believing in the rich fruit of kamma—
This is an offering purified by neither.

Whoever, moral in habit, gives to those of moral habit
A gift rightfully acquired, the mind well pleased,
Firmly believing in the rich fruit of kamma—
I assert this gift to be of abundant fruit.

Whoever, without attachment,[2] gives to those without attachment
A gift rightfully acquired, the mind well pleased,
Firmly believing in the rich fruit of kamma—
I assert this gift to be a gift abundant in gain.

Discourse on the Analysis of Offerings:
The Twelfth

Division on Analysis:
The Fourth

---

[1] *I.e.* with the Teaching. *Miln.* 258 quotes this verse and mentions this Sutta by name.

[2] *MA.* v. 77 says this means a non-returner here, for an arahant is wholly without attachment, *ekantavītarāga*, therefore a gift given by an arahant to an arahant is the chief of gifts. Because of his being without desire or attachment, a deed done by an arahant is neither skilled nor unskilled but remains in the position of its doing.

V. THE DIVISION OF THE SIXFOLD SENSE(-FIELD)
(Saḷāyatanavagga)

143. DISCOURSE ON AN EXHORTATION TO ANĀTHAPIṆḌIKA
(Anāthapiṇḍikovādasutta)

[258] THUS have I heard: At one time the Lord was staying near Sāvatthī in the Jeta Grove in Anāthapiṇḍika's monastery. Now at that time the householder Anāthapiṇḍika was a sick man, in pain, grievously ill. And the householder Anāthapiṇḍika summoned a certain man and said to him: "Come you, my good man, approach the Lord; having approached, in my name salute the Lord's feet with your head and say to him: 'Revered sir, the householder Anāthapiṇḍika is a sick man, in pain, grievously ill; he salutes the Lord's feet with his head.' And then approach the venerable Sāriputta; having approached, in my name salute the venerable Sāriputta's feet with your head and say to him: 'Revered sir, the householder Anāthapiṇḍika . . . salutes the venerable Sāriputta's feet with his head.' And then say: 'Indeed, it would be good, revered sir, if the venerable Sāriputta, out of compassion, would approach the dwelling of the householder Anāthapiṇḍika.'"

When that man had answered the householder Anāthapiṇḍika in assent, saying, "Very well, reverend sir,"[1] he approached the Lord; having approached and greeted the Lord, he sat down at a respectful distance. As he was sitting down at a respectful distance that man spoke thus to the Lord: "Revered sir, the householder Anāthapiṇḍika is a sick man, in pain, grievously ill; he salutes the Lord's feet with his head." And he then approached the venerable Sāriputta; having approached and greeted the venerable Sāriputta, he sat down at a respectful distance. As he was sitting down at a respectful distance that man spoke thus to the venerable Sāriputta: "Revered sir, the householder Anāthapiṇḍika is a sick man . . . he salutes the venerable Sāriputta's feet with his head and speaks to him thus: Indeed it would be good, revered sir, if the venerable Sāriputta, out of compassion, would approach the dwelling of the householder Anāthapiṇḍika."

The venerable Sāriputta consented by becoming silent. Then

---

[1] *bhante*.

the venerable Sāriputta clothed himself and, taking his bowl and robe, approached the dwelling of the householder Anāthapiṇḍika with the venerable Ānanda as his attendant; having approached, [259] he sat down on the appointed seat. As he was sitting down on the appointed seat the venerable Sāriputta spoke thus to the householder Anāthapiṇḍika: " I hope that you, householder, are getting better, I hope you are keeping going, I hope the painful feelings are lessening, not increasing, that a lessening in them is apparent, not an increase ?"

" I am not getting better, revered Sāriputta, I am not keeping going; my painful feelings are increasing, not lessening; an increase in them is apparent, not a lessening. Revered Sāriputta,[1] as a strong man might cleave one's head with a sharp-edged sword, even so, revered Sāriputta, do exceedingly loud winds rend my head. I am not better, revered Sāriputta, I am not keeping going; my grievously painful feelings are increasing, not lessening; an increase in them is apparent, not a lessening. As, revered Sāriputta, a strong man might clamp a turban on one's head with a tight leather strap, even so, revered Sāriputta, do I have very bad headaches. I am not better . . . an increase in them is apparent, not a lessening. As, revered Sāriputta, a skilled cattle-butcher or his apprentice might cut through the stomach with a sharp butcher's knife, even so, revered Sāriputta, do very strong winds cut through my stomach. I am not better . . . an increase in them is apparent, not a lessening. As, revered Sāriputta, two strong men, having taken hold of a weaker man by his limbs, might set fire to him, might make him sizzle up over a charcoal pit, even so, revered Sāriputta, there is a fierce heat in my body. I am not better, revered Sāriputta, I am not keeping going; my painful feelings are increasing, not lessening; an increase in them is apparent, not a lessening."

" Wherefore you, householder, must train yourself thus: (you must think), ' I will not grasp after vision and so will have no consciousness dependent on vision.' This is how you must train yourself, householder. Wherefore you, householder, must train yourself thus: (you must think), ' I will not grasp after hearing . . . smelling . . . tasting . . . body . . . mind . . . material shapes . . . sounds . . . smells . . . tastes . . . touches . . . mental objects and so will have no consciousness dependent on mental objects.' This is how you must train yourself, householder.

---

[1] As at *M*. ii. 192-193.

Wherefore you, householder, must train yourself thus: (you must think), 'I will not grasp after visual consciousness and so will have no consciousness dependent on visual consciousness.' This is how you must train yourself, householder. Wherefore you, householder, must train yourself thus: (you must think), 'I will not grasp after auditory ... olfactory ... gustatory ... bodily ... mental consciousness and so will have no consciousness dependent on mental consciousness.' This is how you must train yourself, householder.

Wherefore you, householder, must train yourself thus: (you must think), 'I will not grasp after visual impact and so will have no consciousness dependent on visual impact.' [260] This is how you must train yourself, householder. Wherefore, you, householder, must train yourself thus: (you must think), 'I will not grasp after auditory ... olfactory ... gustatory ... bodily ... mental impact and so will have no consciousness dependent on mental impact.' This is how you must train yourself, householder.

Wherefore you, householder, must train yourself thus: (you must think), 'I will not grasp after feeling born of visual impact and so will have no consciousness dependent on feeling born of visual impact.' This is how you must train yourself, householder. Wherefore, you, householder, must train yourself thus: (you must think), 'I will not grasp after feeling born of auditory ... olfactory ... gustatory ... bodily ... mental impact and so will have no consciousness dependent on feeling born of mental impact.' This is how you must train yourself, householder.

Wherefore you, householder, must train yourself thus: (you must think), 'I will not grasp after the element of extension and so will have no consciousness dependent on the element of extension' This is how you must train yourself, householder. Wherefore you, householder, must train yourself thus: (you must think), 'I will not grasp after the liquid element ... the element of radiation ... the element of motion ... the element of space ... the element of consciousness and so will have no consciousness dependent on the element of consciousness.' This is how you must train yourself, householder.

Wherefore you, householder, must train yourself thus: (you must think), 'I will not grasp after material shape and so will have no consciousness dependent on material shape.' This is how you must train yourself, householder. Wherefore you, householder, must train yourself thus: (you must think), 'I will not grasp after feeling

... perception ... the habitual tendencies ... consciousness and so will have no consciousness dependent on consciousness.' This is how you must train yourself, householder.

Wherefore you, householder, must train yourself thus: (you must think), 'I will not grasp after the plane of infinite ether and so will have no consciousness dependent on the plane of infinite ether.' This is how you must train yourself, householder. Wherefore you, householder, must train yourself thus: (you must think), 'I will not grasp after the plane of infinite consciousness ... the plane of no-thing ... [261] the plane of neither-perception-nor-non-perception and so will have no consciousness dependent on the plane of neither-perception-nor-non-perception.' This is how you must train yourself, householder.

Wherefore you, householder, must train yourself thus: (you must think), 'I will not grasp after this world and so will have no consciousness dependent on this world.' This is how you must train yourself, householder. Wherefore you, householder, must train yourself thus: (you must think), 'I will not grasp after a world beyond and so will have no consciousness dependent on a world beyond.' This is how you must train yourself, householder.

Wherefore you, householder, must train yourself thus: (you must think), 'As I will not grasp after that which is here seen, heard, sensed, cognised, sought after, pondered over with the mind, I will have no consciousness dependent on it.' This is how you must train yourself, householder."

When this had been said, the householder Anāthapiṇḍika cried and shed tears. Then the venerable Ānanda spoke thus to the householder Anāthapiṇḍika: "Householder, are you holding on or are you sinking, householder?"

"I, revered Ānanda, am not holding on, I am sinking.[1] Although the Teacher and monks who were developing their minds[2] visited

---

[1] It seems necessary here to omit the *na* of Chalmers' text. For Anāthapiṇḍika was on the point of death and already failing or sinking. Otherwise one could translate, "I am not holding on (but) I am not sinking." Or as, "No, Ānanda, I am holding on, I am not sinking." But this appears to be against the context and against grammatical usage, for the plain negative answer, our "No," is never expressed by the word *na*, not.

[2] *manobhāvanīyo bhikkhū*. *Cf. manobhāvaniyo bhikkhu* at *A*. iii. 317, *Vv.* 34. 13; and the same expression, in the genitive plural, at *A*. v. 55, *S*. iii. 1, which *SA*. iii. 249-250 explains by *mana-vaḍḍhanaka*. It is possible that *bhikkhū* in the above *M*. passage should read *bhikkhu*, the reference then being to Sāriputta.

me for a long time, I have never yet heard reasoned talk such as this."

"Reasoned talk such as this, householder, does not (usually) occur for householders clad in white.[1] It is for those that have gone forth, householder, that reasoned talk such as this (usually) occurs."

"Well then, revered Sāriputta, let there occur reasoned talk such as this for householders clad in white. There are, revered Sāriputta, young men of family with but little dust in their eyes who, not hearing *dhamma*, are declining, but they could be learners of *dhamma*."[2]

And when the venerable Sāriputta and the venerable Ānanda had exhorted the householder Anāthapiṇḍika with this exhortation, they rose from their seats and departed. Soon after the venerable Sāriputta and the venerable [262] Ānanda had departed, the householder Anāthapiṇḍika at the breaking up of the body after dying arose in the Tusita group (of *devas*). And when the night was far spent the young *deva*[3] Anāthapiṇḍika, having illumined the whole of the Jeta Grove with his radiant beauty, approached the Lord;[4] having approached and greeted the Lord, he stood at a respectful distance. As he was standing at a respectful distance, the young *deva* Anāthapiṇḍika addressed the Lord in verses:

"This[5] friendly Jeta Grove frequented by the Order of seers,[6]
Dwelt in by the King under Dhamma, is the generator of my joy.

---

[1] This should not be taken to point to any esoteric element in the giving of the Teaching. Many passages could be adduced to show it was open to all who wanted to hear it; see especially *D*. ii. 100 and *S*. iv. 314-316. But as *MA*. v. 80 says, talk on giving was (usually) addressed to householders. This is what they wanted to hear, so why should they receive a talk that did not please them ? *Paṭibhāti* is a semi-technical term; it might be translated here as "vouchsafe": a talk such as this is not (usually) vouchsafed (by monks) for householders: because it is not appropriate, since their mental development is not as a rule sufficiently advanced for them to appreciate it.

[2] As at *M*. i. 168, *Vin*. i. 5, where these words form part of Brahmā Sahampati's plea to the Buddha to teach *dhamma*. Brahmā however says that there are beings, *satta*, with but little dust in their eyes, instead of "young men of family," *kulaputtā*; but it was of these that Anāthapiṇḍika was thinking.

[3] I think *devaputta* may sometimes be a young or new *deva*, one who has just become a *deva*.

[4] *MA*. v. 80 says he wanted to speak praise of "my Jeta Grove," the Order of monks, the Tathāgata, the ariyan Way, and Sāriputta.

[5] As at *S*. i. 33. See notes at *K.S*. i. 46.

[6] *MA*. v. 81 paraphrases "seers," *isi*, by monks, *bhikkhu*.

Deed,[1] knowledge,[2] and Dhamma,[3] the highest moral life[4]—
By these are mortals purified,[5] not by clan nor wealth.
Accordingly the wise man, beholding his own goal,
Seeking Dhamma[6] judiciously, is thus purified therein.[7]
As Sāriputta in wisdom, in morality and calm,[8]
So let whatever monk has gone beyond be excellent in these."

Thus spoke the young *deva* Anāthapiṇḍika. The Lord was approving. And the young *deva* Anāthapiṇḍika thought: "The Lord approves of me," and having greeted the Lord, then and there he vanished keeping his right side towards him. Then the Lord towards the end of that night addressed the monks, saying:

"Monks, when this night was far spent a certain young *deva*, having illumined the whole of the Jeta Grove with his radiant beauty, approached me; having approached and greeted me, he stood at a respectful distance. As he was standing at a respectful distance, this young *deva* addressed me in verses:

'This friendly Jeta Grove ...

... be excellent in these.'

[263] Thus spoke that young *deva*, monks. Thinking, 'The Lord approves of me,' and having greeted me, then and there he vanished keeping his right side towards me."

When this had been said, the venerable Ānanda spoke thus to the Lord: "Now, revered sir, could that have been the young *deva* Anāthapiṇḍika ? Revered sir, the householder Anāthapiṇḍika had unwavering confidence in the venerable Sāriputta."

---

[1] "Here *kamma* is volition (striving) for the Way," *maggacetanā*, *MA.* v. 81. On *cetanā* as *kamma* see M. i. 391, *A.* iii. 415.

[2] *vijjā* is extra-sensory knowledge of the Way, *maggapaññā*, or it is right understanding and purpose (or thought), *MA.* v. 81.

[3] The *dhamma* belonging to concentration, *samādhipakkhikadhamma*. It therefore seems as if *dhamma* here, as sometimes elsewhere, is being used instead of *citta* or *samādhi* to represent the middle one of the three branches of the training: *sīla*, *samādhi* (or, *citta*), *paññā*. Or it means, as recognised at *MA.* v. 81, (right) endeavour, mindfulness and concentration.

[4] "The life of one established in moral conduct is the highest," Or, *sīla* is (right) speech, action and mode of livelihood, *MA.* v. 81.

[5] "Selves are purified by this eightfold Way," according to *MA.* v. 81 which, in its exegesis on *vijjā*, *dhamma* and *sīla*, has presented the factors of the Way.

[6] Either the *dhamma* belonging to concentration, or the *dhamma* of the five *khandhā* on which the teaching of the four truths of anguish centres.

[7] In this ariyan Way, or in these four truths, *MA.* v. 81.

[8] "is the best," *MA.* v. 81.

"It is good, it is good, Ānanda. All that could be obtained by reasoning, Ānanda, has been obtained by you. Ānanda, that young *deva* was Anāthapiṇḍika, no other."

Thus spoke the Lord. Delighted, the venerable Ānanda rejoiced in what the Lord had said.

Discourse on an Exhortation to Anāthapiṇḍika:
The First

144. DISCOURSE ON AN EXHORTATION TO CHANNA

(Channovādasutta)

THUS have I heard: At one time[1] the Lord was staying near Rājagaha in the Bamboo Grove at the squirrels' feeding place. Now at that time the venerable Sāriputta and the venerable Cunda the Great and the venerable Channa were staying on Mount Vulture Peak. At that time the venerable Channa was a sick man, in pain, grievously ill. And the venerable Sāriputta, emerging from solitary meditation towards evening, approached the venerable Cunda the Great; having approached, he spoke thus to the venerable Cunda the Great: "Let us go on, reverend Cunda, and approach the venerable Channa so as to ask about his illness."[2]

"Yes, reverend sir," the venerable Cunda the Great answered the venerable Sāriputta in assent. Then the venerable Sāriputta and the venerable Cunda the Great approached the venerable Channa; having approached, they exchanged greetings with the venerable Channa; [264] having conversed in a friendly and courteous way, they sat down at a respectful distance. As they were sitting down at a respectful distance, the venerable Sāriputta spoke thus to the venerable Channa: "I hope that you, reverend Channa, are getting better, I hope you are keeping going, I hope the painful feelings are lessening, not increasing, that a lessening in them is apparent, not an increase ?"

---

[1] This episode is also recorded at *S.* iv. 55 *ff.*

[2] *MA.* v. 82 says he said this as attending to the sick had been praised by the Lord (*Vin.* i. 302).

"I am not getting better, reverend Sāriputta, I am not keeping going; my grievously painful feelings ...¹ ... are increasing, not lessening; an increase in them is apparent, not a lessening. I will take a knife (to myself), I do not desire life."²

"Do not let the venerable Channa take a knife (to himself). The venerable Channa must go on living. We want the venerable Channa to go on living. If the venerable Channa has no beneficial foods, I will search for beneficial foods for the venerable Channa. If the venerable Channa has no beneficial medicines, I will search for beneficial medicines for the venerable Channa. If the venerable Channa has no suitable attendant, I will attend to the venerable Channa. Do not let the venerable Channa take a knife (to himself). The venerable Channa must go on living. We want the venerable Channa to go on living."

"Reverend Sāriputta, I am not without beneficial foods, I am not without beneficial medicines, nor am I without a suitable attendant. Moreover, reverend Sāriputta, for a long time have I waited on³ the Teacher with satisfaction⁴ (to him), not with lack of satisfaction⁴ (to him). For this, reverend Sāriputta, is suitable in a disciple, that he should wait on the Teacher with satisfaction (to him), not with lack of satisfaction (to him). 'Channa the monk will take a knife (to himself) without incurring blame'⁵—remember this thus, reverend Sāriputta."

"We would question the venerable Channa on a particular matter if the venerable Channa grants us the opportunity for setting forth the question."⁶

"Ask, reverend Sāriputta; having heard (you) we will know (what to say)."

---

¹ As at *M*. iii. 259, above, p. 310.

² *MA*. v. 82 says that as he could not endure the deadly pains and thought of taking a knife (with which to stab himself or cut this throat ?), he was an ordinary person, *puthujjana*.

³ *paricinna*, as at *M*. i. 497 (*M.L.S.* ii. 175).

⁴ *manāpena* . . . *no amanāpena*. According to the Comys. (*e.g. AA*. iii. 287, *SA* i. 78) derived from *appeti*, to flow into, or *appāyati*, to make full, to satisfy.

⁵ *anupavajjaṁ* . . . *sattham āharissati*, lit. he will take an irreproachable, unblamed knife, *i.e.* in the karmic sense. According to *MA*. v. 82 his deed would be *anupapattika*, non-rebirthing, *appaṭisandhika*, not re-linking (as to consciousness). *SA*. ii. 371 reads *anupavattika*, not rolling on (in renewed births).

⁶ As at *M*. iii. 15.

"Reverend Channa, do you regard the eye, visual consciousness, the things cognisable by visual consciousness as 'This is mine, this am I, [265] this is my self'? Reverend Channa, do you regard the ear, auditory consciousness . . . the nose, olfactory consciousness . . . the tongue, gustatory consciousness . . . the body, tactile consciousness . . . the mind, mental consciousness, the things cognisable by mental consciousness as 'This is mine, this am I, this is my self'?"

"Reverend Sāriputta, I regard the eye, visual consciousness, the things cognisable by visual consciousness . . . the mind, mental consciousness, the things cognisable by mental consciousness as 'This is not mine, this am I not, this is not my self.'"

"Reverend Channa, what do you see, what do you understand there is in the eye, in visual consciousness, in the things cognisable by visual consciousness . . . in the mind, in mental consciousness, in the things cognisable by mental consciousness that you regard the eye, visual consciousness, the things cognisable by visual consciousness . . . the mind, mental consciousness, the things cognisable by mental consciousness as 'This is not mine, this am I not, this is not my self'?"

"It is because I see cessation,[1] understand that there is cessation in the eye, reverend Sāriputta, in visual consciousness, in the things cognisable by visual consciousness . . . it is because I see cessation, understand that there is cessation in the mind, reverend Sāriputta, in mental consciousness, in the things cognisable by mental consciousness, that I, reverend Sāriputta, regard the eye, visual consciousness, the things cognisable by visual consciousness . . . the mind, mental consciousness, [266] the things cognisable by mental consciousness as 'This is not mine, this am I not, this is not my self.'"

When this had been said, the venerable Cunda the Great spoke thus to the venerable Channa:[2]

"Wherefore, reverend Channa, this teaching of the Lord should always be attended to: 'For[3] him who clings there is wavering; for him who clings not there is no wavering; if there is no wavering

---

[1] *nirodha*, explained at *MA*. v. 82 = *SA*. ii. 372 as *khayavayaṁ*, destruction and waning.

[2] *SA*. ii. 372 says that Sāriputta, knowing Channa to be at the *puthujjana* stage, was silent and neither said "You are an average person" nor "You are cankerless." Cunda spoke so as to test Channa.

[3] This passage recurs at *Ud*. 81, *UdA*. 398, *Netti*, 65; *cf.* also *S*. ii. 67.

there is impassibility;[1] if there is impassibility there is no yearning;[2] if there is no yearning,[3] there is no coming and going;[4] if there is no coming and going, there is no deceasing and uprising; if there is no deceasing and uprising, there is no 'here' itself nor 'yonder' nor 'in between the two.' This is itself the end of anguish."

Then the venerable Sāriputta and the venerable Cunda the Great, having exhorted the venerable Channa with this exhortation, rose from their seats and departed. And not long after the departure of the venerable Sāriputta and the venerable Cunda the Great, the venerable Channa took a knife (to himself).[5] Then the venerable Sāriputta approached the Lord; having approached and greeted the Lord, he sat down at a respectful distance. As he was sitting down at a respectful distance, the venerable Sāriputta spoke thus to the Lord: "Revered sir, a knife has been taken by the venerable Channa to himself. What is his bourn, what his future state?"

"Was it not face to face with you, Sāriputta, that the monk Channa declared (his) blamelessness?"[6]

"There is, revered sir, a village of the Vajjis called Pubbajira.[7] There are families there who were friends of the venerable Channa, families which sustained[8] him, families to be visited."[9]

"Indeed, Sāriputta, these families were friends of the monk Channa, families who sustained him, families to be visited. As far as this, Sāriputta, I do not say he was to be blamed.[10] But whoever,

---

[1] Of body and mind, and in respect of the obstructions, *MA.* v. 83.
[2] *nati*, as at *M.* i. 115. *MA.* v. 83, *SA.* ii. 372 say *taṇhā*.
[3] *I.e.* for becoming, *MA.* v. 82 = *SA.* ii. 372.
[4] *āgatigati*, some vv. ll. giving *agatigati*. The Comys. says "what is called 'coming,' *āgati*, because of re-linking, what is called 'going,' *gati*, because of decease, these are not." *Cf. āgati gati cuti upapatti* at *D.* i. 162, etc.
[5] He cut his windpipe, but at that moment fell into the fear of dying. Knowing he was a *puthujjana*, he hastily applied insight and, mastering the *saṁkhārā*, attained arahantship and final nibbāna. See *K.S.* iv. 33, *n.* 1.
[6] *anupavajjatā*. [7] *S.* iv. 59 reads Pubbavijjhana, v.l. Pubbavicira.
[8] *suhajjakulāni*. *Suhajja* would appear to be from Skrt. *suhyati*, to satisfy, gladden; rejoice; sustain, support.
[9] *upavajjakulāni*. Comys. explain as families to be approached or visited, *upasaṁkamitabbakulāni*. According to *C.P.D.*, s.v. *anupavajja*, it was Sāriputta who mistook *upavajja* for *upasaṁkamitabba*. He wondered whether, *MA.* v. 83, as Channa had these lay supporters he would have attained final nibbāna in the Lord's teaching. The Lord however said there was no gregariousness (which was not allowed to monks) between Channa and these families. Therefore there was no blame.
[10] *sa-upavajja*.

Sāriputta, lays down this body and grasps after another body, of him I say he is to be blamed.¹ The monk Channa did not do this;² the monk Channa took the knife (to himself) without incurring blame."
Thus spoke the Lord. Delighted, the venerable Sāriputta rejoiced in what the Lord had said.

Discourse on an Exhortation to Channa:
The Second

145. DISCOURSE ON AN EXHORTATION TO PUNNA
(Puṇṇovādasutta)

[267] THUS have I heard: At one time³ the Lord was staying near Sāvatthī in the Jeta Grove in Anāthapiṇḍika's monastery. Then the venerable Puṇṇa,⁴ emerging from solitary meditation towards evening, approached the Lord; having approached and greeted the Lord, he sat down at a respectful distance. As he was sitting down at a respectful distance, the venerable Puṇṇa spoke thus to the Lord: "It would be good, revered sir, if the Lord would exhort me with an exhortation in brief so that I, having heard *dhamma* from the Lord, might abide alone, aloof, diligent, ardent, self-resolute."
"Well then, Puṇṇa, listen, attend carefully and I will speak."
"Yes, revered sir," the venerable Puṇṇa answered the Lord in assent. The Lord spoke thus:
"There are, Puṇṇa, material shapes cognisable by the eye, agreeable, pleasant, liked, enticing, connected with sensual pleasures, alluring. If a monk delights in these,⁵ welcomes them and persists in cleaving to them, then, because he delights in them, welcomes them and persists in cleaving to them, delight uprises in him. I say,

---

¹ *sa-upavajja.*
² *taṁ Channassa bhikkhuno n' atthi,* lit. "this was not (there was not this) for the monk Channa."
³ As at *S.* iv. 60 *ff., Divy.* 37-39.
⁴ Verses at *Thag.* 70. See *ThagA.* i. 167-169 and *MA.* v. 85-92.
⁵ That is, in both the eye and material shapes.

Puṇṇa, that from the uprising of delight is the uprising of anguish. There are, Puṇṇa, sounds cognisable by the ear ... smells cognisable by the nose ... tastes cognisable by the tongue ... touches cognisable by the body ... mental states cognisable by the mind ... I say, Puṇṇa, that from the uprising of delight is the uprising of anguish. And there are, Puṇṇa, material shapes cognisable by the eye ... sounds cognisable by the ear ... smells cognisable by the nose ... tastes cognisable by the tongue ... touches cognisable by the body ... mental states cognisable by the mind, agreeable, pleasant, liked, connected with sensual pleasures, [**268**] alluring. If a monk does not delight in these, does not welcome them or persist in cleaving to them, then, because he does not delight in them, welcome them or persist in cleaving to them, delight is stopped in him. I say, Puṇṇa, that from the stopping of delight is the stopping of anguish.

And in what district will you stay, Puṇṇa, now that you have been exhorted by me with this exhortation in brief?"

"There is a district called Sunāparanta.[1] I will stay there, revered sir, now that I have been exhorted by the Lord with this exhortation in brief."

"Puṇṇa, the people of Sunāparanta are fierce, the people of Sunāparanta are rough. If the people of Sunāparanta revile[2] and abuse you, Puṇṇa, how will it be for you there, Puṇṇa?"

"If the people of Sunāparanta revile and abuse me, revered sir, it will be thus for me there: I will say, 'Goodly indeed are these people of Sunāparanta, indeed very goodly are these people of Sunāparanta in that they do not strike me a blow with their hands.' It will be thus for me here, Lord, it will be thus for me here, Wellfarer."

"But if the people of Sunāparnata do strike you a blow with their hands, Puṇṇa, how will it be for you there, Puṇṇa?"

"If the people of Sunāparanta strike me a blow with their hands, revered sir, it will be thus for me there: I will say, 'Goodly indeed are these people of Sunāparanta, indeed very goodly are these people

---

[1] *MA.* v. 85 says he was a dweller in Sunāparanta, and there were four places there where he stayed. Two, however, were not suitable: the monastery in Samuddagiri was surrounded by magnetic rocks so it was impossible to pace up and down; and at Mātulagiri a huge flock of birds made a noise day and night.

[2] Or, "curse." See *B.D.* ii. 171, *n*. 3, also p. 269; also *B.D.* iii. 344 (*Vin.* iv. 309) where "revile" and "abuse" are defined much as they are at *MA.* v. 85.

of Sunāparanta in that they do not strike me a blow with clods of earth.' It will be thus for me here, Lord, it will be thus for me here, Well-farer."

" But if the people of Sunāparanta do strike you a blow with clods of earth, Puṇṇa, how will it be for you there, Puṇṇa ?"

" If the people of Sunāparanta . . . I will say, ' Goodly indeed are these people . . . in that they do not strike me a blow with a stick '[1] . . . "

[269] " But if the people of Sunāparanta do strike you a blow with a stick . . . ?"

" If the people of Sunāparanta . . . ' . . . in that they do not strike me a blow with a knife ' . . . "

" But if the people of Sunāparanta do strike you a blow with a knife . . . ?"

" If the people of Sunāparanta strike me a blow with a knife . . . ' . . . in that they do not deprive me of life with a sharp knife ' . . . "

" But if the people of Sunāparanta do deprive you of life with a sharp knife . . . ?"

" If the people of Sunāparanta deprive me of life with a sharp knife, revered sir, it will be thus for me there: I will say, ' There are disciples of the Lord who, disgusted by the body and the life-principle and ashamed of them, look about for a knife (with which to kill themselves).[2] I have come upon this very knife without having looked about for it.' It will be thus for me here, Lord, it will be thus for me here, Well-farer."

" It is good, Puṇṇa, it is good. You will be able to live in the district among the people of Sunāparanta possessed as you are of this taming and calm.[3] You, Puṇṇa, now do that for which you deem the time is right."

Then the venerable Puṇṇa, having rejoiced in what the Lord had said and having given thanks for it, rose from his seat and greeted the Lord keeping his right side towards him, packed away his lodging and, taking his bowl and robe, set out on tour for the Sunāparanta district. Walking on tour, he gradually arrived at the Sunāparanta district. While he was there the venerable Puṇṇa stayed in the district among the people of Sunāparanta. And

---

[1] *MA*. v. 85 says a four-handed stick or a club of twigs.

[2] *satthahāraka*, or an assassin. But see Pārājika III (*Vin*. iii. 73) to which *MA*. v. 85 refers.

[3] *damupasama*. *MA*. v. 85 says that in this Sta. *dama* is *khanti*, forbearance or patience, and *upasama* has the same meaning.

during the same rainy season the venerable Puṇṇa established as many as five hundred lay-devotees, as many as five hundred female lay-devotees, and he realised the three knowledges. Then after a time the venerable Puṇṇa attained final nibbāna.[1]

A number of monks approached the Lord; having approached and greeted the Lord, they sat down at a respectful distance. As they were sitting down at a respectful distance, these monks spoke thus to the Lord: " Revered sir, that [270] young man of family[2] named Puṇṇa who was exhorted by the Lord with an exhortation in brief, has died. What is his bourn, what his future state ?"

" Clever, monks, was Puṇṇa the young man of family; he followed after *dhamma* according to the various parts of *dhamma*; and he did not annoy me with questionings about *dhamma*. Puṇṇa the young man of family has gained final nibbāna, monks."

Thus spoke the Lord. Delighted, these monks rejoiced in what the Lord had said.

Discourse on an Exhortation to Puṇṇa:
The Third

146. DISCOURSE ON AN EXHORTATION FROM NANDAKA

(Nandakovādasutta)

THUS have I heard: At one time the Lord was staying near Sāvatthī in the Jeta Grove in Anāthapiṇḍika's monastery. Then Mahāpajā- patī the Gotamid with as many as five hundred nuns approached the Lord; having approached and greeted the Lord, she stood at a respectful distance. As she was standing at a respectful distance, Mahāpajāpatī the Gotamid spoke thus to the Lord: " Revered sir,

---

[1] *MA*. v. 92 says he attained final nibbāna in the element of nibbāna that has no substrate for rebirth remaining. The people reverenced his body for a week and then, having collected sweet scented sticks, they cremated it, took away the remains and built a cetiya.

[2] I do not know why Puṇṇa is here referred to as *kulaputta*. It is perhaps to show he died young.

let the Lord exhort the nuns; revered sir, let the Lord instruct the nuns; revered sir, let the Lord make a talk on *dhamma* for the nuns."

Now at that time the monks who were elders used to exhort the nuns in turn; but the venerable Nandaka[1] did not want to exhort the nuns in (his) turn.[2] So the Lord addressed the venerable Ānanda, saying: "Ānanda, whose turn is it today to exhort the nuns by turn?"

"It is Nandaka's turn, revered sir, to exhort the nuns by turn; but this venerable Nandaka, revered sir, does not want to exhort the nuns in (his) turn." Then the Lord addressed the venerable Nandaka, saying:

"Exhort the nuns, Nandaka; instruct the nuns, Nandaka; do you, brahman,[3] make a talk on *dhamma* for the nuns."

"Yes, revered sir," [271] answered the venerable Nandaka in assent to the Lord. He dressed in the early morning and, taking his bowl and robe, entered Sāvatthī for almsfood. When he had walked for almsfood in Sāvatthī, on returning from the alms-gathering after the meal he approached the King's Monastery[4] without a companion.[5] Those nuns saw the venerable Nandaka coming in the distance, and on seeing him they made ready a seat and set out water for (washing) the feet. The venerable Nandaka sat down on the seat made ready and as he was sitting down he washed his feet. And when those nuns had greeted the venerable Nandaka they sat down at a respectful distance. The venerable Nandaka spoke thus to those nuns as they were sitting down at a respectful distance:

"Sisters, there will be a talk by way of putting questions. Those who understand (each question) should say: 'We understand'; those who do not understand should say: 'We do not understand.'

---

[1] At *A.* i. 25 he is called foremost of those who exhort nuns. Verses at *Thag.* 279-282. *MA.* v. 93-94 says that in a former life he had been head of 500 slaves and Mahāpajāpatī of 500 women slaves, and they were husband and wife. In this life the women were born as her companions and went forth with her.

[2] This was because in a previous birth he had been a king and they his concubines. He feared that anyone with recollection of former "habitations" would know this, and accuse him of wanting to see his former companions again.

[3] A term of high regard. The Buddha knew that only Nandaka could liberate the nuns.

[4] Rājakārāma, built by Pasenadi to the south of the city, corresponding to the Thūpārāma (at Anurādhapura), *MA.* v. 96. See *Jā.* ii. 15 and *D.P.P.N.*

[5] *attadutiya*, with oneself for companion, *i.e.* alone; see *C.P.D.*

But if anyone has any doubt or perplexity I should be questioned about it thus: ' How is this, revered sir ? What is the meaning of that ?' "

" So far, revered sir, we are pleased and satisfied with the master Nandaka in that the master Nandaka invites us."

" What do you think about this, sisters ? Is the eye permanent or impermanent ?"

" Impermanent, revered sir."

" But is what is impermanent, anguish or happiness ?"

" Anguish, revered sir."

" Is it right to regard that which is impermanent, anguish and liable to alteration as, ' This is mine, this am I, this is my self ' ?"

" No, revered sir."

" What do you think about this, sisters ? Is the ear ... the nose ... the tongue ... the body ... the mind permanent or impermanent ? ... Is it right to [272] regard that which is impermanent, anguish and liable to alteration as ' This is mine, this am I, this is my self ' ?"

" No, revered sir. What is the reason for this ? Already, revered sir, by means of perfect intuitive wisdom it has been well seen by us as it really is that ' These six internal sense-fields are impermanent.' "

" It is good, sisters, it is good. For it is thus, sisters, that by means of perfect intuitive wisdom this is seen by an ariyan disciple as it really is. What do you think about this, sisters ? Are material shapes ... sounds ... smells ... tastes ... touches ... mental states permanent or impermanent ? ... Is it right to regard that which is impermanent, anguish and liable to alteration as ' This is mine, this am I, this is my self ' ?"

" No, revered sir. What is the reason for this ? Already, revered sir, by means of perfect intuitive wisdom it has been well seen by us as it really is that ' These six external sense-fields are impermanent.' "

" It is good, sisters, it is good. For it is thus, sisters, that by means of perfect intuitive wisdom this is seen by an ariyan disciple as it really is. What do you think about this, sisters ? Is visual consciousness ... [273] ... auditory consciousness ... olfactory consciousness ... gustatory consciousness ... tactile consciousness ... mental consciousness permanent or impermanent ?"

" Impermanent, revered sir."

" But is what is impermanent, anguish or happiness ?"

" Anguish, revered sir."

"Is it right to regard that which is impermanent, anguish and liable to alteration as 'This is mine, this am I, this is my self'?"

"No, revered sir. What is the reason for this? Already, revered sir, by means of perfect intuitive wisdom it has been well seen by us as it really is that 'These six classes of consciousness are impermanent.'"

"It is good, sisters, it is good. For it is thus, sisters, that by means of perfect intuitive wisdom this is seen by an ariyan disciple as it really is. It is, sisters, like the oil for lighting an oil-lamp which is impermanent and liable to alteration, and like the wick which is impermanent and liable to alteration, and like the flame which is impermanent and liable to alteration, and like the light which is impermanent and liable to alteration. If anyone, sisters, were to speak thus: 'The oil for lighting this oil-lamp is impermanent and liable to alteration, and the wick ... and the flame is impermanent and liable to alteration, but that which is the light—that is permanent, lasting, eternal, not liable to alteration,' speaking thus, sisters, would he be speaking rightly?"

"No, revered sir. What is the reason for this? It is, revered sir, that if the oil for lighting this oil-lamp be impermanent and liable to alteration, and if the wick ... and if the flame be impermanent and liable to alteration, all the more is the light impermanent and liable to alteration."

"Even so, sisters, if anyone should speak thus: 'These six internal sense-fields are impermanent and liable to alteration, but whatever pleasure or pain or neither pain nor pleasure I experience as a result of these six internal sense-fields—that is permanent, lasting, eternal, not liable to alteration,' speaking this, sisters, would he be speaking rightly?"

"No, revered sir. What is the reason for this? As a result of this or that condition, revered sir, these or those feelings arise. [274] From the stopping of this or that condition these or those feelings are stopped."

"It is good, sisters, it is good. For it is thus, sisters, that by means of perfect intuitive wisdom this is seen by an ariyan disciple as it really is. It is, sisters, like the roots of a great, stable and pithy tree ... like the trunk ... the branches and foliage which are impermanent and liable to alteration, and like the shade which is impermanent and liable to alteration. If anyone, sisters, were to speak thus: 'The roots ... the trunk ... the branches and foliage of this great, stable and pithy tree are impermanent and liable to alteration, but that which is its shade—that is permanent, lasting, eternal, not liable to alteration,' speaking thus, sisters, would he be speaking rightly ?"

"No, revered sir. What is the reason for this ? It is, revered sir, that if the roots ... the trunk ... the foliage and branches of this great, stable and pithy tree are impermanent and liable to alteration, all the more is the shade impermanent and liable to alteration."

"Even so, sisters, if anyone should speak thus: 'These six external sense-fields are impermanent and liable to alteration, but whatever pleasure or pain or neither pain nor pleasure I experience as a result of these six external sense-fields—that is permanent, lasting, eternal, not liable to alteration,' speaking thus, sisters, would he be speaking rightly ?"

"No, revered sir. What is the reason for this ? As a result of this or that condition, revered sir, these or those feelings arise. From the stopping of this or that condition these or those feelings are stopped."

"It is good, sisters, it is good. For it is thus, sisters, that by means of perfect intuitive wisdom this is seen by an ariyan disciple as it really is. It is, sisters, as if a clever cattle-butcher or cattle-butcher's apprentice, having killed a cow, should dissect the cow with a butcher's sharp knife without spoiling the flesh within, without spoiling the outer hide, and with the butcher's sharp knife should cut, should cut around, should cut all around whatever tendons, sinews and ligaments there are there within; [275] and having cut, cut around, cut all around and removed the outer hide and, having clothed that cow in that self-same hide again, should then speak thus: 'This cow is conjoined with this hide as before.' Speaking thus, sisters, would he be speaking rightly ?"

"No, revered sir. What is the reason for this ? Although, revered sir, that clever cattle-butcher or cattle-butcher's apprentice, having killed a cow ... having clothed that cow in that self-same hide again, might then speak thus: 'This cow is conjoined with this hide as before,' yet that cow is not conjoined with that hide."

"I have made this simile for you, sisters, so as to illustrate the meaning. This is the meaning here: 'the flesh within,' sisters, is a synonym for the six internal sense-fields. 'The outer hide,' sisters, is a synonym for the six external sense-fields. 'The tendons, sinews and ligaments within,' sisters, is a synonym for delight and attachment. 'The butcher's sharp knife,' sisters, is a synonym for the ariyan intuitive wisdom, the ariyan intuitive wisdom by which one cuts, cuts around and cuts all around the inner defilements, the inner fetters and the inner bonds.

There are, sisters, these seven links in awakening[1] from the development and making much of which a monk, by the destruction of the cankers, having here and now realised by his own super-knowledge the freedom of mind and the freedom through intuitive wisdom that are cankerless, entering on them abides therein. What are the seven? Herein, sisters, a monk develops the link in awakening that is mindfulness and is dependent on aloofness, dependent on detachment, dependent on cessation, ending in abandoning; he develops the link in awakening that is investigation into things ... that is energy ... that is rapture ... that is impassibility ... that is concentration ... he develops the link in awakening that is equanimity and is dependent on aloofness, dependent on detachment, dependent on cessation, ending in abandoning. These, sisters, are the seven links in awakening from the development and making much of which a monk ... entering on them abides therein."

[276] Then the venerable Nandaka, having exhorted the nuns with this exhortation, dismissed them, saying: " Go, sisters, it is time."

Then these nuns, having rejoiced in what the venerable Nandaka had said and having given thanks, rose from their seats, greeted the venerable Nandaka keeping their right sides towards him, and approached the Lord; having approached and greeted the Lord, they stood at a respectful distance. The Lord spoke thus to these nuns as they were standing at a respectful distance: " Go, nuns, it is time." Then these nuns, having greeted the Lord, departed keeping their right sides towards him. Not long after these nuns had departed the Lord addressed the monks, saying:

" Monks, as on an Observance day, a fourteenth, there is neither doubt nor perplexity among the populace as to whether the moon is not full[2] or whether the moon is full, for the moon is then not full, even so, monks, although these nuns were delighted with Nandaka's teaching on *dhamma*, their aspirations were not fulfilled."

Then the Lord addressed the venerable Nandaka, saying: " Well

---

[1] As at *M.* iii. 88. They are spoken of here according to *MA.* v. 96-97 because wisdom alone, without the seven links in awakening, is unable to cut off the defilements.

[2] *ūno chando, i.e.* one day less than full; the fifteenth being the day of the full moon.

then, Nandaka, you may exhort these nuns with this same exhortation again tomorrow."

"Yes, revered sir," the venerable Nandaka answered the Lord in assent.

Then the venerable Nandaka dressed in the early morning towards the end of that night and, taking his bowl and robe, entered Sāvatthī for almsfood ... (*as above, p.* 323 *to p.* 327) ... [**277**] ... " Go, nuns, it is time." Not long after these nuns had departed the Lord addressed the monks, saying:

" Monks, as on an Observance day, a fifteenth, there is neither doubt nor perplexity among the populace as to whether the moon is not full or whether the moon is full, for the moon is then quite full, even so, monks, these nuns were delighted with Nandaka's teaching on *dhamma* and their aspirations were fulfilled. She who is the last nun[1] of these five hundred nuns is a stream-attainer, not liable to the Downfall; she is assured, bound for self-awakening."

Thus spoke the Lord. Delighted, these monks rejoiced in what the Lord had said.

Discourse on an Exhortation from Nandaka:
The Fourth

147. LESSER DISCOURSE ON AN EXHORTATION TO RĀHULA

(Cūḷarāhulovādasutta)

THUS have I heard: At one time[2] the Lord was staying near Sāvatthī in the Jeta Grove in Anāthapiṇḍika's monastery. Then as the Lord was in solitary meditation a reasoning arose in his mind thus: " Mature now in Rāhula are the things[3] that bring freedom to

---

[1] The last of all in so far as excellent qualities, *guṇa*, are concerned is a stream-attainer; the others are once-returners, non-returners and those whose cankers are destroyed, *MA.* v. 97.

[2] This Discourse also occurs at *S.* iv. 105-107.

[3] *dhammā.* Fifteen of them, *i.e.* the five *indriyas*, beginning with *saddhā*, are each purified in three ways; or five faculties of perception, *MA.* v. 98.

III. 277-279   *An Exhortation to Rāhula (Lesser)*   329

maturity.[1] Suppose I were to train Rāhula further in the destruction of the cankers ?" And having dressed in the early morning the Lord, taking his bowl and robe, entered Sāvatthī for almsfood. When he had walked in Sāvatthī for almsfood, on returning from the alms-gathering after the meal he addressed the venerable Rāhula, saying: " Take your piece of cloth for sitting on,[2] Rāhula; we will go to the Blind Men's Grove[3] [**278**] for the day-sojourn."

" Yes, revered sir," answered the venerable Rāhula in assent to the Lord and, taking his piece of cloth for sitting on, he followed closely after the Lord. Now at that time various thousands of *devas* were following the Lord, thinking: " Today the Lord will train the venerable Rāhula further in the destruction of the cankers." Then the Lord plunged into the Blind Men's Grove and sat down on a seat made ready at the root of a tree. And the venerable Rāhula, having greeted the Lord, sat down at a respectful distance. The Lord spoke thus to the venerable Rāhula as he was sitting down at a respectful distance:

" What do you think about this, Rāhula ?   Is the eye . . . are material shapes . . . is visual consciousness . . . [**279**] . . . is impact on the eye permanent or impermanent ? . . . Is the ear . . . the nose . . . the tongue . . . the body . . . the mind . . . are mental states . . . is mental consciousness . . . is impact on the mind permanent or impermanent ?"

" Impermanent, revered sir."

" But is what is impermanent, anguish or happiness ?"

" Anguish, revered sir."

" But is it right to regard that which is impermanent, anguish, liable to alteration as, ' This is mine, that am I, this is my self ' ?"

" No, revered sir."

" What do you think about this, Rāhula ?   Is that which arises as feeling, perception, the habitual tendencies, consciousness because of impact on the eye . . . the ear . . . the nose . . . the tongue . . . the body . . . the mind permanent or impermanent ?"

" Impermanent, revered sir."

" But is what is impermanent, anguish or happiness ?"

" Anguish, revered sir."

---

[1] *vimuttiparipācaniyā*. Mentioned at *MA*. iii. 126. These two sentences are quoted at *DA*. 50. The text should at least have a hyphen between *vimutti* and *paripācaniyā*.

[2] *nisīdana*, defined at *Vin*. iii. 232; see *B.D*. ii. 87, *n*. 2.

[3] *Andhavana*. See *B.D*. ii. 36, *n*. 3.

"And is it right to regard that which is impermanent, anguish, liable to alteration as, ' This is mine, this am I, this is my self ' ?"

"No, revered sir."

"Seeing thus, Rāhula, the instructed disciple of the ariyans turns away from the eye, he turns away from material shapes, he turns away from visual consciousness, he turns away from impact on the eye; and likewise he turns away from that which arises because of impact on the eye as feeling, perception, the habitual tendencies, consciousness. He turns away from the ear, he turns away from sounds; he turns away from the nose, he turns away from smells; he turns away from the tongue, he turns away from tastes; he turns away from the body, he turns away from touches; he turns away from the mind, he turns away from mental states, he turns away from mental consciousness, he turns away from impact on the mind; and likewise he turns away from that which [280] arises because of impact on the mind as feeling, perception, the habitual tendencies, consciousness. In turning away he is dispassionate; by dispassion he is freed; in freedom is the knowledge that he is freed, and he comprehends: Destroyed is birth, brought to a close the Brahma-faring, done is what was to be done, there is no more of being such or so."

Thus spoke the Lord. The venerable Rāhula rejoiced in what the Lord had said. While this exposition was being given the venerable Rāhula's mind was freed from the cankers without grasping. And to those various thousands of *devas* there arose the dustless, stainless vision of *dhamma*[1] that, ' whatever is liable to uprising all that is liable to stopping.'

Lesser Discourse on an Exhortation to Rāhula:
The Fifth

---

[1] *MA.* v. 99 states that in the Exhortation to Upāli and the *Dīghanakha Sutta* this means the first Way; in the *Brahmāyu Sutta* the three fruits; but here the four Ways and the four fruits are to be understood, for some of these *devas* were stream-attainers, some once-returners, non-returners and those whose cankers were destroyed.

148. DISCOURSE ON THE SIX SIXES
(Chachakkasutta)

THUS have I heard: At one time the Lord was staying near Sāvatthī in the Jeta Grove in Anāthapiṇḍika's monastery. While he was there the Lord addressed the monks, saying: "Monks." "Revered One," these monks answered the Lord in assent. The Lord spoke thus:

"I will teach you *dhamma*, monks, lovely in the beginning, lovely in the middle, lovely at the ending. With the spirit and the letter I will proclaim to you the Brahma-faring, utterly complete, quite purified, that is to say the Six Sixes. Listen to it, attend carefully and I will speak."

"Yes, revered sir," these monks answered the Lord in assent. The Lord spoke thus:

"Six internal sense-fields are to be understood, six external sense-fields are to be understood, six classes of consciousness are to be understood, six classes of sensory impingement are to be understood, six classes of feeling are to be understood, six classes of craving are to be understood.

When it is said, 'Six internal sense-fields are to be understood' in reference to what is it said ? It is in reference to the sense-field of eye, the sense-field of ear, the sense-field of nose, the sense-field of tongue, the sense-field of body, the sense-field of mind. When it is said, 'Six internal sense-fields are to be understood' it is said in reference to this. This is the first Six.

[281] When it is said, 'Six external sense-fields are to be understood,' in reference to what is it said ? It is in reference to the sense-field of material shapes, the sense-field of sounds, the sense-field of smells, the sense-field of tastes, the sense-field of touches, the sense-field of mental states. When it is said, 'Six external sense-fields are to be understood,' it is said in reference to this. This is the second Six.

When it is said, 'Six classes of consciousness are to be understood,' in reference to what is it said ? It is in reference to the visual consciousness that arises because of eye and material shapes; the auditory consciousness that arises because of ear and sounds; the olfactory consciousness that arises because of nose and smells; the gustatory consciousness that arises because of tongue and tastes; the bodily consciousness that arises because of body and touches; the mental consciousness that arises because of mind and mental states. When it is said, 'Six classes of consciousness are to be understood,' it is said in reference to this. This is the third Six.

When it is said, 'Six classes of (sense-)impingement are to be understood,' in reference to what is it said? It is in reference to the visual consciousness that arises because of eye and material shapes—the meeting of the three is sensory impingement;[1] the auditory consciousness that arises because of ear and sounds—the meeting of the three is sensory impingement; the olfactory consciousness that arises because of nose and smells—the meeting of the three is sensory impingement; the gustatory consciousness that arises because of tongue and tastes—the meeting of the three is sensory impingement; the bodily consciousness that arises because of body and touches—the meeting of the three is sensory impingement; the mental consciousness that arises because of mind and mental states—the meeting of the three is sensory impingement. When it is said, 'Six classes of sensory impingement are to be understood,' it is said in reference to this. This is the fourth Six.

When it is said, 'Six classes of feeling are to be understood,' in reference to what is it said? It is in reference to the visual consciousness that arises because of eye and material shapes—the meeting of the three is sensory impingement; conditioned by sensory impingement is feeling; the auditory consciousness that arises because of ear and sounds ... the olfactory consciousness that arises because of nose and smells ... the gustatory consciousness that arises because of tongue and tastes ... the bodily consciousness that arises because of body and touches ... the mental consciousness that arises because of mind and mental states—the meeting of the three is sensory impingement; conditioned by sensory impingement is feeling. When it is said, 'Six classes of feeling are to be understood,' it is [282] said in reference to this. This is the fifth Six.

When it is said, 'Six classes of craving are to be understood,' in reference to what is it said? It is in reference to the visual consciousness that arises because of eye and material shapes—the meeting of the three is sensory impingement, conditioned by sensory impingement is feeling, conditioned by feeling is craving; the

---

[1] Cf. M. i. 111.

auditory consciousness that arises because of ear and sounds . . . the olfactory consciousness that arises because of nose and smells . . . the gustatory consciousness that arises because of tongue and tastes . . . the bodily consciousness that arises because of body and touches . . . the mental consciousness that arises because of mind and mental states—the meeting of the three is sensory impingement, conditioned by sensory impingement is feeling, conditioned by feeling is craving. When it is said, 'Six classes of craving are to be understood,' it is said in reference to this. This is the sixth Six.

If anyone should say, 'Eye is self,' that is not fitting.[1] For the arising of the eye is to be seen and its decaying. Since its arising and decaying are to be seen one would thus be brought to the stage of saying: 'Self arises in me and passes away.'[2] Therefore if anyone should say, 'Eye is self,' that is not fitting; in this way eye is not-self. If anyone should say, 'Material shapes are self' . . . 'Visual consciousness is self' . . . 'Impact on the eye is self' . . . 'Feeling is self' [283] . . . therefore if anyone should say, 'Feeling is self,' that is not fitting; in this way eye is not-self, material shapes are not-self, visual consciousness is not-self, impact on the eye is not-self, feeling is not-self. If anyone should say, 'Craving is self' that is not fitting. For the arising of craving is to be seen and its decaying. Since its arising and decaying are to be seen one would thus be brought to the stage of saying: 'Self arises in me and passes away.' Therefore if anyone should say, 'Craving is self,' that is not fitting; in this way eye is not-self, material shapes are not-self, visual consciousness is not-self, impact on the eye is not-self, feeling is not-self, craving is not-self. If anyone should say, 'Ear is self' . . . 'Nose is self' . . . 'Tongue is self' . . . 'Body is self' . . . 'Mind is self' . . . 'Mental states are self' . . . 'Mental consciousness is self' . . . 'Impact on the mind is self,' that is not fitting . . . in this way mind is not-self, mental states are not-self, mental consciousness is not-self, impact on the mind is not-self. If anyone should say, 'Feeling is self,' that is not fitting. For the arising of feeling is to be seen and its decaying. Since [284] its arising and decaying are to be seen one would thus be brought to the stage of saying: 'Self arises in me and passes away.' Therefore if anyone should say, 'Feeling is self,' that is not fitting; in this way mind is not-self, mental states are not-

---

[1] *na uppajjati*, glossed as *na yujjati* at *MA*. v. 100.
[2] *veti*, glossed as *vigacchati nirujjhati* at *MA*. v. 100.

self, mental consciousness is not-self, impact on the mind is not-self, feeling is not-self. If anyone should say, 'Craving is self,' that is not fitting. For the arising of craving is to be seen and ... Therefore if anyone should say, 'Craving is self,' that is not fitting; in this way mind is not-self, mental states are not-self, mental consciousness is not-self, impact on the mind is not-self, feeling is not-self, craving is not-self.

But this, monks, is the course leading to the arising of 'own body': one says with regard to eye ... material shapes ... visual consciousness ... impact on the eye ... feeling ... craving ... ear ... nose ... tongue ... body ... mind ... mental states ... mental consciousness ... impact on the mind ... feeling ... craving that 'This is mine, this am I, this is my self.'

And this, monks, is the course leading to the stopping of 'own body': one says with regard to eye ... material shapes ... visual consciousness ... impact on the eye ... feeling ... craving ... ear ... nose ... tongue ... body ... mind ... mental states ... mental consciousness ... impact on the mind ... feeling [**285**] ... craving that 'This is not mine, this am I not, this is not my self.'

Monks, visual consciousness arises because of eye and material shapes, the meeting of the three is sensory impingement; an experience arises conditioned by sensory impingement that is pleasant or painful or neither painful nor pleasant. He, being impinged on by a pleasant feeling, delights, rejoices and persists in cleaving to it; a tendency to attachment is latent in him.[1] Being impinged on by a painful feeling, he grieves, mourns, laments, beats his breast and falls into disillusion; a tendency to repugnance is latent in him. Being impinged on by a feeling that is neither painful nor pleasant, he does not comprehend the origin nor the going down nor the satisfaction nor the peril of that feeling nor the escape from it as it really is; a tendency to ignorance is latent in him. That he, monks, not getting rid of the tendency to attachment to a pleasant feeling, not driving out the tendency to repugnance for a painful feeling, not rooting out the tendency to ignorance concerning a feeling that is neither painful nor pleasant, not getting rid of ignorance, not making knowledge arise, should here and now be an end-maker of anguish—this situation does not exist.

Monks, auditory consciousness arises because of ear and sounds ... mental consciousness arises because of mind and mental states,

---

[1] For attachment, repugnance and ignorance, *cf. M.* i. 303 *f.*

the meeting of the three is sensory impingement; an experience arises ... (*as above*) ... not getting rid of ignorance, not making knowledge arise, should here and now be an end-maker of anguish —this situation does not exist.

[286] Monks, visual consciousness arises because of eye and material shapes ... auditory consciousness arises because of ear and sounds ... olfactory consciousness arises because of nose and smells ... gustatory consciousness arises because of tongue and tastes ... bodily consciousness arises because of body and touches ... mental consciousness arises because of mind and mental state; the meeting of the three is sensory impingement; an experience arises conditioned by sensory impingement that is pleasant or painful or neither pleasant nor painful. He, being impinged on by a pleasant feeling, does not delight, rejoice or persist in cleaving to it; a tendency to attachment is not latent in him. Being impinged on by a painful feeling, he does not grieve, mourn, lament, beat his breast or fall into disillusion; a tendency to repugnance is not latent in him. Being impinged on by a feeling that is neither painful nor pleasant, he comprehends the origin and the going down and the satisfaction and the peril of that feeling and the escape as it really is, a tendency to ignorance is not latent in him. That he, monks, by getting rid of any tendency to attachment to a pleasant feeling, by driving out any tendency to repugnance for a painful feeling, by rooting out any tendency to ignorance concerning a feeling that is neither painful nor pleasant, by getting rid of ignorance, by making knowledge arise, should here and now be an end-maker of anguish—this situation exists.

Seeing this thus, monks, the instructed disciple of the ariyans turns away from eye, turns away from material shapes, turns away from visual consciousness, turns away from impact on the eye, turns away from feeling, turns away from craving. He turns away from ear, he turns away from sounds ... He turns away from nose, he turns away from smells ... He turns away from tongue, he turns away from tastes ... He turns away from body, he turns away from touches ... He turns away from mind, he turns away from mental states, he turns away from mental consciousness, he turns away from impact on the mind, he turns away from feeling, he turns away from craving. Turning away [287] he is dispassionate; by dispassion he is freed; in freedom is the knowledge that he is freed, and he comprehends: Destroyed is birth, brought to a close the Brahma-faring, done is what was to be done, there is no more of being such or so."

Thus spoke the Lord. Delighted, these monks rejoiced in what the Lord had said. And while this exposition was being given the minds of as many as sixty monks were freed from the cankers without grasping.[1]

Discourse on the Six Sixes:
The Sixth

149. DISCOURSE PERTAINING TO THE GREAT SIXFOLD (SENSE-)FIELD
(Mahāsaḷāyatanikasutta)[2]

THUS have I heard: At one time the Lord was staying near Sāvatthī in the Jeta Grove in Anāthapiṇḍika's monastery. While he was there the Lord addressed the monks, saying: " Monks." " Revered One," these monks answered the Lord in assent. The Lord spoke thus: " I will teach you, monks, the great sixfold (sense-)field. Listen to it, attend carefully and I will speak." " Yes, revered sir," the monks answered the Lord in assent. The Lord spoke thus:

" Monks, (anyone) not knowing, not seeing eye as it really is, not knowing, not seeing material shapes . . . visual consciousness . . . impact on the eye as it really is, and not knowing, not seeing as it really is the experience, whether pleasant, painful or neither painful nor pleasant, that arises conditioned by impact on the eye, is attached to the eye, is attached to material shapes, is attached to

---

[1] *MA.* v. 101 says that besides the sixty monks who became arahants when the Buddha first gave this Discourse, on each occasion of its preaching by Sāriputta or Moggallāna or eighty of the great Elders a like number attained arahantship. Later, each time Maliyadeva, an Elder (see *Mhvs.* p. 262) preached it at sixty different places in Ceylon, sixty monks attained arahantship. Once, after it had been preached by Tipiṭaka-Cūḷanāga, a thousand monks did so.

[2] Some MSS. read Saḷāyatanavibhaṅgasutta, Discourse on the Analysis of the Sixfold Sense-field, but this is the title of *M.* Sta. No. 137; there is no Cūḷa-Sutta of this name, and *mahā* with *saḷāyatanika*, as found in the first paragraph above, appears to refer to the subject-matter rather than to the Discourse itself, as in Sta. No. 136.

visual consciousness, is attached to impact on the eye; and as for that experience, whether pleasant, painful or neither painful nor pleasant, that arises conditioned by impact on the eye—to that too is he attached. While he, observing the satisfaction, is attached, bound and infatuated, the five groups of grasping go on to future accumulation.[1] And his craving, which is connected with again-becoming, accompanied by attachment and delight, finding its pleasure here and there, increases in him. And his physical anxieties increase, [288] and mental anxieties increase, and physical torments increase, and mental torments increase, and physical fevers increase, and mental fevers increase. He experiences anguish of body and anguish of mind.

Monks, (anyone) not knowing, not seeing ear as it really is . . . nose . . . tongue . . . body . . . mind as it really is, not knowing, not seeing mental states as they really are, not knowing, not seeing mental consciousness as it really is, not knowing, not seeing impact on the mind as it really is and not knowing, not seeing as it really is the experience . . . (*as above*) . . . and mental fevers increase. He experiences anguish of body and anguish of mind.

But (anyone), monks, knowing and seeing eye as it really is, knowing and seeing material shapes . . . visual consciousness . . . impact on the eye as it really is, and knowing, seeing as it really is the experience, whether pleasant, painful or neither painful nor pleasant, that arises conditioned by impact on the eye, is not attached to the eye nor to material shapes nor to visual consciousness nor to impact on the eye; and that experience, whether pleasant or painful or neither painful nor pleasant, that arises conditioned by impact on the eye—neither to that is he attached. While he, observing the peril, is not attached, bound or infatuated, the five groups of grasping go on to future diminution.[2] And his craving, which is connected with again-becoming, accompanied by attachment and delight, finding its pleasure here and there, decreases in him. And his physical anxieties decrease, and mental anxieties decrease, and bodily torments . . . and mental torments . . . and bodily fevers decrease, [289] and mental fevers decrease. He experiences happiness of body and happiness of mind.

Whatever is the view of what really is, that is for him right view;[3]

---

[1] *upacaya*, piling up, conservation—karmic in nature.
[2] *apacaya*, falling away.
[3] *MA*. v. 104 says that the sophist, *vitaṇḍavādin*, taking his stand on this Discourse, holds that the transcendental Way is fivefold.

whatever is aspiration for what really is, that is for him right aspiration; whatever is endeavour for what really is, that is for him right endeavour; whatever is mindfulness of what really is, that is for him right mindfulness; whatever is concentration on what really is, that is for him right concentration. And his past acts of body, acts of speech and mode of livelihood have been well purified. So does this ariyan eightfold Way go on to development and fulfilment for him. While this ariyan eightfold Way is being developed by him thus the four arousings of mindfulness also go on to development and fulfilment, and the four right efforts . . . and the four bases of psychic power . . . and the five controlling faculties . . . and the five powers . . . and the seven links in awakening go on to development and fulfilment. And in him these two things occur simultaneously:[1] calm and insight. By superknowledge he understands those things that should be understood by superknowledge; by superknowledge he gets rid of those things that should be got rid of by superknowledge; by superknowledge he develops those things that should be developed by superknowledge; by superknowledge he realises those things that should be realised by superknowledge.

And what, monks, are the things that should be understood by superknowledge? The five groups of grasping is the answer to this, that is to say, grasping after material shape, grasping after feeling, grasping after perception, grasping after the habitual tendencies, grasping after consciousness—these are the things that should be understood by superknowledge. And what are the things, monks, that should be got rid of by superknowledge? Ignorance and the craving for becomings—these are the things that should be got rid of by superknowledge. And what are the things, monks, that should be developed by superknowledge? Calm and insight—these are the things that should be developed by superknowledge. And what, [**290**] monks, are the things that should be realised by superknowledge? Knowledge and freedom—these are the things that should be realised by superknowledge.

And (anyone), monks, knowing and seeing ear as it really is . . . nose . . . tongue . . . body . . . mind as it really is . . . mental states . . . mental consciousness . . . impact on the mind as it really is, and knowing, seeing as it really is the experience, whether pleasant, painful or neither painful nor pleasant, that arises conditioned by impact on the mind, is not attached to the mind nor to mental

---

[1] *yuganandhā ti ekakkhaṇikayugannadhā, MA.* v. 104.

states nor to mental consciousness nor to impact on the mind; and that experience, whether pleasant or painful or neither painful nor pleasant, that arises conditioned by impact on the mind—neither is he attached to that ... and his mental fevers decrease. He experiences happiness of body and happiness of mind.

Whatever is the view of what really is, that is for him right view ... And his past acts of body, acts of speech and mode of livelihood have been well purified. So does this ariyan eightfold Way go on to development and fulfilment for him ... And what, monks, are the things that should be realised by superknowledge ? Knowledge and freedom—these are the things that should be realised by superknowledge."

Thus spoke the Lord. Delighted, these monks rejoiced in what the Lord had said.

Discourse pertaining to the Great Sixfold (Sense-)Field:
The Seventh

150. DISCOURSE TO THE PEOPLE OF NAGARAVINDA

(Nagaravindeyyasutta)

THUS have I heard: At one time, the Lord, walking on tour among the Kosalans together with a large Order of monks, arrived at the brahman village of the Kosalans called Nagaravinda. The brahman householders of Nagaravinda heard it said that " Indeed, the recluse Gotama, gone forth from the Sakyan clan, and walking on tour among the Kosalans together with a large Order of monks, [291] has arrived at Nagaravinda. A lovely reputation concerning the recluse Gotama has gone abroad thus: He is indeed the Lord, perfected one ... It is good to see perfected ones such as this." Then the brahman householders of Nagaravinda approached the Lord; having approached him, some exchanged greetings with the Lord and having conversed in a friendly and courteous way, they sat down at a respectful distance; some, having saluted the Lord with joined palms, sat down at a respectful distance; some, having informed the Lord of their names and clans, sat down at a respectful distance; some, becoming silent, sat down at a respectful distance. The Lord spoke thus to the brahman householders of Nagaravinda as they were sitting down at a respectful distance:

"If, householders, wanderers belonging to other sects should question you thus: 'Householders, what kind of recluses and brahmans should not be revered, reverenced, esteemed or honoured?' you, householders, being questioned thus, could answer thus: 'Those recluses and brahmans who are not devoid of attachment, not devoid of aversion, not devoid of confusion in regard to material shapes cognisable by the eye, whose minds are not inwardly tranquillised, who fare along now evenly, now unevenly[1] in body, speech and thought—recluses and brahmans such as these are not to be revered, reverenced, esteemed or honoured. What is the reason for this? It is that while[2] we, who are not devoid of attachment, not devoid of aversion, not devoid of confusion in regard to material shapes cognisable by the eye, our minds not inwardly tranquillised, fare along now evenly, now unevenly in body, speech and thought, it is yet not seen by them that this even-faring of ours is the higher. Therefore these worthy recluses and brahmans are not to be revered, reverenced, esteemed or honoured. Those recluses and brahmans who are not devoid of attachment . . . confusion in regard to sounds . . . smells . . . tastes . . . touches cognisable by the body . . . mental states cognisable by the mind, whose minds are not inwardly tranquillised, who fare along now evenly, now unevenly in body, speech and thought—recluses and brahmans such as these are not to be revered . . . or honoured. What is the reason for this? It is that while we, who are not devoid of attachment, not devoid of aversion, not devoid of confusion in regard to mental states cognisable by the mind, [292] our minds not inwardly tranquillised, fare along now evenly, now unevenly in body, speech and thought, it is yet not seen by them that this even-faring of ours is the higher. Therefore these worthy recluses and brahmans are not to be revered, reverenced, esteemed or honoured.' If you, householders, are questioned thus, you could answer those wanderers belonging to other sects thus.

But if, householders, wanderers belonging to other sects should question you thus: 'Householders, what kind of recluses and

---

[1] *samavisama*; *MA*. v. 105 says that at times they fare along evenly, at times unevenly.

[2] *pi hi*, though.

brahmans should be revered, reverenced, esteemed and honoured?' you, householders, being questioned thus, could answer thus: 'Those recluses and brahmans who are devoid of attachment, aversion and confusion in regard to material shapes cognisable by the eye, whose minds are inwardly tranquillised, who fare the even-faring[1] in body, speech and thought—recluses and brahmans such as these are to be revered . . . and honoured. What is the reason for this? It is that while we, who are not devoid of attachment, aversion and confusion, our minds not inwardly tranquillised, fare along now evenly, now unevenly in body, speech and thought, it is yet seen by them that this even-faring of ours is the higher. Therefore these worthy recluses and brahmans are to be revered . . . and honoured. Those worthy recluses and brahmans who are devoid of attachment . . . aversion . . . confusion in regard to sounds . . . smells . . . tastes . . . touches cognisable by the body . . . mental states cognisable by the mind, whose minds are inwardly tranquillised, who fare the even-faring in body, speech and thought—recluses and brahmans such as these are to be revered . . . and honoured. What is the reason for this? It is that while we, who are not devoid of attachment . . . aversion . . . confusion, our minds not inwardly tranquillised, fare along now evenly, now unevenly in body, speech and thought, it is yet seen by them that this even-faring of ours is the higher. Therefore these worthy recluses and brahmans are to be revered, reverenced, esteemed and honoured.' If you, householders, are questioned thus, you could answer those wanderers belonging to other sects thus.

If, householders, wanderers belonging to other sects should question you thus: ' But what grounds do the venerable ones[2] have, what is the authority by which you, venerable ones, should speak thus: Certainly, those venerable ones [**293**] are either devoid of attachment or are practising for the driving out of attachment, they are either devoid of aversion or are practising for the driving

---

[1] *samacariyaṁ caranti.*
[2] *ke pan' āyasmantānaṁ ākārā*, lit.: What are the venerable ones' grounds? Here too, in the same sentence, the wanderers appear to address the householders as *āyasmanto*, although this form is both nom. and voc. pl. The householders, on the other hand, appear to address the wanderers both as *āvuso*, " your reverences " (a few lines lower down) and as *āyasmanto*. The question: What grounds do the venerable ones have . . . by which you, venerable ones, should speak thus: *yena tumhe āyasmanto evaṁ vadetha*, is balanced by the answer: These, your reverences, are the grounds . . . by which we, venerable ones, speak thus, *yena mayaṁ āyasmanto evaṁ vadema.*

out of aversion; they are either devoid of confusion or are practising for the driving out of confusion.' If you are questioned thus, householders, you could answer these wanderers belonging to other sects thus: ' Those venerable ones frequent remote lodgings in lonely forest glades. But there are not there material shapes cognisable by the eye, sounds cognisable by the ear, smells cognisable by the nose, tastes cognisable by the tongue, touches cognisable by the body[1] such as having been seen, heard, smelt, tasted or touched over and over again, could delight them. These, your reverences, are the grounds, this is the authority by which we, venerable ones, speak thus: Certainly, those venerable ones are either devoid of attachment or are practising for the driving out of attachment; they are either devoid of aversion or are practising for the driving out of aversion; they are either devoid of confusion or are practising for the driving out of confusion.' If you, householders, are questioned thus, you could answer those wanderers belonging to other sects thus."

When this had been said, the brahman householders of Nagaravinda spoke thus to the Lord: "It is excellent, good Gotama, it is excellent, good Gotama. As, good Gotama, one might set upright what had been upset ... May the revered Gotama accept us as lay-disciples going for refuge from this day forth for as long as life lasts."

Discourse to the People of Nagaravinda:
The Eighth

151. DISCOURSE ON COMPLETE PURITY FOR ALMS-GATHERING
(Piṇḍapātapārisuddhisutta)

THUS have I heard: At one time the Lord was staying near Rājagaha in the Bamboo Grove at the squirrels' feeding place. Then the venerable Sāriputta, emerging from solitary meditation towards

---

[1] *MA*. v. 105 says the five strands of sense-pleasures as such are not meant here, but women; and it quotes *A*. i. 1, " I behold no other single thing that more obsesses a man's mind than a woman."

evening, approached the Lord; having approached and greeted the Lord, he sat down at a respectful distance. The Lord spoke thus to the venerable Sāriputta as he was sitting down at a respectful distance: [**294**] " Your faculties are very bright, Sāriputta, your complexion very pure, very clear. In which abiding are you, Sāriputta, now abiding in the fulness thereof ? "

" Abiding in (the concept of) emptiness do I, revered sir, now abide in the fulness thereof."[1]

" It is good, Sāriputta, it is good. You, Sāriputta, are now indeed abiding in fulness in the abiding of great men.[2] For this is the abiding of great men, Sāriputta, that is to say (the concept of) emptiness. Wherefore, Sāriputta, if a monk should desire: ' May I now abide in fulness in the abiding in (the concept of) emptiness,' that monk should consider thus, Sāriputta: ' On the road by which I entered the village for almsfood or in the part in which I walked for almsfood or on the road by which I left the village after (walking for) almsfood—did I have there in my mind desire or attachment or aversion or confusion or sensory reaction in regard to material shapes cognisable by the eye ?'

If, Sāriputta, a monk while considering knows thus: ' On the road by which I entered the village and in the part . . . I had there in my mind desire . . . or sensory reaction in regard to material shapes cognisable by the eye '—that monk, Sāriputta, should make an effort to get rid of these evil unskilled states themselves.

But if, Sāriputta, a monk while considering knows thus: ' On the road by which I entered the village . . . I had there in my mind no desire or attachment or aversion or confusion or sensory reaction in regard to material shapes cognisable by the eye '—that monk, Sāriputta, with rapture and joy can forsake[3] these, training himself day and night in states that are skilled.

And again, Sāriputta, a monk should consider thus: ' On the road by which I entered the village . . . did I have there in my mind desire or attachment or . . . sensory reaction in regard to sounds cognisable by the ear . . . smells cognisable by the nose . . . tastes cognisable by the tongue . . . touches cognisable by the body . . . mental states cognisable by the mind ?'

---

[1] *Cf. Vin.* ii. 304, and *M.* iii. 104.

[2] This is the abiding of Buddhas, individual Buddhas, Tathāgatas and great disciples, *MA.* v. 106.

[3] *vihātabbaṁ*, from *vijahati*; but *G.S.* iii. 220 (*A.* iii. 307) translates it in parallel passage as though derived from *viharati*.

[**295**] If, Sāriputta, a monk while considering knows thus: ' On the road by which I entered the village . . . I had there in my mind desire . . . or sensory reaction in regard to sounds cognisable by the ear . . . mental states cognisable by the mind '—that monk, Sāriputta, should make an effort to get rid of these evil unskilled states themselves.

But if, Sāriputta, a monk . . . that monk, Sāriputta, with rapture and joy can forsake these, training himself night and day in states that are skilled.

And again, Sāriputta, a monk should consider thus: ' Are the five strands of sense-pleasures got rid of by me ? . . . Are the five hindrances got rid of by me ?' If, Sāriputta, a monk while considering knows thus: ' The five strands of sense-pleasures . . . the five hindrances have not been got rid of by me,' he should make an effort to get rid of them. But if while considering he knows that they have been got rid of, then, Sāriputta, that monk with rapture and joy can forsake them, training himself day and night in states that are skilled.

And again, Sāriputta, a monk should consider thus: ' Do I fully understand the five groups of grasping ?' If while considering he knows that he does not fully understand them, that monk, Sāriputta, should make an effort to understand them fully. But if, Sāriputta, a monk [**296**] while considering knows that he does understand them fully, then, Sāriputta, that monk with rapture and joy can forsake them, training himself day and night in states that are skilled.

And again, Sāriputta, a monk should consider thus: ' Are the four applications of mindfulness developed by me ? . . . Are the four right efforts . . . the four bases of psychic power . . . the five controlling faculties . . . the five powers . . . the seven links in awakening . . . is the ariyan eightfold Way developed by me ?' If, Sāriputta, while a monk is considering he knows in regard to each that it is not developed by him, he should make an effort to develop it. But if, Sāriputta, a monk while considering knows that each is developed by him . . . [**297**] then, Sāriputta, that monk with rapture and joy can forsake them, training himself day and night in states that are skilled.

(*The same with* calm *and* insight.)

And again, Sāriputta, a monk should consider thus: ' Are knowledge and freedom realised by me ?' But if, Sāriputta, a monk while considering knows: ' Knowledge and freedom are not realised by me,' that monk, Sāriputta, should make an effort to realise knowledge and freedom. But if, Sāriputta, that monk while considering knows: ' Knowledge and freedom are realised by me '— that monk, Sāriputta, with rapture and joy can forsake them, training himself day and night in states that are skilled.

Sāriputta, all those recluses and brahmans in the distant past who completely purified themselves for alms-gathering did so only after having reflected over and over again in these ways. And, Sāriputta, all those recluses and brahmans in the distant future who will completely purify themselves for alms-gathering will do so only after having reflected over and over again in these ways. And, Sāriputta, all those recluses and brahmans who at present completely purify themselves for alms-gathering do so only after having reflected over and over again in these ways. Wherefore, Sāriputta, this is how you must train yourself: ' I will completely purify myself for alms-gathering after having reflected over and over again.' This is how you, Sāriputta, must train yourself."

Thus spoke the Lord. Delighted, the venerable Sāriputta rejoiced in what the Lord had said.

Discourse on Complete Purity for Alms-gathering:
The Ninth

152. DISCOURSE ON THE DEVELOPMENT OF THE SENSE-ORGANS[1]

(Indriyabhāvanāsutta)

[**298**] THUS have I heard: At one time the Lord was staying near Kajaṅgalā in the Mukhelu Grove.[2] Then the brahman youth Uttara, a pupil of Pārāsariya,[3] approached the Lord; having approached

---

[1] One of the chief difficulties in this Discourse in the translation of the terms *indriya* and *bhāvanā*. The term *indriya* might be rendered " controlling faculties," as it appears to mean at *Vin.* i. 294 and which is apparently the only other canonical passage where the compound *indriyabhāvanā* occurs as such, although there is also a *M.* context (iii. 81) where we find *pañcannaṁ indriyānaṁ bhāvanānuyogaṁ*, the practice of the development (or, mind-development) of the five controlling faculties: of faith, energy, mindfulness, concentration and wisdom. Since, in these two passages, the *indriyas* are associated at least with some (*Vin.* i. 294), if not all (*M.* iii. 81 *f.*) of the seven groups of the *bodhipakkhiyadhammā* (things helpful to enlightenment), it may be assumed that in such contexts *indriya* means controlling faculty. But on the other hand, *indriya* can also mean sense-organ, and I believe that, from the internal evidence of this Discourse, it has this meaning here. One may usefully *cf. S.* v. 73 *f.* which is partially concerned with *indriyasaṁvara*, control of the sense-organs of eye, etc., for this is a passage that states that whether the material shapes that a monk sees are liked or disliked, he remains unmoved (or, stands firm, *ṭhita*) in body and mind, his mind inwardly well established, *susaṇṭhita*, and freed. And this is presumably tantamount to the " equanimity remains," *upekhā saṇṭhāti*, of our *M.* Sta.

Bhāvanā, the second part of the compound, means developing or producing, with a strong secondary implication that such developing is done by the mind, and is therefore a mind-development such as gives the ariyan control over the sense-data he perceives so that, if he wish, he may abide not perceiving their impurity, etc., but with equanimity in regard to their impingement on him. He therefore trains his sense-organs not to respond in wrong ways to sensory stimuli, and develops such control over them that he will remain unaffected by them and indifferent as to whether he likes them, dislikes them or neither dislikes nor likes. That the impingement of sense-data is inevitable while a man is still alive is nowhere denied in the Pali canon; but response to them, even noticing them may be stopped in deep meditation where all is stilled.

[2] The Grove was full of trees of this name. Variant readings are: Mukheluvana, Muñcelu-, Suveḷu-, and Veḷuvana.

[3] On the possible identity with Pārāpariya (verses at *Thag.* 72ff.) see *Pss. Breth.* p. 295, note; and *DPPN.*, *s.v.* Indriyabhāvanā Sutta and Pārāpariya Thera.

him, he exchanged greetings with the Lord, and when he had conversed in a friendly and courteous way he sat down at a respectful distance. The Lord spoke thus to the brahman youth Uttara, a pupil of Pārāsariya, as he was sitting down at a respectful distance: "Uttara, does Pārāsariya the brahman teach the development of the sense-organs to his disciples?"

"Good Gotama, the brahman Pārāsariya teaches the development of the sense-organs to his disciples."

"But in what way, Uttara, does Pārāsariya the brahman teach the development of the sense-organs to his disciples?"

"As to this, good Gotama, one should not see material shapes with the eye, one should not hear sounds with the ear. It is thus, good Gotama, that the brahman Pārāsariya teaches the development of the sense-organs to his disciples."

"This being so, Uttara, then according to what Pārāsariya the brahman says a blind man must have his sense-organ developed, a deaf man must have his sense-organ developed. For a blind man, Uttara, does not see material shape with his eye, nor does a deaf man hear a sound with his ear."

When this had been said, the brahman youth Uttara, a pupil of Pārāsariya, sat silent, ashamed, his shoulders drooped, his face downcast, brooding, speechless. Then the Lord, knowing that Uttara, a pupil of Pārāsariya, was sitting silent, ashamed . . . brooding, speechless, addressed the venerable Ānanda, saying: "Ānanda, the brahman Pārāsariya teaches his disciples the development of the sense-organs in one way;[1] but in the discipline for an ariyan the incomparable development of the sense-organs is otherwise."[1]

"It is the right time for this, Lord, it is the right time for this, Well-farer, that the Lord [**299**] should teach the incomparable development of the sense-organs (as it is) in the discipline for an ariyan. When the monks have heard the Lord, they will remember."

"Well than, Ānanda, listen, attend carefully and I will speak."

"Yes, revered sir," the venerable Ānanda answered the Lord in assent. The Lord spoke thus:

"And what, Ānanda, is the incomparable development of the sense-organs in the discipline for an ariyan? As to this, Ānanda, when a monk has seen a material shape with the eye there arises what is liked, there arises what is disliked, there arises what is both

---

[1] *aññathā . . . aññathā.*

liked and disliked.[1] He comprehends thus: 'This that is liked is arising in me, this that is disliked is arising, this that is both liked and disliked is arising, and this that arises is because it is constructed, is gross. (But) this is the real, this the excellent, that is to say equanimity.' So whether what is arising in him is liked, disliked or both liked and disliked, it is (all the same) stopped in him, and equanimity remains.[2] Ānanda, it is as if a man with vision, having opened his eyes should close them, or having closed them should open them. Even so, Ānanda, such is the speed, such the swiftness, such the ease with which anything that has arisen, whether it is liked, disliked or both liked and disliked, is (all the same) stopped in him, and equanimity remains. In the discipline for an ariyan, Ānanda, this is called the incomparable development of the sense-organs in regard to material shapes cognisable by the eye.

And again, Ānanda, when a monk has heard a sound with the ear there arises what is liked, there arises what is disliked, there arises what is both liked and disliked. He comprehends thus: ... and equanimity remains. Ānanda, as a strong man can snap his fingers with ease, even so, Ānanda, such is the speed, such the swiftness, such the ease with which anything that has arisen, whether it is liked, disliked or both liked and disliked, is (all the same) stopped in him, and equanimity remains. In the discipline for an ariyan, Ānanda, this is called the incomparable development of the sense-organs in regard to sounds cognisable by the ear.

And again, Ānanda, when a monk has smelt a smell with the nose there arises what is liked ... and equanimity remains. As, [300] Ānanda, the rain-drops slide off a lotus-leaf that is slightly on the slant and do not remain, even so, Ānanda, such is the speed ... with which anything that has arisen ... is stopped in him, and equanimity remains. In the discipline for an ariyan, Ānanda, this is called the incomparable development of the sense-organs in regard to smells cognisable by the nose.

And again, Ānanda, when a monk has tasted a flavour with the tongue there arises what is liked ... and equanimity remains. As, Ānanda, when a fleck of mucus has collected on the tip of his tongue a strong man can easily spit it out, even so, Ānanda, such is the speed ... with which anything that has arisen ... is stopped in him, and equanimity remains. In the discipline for an ariyan, Ānanda, this

---

[1] *manāpāmanāpaṁ.* [2] *upekhā saṇṭhāti.*

is called the incomparable development of the sense-organs in regard to flavours cognisable by the tongue.

And again, Ānanda, when a monk has felt a touch with the body there arises what is liked . . . and equanimity remains. As, Ānanda, a strong man can stretch out his bent arm or can bend back his outstretched arm, even so, Ānanda, such is the speed . . . with which anything that has arisen . . . is stopped in him, and equanimity remains. In the discipline for an ariyan, Ānanda, this is called the incomparable development of the sense-organs in regard to touches cognisable by the body.

And again, Ānanda, when a monk has cognised a mental state with the mind there arises what is liked . . . and equanimity remains. It is, Ānanda, as if a man might let two or three drops of water fall into a red-hot iron vessel daily. Slow, Ānanda, would be the falling of the drops of water, yet quickly would they be destroyed and consumed. Even so, Ānanda, such is the speed . . . with which anything that arises . . . is stopped in him, and equanimity remains. In the discipline for an ariyan, Ānanda, this is called the incomparable development of the sense-organs in regard to mental states cognisable by the mind.

Even so, Ānanda, is the incomparable development of the sense-organs in the discipline for an ariyan.

And what, Ānanda, is a learner's course ? As to this, Ānanda, when a monk has seen a material shape with the eye there arises what is liked, there arises what is disliked, there arises what is both liked and disliked. Because there has arisen what is liked, because there has arisen what is disliked, because there has arisen what is both liked and disliked, he is troubled about it, ashamed of it, loathes it. [301] When he has heard a sound with the ear, smelt a smell with the nose, tasted a flavour with the tongue, felt a touch with the body, cognised a mental state with the mind there arises what is liked, there arises what is disliked, there arises what is both liked and disliked. Because there has arisen what is liked, because there has arisen what is disliked, because there has arisen what is both liked and disliked, he is troubled about it, ashamed of it, loathes it. Just so, Ānanda, is a learner's course.

And what, Ānanda, is the ariyan whose sense-organs are developed ? As to this, Ānanda, when a monk has seen a material shape with the eye . . . heard a sound with the ear . . . smelt a smell with the nose . . . tasted a flavour with the tongue . . . felt a touch with the body . . . cognised a mental state with the mind there arises what is liked, there arises what is disliked, there arises what is both liked and disliked. If he desire thus: ' May I abide not perceiving impurity in impurity,'[1] he abides there not perceiving impurity. If he desire: ' May I abide perceiving impurity in purity,' he abides there perceiving impurity. If he desire: ' May I abide not perceiving impurity in impurity and in purity,' he abides there not perceiving impurity. If he desire: ' May I abide perceiving impurity in purity and impurity,' he abides there perceiving impurity. If he desire: ' May I, having avoided both impurity and purity, [**302**] abide in equanimity, mindful and clearly conscious,' he abides there in equanimity, mindful and clearly conscious. Even so, Ānanda, is the ariyan whose sense-organs are developed.

Thus, Ānanda, there has been taught by me the incomparable development of the sense-organs (as it is) in the discipline for an ariyan, there has been taught a learner's course, there has been taught the ariyan whose sense-organs are developed. Whatever, Ānanda, is to be done out of compassion by a teacher seeking the welfare of his disciples and compassionate for them, that has been done by me for you. These, Ānanda, are the roots of trees, these are empty places. Meditate, Ānanda, do not be slothful, do not be remorseful later. This is our instruction for you."

Thus spoke the Lord. Delighted, the venerable Ānanda rejoiced in what the Lord had said.

Discourse on the Development of the Sense-organs:
The Tenth

Division of the Sixfold (Sense-)field:
The Fifth

TOLD ARE THE FINAL FIFTY

---

[1] At *Pts.* ii. 212 this and the following are called *ariyā iddhi*. The explanations that are given there are found also at *MA.* v. 108.

INDEXES

I.—TOPICS

Abhidhamma, xii, xiv, 25 n.
Abiding (*vihāra*), 154, 156 *f*., 163, 343; in comfort, 53, 180, 202; in ease, 55, 61, 137, 198; in emptiness, 147, 343; in equanimity, 350; in friendliness . . . equanimity, 191; of great men, 343
Action: right, 117, 298; wrong, 117
Activities (*saṅkhārā*), 18; of body, 130; of body, speech, thought, 114 n.; of body, thought, 124 *f*.; of speech, 28, 116
adhimuccati, xx *f*.
Adviser, Treasure of the, 220
Affliction (*upaddava*), for teachers, etc., 159 *ff*.
Ākāsa, see Ether *and* Space
All-knowing, all-seeing, 6
Almsfood, 24 *f*., 103, 199 *ff*., 343; content with, 61, 86 *f*. See also Requisites
Alms-gathering, 345
Aloofness (*viveka*), 21 *ff*., 153 *ff*., 157, 159 *f*., 327; happiness of, 281, 283
Analysis (*vibhaṅga*), x, 233, 235 *f*., 238, 245 *ff*., 264, 271, 277 *f*., 286, 293
Anguish (*dukkha*), xi *f*., 3 *ff*., 10 *ff*., 88, 161, 163, 211 *ff*., 230, 255 *f*., 261, 272, 324 *f*., 329 *f*.; destruction of, xxxi, 88, 157, 292; end of, 318, 334 *f*.; of animal birth, 214; of body and mind, 337; of Niraya, 211 *ff*., origin of, 107; root of, 44; threefold, 209 *ff*.; truths of, 295 *ff*., 301, 314 n.; uprising, stopping of, 320; *with* annoyance, trouble, fret, 278 *ff*., 283 *f*.
Animal(s), 302 *f*.; -birth xxiv, 72, 213 *f*., 224; grass-, dung-eaters, etc., 213 *f*.
Another mode (*apara pariyāya*), 261 *f*.
Approval, disapproval (*apasādana ussādanā*), 278 *ff*., 283

Arahant, xiv, xvii, xxii, xxviii *f*., 20 n., 143 n., 173 n., 305 n.; -ship, xxii *f*., xxx, 24 n., 47 n., 50 n., 51 n., 170 n., 291 n., 318 n., 336 n. See also Perfected one; Perfection
Archery, 52
Ariyan: calm, 292; concentration, 113 *f*.; concentration, freedom, moral habit, wisdom, xxxi, 81; control, 87; deliverance, 51; *dhamma*, 230; disciple, 46 *ff*., 51, 180 *f*., 324 *ff*.; discipline, death in, 43; eightfold Way, 114 *ff*., 123, 338 *f*., 344; mindfulness, 87; moral habit, 87; relinquishment, 292; states (*dhammā*), 158; thought (*citta*), 115 *ff*.; thoughts (*vitakkā*), 157; truth, xxxi, 292; truths, xxvi, 286 n., 295 *ff*.; view, 37; Way, 115, 279; wisdom, 44, 292, 326
Ariyan(s), 264, 266 *f*., 269 *f*., 294, 301, 347 *ff*.; scoffers at, 223 *f*.
Army, fourfold, 218 *f*., 221
Ascetic practices (*dhutaṅga*), 91
Aspiration: (*saṅkappa*), 298, 327 *f*., 338; (*saṅkhāra*), 139 *ff*. See Purpose
Assembly hall, 129, 163 *f*., 235
Attachment: (*āsatti*), 19; (*rāga*), 42 *f*., 63 *f*., 66, 158, 241 *ff*., 326, 337; control of, 68; *with* aversion, confusion, 62, 123, 182, 292, 340 *ff*., 343 *f*.; *with* repugnance, ignorance, 334 *f*.
Attainment (*samāpatti*), 254
Attention, lack of proper (*amanasikāra*), 203 *ff*., 207
Auspicious, the, 233 *ff*., 235 *ff*., 238 *ff*., 245 *ff*.
Awakened One(s), 58 *ff*., 82 *ff*., 109, 162, 230, 286, 293, 303; *with* Dhamma, etc., 301 *f*.
Awakening . (*sambodha*), 157, 159, 202; happiness of, 153; seven

Index of Topics

links in (*bojjhaṅga*), 25, 31, 123 *f.*, 127 *ff.*, 327, 338, 344; thirty-seven things helpful to (*bodhipakkhiyadhammā*), xii, xxix, 25 *n.*, 26 *n.*

Becoming (*bhava*), 192, 280, 291, 298, 338; again-, xxii, 161, 168, 208, 298, 337; canker of, 88, 151; fetter(s) of, 55, 279 *f.*; de-, 291
Beings (*satta*), 13, 223
Bhaddekaratta, xxvi *f.*, 233 *n.*, 245 *n.*
Bile, phlegm, pus, *etc.*, 131, 288
Birth (*jāti*): ended, xviii, xxii; last, 168, 208; *with* ageing and dying, xxxi, 161, 272, 277, 293, 296 (defined); *with* dying, 230; destroyed is birth, *etc.*, 13, 37 *f.*, 69, 81, 88, 151, 174, 291, 330, 334
Blame: without (*anupavajja*), 316, 319; to be blamed (*sa-upavajja*), 318 *f.*; -less(ness) (*anavajja*), 87, 180; (*anupavajjatā*), 318
Bodhisatta, xviii, xxii *f.*, xxv, 164 *ff.*, 202; 's mother, 165 *ff.*
Body, xviii, 53, 124 *f.*, 151, 180, 182, 321, 337; activity (*saṅkhāra*) of, 114 *n.*, 124 *f.*, 130; consciousness-informed, xiv, 68, 85, 89; a feeling limited by, 291 *f.*; mindfulness of, 129 *ff.*; own (*sakkāya*), xi, 15 *n.*, 19, 51, 67, 334; unchastity (*dutthulla*) of, 196
Boundless (*appamāna*), 191 *ff.*
Bourn (*gati*), 210 *f.*, 217, 294, 318, 322; bad, *see* Niraya; good, *see* Heaven
Bowl: six words for, 282; and robe, 294
Brahma; -become, 240; -*vihāra*, xx, 191; -world, xxviii, 62, 138, 197 *n.*
Brahma-farer(s), 36 *f.*, 89, 172, 201, 239 *f.*, 272; affliction for, 159 *ff.*
Brahma-faring, 61, 85, 174, 180, 184 *ff.*, 331; brought to a close *see* Birth destroyed; fundamental to, 238, 246 *f.*
Brahman(s) (and) householders, 221, 339 *ff. See* Nobles; Recluses and brahmans
Breathing in, out, 124 *ff.*, 130
Brief exhortations, statements, utterances, xv *ff.*, xxv *f.*, xxviii, 95, 101 *ff.*, 239 *f.*, 249, 272, 276, 293 *f.*, 319 *f.*.. 322

Buddha(s), xxv *ff.*, 174 *n.*, 263 *n.*
Bull to be tamed, 270
Burden, shed, 55
Burn (*jhāyati*), 196

Calculation (*gananā*), 52
Calm (*upasama*), 321; ariyan, 292; resolve for, 287, 292; (*samatha*) and insight, xxix, 338, 344. *See also* Tranquillity
Cankers (*āsavā*), xviii, xxviii, 88, 114 *ff.*, 154; destroyed, 55, 82 *ff.*, 93, 123, 183, 267 *n.*, 328 *n.*, 330 *n.*; destruction of, 62, 88, 138, 143, 327, 329; freed from, 70, 82 *ff.*, 88, 151, 330, 336; three, 88, 151; -less, 115 *ff.*, 327
Cause, deniers of, 121
Cemetery, 131 *f.*
Cessation: *see* Stopping
Charioteer of men, 264, 270 *f.*
Clinging (*upadhi*), 44 *f.*, 292
Cloth(s): for sitting on, 329; pair of (*dussayuga*), 300 *f.*
Cohesion, element of (*āpodhātu*), 83 *f.*, 105, 131, 287 *f.*, 311
Cold, heat, hunger, *etc.*, 137
Comfort, abiding in, 53, 180, 202
Companion (*dutiya*), 201
Compassion, 25, 51, 124, 161, 191, 198, 269, 309, 350
Comport oneself, 87
Conceit and boasting (*maññussava*), 286, 293
Concentration (*samādhi*), xvi *f.*, xxix, 81, 157, 159, 163 *n.*, 203 *ff.*, 257 *ff.*, 314 *n.*; right, 119, 187 *ff.*, 279, 298 *f.*, 338; threefold, xxii, 207, 208 *n.*; wrong, 185 *ff. See also* Awakening, 7 links in; Meditation
Conditioned Genesis (*paṭiccasamuppāda*), xv, 105, 107
Consciousness (*viññāṇa*), 50, 241 *ff.*, 272 *ff.*, 289; -device, 16; element of, 83 *f.*, 105, 287, 311; evolving (*saṁvattanika*), 47; infinite, 80, 93, 142, 149 *f.*, 268, 271, 290, 312, 317; of what is external, 272 *f.*; six classes, xxviii, 85, 263 *f.*, 310 *f.*, 312, 317, 324 *f.*, 330, 331 *f.*, 334 *f.*, 336 *ff. See also* Material shape (as *khandha*)
Consternation (*chambhitattā*), 203 *ff.*, 207

Construct and think out, to (*abhisaṅkharoti abhisañcetayati*), 291. *See* Effected . . .
Constructed (*saṅkhata*), 18 *f*., 20 *ff*., 290, 348; element, 106
Construction(s) (*saṅkhāra*), 17 *f*., 20 *ff*., 108
Contention (*vivāda*), 25 *ff*.
Cool, to become (*sītibhavati*), 291 *f*.
Course: Middle, xxvi, 278 *f*., 283; learner's, 119, 349; undefiled, 284; wrong, right, 278, 279 *n*., 280, 282 *ff*.
Covering up (as) with grass, 33, 36
Covetous, malevolent, harmful, 98 *f*.
Covetousness, 46 *f*., 53 *f*., 87, 98 *f*., 125 *f*., 156, 292
Cow, 326; swerving, 294
Craving (*taṇhā*), 41, 43 *f*., 69, 234 *n*., 332 *ff*., 337 *f*.; six classes, 331 *f*.; threefold, 298

Dead-ends (*antā*), 278 *f*.
Death (*maraṇa*), liable to, 226; (*maccu*), 233 *ff*., 246
Deathless, -ness (*amata*), xiii, 51, 240
Decision: of the majority (*yebhuyyasikā*), 33; for specific depravity (*tassapāpiyyasikā*), 35
Deeds (*kamma*), 3 *ff*., 8 *ff*., 14, 62, 68, 209 *f*., 212 *ff*., 223, 249, 254 *ff*., 314; evil, 224 *ff*., 229, 257 *f*., 260 *ff*.; great analysis of, 256, 260 *f*.; lovely, 260 *f*.; operative (*bhabba*), *etc*., 262
Defiled (*saraṇa*), 282 *ff*.
Defilements (*kilesa, upakkilesa*), xxii, 161, 327; of the mind, 205 *ff*.
Delight (*nandī*), 320, 326, 337
Deliverance (*vimokkha*), 24, 51; -s, 266 *f*., 270 *n*.
Denotation and connotation, 25 *ff*.
Departed, realm of the, 224
Dependence, to live in (*upanissāya viharati*), 61, 63
Desire (*chanda*), 66, 158, 241 *ff*., 343 *f*.; control of, 68; lack of (*atammayatā*), xv, 92 *f*., 269
Detachment (*virāga*), 11, 69, 156 *f*., 159, 327
Deva(s), xxviii, 165 *f*., 168 *f*., 180, 327 *f*., 245 *ff*., 313 *f*., 329 *f*.; -greatness, 74; -happiness, 222; -hearing, 62, 138; -messengers,

xxv, 224 *ff*.; -*putta*, xxviii, 166 *n*., 168, 245 *n*., 313 *n*.; -vision, xxi *f*., 62, 138, 202 *n*., 220, 223, 257; of Light, 192 *f*., 195 *f*.; of the Thirty-Three, 246; *various classes*, 139 *f*., 142
Devatās, 192 *f*., 195 *ff*., 224 *ff*.
Development (*bhāvanā*), 123 *f*.; of mind (*citta-*), 194 *f*.; of sense-organs (*indriya-*), 347 *ff*.
Dhamma, xiii *ff*., xxiv *ff*., 32 *f*., 67, 82 *ff*., 185, 275, 285 *f*., 293 *f*., 301, 314, 322; ariyan, 230; as support, 60; born of, 81; disquisition on, xvii, 94, 110, 120 *f*., 197; -farer, 90 *ff*.; -faring, 215; -king, 313; learners of, 313; -lord, 240; -master, 198; speaker on, 91; talk on, 201. 235 *f*., 323; to hear, 29, 85, 313, 319; to teach, 24 *f*., 29, 38, 85, 89. 161, 172, 175 *f*., 230, 249, 269 *f*., 278 *ff*., 283, 286, 327, 330; trained, untrained in, 234; vision of, 330; wheel of, xiv, 81, 295 *f*., 299; and discipline, 26 *f*., 30, 52, 86, 96 *f*., 173; Further- (*abhidhamma*), 25. *See also* Refuge
Dialect of the countryside (*janapadanirutti*), 278, 282, 284
Diligent, ardent, self-resolute, xxiii, 130 *ff*., 173, 175 *f*., 201 *ff*., 319
Disciple (*sāvaka*), 159, 161, 269 *f*., 350. *See under* Ariyan
Discipline, the (*vinaya*), 294, 347 *ff*.; to (*vineti*), 53 *f*.
Discourses, 159
Discriminates (*vijānāti*), 289
Dislike and liking (*aratirati*), 137
Dispute (*vivāda*), 31 *ff*.; six sources of, 32
Distress (*duṭṭhulla*), 204 *f*., 207
Do one's time (*kālaṃ karoti*), 212 *f*., 227 *ff*.
Doubt, 202 *ff*., 207. *See also* Hindrances
Dying, time of (*maraṇakāla*), 261 *f*.

Earth (*paṭhavī*), 148 *f*., 192, 195, 218 *f*. *See also* Elements; Extension
Effected and thought out (*abhisaṅkhata abhisañcetayita*), 151. *See* Construct . . .
Efficacies (*iddhi*), four, 217, 221 *f*.

Index of Topics

Effort (*upakkama*), 7 *ff.*, 12 *ff.*; (*padhāna*), four right, 25, 31, 123, 338, 344
Elation (*ubbilla*), 204 *f.*, 207
Elementals, four great (*mahābhūtā*), 67, 83 *n.*
Elements (*dhātu*), xiv *f.*; four, 131; six, 83 *f.*, 105, 286 *f.*, 293, 311; various groups of, 105 *f.*
Elephant: to be tamed, 270; Treasure of, 219
Emptiness (*suññatā*), xviii, xxix, 147 *ff.*, 154 *ff.*, 343
Empty (*suñña*), 48, 147 *ff.*; place(s), 51, 124, 130, 350
Endeavour: right, 116 *ff.*, 187 *ff.*, 298, 314 *n.*, 338; wrong, 185 *ff.*
Energy, 57, 157, 159; too much, too little, 204 *ff.* See also Awakening, 7 links in
Equanimity, xiii, xxx, 11 *ff.*, 28, 50, 124, 191, 208, 265, 268, 274 *f.*, 290, 346 *n.*, 348 *ff.*; connected with multiformity, *etc.*, 268 *f.*; element of, 106; six, 265, 267 *f.*, 287. See also Awakening, seven links in; Meditation(s), the four
Escape (*nissaraṇa*), 17 *ff.*, 64, 78 *ff.* See also Satisfaction, *etc.*
'Eternal is self and the world,' *etc.*, 19 *f.*
Ether (*ākāsa*), 83 *n.*; plane of, 79, 93, 142, 148 *ff.*, 268, 270, 290, 312. See also Space
Even-faring, 215, 340 *f.*
Exalt oneself, to, 29, 89 *ff.*
Exhort, to, 323, 327 *f.*
Exhortation(s) (*ovāda*), xxviii, 57, 313, 318, 319, 322, 327 *f.*
Expectation (*āsā*), 184 *ff.*
Exposition (*uddesa*), 233, 235 *f.*, 238 *ff.*, 245 *ff.*, 264, 271 *f.*, 276, 278, 286
Extension, element of (*paṭhavīdhātu*), 83 *f.*, 105, 131, 287 *f.*, 311
Eye, ear, *etc.*, 84 *f.*, 87, 102, 107, 158, 180, 241 *ff.*, 264 *ff.*, 272 *f.*, 281, 317, 324, 329 *f.*, 331 *ff.*, 336 *ff.*, 340 *ff.*, 343 *f.*, 347 *ff.*; element of, 105
Eye of affection, 200 *f.*

Faculties (*indriya*), five, 25, 31, 123, 338, 344, 346 *n.*
Fair, the (*subha*), 270

Faith (*saddhā*), 56 *f.*, 73, 85, 285; endowed with, 139 *ff.*; lacking in, *etc.*, 71
Family: high, great, *etc.*, 89 *f.*, 222, 249, 252; low, 215, 249, 252; families, 318
Fear(s), 104 *f.*; and dread, 137
Feeling(s) (*vedanā*), 3 *ff.*, 53, 125 *f.*, 169, 180, 182, 212 *f.*, 227 *ff.*, 311, 332 *ff.*; limited by body, *etc.*, 291 *f.*; six classes, 331 *f.*; three, 22 *f.*, 256, 289 *ff.*, 325 *f.*, 334, 337. See also Material Shape (as *khandha*)
Fetters, 327; five, 123, 294; of becoming, 55, 279 *f.*; of satisfaction, 273; three, 123
Fivefold pinion, 212, 227
Flood (*ogha*), crossing the, 50 *f.*
Followed, to be and not to be, 94 *ff.*
Food, xxix *f.*
Fool and the wise, the, 104 *f.*, 209 *ff.*
' For him who clings . . . ,' 317
Forest: perception of, 147; -dweller, *etc.*, 91
Foul, the (*asubha*), 124
Freed (*vimutta*), 55, 69 *f.*, 82 *ff.*, 88, 155 *f.*, 330, 334
Freedom (*vimutti*), xxix, xxxi, 69, 81, 88, 151, 157, 159, 163, 292, 328, 330, 335, 338 *f.*, 344 *f.*; right, wrong, 119 *f.*; of mind, xvii, xx, xxii, 62, 138, 143, 155, 191 *ff.* (boundless, widespread), 208, 327; through knowledge (*vijjā*), 124, 129; through wisdom, xvii, 62, 138, 142, 327
Friendliness (*mettā*), 124, 191, 201; meditation on, 284 *n.*; (*mittavatā*), 161
Friendly terms, 200 *f.*
Fruit (*phala*): of Brahma-faring, 184 *ff.*; of kamma, 305
Fruition (*vipāka*), 258 *f.*, 267. See Ripening
Future, 3 *ff.*, 8 *f.*, 15, 19, 21 *ff.*, 233 *ff.*, 238 *ff.*, 246 *ff.*

Get rid of (*pajahatha*), 268 *f.*
Gift, giving, xxviii, xxx, 71 *ff.*, 302 *ff.*
Giver (*dātā*), a, 251; (*dāyaka*), 304 *f.*
Goal (*attha*), 55, 96, 238, 240, 246 *f.*, 278, 281 *ff.*, 296 (highest); (*niṭṭhā*), 55

Index of Topics

Going beyond (*pāramī*), 81
Going forth, the (*pabbajjā*), 173
Gradual training, *etc.*, 52
Grasp, to, 23, 26 *f.*, 50, 291, 310 *ff.*, 319
Grasping (*upādāna*), xiii, xxviii *ff.*, 20 *f.*, 23, 50, 84 *f.*, 230; disturbed by, 272, 275; five groups of, xiv, 66, 82 *f.*, 158, 297, 337 *f.*, 344; without, 24, 50 *f.*, 70, 82 *ff.*
Greed, aversion, confusion, 90 *ff.*
Grief, suffering, misery, despair (*defined*), 297
Group (*gaṇa*), 153

Habitations, former, 13, 62, 88 *n.*, 138
Habitual tendencies (*saṅkhāra*), *see under* Material Shape (as *khandha*)
' Had it not been . . .', 49 *f.*
Hair of the head, *etc.*, 131, 287
Happiness (*sukha*), 68, 222, 261 *f.*, 269 *f.*, 324, 329; element of, 106; four kinds, 153 *f.*; of body and mind, 337; of heaven, 217 *ff.*; of sense-pleasures, 278 *f.*, 282 *f.*; spiritual (*nirāmisa*), 22 *f.*; threefold, 216 *f.*; to judge, 278, 281
Harmful by nature (*viheṭhakajātika*), 250
Heard much, 61, 91
Heat, condition of, 174 *n.*; with cold, hunger, *etc.*, 182
Heaven (*sagga*), 217, 222 *f.*, 250 *f.*, 257 *ff.*; happinesses of, 217 *ff.*
Hells, 228 *f.*
Hindrances, five, xix, 13, 54, 64, 87 *f.*, 181, 196 *n.*, 344
Homelessness, to go forth into, 56 *f.*, 85, 174, 180, 285, 313
Horse: to be tamed, 270; Treasure of, 219
Householder(s), 160 *f.*, 182, 313, 339 *ff.*; brahmans and, 221 (*see also* Nobles); Treasure of, 220
Human: beings (*manussā*), differences between, 249 *ff.*; form (*manussabhūta*), 249; status (*manussatta*), xxiv *f.*, 215, 222, 229, 250

' I am ', 158
' I am naught of anyone . . .', 49
' I am the doer ', *etc.*, 68, 85, 89
' I am, will (not) be ', *etc.*, 293
' If this is ', *etc.*, 107

Ignorance (*avijjā*), 44, 107, 178, 292, 334 *f.*, 338; canker of, 88, 151; element of, 106; tendency to, 334 *f.*
Illness, liable to, 225
Impermanence, xxviii, xxx, 68, 125, 126 *n.*, 266 *ff.*, 291 *n.*; perception of, 124
Impermanent, 46, 48, 68 *f.*, 151, 266 *ff.*, 291, 324 *ff.*, 329 *f.*
Imperturbability (*āṇañja*), 39 *f.*, 47 *f.*, 51, 155 *f.*
Individuality (*attabhāva*), 94, 100 *f.*
Indolent, 224 *ff.*
Insight (*vipassanā*), 202 *n.*, 233 *n.*, 234 *n.*, 338, 344
Insignificant (*appamattaka*), 212, 215, 222. *See* Trifle
Intentness (*anuyoga*), 280, 282 *f.*
Investigate, to (*upaparikkhati*), 272
Investigating (*vīmaṁsaka*), 105

Jains, xi, 3 *ff.*
Jealousy (*issā*), 251
Jewel, Treasure of, 219
Joy (*somanassa*), 265; six, 265 *f.*, 268, 287

Kamma, 220, 223 *f.*, 249 *n.*, 314 *n.*; fruit of, 305
Key (*apāpuraṇa*), 174
King, 209 *f.*, 216 *ff.*, 226; wheel-rolling, 109, 217 *ff.*; -dom, 192, 194 *f.*
Knife, to take to oneself, 316 *ff.*, 321
Know and see, to, 68, 82 *ff.*, 105 *ff.*, 151, 176, 240, 258
Knowledge (*ñāṇa*), 20, 69, 292, 330, 334; -and-vision, 6, 208; become, 240; false (*micchā*), 258 *ff.*; right, wrong, 119 *f.*
Knowledge (*vijjā*), 314, 334 *f.*, 338 *f.*; connected with, 134, 344; freedom through, 124, 129; the three, 322
Knowledge, profound (*aññā*), 37 *f.*, 55, 81 *ff.*, 123, 161, 173, 269 *f.*

Lay-devotees, -follower(s), 322; acceptance as, 57, 253, 342; female, 322
Learners (*sekha*), 55; 's course, 119, 349
Learning (*suta*), 139 *ff.*

Legal questions (*adhikaraṇa*), 33 ff.
Life-principle (*jīvita*), 291 f., 321;
a feeling limited by, 291 f.
Life-span (*āyu*), 250 f., 253, 290 n.,
291 n.
Light (*ābhā*), 196; *devas* of, 192 f.,
195 f.
Light-radiation, -manifestation, (*obhāsa*), xxii, 202 ff.
Liked and disliked (*manāpāmanāpa*),
347 ff.
Lion-posture, 53, 181
Liquid element, *see* Cohesion
Livelihood, wrong and right, 118, 298;
mode of, 338
Lodgings, 24 f., 103, 153, 246;
content with, 61; remote, 54, 87,
159 ff., 181, 342
Longing (*abhijappā*), 205 ff.
Lord (*bhagavā*), *passim and* 163
(plural), 286; epithets of, 240, 339;
who knows, sees, etc., 59 ff., 82 ff.,
129; 's own son, 81

Mahaggatā cetovimutti, xx f.
Malign One, the (Māra), 158
Man (*purisa*), 286 f.; bad, xiv, 70 ff.,
89 ff.; good, true, xiv f., 70 ff.,
89 ff., 209, 216; to be tamed, 264,
270 f.
Market-town (*nigama*), 103, 147
Mastery (*vasī*), 81
Material shape (*rūpa*), 47 ff., 154,
206 f., 270; appearance (*dassana*)
of, 202 ff.; being too intent on,
205 ff.; element of, 105; perceptions of, 79, 93, 270; reflex image
of, 206; *with four other khandhā*,
17, 66 ff., 82 f., 158, 234 f., 236,
247, 275 f., 297, 311 ff., 330, 338;
with sound, smell, etc., 39, 41 ff.,
53, 84 ff., 87, 102, 105, 107, 158,
180, 241 f., 264 ff., 273, 281, 287,
310, 319 f., 329 f., 331 ff., 336 f.,
340 ff., 343 f., 347 ff.
Material things (*āmisa*), 39 f., 81,
265 f., 295 n.
Mātikā, xxvi f., 241 n., 263 n., 271 n.
Medicines, *see* Requisites
Meditate, meditate absorbed, etc., 64
Meditation(s) (*jhāna*), xxi f., xxxi,
63, 70 n.; emergence from, xviii;
fivefold, 207 n., 208 n.; plane(s) of,
xv, 18; the four, 13, 54 f., 61, 64,
78 f., 88, 92, 132 ff., 137, 155, 182
(two), 273 f., 281, 299
Memories and aspirations (*sarasaṅkappa*), 130 ff., 178
Men: to arise among, 223; of family,
young, 313, 322
Mental objects, states (*dhammā*),
53 f., 126, 181 f., 275 f. *See also*
Material shape *with* sound, smell,
etc.
Mental ranges (*manopavicārā*), 263,
265, 286 f.
Middle Course, xxvi, 278 f., 283
Mind (*citta*), 126, 130 ff., 182, 201,
340 f.; composed, etc., 182; defilements of, 205 f.; development
(*bhāvanā*) of, 194 f., 346 n.; onepointedness of, 175 f.; satisfied with,
etc., 147 ff., 155 f.; to steady, etc.,
155; with, without attachment,
etc., 62, 138; (*cetas*), 62, 78, 82,
150 f., 337; (*manas*), xvi; developing, 312. *See also* Eye, ear, etc.;
Freedom
Mindfulness (*sati*), 44, 54, 57, 87,
130, 285, 327; and clear consciousness, 54, 87, 164 f., 181; four
applications of, xix, xxx, 25, 31,
123 ff., 182, 299, 338, 344; of
body, 129 ff.; of breathing, 124 ff.;
right, 114 ff., 187 ff., 279, 298 f.,
314 n., 338; three arousings of,
xxvii, 263, 269 f.; wrong, 185 ff.
Moderation in eating, xix, xxx, 53,
56 f., 180, 218
Modes for creatures (*sattapadā*), 263,
265, 268
Monks, *passim*; developing their
minds, 312; elders, 191; elders,
newly ordained, 121, 183, 255,
303; not anywhere, 94, 143; of
Kosambī, 197 f.; Order of, 31 ff.,
122 ff., 147, 300, 303; sixty, 70
Moon: full, 65, 70, 122, 327 f.; and
sun, 62, 137, 165, 168
Moral (*sīlavā*), 53, 180
Moral habit(s) (*sīla*), 37, 81, 139 ff.,
157, 159, 163, 302 ff.; *in formula*,
(*a*), 53, 61, (*b*) 301 f.
Mother, father, 224 ff.; to deprive
of life, 108; to respect, 224
Motion, element of (*vāyodhātu*), 83 f.,
105, 131, 287 f., 311
Multiformity (*nānatta*), 268 f.

Index of Topics

Name-and-shape (*nāmarūpa*), 67
Neither - perception - nor - non - perception, 18 *n.*, 40 *f.*, 49 *ff.*, 80, 93, 142, 150 *f.*, 269, 271, 290, 312
Nibbāna, xii *f.*, xxiii, xxxi, 16, 17 *n.*, 20 *n.*, 23, 24 *n.*, 28 *f.*, 51 *n.*, 55 *f.*, 83 *n.*, 108 *n.*, 157, 159, 182, 278 *f.*, 283, 291; attainers of, 123, 163, 294; final, 50, 174, 303, 318 *n.*, 322; perfect, xii, 41; way to, 55 *f.* See also Parinibbāna
Nobles: *with* brahmans, householders, 139, 222; *with* brahmans, merchants, workers, 104
Non-returner, 93 *n.*, 302 *f.*, 305 *n.*, 328 *n.*, 330 *n.*
Nothing (*na kiñci*), 254
No-thing, plane of, 17, 40*f.*, 48 *f.*, 80, 93, 142, 149 *ff.*, 269, 271, 290, 312
Novice, 172
Nuns, xxviii, 154, 172, 303, 322 *ff.*; Order of, 303

Obhāsa, xxi *f.*, 202 *n.*
Obligations (*pātimokkha*), 31, 53, 60 *f.*, 180
Observance day, 60, 65, 70, 122, 217, 327 *f.*
Offence (*āpatti*), 27, 34 *ff.*, 43, 60; to confess an, 36
Offerings (*dakkhiṇā*), 302 *ff.*; purifications of, 304
Old age, liable to, 225
Once-returners, 123, 302 *f.*, 328 *n.*, 330 *n.*
Onslaught on creatures, *etc.*, 71, 73, 85 *f.*, 95, 117, 166, 209, 216, 249, 257, 298, 301
Order(s): both, 303; of monks, 31 *ff.*, 122 *ff.*, 147, 300, 303; of nuns, 303; offering to, 303 *f.* See also Refuge
Ordination (*upasampadā*), 173, 294
Overlord (*issara*), 10, 14

Paccekabuddha(s), xvi, 111 *ff.*, 302 *f.*
Parinibbāna, xii *f.*, xix, xxviii, 58, 174 *n.* See also Nibbāna, final
Past (*atīta*), 4 *ff.*, 19 *ff.*, 233 *ff.*, 238 *ff.*, 246 *ff.*
Peace (*santi*), 286 *f.*, 293
Perception(s) (*saññā*), 16 *ff.*, 47 *ff.*, 80, 124, 147 *ff.*, 169, 170; and feeling, 93, 271; assumption of, 94, 99; of diversity, 205 *ff.*; of material shapes, sensory reactions, *etc.*, 79, 93, 270; of sense-pleasures, 46 *ff.* See also Material shape (*as khandha*)
Perfected ones, 55, 108 *f.*, 119, 123, 174, 302 *f.*, 339. See also Arahant
Perfection (*arahatta*), 55; fruit of, 302
Peril (*ādīnava*), 267, 337. See also Satisfaction
Permanent *etc.*, 193
Persons (*puggala*), four types, 257
Pith (*sāra*), 122, 162
Plane (*āyatana*), 136 *f.*, 266 *f.*
Pleasure and pain (*sukhadukkha*), 10, 14
Possible and impossible (*ṭhānāṭṭhāna*), 105, 107 *ff.*
Potter, 162, 285
Powers (*bala*), five, 25, 31, 123, 338, 344
Present thing(s) (*paccuppanna dhamma*), 233 *ff.*, 236 *f.*, 242 *f.*, 246 *ff.*
Psychic power (*iddhi*), 163; bases of, 25, 31, 123, 338, 344; forms of, 61, 137
Punishment(s) (*kammakāraṇa*), 209 *f.*, 216, 226, 229; (*daṇḍa*), 211, 224
Pupils (*antevāsika*), 159 *ff.*
Purity (*paṭikkūla*), 350
Purpose (*saṅkappa*), wrong, right, 115 *f.* See Aspiration

Quarters (*disā*), eight, 270 *f.*

Radiation, element of (*tejodhātu*), 83 *f.*, 105, 131, 287 *f.*, 311
Raft, Parable of, xvii, xxix
Real (*santa*), 48 *f.*; and excellent, 21, 348
Recluse, the (Gotama), 24 *f.*, 28 *f.*, 41, 43 *f.*, 254, 339
Recluse(s) and/or brahman(s), 3, 15 *ff.*, 71, 73, 100, 104, 120, 152, 165, 168, 184 *ff.*, 224, 230, 251 *f.*, 257 *ff.*, 295, 299, 340 *f.*, 345
Reflex image (*nimitta*), 206
Refuge (threefold), 57, 253, 301, 342
Relinquishment (*cāga*), 139 *ff.*, 298; resolve for, 287, 292; to cultivate, 286 *f.*, 293
Renunciation (*nekkhamma*), 106, 116, 153 *f.*, 157, 176 *ff.*, 281, 283, 298; six joys, *etc.*, of, 265 *ff.*

Requisites, 61, 90, 118 f., 301 f.
Resolves (adhiṭṭhānā), four, 286 f., 292
Restlessness and worry, 196. See also Hindrances
Revere, reverence, etc., to, 61, 63, 252, 340 f.
Right path (ñāya), 182
Ripening (vipāka), 224 ff. See Fruition
Robe-material, 24 f., 103, 153, 171 f.; content with, 61. See also Requisites
Robes, yellow (kāsāva), 304
Rule (dhamma), 60; according to the, 60, 294

Sage (muni), 233, 235 ff., 238 ff., 286, 293
Saṅkhāra, 318 n. See under Activities, Constructions, Material shape (as khandha: 'habitual tendencies'); as aspiration, purpose, xvii, 139 ff.
Satisfaction (assāda), 272 f., 337; with peril, escape, xiv, 24, 67 f., 334
Satisfying things (pasādaniyā dhammā), ten, 61 f.
Schism, 108
Sects: other, xi, 154, 256, 340 ff.
Security (from the bonds), 55, 230
Seen, heard, sensed, etc., 82, 312
Self (attā), xi f., 10, 12, 15 ff., 19 ff., 48, 67 ff., 84, 86, 98, 108, 200, 234 f., 236, 275 f., 333 f.; -awakening, happiness of, 281, 283; -mortification (attakilamatha), 278 ff., 283; -taming, xix, xxvi, xxxi; -torment, etc., 71, 73; not-, 68 f., 84, 333 f.
Sense(s), x, xiii, xxx f.; -impingement (phassa), 67, 107, 263 f., 286 f., 289, 331 f., 346 n.; -reactions, 93, 270, 343 f.
Sense-fields, xiv f., xviii, xxviii f., 24, 44 f., 84 f., 105 ff., 150 ff., 241 n., 286 f.; six internal, six external, 263 f., 324 ff., 331; sixfold, 336
Sense-organs, xix, xxix f., 241 n., 347 ff.; doors of, 53, 56 f., 180
Sense-pleasures (kāma), 46, 63 f., 95 f., 115, 153 n., 157, 166, 170 f., 176 ff., 196 n., 257, 298; canker of, 88, 151; element of, 106; five

strands, 39, 158, 180, 281 f., 344; happiness of, 278 f., 282 f.; perceptions of, 46 ff.; without attachment to, 302 f.; with fine-materiality, etc., 106. See also Hindrances
Sign (nimitta), 154, 272 f.; -less, 150 f.
Similes, xix, 86, 97, 178, 189, 211, 217, 326. See Index II
Six things to be remembered, 36
Skill, unskill, 27 ff., 120, 252
Skilled, unskilled states of mind, things, 4 ff., 12 f., 95 ff., 119 f., 161, 298 f., 343 f.
Sloth and torpor, 196, 203 ff., 207. See also Hindrances
Solitude (ekatta), 147 ff.
Sorrow (domanassa), 265; six, 266 ff., 287
Space, element of (ākāsadhātu), 83 f., 105, 287, 289, 311
Speak slowly, to, 278, 282, 284
Spears, to stab with, 211 f.
Speech: activity of, 28, 116; right, wrong, 116 f., 298; lying, 71, 73, 86, 96 f., 116, 257; secret (raho vāda), 278, 281 ff.; to break into, 201; vexatious, 278, 281, 283 f.; way(s) of, 37, 117
Stability (ṭhita), 286, 293
Statement, four modes of (vohāra), 82
Stone: ornamental, 246; small, 212, 222
Stopping (nirodha), 93, 163 n., 271, 317; liable to, 330
Stream-attainers, 123, 302, 328, 330 n.; -attainment, 295, 302 f.
Striving (padhāna), 7 ff.
Suffuse and pervade, to, xx, 140 f., 191 f., 194 ff.
Suicide, xxviii. See Knife
Super-knowledge (abhiññā), xii, 25, 31, 62, 136, 138, 143, 156 f., 159, 174, 278 f., 283, 327, 338
Support (paṭisaraṇa), 59 f.
Supposition (maññita), 293
Synonym, 44, 326

Talk, inferior, 157
Tamed (danta), 183; man to be (purisadamma), 53, 264, 270 f.; taming (dama), 321
Tastes (rasa), 213 f. See also Eye, ear

Index of Topics

Tathāgata, xiii, xix, xxiv *f.*, xxvii, 14, 16 *ff.*, 38, 44, 52 *ff.*, 56, 81, 85, 108, 154, 162 *f.*, 168, 180 *ff.*, 230, 240, 256, 260, 269 *ff.*, 278 *f.*, 283, 294, 295, 302 *f.*; arises in the world, *etc.*, 13, 160, 179
Teacher (*ācariya*), affliction for, 159 *f.*; (*satthā*), 51, 159 *ff.*, 169, 184, 200, 230, 239 *f.*, 255, 264, 269 *f.*, 272, 285 *f.*, 304, 312, 316, 350; with Dhamma, Order, 32
'That being, this is', 149 *ff.*
'There is not', 121
'There is (no) (result of) gift', *etc.*, 71, 73, 100, 114 *f.*
Thief, 209 *ff.*, 216, 226
'This is (not) mine', *etc.*, 68 *f.*, 288 *f.*, 317, 324 *f.*, 330, 334
Thought (*citta*): arising of, 94, 98; slackened (*santhita*), 273 *ff*. *See* Mind; (*vitakka*), 157, 169
Train oneself, to (*sikkhati*), 25, 152, 286 *f.*, 293, 310 *ff.*, 345
Trainers (*yoggācariya*), 264, 270 *f.*
Training (*sikkhā*), 52, 57, 85; rule(s) of, 53, 60 *f.*, 180; to disavow, 43
Tranquillity (*upasama*), happiness of, 281, 283. *See also* Calm
Transcending, the (*samatikkama*), 268 *f.*
Transgression (*accaya*), 293
Treasures, seven, xxiv, 217 *ff.*
Tree(s), roots of, 51, 54, 124, 130, 191 *ff.*, 325 *f.*, 329, 350
Trifle (*appamattaka*), 27 *f.*, 32
Truth (*sacca*), 258 *ff.*, 292; ariyan, 292; resolve for, 287, 292; to guard, 286 *f.*, 293; -s, ariyan, 295 *ff.*
Turn away from (*nibbindati*), to, 69, 156 *f.*, 159, 330, 335

Unaffected (*avyāseka*), 87
Unconstructed element (*asaṅkhatadhātu*), 106
Undefiled (*araṇa*), 277 *f.*, 283 *f.*
Uniformity (*ekatta*), 268 *f.*
Untroubled (*anavassuta*), 269 *f.*
Unwavering confidence (*aveccapasāda*), 301 *f.*, 314
Uprisings (*uppatti*), 192, 193 *n.*

Verdict: in the presence of, *etc.*, 33 *ff.*
View(s) (*diṭṭhi*): ariyan, 37; assumption of, 94, 99; right, xiv, xvi, xxix, 107 *f.*, 114 *ff.*, 187 *ff.*, 223, 257 *ff.*, 279, 298, 337; wrong, false, xiv, 15 *n.*, 71, 114 *ff.*, 185 *ff.*, 224, 234 *n.*, 257 *ff.*
Vigilance, xix, 53, 56 *f.*, 180 *f.*
Village, 103, 148, 173, 201, 343; -field, 192, 194
Vinaya, expert in, 91
Vision (*cakkhu*), 206 *f.*, 223, 241 *ff.*, 310. *See also* Eye, ear, *etc.*

Wanderer (*paribbājaka*), 254 *ff.*, 340 *ff.*
Wanting little, *etc.*, 157, 159
Way, ix, xii, xv, xxiii *f.*, 32, 58 *f.*, 65; component of, 115 *ff.*; eightfold, xvi *f.*, xxix, 25, 31, 114 *ff.*, 187, 279, 298, 314 *n.*, 338 *f.*, 344; fivefold, 337 *n.*; -follower, xiii, xvii, 59, 65; fourfold, 208 *n.*; -Shower, xiii, 56, 59, 65; tenfold, xvii, xxix, 119
Welcome, a, 58
Wheel: of Dhamma, xiv, 81, 295 *f.*, 299; Treasure of the, 218 *f.*
'Wherefore, because of this ... ', 263, 268
Widespread (*mahaggata*), xx *f.*, 191 *ff.*
Wisdom (*paññā*), 47, 57, 68 *f.*, 93, 115, 126, 139 *ff.*, 157, 159, 163; ariyan, 44, 292, 326; great, 244, 252 *f.*; kinds of, 77; not slothful in, 286 *f.*, 293; perfect, 266 *ff.*, 288 *f.*, 324 *f.*; resolve for, 287, 292. *See also* Freedom
Wise (*paṇḍita*), 104 *f.*; man, 216 *ff.*
Woman (*itthi*), 109; Treasure of, 219 *f.*
Wonderful and marvellous, 163 *ff.*, 171 *ff.*
World: overcome, 46 *f.*; -system, 109, 140 *ff.*, 165, 169; this, beyond, 312; with devas, 104; 'is (not) eternal', *etc.*, 19 *ff.*
Worldly life (*gehasita*), 265 *ff.*
Wrathful (*kodhana*), 251

II.—SIMILES

Bath-attendant, 132
Bird on the wing, 87
Black gum, etc., 57
Blind turtle, xxiv f., 214 f.
Broken rock, 40
Brahmans at sacrifice, 213
Bull's hide, 148

Cattle-butcher, 131, 310, 326

Dog and post, 19
Door-panel, 135
Drops of water, 349

Elephant in jungle, 199
Elephant-taming, 178, 182
Elephant, untamed, tamed, 182 f.
Elephants, horses, etc., tamed, untamed, 176

Fathers and children, 221
Fleck of mucus, 348
Fletcher, 12
Flies on pingo, 193
Full moon, 327 f.

Gambler, 215, 222
Gem on pale cloth, 141
Gold ornament on pale cloth, 141
Goldsmith, 290
Groom and chariot, 137

Heat from two sticks, 289
Heavy stone, 134
House on fire, 104

Jewel on muslin, 168
Jewel on thread, 167

Lotus-pond, 133

Man and own village, 39

Man eating dainties, 40
Man fully clothed, 134
Man gripping quail, 204 f.
Man in love, 11
Man meeting murderers, 203
Man needing oil, milk, etc., 185 ff.
Man seeking treasure, 204
Man with emblic myrobalan, 140 f.
Man with vision, 348
Merchant trading, 19
Milk and water, 200 f.
Mountain-climbing, 177
Mountain-shadows, 210, 216

Oil, lamp, wick, 196, 292; with flame, light, 325
Oil-lamps in house, 192 f.

Palm-tree, 41, 292
Pith, 240
Poisoned arrow, 4, 42
Poisoned goblet, 44
Poisonous snake, 45
Pool of water, 133
Provision-bag, 131

Rain-drops, 348
Roots, etc., of a tree, 325

Sere leaf, 40
Setting upright, etc., 57, 253, 342
Stick, wet and dry, 135
Streams and ocean, 134
Strong man, men, 310, 348, 349
Sun and shade, 21 ff.

Tank, 136
Thoroughbred, 52
Two houses, 223

Water-pot, empty, full, 135 f.
Way to Rājagaha, 56

III.—NAMES

Abhirādana, 183 n.
Abhiya Kaccāna, 193 ff.
Aciravata, 175 f.
Aggivessana, 175 ff.

Ajātasattu, 58
Ākankheyyasutta, xvii
Ānanda, xiii, xv, xxviii, 30 ff., 49 ff., 58 ff., 105 ff., 121, 147 ff., 153 ff.,

Index of Names

164 *ff.*, 235 *ff.*, 255 *ff.*, 300 *ff.*, 310, 312 *ff.*, 347 *ff.*
Anāthapiṇḍika, xxviii, 309, 312 *ff.*; 's monastery, *see under* Sāvatthī
Anuruddha, xix, 121, 190 *ff.*, 200 *ff.*
Avīci, 213 *n.*, 227 *n.*

Bakkula, xviii, 170 *ff.*
Bakkulatheracchariyabbhutasutta, 174 *n.*
Bālakaloṇakāra, 199
Baliharaṇa, 24 *n.*
Bamboo Grove, 58, 63, 170, 175, 183, 254; Eastern, 200
Benares, 295 *f.*, 299
Bhaggava, 285
Bhagu, 199 *f.*
Bhaññas, the, 121
Bhūmija, 183 *ff.*
Bimbisāra, 58 *n.*, 175 *n.*
Blind Men's Grove, 329
Brahmā(s), 104, 109, 120, 165, 169, 295, 299; of world-systems, 140 *ff.*
Brahmā Sahampati, 313 *n.*
Brahmajālasuttanta, xi, xv, 110 *n.*
Brahmāyu-sutta, 330 *n.*
Buddhaghosa, xxiii, xxvi
Buddhavaṃsa, xxiii

Candana, *devaputta*, 245 *ff.*
Chalmers, Lord, 22 *n.*, 35 *n.*, 275 *n.*
Channa, xxviii, 315 *ff.*
Childers, R., 140 *n.*, 251 *n.*
Coral Tree (*pāricchattaka*), 246
Cūḷahatthapadopamasutta, xiv
Cūḷakammavibhaṅga Sutta, ix
Cunda the Great, 121, 315, 317 *f.*
Cunda, novice, 30 *f.*

Dakkhiṇāvisuddhisutta, 303 *n.*
Devadaha, x, 3
Devadahavagga, xi
Devadatta, xxiv *f.*, 227 *n.*
Dhammacakkappavattanasutta, xvi *f.*, xxvi
Dhammapāla, xxiii
Dhānañjāni, xxviii
Dīghanakha-sutta, 330 *n.*
Downfall (*vinipāta*), the, 161, 215, 328

Eastern Monastery, 52, 65
Ekavisajjakasutta, 88 *n.*

Fivetools, carpenter, 190 *ff.*

Gaṇaka-Moggallāna, 52 *ff.*
Ganges, 220
Ghaṭāya, 153
Ghosita's monastery, 197
Gijjhakūṭa, 111
Godhika, xxviii *n.*
Gopaka-Moggallāna, 58 *ff.*
Gotama, 24 *f.*, 52, 55 *ff.*, 58 *ff.*, 63 *f.*, 253, 254, 285 *f.*, 339
Great Forty (*mahācattārīsa*), 120 *f.*
Great Grove, *see* Vesālī
Gulissāni, xviii

Hare, E. M., 202 *n.*
Himalaya, 212, 222

Isigili, xvi, 110 *ff.*
Isipatana, 295 *f.*, 299

Jayasena, xix, 175 *ff.*, 183 *f.*, 189
Jeta Grove, 313. *See under* Sāvatthī
Jeyyasena, 183 *n.*
Jones, J. J., xviii *n.*, xxi, xxxi, 59 *n.*, 165 *n.*

Kaccā(ya)na the Great, xxvi, 121, 239 *f.*, 243 *f.*, 272, 277
Kajaṅgalā, 346
Kālakhemaka, 152 *f.*
Kammassadhamma, 46
Kandarakasutta, xiv
Kapilavatthu, 152, 245, 247, 301
Kappina, 121
Kassapa, Buddha, 173 *n.*, 245 *n.*
Kassapa the Great, 121
Kassapa the Unclothed, 170, 173 *f.*
Kimbila, 200 *f.*
King's monastery, 323
Komudī, 122
Kosalans, 339
Kosambī, 197 *f.*
Kosambiyasutta, 197 *n.*
Koṭṭhita, 121
Kumārapañhā, xxix
Kurus, 46
Kusinārā, 24

Lévi, S., 248 *n.*
Licchavi, 38
Lomasakaṅgiya, 245 *ff.*

Magadha, 58 *f.*, 63, 285
Māgandiya, xii *n.*

Index of Names

Mahācattārīsaka Sutta, ix
Mahākammavibhaṅga Sutta, ix
Mahāpajāpatī, xxviii, 300 f., 322, 323 n.
Mahāpañhā, xxix
Mahāsakuludāyi-sutta, 172 n.
Mahāsaḷāyatanika Sutta, ix ff., xxviii f.
Mahāsatipaṭṭhānasuttanta, 296 n.
Mahāvastu, xviii, xxiii, xxxii
Maliyadeva, 336 n.
Māra(s), xxxi, 46, 104, 109, 120, 134 ff., 165, 169, 295, 299
Migāra's mother, palace of, 52, 65, 70, 121, 147
Milinda, King, xxiv
Moggallāna, 121, 295, 336 n.
Mukhelu Grove, 346
Musīla, 20 n.

Nagaraka, 147
Nagaravinda, 339 ff.
Nandaka, xxviii, 323 ff.
Nandiya, 200 f.
Nāṭaputta, Jain, 6, 29 ff.
Neumann, E. K., xxvi, 35 n., 79 n.
Nigrodha's park, 245, 247
Nikāyas, xvii, xxxii, 119 n.
Niraya Hell, xxiii ff., 72, 109 f., 211, 215, 224, 250 ff., 257 ff.; anguishes of, 211 ff.; Great, 213, 227 ff.; guardians of, 212 f., 224, 227, 229
Nyanatiloka, 202 n.

Padumuttara, Buddha, 173 n.
Pajjota, 58
Pañcakaṅga (Fivetools), 190 ff.
Pañcattayasutta, xi
Paṇḍava mountain, 111
Pārāsariya, 346 f.
Pasenadi, 248 n.
Paṭṭhānakathā, 293 n.
Pāvā, 30
Potali's son, 254 ff.
Poṭṭhapādasutta, 254 n.
Pubbajira, village, 318
Pukkusāti, 285 f., 293 f.
Puṇṇa, xxviii, 319 ff.

Radhakrishnan, S., 15 n.
Rāhula, xxviii, 328 ff.
Rājagaha, 58, 110, 170, 175, 183, 237, 254, 285, 315, 342; way to, 56
Raṭṭhapāla, 221 n.

Revata, 121
Rhys Davids, T. W., 15 n.
Rhys Davids, Mrs., xix n., 248 n.

Sakka, 109, 246 n.
Sakyans, 3, 29, 147, 152, 245, 247, 285, 300
Saḷāyatanavaggā, x, xxvii
Saḷāyatanavibhaṅgasutta, x f., 336 n.
Sāmagāma, 29 f.
Sambhūta, 183 n.
Samiddhi, 237 f., 254 ff.
Sāriputta, xiv f., xviii, xxviii, xxxi, 30 n., 95, 101 ff., 121, 284 n., 295 f., 309 f., 313 f., 315 ff., 336 n., 342 ff.; eulogy of, 77 ff.
Satipaṭṭhānasutta, xvii
Sāvatthī, 15, 52, 65, 70, 77, 81, 89, 94, 104, 113, 121 f., 129, 139, 147, 163, 190, 209, 223, 233, 235, 245 f., 248, 263, 271, 277, 286, 309, 319, 322 f., 328 f., 331
Subha, Todeyya's son, 248 ff.
Subhasutta, 248 n.
Subhūti, 277 n., 279 n., 284
Sumedhā, xxiv
Sunakkhatta, 38 ff.
Sunāparanta, 320 f.

Tapoda, 237
Tipiṭaka-Cūḷanāga, 336 n.
Todeyya, 248 n., 249 n.
Tusita group, 164 f., 167, 313

Udāyin, 255 f.
Ukkala, 120
Upālisutta, 254 n., 330 n.
Upananda, general, 63
Uposatha, elephant, 219
Uttara, 346 f.

Valāha, horse, 219
Vassakāra, 59, 63 f., 70 n.
Vassas, the, 120
Vebhāra, 110 f.
Vepulla mountain, 111, 219 n.
Vesālī, 37, 63
Vetaraṇī, 229 n.
Vibhaṅgavagga, x, xxv
Vinaya-piṭaka, xii, xviii, 88 n.
Vulture Peak, 315

Watt, G., 140 n.
Wood of the Offerings, 24

Yama, xxv, 224 ff., 229

IV.—SOME PALI WORDS IN THE NOTES

ajjhupekkhitar, 126
aññadatthu uyyojaniyapaṭisaṁyuttaṁ yeva kathaṁ kattā hoti, 154
anuggāhakā, 295
abhinibbattayato apariniṭṭhitabhāvāya, 101
araṇa, 277
aratiratisaho, 137
ākāsa, 83
ākāsadhātu, 83
āmake āmakamatte, 162
āmaṇḍa, 140
āyatana, 136
indriya, 346
upavajjakulāni, 318
ummagga, 256
ummujjamāno ayoniso ummujjissati, 256
ekacchigaḷa yuga, 214
obhāsa, 202
kuhanā, 118
gaddūhanamattaṁ, 173
cara vādappamokkhāya, 30
cetaso anābhogo, 79
jhāyati, 196
tayo satipaṭṭhānā, 263, 264
tividhena samādhi, 207, 208

dhamma vijjābhāgiyā, 134
na ca kālaṁ karoti ... 212
niggayha niggayha, 162
nippesikatā, 118
nemittakatā, 118
pavayha pavayha, 162
bālabhūmi, 216
bhavābhava, 25
bhāvanā, 346
matthena āviñjeyya, 186
manussānaṁ yeva sataṁ manussabhūtānaṁ, 249
mahāpaññā, 77
mucchati kāmayati, 160
yathākathaṁ dhāresi, 245
yo sāro so ṭhassati, 162
lapanā, 118
vidhāvati, 270
saṅkhataṁ etaṁ, 290
saṅkhāra, 108, 139
saṁhīrati, 234
samannāgata, 59
sāṇa, 173
sāmāyikā cetovimutti, 154
sārita, 270
hāsupaññā, 77

LIBRARY OF DAVIDSON COLLEGE

Bibliography on Methods of Social and Business Research

William A. Belson, B.A., Ph.D.
Design and direction
and
Beryl-Anne Thompson, B.Sc., Dip.Lib., A.L.A.
Compilation

Prepared with the support of the Nuffield Foundation

A Halsted Press Book

John Wiley & Sons
New York

Published in the U.S.A. by Halsted Press,
a Division of John Wiley & Sons, Inc. New York

Copyright © 1973 by W. A. Belson

All rights reserved. No part of this publication
may be reproduced, stored in a retrieval system,
or transmitted, in any form or by any means,
electronic, mechanical, photocopying, recording
or otherwise, without the prior permission of
the publishers.

ISBN 0 470-85986-5

Library of Congress Catolog Card Number 72-11488

Printed in Great Britain

CONTENTS

Introduction	vii
List of papers	1
Index to subjects	209
List of books	289
List of periodicals	297

INTRODUCTION

The aim of the authors in publishing this Bibliography is to provide a system which will make for ready identification of the published material bearing on a specific or a general aspect of survey methodology, or written by a particular author. The book also serves to update and extend an earlier publication, *A bibliography of papers bearing on the adequacy of techniques used in survey research* by W. A. Belson and C. R. Bell, published by the Market Research Society and Oakwood Press in 1960.

The Bibliography is designed as a flexible tool for information retrieval which will be of value to students and teachers in business studies and in the social sciences; to those engaged in industrial, commercial and social research; to those who buy research as an aid to decision making; to librarians and information officers.

A special feature of this Bibliography is that it contains both a List of Papers and a very detailed Index to the methodological matters they deal with. The list of subject headings used in the Index was developed through a content analysis of a sample of those papers, the indexing being carried out by a panel of research personnel working in industry, the public services, and the Survey Research Centre. The List of Papers is arranged alphabetically by author name and includes over 2000 items which have been given consecutive reference numbers. The Index to Subjects consists of alphabetically listed headings for both broad and specific topics, the broad topics generally being broken down into subgroups referring to specific aspects of the broader topics. These headings and subheadings list the reference numbers of the relevant publications as numbered in the List of Papers. There is extensive cross-referencing and the form of the Index allows the rapid identification of that limited number of papers which deal with some specified aspect, or combination of aspects, of a methodological issue.

The papers presented in the Bibliography are for the most part those published in the period 1930 to 1970. Prior to that period, the number of methodological papers was fairly limited and the task of searching them out was seen both as unrewarding and beyond the budget available for this project. However some of the classics of the period before 1930 have been included.

The papers dealt with in the Bibliography are principally those journal articles, published research reports and conference papers that deal with the techniques of gathering information from population samples in the context of social and business research. Thus it does not include publications concerned with measurement techniques suitable primarily for guiding decisions about individuals as in, for example, vocational guidance testing, personnel selection, personality measurement. The Bibliography also excludes publications of a wholly statistical nature, on the grounds that these have been included in other published bibliographies.

Books that deal in a descriptive manner with the methods and techniques of research have been listed separately.

In the List of Papers full bibliographical descriptions have been made for the entry under the author or principal author. *'See'* references are made from the names of second and third authors to the principle author. In the Index to Subjects *'See'* references are made from unused terms to used terms and there are *'See also'* references to related terms which may provide the reader with relevant material. In the construction of the bibliographical entries for the List of Papers and List of Books we have generally followed the *Anglo-American cataloguing rules* and the *British Standard 1629: 1950* for bibliographical references. We have, however, not followed the rules for typography in their entirety where they were felt to be unnecessarily complex, and we have moved the date of publication to the position normally occupied by the 'date of priority', the two dates being the same in most cases.

The journals and the several other serial publications which were scanned for material referred to in the Bibliography are listed at the end of the book.

The Bibliography project was principally supported by a grant from the Nuffield Foundation and the authors wish to express their deep appreciation to the Foundation for making the project possible.

The Bibliography also received support from the wide consortium of organisations which contribute to the Survey Research Centre through subscriptions and grants. Special grants were received from AGB Research Limited, Marketing Advisory Services Limited and National Opinion Polls Limited. Their help is acknowledged and appreciated.

The following people participated in the subject indexing of papers for the Bibliography: Mrs. T. Anderson, Miss L. Ward, Mr. J. Couzens. Miss D. Sweetland, Miss B. Hynds, Miss A. Malcolm, Mr. J. Nettle, Mr. J. Payne, Mr. F. le Grice, Mrs. A. Stokes, Mr. D. Tomily, Mrs. J. Fiehn, Mr. V. Thompson, Mrs. S. Quinn, Mr. P. Clark, Mr. M. Couzens, Miss C. Closey, Miss. R. Barker and Miss J. Christensen helped in preparing the manuscript for publication. Their contribution is gratefully acknowledged.

April, 1972   W. A. Belson
                                                                   B. A. Thompson

LIST OF PAPERS

1. **ABEL**, Theodore. 1947. The nature and use of biograms. *American Journal of Sociology*, vol. 53, no. 2, pp. 111-118.

2. **ABELSON**, Herbert I. 1966. A 'role rehearsal' technique for exploratory interviewing. *Public Opinion Quarterly*, vol. 30, no. 2, pp. 302-305.

   ABERNATHY, J[ames] R. 1969. *See* GOULD, A. L., SHAH, B. V. and ABERNATHY, J[ames] R. 1969.

   ABERNATHY, James R. 1969. *See* GREENBERG, Bernard G., ABERNATHY, James R. and HORVITZ, Daniel G. 1969.

3. **ABRAHAMS**, Norman M. 1969. Off-quadrant comment. *Journal of Applied Psychology*, vol. 53, no. 1, pp. 66-68.

4. **ABRAMS**, Jack. 1966. An evaluation of alternative rating devices for consumer research. *Journal of Marketing Research*, vol. 3, no. 2, pp. 189-193.

5. **ABRAMS**, Jack. 1969. Reducing the risk of new product marketing strategies testing. *Journal of Marketing Research*, vol. 6, no. 2, pp. 216-220.

6. **ABRAMS**, Mark. 1958. Technical problems in the I.P.A. readership survey. *The Incorporated Statistician*, vol. 8, no. 2, pp. 55-65.

   ABRAMSON, Edward. 1952. *See* ASH, Philip and ABRAMSON, Edward. 1952.

7. **ABRAMSON**, H. A. 1960. Lysergic acid diethylamide (LSD-25), XXX: the questionnaire technique with notes on its use. *Journal of Psychology*, vol. 49, no. 1, pp. 57-65.

8. **ABRUZZINI**, Pompeo. 1967. Measuring language difficulty in advertising copy. *Journal of Marketing*, vol. 31, no. 2, pp. 22-26.

9. **ABT**, Lawrence Edwin. 1949. The analysis of structured clinical interviews. *Journal of Clinical Psychology*, vol. 5, no. 4, pp. 364-370.

10. **ABUL-ELA**, Abdel Latif A., GREENBERG, Bernard G. and HORVITZ, Daniel G. 1967. A multi-proportions randomized response model. *Journal of the American Statistical Association*, vol. 62, no. 319, pp. 990-1008.

11. **ACHENBAUM**, Alvin A., HALEY, Russell I. and GATTY, Ronald. 1967. On-air vs. in-home testing of TV commercials. *Journal of Advertising Research*, vol. 7, no. 4, pp. 15-19.

12. **ACKOFF**, Russell L. and PRITZKER, Leon. 1951. The methodology of survey research. *International Journal of Opinion and Attitude Research*, vol. 5, no. 3, pp. 313-334.

13. **ADAMCZEWSKI**, B. F. M. 1969. Computer processing of market research and media data. *Admap*, vol. 5, no. 4, pp. 180-182, 184.

14. **ADAMEC**, Cenek. 1947. Experiences with an international question. *International Journal of Opinion and Attitude Research*, vol. 1, no. 4, pp. 40-44.

15. **ADAMS**, Henry F. 1930. An objectivity-subjectivity ratio for scales of measurement. *Journal of Social Psychology*, vol. 1, no. 1, pp. 122-134.

16. **ADAMS**, Henry F. 1936. Validity, reliability, and objectivity. *Psychological Monographs*, vol. 47, no. 2, pp. 329-350.

17. **ADAMS**, J. Stacy. 1956. An experiment on question and response bias. *Public Opinion Quarterly*, vol. 20, no. 3, pp. 593-598.

ADAMS, John B. 1958. *See* DEUTSCHMANN, Paul J. and ADAMS, John B. 1958.

18. **ADLER**, Lee, GREENBERG, Allan and LUCAS, Darrell B. 1965. What big agency men think of copy testing methods. *Journal of Marketing Research*, vol. 2, no. 4, pp. 339-345.

19. **ADLER**, Lee. 1966. Confessions of an interview reader. *Journal of Marketing Research*, vol. 3, no. 2, pp. 194-195.

20. **ADLER**, Max K. 1962/63. Sampling and interviewing in industrial research. *Commentary*, no. 9, pp. 3-5.

21. **ADLER**, Max K. 1963. Sampling and interviewing in industrial research, part 2. *Commentary*, no. 11, pp. 20-21.

22. **ADLER**, Max K. 1964. The use of the telephone in industrial market research. *Scientific Business*, vol. 1, no. 4, pp. 336-342.

23. **ADLER**, Max K. 1966. How to conduct readership surveys for the industrial press. *Admap*, October 1966, pp. 454-455.

AGISM, Philip. 1951. *See* ROBINSON, R. A. and AGISM, Philip. 1951.

24. **AGOSTINI**, J[ean]-M[ichel]. 1961. How to estimate unduplicated audiences. *Journal of Advertising Research*, vol. 1, no. 3, pp. 11-14.

25. **AGOSTINI**, J[ean]-M[ichel]. 1962. Analysis of magazine accumulative audience. *Journal of Advertising Research*, vol. 2, no. 4, pp. 24-27.

26. AGOSTINI, J[ean]-M[ichel]. 1964. The case for direct questions on reading habits. *Journal of Advertising Research*, vol. 4, no. 2, pp. 28-33.

27. AGOSTINI, J[ean]-M[ichel]. 1966. A method of market segmentation. *Advertiser's Weekly*, January 7, pp. 22-24.

28. AGOSTINI, Jean-Michel. 1967. The possible role of readership panels in media research and media planning. *The Roy Thomson medals and awards for media research 1966*. London: The Thomson Organisation, 1967. pp. 30-47.

29. AGOSTINI, J[ean]-M[ichel]. 1969. New criteria for classifying informants in market research and media strategy. *Admap*, vol. 5, no. 6, pp. 248, 250, 252-254, 256, 258-260, 262-263.

30. AIKEN, Lewis R., Jr. 1968. Weighting and guessing on varieties of the multiple-choice item. *Educational and Psychological Measurement*, vol. 28, no. 4, pp. 1087-1101.

31. AITCHISON, D. R. 1960. The measurement of the television viewing of individuals. *Commentary*, no. 2, part 2, pp. 7-10.

32. AKE, James N. 1962. A rapid machine procedure for determining scalability of any number of questions. *Public Opinion Quarterly*, vol. 26, no. 1, pp. 121-125.

33. ALDERFER, Clayton P. 1967. Convergent and discriminant validation of satisfaction and desire measures by interviews and questionnaires. *Journal of Applied Psychology*, vol. 51, no. 6, pp. 509-520.

34. ALDERFER, Clayton P. 1968. Comparison of questionnaire responses with and without preceding interviews. *Journal of Applied Psychology*, vol. 52, no. 4, pp. 335-340.

35. ALEXANDER, C. Norman, Jr. 1963. A method for processing sociometric data. *Sociometry*, vol. 26, no. 2, pp. 268-269.

36. ALEXANDER, C. Norman, Jr., and PERRY, Josef. 1967. A new technique for improving cumulative scales. *Public Opinion Quarterly*, vol. 31, no. 1, pp. 110-115.

37. ALEXANDER, S. J., et al. 1955. Studies of motion sickness, X: experimental proof that aviation cadets tell the truth on motion sickness history questionnaires. *Journal of Psychology*, vol. 39, no. 2, pp. 403-409.

ALF, Edward F. 1961. *See* GORDON, Leonard V. and ALF, Edward F. 1961.

38. **ALFORD**, Robert R. 1962. A suggested index of the association of social class and voting. *Public Opinion Quarterly*, vol. 26, no. 3, pp. 417-425.

ALIMENA, Benjamin S. 1949. *See* DONCEEL, Joseph, F., ALIMENA, Benjamin S. and BIRCH, Catherine M. 1949.

39. **ALLEN**, Bernadine V., *et al.* 1965. Effects of warm-cold set on interviewee speech. *Journal of Consulting Psychology*, vol. 29, no. 5, pp. 480-482.

ALLEN, C. N. 1939. *See* OSGOOD, C. E., ALLEN, C. N. and ODBERT, H. S. 1939.

40. **ALLEN**, Irving L. 1966. Detecting respondents who fake and confuse information about question areas on surveys. *Journal of Applied Psychology*, vol. 50, no. 6, pp. 523-528.

41. **ALLEN**, R. G. D. 1964. Sampling for current economic statistics. *Journal of the Royal Statistical Society, series A*, vol. 127, part 1, pp. 76-88.

42. **ALLISON**, Harry E., ZWICK, Charles J. and BRINSER, Ayres. 1958. Recruiting and maintaining a consumer panel. *Journal of Marketing*, vol. 22, no. 4, pp. 377-390.

43. **ALLISON**, Roger B., *Jr.* 1963. Using adverbs as multipliers in semantic differentials. *Journal of Psychology*, vol. 56, no. 1, pp. 115-117.

44. **ALPER**, Thelma G. and KORCHIN, Sheldon J. 1952. Memory for socially relevant material. *Journal of Abnormal and Social Psychology*, vol. 47, no. 1, pp. 25-37.

45. **AMERICAN MARKETING ASSOCIATION**. Committee on Marketing Research Techniques. 1946. Design, size, and validation of sample for market research. *Journal of Marketing*, vol. 10, no. 3, pp. 221-234.

46. **AMERICAN MARKETING ASSOCIATION**. Committee on Marketing Research Techniques. 1949. Tabulation planning and tabulation techniques. *Journal of Marketing*, vol. 13, no. 3, pp. 330-355.

47. **ANA**: probing ad effectiveness. 1964. *Printer's Ink*, vol. 287, no. 6, pp. 43-44.

48. **ANDERSON**, Dale. 1952. Roper's field interviewing organization. *Public Opinion Quarterly*, vol. 16, no. 2, pp. 263-272.

ANDREWS, Frank M. 1964. *See* PELZ, Donald C. and ANDREWS, Frank M. 1964.

49. ANDREWS, Frank M., MORGAN, James N. and SONQUIST, John A. 1969. Multiple classification analysis: a report on a computer program for multiple regression using categorical predictors. Ann Arbor, Michigan: University of Michigan, Survey Research Center, 1969. 211pp.

50. ANDREWS, Lee. 1949. The interviewer problem in market research. *Journal of Marketing*, vol. 13, no. 4, pp. 522-524.

51. ANDREWS, Lee. 1953. Court decree on the 'cheater problem'. *Journal of Marketing*, vol. 18, no. 2, pp. 167-169.

52. ANDREWS, Leonora de Lima. 1949. That dreadful interviewer problem again. *International Journal of Opinion and Attitude Research*, vol. 3, no. 4, pp. 587-590.

53. ANDRIESSENS, Jacques E. 1966. An experiment in media research. *Journal of Advertising Research*, vol. 6, no. 4, pp. 19-24.

54. ARGYRIS, Chris. 1952. Diagnosing defenses against the outsider. *Journal of Social Issues*, vol. 8, no. 3, pp. 24-34.

55. ARNOLD, Rome G. 1964. The interview in jeopardy: a problem in public relations. *Public Opinion Quarterly*, vol. 28, no. 1, pp. 119-123.

ARNOLD, William E. 1967. *See* McCROSKEY, James C., PRICHARD, Samuel V. O. and ARNOLD, William E. 1967.

56. ARRINGTON, Ruth E. 1932. Some technical aspects of observer reliability as indicated in studies of the 'talkies'. *American Journal of Sociology*, vol. 38, no. 3, pp. 409-417.

57. ARTHUR, A. Z. 1966. Response bias in the semantic differential. *British Journal of Social and Clinical Psychology*, vol. 5, no. 2, pp. 103-107.

58. ASCH, S. E. 1948. The doctrine of suggestion, prestige and imitation in social psychology. *Psychological Review*, vol. 55, no. 5, pp. 250-276.

ASH, Philip. 1951. *See* KURTZ, Albert K., JASPEN, Nathan and ASH, Philip. 1951.

59. ASH, Philip and ABRAMSON, Edward. 1952. The effect of anonymity on attitude-questionnaire response. *Journal of Abnormal and Social Psychology*, vol. 47, no. 3, pp. 722-723.

ASSAEL, Henry. 1966. *See* EASTLACK, J. O., *Jr.* and ASSAEL, Henry. 1966.

60. **ASSAEL**, Henry. 1967. Comparison of brand share data by three reporting systems. *Journal of Marketing Research*, vol. 4, no. 4, pp. 400-401.

61. **ATCHLEY**, Robert C. 1968. A qualification of test factor standardization: a methodological note. *Social Forces*, vol. 47, no. 1, pp. 84-85.

    ATHANASOPOULOS, Demetrios A. 1970. *See* HOCHSTIM, Joseph R. and ATHANASOPOULOS, Demetrios A. 1970.

62. **ATHEY**, K. R., *et al.* 1960. Two experiments showing the effect of the interviewer's racial background on responses to questionnaires concerning racial issues. *Journal of Applied Psychology*, vol. 44, no. 4, pp. 244-246.

63. **ATKINSON**, Jean. 1968. Handbook for interviewers: a manual for Government Social Survey interviewing staff, describing practise and procedures on structured interviewing. London: H.M.S.O., 1968. 165pp.

64. **ATTNEAVE**, Fred. 1949. A method of graded dichotomies for the scaling of judgments. *Psychological Review*, vol. 56, no. 6, pp. 334-340.

65. **AUDITS OF GREAT BRITAIN.** 1965. Instructions for the random route procedure. Eastcote, Middlesex: Audits of Great Britain, 1965. 5pp.

    AUERBACH, Barbara K. 1963. *See* STOCK, J. Stevens and AUERBACH, Barbara K. 1963.

66. **AULD**, Frank, *Jr.*, and WHITE, Alice M. 1956. Rules for dividing interviews into sentences. *Journal of Psychology*, vol. 42, no. 2, pp. 273-281.

67. **AUSTIN**, Richard B., *Jr.* 1964. Volunteering as a function of induced social forces. *Journal of Social Psychology*, vol. 62, no. 1, pp. 57-64.

    AXELROD, Joel. 1961. *See* STEVENS, Bill and AXELROD, Joel. 1961.

68. **AXELROD**, Joel N. 1964. Reducing advertising failures by concept testing. *Journal of Marketing*, vol. 28, no. 4, pp. 41-44.

69. **AXELROD**, Joel N. 1968. Attitude measures that predict purchase. *Journal of Advertising Research*, vol. 8, no. 1, pp. 3-17.

    AXELROD, Morris, 1956. *See* CANNELL, Charles F. and AXELROD, Morris. 1956.

70. AXELROD, Morris and CANNELL, Charles F. 1959/60. A research note on an attempt to predict interviewer effectiveness. *Public Opinion Quarterly*, vol. 23, no. 4, pp. 571-576.

71. AXELROD, Morris, MATTHEWS, Donald R. and PROTHRO, James W. 1962. Recruitment for survey research on race problems in the South. *Public Opinion Quarterly*, vol. 26, no. 2, pp. 254-262.

72. AXELROD, Morris 1964. An experimental attempt to reduce field costs by limiting callbacks and increasing cluster size. *AMERICAN STATISTICAL ASSOCIATION. Proceedings of the Social Statistics Section*, 1964. pp. 32-40.

AYLWARD, Merriam 1956. *See* DUNNETTE, Marvin D., UPHOFF, Walter and AYLWARD, Merriam. 1956.

73. AZRIN, N. H., HOLZ, W. and GOLDIAMOND, I. 1961. Response bias in questionnaire reports. *Journal of Consulting Psychology*, vol. 25, no. 4, pp. 324-326.

74. BABCHUK, Nicholas and GORDON, C. Wayne. 1958. The child as a prototype of the naive informant in the interview situation. *American Sociological Review*, vol. 23, no. 2, pp. 196-198.

75. BACHELDER, Joseph, *chairman*. 1955. Motivation research: I. *Public Opinion Quarterly*, vol. 19, no. 4, pp. 431-433.

76. BACHRACK, Stanley D. and SCOBLE, Harry M. 1967. Mail questionnaire efficiency: controlled reduction of nonresponse. *Public Opinion Quarterly*, vol. 31, no. 2, pp. 265-271.

77. BACK, Kurt W. 1956. The well-informed informant. *Human Organization*, vol. 14, no. 4, pp. 30-33.

BACK, Kurt W. 1956. *See* STANTON, Howard, BACK, Kurt W. and LITWAK, Eugene. 1956.

78. BACK, Kurt W. and GERGEN, Kenneth J. 1963. Idea orientation and ingratiation in the interview: a dynamic model of response bias. *AMERICAN STATISTICAL ASSOCIATION. Proceedings of the Social Statistics Section*, 1963. pp. 284-288.

BACK, Kurt W. 1966. *See* BROOKOVER, Linda and BACK, Kurt W. 1966.

BACK, Kurt W. 1966. *See* GERGEN, Kenneth J. and BACK, Kurt W. 1966.

79. BADER, Carolyn F. 1948. Solve the field problem first. *International Journal of Opinion and Attitude Research*, vol. 2, no. 1, pp. 97-99.

80. **BAEHR**, Melany E. 1953. A simplified procedure for the measurement of employee attitudes. *Journal of Applied Psychology*, vol. 37, no. 3, pp. 163-167.

BAGGALEY, Andrew R. 1956. *See* CATTELL, Raymond B. and BAGGALEY, Andrew R. 1956.

81. **BAGGALEY**, Andrew R. 1960. Some remarks on scales of measurement and related topics. *Journal of General Psychology*, vol. 62, no. 1, pp. 141-145.

82. **BAIER**, Donald E. 1951. Reply to Travers' 'A critical review of the validity and rationale of the forced-choice technique'. *Psychological Bulletin*, vol. 48, no. 5, pp. 421-434.

83. **BAILAR**, Barbara A. 1968. Recent research in reinterview procedures. *Journal of the American Statistical Association*, vol. 68, no. 321, pp. 41-63.

84. **BAILAR**, Barbara A. and DALENIUS, Tore. 1969. Estimating the response variance components of the U.S. Bureau of the Census' survey model. *Sankhya, series B*, vol. 31, part 3, pp. 341-360.

85. **BAIN**, Read. 1931. Stability in questionnaire response. *American Journal of Sociology*, vol. 37, no. 3, pp. 445-453.

BAIN, Robert K. 1961. *See* MASON, Ward S., DRESSEL, Robert J. and BAIN, Robert K. 1961.

86. **BAKAN**, David. 1966. The test of significance in psychological research. *Psychological Bulletin*, vol. 66, no. 6, pp. 423-437.

87. **BAKAN**, Paul. 1956. The collection and use of retrospective data. *Journal of Psychology*, vol. 41, no. 2, pp. 369-378.

BAKER, Elizabeth Lauh. 1971. *See* SONQUIST, John A., BAKER, Elizabeth Lauh and MORGAN, James N. 1971.

BAKER, Kenneth H. 1942. *See* STANTON, Frank [N.] and BAKER, Kenneth H. 1942.

88. **BAKER**, P. R. 1965. The validation of new research techniques. *Commentary*, vol. 7, no. 3, pp. 176-183.

BALABAN, V. 1961. *See* MACURA, M. and BALABAN, V. 1961.

89. **BALAN**, Jorge, *et al.* 1969. A computerized approach to the processing and analysis of life histories obtained in sample surveys. *Behavioral Science*, vol. 14, no. 2, pp. 105-120.

90. **BALES**, Robert F. and GERBRANDS, Henry. 1948. The 'interaction recorder': an apparatus and check list for sequential content

analysis of social interaction. *Human Relations*, vol. 1, no. 4, pp. 456-463.

91. BALINSKY, Benjamin, BLUM, Milton L. and DUTKA, Solomon. 1951. The coefficient of agreement in determining product preferences. *Journal of Applied Psychology*, vol. 35, no. 5, pp. 348-351.

92. BALL, John C. 1967. The reliability and validity of interview data obtained from 59 narcotic drug addicts. *American Journal of Sociology*, vol. 72, no. 6, pp. 650-654.

93. BALLWEG, John A. 1969. Husband-wife response similarities on evaluative and non-evaluative survey questions. *Public Opinion Quarterly*, vol. 33, no. 2, pp. 249-254.

94. BANCROFT, Gertrude. 1940. Consistency of information from records and interviews. *Journal of the American Statistical Association*, vol. 35, no. 210, part 1, pp. 377-381.

95. BANCROFT, Gertrude and WELCH, Emmett H. 1946. Recent experience with problems of labor force measurement. *Journal of the American Statistical Association*, vol. 41, no. 235, pp. 303-312.

96. BANKS, J. A. 1957. The group discussion as an interview technique. *Sociological Review*, vol. 5, no. 1, pp. 75-84.

97. BANKS, Seymour. 1957. How and why ad scores vary. *Printer's Ink*, vol. 260, no. 10, pp. 19-22.

98. BANKS, Seymour. 1964. Designing marketing research to increase validity. *Journal of Marketing*, vol. 28, no. 4, pp. 32-40.

99. BANKS, Seymour. 1965. Latin square experiments. *Journal of Advertising Research*, vol. 5, no. 3, pp. 37-46.

100. BANTA, Thomas J. 1961. Social attitudes and response styles. *Educational and Psychological Measurement*, vol. 21, no. 3, pp. 543-557.

BARAKAT, Mohamed K. 1959. *See* HUDSON, Bradford B., BARAKAT, Mohamed K. and LaFORGE, Rolfe. 1959.

101. BARBAN, Arnold M. and CUNDIFF, Edward W. 1964. Negro and White response to advertising stimuli. *Journal of Marketing Research*, vol. 1, no. 4, pp. 53-56.

102. BARBER, Jane. 1962. Interviewer training—does it pay dividends? *Commentary*, no. 8, pp. 17-19.

103. **BARBER**, Theodore Xenophon and **SILVER**, Maurice J. 1968. Fact, fiction, and the experimenter bias effect. *Psychological Bulletin*, vol. 70, no. 6, part 2, pp. 1-29.

104. **BARBER**, Theodore Xenophon and **SILVER**, Maurice J. 1968. Pitfalls in data analysis and interpretation: a reply to Rosenthal. *Psychological Bulletin*, vol. 70, no. 6, part 2, pp. 48-62.

105. **BARBER**, Theodore Xenophon. 1969. Invalid arguments, postmortem analyses, and the experimenter bias effect. *Journal of Consulting and Clinical Psychology*, vol. 33, no. 1, pp. 11-14.

106. **BARBER**, Theodore Xenophon, *et al.* 1969. Five attempts to replicate the experimenter bias effect. *Journal of Consulting and Clinical Psychology*, vol. 33, no. 1, pp. 1-6.

107. **BARCLAY**, William D. 1962. Why aren't portfolio tests here to stay? *Journal of Marketing*, vol. 26, no. 3, pp. 73-75.

108. **BARCLAY**, William D. 1963. A probability model for early prediction of new product market success. *Journal of Marketing*, vol. 27, no. 1, pp. 63-68.

109. **BARCLAY**, William D. 1964. The semantic differential as an index of brand attitude. *Journal of Advertising Research*, vol. 4, no. 1, pp. 30-33.

110. **BARIOUX**, Max. 1952. A method for the selection, training and evaluation of interviewers. *Public Opinion Quarterly*, vol. 16, no. 1, pp. 128-130.

111. **BARKLEY**, Key Lee. 1931. The development of a new method for determining the relative efficiencies of advertisements in magazines. *Journal of Applied Psychology*, vol. 15, no. 4, pp. 390-410.

112. **BARKLEY**, Key Lee. 1932. The demonstration of a new method for determining the relative efficiencies of advertisements in magazines. *Journal of Applied Psychology*, vol. 16, no. 1, pp. 74-90.

113. **BARLOW**, Robin, **MORGAN**, James [N.] and **WIRICK**, Grover. 1960. A study of validity in reporting medical care in Michigan. *AMERICAN STATISTICAL ASSOCIATION. Proceedings of the Social Statistics Section*, 1960. pp. 54-65.

114. **BARNETTE**, W. Leslie, *Jr.* 1950. The non-respondent problem in questionnaire research. *Journal of Applied Psychology*, vol. 34, no. 6, pp. 397-398.

115. **BARR**, Alexander. 1957. Differences between experienced interviewers. *Applied Statistics*, vol. 6, no. 3, pp. 180-188.

116. **BARRETT**, Gerald V., SVETLIK, Byron and PRIEN, Erich P. 1967. Validity of the job-concept interview in an industrial setting. *Journal of Applied Psychology*, vol. 51, no. 3, pp. 233-235.

117. **BARTHOLOMEW**, D. J. 1961. A method of allowing for 'not-at-home' bias in sample surveys. *Applied Statistics*, vol. 10, no. 1, pp. 52-59.

118. **BARTLETT**, Claude J., QUAY, Lorene Childs and WRIGHTSMAN, Lawrence S., Jr. 1960. A comparison of two methods of attitude measurement: Likert-type and forced choice. *Educational and Psychological Measurement*, vol. 20, no. 4, pp. 699-704.

   BARTLEY, S. Howard. 1960. *See* NELSON, Thomas M., BARTLEY, S. Howard and DeHARDT, Doris. 1960.

119. **BARTON**, J. Allen. 1958. Asking the embarrassing question. *Public Opinion Quarterly*, vol. 22, no. 2, pp. 67-68.

120. **BARTON**, Samuel G. 1947. A working system for the socio-economic classification of a national sample of families. *Journal of Marketing*, vol. 11, no. 4, pp. 364-366.

121. **BATES**, Brian and BERMINGHAM, John. 1968. Short term diaries: their use in collecting detailed consumption data. *EUROPEAN SOCIETY FOR OPINION AND MARKETING RESEARCH. Congress, XXI, Opatija, 1968. Papers...* Brussels: ESOMAR, 1968. pp. 651-667.

122. **BATSON**, E. 1951. A note on certain internal checks employed by the Social Survey of Cape Town. *Journal of Social Research, Pretoria*, vol. 2, no. 2, pp. 112-117.

123. **BAUER**, E. Jackson. 1947. Response bias in a mail survey. *Public Opinion Quarterly*, vol. 11, no. 4, pp. 594-600.

124. **BAUER**, Rainald K. and MEISSNER, Frank. 1963. Structures of mail questionnaires: test of alternatives. *Public Opinion Quarterly*, vol. 27, no. 2, pp. 307-311.

   BAUER, Raymond A. 1956. *See* ZIMMERMAN, Claire and BAUER, Raymond A. 1956.

125. **BAUERNFEIND**, Robert H. 1955. Measuring children's strength of response to attitude items. *Educational and Psychological Measurement*, vol. 15, no. 1, pp. 63-70.

126. **BAXTER**, Richard. 1964. An inquiry into the misuse of the survey technique by sales solicitors. *Public Opinion Quarterly*, vol. 28, no. 1, pp. 124-134.

127. **BAXTER**, Robert E. 1943. Use both mail-type questionnaire and personal interviews in readership research. *Printer's Ink*, vol. 203, no. 6, pp. 24, 28, 80, 82.

BAYTON, James A. 1954. *See* CLEMENTS, Forrest E., BAYTON, James A. and BELL, Hugh P. 1954.

BEAL, George M. 1958. *See* ROGERS, Everett M. and BEAL, George M. 1958.

128. **BEATON**, D. C. 1967. The development of market research in south east Asia. *Commentary*, vol. 9, no. 2, pp. 61-67.

BECKER, Gilbert. 1965. *See* BROCK, Timothy C. and BECKER, Gilbert. 1965.

129. **BECKER**, Howard S. 1954. A note on interviewing tactics. *Human Organization*, vol. 12, no. 4, pp. 31-32.

130. **BECKER**, Howard S. 1956. Interviewing medical students. *American Journal of Sociology*, vol. 62, no. 2, pp. 199-201.

131. **BECKER**, Howard S. 1958. Problems of inference and proof in participant observation. *American Sociological Review*, vol. 23, no. 6, pp. 652-660.

132. **BECKER**, Howard S. and GEER, Blanche. 1958. Participant observation and interviewing: a comparison. *Human Organization*, vol. 16, no. 3, pp. 28-32.

133. **BECKER**, Howard S. and GEER, Blanche. 1958. 'Participant observation and interviewing': a rejoinder. *Human Organization*, vol. 17, no. 2, pp. 39-40.

BECKER, Wesley C. 1958. *See* FREY, Allan H. and BECKER, Wesley C. 1958.

134. **BECKNELL**, James C. *Jr.*, and MAHER, Howard. 1962. Utilization of factor analysis for image clarification and analysis. *Public Opinion Quarterly*, vol. 26, no. 4, pp. 658-663.

135. **BECKNELL**, James C., Jr. 1965. Utilizing pre-testing devices to reduce variance in advertising experiments. *ADVERTISING RESEARCH FOUNDATION. Annual Conference, 11th, New York City, 1965. Proceedings* . . . New York: Advertising Research Foundation, 1965. pp. 34-38.

136. **BEILIN**, Harry and WERNER, Emmy E. 1957. Interviewing availability of a follow-up sample of rural youth. *Public Opinion Quarterly*, vol. 21, no. 3, pp. 380-384.

137. **BELDEN**, Joe, STEMBER, Herbert and HOCHSTIM, Joseph [R.] 1951. Interviewer bias and what to do about it. *Public Opinion Quarterly*, vol. 15, no. 4, pp. 774-778.

    BELDO, Leslie A. 1953. *See* JONES, Robert L. and BELDO, Leslie A. 1953.

    BELFORD, R. J. 1962. *See* KIRSCH, Arthur D., BERGER, Philip K. and BELFORD, R. J. 1962.

138. **BELKIN**, Marvin and LIEBERMAN, Seymour. 1967. Effect of question wording on response distribution. *Journal of Marketing Research*, vol. 4, no. 3, pp. 312-313.

139. **BELL**, C. R. 1961. Psychological versus sociological variables in studies of volunteer bias in surveys. *Journal of Applied Psychology*, vol. 45, no. 2, pp. 80-85.

140. **BELL**, C. R. 1962. Personality characteristics of volunteers for psychological studies. *British Journal of Social and Clinical Psychology*, vol. 1, part 2, pp. 81-95.

    BELL, Hugh P. 1954. *See* CLEMENTS, Forrest E., BAYTON, James A. and BELL, Hugh P. 1954.

141. **BELL**, Richard Q. 1962. Isolation of elevation and scatter components in personality and attitude questionnaires. *Educational and Psychological Measurement*, vol. 22, no. 4, pp. 699-713.

142. **BELLOC**, Nedra B. 1954. Validation of morbidity survey data by comparison with hospital records. *Journal of the American Statistical Association*, vol. 49, no. 268, pp. 832-846.

143. **BELSON**, William A. 1956. A technique for studying the effects of a television broadcast. *Applied Statistics*, vol. 5, no. 3, pp. 195-202.

144. **BELSON**, William A. 1958. Measuring the effects of television: a description of method. *Public Opinion Quarterly*, vol. 22, no. 1, pp. 11-18.

145. **BELSON**, William A. 1958. New developments in audience research methods. *American Journal of Sociology*, vol. 64, no. 2, pp. 174-179.

146. **BELSON**, W[illiam] A. 1959. Matching and prediction in the social sciences. *Nature*, vol. 183, no. 46631, pp. 772.

147. **BELSON**, William A. 1959. Matching and prediction on the

principle of biological classification. *Applied Statistics*, vol. 8, no. 2, pp. 65-75.

148. BELSON, William A. 1959. Research for programme planning in television. London: Association Television Ltd., 1959. 15pp. (*ATV technical research studies, no. 3*).

149. BELSON, William A. 1959. Scientific matching made easy. *Commentary*, no. 1, pp. 8-13.

150. BELSON, William A. 1960. Volunteer bias in test-room groups. *Public Opinion Quarterly*, vol. 24, no. 1, pp.115-126.

151. BELSON, William A. 1961. Matching and prediction on the principle of biological classification. *Commentary*, no. 5, pp. 6-18.

152. BELSON, W[illiam] A. 1961. Techniques for measuring the effects of exposure to the mass media. *Business Review*, May, 1961, pp. 109-114.

153. BELSON, William [A.] and DUNCAN, Judith A. 1962. A comparison of the check-list and the open response questioning systems. *Applied Statistics*, vol. 2, no. 2, pp. 120-132.

154. BELSON, William A. 1963. A reply to Parker's note. *Public Opinion Quarterly*, vol. 27, no. 2, pp. 321-329.

155. BELSON, William A. 1963. Accuracy levels in a national readership survey. *MARKET RESEARCH SOCIETY. Research in advertising.* London: Market Research Society with the Oakwood Press, 1963. pp. 82-93.

156. BELSON, William A. 1963. Group testing in market research. *Journal of Advertising Research*, vol. 3, no. 2, pp. 39-43.

157. BELSON, William A. 1963. Tape recording: its effect upon accuracy of response in survey interviews. London: London School of Economics, Survey Research Unit, 1963. 24pp.

158. BELSON, W[illiam] A. 1963. The best method of classifying informants in media studies, having regard to the end-usage of such studies for marketing purposes. *The Roy Thomson medals and awards for media research 1963*. London: The Thomson Organisation, 1963. pp. 9-30.

159. BELSON, William A. 1965. Increasing the power of research to guide advertising decisions. *Journal of Marketing*, vol. 29, no. 2, pp. 35-42.

160. BELSON, William A. 1966. The effects of reversing the presentation order of verbal rating scales. *Journal of Advertising Research*, vol. 6, no. 4, pp. 30-37.

161. BELSON, William A. 1967. Tape recording: its effect on accuracy of response in survey interviews. *Journal of Marketing Research*, vol. 4, no. 3, pp. 253-260.

162. BELSON, William A. 1968. Respondent understanding of survey questions. *Polls*, vol. 3, no. 4, pp. 1-13.

163. BELSON, W[illiam] [A.], MILLERSON, G. L. and DIDCOTT, P[eter] J. 1968. The development of a procedure for eliciting information from boys about the nature and extent of their stealing. London: London School of Economics, Survey Research Centre, 1968. vi, 337pp.

164. BELSON, William A. 1969. Measuring the influence of television programmes and campaigns. *Advancement of Science*, vol. 25, no. 126, pp. 422-429.

165. BELSON, William A. and QUINN, Susan B. 1969. The semantic differential scaling system in market research, III: interviewer deviations from instructions. London: London School of Economics, Survey Research Centre, 1969. v, 84pp.

166. BELSON, William A. and YULE, V. R. 1969. The semantic differential scaling system in market research, II: accuracy of ratings. London: London School of Economics, Survey Research Centre, 1969. vi, 103pp.

BELSON, William A. 1969. *See* QUINN, Susan B. and BELSON, William A. 1969.

BELSON, William A. 1970. *See* QUINN, Susan B. and BELSON, William A. 1970.

167. BELT, Jorge. 1963. The technique of non-directive interviews. *Scientific Business*, vol. 1, no. 3, pp. 245-248.

168. BENDIG, A. W. 1953. The reliability of self-rating as a function of the amount of verbal anchoring and the number of categories on the scale. *Journal of Applied Psychology*, vol. 37, no. 1, pp. 38-41.

169. BENDIG, A. W. 1954. Reliability and the number of rating scale categories. *Journal of Applied Psychology*, vol. 38, no. 1, pp. 38-40.

170. BENDIG, A. W. 1954. Reliability of short rating scales and the heterogeneity of the rated stimuli. *Journal of Applied Psychology*, vol. 38, no. 3, pp. 167-170.

171. BENGSTON, Roger and BRENNER, Henry. 1964. Product test results using three different methodologies. *Journal of Marketing Research*, vol. 1, no. 4, pp. 49-52.

172. **BENJAMIN**, B. 1954/55. Quality of response in census taking. *Population Studies*, vol. 8, no. 3, pp. 288-293.

173. **BENJAMIN**, B. 1960. Statistical problems connected with the 1961 population census. *Journal of the Royal Statistical Society, series A*, vol. 123, part 4, pp. 413-426.

174. **BENJAMIN**, Kurt. 1947. Problems of multiple-punching with Hollerith machines. *Journal of the American Statistical Association*, vol. 42, no. 237, pp. 46-71.

175. **BENJAMIN**, Kurt. 1950. On coding and tabulating errors. *Public Opinion Quarterly*, vol. 14, no. 2, pp. 385-386.

176. **BENJAMIN**, W. 1968. How accurate a sample when drawn from the electoral register. *Commentary*, vol. 10, no. 1, pp. 58-59.

177. **BENNETT**, Archibald S. 1945. Some aspects of preparing questionnaires. *Journal of Marketing*, vol. 10, no. 2, pp. 175-179.

178. **BENNETT**, Archibald S. 1947. How good are local interviewers in market research? *Printer's Ink*, vol. 221, no. 3, pp. 70, 72, 74.

179. **BENNETT**, Archibald S. 1948. Observations on the so-called cheater problem among field interviewers. *International Journal of Opinion and Attitude Research*, vol. 2, no. 1, pp. 89-96.

180. **BENNETT**, Archibald S. 1948. Toward a solution to the 'cheater problem' among part-time research investigators. *Journal of Marketing*, vol. 12, no. 4, pp. 470-474.

BENNETT, John W. 1957. *See* RYCHLAK, Joseph K., MUSSEN, Paul H. and BENNETT, John W. 1957.

181. **BENNEY**, Mark and HUGHES, Everett C. 1956. Of sociology and the interview: editorial preface. *American Journal of Sociology*, vol. 62, no. 2, pp. 137-142.

182. **BENNEY**, Mark, RIESMAN, David and STAR, Shirley, A. 1956. Age and sex in the interview. *American Journal of Sociology*, vol. 62, no. 2, pp. 143-152.

BENSMAN, J. 1954. *See* VIDICH, A. and BENSMAN, J. 1954.

183. **BENSON**, Edward G. 1940. Three words. *Public Opinion Quarterly*, vol. 4, no. 1, pp. 130-134.

184. **BENSON**, Lawrence E. 1941. Studies in secret-ballot technique. *Public Opinion Quarterly*, vol. 5, no. 1, pp. 79-82.

185. **BENSON**, Lawrence E. 1946. Mail surveys can be valuable. *Public Opinion Quarterly*, vol. 10, no. 2, pp. 234-241.

186. BENSON, Purnell H. 1955. A model for the analysis of consumer preference and an exploratory test. *Journal of Applied Psychology*, vol. 39, no. 5, pp. 375-381.

187. BENSON, P[urnell] H. 1956. The marginal preference model: scope for application. *Journal of Marketing*, vol. 21, no. 2, pp. 171-174.

188. BENSON, Purnell H. and BENTLEY, Evelyn. 1957. Sources of sampling bias in sex studies. *Public Opinion Quarterly*, vol. 21, no. 3, pp. 388-394.

189. BENSON, Purnell H. 1964. Eliminating consumer biases in survey data by balanced tabulation. *Journal of Marketing Research*, vol. 1, no. 4, pp. 66-71.

190. BENSON, Purnell H. 1969. A paired comparison approach to evaluating interviewer performance. *Journal of Marketing Research*, vol. 6, no. 1, pp. 66-70.

191. BENSON, Sherwood, BOOMAN, Wesley P. and CLARK, Kenneth E. 1951. A study of interview refusals. *Journal of Applied Psychology*, vol. 35, no. 2, pp. 116-119.

BENTLEY, Evelyn. 1957. *See* BENSON, Purnell H. and BENTLEY, Evelyn. 1957.

BERDY, D[avid]. 1967. *See* GOODSON, C. and BERDY, D[avid]. 1967.

192. BERDY, David. 1969. Order effects in taste tests. *Journal of the Market Research Society*, vol. 11, no. 4, pp. 361-371.

BERG, Irwin A. 1951. *See* CAREY, James F., *Jr.*, BERG, Irwin A. and VAN DUSEN, A. C. 1951.

193. BERG, Irwin A. and RAPAPORT, Gerald M. 1954. Response bias in an unstructured questionnaire. *Journal of Psychology*, vol. 38, no. 2, pp. 475-481.

194. BERG, Irwin A. 1955. Response bias and personality: the deviation hypothesis. *Journal of Psychology*, vol. 40, no. 1, pp. 61-72.

BERGER, Philip K. 1962. *See* KIRSCH, Arthur D., BERGER, Philip K. and BELFORD, R. J. 1962.

195. BERKSON, Joseph. 1941. A punch card designed to contain written data and coding. *Journal of the American Statistical Association*, vol. 36, no. 216, pp. 535-538.

BERMINGHAM, John. 1968. *See* BATES, Brian and BERMINGHAM, John. 1968.

BERNBERG, Raymond E. 1950. *See* WESCHLER, Irving R. and BERNBERG, Raymond E. 1950.

196. **BERNBERG**, Raymond E. 1951. The direction of perception technique of attitude measurement. *International Journal of Opinion and Attitude Research*, vol. 5, no. 3, pp. 397-406.

197. **BERROL**, Edward and HOLMES, Olive. 1952/53. Survey and area approaches to international communications research. *Public Opinion Quarterly*, vol. 16, no. 4, pp. 567-578.

BERSHAD, Max A. 1959. *See* HANSEN, Morris H., HURWITZ, William N. and BERSHAD, Max A. 1959.

BERSHAD, Max A. 1961. *See* HANSEN, Morris H., HURWITZ, William N. and BERSHAD, Max A. 1961.

198. **BERSHAD**, Max A. and TEPPING, Benjamin J. 1969. The development of household sample surveys. *Journal of the American Statistical Association*, vol. 64, no. 328, pp. 1134-1140.

199. **BEUM**, Corlin O. and CRISWELL, Joan H. 1947. Application of machine tabulation methods to sociometric data. *Sociometry*, vol. 10, no. 3, pp. 227-232.

200. **BEVILLE**, H. M., *Jr.* 1940. The ABCD's of radio audiences. *Public Opinion Quarterly*, vol. 4, no. 2, pp. 195-206.

201. **BEVILLE**, H. M., *Jr.* 1949. Surveying radio listeners by use of a probability sample. *Journal of Marketing*, vol. 14, no. 3, pp. 373-378.

202. **BEVIS**, Joseph C. 1945. Management of field staffs in the opinion research field. *Journal of the American Statistical Association*, vol. 40, no. 230, pp. 245-246.

203. **BEVIS**, Joseph C. 1948. Economical incentive used for mail questionnaire. *Public Opinion Quarterly*, vol. 12, no. 3, pp. 492-493.

204. **BEVIS**, Joseph C. 1949. Interviewing with tape recorders. *Public Opinion Quarterly*, vol. 13, no. 4, pp. 629-634.

BIDWELL, Charles E. 1959. *See* JACKSON, David M. and BIDWELL, Charles E. 1959.

205. **BIEL**, Alexander L. 1967. Abuses of survey research techniques: the phony interview. *Public Opinion Quarterly*, vol. 31, no. 2, pp. 298.

206. **BIGELOW**, Charles L. 1947. Confusion control in poster readership study. *Journal of Applied Psychology*, vol. 31, no. 6, pp. 626-633.

207. **BIGELOW**, Charles L. 1948. Elements of confusion in newspaper readership study. *Journal of Marketing*, vol. 12, no. 3, pp. 337-347.
208. **BILLEWICZ**, W. Z. 1965. The efficiency of matched samples: an empirical investigation. *Biometrics*, vol. 21, no. 3, pp. 623-644.

   BIRCH, Catherine M. 1949. *See* DONCEEL, Joseph F., ALIMENA, Benjamin S. and BIRCH, Catherine M. 1949.

   BIRD, Kermit. 1958. *See* FRAZIER, George and BIRD, Kermit. 1958.

   BIRD, M. 1967. *See* JOYCE, T[imothy] and BIRD, M. 1967.

209. **BIRDWHISTELL**, Ray L. 1952. Body motion research and interviewing. *Human Organization*, vol. 11, no. 1, pp. 37-38.
210. **BIRMINGHAM**, W. B. and JAHODA, G. 1955. A pre-election survey in a semi-literate society. *Public Opinion Quarterly*, vol. 19, no. 2, pp. 140-152.
211. **BIRNBAUM**, Z. W. and SIRKEN, Monroe G. 1950. Bias due to non-availability in sampling surveys. *Journal of American Statistical Association*, vol. 45, no. 249, pp. 98-111.
212. **BIRNBAUM**, Z. W. and SIRKEN, Monroe G. 1950. On the total error due to non-interview and to random sampling. *International Journal of Opinion and Attitude Research*, vol. 4, no. 2, pp. 179-191.
213. **BIRT**, E. M. and BROGREN, R. H. 1964. Minimizing number of interviews through sequential sampling. *Journal of Marketing Research*, vol. 1, no. 1, pp. 65-67.
214. **BJERSTEDT**, Ake. 1961. The five-step intersubject interview technique in psychological research. *Journal of Psychology*, vol. 51, no. 2, pp. 273-278.
215. **BLACK**, Percy. 1956. Two 'why's?' in the market place. *Journal of Marketing*, vol. 21, no. 2, pp. 163-170.

   BLACKWELL, Roger D. 1969. *See* ENGEL, James F., KOLLAT, David T. and BLACKWELL, Roger D. 1969.

   BLAINE, Harry R. 1966. *See* SCHWIRIAN, Kent P. and BLAINE, Harry R. 1966.

216. **BLAIR**, William S. 1966. Observed vs. reported behavior in magazine reading: an investigation of the editorial interest method. *ADVERTISING RESEARCH FOUNDATION. Annual Conference, 12th, New York City, 1966. Proceedings...* New York: Advertising Research Foundation, 1966. pp. 66-68.

217. **BLAKE**, Robert R., *et al.* 1956. Volunteering as an avoidance act. *Journal of Abnormal and Social Psychology*, vol. 53, no. 2, pp. 154-156.

218. **BLALOCK**, H[ubert] M., *Jr.* 1961. Correlation and causality: the multivariate case. *Social Forces*, vol. 39, no. 3, pp. 246-251.

219. **BLALOCK**, Hubert M., *Jr.* 1962. Further observations on asymmetric causal models. *American Sociological Review*, vol. 27, no. 4, pp. 542-545.

220. **BLALOCK**, H[ubert] M., *Jr.* 1963. Correlated independent variables: the problem of multicollinearity. *Social Forces*, vol. 42, no. 2, pp. 233-237.

221. **BLALOCK**, H[ubert] M., *Jr.* 1963. Making causal inferences for unmeasured variables from correlations among indicators. *American Journal of Sociology*, vol. 69, no. 1, pp. 53-62.

222. **BLALOCK**, H[ubert] M., *Jr.* 1965. Some implications of random measurement error for causal inferences. *American Journal of Sociology*, vol. 71, no. 1, pp. 37-47.

223. **BLALOCK**, Hubert M., *Jr.* 1965. Theory building and the statistical concept of interaction. *American Sociological Review*, vol. 30, no. 4, pp. 374-380.

224. **BLALOCK**, Hubert M. 1967. Causal inferences in natural experiments: some complications in matching designs. *Sociometry*, vol. 30, no. 3, pp. 300-315.

225. **BLALOCK**, Hubert M., *Jr.* 1969. Multiple indicators and the causal approach to measurement error. *American Journal of Sociology*, vol. 75, no. 2, pp. 264-272.

226. **BLANC**, Haim. 1956. Multilingual interviewing in Israel. *American Journal of Sociology*, vol. 62, no. 2, pp. 205-209.

BLANKENSHIP, Albert B. 1939. *See* ROSLOW, Sydney and BLANKENSHIP, Albert B. 1939.

227. **BLANKENSHIP**, Albert B. 1940. Does the question form influence public opinion poll results? *Journal of Applied Psychology*, vol. 24, no. 1, pp. 27-30.

228. **BLANKENSHIP**, Albert B. 1940. Pre-testing a questionnaire for a public opinion poll. *Sociometry*, vol. 3, no. 3, pp. 263-269.

229. **BLANKENSHIP**, Albert B. 1940. The case for and against the public opinion poll. *Journal of Marketing*, vol. 5, no. 2, pp. 110-113.

230. **BLANKENSHIP**, Albert B. 1940. The choice of words in poll questions. *Sociology and Social Research*, vol. 25, no. 1, pp. 12-18.

231. **BLANKENSHIP**, Albert B. 1940. The effect of the interviewer upon the response in a public opinion poll. *Journal of Consulting Psychology*, vol. 4, no. 4, pp. 134-136.

232. **BLANKENSHIP**, Albert B. 1940. The influence of the question form upon the response in a public opinion poll. *Psychological Record*, vol. 3, no. 23, pp. 349-422.

233. **BLANKENSHIP**, Albert B. 1940. The 'sample' study in opinion research. *Sociometry*, vol. 3, no. 3, pp. 271-276.

234. **BLANKENSHIP**, Albert B. 1941. A correction. *Journal of Applied Psychology*, vol. 25, no. 1, pp. 124-127.

235. **BLANKENSHIP**, A[lbert] B. 1942. Psychological difficulties in measuring consumer preference. *Journal of Marketing*, vol. 6, no. 4, (ii), pp. 66-75.

236. **BLANKENSHIP**, Albert B. 1942. These opinion polls again! *Sociometry*, vol. 5, no. 1, pp. 89-101.

237. **BLANKENSHIP**, A[lbert] B., et al. 1947. Survey on problems of interviewer cheating. *International Journal of Opinion and Attitude Research*, vol. 1, no. 3, pp. 93-106.

238. **BLANKENSHIP**, A[lbert] B. 1948. What happened to the polls? *International Journal of Opinion and Attitude Research*, vol. 2, no. 3, pp. 321-328.

239. **BLANKENSHIP**, A[lbert] B. 1949. A source of interviewer bias. *International Journal of Opinion and Attitude Research*, vol. 3, no. 1, pp. 95-98.

240. **BLANKENSHIP**, Albert B., et al. 1949. Questionnaire preparation and interviewer technique. *Journal of Marketing*, vol. 14, no. 3, pp. 399-433.

BLANKENSHIP, A[lbert] B. 1951. *See* PARADISE, L. M. and BLANKENSHIP, A[lbert] B. 1951.

241. **BLANKENSHIP**, A[lbert] B. 1964. Some aspects of ethics in marketing research. *Journal of Marketing Research*, vol. 1, no. 2, pp. 26-31.

242. **BLANKENSHIP**, A[lbert] B. 1966. Let's bury paired comparisons. *Journal of Advertising Research*, vol. 16, no. 1, pp. 13-17.

243. **BLAU**, Peter M. 1955. Determining the dependent variable in

certain correlations. *Public Opinion Quarterly*, vol. 19, no. 1, pp. 100-105.

BLINN, Elaine. 1970. *See* TIFFANY, Donald W., COWAN, James R. and BLINN, Elaine. 1970.

244. **BLOOD**, Robert O., *Jr.* 1955. Respondent reactions to ambiguous items in an attitude scale. *Journal of Abnormal and Social Psychology*, vol. 50, no. 3, pp. 402-403.

245. **BLUM**, Fred H. 1952. Getting individuals to give information to the outsider. *Journal of Social Issues*, vol. 8, no. 3, pp. 35-42.

BLUM, Milton L. 1951. *See* BALINSKY, Benjamin, BLUM, Milton L. and DUTKA, Solomon. 1951.

246. **BLUMENFELD**, Warren S. 1966. A research note on the method of error-choice. *Educational and Psychological Measurement*, vol. 26, no. 4, pp. 847-851.

247. **BLUMER**, Herbert. 1948. Public opinion and public opinion polling. *American Sociological Review*, vol. 13, no. 5, pp. 542-554.

248. **BLUNDEN**, R. M. 1966. Sampling frames. *Commentary*, vol. 8, no. 2, pp. 101-112.

BODINE, Adolph J. 1951. *See* KAHN, Lessing A. and BODINE, Adolph J. 1951.

249. **BOEK**, Walter E. and LADE, James H. 1963. A test of the usefulness of the post-card technique in a mail questionnaire study. *Public Opinion Quarterly*, vol. 27, no. 3, pp. 303-306.

250. **BOGARDUS**, Emory S. 1934. Interviewing as a social process. *Sociology and Social Research*, vol. 19, no. 1, pp. 70-75.

251. **BOGART**, Leo. 1957/58. Measuring the effectiveness of an overseas information campaign: a case history. *Public Opinion Quarterly*, vol. 21, no. 4, pp. 475-498.

252. **BOGART**, Leo. 1967. No opinion, don't know and maybe no answer. *Public Opinion Quarterly*, vol. 31, no. 3, pp. 331-345.

253. **BOGUE**, Donald J. 1965. The pros and cons of 'self-enumeration'. *Demography*, vol. 2, pp. 600-626.

254. **BOOKER**, H. S. and DAVID, S. T. 1952. Differences in results obtained by experienced and inexperienced interviewers. *Journal of Royal Statistical Society, series A,* vol. 15, part 2, pp. 232-257.

BOOMAN, Welsey P. 1951. *See* BENSON, Sherwood, BOOMAN, Wesley P. and CLARK, Kenneth E. 1951.

255. **BOPEGAMAGE**, A. 1966. A methodological problem in Indian urban sociological research. *Sociological and Social Research*, vol. 50, no. 2, pp. 236-240.

256. **BORG**, Lloyd E. 1948. Interviewing school. *International Journal of Opinion and Attitude Research*, vol. 2, no. 3, pp. 393-400.

257. **BORGATTA**, Edgar F. and HAYS, David G. 1952. Some limitations on the arbitrary classification of non-scale response patterns in a Guttman scale. *Public Opinion Quarterly*, vol. 16, no. 3, pp. 410-416.

258. **BORGATTA**, Edgar F. 1955. An error ratio for scalogram analysis. *Public Opinion Quarterly*, vol. 19, no. 1, pp. 96-100.

BORGATTA, Edgar F. 1956. *See* HENRY, Andrew F. and BORGATTA, Edgar F. 1956.

259. **BORGATTA**, Edgar F. 1957. Cumulative scaling as a routine procedure with the IBM 101. *Sociometry*, vol. 20, no. 4, pp. 317-325.

260. **BORUS**, Michael [E.] 1966. Response error in survey reports of earnings information. *Journal of the American Statistical Association*, vol. 61, no. 315, pp. 729-738.

261. **BORUS**, Michael E. 1970. Response error and questioning technique in surveys of earnings information. *Journal of the American Statistical Association*, vol. 65, no. 330, pp. 566-575.

262. **BOSS**, Jean-Francois. 1968. Experiments in merging surveys. *EUROPEAN SOCIETY FOR OPINION AND MARKETING RESEARCH. Congress, XXI, Opatija, 1968. Papers . . .* Brussels: ESOMAR, 1968. pp. 379-385.

263. **BOUDON**, Raymond. 1965. A method of linear causal analysis: dependence analysis. *American Sociological Review*, vol. 30, no. 3, pp. 365-374.

BOWER, Robert T. 1952/53. *See* ERVIN, Susan and BOWER, Robert T. 1952/53.

264. **BOWMAN**, Claude C. 1952. A sour note on questionnaires. *American Sociological Review*, vol. 17, no. 3, p. 362.

265. **BOX**, Kathleen and THOMAS, Geoffrey. 1944. The Wartime Social Survey. *Journal of the Royal Statistical Society*, vol. 107, parts 3-4, pp. 151-177. Discussion . . . pp. 179-189.

BOYD, Harper. 1951. *See* WOMER, Stanley and BOYD, Harper. 1951.

266. **BOYD**, Harper W., *Jr.* and WESTFALL, Ralph. 1955. Interviewers as a source of error in surveys. *Journal of Marketing*, vol. 19, no. 4, pp. 311-324.

BOYD, Harper W., *Jr.* 1957. *See* WESTFALL, Ralph L., BOYD, Harper W., *Jr.* and CAMPBELL, Donald T. 1957.

267. **BOYD**, Harper W., *Jr.* and WESTFALL, Ralph. 1965. Interviewer bias revisited. *Journal of Marketing Research*, vol. 2, no. 1, pp. 58-63.

268. **BOYLE**, Richard P. 1966. Causal theory and statistical measures of effect: a convergence. *American Sociological Review*, vol. 31, no. 6, pp. 843-851.

269. **BRADBURN**, Norman M. and MASON, William M. 1964. The effect of question order on responses. *Journal of Marketing Research*, vol. 1, no. 4, pp. 57-61.

270. **BRADBURN**, Norman M. 1969. Selecting the questions to be asked. *AMERICAN STATISTICAL ASSOCIATION. Proceedings of the Social Statistics Section*, 1969. pp. 178-181.

BRADLEY, Joseph E. 1957. *See* LYSAKER, Richard L. and BRADLEY, Joseph E. 1957.

271. **BRADT**, Kenneth. 1955. The usefulness of a post card technique in a mail questionnaire study. *Public Opinion Quarterly*, vol. 19, no. 2, pp. 218-222.

272. **BRADY**, Dorothy S. 1954. The Kinsey report on females. *Journal of the American Statistical Association*, vol. 49, no. 268, pp. 696-705.

BRAINE, R. L. 1967. *See* FROST, W. A. K. and BRAINE, R. L. 1967.

273. **BRENNAN**, Robert D. 1958. Trading stamps as an incentive in mail surveys. *Journal of Marketing*, vol. 22, no. 3, pp. 306-307.

BRENNER, Henry. 1964. *See* BENGSTON, Roger and BRENNER, Henry. 1964.

BRESSLER, Marvin. 1958. *See* KEPHART, William M. and BRESSLER, Marvin. 1958.

274. **BRICHLER**, M. 1958. Classification of the population by social and economic characteristics: the French experience and international recommendations. *Journal of the Royal Statistical Society*, series A, vol. 121, part 2, pp. 161-189. Discussion on M. Brichler's paper, pp. 189-195.

275. **BRIGGS**, Peter F. WIRT, Robert D. and JOHNSON, Rochelle. 1961. An application of prediction tables to the study of delinquency. *Journal of Consulting Psychology*, vol. 25, no. 1, pp. 46-50.

BRIGHT, Margaret. 1957. *See* KINCAID, Harry V. and BRIGHT, Margaret. 1957.

BRIGHT, Margaret. 1957. *See* KINCAID, Harry V. and BRIGHT, Margaret. 1957.

BRINSER, Ayres. 1958. *See* ALLISON, Harry E., ZWICK, Charles J. and BRINSER, Ayres. 1958.

276. **BRINTON**, James E. 1957. Subscriber vs. non-subscriber method for studying effects. *Journalism Quarterly*, vol. 34, Winter 1957, pp. 92-93.

277. **BRINTON**, James E. and DANIELSON, Wayne A. 1958. A factor analysis of language elements affecting readability. *Journalism Quarterly*, vol. 35, Fall, pp. 420-426.

278. **BRINTON**, James E. 1961. Deriving an attitude scale from semantic differential data. *Public Opinion Quarterly*, vol. 25, no. 2, pp. 289-295.

BRISTER, David M. 1967. *See* WEBB, James T. and BRISTER, David M. 1967.

BRITT, Steuart Henderson. 1947. *See* EDGERTON, Harold A., BRITT, Steuart Henderson and NORMAN, Ralph D. 1947.

279. **BRITT**, Steuart Henderson. 1955. Four hazards of motivation research: how to avoid them. *Printer's Ink*, vol. 251, no. 11, pp. 40, 45, 48.

280. **BRITTON**, Joseph H. and BRITTON, Jean Oppenheimer. 1951. Factors in the return of questionnaires mailed to older persons. *Journal of Applied Psychology*, vol. 35, no. 1, pp. 57-60.

BRITTON, Jean Oppenheimer. 1951. *See* BRITTON, Joseph H. and BRITTON, Jean Oppenheimer. 1951.

281. **BROADBENT**, Simon and MOONEY, Peter. 1968. Can informant claims on product purchase made at an interview be used for media planning? *Admap,* vol. 4, no. 11, pp. 544-547.

282. **BROADBENT**, Simon and MASSON, Peter. 1969. Informant classification in media and product surveys, part 1. *Admap,* vol. 5, no. 1, pp. 18, 20-22, 24, 26.

283. **BROADBENT**, Simon and MASSON, Peter. 1969. Informant classification in media and product surveys, part 2. *Admap*, vol. 5, no. 2, pp. 52-54, 56-57, 76.

BROADBENT, Simon. 1970. *See* SEGNIT, Susanna and BROADBENT, Simon. 1970.

284. **BROCK**, Timothy C. and BECKER, Gilbert. 1965. Birth order and subject recruitment. *Journal of Social Psychology*, vol. 65, no. 1, pp. 63-66.

285. **BROEN**, William E., *Jr.* and WIRT, Robert D. 1958. Varieties of response sets. *Journal of Consulting Psychology*, vol. 22, no. 3, pp. 237-240.

286. **BROGDEN**, Hubert E. and TAYLOR, Erwin K. 1950. The theory and classification of criterion bias. *Educational and Psychological Measurement*, vol. 10, no. 2, pp. 159-186.

BROGREN, R. H. 1964. *See* BIRT, E. M. and BROGREN, R. H. 1964.

287. **BROOK**, Caspar. 1963. Testing by consumers. *The Statistician*, vol. 13, no. 1, pp. 33-43.

288. **BROOKOVER**, Linda and BACK, Kurt W. 1966. Time sampling as a field technique. *Human Organization*, vol. 25, no. 1, pp. 64-70.

289. **BROTHERTON**, P. A. 1968. The use of the diary technique for measuring product usage. Bradford: University of Bradford, Management Centre, 1968. 48ff. (*Research dissertation in marketing series, no. 5*).

290. **BROWER**, Daniel. 1948. The role of incentive in psychological research. *Journal of General Psychology*, vol. 39, no. 1, pp. 145-147.

BROWN, Donald E. 1949. *See* HARRELL, Thomas W., BROWN, Donald E. and SCHRAMM, Wilbur. 1949.

291. **BROWN**, Geo[rge] H. 1947. A comparison of sampling methods. *Journal of Marketing*, vol. 11, no. 4, pp. 331-337.

292. **BROWN**, George H. 1950. Measuring consumer attitudes toward products. *Journal of Marketing*, vol. 14, no. 5, pp. 691-698.

293. **BROWN**, J. Marshall. 1955. Respondents rate public opinion interviewers. *Journal of Applied Psychology*, vol. 39, no. 2, pp. 96-102.

294. **BROWN**, Michael M. 1965. Readership estimates: concord or dissonance? *Commentary*, vol. 7, no. 2, pp. 75-81.

295. BROWN, Michael M. 1968. Pre-testing press advertisements. *Admap*, vol. 4, no. 3, pp. 112-114, 116, 118, 120-121.

296. BROWN, Morton L. 1965. Use of a postcard query in mail surveys. *Public Opinion Quarterly*, vol. 29, no. 4, pp. 635-637.

297. BROWN, Nicholas. 1960. Consumer placement blind testing. *Commentary*, no. 3, pp. vi-ix.

298. BROWN, Rex V. 1967. Evaluation of total survey error. *Journal of Marketing Research*, vol. 4, no. 2, pp. 117-127.

BROWN, Roger W. 1956. *See* HILDUM, Donald C. and BROWN, Roger W. 1956.

299. BROWNLEE, K. A. 1957. A note on the effects of nonresponse on surveys. *Journal of the American Statistical Association*, vol. 52, no. 277, pp. 29-32.

300. BRUNK, Max E. and FEDERER, Walter T. 1953. Experimental designs and probability sampling in marketing research. *Journal of the American Statistical Association*, vol. 48, no. 263, pp. 440-452.

301. BRUNNER, G. Allen and CARROLL, Stephen, J., *Jr.* 1967. The effect of prior telephone appointments on completion rates and response content. *Public Opinion Quarterly*, vol. 31, no. 4, pp. 652-654.

302. BRUNNER, G. Allen and CARROLL, Stephen J., *Jr.* 1969. Weekday evening interviews of employed persons are better. *Public Opinion Quarterly*, vol. 33, no. 2, pp. 265-267.

303. BRYAN, Alice I. and WILKE, Walter H. 1942. Audience tendencies in rating public speakers. *Journal of Applied Psychology*, vol. 26, no. 3, pp. 371-381.

BRYAN, Sam Dunn. 1963. *See* DANIELSON, Wayne A. and BRYAN, Sam Dunn. 1963.

304. BRYANT, Eugene C., GARDNER, Isaac, *Jr.*, and GOLDMAN, Morton. 1966. Responses on racial attitudes as affected by interviewers of different ethnic groups. *Journal of Social Psychology*, vol. 70, no. 1, pp. 95-100.

305. BUCHER, Rue, FRITZ, Charles E. and QUARANTELLI, E. L. 1956. Tape recorded interviews in social research. *American Sociological Review*, vol. 21, no. 3, pp. 359-364.

306. BUCHER, Rue, FRITZ, Charles E. and QUARANTELLI, E. L. 1956. Tape recorded research: some field and data processing problems. *Public Opinion Quarterly*, vol. 20, no. 2, pp. 427-439.

307. BUCK, S. F. 1960. A method of estimation of missing values in multivariate data suitable for use with an electronic computer. *Journal of the Royal Statistical Society, series B*, vol. 22, no. 2, pp. 302-306.

308. BUCK, S. F. 1966. A new look at old data. *Commentary*, vol. 8, no. 4, pp. 263-277.

309. BUCK, S. F. 1966. Problems and procedures in continuous sampling. *Commentary*, vol. 8, no. 2, pp. 92-100.

310. BUCK, S. F. and WEST, M. J. 1968. Consistency of purchasing and television viewing behaviour: optimum periods for study. *Commentary*, vol. 10, no. 4, pp. 234-252.

311. BUCKHOUT, Robert and ROSENBERG, Milton J. 1966. Verbal reinforcement and attitude change. *Psychological Reports*, vol. 18, no. 3, pp. 691-694.

312. BUDD, Richard W. 1964. Attention score: a device for measuring news 'play'. *Journalism Quarterly*, vol. 41, no. 2, pp. 259-262.

313. BUGELSKI, B. R. 1949. A note on Grant's discussion of the latin square principle in the design of experiments. *Psychological Bulletin*, vol. 46, no. 1, pp. 49-50.

314. BURCHINAL, Lee G. 1960. Personality characteristics and sample bias. *Journal of Applied Psychology*, vol. 44, no. 3, pp. 172-174.

BURGER, Philip C. 1967. *See* PESSEMIER, Edgar A., BURGER, Philip C. and TIGERT, Douglas J. 1967.

BURKE, C[letus] J. 1947. *See* MEIER, Norman C. and BURKE, C[letus] J. 1947.

BURKE, C[letus] J. 1949. *See* LEWIS, Don and BURKE, C[letus] J. 1949.

BURKHEAD, C. E. 1949. *See* SCHOLL, J. C. and BURKHEAD, C. E. 1949.

315. BURTT, Harold E. and GASKILL, Harold V. 1932. Suggestibility and the form of the question. *Journal of Applied Psychology*, vol. 16, no. 4, pp. 358-373.

316. BURTT, Harold E. 1941. The association reaction as a measurement of attitude. *Journal of Social Psychology*, vol. 14, no. 2, pp. 363-368.

317. BURWEN, Leroy S., CAMPBELL, Donald T. and KIDD, Jerry. 1956. The use of a sentence completion test in measuring attitudes toward superiors and subordinates. *Journal of Applied Psychology*, vol. 40, no. 4, pp. 248-250.

318. **BUSH**, Chilton R. 1960. A system of categories for general news content. *Journalism Quarterly*, vol. 37, no. 2, pp. 206-210.

319. **BUSH**, Chilton R. 1960. Content and 'mise en valeur': attention as effect. *Journalism Quarterly*, vol. 37, no. 3, pp. 435-437.

320. **BUTCHER**, H. J. 1956. A note on the scale product and related methods of scoring attitude scales. *British Journal of Psychology*, vol. 47, part 2, pp. 133-139.

   BUTCHER, H. J. 1962. See CATTELL, R. B., HORN, J. and BUTCHER, H. J. 1962.

   BUTLER, Bruce V. 1955. See GENGERELLI, J. A. and BUTLER, Bruce V. 1955.

   BUTLER, Edgar W. 1965. See MERCER, Jane R. and BUTLER, Edgar W. 1965.

321. **BUTLER**, John M. 1948. On the role of directive and non-directive techniques in the counselling process. *Educational and Psychological Measurement*, vol. 8, no. 2, pp. 201-209.

322. **BYHAM**, William C. and PERLOFF, Robert. 1965. Recall of product purchase and use after six years. *Journal of Advertising Research*, vol. 5, no. 3, pp. 16-19.

323. **BYNNER**, J. M. [196-]. Preparing questionnaire data in order to carry out a factor analysis. London: Office of Population Censuses and Surveys, Social Survey Division, [196–]. 2pp. (*Methodological series, M126*).

   BYNNER, J. M. 1968. See PARKER, S. R. and BYNNER, J. M. 1968.

324. **CAFFREY**, Bernard and CAPEL, William C. 1968. The predictive value of neutral positions in opinion and attitude research. *Journal of Psychology*, vol. 69, no. 2, pp. 145-154.

325. **CAFFYN**, John M. 1964. Psychological laboratory techniques in copy research. *Journal of Advertising Research*, vol. 4, no. 4, pp. 45-50.

326. **CAFFYN**, John [M.] and LOYD, Alison. 1968. Predicting effects of brand name and consumer proposition on consumer purchase decisions: a case history. *Admap*. vol. 4, no. 11, pp. 538, 540-542, 556.

327. **CAHALAN**, Don, and MEIER, Norman C. 1939. The validity of mail-ballot polls. *Psychological Record*, vol. 3, no. 1, pp. 3-11.

328. **CAHALAN**, Don, TAMULONIS, Valerie and VERNER, Helen W. 1947. Interviewer bias involved in certain types of opinion survey

questions. *International Journal of Opinion and Attitude Research*, vol. 1, no. 1, pp. 63-77.

329. **CAHALAN**, Don. 1949. Implications to the social sciences of the 1948 mispredictions. *International Journal of Opinion and Attitude Research*, vol. 3, no. 2, pp. 157-168.

330. **CAHALAN**, Don. 1951. Effectiveness of a mail questionnaire technique in the Army. *Public Opinion Quarterly*, vol. 15, no. 3, pp. 575-578.

331. **CAHALAN**, Don. 1960. Measuring newspaper readership by telephone: two comparisons with face-to-face interviews. *Journal of Advertising Research*, vol. 1, no. 2, pp. 1-6.

332. **CAHALAN**, Don. 1968. Correlates of respondent accuracy in the Denver validity study. *Public Opinion Quarterly*, vol. 32, no. 4, pp. 607-621.

333. **CALLENDER**, Martin. 1966. Industrial research for exports in Europe. *Commentary*, vol. 8, no. 3, pp. 199-204.

334. **CAMPBELL**, Albert A. 1945. Two problems in the use of the open question. *Journal of Abnormal and Social Psychology*, vol. 40, no. 3, pp. 340-343.

335. **CAMPBELL**, Angus. 1946. Polling, open interviewing, and the problem of interpretation. *Journal of Social Issues*, vol. 2, no. 4, pp. 67-71.

336. **CAMPBELL**, Angus. 1948. Attitude stability and change; a re-interview study of the national population. *American Psychologist*, vol. 3, no. 7, pp. 272.

337. **CAMPBELL**, Donald T. 1949. Bias in mail surveys. *Public Opinion Quarterly*, vol. 13, no. 4, pp. 562.

338. **CAMPBELL**, Donald T. 1950. The indirect assessment of social attitudes. *Psychological Bulletin*, vol. 47, no. 1, pp. 15-38.

339. **CAMPBELL**, Donald T. and MOHR, Phillip J. 1950. The effect of ordinal position upon responses to items in a check list. *Journal of Applied Psychology*, vol. 34, no. 1, pp. 62-67.

CAMPBELL, Donald T. 1950. *See* WYATT, Dale F. and CAMPBELL, Donald T. 1950.

340. **CAMPBELL**, Donald T. 1955. The informant in quantitative research. *American Journal of Sociology*, vol. 60, no. 4, pp. 339-342.

CAMPBELL, Donald T. 1956. *See* BURWEN, Leroy S., CAMPBELL, Donald T. and KIDD, Jerry. 1956.

341. **CAMPBELL**, Donald T. 1957. Factors relevant to the validity of experiments in social settings. *Psychological Bulletin*, vol. 54, no. 4, pp. 297-312.

342. **CAMPBELL**, Donald T. and TYLER, Bonnie B. 1957. The construct validity of work-group morale measures. *Journal of Applied Psychology*, vol. 41, no. 2, pp. 91-92.

CAMPBELL, Donald T. 1957. *See* WESTFALL, Ralph L., BOYD Harper, W., *Jr.* and CAMPBELL, Donald T. 1957.

CAMPBELL, Donald T. 1960. *See* MAHER, Brendan A., WATT, Norman, and CAMPBELL, Donald T. 1960.

CAMPBELL, Donald T. 1960. *See* THISTLETHWAITE, Donald L. and CAMPBELL, Donald T. 1960.

CAMPBELL, Donald T. 1965. *See* HICKS, Jack M. and CAMPBELL, Donald T. 1965.

343. **CAMPBELL**, Donald T., SIEGMAN, Carole R. and REES, Matilda B. 1967. Direction-of-wording effects in the relationships between scales. *Psychological Bulletin*, vol. 68, no. 5, pp. 293-303.

344. **CAMPBELL**, Donald T. 1968. A cooperative multinational opinion sample exchange. *Journal of Social Issues*, vol. 24, no. 2, pp. 245-256.

CAMPBELL, Donald T. 1969. *See* WINCH, Robert F. and CAMPBELL, Donald T. 1969.

345. **CAMPBELL**, Ernest Q. and KERCKHOFF, Alan C. 1957. A critique of the concept 'universe of attributes'. *Public Opinion Quarterly*, vol. 21, no. 2, pp. 295-303.

346. **CAMPBELL**, Ernest Q. 1962. Scale and intensity analysis in the study of attitude change. *Public Opinion Quarterly*, vol. 26, no. 2, pp. 227-235.

347. **CAMPBELL**, James W. 1948. An attitude survey in a typical manufacturing firm. *Personnel Psychology*, vol. 1, no. 1, pp. 31-39.

348. **CAMPBELL**, Roy H. 1965. A managerial approach to advertising measurement. *Journal of Marketing*, vol. 29, no. 4, pp. 1-6.

349. **CANNELL**, Charles F. and KAHN, Robert L. 1953. The collection of data by interviewing. *FESTINGER, L. and KATZ, D., eds. Research methods in the behavioral sciences.* New York: Dryden Press, 1953, pp. 327-379.

350. **CANNELL**, Charles F. and AXELROD, Morris. 1956. The respondent reports on the interview. *American Journal of Sociology*, vol. 62, no. 2, pp. 177-181.

CANNELL, Charles F. 1959/60. *See* AXELROD, Morris and CANNELL, Charles F. 1959/60.

351. **CANNELL**, Charles F. and FOWLER, Floyd J. 1963. Comparison of a self-enumerative procedure and a personal interview: a validity study. *Public Opinion Quarterly*, vol. 27, no. 2, pp. 250-264.

352. **CANNELL**, Charles F. and FOWLER, Floyd J., *Jr.* 1964. A note on interviewer effect in self-enumerative procedures. *American Sociological Review*, vol. 29, no. 2, pp. 270.

353. **CANNELL**, Charles F. and MARQUIS, Kent H. 1966. An experimental study comparing three interviewing techniques in the NHS-HIS. Ann Arbor, Michigan: University of Michigan, Survey Research Center, 1966. iii, 59ff.

354. **CANNELL**, Charles F. and MARQUIS, Kent H. 1967. Effect of some experimental interviewing techniques on reporting in the health interview survey. Ann Arbor, Michigan: University of Michigan, Survey Research Center, 1967. 89pp.

355. **CANNELL**, Charles F. and KAHN, Robert L. 1968. Interviewing. *LINDZEY, Gardner and ARONSON, Elliot, eds. The handbook of social psychology*. 2nd ed. Reading, Massachusetts; London: Addison-Wesley, 1968. v.2. pp. 526-595.

CANNELL, Charles F. 1968. *See* NATIONAL CENTER FOR HEALTH STATISTICS. Vital and Health Statistics. 1968.

356. **CANTER**, Ralph R., *Jr.* 1951. The use of extended control-group designs in human relations studies. *Psychological Bulletin*, vol. 48, no. 4, pp. 340-347.

357. **CANTER**, Stanley D. 1967. Alternative criteria in evaluating TV commercials. *ADVERTISING RESEARCH FOUNDATION. Annual Conference, 13th, New York City, 1967. Proceedings...* New York: Advertising Research Foundation, 1967. pp. 70-77.

358. **CANTRIL**, Hadley, *ed.* 1937. Technical research. *Public Opinion Quarterly*, vol. 1, no. 1, pp. 105-109.

CANTRIL, Hadley. 1937. *See* KATZ, Daniel and *CANTRIL, Hadley*, 1937.

359. **CANTRIL**, Hadley. 1940. Experiments in the wording of questions. *Public Opinion Quarterly*, vol. 4, no. 2, pp. 330-332.

360. **CANTRIL**, Hadley. 1944. The use of breakdowns. *CANTRIL, Hadley, et al. Gauging public opinion.* Princeton: Princeton University Press; London: H. Milford, Oxford University Press, 1944. pp.175-194.

361. **CANTRIL**, Hadley and FRIED, Edrita. 1944. The meaning of questions. *CANTRIL, Hadley, et al. Gauging public opinion.* Princeton: Princeton University Press; London: H. Milford, Oxford University Press, 1944. pp. 3-22.

362. **CANTRIL**, Hadley, *et al.* 1944. The use of small samples. *CANTRIL, Hadley, et al.Gauging public opinion.* Princeton: Princeton University Press; London: H. Milford, Oxford University Press, 1944. pp. 150-171.

    CANTRIL, Hadley. 1944. *See* MOSTELLER, Frederick and CANTRIL, Hadley, 1944.

    CANTRIL, Hadley. 1944. *See* RUGG, Donald and CANTRIL, Hadley. 1944.

363. **CANTRIL**, Hadley. 1945. Do different polls get the same results? *Public Opinion Quarterly*, vol. 9, no. 1, pp. 61-69.

    CANTRIL, Hadley. 1945. *See* WILLIAMS, Frederick and CANTRIL, Hadley. 1945.

364. **CANTRIL**, Hadley. 1946. The intensity of an attitude. *Journal of Abnormal and Social Psychology*, vol. 41, no. 2, pp. 129-135.

    CANTRIL, Hadley. 1949. *See* HASTORF, Albert H. and CANTRIL, Hadley. 1949.

365. **CAPEL**, W[illiam] C. 1967. Continuities and discontinuities in attitudes of the same persons measured through time. *Journal of Social Psychology*, vol. 73, no. 1, pp. 125-136.

    CAPEL, William C. 1968. *See* CAFFREY, Bernard and CAPEL, William C. 1968.

366. **CAPLOW**, Theodore. 1956. The dynamics of information interviewing. *American Journal of Sociology*, vol. 62, no. 2, pp. 165-171.

367. **CAPRA**, Paul C. and DITTES, James E. 1962. Birth order as a selective factor among volunteer subjects. *Journal of Abnormal and Social Psychology*, vol. 64, no. 4, pp. 302.

    CAPT, Katherine G. 1948. *See* REED, Vergil D., CAPT, Katherine G. and VITRIOL, Herbert A. 1948.

368. **CAREY**, James F., *Jr.*, BERG, Irwin A. and VAN DUSEN, A. C. 1951. Reliability of ratings of employee satisfaction based on written interview records. *Journal of Applied Psychology*, vol. 3, no. 4, pp. 252-255.

CARLSON, J. Spencer. 1959. *See* FINK, Joseph and CARLSON, J. Spencer. 1959.

CARMONE, Frank J. 1969. *See* GREEN, Paul E. and CARMONE, Frank J. 1969.

CARMONE, Frank J. 1969. *See* GREEN, Paul E., CARMONE, Frank J. and FOX, Leo B. 1969.

369. **CARPER**, James and DOOB, Leonard W. 1953/54. Intervening responses between questions and answers in attitude surveys. *Public Opinion Quarterly*, vol. 17, no. 4, pp. 511-519.

CARROLL, Stephen J., *Jr.* 1967. *See* BRUNNER, G. Allen and CARROLL, Stephen J., *Jr.* 1967.

CARROLL, Stephen J., *Jr.* 1969. *See* BRUNNER, G. Allen and CARROLL, Stephen J., *Jr.* 1969.

370. **CARTER**, Launor F. 1963. Survey results and public policy decisions. *Public Opinion Quarterly*, vol. 27, no. 4, pp. 549-557.

371. **CARTER**, Roy E., *Jr.* 1955. Cross-cultural application of four Flesch formulas. *Journalism Quarterly*, vol. 32, Fall, pp. 487-489.

372. **CARTER**, Roy E., *Jr.* 1955. The content response code: a pre-testing procedure. *Journalism Quarterly*, vol. 32, Spring, pp. 147-160.

373. **CARTER**, Roy E., *Jr.* and TROLDAHL, Verling C. 1962. Use of a recall criterion in measuring the educational television audience. *Public Opinion Quarterly*, vol. 26, no. 1, pp. 114-121.

374. **CARTER**, Roy E., *Jr.*, TROLDAHL, Verling C. and SCHUNEMAN, R. Smith. 1963. Interviewer bias in selecting households. *Journal of Marketing*, vol. 27, no. 2, pp. 27-34.

375. **CARTER**, Roy E., *Jr.* and MACDONALD, Neil. 1964. Recognition responses as related to more general reader claims. *Journalism Quarterly*, vol. 41, no. 4, pp. 578-580.

CARTER, Roy E., *Jr.* 1964. *See* TROLDAHL, Verling C. and CARTER, Roy E., *Jr.* 1964.

376. **CARTER**, Roy E., *Jr.* and KLINE, F. Gerald. 1968. An experi-

mental study of two methods of gathering newspaper readership data. *Journalism Quarterly*, vol. 45, no. 2, pp. 118-122.

CARTWRIGHT, Ann. 1951. *See* GRAY, P. G. and CARTWRIGHT, Ann. 1951.

377. **CARTWRIGHT**, Ann. 1957. The effect of obtaining information from different informants on a family morbidity inquiry. *Applied Statistics*, vol. 6, no. 1, pp. 18-25.

378. **CARTWRIGHT**, Ann and TUCKER, Wyn. 1967. An attempt to reduce the number of calls on an interview inquiry. *Public Opinion Quarterly*, vol. 31, no. 2, pp. 299-302.

379. **CASH**, William S. and MOSS, Abigail J. 1969. Methodology study for determining the optimum recall period for the reporting of motor vehicle accidental injuries. *AMERICAN STATISTICAL ASSOCIATION. Proceedings of the Social Statistics Section*, 1969. pp. 364-378.

380. **CASSADY**, Ralph, Jr. 1942. Discussion. *Journal of Marketing*, vol. 6, no. 4, part 2, pp. 87-88.

381. **CASSADY**, Ralph, Jr. 1945. Statistical sampling techniques and marketing research. *Journal of Marketing*, vol. 9, no. 4, pp. 317-341.

CASSIDY, Sally W. 1956. *See* HOFFMAN, Nicholas von and CASSIDY, Sally W. 1956.

382. **CASTLE**, Peter F. C. 1953. A note on the scale-product technique of attitude scale construction. *Occupational Psychology*, vol. 27, no. 2, pp. 104-108.

383. **CATALDO**, Everett F., *et al.* 1970. Card sorting as a technique for survey interviewing. *Public Opinion Quarterly*, vol. 34, no. 2, pp. 202-215.

CATEORA, Philip R. 1963. *See* DOMMERMUTH, William P. and CATEORA, Philip R. 1963.

384. **CATTELL**, R[aymond] B., *et al.* 1949. The objective measurement of attitudes. *British Journal of Psychology*, vol. 40, part 2, pp. 81-90.

385. **CATTELL**, Raymond B. 1952. The three basic factor-analytic research designs – their interrelations and derivatives. *Psychological Bulletin*, vol. 49, no. 5, pp. 499-520.

386. **CATTELL**, Raymond B. and BAGGALEY, Andrew R. 1956. The objective measurement of attitude motivation: development and

evaluation of principles and devices. *Journal of Personality*, vol. 24, no. 4, pp. 401-423.

387. **CATTELL**, R[aymond] B., HORN, J. and BUTCHER, H. J. 1962. The dynamic structure of attitudes in adults: a description of some established factors and of their measurement by the motivational analysis test. *British Journal of Psychology*, vol. 53, no. 1, pp. 57-69.

CATTON, William R., Jr. 1957. See DeFLEUR, Melvin L. and CATTON, William R., Jr. 1957.

CATTON, William R., Jr. 1959. See LARSON, Richard F. and CATTON, William R., Jr. 1959.

388. **CAUTER**, Tom. 1956. Some aspects of classification data in market research. *The Incorporated Statistician*, vol. 6, nos. 3 and 4, pp. 133-144.

CAVALLI-SFORZA, L. L. 1965. See EDWARDS, A. W. F. and CAVALLI-SFORZA, L. L. 1965.

389. **CAVAN**, Ruth Shonle. 1929. Interviewing for life history material. *American Journal of Sociology*, vol. 35, no. 1, pp. 100-115.

390. **CAVAN**, Ruth Shonle. 1933. The questionnaire in a sociological research project. *American Journal of Sociology*, vol. 38, no. 2, pp. 721-727.

391. **CAWL**, Franklin R. 1943. The continuing panel technique. *Journal of Marketing*, vol. 8, no. 1, pp. 45-50.

392. **CEGLIA**, Salvatore. 1968. Data collecting systems for a consumer panel in the field of semi-durable goods. *EUROPEAN SOCIETY FOR OPINION AND MARKETING RESEARCH. Congress, XXI, Opatija, 1968. Papers...* Brussels: ESOMAR, 1968, pp. 669-695.

393. **CENTERS**, Richard. 1963. A laboratory adaption of the conversational procedure for the conditioning of verbal operants. *Journal of Abnormal and Social Psychology*, vol. 67, no. 4, pp. 334-339.

394. **CHABOT**, James. 1950. A simplified example of the use of matrix multiplication for the analysis of sociometric data. *Sociometry*, vol. 13, no. 2, pp. 131-140.

395. **CHAFFEE**, Steven H. and McLEOD, Jack M. 1968. Sensitization in panel design: a co-orientational experiment. *Journalism Quarterly*, vol. 45, no. 1, pp. 661-669.

396. **CHAMPION**, Dean J. and SEAR, Alan M. 1969. Questionnaire

response rate: a methodological analysis. *Social Forces*, vol. 47, no. 3, pp. 335-339.

397. **CHAMPNEY**, Horace and **MARSHALL**, Helen. 1939. Optimal refinement of the rating scale. *Journal of Applied Psychology*, vol. 23, no. 3, pp. 323-331.

398. **CHANDLER**, Margaret. 1954. An evaluation of the group interview. *Human Organization* vol. 13, no. 2, pp. 26-28.

    CHANNON, C. 1966. *See* JOYCE, T[imothy] and CHANNON, C. 1966.

399. **CHAPIN**, F. Stuart. 1943. Some problems in field interviews when using the control group technique in studies in the community. *American Sociological Review*, vol. 8, no. 1, pp. 63-68.

400. **CHAPIN**, F. Stuart. 1948. The role of experimental designs in public opinion research. *International Journal of Opinion and Attitude Research*, vol. 2, no. 3, pp. 333-340.

401. **CHAPIN**, F. Stuart. 1955. Some new tools of statistical analysis and some applications of older tools. *Sociometry*, vol. 18, no. 4, pp, 703-711.

    CHAPMAN, P. J. 1951. *See* COCHRANE, A. L., CHAPMAN, P. J. and OLDHAM, P. D. 1951.

402. **CHAPPELL**, Matthew N. 1942. Factors influencing recall of radio programs. *Public Opinion Quarterly*, vol. 6, no. 1, pp. 107-114.

403. **CHAPPLE**, Albert W. 1956. Do's and don'ts for increasing response. *Printer's Ink*, vol. 255, no. 5, pp. 60, 63-64, 66.

404. **CHEIN**, Isidor. 1949. On evaluating self-surveys. *Journal of Social Issues*, vol. 5, no. 2, pp. 56-63.

405. **CHEVRY**, Gabriel. 1949. Control of a general census by means of an area sampling method. *Journal of the American Statistical Association*, vol. 44, no. 247, pp. 373-379.

406. **CHIEN**, Robert I. 1964. Testing prescription drug promotions. *Journal of Advertising Research*, vol. 4, no. 3, pp. 9-11.

407. **CHOKEL**, Frank J. and **PAYNE**, Stanley L. 1951. A pitfall in cluster samples. *Journal of Marketing*, vol. 15, no. 3, pp. 329-331.

408. **CHRISTOPHER**, Martin. 1969. Cluster analysis and market segmentation. *British Journal of Marketing*, vol. 3, Summer, pp. 99-102.

409. **CHU**, Godwin C. 1964. Problems of cross-cultural communication research. *Journalism Quarterly*, vol. 41, no. 4, pp. 557-562.

410. **CIRLIN**, Bernard D. and PETERMAN, Jack N. 1947. Pre-testing a motion picture: a case history. *Journal of Social Issues*, vol. 3, no. 3, pp. 39-41.

CISIN, Ira H. 1948. *See* ELINSON, Jack and CISIN, Ira H. 1948.

411. **CITRON**, Leonard. 1962. Research into the U.K. cinema advertising audience. *Commentary*, no. 8, pp. 13-16.

CLANCY, Kevin J. 1970. *See* PHILLIPS, Derek L. and CLANCY, Kevin J. 1970.

412. **CLARE**, Donald A. 1968. Language medium and responses to the semantic differential. *Journal of Social Psychology*, vol. 76, no. 2, pp. 271-272.

413. **CLARK**, Alexander L. and WALLIN, Paul. 1955. The accuracy of husbands' and wives' reports of the frequency of marital coitus. *American Sociological Review*, vol. 20, no. 2, pp. 165-173.

414. **CLARK**, E. L. 1926. Value of student interviews. *Journal of Personnel Research*, vol. 5, no. 5, pp. 204-207.

415. **CLARK**, John P. and TIFFT, Larry L. 1966. Polygraph and interview validation of self-reported deviant behaviour. *American Sociological Review*, vol. 31, no. 4, pp. 516-523.

416. **CLARK**, Kenneth E. and KRIEDT, Philip H. 1948. An application of Guttman's new scaling techniques to an attitude questionnaire. *Educational and Psychological Measurement*, vol. 8, no. 2, pp. 215-223.

417. **CLARK**, Kenneth E. 1949. A note on the meaning of poll results. *International Journal of Opinion and Attitude Research*, vol. 3, no. 1, pp. 109-112.

CLARK, Kenneth E. 1949. *See* KRIEDT, Philip H. and CLARK, Kenneth E. 1949.

CLARK, Kenneth E. 1951. *See* BENSON, Sherwood, BOOMAN, Wesley P. and CLARK, Kenneth E. 1951.

CLARK, Margaret Leitner. 1968. *See* CLEVENGER, Theodore, *Jr.*, LAZIER, Gilbert A. and CLARK, Margaret Leitner. 1968.

418. **CLARKE**, T. J. 1967. Product testing in new product development. *Commentary*, vol. 9, no. 3, pp. 135-146.

419. **CLARKSON**, Eleanor P. 1949. Some suggestions for field research supervisors. *Journal of Marketing*, vol. 13, no. 3, pp. 321-329.

420. **CLARKSON**, Eleanor P. 1950. The problem of honesty. *International Journal of Opinion and Attitude Research*, vol. 4, no. 1, pp. 84-90.

421. **CLAUSEN**, Aage R. 1968. Response validity: vote report. *Public Opinion Quarterly*, vol. 32, no. 4, pp. 588-606.

422. **CLAUSEN**, John A. and FORD, Robert N. 1947. Controlling bias in mail questionnaires. *Journal of the American Statistical Association*, vol. 42, no. 240, pp. 497-511.

423. **CLAYCAMP**, H. J. and McCLELLAND, C. W. 1968. Estimating reach and the magic of K. *Journal of Advertising Research*, vol. 8, no. 2, pp. 44-51.

424. **CLEMENS**, John. 1965. Page and advertisement readership studies: the problems of validation. *Commentary*, vol. 7, no. 3, pp. 150-158.

425. **CLEMENS**, John and DUNCAN-JONES, Paul. 1965. The use of the semantic differential in media research. *Admap*, July. pp. 399-401.

426. **CLEMENS**, John and THORNTON, Crossley. 1968. Evaluating non-existent products. *Admap*, vol. 4, no. 5, pp. 232-235.

427. **CLEMENTS**, Forrest E., BAYTON, James A. and BELL, Hugh P. 1954. Method of single stimulus determinations of taste preference. *Journal of Applied Psychology*, vol. 38, no. 6, pp. 446-451.

428. **CLEVENGER**, Theodore, *Jr.,* LAZIER, Gilbert A. and CLARK, Margaret Leitner. 1968. The influence of certain factors on response to the semantic differential. *Public Opinion Quarterly*, vol. 32, no. 4, pp. 675-679.

429. **CLOVER**, Vernon T. 1950. Measuring firmness with which opinions are held. *Public Opinion Quarterly*, vol. 14, no. 2, pp. 338-340.

430. **CLUNIES-ROSS**, Charles. 1970. Multidimensional techniques in market research. *MARKET RESEARCH SOCIETY. Annual Conference, Brighton, March 15th-17th, 1970. Conference papers.* Southampton: Hobb [London: Market Research Society], 1970, pp. 111-124.

431. **COALE**, Ansley J. and STEPHAN, Frederick F. 1962. The case of the Indians and the teen-age widows. *Journal of the American Statistical Association*, vol. 57, no. 298, pp. 338-347.

432. **COBLINER**, W. Godfrey. 1951/52. On the place of projective tests in opinion and attitude surveys. *International Journal of Opinion and Attitude Research*, vol. 5, no. 4, pp. 480-490.

433. **COCHRAN**, William G., MOSTELLER, Frederick and TUKEY, John W. 1953. Statistical problems of the Kinsey report. *Journal of the American Statistical Association*, vol. 48, no. 264, pp. 673-716.

434. **COCHRAN**, W[illiam] G. 1965. The planning of observational studies of human populations. *Journal of the Royal Statistical Society, series A*, vol. 128, part 2, pp. 234-265.

435. **COCHRANE**, A. L., CHAPMAN, P. J. and OLDHAM, P. D. 1951. Observers' errors in taking medical histories. *The Lancet*, vol. 260, May 5th, pp. 1007-1009.

436. **COFFIN**, Thomas E. 1963. A pioneering experiment in assessing advertising effectiveness. *Journal of Marketing*, vol. 27, no. 3, pp. 1-10.

COHEN, Jacob. 1967. *See* NEFF, Walter S. and COHEN, Jacob. 1967.

437. **COHEN**, Louis. 1966. The level of consciousness: a dynamic approach to the recall technique. *Journal of Marketing Research*, vol. 3, no. 2, pp. 142-148.

438. **COHEN**, Louis. 1967. Use of paired-comparison analysis to increase statistical power of ranked data. *Journal of Marketing Research*, vol. 4, no. 3, pp. 309-311.

COHEN, Nathan E. 1949. *See* LAMBERT, Benjamin W. and COHEN, Nathan E. 1949.

439. **COHEN**, Samuel E. and LIPSTEIN, Benjamin. 1956. Response errors in the collection of wage statistics by mail questionnaire. *Journal of the American Statistical Association*, vol. 49, no. 266, pp. 240-250.

440. **COLE**, Dorothy E. 1956. Field work in sample surveys of household income and expenditure. *Applied Statistics*, vol. 5, no. 1, pp. 49-61.

441. **COLE**, Dorothy and UTTING, J. E. G. 1956. Estimating expenditure, saving and income from household budgets. *Journal of the Royal Statistical Society, series A*, vol. 119, part 4, pp. 371-387. Discussion on the paper by Mrs. Cole and Mr. Utting, pp. 387-392.

442. **COLEMAN**, James S. 1957. Multidimensional scale analysis. *American Journal of Sociology*, vol. 63, no. 3, pp. 253-263.

443. **COLEMAN**, James S. 1958/59. Relational analysis: the study of social organizations with survey methods. *Human Organization*, vol. 17, no. 4, pp. 28-36.

444. **COLEMAN**, James S. and MACRAE, Duncan, *Jr.* 1960. Electronic processing of sociometric data for groups up to 1,000 in size. *American Sociological Review*, vol. 25, no. 5, pp. 722-727.

COLLINS, B. J. K. 1968. *See* PARFITT, J[ohn] H. and COLLINS, B. J. K. 1968.

445. **COLLINS**, Gwyn. 1961. Analysis of variance. *Journal of Advertising Research*, vol. 1, no. 6, pp. 40-46.

446. **COLLINS**, Gwyn. 1961. Correlation and regression. *Journal of Advertising Research*, vol. 1, no. 4, pp. 36-40.

447. **COLLINS**, Gwyn. 1961. Factor analysis. *Journal of Advertising Research*, vol. 1, no. 6, pp. 28-32.

448. **COLLINS**, Gwyn. 1961. On methods. *Journal of Advertising Research*, vol. 1, no. 3, pp. 28-33.

449. **COLLINS**, J. and NELSON, B. 1966. Interviewing the married couple. *Journal of Psychology*, vol. 8, no. 3, pp. 46-51.

450. **COLLINS**, Leslie and MONTGOMERY, Caroline. 1969. The origins of motivational research. *British Journal of Marketing*, vol. 3, Summer, pp. 103-113.

451. **COLLINS**, Leslie and MONTGOMERY, Caroline. 1970. Whatever happened to motivation research? end of the messianic hope. *Journal of the Market Research Society*. vol. 12, no. 1, pp. 1-11.

COLLINS, Martin. 1968. *See* MONK, Donald and COLLINS, Martin. 1968.

COLLINS, Sy. 1966. *See* GREENBERG, Allan and COLLINS, Sy. 1966.

452. **COLLINS**, W. Andrew. 1970. Interviewers' verbal idiosyncrasies as a source of bias. *Public Opinion Quarterly*, vol. 34, no. 3, pp. 416-422.

COLOMBOTOS, John. 1968. *See* DOHRENWEND, Barbara Snell, COLOMBOTOS, John and DOHRENWEND, Bruce P. 1968.

COMREY, Andrew L. 1954. *See* WILSON, Robert C. and COMREY, Andrew L. 1954.

CONNELLY, Gordon M. 1942. *See* FIELD, Harry H. and CONNELLY, Gordon M. 1942.

453. **CONNELLY**, Gordon M. 1945. Now let's look at the real problem: validity. *Public Opinion Quarterly*, vol. 9, no. 1, pp. 51-60.

CONNELLY, Gordon M. 1948. *See* HARRIS, Natalie and CONNELLY, Gordon M. 1948.

454. **CONNER**, James R. and WELSCH, Delane E. 1968. Use of domain estimators with unequal probability in sample surveys. *Journal of the American Statistical Association*, vol. 63, no. 328, pp. 984-992.

455. **CONRAD**, Herbert S. 1946. Some principle of attitude-measurement: a reply to 'Opinion-attitude methodology'. *Psychological Bulletin*, vol. 43, no. 6, pp. 570-589.

456. **CONSTERDINE**, Guy. 1968. AMPS TV diaries: is a running-in period really necessary? *Admap*, vol. 4, no. 2, pp. 80-84.

457. **CONSTERDINE**, Guy. 1968. Outdoor research. *Admap*, vol. 4, no. 9, pp. 391-392.

458. **CONSTERDINE**, Guy. 1968. Reading intensity. *Admap*, vol. 4, no. 8, pp. 339-340.

459. **CONSTERDINE**, Guy. 1968. Some recent evidence on television audience research. *Commentary*, vol. 10, no. 1, pp. 38-53.

460. **COOK**, Stuart W. and WELCH, Alfred C. 1940. Methods of measuring the practical effect of polls of public opinion. *Journal of Applied Psychology*, vol. 24, no. 4, pp. 441-454.

461. **COOK**, Stuart W. and SELLTIZ, Claire. 1964. A multiple-indicator approach to attitude measurement. *Psychological Bulletin*, vol. 62, no. 1, pp. 36-55.

462. **COOLEY**, William W. and JONES, Kenneth J. 1964. Computer systems for multivariate statistical analysis. *Educational and Psychological Measurement*, vol. 24, no. 3, pp. 645-653.

463. **COOMBS**, Lolagene and FREEDMAN, Ronald. 1964. Use of telephone interviews in a longitudinal fertility study. *Public Opinion Quarterly*, vol. 28, no. 1, pp. 112-117.

464. **COOPER**, C. A. [196–]. Recruitment and initial training of interviewers for the Passenger Survey. London: Office of Population Censuses and Surveys, Social Survey Division, [196–]. 8pp. (*Methodological series, M109*).

465. **COOPER**, Sanford L. 1964. Random sampling by telephone – an improved method. *Journal of Marketing Research*, vol. 1, no. 4, pp. 45-48.

466. **COPLAND**, Brian D. 1960. Exposure and communication measures of outdoor advertising in Britain. *Journal of Advertising Research*, vol. 1, no. 1, pp. 13-17.

467. **COPLAND**, Brian [D.] 1960. Outdoor indecision. *Commentary*, no. 2, part 2, pp. 11-17.

468. **CORBALLY**, John E., *Jr.* 1956. The critical incident technique and educational research. *Educational Research Bulletin*, vol. 35, no. 3, pp. 57-62.

CORBIN, Horace H., *Jr.* 1938. *See* JENKINS, John G. and CORBIN, Horace H., *Jr.* 1938.

CORBY, Philip G. 1940. *See* ROSLOW, Sydney, WULFECK, Wallace H. and CORBY, Philip G. 1940.

469. **CORDELL**, Warren N. and RAHMEL, Henry A. 1962. Are Nielsen ratings affected by non-cooperation, conditioning or response error? *Journal of Advertising Research*, vol. 2, no. 3, pp. 45-49.

470. **COREY**, Stephen M. 1937. Signed versus unsigned attitude questionnaires. *Journal of Educational Psychology*, vol. 28, no. 2, pp. 144-148.

CORLETT, T[homas]. 1950. *See* GRAY, P[ercy] G. CORLETT, T[homas] and FRANKLAND, Pamela. 1950.

CORLETT, T[homas]. 1950. *See* GRAY, P[ercy] G. and CORLETT, T[homas]. 1950.

CORLETT, T[homas]. 1951. *See* GRAY, P[ercy] G., CORLETT, T[homas] and JONES, Pamela. 1951.

471. **CORLETT**, Thomas. 1952. A use for the jury qualification in sample design. *Applied Statistics*, vol. 1, no. 1, pp. 34-36.

472. **CORLETT**, Thomas. 1953. A change in the proportion of jurors. *Applied Statistics*, vol. 2, no. 3, pp. 193-195.

473. **CORLETT**, Thomas and EDWARDS, Frederick. 1955. Sampling methods. *The Incorporated Statistician*, vol. 5, no. 4, (supplement), pp. 16-36.

474. **CORLETT**, T[homas]. 1960/61. Designing a national probability sample of retail outlets. *Commentary*, no. 4, pp. 31-36.

475. **CORLETT**, T[homas]. 1963. Rapid methods of estimating standard errors of stratified multi-stage samples: a preliminary investigation. *The Statistician*, vol. 13, no. 1, pp. 5-16.

476. **CORLETT**, Thomas. 1964. The IPA national readership survey: some problems and possible solutions. *Journal of Advertising Research*, vol. 4, no. 4, pp. 4-10.

477. **CORLETT**, T[homas]. 1965. Sampling errors in practice. *Commentary*, vol. 7, no. 3, pp. 127-138.

CORMAN, T. 1969. *See* HART, H.'t., CORMAN, T. and ZEE, H. van der. 1969.

478. **CORNFIELD**, Jerome. 1942. On certain biases in samples of human populations. *Journal of the American Statistical Association*, vol. 37, no. 217, pp. 63-68.

479. **CORSINI**, Raymond J. 1948. The pin prick method of secret balloting. *Journal of Applied Psychology*, vol. 32, no. 6, p. 641.

480. **COUCH**, Arthur and KENISTON, Kenneth. 1960. Yeasayers and naysayers: agreeing response set as a personality variable. *Journal of Abnormal and Social Psychology*, vol. 60, no. 2, pp. 151-174.

481. **COUTANT**, F. R. 1939. Determining the appeal of special features of a radio program. *Journal of Applied Psychology*, vol. 23, no. 1, pp. 54-57.

482. **COVNER**, Bernard J. 1944. Studies in phonographic recordings of verbal material, IV: written reports of interviews. *Journal of Applied Psychology*, vol. 28, no. 2, pp. 89-98.

COWAN, Frederic J., *Jr.* 1966. *See* STRICKLAND, Lloyd H. and COWAN, Frederic J., *Jr.* 1966.

COWAN, James R. 1970. *See* TIFFANY, Donald W., COWAN, James R. and BLINN, Elaine. 1970.

483. **COWLING**, A. B. 1966. A scale for measuring intensity of readership. *Admap*, February, pp. 210-211.

484. **COX**, William E., *Jr.* 1966. Response patterns to mail surveys. *Journal of Marketing Research*, vol. 3, no. 4, pp. 392-397.

CRANE, Wilder W. 1964. *See* HUNT, William H., CRANE, Wilder W. and WAHIKE, John C. 1964.

485. **CRESPI**, Irving. 1961. Use of a scaling technique in surveys. *Journal of Marketing*, vol. 25, no. 5, pp. 69-72.

486. **CRESPI**, Leo [P.] and RUGG, Donald. 1940. Poll data and the study of opinion determinants. *Public Opinion Quarterly*, vol. 4, no. 2, pp. 273-276.

487. **CRESPI**, Leo P. 1945/46. The cheater problem in polling. *Public Opinion Quarterly*, vol. 9, no. 4, pp. 431-445.

488. **CRESPI**, Leo P. 1946. Further observations on the 'cheater' problem. *Public Opinion Quarterly*, vol. 10, no. 4, pp. 646-649.

489. **CRESPI**, Leo P. 1946. 'Opinion-attitude methodology' and the polls – a rejoinder. *Psychological Bulletin*, vol. 43, no. 6, pp. 562-569.

490. **CRESPI**, Leo P. 1948. The interview effect in polling. *Public Opinion Quarterly*, vol. 12, no. 1, pp. 99-111.

491. **CRESPI**, Leo P. 1948/49. Elections and poll validity. *International Journal of Opinion and Attitude Research*, vol. 2, no. 4, pp. 481-488.

492. **CRESPI**, Leo P. 1950. The influence of military government sponsorship in German opinion polling. *International Journal of Opinion and Attitude Research*, vol. 4, no. 2, pp. 151-178.

CRISWELL, Joan H. 1947. *See* BEUM, Corlin O. and CRISWELL, Joan H. 1947.

493. **CROCKETT**, Walter H. and NIDORF, Louis J. 1967. Individual differences in responses to the semantic differential. *Journal of Social Psychology*, vol. 73, no. 2, pp. 211-218.

494. **CRONBACH**, Lee J. 1950. Further evidence on response sets and test design. *Educational and Psychological Measurement*, vol. 10, no. 1, pp. 3-31.

495. **CRONBACH**, Lee J. and MEEHL, Paul E. 1955. Construct validity in psychological tests. *Psychological Bulletin*, vol. 52, no. 4, pp. 281-302.

496. **CROOG**, Sydney H. 1961. Ethnic origins, educational level, and responses to a health questionnaire. *Human Organization*, vol. 20, no. 2, pp. 65-69.

497. **CROSBY**, Richard W. 1969. Attitude measurement in a bilingual culture. *Journal of Marketing Research*, vol. 6, no. 4, pp. 421-426.

498. **CROSSLEY**, Archibald M. 1937. Measuring public opinion. *Journal of Marketing*, vol. 1, no. 3, pp. 272-274.

499. **CROSSLEY**, Archibald M. 1937. Straw polls in 1936. *Public Opinion Quarterly*, vol. 1, no. 1, pp. 24-35.

500. **CROSSLEY**, Archibald M. 1941. Methods tested during 1940 campaign. *Public Opinion Quarterly*, vol. 5, no. 1, pp. 83-86.

CROSSLEY, Helen M. 1950. *See* PARRY, Hugh J. and CROSSLEY, Helen M. 1950.

501. CROSSLEY, Helen M. and FINK, Raymond. 1951. Response and non-response in a probability sample. *International Journal of Opinion and Attitude Research*, vol. 5, no. 1, pp. 1-19.

CROWN, S. 1949. *See* EYSENCK, H[ans] J. and CROWN, S. 1949.

502. CRUM, W. L. 1933. On analytical interpretation of straw-vote samples. *Journal of the American Statistical Association*, vol. 28, no. 182, pp. 152-163.

503. CRUTCHFIELD, Richard S. and GORDON, Donald A. 1947. Variations in respondents' interpretations of an opinion-poll question. *International Journal of Opinion and Attitude Research*, vol. 1, no. 3, pp. 1-12.

504. CUBER, John F. and GERBERICH, John B. 1946. A note on consistency in questionnaire responses. *American Sociological Review*, vol. 11, no. 1, pp. 13-15.

505. CUDRIN, Jay M. 1969. Intelligence of volunteers as research subjects. *Journal of Consulting and Clinical Psychology*, vol. 33, no. 4, pp. 501-503.

CUNDIFF, Edward W. 1964. *See* BARBAN, Arnold M. and CUNDIFF, Edward W. 1964.

506. CURTIS, Alberta. 1939. The reliability of a report on listening habits. *Journal of Applied Psychology*, vol. 23, no. 1, pp. 127-130.

507. CURTIS, Richard F. and JACKSON, Elton F. 1962. Multiple indicators in survey research. *American Journal of Sociology*, vol. 68, no. 2, pp. 195-204.

508. DALENIUS, Tore. 1961. Treatment of the non-response problem. *Journal of Advertising Research*, vol. 1, no. 5, pp. 1-7.

509. DALENIUS, Tore. 1965. Time and survey design. *Journal of Advertising Research*, vol. 5, no. 3, pp. 2-5.

DALENIUS, Tore. 1969. *See* BAILAR, Barbara A. and DALENIUS, Tore. 1969.

DALY, Joseph F. 1937. *See* FURFEY, Paul Hanly and DALY, Joseph F. 1937.

DAMES, Joel. 1962. *See* WELLS, William D. and DAMES, Joel. 1962.

510. **DANIELSON**, Wayne A. 1957. A data reduction method for scaling dichotomous items. *Public Opinion Quarterly*, vol. 21, no. 3, pp. 377-379.

DANIELSON, Wayne A. 1958. *See* BRINTON, James E. and DANIELSON, Wayne A. 1958.

511. **DANIELSON**, Wayne A. and BRYAN, Sam Dunn. 1963. Computer automation of two readability formulas. *Journalism Quarterly*, vol. 40, no. 2, pp. 201-206.

512. **DANIELSON**, Wayne A. and MULLEN, James J. 1965. A basic space unit for newspaper content analysis. *Journalism Quarterly*, vol. 42, no. 1, pp. 108-110.

513. **DAVENPORT**, John Scott, PARKER, Edwin B. and SMITH, Stewart A. 1962. Measuring readership of newspaper advertisements. *Journal of Advertising Research*, vol. 2, no. 4, pp. 2-9.

DAVENPORT, John Scott. 1963. *See* PARKER, Edwin B., SMITH, Stewart A. and DAVENPORT, John Scott. 1963.

DAVID, Mort. 1961. *See* MARDER, Eric and DAVID, Mort. 1961.

DAVID, S. T. 1952. *See* BOOKER, H. S. and DAVID, S. T. 1952.

DAVIDSON, Helen H. 1953. *See* KRUGLOV, Lorraine P. and DAVIDSON, Helen H. 1953.

DAVIE, James S. 1954. *See* HARE, A. Paul and DAVIE, James S. 1954.

514. **DAVIS**, F. James and HAGEDORN, Robert. 1954. Testing the reliability of systematic field observations. *American Sociological Review*, vol. 19, no. 3, pp. 345-348.

515. **DAVIS**, James A. 1958. On criteria for scale relationship. *American Journal of Sociology*, vol. 63, no. 4, pp. 371-380.

DAVIS, John D. 1966. *See* HELLER, Kenneth, DAVIS, John D. and MYERS, Roger A. 1966.

DAWIS, Rene V. 1960. *See* WEISS, David J. and DAWIS, Rene V. 1960.

DAWIS, Rene V. 1968. *See* FISHER, Stephen T., WEISS, David J. and DAWIS, Rene V. 1968.

516. **DAY**, Alice B. 1948. Consumer panels react well to friendly, personal letters. *Printer's Ink*, vol. 225, no. 9, pp. 38-39, 75, 78.

517. **DAY**, D. J. and DUNN, Jennifer E. 1969. Estimating the audience for advertising on the outside of London buses. *Applied Statistics*, vol. 18, no. 3, pp. 209-220.

518. **DAY**, Daniel [D.] 1940. Methods in attitude research. *American Sociological Review*, vol. 5, no. 3, pp. 395-410.

519. **DAY**, Daniel D. 1941. Methodological problems in attitude research. *Journal of Social Psychology*, vol. 14, no. 1, pp. 165-179.

520. **DAY**, Ralph L. 1965. Systematic paired comparisons in preference analysis. *Journal of Marketing Research*, vol. 2, no. 4, pp. 406-412.

521. **DAY**, Ralph L. 1968. Preference distribution analysis: a rejoinder. *Journal of Marketing Research*, vol. 5, no. 4, pp. 438-441.

522. **DAY**, Ralph L. 1968. Preference tests and the management of product features. *Journal of Marketing*, vol. 32, no. 3, pp. 24-29.

523. **DAY**, Ralph L. 1969. Position bias in paired product tests. *Journal of Marketing Research*, vol. 6, no. 1, pp. 98-100.

524. **DEAN**, John P. and WHYTE, William Foote. 1958. How do you know if the informant is telling the truth? *Human Organization*, vol. 17, no. 2, pp. 34-38.

525. **DEEMER**, Walter L., *Jr.* 1948. The use of mark sensing in a large scale testing program. *Journal of the American Statistical Association*, vol. 43, no. 241, pp. 40-52.

526. **DeFLEUR**, Melvin L. and CATTON, William R., *Jr.* 1957. The limits of determinacy in attitude measurement. *Social Forces*, vol. 35, no. 4, pp. 295-300.

DeHARDT, Doris. 1960. *See* NELSON, Thomas M., BARTLEY, S. Howard and DeHARDT, Doris. 1960.

DeLOTT, Jack. 1952. *See* WOODWARD, Julian L. and DeLOTT, Jack. 1952.

527. **DEMING**, W. Edwards and GEOFFREY, Leon. 1941. On sample inspection in the processing of census returns. *Journal of the American Statistical Association*, vol. 36, no. 215, pp. 351-360.

528. **DEMING**, W. Edwards, TEPPING, Benjamin J. and GEOFFREY, Leon. 1942. Errors in card punching. *Journal of the American Statistical Association*, vol. 37, no. 220, pp. 525-536.

DEMING, W. Edwards. 1943. *See* HANSEN, Morris H. and DEMING, W. Edwards. 1943.

529. **DEMING**, W. Edwards. 1944. On errors in surveys. *American Sociological Review*, vol. 9, no. 4, pp. 359-369.

530. **DEMING**, W. Edwards. 1947. Some criteria for judging the quality of surveys. *Journal of Marketing*, vol. 12, no. 2, pp. 145-157.

DEMING, W. Edwards. 1949. *See* HANSEN, Morris H. and DEMING, W. Edwards. 1949.

531. **DEMING**, W. Edwards. 1953. On a probability mechanism to attain an economic balance between the resultant error of response and the bias of nonresponse. *Journal of the American Statistical Association*, vol. 48, no. 264, pp. 743-772.

532. **DEMING**, W. Edwards. 1953. On the distinction between enumerative and analytic surveys. *Journal of the American Statistical Association*, vol. 48, no. 262, pp. 244-255.

533. **DEMING**, W. Edwards. 1954. On the presentation of the results of sample surveys as legal evidence. *Journal of the American Statistical Association*, vol. 49, no. 268, pp. 814-825.

534. **DEMING**, W. Edwards. 1956. On simplifications of sampling design through replication with equal probabilities and without stages. *Journal of the American Statistical Association*, vol. 51, no. 273, pp. 24-53.

535. **DEMING**, W. Edwards. 1961. Uncertainties in statistical data, and their relation to the design and management of statistical surveys and experiments. *Bulletin of the International Statistical Institute*, vol. 38, no. 4, pp. 365-383.

DENERLEY, R. A. 1955. *See* MARRIOTT, R. and DENERLEY, R. A. 1955.

DENERLEY, R. A. 1955. *See* MARRIOTT, R. and DENERLEY, R. A. 1955.

536. **DERI**, Susan, *et al.* 1948. Techniques for the diagnosis and measurement of intergroup attitudes and behavior. *Psychological Bulletin*, vol. 45, no. 3, pp. 248-271.

537. **DEUTSCHER**, Irwin. 1956. Physicians' reactions to a mailed questionnaire: a study in 'resistentialism'. *Public Opinion Quarterly*, vol. 20, no. 3, pp. 599-604.

538. **DEUTSCHMANN**, Paul J. and ADAMS, John B. 1958. Testing representativeness of mail samples of newspapers. *Journalism Quarterly*, vol. 35, no. 3, pp. 351-352.

539. **DeWICK**, Henry N. 1935. The relative recall effectiveness of visual and auditory presentation of advertising material. *Journal of Applied Psychology*, vol. 19, no. 3, pp. 245-264.

540. **DEXTER**, Lewis A[nthony]. 1939. An attempt to measure change of attitude as a result of hearing speakers. *Sociometry*, vol. 2, no. 2, pp. 76-83.

541. **DEXTER**, Lewis Anthony. 1956. Role relationships and conceptions of neutrality in interviewing. *American Journal of Sociology*, vol. 62, no. 2, pp. 153-157.

542. **DIAB**, Lutfy N. 1965. Studies in social attitudes, III: attitude assessment through the semantic-differential technique. *Journal of Social Psychology*, vol. 67, no. 2, pp. 303-314.

DIDCOTT, P[eter] J. 1968. *See* BELSON, W[illiam] [A.], MILLERSON, G. L. and DIDCOTT, P[eter] J. 1968.

543. **DIDCOTT**, Peter [J.] 1969. Field strategies and response bias in a survey of adolescent boys. London: London School of Economics and Political Science, Survey Research Centre, 1969. 94pp.

DIETRICH, Donald H. 1941. *See* SYMONDS, Percival M. and DIETRICH, Donald H. 1941.

544. **DIETSCH**, R. W. and GURNEE, Herbert. 1948. Cumulative effect of a series of campaign leaflets. *Journal of Applied Psychology*, vol. 32, no. 2, pp. 189-194.

545. **DINERMAN**, Helen, *chairman*. 1957. The analysis of quantitative data: four analysts assess the same questionnaire returns. *Public Opinion Quarterly*, vol. 21, no. 3, pp. 424-427.

DINGMAN, Harvey F. 1960. *See* WINDLE, Charles D. and DINGMAN, Harvey F. 1960.

DITTES, James E. 1962. *See* CAPRA, Paul C. and DITTES, James E. 1962.

546. **DiVESTA**, Francis J. 1954. Problems in the use of questionnaires for studying the effectiveness of educational programs. *Educational and Psychological Measurement*, vol. 14, no. 1, pp. 138-150.

DIXON, Theodore R. 1968. *See* SMITH, Edward W. L. and DIXON, Theodore R. 1968.

547. **DODD**, Stuart C. 1944. On reliability in polling: a sociometric study of errors of polling in war zones. *Sociometry*, vol. 7, no. 3, pp. 265-282.

548. **DODD**, Stuart C. 1947. Standards for surveying agencies. *Public Opinion Quarterly*, vol. 11, no. 1, pp. 115-130.

549. **DODD**, Stuart C. 1948. A simple test for predicting opinions from their subclasses. *International Journal of Opinion and Attitude Research*, vol. 2, no. 1, pp. 1-21.

550. **DODD**, Stuart C., *chairman*. 1950. Research on scaling techniques. *Public Opinion Quarterly*, vol. 14, no. 4, pp. 845-852.

551. **DODD**, Stuart C. 1952. Testing message diffusion from person to person. *Public Opinion Quarterly*, vol. 16, no. 2, pp. 247-262.

552. **DOHERTY**, Judith. 1969. An example of multi-population cluster sampling. London: Office of Population Censuses and Surveys, Social Survey Division, 1969. 23pp. (*Methodological series, M145*).

553. **DOHRENWEND**, Barbara S[nell] and RICHARDSON, Stephen A. 1956. Analysis of the interviewer's behavior. *Human Organization*, vol. 15, no. 2, pp. 29-32.

554. **DOHRENWEND**, Barbara Snell and RICHARDSON, Stephen A. 1963. Directiveness and nondirectiveness in research interviewing: a reformulation of the problem. *Psychological Bulletin*, vol. 60, no. 5, pp. 475-485.

555. **DOHRENWEND**, Barbara Snell and RICHARDSON, Stephen A. 1964. A use for leading questions in research interviewing. *Human Organization*, vol. 23, no. 1, pp. 76-77.

556. **DOHRENWEND**, Barbara Snell. 1965. Some effects of open and closed questions on respondents' answers. *Human Organization*, vol. 24, no. 2, pp. 175-184.

557. **DOHRENWEND**, Barbara Snell, *et al.* 1967. Factors interacting with birth order in self-selection among volunteer subjects. *Journal of Social Psychology*, vol. 72, no. 1, pp. 125-128.

558. **DOHRENWEND**, Barbara Snell, COLOMBOTOS, John and DOHRENWEND, Bruce P. 1968. Social distance and interviewer effects. *Public Opinion Quarterly*, vol. 32, no. 3, pp. 410-422.

559. **DOHRENWEND**, Barbara Snell and DOHRENWEND, Bruce P. 1968. Sources of refusals in surveys. *Public Opinion Quarterly*, vol. 32, no. 1, pp. 74-83.

560. **DOHRENWEND**, Barbara Snell, WILLIAMS, J. Allen, *Jr.*, and WEISS, Carol H. 1969. Interviewer biasing effects: toward a reconciliation of findings. *Public Opinion Quarterly*, vol. 33, no. 1, pp. 121-129.

DOHRENWEND, Bruce P. 1968. *See* DOHRENWEND, Barbara Snell, COLOMBOTOS, John and DOHRENWEND, Bruce P. 1968.

DOHRENWEND, Bruce P. 1968. *See* DOHRENWEND, Barbara Snell and DOHRENWEND, Bruce P. 1968.

561. **DOLLARD**, John. 1938. The life history in community studies. *American Sociological Review*, vol. 3, no. 5, pp. 724-737.

562. **DOLLARD**, John. 1948. Under what conditions do opinions predict behavior? *Public Opinion Quarterly*, vol. 12, no. 4, pp. 623-632.

563. **DOMMERMUTH**, William P. and CATEORA, Philip R. 1963. Can refusals by respondents be decreased. *Journal of Marketing*, vol. 27, no. 3, pp. 74-76.

564. **DONALD**, Marjorie N. 1960. Implications of non-response for the interpretation of mail questionnaire data. *Public Opinion Quarterly*, vol. 24, no. 1, pp. 99-114.

565. **DONCEEL**, Joseph F., ALIMENA, Benjamin S. and BIRCH, Catherine M. 1949. Influence of prestige suggestion on the answers of a personality inventory. *Journal of Applied Psychology*, vol. 33, no. 4, pp. 352-355.

DOOB, Leonard W. 1953/54. *See* CARPER, James and DOOB, Leonard W. 1953/54.

566. **DOOB**, Leonard W. 1957/58. The use of different test items in nonliterate societies. *Public Opinion Quarterly*, vol. 21, no. 4, pp. 499-504.

567. **DOTSON**, Floyd. 1954. Intensive interviewing in community research. *Journal of Educational Sociology*, vol. 27, no. 5, pp. 225-230.

568. **DOWNHAM**, J. S. 1954. Social class in sample surveys. *The Incorporated Statistician*, vol. 5, no. 1, pp. 17-38.

569. **DOWNHAM**, J. S. 1955. The function of coding. *The Incorporated Statistician*, vol. 5, no. 4, (supplement), pp. 73-81.

570. **DRAPER**, Norman R., HUNTER, William G. and TIERNEY, David E. 1969. Analyzing paired comparison tests. *Journal of Marketing Research*, vol. 6, no. 4, pp. 477-480.

571. **DRAYTON**, Leslie E. 1954. Bias arising in wording consumer questionnaires. *Journal of Marketing*, vol. 19, no. 2, pp. 140-145.

DREGER, Ralph Mason. 1954. *See* SWEETLAND, Anders and DREGER, Ralph Mason. 1954.

DRESSEL, Robert J. 1961. *See* MASON, Ward S., DRESSEL, Robert J. and BAIN, Robert K. 1961.

572. **DRINKWATER**, Barbara L. 1965. A comparison of the direction-of-perception technique with the Likert method in the measurement of attitudes. *Journal of Social Psychology*, vol. 67, no. 2, pp. 189-196.

573. **DROBA**, D. D. 1931. Methods used for measuring public opinion. *American Journal of Sociology*, vol. 37, no. 3, pp. 410-423.

574. **DUDEK**, Frank J. 1964. Relations among television rating indices. *Journal of Advertising Research*, vol. 4, no. 3, pp. 24-28.

DUNCAN, Judith A. 1962. *See* BELSON, William [A.] and DUNCAN, Judith A. 1962.

DUNCAN-JONES, Paul. 1965. *See* CLEMENS, John and DUNCAN-JONES, Paul. 1965.

575. **DUNCAN-JONES**, Paul. 1971. Canonical scoring of survey data. Paper read to the annual conference of the Market Research Society, Brighton, March 1971. 15, [8] ff.

DUNHAM, Ruth E. 1959. *See* SAGEN, O. K., DUNHAM, Ruth E. and SIMMONS, Walt R. 1959.

576. **DUNLAP**, Jack W. and KROLL, Abraham. 1939. Observations on the methodology in attitude scales. *Journal of Social Psychology*, vol. 10, no. 4, pp. 475-487.

DUNN, Jennifer E. 1969. *See* Day, D. J. and DUNN, Jennifer E. 1969.

DUNN, S. Watson. 1967. *See* LORIMOR, E. S. and DUNN, S. Watson. 1967.

577. **DUNNETTE**, Marvin D. and HENEMAN, Herbert G., *Jr.* 1956. Influence of scale administration on employee attitude responses. *Journal of Applied Psychology*, vol. 40, no. 2, pp. 73-77.

578. **DUNNETTE**, Marvin D., UPHOFF, Walter and AYLWARD, Merriam. 1956. The effect of lack of information on the undecided response in attitude surveys. *Journal of Applied Psychology*, vol. 40, no. 3, pp. 150-153.

DUNNINGTON, Richard A. 1967. *See* KLEIN, Stuart M., MAHER, John R. and DUNNINGTON, Richard A. 1967.

579. **DUNPHY**, Dexter C., STONE, Philip J. and SMITH, Marshall S. 1965. The General Inquirer: further developments in a computer system for content analysis of verbal data in the social sciences. *Behavioral Science*, vol. 10, no. 4, pp. 468-480.

580. **DURANT**. Henry. 1946. The 'cheater' problem. *Public Opinion Quarterly*, vol. 10, no. 2, pp. 288-291.

581. **DURANT**, Henry. 1951/52. Experiences of random (probability) sampling. *Public Opinion Quarterly*, vol. 15, no. 4, pp. 765-766.

582. **DURANT**, Henry. 1954. The Gallup poll and some of its problems. *The Incorporated Statistician,* vol. 5, no. 2, pp. 101-110. Discussion, pp. 110-112.

583. **DURANT**, Henry and MAAS, Irene. 1956. Who doesn't answer? A symposium on the problems of bias through non-returns in questionnaire surveys and follow-up conducted by post. *Bulletin of the British Psychological Society*, no. 29, pp. 33-34.

584. **DURANT**, Henry and SIMMONS, Martin. 1968. The paradox of memory in market research. *Commentary*, vol. 10, no. 4, pp. 253-263.

585. **DURBIN**, J. and STUART, A[lan]. 1951. Differences in response rates of experienced and inexperienced interviewers. *Journal of the Royal Statistical Society, series A,* vol. 114, part 2, pp. 163-195. Discussion on the paper by Mr. Durbin and Mr. Stuart, pp. 196-206.

586. **DURBIN**, J. 1954. Non-response and call-backs in surveys. *Bulletin of the International Statistical Institute*, vol. 34, part 2, pp. 72-86.

587. **DURBIN**, J. and STUART, A[lan]. 1954. An experimental comparison between coders. *Journal of Marketing*, vol. 19, no. 1, pp. 54-66.

588. **DURBIN**, J. and STUART, A[lan]. 1954. Callbacks and clustering in sample surveys: an experimental study. *Journal of the Royal Statistical Society, series A*, vol. 117, part 4, pp. 387-418. Discussion on the paper by Mr. Durbin and Mr. Stuart, pp. 418-428.

DUTFIELD, Jon. 1966. *See* CONSTERDINE, Guy and DUTFIELD, Jon. 1966.

DUTKA, Solomon. 1951. *See* BALINSKY, Benjamin, BLUM, Milton L. and DUTKA, Solomon. 1951.

DUTKOWSKI, John. 1952/53. *See* SHELDON, Richard C. and DUTKOWSKI, John. 1952/53.

589. **DVORAK**, Beatrice, FOX, Frances C. and MEIGH, Charles. 1952 Tests for field survey interviewers. *Journal of Marketing*, vol. 16, no. 3, part 1, pp. 301-306.

EAPEN, A. T. 1959. *See* LANSING, John B. and EAPEN, A. T. 1959.

590. **EASTLACK**, J. O., *Jr.* 1964. Consumer flavor preference factors in food product design. *Journal of Marketing Research*, vol. 1, no. 1, pp. 38-42.

591. EASTLACK, J. O., Jr. 1964. Recall of advertising by two telephone samples. *Journal of Advertising Research*, vol. 4, no. 1, pp. 25-29.

592. EASTLACK, J. O., Jr. and ASSAEL, Henry. 1966. Better telephone surveys through centralized interviewing. *Journal of Advertising Research*, vol. 6, no. 1, pp. 2-7.

EBERHART, John C. 1947. *See* SHAPIRO, Sam and EBERHART, John C. 1947.

593. ECKLER, A. Ross and PRITZKER, Leon. 1951. Measuring the accuracy of enumerative surveys. *Bulletin of the International Statistical Institute*, vol. 33, no. 4, pp. 7-24.

594. ECKLER, A. Ross. 1953. Extent and character of errors in the 1950 census. *The American Statistician*, vol. 7, no. 5, pp. 15-21.

595. ECKLER, A. Ross and HURWITZ, William N. 1958. Response variance and biases in censuses and surveys. *Bulletin of the International Statistical Institute*, vol. 36, no. 4, pp. 12-35.

596. ECKSTRAND, Gordon and GILLILAND, A. R. 1948. The psychogalvanometric method for measuring the effectiveness of advertising. *Journal of Psychology*, vol. 32, no. 4, pp. 415-425.

597. EDGERTON, Harold A., BRITT, Steuart Henderson and NORMAN, Ralph D. 1947. Objective differences among various types of respondents to a mailed questionnaire. *American Sociological Review*, vol. 12, no. 4, pp. 435-444.

598. EDGINGTON, Eugene S. 1966. Statistical inference and non-random samples. *Psychological Bulletin*, vol. 66, no. 6, pp. 485-487.

599. EDMISTON, Vivian. 1944. The group interview. *Journal of Educational Research*, vol. 37, no. 8, pp. 593-601.

600. EDSALL, Richard L. 1943. A method of measuring effectiveness of business and trade paper advertising. *Journal of Marketing*, vol. 7, no. 3, pp. 208-209.

601. EDSALL, Richard L. 1958. Getting 'not-at-homes' to interview themselves. *Journal of Marketing*, vol. 23, no. 2, pp. 184-185.

602. EDWARDS, Allen L. 1946. A critique of 'neutral' items in attitude scales constructed by the method of equal appearing intervals. *Psychological Review*, vol. 53, no. 3, pp. 159-169.

603. EDWARDS, Allen L. and KENNEY, Kathryn Claire. 1946. A comparison of the Thurstone and Likert techniques of attitude scale construction. *Journal of Applied Psychology*, vol. 30, no. 1, pp. 72-83.

604. **EDWARDS**, Allen L. 1948. On Guttman's scale analysis. *Educational and Psychological Measurement*, vol. 8, no. 3, pp. 313-318.
605. **EDWARDS**, Allen L. and KILPATRICK, Franklin P. 1948. A technique for the construction of attitude scales. *Journal of Applied Psychology*, vol. 32, no. 4, pp. 374-384.
606. **EDWARDS**, Allen L. 1956. A technique for increasing the reproducibility of cumulative attitude scales. *Journal of Applied Psychology*, vol. 40, no. 4, pp. 263-265.
607. **EDWARDS**, A. W. F. and CAVALLI-SFORZA, L. L. 1965. A method for cluster analysis. *Biometrics*, vol. 21, no. 2, pp. 362-375.
608. **EDWARDS**, Frederick. 1953. Aspects of random sampling for a commercial survey. *The Incorporated Statistician*, vol. 4, no. 1, pp. 9-25. Discussion, pp. 25-26.

EDWARDS, Frederick. 1955. *See* CORLETT, Thomas and EDWARDS, Frederick. 1955.

609. **EHRENBERG**, A. S. C. 1959. The relative merits of independent matched samples and of the panel technique for before-and-after studies. *Commentary*, no. 1, pp. 1-7.
610. **EHRENBERG**, A. S. C. 1960. A study of some potential biases in the operation of a consumer panel. *Applied Statistics*, vol. 9, no. 1, pp. 20-27.
611. **EHRENBERG**, A. S. C. and SHEWAN, J. M. 1960. The development and use of a taste panel technique − a review. *Occupational Psychology*, vol. 34, no. 4, pp. 241-248.
612. **EHRENBERG**, A. S. C. 1961. 'A comparison of estimates from the nights-at-home formulas with estimates from six calls: an Advertising Research Foundation report': critical review ... *Commentary*, no. 6, pp. 45-49.
613. **EHRENBERG**, A. S. C. 1961. How reliable is aided recall of TV viewing? *Journal of Advertising Research*, vol. 1, no. 4, pp. 29-31.

EHRENBERG, A. S. C. 1961. *See* MONK, D. M. and EHRENBERG, A. S. C. 1961.

614. **EHRENBERG**, A. S. C. 1962. Some questions about factor analysis. *The Statistician*, vol. 12, no. 3, pp. 191-208.
615. **EHRENBERG**, A. S. C. 1963. A review of 7-day recall. *Commentary*, no. 12, pp. 3-18.
616. **EHRENBERG**, A. S. C. 1963. On matching and experimental

design. *MARKET RESEARCH SOCIETY. New developments in research.* London: Market Research Society with The Oakwood Press, 1963. pp. 82-98.

617. **EHRENBERG**, A. S. C. 1964. A comparison of TV audience measures. *Journal of Advertising Research*, vol. 4, no. 4, pp. 11-16.

618. **EHRENBERG**, A. S. C. and TWYMAN, W. A. 1967. On measuring television audiences. *Journal of the Royal Statistical Society, series A*, vol. 130, part 1, pp. 1-59.

619. **EHRENBERG**, A. S. C. 1968. The time and the place for readership panels. *Journal of Advertising Research*, vol. 8, no. 2, pp. 19-22.

620. **EHRLICH**, June Sachar and RIESMAN, David. 1961. Age and authority in the interview. *Public Opinion Quarterly*, vol. 25, no. 1, pp. 39-56.

621. **EISENBERG**, Philip. 1945. Two methods for combining attitudes of like, indifference and dislike into one score. *Journal of Applied Psychology*, vol. 29, no. 3, pp. 246-251.

622. **EKMAN**, Paul. 1964. Body position, facial expression, and verbal behavior during interviews. *Journal of Abnormal and Social Psychology*, vol. 68, no. 3, pp. 295-301.

623. **EL-BADRY**, M. A. and STEPHAN, F. F. 1955. On adjusting sample tabulations to census counts. *Journal of the American Statistical Association*, vol. 50, no. 271, pp. 738-762.

624. **EL-BADRY**, M. A. 1956. A sampling procedure for mailed questionnaires. *Journal of the American Statistical Association*. vol. 51, no. 274, pp. 209-227.

625. **EL-BADRY**, M. A. 1961. Failure of enumerators to make entries of zero: errors in recording childless cases in population censuses. *Journal of the American Statistical Association*, vol. 56, no. 296, pp. 909-924.

626. **ELECTRONIC** test of in-home TV viewing among those families who fail to respond to the doorbell. 1968. New York: Advertising Research Foundation, 1968. 14pp. (*Arrowhead study, no. 8*).

ELIASBERG, Jay. 1969. *See* METZNER, Gale D., GLASSER, Gerald J. and ELIASBERG, Jay. 1969.

627. **ELINSON**, Jack and CISIN, Ira H. 1948. Detection of interviewer cheating through scale technique. *Public Opinion Quarterly*, vol. 12, no. 2, pp. 325.

628. **ELINSON**, Jack and **HAINES**, Valerie T. 1950. Role of anonymity in attitude surveys. *American Psychologist*, vol. 5, no. 7, pp. 315.

629. **ELKIND**, David. 1960. Interviewing children in a school setting. *Journal of Psychology*, vol. 50, no. 1, pp. 111-117.

630. **ELLIOTT**, Frank R. 1937. Memory effects from poster, radio and television modes of advertising an exhibit. *Journal of Applied Psychology*, vol. 21, no. 5, pp. 504-512.

631. **ELLIOTT**, Frank R. 1937. Memory for trade names presented in screen, radio and television advertisements. *Journal of Applied Psychology*, vol. 21, no. 6, pp. 653-667.

632. **ELLIS**, Albert. 1947. Questionnaire versus interview methods in the study of human love relationships. *American Sociological Review*, vol. 12, no. 5, pp. 541-553.

633. **ELLIS**, Albert. 1948. Questionnaire versus interview methods in the study of human love relationships, II: uncategorized responses. *American Sociological Review*, vol. 13, no. 1, pp. 61-65.

634. **ELLIS**, Robert A., **LANE**, W. Clayton and **OLESEN**, Virginia. 1963. The index of class position: an improved intercommunity measure of stratification. *American Sociological Review*, vol. 28, no. 2, pp. 271-277.

635. **ELLSON**, Douglas G. and **ELLSON**, Elizabeth Cox. 1953. Historical note on the rating scale. *Psychological Bulletin*, vol. 50, no. 5, pp. 383-384.

ELLSON, Elizabeth Cox. 1953. *See* ELLSON, Douglas G. and ELLSON, Elizabeth Cox. 1953.

636. **ELLWOOD**, Charles A. 1933. Observation and the survey method in sociology. *Social Forces*, vol. 12, no. 1, pp. 51-57.

637. **EMMETT**, B. P. 1966. The design of investigations into the effects of radio and television programmes and other mass communications. *Journal of the Royal Statistical Society, series A*, vol. 129, part 1, pp. 26-49. Discussion ... pp. 50-59.

638. **EMMETT**, B. P. 1968. The exploration of inter-relationships in survey data. *Commentary*, vol. 10, no. 2, pp. 65-77.

EMPEY, L. T. 1956. *See* SLOCUM, W. L., EMPEY, L. T. and SWANSON, H. S. 1956.

639. **ENGEL**, Gerald, **O'SHEA**, Harriet E. and **MENDENHALL**, John H. 1958. 'Projective' responses to a news article: a study in aspects of bias. *Journal of Psychology*, vol. 46, no. 2, pp. 309-317.

640. **ENGEL**, James F. 1962. Tape recorders in consumer research. *Journal of Marketing*, vol. 26, no. 2, pp. 73-74.

641. **ENGEL**, James F. and WALES, Hugh G. 1962. Spoken versus pictured questions on taboo topics. *Journal of Advertising Research*, vol. 2, no. 1, pp. 11-17.

642. **ENGEL**, James F. and WALES, Hugh G. 1963. Rejoinder to Wenderoth. *Journal of Advertising Research*, vol. 3, no. 1, pp. 43-44.

643. **ENGEL**, James F., KOLLAT, David T. and BLACKWELL, Roger D. 1969. Personality measures and market segmentation. *Business Horizons*, vol. 12, no. 3, pp. 61-70.

644. **ENGELHART**, Max D. 1930. Techniques used in securing equivalent groups. *Journal of Educational Research*, vol. 22, no. 2, pp. 103-109.

645. **ENGLAND**, L. R. 1948. Capital punishment and open-end questions. *Public Opinion Quarterly*, vol. 12, no. 3, pp. 412-416.

646. **ENTWISLE**, Doris R. 1961. Interactive effects of pretesting. *Educational and Psychological Measurement*, vol. 21, no. 3, pp. 607-620.

EPLEY, Robert J. 1966. *See*, SESSIONS, Frank Q., EPLEY, Robert J. and MOE, Edward O. 1966.

647. **ERDOS**, Paul L. 1948. Planning the questionnaire for tabulation. *International Journal of Opinion and Attitude Research*, vol. 2, no. 3, pp. 401-408.

648. **ERDOS**, Paul L. 1957. How to get higher returns from your mail surveys. *Printer's Ink*, vol. 258, no. 8, pp. 30-31.

649. **ERDOS**, Paul L. 1957. Successful mail surveys: high returns and how to get them. *Printer's Ink*, vol. 258, no. 9, pp. 56-58, 60.

ERHMANN, J. C. 1952. *See* KING, G. F., EHRMANN, J. C. and JOHNSON, D. M. 1952.

650. **ERICSON**, W. A. 1967. Optimal sample design with nonresponse. *Journal of the American Statistical Association*, vol. 62, no. 317, pp. 63-78.

651. **ERVIN**, Susan and BOWER, Robert T. 1952/53. Translation problems in international surveys. *Public Opinion Quarterly*, vol. 16, no. 4, pp. 595-604.

652. EVAN, William M. and MILLER, James R. 1969. Differential effects on response bias of computer vs. conventional administration of a social science questionnaire: an exploratory methodological experiment. *Behavioral Science*, vol. 14, no. 3, pp. 216-227.

653. EVANS, Franklin B. 1961. On interviewer cheating. *Public Opinion Quarterly*, vol. 25, no. 1, pp. 126-127.

EVANS, Mary C. 1946. *See* FREIBERG, Albert D., VAUGHN, Charles L. and EVANS, Mary C. 1946.

654. EVANS, W. Duane. 1958. The control of non-sampling errors in social and economic surveys. *Bulletin of the International Statistical Institute* vol. 36, no. 2, pp. 36-43.

EVITTS, Mary Sue. 1961. *See* WRIGHT, Benjamin and EVITTS, Mary Sue. 1961.

655. EYSENCK, H[ans] J. and CROWN, S. 1949. An experimental study in opinion-attitude methodology. *International Journal of Opinion and Attitude Research*, vol. 3, no. 1, pp. 47-86.

656. EYSENCK, Hans J. 1952. Uses and abuses of factor analysis. *Applied Statistics*, vol. 1, no. 1, pp. 45-49.

657. EZEKIEL, Mordecai. 1932. 'Student's' method for measuring the significance of a difference between matched groups. *Journal of Educational Psychology*, vol. 23, no. 6, pp. 446-450.

FADNER, Raymond H. 1943. *See* JANIS, Irving L., FADNER, Raymond H. and JANOWITZ, Morris. 1943.

658. FAN, C. T., MULLER, Mervin E. and REZUCHA, Ivan. 1962. Development of sampling plans by using sequential (item by item) selection techniques and digital computers. *Journal of the American Statistical Association*, vol. 57, no. 298, pp. 387-402.

FANNING, John. 1969. *See* GREGORY, William and FANNING, John. 1969.

659. FARBER, Bernard. 1963. Response falsification and spurious correlation in survey research. *American Sociological Review*, vol. 28, no. 1, pp. 123-130.

660. FARBER, Maurice Lee. 1941. Prison research: techniques and methods. *Journal of Social Psychology*, vol. 14, no. 2, pp. 295-310.

FARNSWORTH, Paul R. 1934. *See* SAADI, Mitchel and FARNSWORTH, Paul R. 1934.

661. FASTEAU, Herman H., INGRAM, J. Jack and MINTON, George. 1964. Control of quality of coding in the 1960 censuses. *Journal of the American Statistical Association*, vol. 59, no. 305, pp. 120-132.

662. **FAY**, Paul J. and MIDDLETON, Warren C. 1941. Indirect measurement of listeners' preferences for men and women commercial announcers. *Journal of Applied Psychology*, vol. 25, no. 5, pp. 558-572.

FEARING, Franklin. 1953. *See* SPIEGELMAN, Marvin, TERWILLIGER, Carl and FEARING, Franklin. 1953.

FEDER, Walda. 1962. *See* GOLDSTEIN, Michael J., HIMMELFARB, Samuel and FEDER, Walda. 1962.

FEDERER, Walter T. 1953. *See* BRUNK, Max E. and FEDERER, Walter T. 1953.

663. **FEDERIGHI**, Enrico. 1950. The use of chi-square in small samples. *American Sociological Review*, vol. 15, no. 6, pp. 777-779.

664. **FELDMAN**, J. J., HYMAN, Herbert and HART, C. W. 1951/52. A field study of interviewer effects on the quality of survey data. *Public Opinion Quarterly*, vol. 15, no. 4, pp. 734-761.

FELDT, Allan. 1959. *See* SHARP, Harry and FELDT, Allan. 1959.

665. **FELLEGI**, I. P. 1964. An analysis of response variance. *Bulletin of the International Statistical Institute*, vol. 40, no. 2, pp. 758-759.

666. **FELLEGI**, I. P. 1964. Response variance and its estimation. *Journal of the American Statistical Association*, vol. 59, no. 308, pp. 1016-1041.

667. **FERBER**, Robert. 1948. The problem of bias in mail returns: a solution. *Public Opinion Quarterly*, vol. 12, no. 4, pp. 669-676.

668. **FERBER**, Robert. 1948. Weekly versus monthly consumer purchase panels. *Journal of Marketing*, vol. 13, no. 2, pp. 223-224.

669. **FERBER**, Robert. 1948. Which — mail questionnaires or personal interviews? *Printer's Ink*, vol. 222, no. 7, pp. 44-47, 61, 64, 66.

670. **FERBER**, Robert. 1949. A rejoinder. *Public Opinion Quarterly*, vol. 13, no. 4, pp. 562-563.

671. **FERBER**, Robert. 1950. Further comment. *Public Opinion Quarterly*, vol. 14, no. 1, pp. 196-197.

672. **FERBER**, Robert. 1950. More on bias in mail surveys. *Public Opinion Quarterly*, vol. 14, no. 1, pp. 193-196.

673. **FERBER**, Robert. 1952. Order bias in a mail survey. *Journal of Marketing*, vol. 17, no. 2, pp. 171-178.

674. **FERBER**, Robert and WALES, Hugh G. 1952. Detection and correction of interviewer bias. *Public Opinion Quarterly*, vol. 16, no. 1, pp. 107-127.

675. FERBER, Robert. 1953. Observations on a consumer panel operation. *Journal of Marketing*, vol. 17, no. 3, pp. 246-259.

676. FERBER, Robert. 1955. Gradational adjectives in market surveys. *Journal of Applied Psychology*, vol. 39, no. 3, pp. 173-177.

677. FERBER, Robert. 1955. On the reliability of responses secured in sample surveys. *Journal of the American Statistical Association*, vol. 50, no. 271, pp. 788-810.

678. FERBER, Robert. 1956. The effect of respondent ignorance on survey results. *Journal of the American Statistical Association*, vol. 51, no. 276, pp. 576-586.

679. FERBER, Robert and WALES, Hugh G. 1963. A new way to measure journal readership. *Journal of Advertising Research*, vol. 3, no. 3, pp. 9-16.

680. FERBER, Robert. 1964. Does a panel operation increase the reliability of survey data: the case of consumer savings. *AMERICAN STATISTICAL ASSOCIATION. Proceedings of the Social Statistics Section*, 1964. pp. 210-216.

681. FERBER, Robert. 1965. The reliability of consumer surveys of financial holdings: time deposits. *Journal of the American Statistical Association*, vol. 60, no. 309, pp. 148-163.

682. FERBER, Robert. 1966. Item nonresponse in a consumer survey. *Public Opinion Quarterly*, vol. 30, no. 3, pp. 399-415.

683. FERBER, Robert. 1966. The reliability of consumer surveys of financial holdings: demand deposits. *Journal of the American Statistical Association*, vol. 61, no. 313, pp. 91-103.

684. FERGUSON, H. H. 1937. Food industry: the investigation of consumers' taste preferences. *Human Factor*, vol. 11, no. 11, pp. 399-405.

685. FERGUSON, Leonard W. 1935. The influence of individual attitudes on construction of an attitude scale. *Journal of Social Psychology*, vol. 6, no. 1, pp. 115-117.

686. FERGUSON, Leonard W. 1935. Two methods of representing the distribution of an attitude in a group. *Journal of Social Psychology*, vol. 6, no. 4, pp. 474-479.

687. FERGUSON, Leonard W. 1939. The requirements of an adequate attitude scale. *Psychological Bulletin*, vol. 36, no. 8, pp. 665-673.

688. FERRABY, J. G. 1944. The validity of public opinion survey results. *Sociological Review*, vol. 36, nos. 1-4, pp. 43-49.

689. **FERRISS**, Abbott L. 1951. A note on stimulating response to questionnaires. *American Sociological Review*, vol. 16, no. 2, pp. 247-249.

690. **FESTINGER**, Leon. 1947. The treatment of qualitative data by 'scale analysis'. *Psychological Bulletin*, vol. 44, no. 2, pp. 149-161.

691. **FIELD**, Harry H. and CONNELLY, Gordon M. 1942. Testing polls in official election booths. *Public Opinion Quarterly*, vol. 6, no. 4, pp. 610-616.

692. **FIELD**, J. G. 1967. The study of preferences in market research. *EUROPEAN SOCIETY FOR OPINION AND MARKETING RESEARCH/WORLD ASSOCIATION FOR PUBLIC OPINION RESEARCH. Congress, XX, Vienna, 1967. ESOMAR WAPOR Congress 1967*. Brussels: ESOMAR, 1967. pp. 455-467.

693. **FIELD**, Joan Bissey. 1955. The effects of praise in a public opinion poll. *Public Opinion Quarterly*, vol. 19, no. 1, pp. 85-91.

694. **FIELD** methods and techniques. 1949. *Human Organization*, vol. 8, no. 1, pp. 26-27.

695. **FIELD** methods and techniques. 1949. *Human Organization*, vol. 8, no. 2, pp. 22-24.

696. **FIELD** methods and techniques. 1949. *Human Organization*, vol. 8, no. 3, pp. 27-29.

697. **FIELD** methods and techniques. 1949. *Human Organization*, vol. 8, no. 4, pp. 29-30.

698. **FIELD** methods and techniques. 1949. *Human Organization*, vol. 9, no. 1, pp. 29-30.

699. **FINE**, Bernard J. and HAGGARD, Donald F. 1958. Contextual effects in scaling. *Journal of Applied Psychology*, vol. 42, no. 4, pp. 247-251.

700. **FINK**, Joseph and CARLSON, J. Spencer. 1959. Tetrachoric correlations – thirty an hour! *Journal of Educational Research*, vol. 52, no. 7, pp. 273-275.

   FINK, Raymond. 1951. *See* CROSSLEY, Helen M. and FINK, Raymond. 1951.

701. **FINK**, Raymond. 1960. The retrospective question. *Public Opinion Quarterly*, vol. 24, no. 1, pp. 143-148.

702. **FISCHER**, Robert P. 1946. Signed versus unsigned personal questionnaires. *Journal of Applied Psychology*, vol. 30, no. 3, pp. 220-225.

703. **FISHBEIN**, Martin and RAVEN, Bertram H. 1962. The AB scales: an operational definition of belief and attitude. *Human Relations*, vol. 51, no. 1, pp. 35-43.

704. **FISHER**, Herbert. 1950. Interviewer bias in the recording operation. *International Journal of Opinion and Attitude Research*, vol. 4, no. 3, pp. 391-411.

705. **FISHER**, Stephen T., WEISS, David J., and DAWIS, Rene V. 1968. A comparison of Likert and pair comparisons techniques in multivariate attitude scaling. *Educational and Psychological Measurement*, vol. 28, no. 1, pp. 81-94.

706. **FISK**, George. 1950. Interviewer ratings of respondent interest of sample surveys. *Journal of Marketing*, vol. 14, no. 5, pp. 725-730.

FISKE, Marjorie. 1938. *See* LAZARSFELD, Paul and FISKE, Marjorie. 1938.

707. **FISKE**, Marjorie and HANDEL, Leo. 1946. Motion picture research: content and audience analysis. *Journal of Marketing*, vol. 11, no. 2, pp. 129-134.

708. **FISKE**, Marjorie and HANDEL, Leo. 1946. Motion picture research: response analysis. *Journal of Marketing*, vol. 11, no. 3, pp. 273-280.

709. **FISKE**, Marjorie and HANDEL, Leo. 1947. New techniques for studying the effectiveness of films. *Journal of Marketing*, vol. 11, no. 4, pp. 390-393.

710. **FLANAGAN**, John C. 1954. The critical incident technique. *Psychological Bulletin*, vol. 51, no. 4, pp. 327-358.

711. **FLEISHMAN**, Edwin A. 1951. An experimental consumer panel technique. *Journal of Applied Psychology*, vol. 35, no. 2, pp. 133-135.

712. **FLEISHMAN**, Edwin A. 1953. The measurement of leadership attitudes in industry. *Journal of Applied Psychology*, vol. 37, no. 3, pp. 153-158.

713. **FLEISS**, Marjorie. 1940. The panel as an aid in measuring effects of advertising. *Journal of Applied Psychology*, vol. 24, no. 6, pp. 685-695.

714. **FLETCHER**, Robert. 1969. Reading behaviour reconsidered. *EUROPEAN SOCIETY FOR OPINION AND MARKETING RESEARCH. Congress, XXII, Amsterdam, 1969. Papers* ... Brussels: ESOMAR, 1969. pp. 535-554.

FLOWERMAN, Samuel H. 1950. *See* STEWART, Naomi and FLOWERMAN, Samuel H. 1950.

715. **FOA**, Uriel G. 1950. Scale and intensity analysis in opinion research. *International Journal of Opinion and Attitude Research*, vol. 4, no. 2, pp. 192-208.

716. **FOA**, Uriel G. 1950. Scale and intensity analysis in sociometric research. *Sociometry*, vol. 13, no. 4, pp. 358-362.

FOA, Uriel G. 1951. *See* GUTTMAN, Louis and FOA, Uriel G. 1951.

717. **FOLEY**, John P., *Jr.* 1944. The use of the free association technique in the investigation of the stimulus value of trade names. *Journal of Applied Psychology*, vol. 28, no. 5, pp. 431-435.

718. **FORD**, Neil M. 1967. The advance letter in mail surveys. *Journal of Marketing Research*, vol. 4, no. 2, pp. 202-204.

719. **FORD**, Neil M. 1968. Questionnaire appearance and response rates in mail surveys. *Journal of Advertising Research*, vol. 8, no. 3, pp. 43-46.

720. **FORD**, Neil M. 1969. Consistency of responses in a mail survey. *Journal of Advertising Research*, vol. 9, no. 4, pp. 31-33.

721. **FORD**, Robert N. 1940. Scaling White-Negro experiences by the method of equal-appearing intervals. *Sociometry*, vol. 3, no. 4, pp. 343-352.

722. **FORD**, Robert N. 1941. Scaling experience by a multiple-response technique: a study of White-Negro contacts. *American Sociological Review*, vol. 6, no. 1, pp. 9-23.

FORD, Robert N. 1947. *See* CLAUSEN, John A. and FORD, Robert N. 1947.

723. **FORD**, Robert N. and ZEISEL, Hans. 1949. Bias in mail surveys cannot be controlled by one mailing. *Public Opinion Quarterly*, vol. 13, no. 3, pp. 495-501.

724. **FORD**, Robert N. 1950. A rapid scoring procedure for scaling attitude questions. *Public Opinion Quarterly*, vol. 14, no. 3, pp. 507-532.

725. **FORD**, Robert N. and ZEISEL, Hans. 1950. A rejoinder. *Public Opinion Quarterly*, vol. 14, no. 1, p. 196.

FORLANO, G. 1937. *See* PINTNER, R. and FORLANO, G. 1937.

726. **FOTHERGILL**, J. E. and WILKINS, L[eslie] T. 1953. Analysis and interpretation. London: Office of Population Censuses and Surveys, Social Survey Division, 1953. 21pp. (*Methodological series, M68*).

727. **FOTHERGILL**, J. E. and WILLCOCK, H. D. 1953. Interviewers and interviewing. London: Office of Population Censuses and Surveys, Social Survey Division, 1953. 15pp. (*Methodological series, M69*).

728. **FOTHERGILL**, J. E. and WILKINS, L[eslie] T. 1955. Analysis and interpretation. *The Incorporated Statistician*, vol. 5, no. 4, pp. 93-117.

729. **FOTHERGILL**, J. E. and WILLCOCK, H. D. 1955. Interviewers and interviewing. *The Incorporated Statistician*, vol. 5, no. 4, (supplement), pp. 37-56.

730. **FOTHERGILL**, J. E. and WILLCOCK, H. D. 1956. Interviewers and interviewing. *EDWARDS, F., ed. Readings in market research*. London: British Market Research Bureau, 1956. pp. 63-78.

731. **FOTHERGILL**, Jack and JOYCE, Timothy. 1967. A continuing system for planning and evaluating advertising campaigns. *ADVERTISING RESEARCH FOUNDATION. Annual Conference, 13th, New York City, 1967. Proceedings* ... New York: Advertising Research Foundation, 1967. pp. 54-61.

FOTION, Nicholas G. 1962. *See* MAGID, Frank N., FOTION, Nicholas G. and GOLD, David. 1962.

732. **FOUR** effective ways for testing copy. 1958. *Printer's Ink*, vol. 264, no. 7, pp. 62-64.

FOWLER, Floyd J., *Jr.* 1963. *See* CANNELL, Charles F. and FOWLER, Floyd J., *Jr.* 1963.

FOWLER, Floyd J., *Jr.* 1964. *See* CANNELL, Charles F. and FOWLER, Floyd J., *Jr.* 1964.

FOX, Frances C. 1952. *See* DVORAK, Beatrice, FOX, Frances C. and MEIGH, Charles. 1952.

FOX, Leo B. 1969. *See* GREEN, Paul E., CARMONE, Frank J. and FOX, Leo B. 1969.

733. **FOX**, Peter D. 1963. Noncooperation bias in television ratings. *Public Opinion Quarterly*, vol. 27, no. 2, pp. 312-314.

734. **FRANCEL**, E. G. 1966. Mail-administered questionnaires: a success story. *Journal of Marketing Research*, vol. 3, no. 1, pp. 89-91.

735. **FRANK**, Marji. 1948. Measurement and elimination of confusion elements in recognition surveys. *Journal of Marketing*, vol. 12, no. 3, pp. 362-364.

736. **FRANK**, Ronald E., MASSY, William F. and MORRISON, Donald G. 1965. Bias in multiple discriminant analysis. *Journal of Marketing Research*, vol. 2, no. 3, pp. 250-258.

FRANK, Ronald E. 1966. *See* MORRISON, Donald G., FRANK, Ronald E. and MASSY, William F. 1966.

737. **FRANK**, Ronald E. and GREEN, Paul E. 1968. Numerical taxonomy in marketing analysis: a review article. *Journal of Marketing Research*, vol. 5, no. 1, pp. 83-98.

738. **FRANKEL**, Lester R. 1960. How incentives and subsamples affect the precision of mail surveys. *Journal of Advertising Research*, vol. 1, no. 1, pp. 1-3.

739. **FRANKEL**, Lester R. 1960. Rejoinder. *Journal of Advertising Research*, vol. 1, no. 2, pp. 23-24.

FRANKLAND, Pamela. 1950. *See* GRAY, P[ercy] G., CORLETT, T[homas] and FRANKLAND, Pamela. 1950.

740. **FRANZEN**, Raymond. 1942. Inequalities which affect scores of advertisements. *Journal of Marketing*, vol. 6, no. 4, part 2, pp. 128-132.

741. **FRANZEN**, Raymond and POLITZ, Alfred. 1942. Method for determining number of readers per copy of a magazine circulation. *Journal of Applied Psychology*, vol. 26, no. 4, pp. 477-481.

742. **FRANZEN**, Raymond and LAZARSFELD, Paul F. 1945. Mail questionnaire as a research problem. *Journal of Psychology*, vol. 20, no. 2, pp. 293-320.

FRANZEN, Raymond. 1948. *See* WOODWARD, Julian L. and FRANZEN, Raymond. 1948.

743. **FRANZEN**, Raymond and WILLIAMS, Robert. 1956. A method for measuring error due to variance among interviewers. *Public Opinion Quarterly*, vol. 20, no. 3, pp. 587-592.

744. **FRAZIER**, George and BIRD, Kermit. 1958. Increasing the response of a mail questionnaire. *Journal of Marketing*, vol. 23, no. 2, pp. 186-187.

745. **FREEDMAN**, Ronald. 1950. Incomplete matching in ex post facto studies. *American Journal of Sociology*, vol. 55, no. 5, pp. 485-487.

FREEDMAN, Ronald. 1964. *See* COOMBS, Lolagene and FREEDMAN, Ronald. 1964.

FREEMAN, P. R. 1966. *See* POULTON, E. C. and FREEMAN, P. R. 1966.

FREIBERG, A[lbert] D. 1942. *See* LINK, Henry C. and FREIBERG, A[lbert] D. 1942.

746. FREIBERG, Albert D., VAUGHN, Charles L. and EVANS, Mary C. 1946. Effect of interviewer bias upon questionnaire results obtained with a large number of investigators. *American Psychologist*, vol. 1, no. 7, pp. 243.

FRENCH, Gilbert M. 1963. *See* MALMSTROM, Edward J. and FRENCH, Gilbert M. 1963.

747. FREUND, R. J. and HARTLEY, H. O. 1965. A procedure for automatic data editing. *AMERICAN STATISTICAL ASSOCIATION. Proceedings of the Social Statistics Section*, 1965. pp. 272-279.

748. FREUND, R. J. and HARTLEY, H. O. 1967. A procedure for automatic data editing. *Journal of the American Statistical Association*, vol. 62, no. 318, pp. 341-352.

749. FREY, Allan H. and BECKER, Wesley C. 1958. Some personality correlates of subjects who fail to appear for experimental appointments. *Journal of Consulting Psychology*, vol. 22, no. 3, pp. 164.

FRIED, Edrita. 1944. *See* CANTRIL, Hadley and FRIED, Edrita. 1944.

750. FRIEDMAN, Pearl. 1942. A second experiment on interviewer bias. *Sociometry*, vol. 5, no. 4, pp. 378-381.

751. FRISBIE, Bruce and SUDMAN, Seymour. 1968. The use of computers in coding free responses. *Public Opinion Quarterly*, vol. 32, no. 2, pp. 216-232.

FRITZ, Charles E. 1956. *See* BUCHER, Rue, FRITZ, Charles E. and QUARANTELLI, E. L. 1956.

FRITZ, Charles E. 1956. *See* BUCHER, Rue, FRITZ, Charles E. and QUARANTELLI, E. L. 1956.

752. FROST, W. A. K. and BRAINE, R. L. 1967. The application of the repertory grid technique to problems in market research. *Commentary*, vol. 9, no. 3, pp. 161-175.

753. FULCHER, John S. and ZUBIN, Joseph. 1942. The item analyzer:

a mechanical device for treating the four fold table in large samples. *Journal of Applied Psychology*, vol. 26, no. 4, pp. 511-522.

754. FUNKHOUSER, G. Ray and PARKER, Edwin B. 1968. Analyzing coding reliability: the random-systematic-error coefficient. *Public Opinion Quarterly*, vol. 32, no. 1, pp. 122-128.

755. FURFEY, Paul Hanly and DALY, Joseph F. 1937. A criticism of factor analysis as a technique of social research. *American Sociological Review*, vol. 2, no. 2, pp. 178-186.

756. FURLONG, E. J. 1948. Memory. *Mind*, vol. 57, no. 225, pp. 16-44.

757. FYOCK, James A. 1968. Content analysis of films: new slant on an old technique. *Journalism Quarterly*, vol. 45, no. 1, pp. 687-691.

758. GADDIS, L. Wesley. 1959. Questionnaire analysis program. *Educational and Psychological Measurement*, vol. 19, no. 3, pp. 435-437.

759. GAGE, N. L. and REMMERS, H. H. 1948. Opinion polling and marked-sensed punch cards. *Journal of Applied Psychology*, vol. 32, no. 1, pp. 88-91.

760. GAITO, John. 1961. Repeated measurements designs and counterbalancing. *Psychological Bulletin*, vol. 58, no. 1, pp. 46-54.

761. GALES, Kathleen. 1957. Discriminant functions of socio-economic class. *Applied Statistics*, vol. 6, no. 2, pp. 123-132.

762. GALES, Kathleen and KENDALL, M. G. 1957. An inquiry concerning interviewer variability. *Journal of the Royal Statistical Society, series A*, vol. 120, part 2, pp. 121-147.

763. GALLUP, George [H.] 1930. A scientific method for determining reader-interest. *Journalism Quarterly*, vol. 7, no. 1, pp. 1-13.

764. GALLUP, George [H.] 1941. Question wording in public opinion polls: comments on points raised by Mr. Stagner. *Sociometry*, vol. 4, no. 3, pp. 259-268.

765. GALLUP, George [H.] 1947. The quintamensional plan of question design. *Public Opinion Quarterly*, vol. 11, no. 3, pp. 385-393.

766. GALLUP, George H., *et al.* 1949. Unsettled problems of the sampling survey methodology. MEIER, Norman C. and SAUNDERS, Harold W., eds. *The polls and public opinion.* New York: Holt, 1949. pp. 314-334.

767. GALT, William E. 1955. Trends in the study of memory. ROBACK, A. A., ed. *Present-day psychology.* New York: Philosophical Library, 1955. pp. 117-133.

768. **GANLY**, Raymond H. 1948. Consumer panel shows apparel-home furnishings buying in New York department stores. *Printer's Ink*, vol. 223, no. 12, pp. 34-36.

769. **GANLY**, Raymond H. 1949. Market research project employs split-panel technique. *Printer's Ink*, vol. 227, no. 7, pp. 45, 48.

770. **GARBER**, C. W., Jr. 1951. Play techniques for interviewing on durable goods. *Public Opinion Quarterly*, vol. 15, no. 1, pp. 139-140.

GARDNER, Isaac, Jr. 1966. *See* BRYANT, Eugene C., GARDNER, Isaac, Jr. and GOLDMAN, Morton. 1966.

GARFINKLE, Norton. 1962. *See* GREENBERG, Allan and GARFINKLE, Norton. 1962.

771. **GARRETT**, Henry E. and ZUBIN, Joseph. 1943. The analysis of variance in psychological research. *Psychological Bulletin*, vol. 40, no. 4, pp. 233-267.

GASKILL, Harold V. 1932. *See* BURTT, Harold E. and GASKILL, Harold V. 1932.

772. **GASKILL**, Harold V. and HOLCOMB, Richard L. 1936. The effectiveness of appeal in radio advertising: a technique with some typical results. *Journal of Applied Psychology*, vol. 20, no. 3, pp. 325-339.

GATEWOOD, Robert D. 1967. *See* HINRICHS, John R. and GATEWOOD, Robert D. 1967.

GATTY, Ronald. 1967. *See* ACHENBAUM, Alvin A., HALEY, Russell I. and GATTY, Ronald. 1967.

773. **GAUDET**, Hazel. 1939. The favorite radio program. *Journal of Applied Psychology*, vol. 23, no. 1, pp. 115-126.

774. **GAUDET**, Hazel and WILSON, E[lmo] C. 1940. Who escapes the personal investigator? *Journal of Applied Psychology*, vol. 24, no. 6, pp. 773-777.

GEER, Blanche. 1958. *See* BECKER, Howard S. and GEER, Blanche. 1958.

GEER, Blanche. 1958. *See* BECKER, Howard S. and GEER, Blanche. 1958.

775. **GENGERELLI**, J. A. and BUTLER, Bruce V. 1955. A method for comparing the profiles of several population samples. *Journal of Psychology*, vol. 40, no. 2, pp. 247-268.

776. **GENGERELLI**, J. A. 1963. A method for detecting subgroups in a population and specifying their membership. *Journal of Psychology*, vol. 55, no. 2, pp. 457-468.

GEOFFREY, Leon. 1941. *See* DEMING, W. Edwards and GEOFFREY, Leon. 1941.

GEOFFREY, Leon. 1942. *See* DEMING, W. Edwards, TEPPING, Benjamin J. and GEOFFREY, Leon. 1942.

777. **GEORGE**, F. H. 1953. 'Either-or' questions in series. *British Journal of Psychology*, vol. 44, part 3, pp. 243-247.

GERBERICH, John B. 1946. *See* CUBER, John F. and GERBERICH, John B. 1946.

778. **GERBERICH**, John B. 1947. A study of the consistency of informant responses to questions in a questionnaire. *Journal of Educational Psychology*, vol. 38, no. 5, pp. 299-306.

GERBRANDS, Henry. 1948. *See* BALES, Robert F. and GERBRANDS, Henry. 1948.

GERGEN, Kenneth J. 1963. *See* BACK, Kurt W. and GERGEN, Kenneth J. 1963.

779. **GERGEN**, Kenneth J. and BACK, Kurt W. 1966. Communication in the interview and the disengaged respondent. *Public Opinion Quarterly*, vol. 30, no. 3, pp. 385-398.

780. **GERSON**, Earle J. 1969. Methodological and interviewing problems in household surveys of employment problems in urban poverty neighborhoods. *AMERICAN STATISTICAL ASSOCIATION. Proceedings of the Social Statistics Section*, 1969. pp. 19-23.

781. **GETZELS**, J. W. and WALSH, J. J. 1958. The method of paired direct and projective questionnaires in the study of attitude structure and socialization. *Psychological Monographs*, vol. 72, no. 1, pp. 1-34.

782. **GHISELLI**, Edwin E. 1939. All or none versus graded response questionnaires. *Journal of Applied Psychology*, vol. 23, no. 3, pp. 405-413.

783. **GHISELLI**, Edwin E. 1940. Some further points on public opinion polls. *Journal of Marketing*, vol. 5, no. 2, pp. 115-119.

784. **GHISELLI**, Edwin E. 1941. The measurement of trade name familiarity. *Journal of Applied Psychology*, vol. 25, no. 1, pp. 97-100.

785. **GHISELLI,** Edwin E. 1941. The problem of question form in the measure of sales by consumer interviews. *Journal of Marketing*, vol. 6, no. 2, pp. 170–171.

786. **GIBBINS,** K. 1968. Response sets and the semantic differential. *British Journal of Social and Clinical Psychology*, vol. 7, part 4, pp. 253-263.

GILLILAND, A. R. 1948. *See* ECKSTRAND, Gordon and GILLILAND, A. R. 1948.

GLASSER, Gerald J. 1969. *See* METZNER, Gale D., GLASSER, Gerald J. and ELIASBERG, Jay. 1969.

787. **GLASER,** William A. 1966. International mail surveys of informants. *Human Organization*, vol. 25, no. 1, pp. 78-86.

GLAZER, Nathan. 1948. *See* RIESMAN, David and GLAZER, Nathan. 1948.

GLAZER, Nathan. 1950/51. *See* RIESMAN, David and GLAZER, Nathan. 1950/51.

GLAZER, Nathan. 1951. *See* RIESMAN, David and GLAZER, Nathan. 1951.

GLESER, Goldine C. 1964. *See* CRONBACH, Lee J. and GLESER, Goldine C. 1964.

788. **GLOCK,** Charles Y[oung]. 1951. Some applications of the panel method to the study of social change. *AMERICAN SOCIETY FOR TESTING MATERIALS. Annual meeting, 54th Atlantic City, N.J., 1951. Symposium on measurement of consumer wants.* Philadelphia: American Society for Testing Materials, 1952. pp. 46-54.

789. **GLOCK,** Charles Young. 1952. Participation bias and re-interview effect in panel studies. *Dissertation Abstracts*, vol. 12, no. 5, pp. 756.

GOLD, David. 1962. *See* MAGID, Frank N., FOTION, Nicholas G. and GOLD, David. 1962.

GOLDFRIED, Marvin R. 1965. *See* GREEN, Russel F. and GOLDFRIED, Marvin R. 1965.

GOLDIAMOND, I. 1961. *See* AZRIN, N. H., HOLZ, W. and GOLDIAMOND, I. 1961.

790. **GOLDMAN,** Alfred E. 1962. The group depth interview. *Journal of Marketing*, vol. 26, no. 3, pp. 61-68.

GOLDMAN, Morton. 1966. *See* BRYANT, Eugene C., GARDNER, Isaac, *Jr.* and GOLDMAN, Morton, 1966.

791. **GOLDMAN-EISLER**, Frieda. 1955. Speech-breathing activity — a measure of tension and affect during interviews. *British Journal of Psychology*, vol. 46, part 1, pp. 53-63.

GOLDSEN, Rose K. 1958. *See* RALIS, Max, SUCHMAN, Edward A. and GOLDSEN, Rose K. 1958.

792. **GOLDSTEIN**, Hyman and KROLL, Bernard H. 1957. Methods of increasing mail response. *Journal of Marketing*, vol. 22, no. 1, pp. 55-57.

793. **GOLDSTEIN**, H. 1968. Longitudinal studies and the measurement of change. *The Statistician*, vol. 18, no. 2, pp. 93-117.

794. **GOLDSTEIN**, H. 1970. Data processing for longitudinal studies. *Applied Statistics*, vol. 19, no. 2, pp. 145-151.

795. **GOLDSTEIN**, Jacob. 1959. The relative advantages and limitations of the panel and successive-sample techniques in the analysis of opinion change. *Journal of Social Psychology*, vol. 50, no. 2, pp. 305-320.

796. **GOLDSTEIN**, Michael J., HIMMELFARB, Samuel and FEDER, Walda. 1962. A further study of the relationship between response bias and perceptual defense. *Journal of Abnormal and Social Psychology*, vol. 64, no. 1, pp. 56-62.

797. **GOODHARDT**, G. J. 1968. The duplication of television viewing between and within channels. *EUROPEAN SOCIETY FOR OPINION AND MARKETING RESEARCH. Congress, XXI, Opatija, 1968. Papers* . . . Brussels: ESOMAR, 1968. pp. 289-306.

GOODMAN, Charles. 1939. *See* SCHANCK, R. L. and GOODMAN, Charles. 1939.

GOODMAN, Leo A. 1963. *See* TOWERS, Irwin M., GOODMAN, Leo A. and ZEISEL, Hans. 1963.

798. **GOODMAN**, Roe and MACCOBY, Eleanor E. 1948. Sampling methods and sampling errors in surveys of consumer finances. *International Journal of Opinion and Attitude Research*, vol. 2, no. 3, pp. 349-360.

799. **GOODSON**, C. and BERDY, D[avid]. 1967. Memory in advertising. *Admap*, vol. 3, no. 6, pp. 261-263.

GORDON, C. Wayne. 1958. *See* BABCHUK, Nicholas and GORDON, C. Wayne. 1958.

800. **GORDON**, Chad. 1963. A note on computer programs for Guttman scaling. *Sociometry*, vol. 26, no. 1, p. 129.

GORDON, Donald A. 1947. *See* CRUTCHFIELD, Richard S. and GORDON, Donald A. 1947.

GORDON, Gerald. 1958. *See* LEVINE, Sol and GORDON, Gerald. 1958.

801. GORDON, Leonard V. and ALF, Edward F. 1961. An analysis of errors made in marking an interest inventory. *Journal of General Psychology*, vol. 65, no. 2, pp. 261-268.

802. GORDON, Raymond L. 1956. Dimensions of the depth interview. *American Journal of Sociology*, vol. 62, no. 2, pp. 158-164.

803. GORDON, Robert A. 1968. Issues in multiple regression. *American Journal of Sociology*, vol. 73, no. 5, pp. 592-616.

804. GORDON, W. D. 1963. Double interview. *MARKET RESEARCH SOCIETY. New developments in research*. London: Market Research Society with The Oakwood Press, 1963. pp. 121–125.

805. GOSNELL, Harold F. and PEARSON, Norman. 1939. The study of voting behavior by correlational techniques. *American Sociological Review*, vol. 4, no. 6, pp. 809-815.

806. GOSNELL, Harold F. and GRAZIA, Sebastian de. 1942. A critique of polling methods. *Public Opinion Quarterly*, vol. 6, no. 3, pp. 378-390.

807. GOULD, A. L., SHAH, B. V. and ABERNATHY, J[ames] R. 1969. Unrelated question randomized response techniques with two trials per respondent. *AMERICAN STATISTICAL ASSOCIATION. Proceedings of the Social Statistics Section*, 1969. pp. 351-359.

808. GOWER, J. C. 1967. A comparison of some methods of cluster analysis. *Biometrics*, vol. 23, no. 4, pp. 623-637.

809. GRAHAM, Milton D. 1954. The effectiveness of photographs as a projective device in an international attitudes survey, 1: responses of 680 Britons to 10 photographs of American types. *Journal of Social Psychology*, vol. 40, no. 1, pp. 93-120.

GRAHAM, William K. 1965. *See* KOMORITA, S. S. and GRAHAM, William K. 1965.

810. GRANT, David A. 1944. On 'The analysis of variance in psychological research'. *Psychological Bulletin*, vol. 41, no. 3, pp. 158-166.

GRAY, Louis N. 1969. *See* MARTIN, J. David and GRAY, Louis N. 1969.

811. **GRAY**, P[ercy] G. and CORLETT, T[homas]. 1950. Sampling for the Social Survey. *Journal of the Royal Statistical Society, series A*, vol. 31, part 2, pp. 150-199. Discussion . . . pp. 200-206.

812. **GRAY**, P[ercy] G., CORLETT, T[homas] and FRANKLAND, Pamela. 1950. The register of electors as a sampling frame. London: Office of Population Censuses and Surveys, Social Survey Division, 1950. 19pp. (*Methodological series, M59*).

813. **GRAY**, P[ercy] G. and CARTWRIGHT, Ann. 1951. Some effects of using a two month memory period on the Survey of Sickness. London: Office of Population Censuses and Surveys, Social Survey Division, 1951. 4pp. (*Methodological series, M41*).

814. **GRAY**, P[ercy] G., CORLETT, T[homas] and JONES, Pamela. 1951. The proportion of jurors as an index of the economic status of a district. London: Office of Population Censuses and Surveys, Social Survey Division, 1951. 9pp. (*Methodological series, M60*).

815. **GRAY**, P[ercy] G., and HARRIS, Amelia [I.] 1951. Some notes on postal checks. London: Office of Population Censuses and Surveys, Social Survey Division, 1951. 3pp. (*Methodological series, M44*).

816. **GRAY**, Percy G. 1955. The memory factor in social surveys. *Journal of the American Statistical Association*, vol. 50, no. 270, pp. 344-363.

817. **GRAY**, Percy G. 1956. Examples of interviewer variability taken from two sample surveys. *Applied Statistics*, vol. 5, no. 2, pp. 73-85.

818. **GRAY**, Percy G. 1957. A sample survey with both a postal and an interview stage. *Applied Statistics*, vol. 6, no. 2, pp. 139-153.

819. **GRAY**, Sheila. 1970. The electoral register: practical information for use when drawing samples, both for interview and postal surveys. London: Office of Population Censuses and Surveys, Social Survey Division, 1970. 18pp. (*Methodological series, M151*).

GRAZIA, Sebastian de. 1942. *See* GOSNELL, Harold F. and GRAZIA, Sebastian de. 1942.

820. **GREAT BRITAIN**. General Register Office. 1961. Electronic data processing and the Census. *Commentary*, no. 5, pp. 33-38.

821. **GREB**, Gordon B. 1959. Surveying public opinion by 'beeper' telephone. *Journalism Quarterly*, vol. 36, Winter, pp. 67-68.

GREELY, Andrew. 1965. *See* SUDMAN, Seymour, GREELEY, Andrew and PINTO, Leonard. 1965.

GREEN, Paul E. 1968. *See* FRANK, Ronald E. and GREEN, Paul E. 1968.

822. GREEN, Paul E. and CARMONE, Frank J. 1969. Multidimensional scaling: an introduction and comparison of nonmetric unfolding techniques. *Journal of Marketing Research*, vol. 6, no. 3, pp. 330-341.

823. GREEN, Paul E. and RAO, Vithala R. 1969. A note on proximity measures and cluster analysis. *Journal of Marketing Research*, vol. 6, no. 3, pp. 359-364.

824. GREEN, Paul E. and RAO, Vithala R. 1970. Rating scales and information recovery — how many scales and response categories to use? *Journal of Marketing*, vol. 34, no. 3, pp. 33-39.

825. GREEN, Russel F. and GOLDFRIED, Marvin R. 1965. On the bipolarity of semantic space. *Psychological Monographs*, vol. 79, no. 6, pp. 1-31.

826. GREENBERG, Allan. 1949. A method for coding questionnaires in market surveys. *Journal of Marketing*, vol. 14, no. 3, pp. 456-458.

827. GREENBERG, Allan. 1955. Matched samples. *Journal of Marketing*, vol. 18, no. 3, pp. 241-245.

828. GREENBERG, Allan and LISSANCE, Daniel. 1955. The accuracy of a journalistic poll. *Public Opinion Quarterly*, vol. 19, no. 1, pp. 45-52.

829. GREENBERG, Allan and MANFIELD, Manuel N. 1957. On the reliability of mail questionnaires in product tests. *Journal of Marketing*, vol. 21, no. 3, pp. 342-345.

830. GREENBERG, Allan. 1958. Validity of a brand-awareness question. *Journal of Marketing*, vol. 23, no. 2, pp. 182-184.

831. GREENBERG, Allan. 1959. Pictorial stereotypes in a projective test. *Journal of Marketing*, vol. 24, no. 2, pp. 72-74.

832. GREENBERG, Allan and GARFINKLE, Norton. 1962. Delayed recall of magazine articles. *Journal of Advertising Research*, vol. 2, no. 1, pp. 28-31.

833. GREENBERG, Allan. 1963. Paired comparisons vs. monadic tests. *Journal of Advertising Research*, vol. 3, no. 4, pp. 44-49.

GREENBERG, Allan. 1965. *See* ADLER, Lee, GREENBERG, Allan and LUCAS, Darrell B. 1965.

834. GREENBERG, Allan and COLLINS, Sy. 1966. Paired comparison taste tests: some food for thought. *Journal of Marketing Research*, vol. 3, no. 1, pp. 76-80.

835. **GREENBERG**, Arthur L. 1956. Respondent ego-involvement in large-scale surveys. *Journal of Marketing*, vol. 20, no. 4, pp. 390-393.

GREENBERG, Bernard G. 1967. *See* ABUL-ELA, Abdel Latif A., GREENBERG, Bernard G. and HORVITZ, Daniel G. 1967.

836. **GREENBERG**, Bernard G., ABERNATHY, James R. and HORVITZ, Daniel G. 1969. Application of the randomized response technique in obtaining quantitative data. *AMERICAN STATISTICAL ASSOCIATION. Proceedings of the Social Statistics Section*, 1969. pp. 40-43.

837. **GREENE**, Jerome D. and STOCK, J. Stevens. 1966. Brand attitudes as measures of advertising effects. *Journal of Advertising Research*, vol. 6, no. 2, pp. 14-22.

838. **GREENE**, Stanley. 1966. Some recent dicennial census occupational experimental work. *AMERICAN STATISTICAL ASSOCIATION. Proceedings of the Social Statistics Section*, 1966. pp. 193-198.

GREENE, W. F. 1961. *See* PURVIS, L. E. and GREENE, W. F. 1961.

839. **GREENHALGH**, C. 1966. Some techniques and interesting results in discrimination testing. *Commentary*, vol. 8, no. 4, pp. 215-236.

840. **GREENHALGH**, C. 1970. Discrimination testing: further results and developments. *EUROPEAN SOCIETY FOR OPINION AND MARKETING RESEARCH. Congress, XXIII, Barcelona, 1970. Papers* . . . Amsterdam: ESOMAR, 1970. pp. 181-199.

841. **GREGORY**, William. 1961. Aided recall – a new approach. *EUROPEAN SOCIETY FOR OPINION AND MARKETING RESEARCH/ WORLD ASSOCIATION FOR PUBLIC OPINION RESEARCH. Congress, VII, Baden-Baden, 1961. Marketing and sociological research in the future: needs and prospects*. 32pp. Mimeo.

842. **GREGORY**, William and FANNING, John. 1969. Researching research: the market for TV commercials pre-testing. *EUROPEAN SOCIETY FOR OPINION AND MARKETING RESEARCH. Congress, XXII, Amsterdam, 1969. Papers* . . . Brussels: ESOMAR, 1969. pp. 467-485.

843. **GREGSON**, R. A. M. 1960. Bias in the measurement of food preferences by triangular tests. *Occupational Psychology*, vol. 34, no. 5, pp. 249-257.

844. **GREGSON**, R. A. M. 1963. Validation problems in interpreting preference responses to mixed food qualities. *Applied Statistics*, vol. 12, no. 1, pp. 1-13.

845. **GREY**, David L. 1967. Interviewing at the Court. *Public Opinion Quarterly*, vol. 31, no. 2, pp. 285-289.

846. **GROSS**, Edward. 1959. The occupational variable as a research category. *American Sociological Review*, vol. 24, no. 5, pp. 640-649.

847. **GROSS**, Edwin J. 1964. The effect of question sequence on measures of buying interest. *Journal of Advertising Research*, vol. 4, no. 3, pp. 40-41.

848. **GROSS**, Neal and MASON, Ward S. 1953. Some methodological problems of eight-hour interviews. *American Journal of Sociology*, vol. 59, no. 3, pp. 197-204.

849. **GRUBER**, Alin and LINDBERG, Barbara. 1966. Sensitivity, reliability and consumer taste testing. *Journal of Marketing Research*, vol. 3, no. 3, pp. 235-238.

850. **GRUBER**, Alin and LINDBERG, Barbara. 1969. Reaffirmation and a reply. *Journal of Marketing Research*, vol. 6, no. 1, pp. 105-106.

851. **GUEST**, L[ester]. 1942. Last vs. usual purchase questions. *Journal of Applied Psychology*, vol. 26, no. 2, pp. 180-186.

852. **GUEST**, Lester. 1945. Magazine vs. personal interview votes in the consumer jury advertising test. *Journal of Applied Psychology*, vol. 29, no. 5, pp. 399-406.

853. **GUEST**, Lester. 1947. A study of interviewer competence. *International Journal of Opinion and Attitude Research*, vol. 1, no. 4, pp. 17-30.

854. **GUEST**, Lester. 1948/49. Have these sources of polling error been fully explored? *International Journal of Opinion and Attitude Research*, vol. 2, no. 4, pp. 507-509.

855. **GUEST**, Lester. 1949. Degrees of freedom in opinion research. *International Journal of Opinion and Attitude Research*, vol. 3, no. 3, pp. 409-413.

856. **GUEST**, Lester and NUCKOLS, Robert. 1950. A laboratory experiment in recording in public opinion interviewing. *International Journal of Opinion and Attitude Research*, vol. 4, no. 3, pp. 336-352.

GUEST, Lester. 1951. *See* LINDZEY, Gardner E. and GUEST, Lester. 1951.

857. **GUEST**, Lester. 1954. A new training method for opinion interviewers. *Public Opinion Quarterly*, vol. 18, no. 3, pp. 287-299.

858. **GUEST**, Lester. 1962. A comparison of two-choice and four-choice questions. *Journal of Advertising Research*, vol. 2, no. 1, pp. 32-34.

859. **GUETZKOW**, Harold. 1950. Unitizing and categorizing problems in coding qualitative data. *Journal of Clinical Psychology*, vol. 6, no. 1, pp. 47-58.

GUILFORD, J. P. 1936. *See* HACKMAN, R. B. and GUILFORD, J. P. 1936.

860. **GUILFORD**, J. P. 1952. When not to factor analyze. *Psychological Bulletin*, vol. 49, no. 1, pp. 26-37.

861. **GUILFORD**, J. P. and ZIMMERMAN, Wayne S. 1963. Some variable-sampling problems in the rotation of axes in factor analysis. *Psychological Bulletin*, vol. 60, no. 3, pp. 289-301.

862. **GUION**, Robert M. 1954. Regression analysis: prediction from classified variables. *Psychological Bulletin*, vol. 51, no. 5, pp. 505-510.

GULLAHORN, Jeanne E. 1959. *See* GULLAHORN, John T. and GULLAHORN, Jeanne E. 1959.

863. **GULLAHORN**, Jeanne E. and GULLAHORN, John T. 1963. An investigation of the effects of three factors on response to mail questionnaires. *Public Opinion Quarterly*, vol. 27, no. 2, pp. 294-296.

864. **GULLAHORN**, Jeanne E. and GULLAHORN, John T. 1968. The utility of applying both Guttman and factor analysis to survey data. *Sociometry*, vol. 31, no. 2, pp. 213-218.

865. **GULLAHORN**, John T. and GULLAHORN, Jeanne E. 1959. Increasing returns from non-respondents. *Public Opinion Quarterly*, vol. 23, no. 1, pp. 119-121.

GULLAHORN, John T. 1963. *See* GULLAHORN, Jeanne E. and GULLAHORN, John T. 1963.

GULLAHORN, John T. 1968. *See* GULLAHORN, Jeanne E. and GULLAHORN, John T. 1968.

866. **GULLIKSEN**, Harold. 1946. Paired comparisons and the logic of measurement. *Psychological Review*, vol. 53, no. 4, pp. 199-213.

GURNEE, Herbert. 1948. *See* DIETSCH, R. W. and GURNEE, Herbert. 1948.

GURNEY, Margaret. 1946. *See* HANSEN, Morris H., HUTWITZ, William N. and GURNEY, Margaret. 1946.

867. **GUSFIELD**, Joseph R. and SCHWARTZ, Michael. 1963. The meanings of occupational prestige: reconsideration of the NORC scale. *American Sociological Review*, vol. 28, no. 2, pp. 265-271.

868. **GUTHRIE**, Harold W. 1965. Some methodological issues in validation studies. *AMERICAN STATISTICAL ASSOCIATION. Proceedings of the Social Statistics Section*, 1965. pp. 193-196.

GUTTMAN, Isaiah. 1965. *See* RAJU, Nambury S. and GUTTMAN, Isaiah. 1965.

869. **GUTTMAN**, Louis. 1944. A basis for scaling qualitative data. *American Sociological Review*, vol. 9, no. 2, pp. 139-150.

870. **GUTTMAN**, Louis. 1947. On Festinger's evaluation of scale analysis. *Psychological Bulletin*, vol. 44, no. 5, pp. 451-465.

871. **GUTTMAN**, Louis. 1947. The Cornell technique for scale and intensity analysis. *Educational and Psychological Measurement*, vol. 7, no. 2, pp. 247-279.

872. **GUTTMAN**, Louis and SUCHMAN, Edward A. 1947. Intensity and a zero point for attitude analysis. *American Sociological Review*, vol. 12, no. 1, pp. 57-67.

GUTTMAN, Louis. 1947. *See* SUCHMAN, Edward A. and GUTTMAN, Louis. 1947.

873. **GUTTMAN**, Louis and FOA, Uriel G. 1951. Social contact and an intergroup attitude. *Public Opinion Quarterly*, vol. 15, no. 1, pp. 43-53.

874. **GUTTMAN**, Louis, *chairman*. 1956. Application of scaling to market research. *Public Opinion Quarterly*, vol. 20, no. 4, pp. 767-768.

GUZE, Samuel B. 1956. *See* MATARAZZO, Joseph D., SASLOW, George and GUZE, Samuel B. 1956.

875. **HABER**, Lawrence D. 1966. Evaluating response error in the reporting of the income of the aged: benefit income. *AMERICAN STATISTICAL ASSOCIATION. Proceedings of the Social Statistics Section*, 1966. pp. 412-419.

876. **HABERMAN**, Paul W. and SHEINBERG, Jill. 1966. Education reported in interviews: an aspect of survey content error. *Public Opinion Quarterly*, vol. 30, no. 2, pp. 295-301.

877. **HACKMAN**, R. B. and GUILFORD, J. P. 1936. A study of the 'visual fixation' method of measuring attention value. *Journal of Applied Psychology*, vol. 20, no. 1, pp. 44-59.

878. **HADLEY**, Howard D. 1951. Effect of reading and interview fatigue upon readership of magazine advertising. *Journal of Applied Psychology*, vol. 35, no. 6, pp. 424-429.

879. **HAGBURG**, Eugene C. 1968. Validity of questionnaire data: reported and observed attendance in an adult education program. *Public Opinion Quarterly*, vol. 32, no. 3, pp. 453-456.

HAGEDORN, Robert. 1954. *See* DAVIS, F. James and HAGEDORN, Robert. 1954.

HAGGARD, Donald F. 1958. *See* FINE, Bernard J. and HAGGARD, Donald F. 1958.

HAINES, Valerie T. 1950. *See* ELINSON, Jack and HAINES, Valerie T. 1950.

880. **HAIRE**, Mason. 1950. Projective techniques in marketing research. *Journal of Marketing*, vol. 14, no. 5, pp. 649-656.

881. **HALDANE**, Ian R. 1969. The pattern of television viewing. *Commentary*, vol. 11, no. 1, pp. 1-5.

882. **HALDANE**, Ian R. 1970. Measuring television audience reactions. *MARKET RESEARCH SOCIETY. Annual Conference, Brighton, March 15th-17th, 1970. Conference papers.* [London: Market Research Society], 1970. pp. 59-85.

HALEY, Russell I. 1967. *See* ACHENBAUM, Alvin A., HALEY, Russell I. and GATTY, Ronald. 1967.

883. **HALL**, J. and MOSER, C. A. 1954. Social grading of occupations. *GLASS, D., ed. Social mobility in Britain.* London: Routledge and Kegan Paul, 1954. pp. 1-18.

HALL, Nason E. 1963. *See* HILL, Richard J. and HALL, Nason E. 1963.

884. **HALLER**, Terry P. 1966. Let's not bury paired comparisons. *Journal of Advertising Research*, vol. 6, no. 3, pp. 29-30.

HALLONQUIST, Tore. 1950. *See* PEATMAN, John Gray and HALLONQUIST, Tore. 1950.

885. **HALPERN**, Richard S. 1967. Application of pupil response to before-and-after experiments. *Journal of Marketing Research*, vol. 4, no. 3, pp. 320-321.

886. **HAMEL**, La Verne and REIF, Hans G. 1952. Should attitude questionnaires be signed? *Personnel Psychology*, vol. 5, no. 2, pp. 87-91.

887. **HAMILTON**, Max. 1968. Some notes on rating scales. *The Statistician*, vol. 18, no. 1, pp. 11-17.

888. **HAMMOND**, Kenneth R. 1948. Measuring attitudes by error-choice: an indirect method. *Journal of Abnormal and Social Psychology*, vol. 41, no. 1, pp. 38-48.

889. **HAMMOND**, Kenneth R. 1948. Subject and object sampling – a note. *Psychological Bulletin*, vol. 45, no. 6, pp. 530-533.

890. **HANAWALT**, Nelson G. and RUTTIGER, Katherine Ford. 1944. The effect of an audience on remembering. *Journal of Social Psychology*, vol. 19, no. 2, pp. 259-272.

891. **HAND**, Jack. 1953. A method of weighting attitude scale items from subject responses. *Journal of Clinical Psychology*, vol. 9, no. 1, pp. 37-39.

HANDEL, Leo. 1946. *See* FISKE, Marjorie and HANDEL, Leo. 1946.

HANDEL, Leo. 1946. *See* FISKE, Marjorie and HANDEL, Leo. 1946.

HANDEL, Leo. 1947. *See* FISKE, Marjorie and HANDEL, Leo. 1947.

892. **HANDEL**, Leo A. 1950. Don't let yes men sabotage your audience research. *Printer's Ink*, vol. 232, no. 4, pp. 32-33.

893. **HANER**, Charles F. and MEIER, Norman C. 1951. The adaptability of area-probability sampling to public opinion measurement. *Public Opinion Quarterly*, vol. 15, no. 2, pp. 335-352.

894. **HANSEN**, Morris H. and HURWITZ, William N. 1942. Relative efficiencies of various sampling units in population inquiries. *Journal of the American Statistical Association*, vol. 37, no. 217, pp. 89-94.

895. **HANSEN**, Morris H. and DEMING, W. Edwards. 1943. On some census aids to sampling. *Journal of the American Statistical Association*, vol. 38, no. 223, pp. 353-357.

HANSEN, Morris H. 1944. *See* HAUSER, Philip M. and HANSEN, Morris H. 1944.

896. **HANSEN**, Morris H. and HAUSER, Philip M. 1945. Area sampling – some principles of sample design. *Public Opinion Quarterly*, vol. 9, no. 2, pp. 183-193.

897. **HANSEN**, Morris H. and HURWITZ, William N. 1946. The

problem of non-response in sample surveys. *Journal of the American Statistical Association*, vol. 41, no. 236, pp. 517-529.

898. HANSEN, Morris H., HURWITZ, William N. and GURNEY, Margaret. 1946. Problems and methods of the sample survey of business. *Journal of the American Statistical Association*, vol. 41, no. 234, pp. 173-189.

899. HANSEN, Morris H. and DEMING, W. Edwards. 1949. On an important limitation to the use of data from samples. *Bulletin of the International Statistical Institute*, vol. 32, part 2, pp. 214-219.

900. HANSEN, Morris H. and HURWITZ, William N. 1949. Dependable samples for market surveys. *Journal of Marketing*, vol. 14, no. 3, pp. 363-372.

901. HANSEN, Morris H., *et al.* 1951. Response errors in surveys. *Journal of the American Statistical Association*, vol. 46, no. 254, pp. 147-190.

902. HANSEN, Morris H., HURWITZ, William N. and PRITZKER, Leon 1953. The accuracy of census results. *American Sociological Review*, vol. 18, no. 4, pp. 416-423.

903. HANSEN, Morris H. and STEINBERG, Joseph. 1956. Control of errors in surveys. *Biometrics*, vol. 12, no. 4, pp. 462-474.

904. HANSEN, Morris H., HURWITZ, William N. and BERSHAD, Max A. 1959. Measurement errors in censuses and surveys. *AMERICAN STATISTICAL ASSOCIATION. Proceedings of the Social Statistics Section*, 1959. pp. 2-5.

905. HANSEN, Morris H., HURWITZ, William N. and BERSHAD, Max A. 1961. Measurement errors in censuses and surveys. *Bulletin of the International Statistical Institute*, vol. 38, no. 2, pp. 359-374.

906. HANSEN, Morris H., HURWITZ, William N. and JABINE, Thomas B. 1961. The use of imperfect lists for probability sampling at the U.S. Bureau of the Census. *Bulletin of the International Statistical Institute*, vol. 40, no. 1, pp. 497-517.

907. HANSON, Robert H. and MARKS, Eli S. 1958. Influence of the interviewer on the accuracy of survey results. *Journal of the American Statistical Association*, vol. 53, no. 283, pp. 635-655.

908. HARDEN, Edward. 1967. On the panels. *Admap*, vol. 3, no. 6, pp. 281-283.

909. HARDIN, Einar and HERSHEY, Gerald L. 1960. Accuracy of employee reports on changes in pay. *Journal of Applied Psychology*, vol. 44, no. 4, pp. 269-275.

910. **HARDING**, John. 1944. Refusals as a source of bias. *CANTRIL, Hadley, et al. Gauging public opinion*. Princeton: Princeton University Press; London: H. Milford, Oxford University Press, 1944. pp. 119-123.

911. **HARDING**, John. 1944. The measurement of civilian morale. *CANTRIL, Hadley, et al. Gauging public opinion*. Princeton: Princeton University Press; London: H. Milford, Oxford University Press, 1944, pp. 233-258. Appendix, pp. 261-285.

912. **HARDING**, John. 1949. Some basic principles of self-surveys. *Journal of Social Issues*, vol. 5, no. 2, pp. 21-29.

913. **HARE**, A. Paul and **DAVIE**, James S. 1954. The group interview: its use in a study of undergraduate culture. *Sociology and Social Research*, vol. 39, no. 2, pp. 81-87.

914. **HARE**, A. Paul. 1960. Interview responses: personality or conformity. *Public Opinion Quarterly*, vol. 24, no. 4, pp. 679-685.

915. **HARRELL**, Thomas W., **BROWN**, Donald E. and **SCHRAMM**, Wilbur. 1949. Memory in radio news listening. *Journal of Applied Psychology*, vol. 33, no. 3, pp. 265-274.

916. **HARRIMAN**, Philip L. 1935. An objective technique for beginning the interview with certain types of adults. *Journal of Applied Psychology*, vol. 19, no. 5, pp. 717-724.

917. **HARRIS**, Amelia [I.] 1951. Detectable errors and omissions on schedules. London: Office of Population Censuses and Surveys, Social Survey Division, 1951. 4pp. (*Methodological series, M39*).

HARRIS, Amelia [I.] 1951. *See* GRAY, P[ercy] G. and HARRIS, Amelia [I.] 1951.

918. **HARRIS**, Amelia I. 1953. The work of a coding section. London: Office of Population Censuses and Surveys, Social Survey Division, 1953. 9pp. (*Methodological series, M67*).

919. **HARRIS**, Amelia [I.] and **WILKINS**, L[eslie] T. 1953. A note on intensity measurement. London: Office of Population Censuses and Surveys, Social Survey Division, 1953. 5pp. (*Methodological series, M66*).

920. **HARRIS**, Amelia I. 1955. The work of a coding section. *The Incorporated Statistician*, vol. 5, no. 4 (supplement) pp. 82-92.

921. **HARRIS**, Amelia I. 1963. Some problems in using sample survey techniques among older people. London: Office of Population Censuses and Surveys, Social Survey Division, 1963. 11pp. (*Methodological series, M108*).

922. **HARRIS**, Amelia I., HUGHES, Gwenda and SEARS, Angela. 1963. A preliminary study of interviewer's response rates on a large-scale survey. London: Office of Population Censuses and Surveys, Social Survey Division, 1963. 7pp. (*Methodological series, M110*).

923. **HARRIS**, Chester W. 1964. Some recent developments in factor analysis. *Educational and Psychological Measurement*, vol. 24, no. 2, pp. 193-206.

924. **HARRIS**, Lawrence. 1965. A note on the distinction between enumerative and analytical surveys for business decisions. *The American Statistician*, vol. 19, no. 5, pp. 29.

925. **HARRIS**, Louis. 1956. Some observations on election behavior research. *Public Opinion Quarterly*, vol. 20, no. 2, pp. 379-391.

926. **HARRIS**, Louis. 1957. Election polling and research. *Public Opinion Quarterly*, vol. 21, no. 1, pp. 108-116.

927. **HARRIS**, Muriel. 1952. Interviewer research, paper I: some facts about interviewer turnover: an examination of turnover in relation to interviewer grades. London: Office of Population Censuses and Surveys. Social Survey Division, 1952. 4pp. (*Methodological series, M47a*).

928. **HARRIS**, Muriel. 1952. Interviewer research, paper I: some facts available about interviewers at time of selection reviewed in relation to turnover. London: Office of Population Censuses and Surveys, Social Survey Division, 1952. 4pp. (*Methodological series, M47b*).

929. **HARRIS**, Muriel. 1952. Interviewer research, paper VI: the grading of interviewers: an examination of visible and concealed interviewer error as revealed by the grading tests, and some suggestions for future grading procedure. London: Office of Population Censuses and Surveys, Social Survey Division, 1952. 5pp. (*Methodological series, M52*).

930. **HARRIS**, Natalie and CONNELLY, Gordon M. 1948. Introducing a symposium on interviewing problems. *International Journal of Opinion and Attitude Research*, vol. 2, no. 1, pp. 69-84.

HARRIS, Paul, 1970. *See* SAMPSON, Peter [M. J.] and HARRIS, Paul. 1970.

931. **HARRISON**, P. J. 1968. A method of cluster analysis and some applications. *Applied Statistics*, vol. 17, no. 3, pp. 226-236.

932. **HARRISON**, Tom. 1947. A British view on 'cheating'. *Public Opinion Quarterly*, vol. 11, no. 1, pp. 172-173.

933. **HART**, Clyde W. 1948. Bias in interviewing in studies of opinions, attitudes, and consumer wants. *Proceedings of the American Philosophical Society*, vol. 92, no. 5, pp. 399-404.

934. **HART**, Clyde W. 1951. Interviewer bias. *AMERICAN SOCIETY FOR TESTING MATERIALS. Annual meeting, 54th, Atlantic City, N.J., 1951. Symposium on measurement of consumer wants.* Philadelphia: American Society for Testing Materials, 1952. pp. 38-45.

HART, C. W. 1951/52. *See* FELDMAN, J. J., HYMAN, Herbert and HART, C. W. 1951/52.

935. **HART**, H. 't., CORMAN, T. and ZEE, H. van der. 1969. Measuring level of consumption: an alternative to classification of socio-economic status. *EUROPEAN SOCIETY FOR OPINION AND MARKETING RESEARCH. Congress, XXII, Amsterdam, 1969. Papers . . .* Brussels: ESOMAR, 1969. pp. 279-300.

936. **HART**, Hornell. 1949. A rapid test of significance for differences between percentages. *Social Forces*, vol. 27, no. 4, pp. 401-408.

HARTER, Susan. 1965. *See* MILGRAM, Stanley, MANN, Leon and HARTER, Susan. 1965.

HARTLEY, H. O. 1965. *See* FREUND, R. J. and HARTLEY, H. O. 1965.

HARTLEY, H. O. 1967. *See* FREUND, R. J. and HARTLEY, H. O. 1967.

937. **HARVEY**, Bill. 1968. Nonresponse in TV meter panels. *Journal of Advertising Research*, vol. 8, no. 2, pp. 24-27.

938. **HASKINS**, Jack B. 1960. Comment on 'How incentives and subsamples affect the precision of mail surveys'. *Journal of Advertising Research*, vol. 1, no. 2, pp. 22-23.

939. **HASKINS**, Jack B. 1960. Pre-testing editorial items and ideas for reader interest. *Journalism Quarterly*, vol. 37, no. 2, pp. 224-230.

940. **HASTORF**, Albert H. and CANTRIL, Hadley. 1949. Some psychological errors in polling – a few guides for opinion interpretation. *Journal of Educational Psychology*, vol. 40, no. 1, pp. 57-60.

941. **HASTORF**, A[lbert] H. and PIPER, G. W. 1951. A note on the effect of explicit instructions on prestige suggestion. *Journal of Social Psychology*, vol. 33, no. 2, pp. 289-293.

942. **HATHAWAY**, S. R. and WELCH, A[lfred] C. 1934. Does guessing distort the results of the method of triple associates? *Journal of Applied Psychology*, vol. 18, no. 6, pp. 793-798.

943. **HATT**, Paul K. 1950. Occupation and social stratification. *American Journal of Sociology*, vol. 55, no. 6, pp. 533-543.

944. **HAUCK**, Mathew. 1964. Interviewer compensation on consumer surveys. *Commentary*, no. 14, pp. 15-18.

HAUG, Arne F. 1969. *See* MYERS, James H. and HAUG, Arne F. 1969.

945. **HAUSER**, Philip M. and HANSEN, Morris H. 1944. On sampling in market surveys. *Journal of Marketing*, vol. 9, no. 1, pp. 26-31.

HAUSER, Philip M. 1945. *See* HANSEN, Morris H. and HAUSER, Philip M. 1945.

946. **HAUSER**, Philip M. *chairman*. 1948. Standards in public opinion research. *Public Opinion Quarterly*, vol. 12, no. 4, pp. 812-818.

947. **HAY**, Edward N. 1958. A simple method of recording paired comparisons. *Journal of Applied Psychology*, vol. 42, no. 2, pp. 139-140.

HAYES, Donald P. 1957. *See* MANNICHE, Erik and HAYES, Donald P. 1957.

948. **HAYES**, Donald P. 1964. Item order and Guttman scales. *American Journal of Sociology*, vol. 70, no. 1, pp. 51-58.

HAYNES, John G. 1957. *See* PERYAM, David R. and HAYNES, John G. 1957.

HAYS, David G. 1952. *See* BORGATTA, Edgar F. and HAYS, David G. 1952.

949. **HEADS**, J. and THRIFT, H. J. 1966. Notes on a study in postal response rates. *Commentary*, vol. 8, no. 4, pp. 257-262.

HEALY, M. J. R. 1962. *See* YATES, F. and HEALY, M. J. R. 1962.

950. **HEATH**, Andrew M. 1950. A demonstration of bias in a mail questionnaire. *Printer's Ink*, vol. 232, no. 12, pp. 36-37.

951. **HEATH**, Robert W. 1958. A machine method of computing Guttman's coefficient of reproducibility with a large sample. *Journal of Applied Psychology*, vol. 42, no. 3, pp. 204-205.

952. **HEATON**, Eugene E., *Jr*. 1965. Increasing mail questionnaire returns with a preliminary letter. *Journal of Advertising Research*, vol. 5, no. 4, pp. 36-39.

953. **HEBERLE**, Rudolf. 1951. On the use of questionnaires in research: open letter to a graduate student. *American Sociological Review*, vol. 16, no. 4, p. 549.

HEIL, L. M. 1939. *See* ROOS, F. J. and HEIL, L. M. 1939.

954. **HELLER**, Frank A. 1969. Group feedback analysis: a method of field research. *Psychological Bulletin*, vol. 72, no. 2, pp. 108-117.

955. **HELLER**, Kenneth, DAVIS, John D. and MYERS, Roger A. 1966. The effects of interviewer style in a standardized interview. *Journal of Consulting Psychology*, vol. 30, no. 6, pp. 501-508.

956. **HELLER**, Norman. 1951. Moran's 'Measuring exposure to advertisements'. *Journal of Applied Psychology*, vol. 35, no. 1, pp. 77-78.

957. **HENDRICKS**, Walter A. 1944. The relative efficiencies of groups of farms as sampling units. *Journal of the American Statistical Association*, vol. 39, no. 227, pp. 366-376.

958. **HENDRICKS**, Walter A. 1949. Adjustment for bias caused by non-response in mailed surveys. *Agricultural Economics Research*, vol. 1, part 2, pp. 52-56.

959. **HENEMAN**, Herbert G., *Jr.* and PATERSON, Donald G. 1949. Refusal rates and interviewer quality. *International Journal of Opinion and Attitude Research*, vol. 3, no. 3, pp. 392-398.

HENEMAN, Herbert G., *Jr.* 1956. *See* DUNNETTE, Marvin D. and HENEMAN, Herbert G., *Jr.* 1956.

HENKEL, Ramon E. 1969. MORRISON, Denton E. and HENKEL, Ramon E. 1969.

960. **HENRY**, Andrew F. 1952. A method of classifying non-scale response patterns in a Guttman scale. *Public Opinion Quarterly*, vol. 16, no. 1, pp. 94-106.

961. **HENRY**, Andrew F. and BORGATTA, Edgar F. 1956. A consideration of some problems of content identification in scaling. *Public Opinion Quarterly*, vol. 20, no. 2, pp. 457-469.

962. **HENRY**, Harry. 1954. Some techniques for simulating actuality in opinion enquiries. Paper read to the 9th annual conference of the American Association for Public Opinion Research and the World Association for Public Opinion Research, Asbury Park, N.J., April 1954. 12ff. Mimeo.

963. **HENRY**, Harry. 1954. The importance of controlling investigators. Paper read to the annual conference of the European Society for Opinion and Marketing Research, Ostende, 1954. 7ff. Mimeo.

964. **HENRY**, Harry. 1956. Questionnaire design. Lecture, delivered at the Market Research Society's Annual Summer School, Oxford, 2nd July, 1956. 8ff. Mimeo.

965. **HENRY**, Harry. 1962. Belson's studies in readership. *Journal of Advertising Research*, vol. 2, no. 2, pp. 9-14.

966. **HERSEN**, Michel. 1967. Experimentally induced response biases as a function of positive and negative wording. *Journal of Experimental Psychology*, vol. 74, no. 4, pp. 588-590.

HERSHEY, Gerald L. 1960. *See* HARDIN, Einar and HERSHEY, Gerald L. 1960.

967. **HERZOG**, Elizabeth G. 1947. Pending perfection: a qualitative complement to quantitative methods. *International Journal of Opinion and Attitude Research*, vol. 1, no. 3, pp. 31-48.

HESS, Irene. 1958. *See* KISH, Leslie and HESS, Irene. 1958.

HESS, Irene. 1959. *See* KISH, Leslie and HESS, Irene. 1959.

968. **HESS**, Robert D. and HINK, Douglas L. 1959. A comparison of forced vs. free Q-sort procedure. *Journal of Educational Research*, vol. 53, no. 3, pp. 83-90.

HESS, Irene. 1959. *See* KISH, Leslie and HESS, Irene. 1959.

HEVNER, Kate. 1933. *See* SEASHORE, Robert H. and HEVNER, Kate. 1933.

969. **HICKS**, J. W. and KOHLS, R. L. 1955. Memomotion study as a method of measuring consumer behavior. *Journal of Marketing*, vol. 20, no. 2, pp. 168-170.

970. **HICKS**, Jack M. and CAMPBELL, Donald T. 1965. Zero-point scaling as affected by social object, scaling method, and context. *Journal of Personality and Social Psychology*, vol. 2, no. 6, pp. 793-808.

971. **HIGHMAN**, Arthur. 1955. The audited self-administered questionnaire. *Journal of Marketing*, vol. 20, no. 2, pp. 155-159.

972. **HILDUM**, Donald C. and BROWN, Roger W. 1956. Verbal reinforcement and interviewer bias. *Journal of Abnormal and Social Psychology*, vol. 53, no. 1, pp. 108-111.

973. **HILGARD**, Ernest R. and PAYNE, Stanley L. 1944. Those not at home: riddle for pollsters. *Public Opinion Quarterly*, vol. 8, no. 2, pp. 254-261.

974. **HILL**, P. B. 1970. Multi-variate analysis – what pay-off for the marketing man? *MARKET RESEARCH SOCIETY. Annual Conference, Brighton, March 15th 17th, 1970. Conference papers.* [London: Market Research Society], 1970. pp. 177-187.

975. **HILL**, Richard J. 1953. A note on inconsistency in paired comparison judgments. *American Sociological Review*, vol. 18, no. 5, pp. 564-566.

976. **HILL**, Richard J. and HALL, Nason E. 1963. A note on rapport and the quality of interview data. *Southwestern Social Science Quarterly*, vol. 44, no. 3, pp. 247-255.

> **HILL**, Richard J. 1967. *See* TITTLE, Charles R. and HILL, Richard J. 1967.

977. **HILL**, R. W. 1969. Some reflections on consumer panels. *British Journal of Marketing*, vol. 3, Summer, pp. 63-75.

978. **HIMELSTEIN**, Philip. 1956. Taylor scale characteristics of volunteers and nonvolunteers for psychological experiments. *Journal of Abnormal and Social Psychology*, vol. 52, no. 2, pp. 138-139.

979. **HIMLER**, Leonard E. 1947. Basic principles and techniques of interviewing and counselling. *Industrial Medicine*, vol. 16, no. 11, pp. 529-534.

> **HIMMELFARB**, Samuel. 1962. *See* GOLDSTEIN, Michael J., HIMMELFARB, Samuel and FEDER, Walda. 1962.

980. **HIMMELFARB**, Samuel. 1969. The stability of attitude item scale values. *Journal of Social Psychology*, vol. 77, no. 1, pp. 107-111.

981. **HINCKLEY**, E. D. 1932. The influence of individual opinion on construction of an attitude scale. *Journal of Social Psychology*, vol. 3, no. 3, pp. 283-295.

982. **HINCKLEY**, E. D. 1963. A follow-up study on the influence of individual opinion on the construction of an attitude scale. *Journal of Abnormal and Social Psychology*, vol. 67, no. 3, pp. 290-292.

> **HINK**, Douglas L. 1959. *See* HESS, Robert D. and HINK, Douglas L. 1959.

983. **HINRICHS**, John R. and GATEWOOD, Robert D. 1967. Differences in opinion-survey response patterns as a function of different methods of survey administration. *Journal of Applied Psychology*, vol. 51, no. 6, pp. 497-502.

984. **HOBART**, Donald M. 1943. Occupational classification for market research. *Journal of Marketing*, vol. 7, no. 3, pp. 367-373.

985. **HOCHSTIM**, Joseph R. and SMITH, Dilman M. K. 1948. Area sampling or quota control? – three sampling experiments. *Public Opinion Quarterly*, vol. 12, no. 1, pp. 73-80.

HOCHSTIM, Joseph [R.] 1951. *See* BELDEN, Joe, STEMBER, Herbert and HOCHSTIM, Joseph [R.] 1951.

HOCHSTIM, Joseph R. 1951. *See* STOCK, J. Stevens and HOCHSTIM, Joseph R. 1951.

986. HOCHSTIM, Joseph R. 1967. A critical comparison of three strategies of collecting data from households. *Journal of the American Statistical Association*, vol. 62, no. 319, pp. 976-989.

987. HOCHSTIM, Joseph R. and ATHANASOPOULOS, Demetrios A. 1970. Personal follow-up in a mail survey: its contribution and its cost. *Public Opinion Quarterly*, vol. 34, no. 1, pp. 69-81.

988. HODGE, Robert W. and SIEGEL, Paul M. 1966. The classification of occupations: some problems of sociological interpretation. *AMERICAN STATISTICAL ASSOCIATION. Proceedings of the Social Statistics Section*, 1966. pp. 176-192.

989. HOFFMAN, Nicholas von and CASSIDY, Sally W. 1956. Interviewing Negro Pentecostals. *American Journal of Sociology*, vol. 62. no. 2, pp. 195-197.

990. HOFSTAETTER, Peter R. 1950. The actuality of questions. *International Journal of Opinion and Attitude Research*, vol. 4, no. 1, pp. 16-26.

991. HOFSTAETTER, Peter R. 1953. The actuality measure in the study of public opinion. *Journal of Applied Psychology*, vol. 37, no. 4, pp. 281-287.

992. HOGG, Margaret H. 1930. Sources of incomparability and error in employment-unemployment surveys. *Journal of American Statistical Association*, vol. 25, no. 171, pp. 284-294.

993. HOGUE, Gerald. 1956/57. Directional probe symbol X as an aid in interview control. *Public Opinion Quarterly*, vol. 20, no. 4, pp. 718-719.

994. HOINVILLE, Gerald and JOWELL, Roger. 1969. Classification manual for household interview surveys in Gt. Britain. London: Social and Community Planning Research, 1969. v,73pp.

995. HOINVILLE, Gerald and JOWELL, Roger. 1969. Guidebook on interviewing procedures. London: Social and Community Planning Research, 1969. 99pp.

HOLLANDER, E. P. 1956. *See* WEBB, Wilse B. and HOLLANDER, E. P. 1956.

HOLMAN, David C. 1967. *See* MATARAZZO, Joseph D. HOLMAN, David C. and WIENS, Arthur N. 1967.

996. HOLMES, C. 1969. Construction and stratification of a sampling frame of primary sampling units. *The Statistician*, vol. 19, no. 1, pp. 31-47.

HOLMES, Olive. 1952/53. *See* BERROL, Edward and HOLMES, Olive. 1952/53.

HOLT, Robert R. 1946. *See* MACCOBY, Eleanor E. and HOLT, Robert R. 1946.

HOLZ, W. 1961. *See* AZRIN, N. H., HOLZ, W. and GOLDIAMOND, I. 1961.

997. HOOFNAGLE, William S. 1963. The effectiveness of advertising for farm products. *Journal of Advertising Research*, vol. 3, no. 4, pp. 2-6.

998. HOOFNAGLE, William S. 1965. Experimental designs in measuring the effectiveness of promotion. *Journal of Marketing Research*, vol. 2, no. 2, pp. 154-162.

999. HOPE, K. 1969. Complete analysis: a method of interpreting multi-variate data. *Journal of the Market Research Society*, vol. 11, no. 3, pp. 201-213.

1000. HOPPE, Donald A. 1952. Certain factors found to improve mail survey returns. *Proceedings of the Iowa Academy of Science*, vol. 59, pp. 374-376.

HORN, J. 1962. *See* CATTELL, R[aymond] B., HORN, J. and BUTCHER, H. J. 1962.

1001. HOROWITZ, C. Morris. 1960. Card tabulation by adding machine. *The American Statistician*, vol. 14, no. 2, pp. 21, 25.

1002. HORST, Paul. 1935. Measuring complex attitudes. *Journal of Social Psychology*, vol. 6, no. 3, pp. 369-374.

1003. HORTON, Mary. 1963. A survey by telephone. London: Office of Population Censuses and Surveys, Social Survey Division, 1963. 19pp. (*Methodological series, M106*).

1004. HORVITZ, D[aniel] G., SHAH, B. V. and SIMMONS, Walt R. 1967. The unrelated question randomized response model. *AMERICAN STATISTICAL ASSOCIATION. Proceedings of the Social Statistics Section*, 1967. pp. 65-72.

HORVITZ, Daniel G. 1967. *See* ABUL-ELA, Abdel Latif A., GREENBERG, Bernard G. and HORVITZ, Daniel G. 1967.

HORVITZ, Daniel G. 1969. *See* GREENBERG, Bernard G., ABERNATHY, James R. and HORVITZ, Daniel G. 1969.

1005. HOUSEHOLDS: magazines' new ad yardstick. 1959. *Printer's Ink*, vol. 268, no. 2, pp. 76, 78.

1006. HOUSEMAN, Earl E. 1949. Designs of samples for surveys. *Agricultural Economics Research*, vol. 1, part 1, pp. 3-10.

1007. HOW consumers edit Breck's TV commercials. 1960. *Printer's Ink*, vol. 271, no. 8, pp. 48-49.

1008. HOW effective are mail questionnaires? 1959. *Printer's Ink*, vol. 267, no. 9, pp. 85-86.

HOY, K. E. 1951. *See* WILLCOCK, H. D. and HOY, K. E. 1951.

1009. HUBBARD, Alfred W. 1950. Phrasing questions. *Journal of Marketing*, vol. 15, no. 1, pp. 48-56.

1010. HUBBARD, Alfred W. 1954. Closed versus open-end code schemes. *Journal of Marketing*, vol. 19, no. 1, pp. 71-74.

1011. HUBBARD, Alfred W. 1954. Which recall aid will obtain reliable information. *Journal of Marketing*, vol. 18, no. 4, pp. 396-398.

1012. HUDSON, Bradford B., BARAKAT, Mohamed K. and LaFORGE, Rolfe. 1959. Problems and methods of cross-cultural research. *Journal of Social Issues*, vol. 15, no. 3, pp. 5-19.

1013. HUEY, George H. H. 1947. Some principles of field administration in large-scale surveys. *Public Opinion Quarterly*, vol. 11, no. 2, pp. 254-263.

1014. HUGHES, Charles J. 1964. Why bother to decrease interview refusals. *Journal of Marketing*, vol. 28, no. 2, pp. 67.

HUGHES, Everett C. 1956. *See* BENNEY, Mark and HUGHES, Everett C. 1956.

1015. HUGHES, G. David. 1967. Selecting scales to measure attitude change. *Journal of Marketing Research*, vol. 4, no. 1, pp. 85-87.

1016. HUGHES, G. David. 1969. Some confounding effects of forced-choice scales. *Journal of Marketing Research*, vol. 6, no. 2, pp. 223-226.

HUGHES, Gwenda. 1963. *See* HARRIS, Amelia I., HUGHES, Gwenda and SEARS, Angela. 1963.

1017. HULETT, J. E., *Jr*. 1938. Interviewing in social research: basic problems of the first field trip. *Social Forces*, vol. 16, no. 3, pp. 358-366.

1018. HUND, James M. 1959. Changing role in the interview situation. *Public Opinion Quarterly*, vol. 23, no. 2, pp. 236-246.

1019. **HUNT**, Audrey. 1966. The effects of weighting on precision. London: Office of Population Censuses and Surveys, Social Survey Division. 14pp. (*Methodological series, M132*).

1020. **HUNT**, Richard A. 1970. A computer procedure for item-scale analysis. *Educational and Psychological Measurement*, vol. 30, no. 1, pp. 133-135.

1021. **HUNT**, William H., CRANE, Wilder W. and WAHIKE, John C. 1964. Interviewing political elites in cross-cultural comparative research. *American Journal of Sociology*, vol. 70, no. 1, pp. 59-68.

HUNTER, William G. 1969. *See* DRAPER, Norman R., HUNTER, William G. and TIERNEY, David E. 1969.

HURWITZ, William N. 1942. *See* HANSEN, Morris H. and HURWITZ, William N. 1942.

HURWITZ, William N. 1946. *See* HANSEN, Morris H. and HURWITZ, William N. 1946.

HURWITZ, William N. 1946. *See* HANSEN, Morris H., HURWITZ, William N. and GURNEY, Margaret. 1946.

HURWITZ, William N. 1949. *See* HANSEN, Morris H. and HURWITZ, William N. 1949.

HURWITZ, William N. 1953. *See* HANSEN, Morris H., HURWITZ, William N. and PRITZKER, Leon, 1953.

HURWITZ, William N. 1958. *See* ECKLER, A. Ross and HURWITZ, William N. 1958.

HURWITZ, William N. 1959. *See* HANSEN, Morris H., HURWITZ, William N. and BERSHAD, Max A. 1959.

HURWITZ, William N. 1961. *See* HANSEN, Morris H., HURWITZ, William N. and BERSHAD, Max A. 1961.

HURWITZ, William N. 1961. *See* HANSEN, Morris H., HURWITZ, William N. and JABINE, Thomas B. 1961.

1022. **HUTCHINSON**, Bertram. 1949. Some problems of measuring the intensiveness of opinion and attitude. *International Journal of Opinion and Attitude Research*, vol. 3, no. 2, pp. 123-131.

1023. **HVISTENDAHL**, J. K. 1961. Headline readability measured in content. *Journalism Quarterly*, vol. 38, no. 2, pp. 226-228.

1024. **HYMAN**, Herbert. 1944/45. Do they tell the truth? *Public Opinion Quarterly*, vol. 8, no. 4, pp. 557-559.

1025. HYMAN, Herbert. 1945. Community background in public opinion research. *Journal of Abnormal and Social Psychology*, vol. 40, no. 4, pp. 411-413.

1026. HYMAN, Herbert and SHEATSLEY, Paul B. 1948. The Kinsey report and survey methodology. *International Journal of Opinion and Attitude Research*, vol. 2, no. 2, pp. 183-195.

1027. HYMAN, Herbert. 1949. Inconsistencies as a problem in attitude measurement. *Journal of Social Issues*, vol. 5, no. 3, pp. 38-42.

1028. HYMAN, Herbert. 1949. Isolation, measurement, and control of interviewer effect. *Social Science Research Council Items*, vol. 3, no. 2, pp. 15-17.

HYMAN, Herbert. 1949. *See* MANHEIMER, Dean and HYMAN, Herbert. 1949.

HYMAN, Herbert. 1949. *See* STEMBER, Herbert and HYMAN, Herbert. 1949.

HYMAN, Herbert. 1949/50. *See* STEMBER, Herbert and HYMAN, Herbert. 1949/50.

HYMAN, Herbert. 1949/50. *See* STEMBER, Herbert and HYMAN, Herbert. 1949/50.

1029. HYMAN, Herbert. 1950. Problems in the collection of opinion-research data. *American Journal of Sociology*, vol. 55, no. 4, pp. 362-370.

HYMAN, Herbert. 1950. *See* SMITH, Harry L. and HYMAN, Herbert. 1950.

1030. HYMAN, Herbert. 1951. Interviewing as a scientific procedure. LERNER, Daniel and LASSWELL, Harold D., eds. *The policy sciences*. Stanford, California: Stanford University Press, 1951 (1965 reprint). pp. 203-216.

HYMAN, Herbert. 1951/52. *See* FELDMAN, J. J., HYMAN, Herbert and HART, C. W. 1951/52.

1031. HYMAN, Herbert H., LEVINE, Gene N. and WRIGHT, Charles R. 1967. Studying expert informants by survey methods: a cross-national inquiry. *Public Opinion Quarterly*, vol. 31, no. 1, pp. 9-26.

IKEDA, Kiyoshi. 1967. *See* YINGER, J. Milton, IKEDA, Kiyoshi and LAYCOCK, Frank. 1967.

INDUSTRIAL HEALTH RESEARCH BOARD. 1938. *See* VERNON, P. E. 1938.

1032. **INGHAM**, J. G. 1952. Memory and intelligence. *British Journal of Psychology,* vol. 43, part 1, pp. 20-32.

1033. **INGLEDEW**, Gwen E. 1952. Interviewer research, paper VIII: interviewers on interviewers. London: Office of Population Censuses and Surveys, Social Survey Division, 1952. 8pp. *(Methodological series, M54).*

1034. **INGLIS**, Jim and JOHNSON, Douglas [J.] 1969. Some observations on, and developments in the analysis of multivariate survey data. *EUROPEAN SOCIETY FOR OPINION AND MARKETING RESEARCH. Congress, XXII, Amsterdam, 1969. Papers...* Brussels: ESOMAR, 1969. pp. 125-157.

INGLIS, Ruth A. 1942. *See* LUDEKE, Herbert C. and INGLIS, Ruth A. 1942.

INGRAM, J. Jack. 1964. *See* FASTEAU, Herman H., INGRAM, J. Jack and MINTON, George. 1964.

1035. **INKELES**, A. and ROSSI, P. H. 1956. National comparisons of occupational prestige. *American Journal of Sociology,* vol. 61. no. 4, pp. 329-339.

INKELES, Alex. 1957. *See* ROSSI, Peter H. and INKELES, Alex. 1957.

1036. **IRELAN**, Lola M. 1969. The older person as a survey respondent. *AMERICAN STATISTICAL ASSOCIATION. Proceedings of the Social Statistics Section,* 1969. pp. 347-350.

IRISH, Donald P. 1967. *See* KNUDSEN, Dean D., POPE, Hallowell and IRISH, Donald P. 1967.

1037. **ISAACSON**, H. L., KOENIGSBERG, A. and SMITH, H. 1967. Mail survey research in Britain: an experiment in incentives. *Commentary,* vol. 9, no. 4, pp. 213-219.

1038. **ITO**, Rikuma. 1967. Differential attitudes of new car buyers. *Journal of Advertising Research,* vol. 7, no. 1, pp. 38-42.

JABINE, Thomas B. 1961. *See* HANSEN, Morris H., HURWITZ, William N. and JABINE, Thomas B. 1961.

1039. **JABINE**, Thomas B. and ROTHWELL, Naomi D. 1970. Split-panel tests of census and survey questionnaires. *AMERICAN STATISTICAL ASSOCIATION. Proceedings of the Social Statistics Section,* 1970. pp. 1-10.

1040. **JACKSON**, David M. and BIDWELL, Charles E. 1959. A modification of Q-technique. *Educational and Psychological Measurement,* vol. 19, no. 2, pp. 221-232.

JACKSON, Elton F. 1962. *See* CURTIS, Richard F. and JACKSON, Elton F. 1962.

1041. JACKSON, Peter J. 1966. Case history evidence of errors associated with non-response in industrial market research. *Commentary*, vol. 8, no. 3, pp. 174-192.

JACKSON, Stuart. 1960. *See* SCOTT, Christopher and JACKSON, Stuart. 1960.

1042. JACOBI, John E. and WALTERS, S. George. 1958. Time sequence and the response error. *Sociological Review*, vol. 6, no. 2, pp. 229-239.

1043. JAEGAR, Carol M. and PENNOCK, Jean L. 1961. An analysis of consistency of response in household surveys. *Journal of the American Statistical Association*, vol. 56, no. 294, pp. 320-327.

JAHODA, G. 1955. *See* BIRMINGHAM, W. B. and JAHODA, G. 1955.

1044. JANIS, Irving L., FADNER, Raymond H. and JANOWITZ, Morris. 1943. The reliability of a content analysis technique. *Public Opinion Quarterly*, vol. 7, no. 2, pp. 293-296.

JANOWITZ, Morris. 1943. *See* JANIS, Irving L., FADNER, Raymond H. and JANOWITZ, Morris. 1943.

1045. JANOWITZ, Morris, *chairman*. 1951. The role of content analysis in opinion and communications research. *Public Opinion Quarterly*, vol. 15, no. 4, pp. 782-788.

JASPEN, Nathan. 1951. *See* KURTZ, Albert K., JASPEN, Nathan and ASH, Philip. 1951.

1046. JENKINS, John G. 1938. Dependability of psychological brand barometers, I: the problem of reliability. *Journal of Applied Psychology*, vol. 22, no. 1, pp. 1-7.

1047. JENKINS, John G. and CORBIN, Horace H., *Jr*. 1938. Dependability of psychological brand barometers, II: the problem of validity. *Journal of Applied Psychology*, vol. 22, no. 3, pp. 252-260.

JENKINS, William O. 1948. *See* POSTMAN, Leo, JENKINS, William O. and POSTMAN, Dorothy L. 1948.

1048. JESSEN, R. J. 1961. A switch-over experimental design to measure advertising effect. *Journal of Advertising Research*, vol. 1, no. 3, pp. 15-22.

JOHNS, S. 1968. *See* LOVELL, M. R. C., JOHNS, S. and RAMPLEY, B. 1968.

JOHNSON, D. M. 1952. *See* KING, G. F., ERHMANN, J. C. and JOHNSON, D. M. 1952.

1049. **JOHNSON**, Douglas J. and PEATE, John L. 1966. The estimation of television viewing frequency. *Admap*, July/August, pp. 394-396.

1050. **JOHNSON**, Doug[las] J. and PEATE, John [L.] 1968. Holiday research: the development and use of a model of the decision making process. *Admap*, vol. 4, no. 1, pp. 5-10.

JOHNSON, Douglas [J.] 1969. *See* INGLIS, Jim and JOHNSON, Douglas [J.] 1969.

JOHNSON, Rochelle. 1961. *See* BRIGGS, Peter F., WIRT, Robert D. and JOHNSON, Rochelle. 1961.

1051. **JOHNSON**, Stephen C. 1967. Hierarchical clustering schemes. *Psychometrika*, vol. 32, no. 3, pp. 241-254.

1052. **JONES**, Charles O. 1959. Notes on interviewing members of the House of Representatives. *Public Opinion Quarterly* vol. 23, no. 3, pp. 404-406.

1053. **JONES**, D. Caradog. 1941. Evolution of the social survey in England since Booth. *American Journal of Sociology*, vol. 46, no. 6, pp. 818-825.

1054. **JONES**, Howard L. 1968. The analysis of variance of data from stratified subsamples. *Journal of the American Statistical Association*, vol. 63, no. 321, pp. 64-86.

JONES, Kenneth J. 1964. *See* COOLEY, William W. and JONES, Kenneth J. 1964.

1055. **JONES**, Kenneth J. 1968. Problems of grouping individuals and the method of modality. *Behavioral Science*, vol. 13, no. 6, pp. 496-511.

JONES, Lyle V. 1957. *See* THURSTONE, L. L. and JONES, Lyle V. 1957.

1056. **JONES**, Lyle V. 1959. Some invariant findings under the method of successive intervals. *American Journal of Psychology*, vol. 72, no. 2, pp. 210-220.

JONES, Pamela. 1951. *See* GRAY, P[ercy] G., CORLETT, T[homas] and JONES, Pamela. 1951.

1057. **JONES**, P[eter] I. 1968. Intensity of reading data – some experimental evidence. *Admap*, vol. 4, no. 6, pp. 286-287.

1058. JONES, Robert L. and BELDO, Leslie A. 1953. Methodological improvements in readership data gathering. *Journalism Quarterly*, vol. 30, Summer, pp. 345-353.

1059. JONGE, W. J. de and STAPEL, J[an]. 1968. De-exaggerating single call interview data. *Admap*, vol. 4, no. 3, pp. 150-151.

1060. JORDAN, Nehemiah. 1965. The 'asymmetry' of 'liking' and 'disliking': a phenomenon meriting further reflection and research. *Public Opinion Quarterly*, vol. 29, no. 2, pp. 315-322.

JOWELL, Roger. 1969. *See* HOINVILLE, Gerald and JOWELL, Roger. 1969.

JOWELL, Roger. 1969. *See* HOINVILLE, Gerald and JOWELL, Roger. 1969.

1061. JOYCE, Timothy. 1963. An approach to measuring the achievement of advertising. *The Statistician*, vol. 13, no. 2, pp. 103-116.

1062. JOYCE, Timothy. 1963. Techniques of brand image measurement. *MARKET RESEARCH SOCIETY. New developments in research.* London: Market Research Society with the Oakwood Press, 1963. pp. 45-63.

1063. JOYCE, T[imothy] and CHANNON, C. 1966. Classifying market survey respondents. *Applied Statistics*, vol. 15, no. 3, pp. 191-215.

1064. JOYCE, Timothy. 1967. A new technique for studying reading behaviour. *Admap*, vol. 3, no. 6, pp. 235-236, 238.

1065. JOYCE, Timothy. 1967. Examples of experimental work with media panels. *Admap*, vol. 3, no. 8, pp. 347-350, 352.

1066. JOYCE, T[imothy] and BIRD, M. 1967. The use of panels for the collection of readership data. *The Roy Thomson medals and awards for media research 1966.* London: The Thomson Organisation, 1967. pp. 49-70.

JOYCE, Timothy. 1967. *See* FOTHERGILL, Jack and JOYCE, Timothy. 1967.

1067. JUDD, Robert C. 1966. Telephone usage and survey research. *Journal of Advertising Research*, vol. 6, no. 4, pp. 38-39.

1068. JUNG, Allen F. 1961. Interviewer differences among automobile purchasers. *Applied Statistics*, vol. 10, no. 1, pp. 93-97.

1069. JUNG, Allen F. 1964. Shopping techniques for collecting price data. *Public Opinion Quarterly*, vol. 28, no. 2, pp. 303-311.

1070. **JUSTER**, F. Thomas. 1966. Consumer buying intentions and purchase probability: an experiment in survey design. *Journal of the American Statistical Association*, vol. 61, no. 315, pp. 658-696.

1071. **KAATZ**, Ronald B. 1963. Improving Agostini's formula for net audience. *Journal of Advertising Research*, vol. 3, no. 3, pp. 43-44.

KAESS, Walter. 1955. *See* RIGGS, Margaret M. and KAESS, Walter. 1955.

1072. **KAHN**, Lessing A. and SUCHMAN, Edward A. 1949/50. The construction and operation of scalogram boards. *International Journal of Opinion and Attitude Research*, vol. 3, no. 4, pp. 530-546.

1073. **KAHN**, Lessing A. and BODINE, Adolph J. 1951. Guttman scale analysis by means of IBM equipment. *Educational and Psychological Measurement*, vol. 11, no. 2, pp. 298-314.

KAHN, Robert L. 1953. *See* CANNELL, Charles F. and KAHN, Robert L. 1953.

KAHN, Robert L. 1968. *See* CANNELL, Charles F. and KAHN, Robert L. 1968.

1074. **KAHNEMAN**, Daniel. 1965. Control of spurious association and the reliability of the controlled variable. *Psychological Bulletin*, vol. 64, no. 5, pp. 326-329.

1075. **KALTON**, G. 1968. Standardization: a technique to control for extraneous variables. *Applied Statistics*, vol. 17, no. 2, pp. 118-136.

KAMEN, Joseph M. 1959. *See* PILGRIM, Francis J. and KAMEN, Joseph M. 1959.

KAMENETZKY, Joe. 1958. *See* SCHUTZ, Howard G. and KAMENETZKY, Joe. 1958.

1076. **KARLSSON**, Hakan K. E. 1968. Postal contact: a methodological or practical economic dilemma. *EUROPEAN SOCIETY FOR OPINION AND MARKETING RESEARCH. Congress, XXI, Opatija, 1968. Papers...* Brussels: ESOMAR, 1968. pp. 149-173.

1077. **KAROL**, John J. 1937. Measuring radio audiences. *Public Opinion Quarterly*, vol. 1, no. 2, pp. 92-96.

1078. **KARSLAKE**, James Spier. 1940. The Purdue eye-camera: a practical apparatus for studying the attention value of advertisements. *Journal of Applied Psychology*, vol. 24, no. 4, pp. 417-440.

1079. **KASSARJIAN**, Harold H. and NAKANISHI, Masao. 1967. A study of selected opinion measurement techniques. *Journal of Marketing Research*, vol. 4, no. 2, pp. 148-153.

1080. KATONA, George. 1949. Financial surveys among consumers. *Human Relations*, vol. 2, no. 1, pp. 3-11.

1081. KATZ, Daniel. 1937. Attitude measurement as a method in social psychology. *Social Forces*, vol. 15, no. 4, pp. 479-482.

1082. KATZ, Daniel and CANTRIL, Hadley. 1937. Public opinion polls. *Sociometry*, vol. 1, nos. 1 & 2, pp. 155-179.

1083. KATZ, Daniel. 1940. Three criteria: knowledge, conviction, and significance. *Public Opinion Quarterly*, vol. 4, no. 2, pp. 277-284.

1084. KATZ Daniel. 1941. The effect of the social status, or membership character, of the interviewer upon his findings. *Psychological Bulletin*, vol. 38, no. 7, p. 540.

1085. KATZ, Daniel. 1942. Do interviewers bias poll results? *Public Opinion Quarterly*, vol. 6, no. 2, pp. 248-268.

1086. KATZ, Daniel. 1944. The measurement of intensity. *CANTRIL, Hadley, et al. Gauging public opinion*. Princeton: Princeton University Press; London: H. Milford, Oxford University Press, 1944. pp. 51-65.

1087. KATZ, Daniel. 1946. Survey technique and polling procedure as methods in social science. *Journal of Social Issues*, vol. 2, no. 4, pp. 62-66.

1088. KATZ, Daniel. 1946. The interpretation of survey findings. *Journal of Social Issues*, vol. 2, no. 2, pp. 33-44.

1089. KATZ, Daniel. 1948/49. Polling methods and the 1948 polling failure. *International Journal of Opinion and Attitude Research*, vol. 2, no. 4, pp. 469-480.

1090. KATZ, Daniel. 1949. An analysis of the 1948 polling predictions. *Journal of Applied Psychology*, vol. 33, no. 1, pp. 15-28.

1091. KATZ, Daniel. 1950. Survey techniques in the evaluation of morale. *MILLER, James Grier, ed. Experiments in social process: a symposium on social psychology*. New York, London: McGraw-Hill, 1950. pp. 65-77.

1092. KATZ, Elihu, et al. 1969. Petitions and prayers: a method for the content analysis of persuasive appeals. *Social Forces*, vol. 47, no. 4, pp. 447-463.

1093. **KATZ**, Leo. 1947. On the matric analysis of sociometric data. *Sociometry*, vol. 10, no. 3, pp. 233-241.

1094. **KATZ**, Leo. 1950. Punched card technique for the analysis of multiple level sociometric data. *Sociometry*, vol. 13, no. 2, pp. 108-122.

1095. **KATZ**, Samuel. 1958. An interviewer tells how to avoid getting wrong answers from research. *Printer's Ink*, vol. 262, no. 2, pp. 73-74.

1096. **KAY**, Herbert. 1955. Notes on a Sunday newspaper readership survey technique. *Journalism Quarterly*, vol. 32, Winter, pp. 76-77, 118.

1097. **KAY**, Herbert. 1959. A new approach to projective testing in survey research. *Public Opinion Quarterly*, vol. 23, no. 2, pp. 267-278.

1098. **KAY**, Lillian Wald and **SCHICK**, Jane Holtzberg. 1945. Role-practice in training depth interviewers. *Sociometry*, vol. 8, no. 1, pp. 82-85.

1099. **KEANE**, John G. 1963. Low cost, high return mail surveys. *Journal of Advertising Research*, vol. 3, no. 3, pp. 28-30.

1100. **KEARL**, Bryant [E.] 1957. The non-reader in a magazine readership survey. *Journalism Quarterly*, vol. 34, Fall, pp. 475-480.

KEARL, Bryant E. 1968. *See* POWERS, Richard D. and KEARL, Bryant E. 1968.

1101. **KEATING**, Elizabeth, **PATERSON**, Donald G. and **STONE**, C. Harold. 1950. Validity of work histories obtained by interview. *Journal of Applied Psychology*, vol. 34, no. 1, pp. 6-11.

1102. **KELLEY**, Harold H. 1949. The warm-cold variable in first impressions of persons. *Journal of Personality*, vol. 18, no. 4, pp. 431-439.

1103. **KELLEY**, H[arold] H., *et al.* 1955. The influence of judges' attitudes in three methods of attitude scaling. *Journal of Social Psychology*, vol. 42, no. 1, pp. 147-158.

1104. **KELLY**, Joe. 1964. The study of executive behaviour by activity sampling. *Human Relations*, vol. 17, no. 3, pp. 277-287.

KELLY, Robert F. 1964. *See* TYLER, Vernon O., *Jr.*, and KELLY, Robert F. 1964.

1105. **KELLY**, Robert F. and STEPHENSON, Ronald. 1967. The semantic differential: an information source for designing retail patronage appeals. *Journal of Marketing*, vol. 31, no. 4, pp. 43-47.

1106. **KELMAN**, Herbert C. 1967. Human use of human subjects: the problem of deception in social psychological experiments. *Psychological Bulletin*, vol. 67, no. 1, pp. 1-11.

1107. **KEMPER**, Raymond A. and THORNDIKE, Robert L. 1951. Interview vs. secret ballot in the survey administration of a personality inventory. *American Psychologist*, vol. 6, no. 7, pp. 362.

1108. **KEMPTHORNE**, O. 1946. The use of a punched-card system for the analysis of survey data, with special reference to the analysis of the National Farm Survey. *Journal of the Royal Statistical Society*, vol. 109, part 3, pp. 284-295.

1109. **KEMSLEY**, W. F. F. 1952. Estimating individual expenditure from family totals. *Applied Statistics*, vol. 1, no. 3, pp. 192-201.

1110. **KEMSLEY**, W. F. F. 1959. Designing a budget survey. *Applied Statistics*, vol. 8, no. 2, pp. 114-123.

1111. **KEMSLEY**, W. F. F. 1960. Interviewer variability and a budget survey. *Applied Statistics*, vol. 9, no. 2, pp. 122-129.

1112. **KEMSLEY**, W. F. F. and NICHOLSON, J. L. 1960. Some experiments in methods of conducting family expenditure surveys. *Journal of the Royal Statistical Society, series A*, vol. 123, part 3, pp. 307-328.

1113. **KEMSLEY**, W. F. F. 1965. Interviewer variability in expenditure surveys. *Journal of the Royal Statistical Society, series A*, vol. 128, part 1, pp. 118-139.

1114. **KEMSLEY**, W. F. F. 1966. Sampling errors in the Family Expenditure Survey. London: Office of Population Censuses and Surveys, Social Survey Division, 1966. 13pp. (*Methodological series, M122*).

1115. **KEMSLEY**, W. F. F. 1969. Income question – a simplified version of the F.E.S. questions for use in other surveys. London: Office of Population Censuses and Surveys, Social Survey Division, 1969. 6pp. (*Methodological series, M147*).

1116. **KENDALL**, M. G. 1950. Factor analysis as a statistical technique. KENDALL, M. G. and SMITH, Babington B. Factor analysis. *Journal of the Royal Statistical Society, series B*, vol. 12, no. 1, pp. 60-73.

1117. KENDALL, M. G. 1952. A classification of the sampling process. *The Incorporated Statistician*, vol. 3, no. 10, pp. 41-47.

KENDALL, M. G. 1957. *See* GALES, Kathleen and KENDALL, M. G. 1957.

KENDALL, Patricia L. 1946. *See* MERTON, Robert K. and KENDALL, Patricia L. 1946.

1118. KENDALL, Patricia L. and LAZARSFELD, Paul F. 1950. Problems of survey analysis. *MERTON, Robert K. and LAZARSFELD, Paul F. Continuities in social research: studies in the scope and method of 'The American soldier'.* Glencoe, Illinois: Free Press, 1950. pp. 133-196.

KENISTON, Kenneth. 1960. *See* COUCH, Arthur and KENISTON, Kenneth. 1960.

KENNEY, Kathryn Claire. 1946. *See* EDWARDS, Allen L. and KENNEY, Kathryn Claire. 1946.

1119. KEPHART, N. C. and OLIVER, James E. 1952. A punched card procedure for use with the method of paired comparisons. *Journal of Applied Psychology*, vol. 36, no. 1, pp. 47-48.

1120. KEPHART, William M. and BRESSLER, Marvin. 1958. Increasing the responses to mail questionnaires: a research study. *Public Opinion Quarterly*, vol. 22, no. 2, pp. 123-132.

1121. KERBY, Joe Kent. 1967. Semantic generalization in the formation of consumer attitudes. *Journal of Marketing Research*, vol. 4, no. 3, pp. 314-317.

KERCKHOFF, Alan C. 1957. *See* CAMPBELL, Ernest Q. and KERCKHOFF, Alan C. 1957.

1122. KESWICK, Gordon M. and COREY, Lawrence G. 1961. A sensitive measure of ad exposure. *Journal of Advertising Research*, vol. 1, no. 6, pp. 12-16.

KIDD, Jerry. 1956. *See* BURWEN, Leroy S., CAMPBELL, Donald T. and KIDD, Jerry. 1956.

1123. KILDEGAARD, Ingrid C. 1962. Comments on Mr. Ehrenberg's review of 'A comparison of estimates from the nights-at-home formula with estimates from six calls.' *Commentary*, no. 7 pp. 40-41.

1124. KILDEGAARD, Ingrid C. 1965. How consumers misreport what they spent. *Journal of Advertising Research*, vol. 5, no. 2, pp. 51-55.

1125. **KILDEGAARD**, Ingrid C. 1966. Checking the checkers. *Journal of Advertising Research*, vol. 6, no. 3, pp. 51-53.

1126. **KILDEGAARD**, Ingrid C. 1966. Rejoinder. *Journal of Advertising Research*, vol. 6, no. 4, pp. 40-41.

1127. **KILDEGAARD**, Ingrid C. 1966. Telephone trends. *Journal of Advertising Research*, vol. 6, no. 2, pp. 56-60.

KILPATRICK, Franklin P. 1948. *See* EDWARDS, Allen L. and KILPATRICK, Franklin P. 1948.

1128. **KIMBALL**, Andrew E. 1961. Increasing the rate of return in mail surveys. *Journal of Marketing*, vol. 25, no. 6, pp. 63-64.

1129. **KIMMEL**, Herbert D. 1956. The relationship between chi square and size of sample in two-celled tables. *Journal of Applied Psychology*, vol. 40, no. 1, pp. 61-62.

1130. **KIMMEL**, Herbert D. 1956. The relationship between chi square and size of sample: the general case. *Journal of Applied Psychology*, vol. 40. no. 6, pp. 415-416.

1131. **KINARD**, A. J. 1955. Randomizing error in multiple-choice questions. *Journal of Marketing*, vol. 19, no. 3, pp. 260-263.

1132. **KINCAID**, Harry V. and BRIGHT, Margaret. 1957. Interviewing the business elite. *American Journal of Sociology*, vol. 63, no. 3, pp. 304-311.

1133. **KINCAID**, Harry V. and BRIGHT, Margaret. 1957. The tandem interview: a trial of the two-interviewer team. *Public Opinion Quarterly*, vol. 21, no. 2, pp. 304-312.

1134. **KING**, David J. and LAU, Alan W. 1963. A comparison of three scaling techniques in estimating the accuracy of written recall. *Journal of General Psychology*, vol. 69, no. 2, pp. 203-207.

1135. **KING**, G. F., ERHMANN, J. C. and JOHNSON, D. M. 1952. Experimental analysis of the reliability of observations of social behavior. *Journal of Social Psychology*, vol. 35, no. 2, pp. 151-160.

1136. **KING**, Morton B., Jr. 1944. Reliability of the idea-centered question in interview schedules. *American Sociological Review*, vol. 9, no. 1, pp. 57-64.

1137. **KINSEY**, Alfred C., *et al*. 1955. The Cochran-Mosteller-Tukey report on the Kinsey study: a symposium. *Journal of the American Statistical Association*, vol. 50, no. 271, pp. 811-829.

1138. KINTZ, B. L., et al. 1965. The experimenter effect. *Psychological Bulletin*, vol. 63, no. 4, pp. 223-232.

1139. KIRCHNER, Wayne K. and UPHOFF, Walter H. 1955. The effect of grouping scale items in union-attitude measurement. *Journal of Applied Psychology*, vol. 39, no. 3, pp. 182-183.

1140. KIRKPATRICK, Clifford and STONE, Sarah. 1935. Attitude measurement and the comparison of generations. *Journal of Applied Psychology*, vol. 19, no. 5, pp. 564-582.

1141. KIRKPATRICK, Clifford. 1936. Assumptions and methods in attitude measurements. *American Sociological Review*, vol. 1, no. 1, pp. 75-88.

1142. KIRSCH, Arthur D., BERGER, Philip K. and BELFORD, R. J. 1962. Are reports of brands bought last reliable and valid? *Journal of Advertising Research*, vol. 2, no. 2, pp. 34-36.

1143. KISER, Clyde V. 1934. Pitfalls in sampling for population study. *Journal of the American Statistical Association*, vol. 29, no. 187, pp. 250-256.

1144. KISH, Leslie. 1949. A procedure for objective respondent selection within the household. *Journal of the American Statistical Association*, vol. 44, no. 247, pp. 380-387.

1145. KISH, Leslie. 1952. A two-stage sample of a city. *American Sociological Review*, vol. 17, no. 6, pp. 761-769.

1146. KISH, Leslie and LANSING, John B. 1954. Response errors in estimating the value of homes. *Journal of the American Statistical Association*, vol. 49, no. 267, pp. 520-538.

1147. KISH, Leslie. 1957. Confidence intervals for clustered samples. *American Sociological Review*, vol. 22, no. 2, pp. 154-165.

1148. KISH, Leslie and HESS, Irene. 1958. On noncoverage of sample dwellings. *Journal of the American Statistical Association*, vol. 53, no. 282, pp. 509-524.

1149. KISH, Leslie and HESS, Irene. 1959. A 'replacement' procedure for reducing the bias of nonresponse. *The American Statistician*, vol. 13, no. 4, pp. 17-19.

1150. KISH, Leslie and HESS, Irene. 1959. Some sampling techniques for continuing survey operations. *AMERICAN STATISTICAL ASSOCIATION. Proceedings of the Social Statistics Section*, 1959. pp. 139-143.

1151. KISH, Leslie and SLATER, Carol W. 1960. Two studies of interviewer variance of socio-psychological variables. *AMERICAN STATISTICAL ASSOCIATION. Proceedings of the Social Statistics Section,* 1960. pp. 66-70.

1152. **KISH**, Leslie. 1962. Studies of interviewer variance for attitudinal variables. *Journal of the American Statistical Association,* vol. 57, no. 297, pp. 92-115.

1153. **KISH**, Leslie. 1965. Sampling organizations and groups of unequal sizes. *American Sociological Review,* vol. 30, no. 4, pp. 564-572.

1154. **KJELDERGAARD**, Paul M. 1961. Attitudes towards newscasters as measured by the semantic differential: a descriptive case. *Journal of Applied Psychology,* vol. 45, no. 1, pp. 35-40.

1155. **KLARE**, George R. 1950. Understandability and indefinite answers to public opinion questions. *International Journal of Opinion and Attitude Research,* vol. 4, no. 1, pp. 91-96.

1156. **KLEIN**, L. R. and MORGAN, J. N. 1951. Results of alternative statistical treatments of sample survey data. *Journal of the American Statistical Association,* vol. 46, no. 256, pp. 442-460.

1157. **KLEIN**, Stuart M., MAHER, John R. and DUNNINGTON, Richard A. 1967. Differences between identified and anonymous subjects in responding to an industrial opinion survey. *Journal of Applied Psychology,* vol. 51, no. 2, pp. 152-160.

KLINE, Gerald. 1968. *See* CARTER, Roy E., *Jr.* and KLINE, Gerald. 1968.

1158. **KLINGEMANN**, Hans Dieter and PAPPI, Franz Urban. 1968. Possibilities and problems of cumulated surveys. *EUROPEAN SOCIETY FOR OPINION AND MARKETING RESEARCH. Congress, XXI, Opatija, 1968. Papers . . .* Brussels: ESOMAR, 1968. pp. 499-519.

1159. **KLUCKHOHN**, Florence R. 1940. The participant-observer technique in small communities. *American Journal of Sociology,* vol. 46, no. 3, pp. 331-343.

KNOTT, Joseph K. 1969. SPIERS, Emmett F. and KNOTT, Joseph K. 1969.

1160. **KNOWER**, Franklin H. 1951/52. An inventory of public opinion pollers' interviewing problems. *International Journal of Opinion and Attitude Research,* vol. 5, no. 2, pp. 221-228.

1161. **KNOWLES**, J. B. 1963. Acquiescence response set and the questionnaire measurement of personality. *British Journal of Social and Clinical Psychology,* vol. 2, part 2, pp. 131-137.

1162. **KNOX**, John B. 1951. Maximizing responses to mail questionnaires: a new technique. *Public Opinion Quarterly*, vol. 15, no. 2, pp. 366-367.

1163. **KNUDSEN**, Dean D., POPE, Hallowell and IRISH, Donald P. 1967. Response differences to questions on sexual standards: an interview-questionnaire comparison. *Public Opinion Quarterly*, vol. 31, no. 2, pp. 290-297.

1164. **KNUTSON**, Andie L. 1945. Japanese opinion surveys: the special need and the special difficulties. *Public Opinion Quarterly*, vol. 9, no. 2, pp. 313-319.

KOENIGSBERG, A. 1967. *See* ISAACSON, H. L., KOENIGSBERG, A. and SMITH, H. 1967.

KOHLS, R. L. 1955. *See* HICKS, J. W. and KOHLS, R. L. 1955.

KOLLAT, David T. 1969. *See* ENGEL, James F., KOLLAT, David T. and BLACKWELL, Roger D. 1969.

1165. **KOMORITA**, S. S. 1963. Attitude content, intensity, and the neutral point on a Likert scale. *Journal of Social Psychology*, vol. 61, no. 2, pp. 327-334.

1166. **KOMORITA**, S. S. and GRAHAM, William K. 1965. Number of scale points and the reliability of scales. *Educational and Psychological Measurement*, vol. 25, no. 4, pp. 987-995.

1167. **KONING**, Co de. 1964. Effective techniques in industrial marketing research. *Journal of Marketing*, vol. 28, no. 2, pp. 57-61.

KORCHIN, Sheldon J. 1952. *See* ALPER, Thelma G. and KORCHIN, Sheldon J. 1952.

1168. **KORNHAUSER**, Arthur. 1947. The problem of bias in opinion research. *International Journal of Opinion and Attitude Research*, vol. 1, no. 4, pp. 1-16.

1169. **KORNHAUSER**, Arthur. 1948. Experience with a poll of experts: the problems and the possibilities. *Public Opinion Quarterly*, vol. 12, no. 3, pp. 399-411.

1170. **KRACAUER**, Siegfried. 1952/53. The challenge of qualitative content analysis. *Public Opinion Quarterly*, vol. 16, no. 4, pp. 631-642.

1171. **KRAUSE**, Merton S. 1965. Role-deviant respondent sets and resulting bias, their detection and control in the survey interview. *Journal of Social Psychology*, vol. 67, no. 1, pp. 163-183.

KRIEDT, Philip H. 1948. *See* CLARK, Kenneth E. and KRIEDT, Philip H. 1948.

1172. **KRIEDT**, Philip H. and CLARK, Kenneth E. 1949. 'Item analysis' versus 'scale analysis'. *Journal of Applied Psychology*, vol. 33, no. 2, pp. 114-121.

1173. **KRIEGER**, Margery H. 1964. A control for social desirability in a semantic differential. *British Journal of Social and Clinical Psychology*, vol. 3, part 2, pp. 94-103.

KRIESBERG, Martin. 1952. *See* VOIGT, Robert B. and KRIESBERG, Martin. 1952.

1174. **KROEGER**, Arthur. 1954. A device for simplifying tabulation. *Journal of Marketing*, vol. 18, no. 3, pp. 285-287.

1175. **KROEGER**, Henry J. 1947. The usefulness of the multiple-choice question. *International Journal of Opinion and Attitude Research*, vol. 1, no. 1, pp. 102-105.

KROLL, Abraham. 1939. *See* DUNLAP, Jack W. and KROLL, Abraham. 1939.

KROLL, Bernard H. 1957. *See* GOLDSTEIN, Hyman and KROLL, Bernard H. 1957.

1176. **KRUGLOV**, Lorraine P. and DAVIDSON, Helen H. 1953. The willingness to be interviewed: a selective factor in sampling. *Journal of Social Psychology*, vol. 38, no. 1, pp. 39-47.

1177. **KRUGMAN**, Herbert E. 1956/57. An historical note on motivation research. *Public Opinion Quarterly*, vol. 20, no. 4, pp. 719-723.

1178. **KRUGMAN**, Herbert E. 1960. The 'Draw a supermarket' technique. *Public Opinion Quarterly*, vol. 24, no. 1, pp. 148-149.

1179. **KRUGMAN**, Herbert E. 1962. The learning of consumer preference. *Journal of Marketing*, vol. 26, no. 2, pp. 31-33.

1180. **KRUGMAN**, Herbert E. 1964. Some applications of pupil measurement. *Journal of Marketing Research*, vol. 1, no. 4, pp. 15-19.

1181. **KRUGMAN**, Herbert E. 1965. A comparison of physical and verbal responses to television commercials. *Public Opinion Quarterly*, vol. 29, no. 2, pp. 323-325.

1182. **KRUGMAN**, Herbert E. 1966. The measurement of advertising involvement. *Public Opinion Quarterly*, vol. 30, no. 4, pp. 583-596.

1183. **KRUSKAL**, J. B. 1964. Nonmetric multidimensional scaling: a numerical method. *Psychometrika*, vol. 29, no. 2, pp. 115-129.

1184. **KUBANY**, Albert J. 1965. A validation study of the error-choice technique using attitudes on national health insurance. *Educational and Psychological Measurement*, vol. 13, no. 2, pp. 157-163.

1185. **KULIK**, James A. 1968. Disclosure of delinquent behaviour under conditions of anonymity and nonanonymity. *Journal of Consulting and Clinical Psychology*, vol. 32, no. 5, pp. 506-509.

1186. **KUMATA**, Hideya and SCHRAMM, Wilbur. 1956. A pilot study of cross-cultural meaning. *Public Opinion Quarterly*, vol. 20, no. 1, pp. 229-238.

1187. **KURTZ**, Albert K., JASPEN, Nathan and ASH, Philip. 1951. An efficient method of partitioning populations among control and experimental groups. *Educational and Psychological Measurement*, vol. 11, no. 4, part 1, pp. 578-586.

1188. **KWEREL**, Seymour M. 1969. Estimating unduplicated audience and exposure distribution. *Journal of Advertising Research*, vol. 9, no. 2, pp. 46-53.

1189. **LABOVITZ**, Sanford I. 1965. Methods for control with small sample size. *American Sociological Review*, vol. 30, no. 2, pp. 243-249.

LADE, James H. 1963. *See* BOEK, Walter E. and LADE, James P. 1963.

LaFORGE, Rolfe. 1959. *See* HUDSON, Bradford B., BARAKAT, Mohamed K. and LaFORGE, Rolfe. 1959.

1190. **LaFORGE**, Rolfe. 1967. Confidence intervals or tests of significance in scientific research? *Psychological Bulletin*, vol. 68, no. 6, pp. 446-447.

LAHIRI, D. B. 1961. *See* MAHALANOBIS, P. C. and LAHIRI, D. B. 1961.

1191. **LAMBERT**, Benjamin W. and COHEN, Nathan E. 1949. A comparison of different types of self-surveys. *Journal of Social Issues*, vol. 5, no. 2, pp. 46-55.

1192. **LAMBERTH**, Denis L. and WILKINS, Leslie T. 1952. Design and analysis in prediction surveys. London: Office of Population Censuses and Surveys, Social Survey Division, 1952. 7pp. (*Methodological series, M55*).

1193. **LAMBERTH**, D[enis] L. 1952. Schedule layout. London: Office of Population Censuses and Surveys, Social Survey Division, 1952. 16pp. (*Methodological series, M57*).

1194. **LAMBERTH**, D[enis] L. 1952. Some effects of bonus payments in interviewer performance. London: Office of Population Censuses and Surveys, Social Survey Division, 1952. 13pp. (*Methodological series, M56*).

1195. **LANA,** Robert E. 1964. The influence of the pretest on order effects in persuasive communications. *Journal of Abnormal and Social Psychology,* vol. 69, no. 3, pp. 337-341.

1196. **LANA,** Robert E. 1966. Inhibitory effects of a pretest on opinion change. *Educational and Psychological Measurement,* vol. 26, no. 1, pp. 139-150.

1197. **LANDFIELD,** A. W. 1968. The extremity rating revisited within the context of personal construct theory. *British Journal of Social and Clinical Psychology,* vol. 7, part 2, pp. 135-139.

1198. **LANDIS,** Jack B. 1962. Multiple regression analysis – the easy way. *Journal of Advertising Research,* vol. 2, no. 1, pp. 35-42.

1199. **LANDIS,** Jack B. 1965. Exposure probabilities as measures of media audiences. *Journal of Advertising Research,* vol. 5, no. 3, pp. 24-29.

1200. **LANDSBERGER,** Henry A. and **SAAVEDRA,** Antonio. 1967. Response set in developing countries. *Public Opinion Quarterly,* vol. 31, no. 2, pp. 214-229.

LANE, W. Clayton. 1963. *See* ELLIS, Robert A., LANE, W. Clayton and OLESON, Virginia. 1963.

LANNON, J. M. 1968. *See* LOVELL, M. R. C. and LANNON, J. M. 1968.

LANSING, John B. 1954. *See* KISH, Leslie and LANSING, John B. 1954.

1201. **LANSING,** John B. and **EAPEN,** A. T. 1959. Dealing with missing information in surveys. *Journal of Marketing,* vol. 24, no. 2, pp. 21-27.

LARSEN, Otto N. 1949. *See* LUNDBERG, George A. and LARSEN, Otto N. 1949.

1202. **LARSEN,** Otto N. 1952. The comparative validity of telephone and face-to-face interviews in the measurement of message diffusion from leaflets. *American Sociological Review,* vol. 17, no. 4, pp. 471-476.

1203. **LARSON,** Richard F. and **CATTON,** William R., *Jr.* 1959. Can the mail-back bias contribute to a study's validity? *American Sociological Review,* vol. 24, no. 2, pp. 243-245.

LAU, Alan W. 1963. *See* KING, David J. and LAU, Alan W. 1963.

1204. **LAURENT,** André. 1969. Effects of an extensive questionnaire and a diary procedure on health reporting. Ann Arbor, Michigan: University of Michigan, Survey Research Center, 1969. 134pp.

1205. LAURENT, Charles K. and PARRA, A. Aquileo. 1968. Use of mail questionnaires in Colombia. *Journal of Marketing Research*, vol. 5, no. 1, pp. 101-103.

1206. LAVIDGE, Robert J. and STEINER, Gary A. 1961. A model for predictive measurements of advertising effectiveness. *Journal of Marketing*, vol. 25, no. 6, pp. 59-62.

1207. LAWSON, Faith. 1949. Varying group responses to postal questionnaires. *Public Opinion Quarterly*, vol. 13, no. 1, pp. 114-116.

LAYBOURN, G. P. 1949. *See* LONGSTAFF, H. P. and LAYBOURN, G. P. 1949.

LAYCOCK, Frank. 1967. *See* YINGER, J. Milton, IKEDA, Kiyoshi and LAYCOCK, Frank. 1967.

1208. LAZARSFELD, Paul F. 1935. The art of asking why in marketing research: three principles underlying the formulation of questionnaires. *National Marketing Review*, vol. 1, no. 1, pp. 26-38.

1209. LAZARSFELD, Paul F. 1937. The use of detailed interviews in market research. *Journal of Marketing*, vol. 2, no. 1, pp. 3-8.

1210. LAZARSFELD, Paul [F.] and FISKE. Marjorie. 1938. The 'panel' as a new tool for measuring opinion. *Public Opinion Quarterly*, vol. 2, no. 4, pp. 596-612.

1211. LAZARSFELD, P[aul] F. 1939. Interchangeability of indices in the measurement of economic influences. *Journal of Applied Psychology*, vol. 23, no. 1, pp. 33-45.

1212. LAZARSFELD, Paul F. 1940. 'Panel' studies. *Public Opinion Quarterly*, vol. 4, no. 1, pp. 122-128.

1213. LAZARSFELD, Paul F. 1940. The use of mail questionnaires to ascertain the relative popularity of network stations in family listening surveys. *Journal of Applied Psychology*, vol. 24, no. 6, pp. 802-816.

1214. LAZARSFELD, Paul F. 1941. Repeated interviews as a tool for studying changes in opinion and their causes. *American Statistical Association Bulletin*, vol. 2, no. 1, pp. 3-7.

1215. LAZARSFELD, Paul F. 1944. The controversy over detailed interviews – an offer for negotiation. *Public Opinion Quarterly*, vol. 8, no. 1, pp. 38-60.

LAZARSFELD, Paul F. 1945. *See* FRANZEN, Raymond and LAZARSFELD, Paul F. 1945.

1216. LAZARSFELD, Paul F. 1948. The use of panels in social research. *Proceedings of the American Philosophical Society,* vol. 92, no. 5, pp. 405-410.

LAZARSFELD, Paul F. 1950. *See* KENDALL, Patricia L. and LAZARSFELD, Paul F. 1950.

1217. LAZERWITZ, Bernard. 1964. A sample of a scattered group. *Journal of Marketing Research,* vol. 1, no. 1, pp. 68-71.

LAZIER, Gilbert A. 1968. *See* CLEVENGER, Theodore, Jr., LAZIER, Gilbert A. and CLARK, Margaret Leitner. 1968.

1218. LE MESURIER, T. H. F. T. 1954. Problems in maintaining and continuing basis. *ESOMAR Journal,* no. 1, pp. 73-80.

1219. LE ROUX, A. A. 1968. A method of detecting errors of classification by respondents to postal enquiries. *Applied Statistics,* vol. 17, no. 1, pp. 64-69.

1220. LEAHY, Alice M. 1931. Punching psychological and sociological data on Hollerith cards. *Journal of Applied Psychology,* vol. 15, no. 2, pp. 199-207.

1221. LEDGERWOOD, Richard. 1932. Measurement of the appeal of performances in the theater. *Journal of Applied Psychology,* vol. 16, no. 4, pp. 403-405.

1222. LEE, Alfred McClung. 1947. Sociological theory in public opinion and attitude studies. *American Sociological Review,* vol. 12, no. 3, pp. 312-323.

1223. LEE, Alfred McClung. 1949. Implementation of opinion survey standards. *Public Opinion Quarterly,* vol. 13, no. 4, pp. 645-652.

LEGGETT, John C. 1960. *See* LENSKI, Gerhard E. and LEGGETT, John C. 1960.

1224. LEIGHTON, Alexander H., *et al.* 1943. Assessing public opinion in a dislocated community. *Public Opinion Quarterly,* vol. 7, no. 4, pp. 652-668.

1225. LENSKI, Gerhard E. and LEGGETT, John C. 1960. Caste, class, and deference in the research interview. *American Journal of Sociology,* vol. 65, no. 5, pp. 463-467.

1226. LENTZ, Theodore F., Jr. 1934. Reliability of opinionaire technique studied intensively by the retest method. *Journal of Social Psychology,* vol. 5, no. 3, pp. 338-363.

1227. **LERNER**, Daniel. 1956. Interviewing Frenchmen. *American Journal of Sociology,* vol. 62, no. 2, pp. 187-194.

1228. **LESTER**, A. M. 1949. The edge marking of statistical cards. *Journal of the American Statistical Association,* vol. 44, no. 246, pp. 293-294.

1229. **LESTER**, David. 1969. The subject as a source of bias in psychological research. *Journal of General Psychology,* vol. 81, no. 2, pp. 237-248.

1230. **LEVENTHAL**, Howard and NILES, Patricia. 1964. A field experiment on fear arousal with data on the validity of questionnaire measures. *Journal of Personality,* vol. 32, no. 3, pp. 459-479.

1231. **LEVIN**, Harry. 1954. The influence of fullness of interview on the reliability, discriminability, and validity of interview judgments. *Journal of Consulting Psychology,* vol. 18, no. 4, pp. 303-306.

1232. **LEVIN**, Joseph. 1965. Three-mode factor analysis. *Psychological Bulletin,* vol. 64, no. 6, pp. 442-452.

1233. **LEVINE**, Gustav. 1961. The effects of two verbal techniques on the expression of feelings. *Journal of Consulting Psychology,* vol. 25, no. 3, pp. 270-271.

LEVINE, Gene N. 1967. *See* HYMAN, Herbert H., LEVINE, Gene N. and WRIGHT, Charles R. 1967.

1234. **LEVINE**, Jerome M. and MURPHY, Gardner. 1943. The learning and forgetting of controversial material. *Journal of Abnormal and Social Psychology,* vol. 38, no. 4, pp. 507-517.

1235. **LEVINE**, Sol and GORDON, Gerald. 1958. Maximizing returns on mail questionnaires. *Public Opinion Quarterly,* vol. 22, no. 4, pp. 568-575.

LEVITT, Eugene E. 1962. *See* LUBIN, Bernard., LEVITT, Eugene E. and ZUCKERMAN, Marvin. 1962.

1236. **LEVY**, Leon H. 1969. Reflections on replications and the experimenter bias effect. *Journal of Consulting and Clinical Psychology,* vol. 33, no. 1, pp. 15-17.

1237. **LEWIS**, Don and BURKE, C [letus] J. 1949. The use and misuse of the chi-square test. *Psychological Bulletin,* vol. 46, no. 6, pp. 433-489.

1238. **LEWIS**, Harrie F. 1948. A comparison of consumer responses to weekly and monthly purchase panels. *Journal of Marketing,* vol. 12, no. 4, pp. 449-454.

1239. **LEWIS**, Leon. 1966. Development of a convertibility list between the D.O.T. and census classification systems. *AMERICAN STATISTICAL ASSOCIATION. Proceedings of the Social Statistics Section,* 1966. pp. 204-206.

1240. **LEWY**, Arieh. 1968. A routine for detecting data cards out of sequence in standard programs. *Educational and Psychological Measurement,* vol. 28, no. 1, pp. 171-175.

1241. **LEZNOFF**, Maurice. 1956. Interviewing homosexuals. *American Journal of Sociology,* vol. 62, no. 2, pp. 202-204.

LIEBERMAN, Seymour. 1967. *See* BELKIN, Marvin and LIEBERMAN, Seymour. 1967.

1242. **LIENAU**, C. C. 1941. Selection, training and performance of the National Health Survey field staff. *American Journal of Hygiene, section A,* vol. 34, no. 3, pp. 110-132.

1243. **LIKERT**, Rensis. 1932. A technique for the measurement of attitudes. *Archives of Psychology,* no. 140, pp. 1-55.

1244. **LIKERT**, Rensis, ROSLOW, Sydney and MURPHY, Gardner. 1934. A simple and reliable method of scoring the Thurstone attitude scales. *Journal of Social Psychology,* vol. 5, no. 2, pp. 228-238.

1245. **LIKERT**, Rensis. 1936. A method for measuring the sales influence of a radio program. *Journal of Applied Psychology,* vol. 20, no. 2, pp. 175-182.

1246. **LIKERT**, Rensis, 1947. The sample interview survey: a fundamental research tool of the social sciences. *DENNIS, Wayne, et al. Current trends in psychology.* Pittsburgh: University of Pittsburgh Press, 1947. pp. 196-225.

1247. **LIKERT**, Rensis. 1948. The polls: straw votes or scientific instruments. *American Psychologist,* vol. 3, no. 12, pp. 556-557.

1248. **LIKERT**, Rensis. 1950. The sample interview survey as a research tool to study motivation. *REYMERT, Martin L., ed. Feelings and emotions: the Mooseheart symposium.* New York, London: McGraw-Hill, 1950. pp. 523-530.

1249. **LIKERT**, Rensis. 1951. The sample interview survey as a tool of research and policy formation. *LERNER, Daniel and LASSWELL, Harold D., eds. The policy sciences.* Stanford, California: Stanford University Press, 1951. pp. 233-251.

LINDBERG, Barbara. 1966. *See* GRUBER, Alin and LINDBERG, Barbara. 1966.

LINDBERG, Barbara. 1969. *See* GRUBER, Alin and LINDBERG, Barbara. 1969.

1250. **LINDGREN**, Henry Clay. 1954. The use of a sentence completion test in measuring attitudinal changes among college freshmen. *Journal of Social Psychology,* vol. 40, no. 1, pp. 79-92.

1251. **LINDQUIST**, E. F. 1931. The significance of a difference between 'matched' groups. *Journal of Educational Psychology,* vol. 22, no. 3, pp. 197-204.

1252. **LINDQUIST**, E. F. 1940. Sampling in educational research. *Journal of Educational Psychology,* vol. 31, no. 8, pp. 561-574.

1253. **LINDSLEY**, Ogden R. 1962. A behavioral measure of television viewing. *Journal of Advertising Research,* vol. 2, no. 3, pp. 2-12.

1254. **LINDSLEY**, Ogden R. 1963. Rejoiner to Sicher: evaluation or procrastination? *Journal of Advertising Research,* vol. 3, no. 1, pp. 47-49.

1255. **LINDZEY**, Gardner [E.] 1951. A note on interviewer bias. *Journal of Applied Psychology,* vol. 35, no. 3, pp. 182-184.

1256. **LINDZEY**, Gardner E. and GUEST, Lester. 1951. To repeat — check lists can be dangerous. *Public Opinion Quarterly,* vol. 15, no. 2, pp. 355-358.

1257. **LINK**, Henry C. 1934. A new method for testing advertising and a psychological sales barometer. *Journal of Applied Psychology,* vol. 18, no. 1, pp. 1-26.

1258. **LINK**, Henry C. 1937. How many interviews are necessary for results of a certain accuracy. *Journal of Applied Psychology,* vol. 21, no. 1, pp. 1-17.

1259. **LINK**, Henry C. and FREIBERG, A. D. 1942. The problem of validity vs. reliability in public opinion polls. *Public Opinion Quarterly,* vol. 6, no. 1, pp. 87-98.

1260. **LINK**, Henry C. 1943. An experiment in depth interviewing on the issue of internationalism vs. isolationism. *Public Opinion Quarterly,* vol. 7, no. 2, pp. 267-279.

1261. **LINK**, Henry C. 1947. Some milestones in public opinion research. *Journal of Applied Psychology,* vol. 31, no. 3, pp. 225-234.

LINN, Robert L. 1970. *See* WERTS, Charles E. and LINN, Robert L. 1970.

1262. **LINSKY**, Arnold S. 1965. A factorial experiment in inducing responses to a mail questionnaire. *Sociology & Social Research,* vol. 49, no. 2, pp. 183-189.

LIPSTEIN, Benjamin. 1956. *See* COHEN, Samuel E. and LIPSTEIN, Benjamin. 1956.

LISSANCE, Daniel. 1955. *See* GREENBERG, Allan and LISSANCE, Daniel. 1955.

LITTLE, Robert T. 1961. *See* SIMMONS, Walt R., LITTLE, Robert T. and MADIGAN, Eleanor L. 1961.

1263. LITWAK, Eugene. 1956. A classification of biased questions. *American Journal of Sociology*, vol. 63, no. 2, pp. 182-186.

LITWAK, Eugene. 1956. *See* STANTON, Howard, BACK, Kurt W. and LITWAK, Eugene. 1956.

LO SCIUTO, Leonard A. 1966. *See* WELLS, William D. and LO SCIUTO, Leonard A. 1966.

LO SCIUTO, Leonard A. 1967. *See* WELLS, William D. and LO SCIUTO, Leonard A. 1967.

1264. LOCKLEY, Lawrence C. and WATSON, Alfred N. 1940. Some fundamental considerations in the conduct of polls. *Journal of Marketing*, vol. 5, no. 2, pp. 113-115.

1265. LOEVINGER, Jane. 1948. The technic of homogeneous tests compared with some aspects of 'scale analysis' and factor analysis. *Psychological Bulletin*, vol. 45, no. 6, pp. 507-529.

1266. LOHMAN, Joseph D. 1937. The participant observer in community studies. *American Sociological Review*, vol. 2, no. 6, pp. 890-897.

1267. LONDON SCHOOL OF ECONOMICS. Survey Research Centre. 1966. Respondent understanding of questions in the interview, part I. London: London School of Economics, Survey Research Centre, 1966. iii, 349pp.

1268. LONDON SCHOOL OF ECONOMICS. Survey Research Centre. 1966. Respondent understanding of questions in the survey interview, part II. London: London School of Economics, Survey Research Centre, 1966. 218pp.

1269. LONDON SCHOOL OF ECONOMICS. Survey Research Centre 1966. The ability of respondents to recall their purchases of chocolate confectionery. London: London School of Economics, Survey Research Centre, 1966. 52pp.

1270. LONDON SCHOOL OF ECONOMICS. Survey Research Centre. 1967. The semantic differential scaling system in market research, I: order effects. London: London School of Economics, Survey Research Centre, 1967. iv, 75pp.

LONDON SCHOOL OF ECONOMICS. Survey Research Centre. *See also* LONDON SCHOOL OF ECONOMICS. Survey Research Unit.

1271. **LONDON SCHOOL OF ECONOMICS.** Survey Research Unit. 1965. A study of the effects of reversing the order of presentation of verbal rating scales. London: London School of Economics, Survey Research Unit, 1965. 67pp.

LONDON SCHOOL OF ECONOMICS. Survey Research Unit. *See also* LONDON SCHOOL OF ECONOMICS. Survey Research Centre.

LONG, Barbara H. 1965. *See* ZILLER, Robert C. and LONG, Barbara H. 1965.

1272. **LONGSTAFF**, H. P. 1939. A method for determining the entertainment value of radio programs. *Journal of Applied Psychology* vol. 23, no. 1, pp. 46-54.

1273. **LONGSTAFF**, H. P. and LAYBOURN, G. P. 1949. What do readership studies really prove? *Journal of Applied Psychology,* vol. 33, no. 6, pp. 585-593.

1274. **LONGWORTH**, Donald S. 1953. Use of a mail questionnaire. *American Sociological Review,* vol. 18, no. 3, pp. 310-313.

1275. **LORGE**, Irving. 1936. Prestige, suggestion, and attitudes. *Journal of Social Psychology,* vol. 7, no. 4, pp. 386-402.

1276. **LORIMOR**, E. S. and DUNN, S. Watson. 1967. Four measures of cross-cultural advertising effectiveness. *Journal of Advertising Research,* vol. 7, no. 4, pp. 11-13.

1277. **LORR**, Maurice and RADHAKRISHNAN, Belur K. 1967. A comparison of two methods of cluster analysis. *Educational and Psychological Measurement,* vol. 27, no. 1, pp. 47-53.

1278. **LOVELL**, M. R. C., JOHNS, S. and RAMPLEY, B. 1968. The pre-testing of press advertisements. *Admap,* vol. 4, no. 3, pp. 90, 92-94, 96-98, 100-102, 104, 107-108, 110-111.

1279. **LOVELL**, M. R. C. and LANNON, J. M. 1968. Difficulties with recall. *Commentary,* vol. 10, no. 3, pp. 172-185.

1280. **LOWE**, Francis E. and McCORMICK, Thomas C. 1955. Some survey sampling biases. *Public Opinion Quarterly,* vol. 19, no. 3, pp. 303-315.

LOYD, Alison. 1968. *See* CAFFYN, John [M.] and LOYD, Alison. 1968.

1281. **LUBIN**, Bernard, **LEVITT**, Eugene E. and **ZUCKERMAN**, Marvin. 1962. Some personality differences between responders and non-responders to a survey questionnaire. *Journal of Consulting Psychology*, vol. 26, no. 2, pp. 192.

1282. **LUCAS**, D[arrell] B. and **MURPHY**, M. J. 1939. False identification of advertisements in recognition tests. *Journal of Applied Psychology*, vol. 23, no. 2, pp. 264-269.

1283. **LUCAS**, D[arrell] B. 1940. A rigid technique for measuring the impression values of specific magazine advertisements. *Journal of Applied Psychology*, vol. 24, no. 6, pp. 778-790.

1284. **LUCAS**, D[arrell] B. 1942. A controlled recognition technique for measuring magazine advertising audiences. *Journal of Marketing*, vol. 6, no. 4, part 2, pp. 133-136.

1285. **LUCAS**, Darrell B. 1960. The ABCs of ARF's PARM. *Journal of Marketing*, vol. 25, no. 1, pp. 9-20.

LUCAS, Darrell B. 1965. *See* ADLER, Lee, GREENBERG, Allan and LUCAS, Darrell B. 1965.

1286. **LUDEKE**, Herbert C. and **INGLIS**, Ruth A. 1942. A technique for validating interviewing methods in reader research. *Sociometry*, vol. 5, no. 2, pp. 109-122.

1287. **LUDEKE**, Herbert C. 1945. A test of two methods commonly used in reader-interest surveys. *Journal of Marketing*, vol. 10, no. 2, pp. 171-173.

LUMB, Frederick. 1969. *See* WILLS, Gordon, LUMB, Frederick and WILSON, Richard M.S. 1969.

1288. **LUMSDEN**, James. 1961. The construction of unidimensional tests. *Psychological Bulletin*, vol. 58, no. 2, pp. 122-131.

1289. **LUNDBERG**, George A. 1940. The measurement of socioeconomic status. *American Sociological Review*, vol. 5, no. 1, pp. 29-39.

1290. **LUNDBERG**, George A. and **LARSEN**, Otto N. 1949. Characteristics of hard-to-reach individuals in field surveys. *Public Opinion Quarterly*, vol. 13, no. 3, pp. 487-494.

1291. **LUNN**, J. A. 1969. Perspectives in attitude research: methods and applications. *Commentary*, vol. 11, no. 3, pp. 201-213.

1292. **LURIE**, Walter A. 1937. Statistics and public opinion. *Public Opinion Quarterly*, vol. 1, no. 4, pp. 78-83.

1293. **LURIE**, Walter A. 1938. The measurement of prestige and prestige-suggestibility. *Journal of Social Psychology*, vol. 9, no. 2, pp. 219-225.

1294. **LYDGATE**, William, *et al.* 1951. New techniques in questioning. *Public Opinion Quarterly*, vol. 15, no. 4, pp. 788-793.

1295. **LYLE**, Jack. 1960. Semantic differential scales for newspaper research. *Journalism Quarterly*, vol. 37, no. 4, pp. 559-562.

1296. **LYLE**, Jack. 1965. Attitude measurement in communication research. *Journalism Quarterly*, vol. 42, no. 4, pp. 606-614.

1297. **LYSAKER**, Richard L. and BRADLEY, Joseph E. 1957. What is a pictorial projective technique? *Journal of Marketing*, vol. 21, no. 3, pp. 339-340.

MAAS, Irene. 1956. *See* DURANT, Henry and MAAS, Irene. 1956.

1298. **McCALL**, George J. and SIMMONS, J. L. 1966. A new measure of attitudinal opposition. *Public Opinion Quarterly*, vol. 30, no. 2, pp. 271-278.

McCANDLESS, Boyd. 1940. *See* SUCHMAN, Edward A. and McCANDLESS, Boyd. 1940.

McCARTHY, Philip J. 1942. *See* MOSTELLER, Frederick and McCARTHY, Philip J. 1942.

1299. **McCARTHY**, Philip [J.] *chairman.* 1948. Experiences with probability sampling in private agencies: I. *Public Opinion Quarterly*, vol. 12, no. 4, pp. 792-799.

1300. **McCARTHY**, Philip J. and STEPHAN, Frederick F. 1951. Area sampling. *American Statistician*, vol. 5, no. 1, pp. 20-21.

1301. **McCARTHY**, Philip J. 1966. Replication: an approach to the analysis of data from complex surveys: development and evaluation of a replication technique for estimating variance. Washington, D. C.: U.S. Department of Health, Education and Welfare, Public Health Service, 1966. 38 pp. (*Public Health Service Publication no. 1000 – series 2 – no. 14*).

1302. **McCARTHY**, Philip J. 1969. Pseudo replication: half samples. *Review of the International Statistical Institute*, vol. 37, no. 3, pp. 239-264.

McCLELLAND, C. W. 1968. *See* CLAYCAMP, H. J. and McCLELLAND, C. W. 1968.

1303. **MACCOBY**, Eleanor E. and HOLT, Robert R. 1946. How surveys are made. *Journal of Social Issues*, vol. 2, no. 2, pp. 45-57.

1304. **MACCOBY**, Eleanor E. 1947. Interviewing problems in financial surveys. *International Journal of Opinion and Attitude Research,* vol. 1, no. 1, pp. 31-39.

MACCOBY, Eleanor E. 1948. *See* GOODMAN, Roe and MACCOBY, Eleanor E. 1948.

1305. **MACCOBY**, Eleanor E. and MACCOBY, Nathan. 1954. The interview: a tool of social science. *LINDZEY, Gardner, ed. Handbook of social psychology.* Cambridge, Mass.: Addison Wesley, 1954. pp. 449-487.

1306. **MACCOBY**, Eleanor E. 1956. Pitfalls in the analysis of panel data: a research note on some technical aspects of 'Voting'. *American Journal of Sociology,* vol. 61, no. 4, pp. 359-362.

MACCOBY, Nathan. 1954. *See* MACCOBY, Eleanor E. and MACCOBY, Nathan. 1954.

1307. **McCORD**, Hallack. 1951. Discovering the 'confused' respondent: a possible projective method. *Public Opinion Quarterly,* vol. 15, no. 2, pp. 363-366.

1308. **McCORMICK**, Thomas C. 1938. On the amount of error in sociological data. *American Sociological Review,* vol. 3, no. 3, pp. 328-332.

1309. **McCORMICK**, Thomas C. and SCHMID, Robert C. 1941. A system of attitude experiments. *Social Forces,* vol. 19, no. 3, pp. 351-356.

1310. **McCORMICK**, Thomas C. 1945. Simple percentage analysis of attitude questionnaires. *American Journal of Sociology,* vol. 50, no. 5, pp. 390-395.

1311. **McCORMICK**, Thomas C. 1948. A rationale for scaling unordered attributes. *American Journal of Sociology,* vol. 54, no. 1, pp. 31-35.

McCORMICK, Thomas C. 1955. *See* LOWE, Francis E. and McCORMICK, Thomas C. 1955.

1312. **McCROSKEY**, James C., PRICHARD, Samuel V. O. and ARNOLD, William E. 1967. Attitude intensity and the neutral point on semantic differential scales. *Public Opinion Quarterly,* vol. 31, no. 4, pp. 642-645.

1313. **McCROSSAN**, L. 1968. The uses of free and semi-structured interviewing in the pre-pilot stages of a survey. London: Office of Population Censuses and Surveys, Social Survey Division, 1968. 3pp. (*Methodological series, M143*).

1314. **McDONAGH**, Edward C. and ROSENBLUM, A. Leon. 1965. A comparison of mailed questionnaires and subsequent structured interviews. *Public Opinion Quarterly,* vol. 29, no. 1, pp. 131-136.

MACDONALD, Neil. 1964. *See* CARTER, Roy E., Jr. and MACDONALD, Neil. 1964.

McFANN, Howard. 1955. *See* WINDLE, Charles, McFANN, Howard and WARD, Joseph. 1955.

1315. **McGEE**, Reece. 1961. A test for halo effect in ranked data. *South-Western Social Science Quarterly*, vol. 42, part 3, pp. 280-284.

1316. **McGEE**, Richard K. 1962. The relationship between response style and personality variables, I: the measurement of response acquiescence. *Journal of Abnormal and Social Psychology,* vol. 64, no. 3, pp. 229-233.

1317. **McGINNIES**, Elliott. 1956. A method for matching anonymous questionnaire data with group discussion material. *Journal of Abnormal and Social Psychology,* vol. 52, no. 1, pp. 139-140.

1318. **McGINNIS**, Robert. 1953. Scaling interview data. *American Sociological Review,* vol. 18, no. 5, pp. 514-521.

1319. **McGLATHERY**, Donald G. 1967. Claimed frequency vs. editorial-interest measures of repeat magazine audiences. *Journal of Advertising Research*, vol. 7, no. 1, pp. 7-15.

McGLOUGHLIN, Ivor. 1968. *See* PARFITT, John and McGLOUGHLIN, Ivor. 1968.

1320. **McGUIGAN**, F. J. 1963. The experimenter: a neglected stimulus object. *Psychological Bulletin,* vol. 60, no. 4, pp. 421-428.

1321. **McKENNELL**, A. C. [196-]. Some uses of factor analysis in social survey work. London: Office of Population Censuses and Surveys, Social Survey Division, [196–]. 3pp. (*Methodological series, M125*).

1322. **McKENNELL**, A. C. and THOMAS, R. K. [196-]. Towards an optimum procedure for scalogram analysis. London: Office of Population Censuses and Surveys, Social Survey Division, [196–]. 14pp. (*Methodological series, M128*).

1323. **McKENNELL**, A. C. 1965. Correlational analysis of social survey data. London: Office of Population Censuses and Surveys, Social Survey Division, 1965. 25pp. (*Methodological series, M114*).

1324. **McKENNELL**, A. C. and THOMAS, R. K. 1968. A simple computer method for the analysis of response patterns and attribute space. London: Office of Population Censuses and Surveys, Social Survey Division, 1968. 8pp. (*Methodological series, M141*).

1325. McKENNELL, A. C. 1968. Use of coefficient alpha in constructing attitude and similar scales. London: Office of Population Censuses and Surveys, Social Survey Division, 1968. 9pp. (*Methodological series, M139*).

McKENNELL, A. C. 1968. *See* THOMAS, R. K. and McKENNELL, A. C. 1968.

1326. McKENNELL, A. C. 1969. Methodological problems in a survey of aircraft noise annoyance. *The Statistician*, vol. 19, no. 1, pp. 1-29.

1327. McKENNELL, A. [C.] 1970. Attitude measurement: use of coefficient alpha with cluster or factor analysis. *Sociology*, vol. 4, no. 2, pp. 227-245.

McKEON, Alfred J. 1953. *See* PRICE, Orville O. and McKEON, Alfred J. 1953.

1328. McKINNEY, Fred. 1935. Retroactive inhibition in advertising. *Journal of Applied Psychology*, vol. 19, no. 1, pp. 59-66.

1329. MACLEAN, Malcolm S., Jr. 1965. Some multivariate designs for communications research. *Journalism Quarterly*, vol. 42, no. 4, pp. 614-622.

McLEOD, Jack M. 1968. *See* CHAFFEE, Steven H. and McLEOD, Jack M. 1968.

McMILLAN, Robert K. 1965. *See* McNIVEN, Malcolm A. and McMILLAN, Robert K. 1965.

1330. McNEMAR, Quinn. 1940. Sampling in psychological research. *Psychological Bulletin*, vol. 37, no. 6, pp. 331-365.

1331. McNEMAR, Quinn. 1946. Opinion-attitude methodology. *Psychological Bulletin*, vol. 43, no. 4, pp. 289-374.

1332. McNEMAR, Quinn. 1947. Response to Crespi's rejoinder and Conrad's reply to appraisal of opinion-attitude methodology. *Psychological Bulletin*, vol. 44, no. 2, pp. 171-176.

1333. McNEMAR, Quinn. 1951. On the use of latin squares in psychology. *Psychological Bulletin*, vol. 48, no. 5, pp. 398-401.

1334. McNEMAR, Quinn. 1969. Moderation of a moderator technique. *Journal of Applied Psychology*, vol. 53, no. 1, pp. 69-72.

1335. **McNIVEN**, Malcolm A. and **McMILLAN**, Robert K. 1965. Telecentral communication – an innovation in survey research. *ADVERTISING RESEARCH FOUNDATION. Annual Conference, 11th, New York City, 1965. Proceedings...* New York: Advertising Research Foundation, 1965. pp. 58-64.

1336. **McPEAK**, William. 1945. Problems of field management in army opinion research. *Journal of the American Statistical Association*, vol. 40, no. 230, pp. 247-248.

1337. **McQUITTY**, Louis L. 1960. Hierarchical syndrome analysis. *Educational and Psychological Measurement*, vol. 20, no. 2, pp. 293-304.

1338. **McQUITTY**, Louis L. 1961. A method for selecting patterns to differentiate categories of people. *Educational and Psychological Measurement*, vol. 21, no. 1, pp. 85-94.

1339. **McQUITTY**, Louis L. 1964. Capabilities and improvements of linkage analysis as a clustering method. *Educational and Psychological Measurement*, vol. 24, no. 3, pp. 441-456.

1340. **MACRAE**, Duncan, *Jr.* 1960. Direct factor analysis of sociometric data. *Sociometry*, vol. 23, no. 4, pp. 360-371.

MACRAE, Duncan, *Jr.* 1960. *See* COLEMAN, James S. and MACRAE, Duncan, *Jr.* 1960.

1341. **McTAVISH**, Donald G. 1964. A method for more reliably coding detailed occupations into Duncan's socio-economic categories. *American Sociological Review*, vol. 29, no. 3, pp. 402-406.

1342. **McTAVISH**, Ronald. 1964. Assessing the effectiveness of advertising. *Scientific Business*, vol. 2, no. 1, pp. 84-92.

1343. **MACURA**, M. and **BALABAN**, V. 1961. Yugoslav experience in evaluation of population censuses and sampling. *Bulletin of the International Statistical Institute*, vol. 38, no. 2, pp. 375-399.

MADIGAN, Eleanor L. 1961. SIMMONS, Walt R., LITTLE, Robert T. and MADIGAN, Eleanor L. 1961.

1344. **MADOW**, Lillian H. 1946. Systematic sampling and its relation to other sampling designs. *Journal of the American Statistical Association*, vol. 41, no. 234, pp. 204-217.

1345. **MADOW**, Lillian H. 1950. On the use of the county as the primary sampling unit for state estimates. *Journal of the American Statistical Association*, vol. 45, no. 249, pp. 30-47.

1346. **MADOW**, William G. 1965. On some aspects of response error measurement. *AMERICAN STATISTICAL ASSOCIATION. Proceedings of the Social Statistics Section*, 1965. pp. 182-192.

1347. **MAGID**, Frank N., FOTION, Nicholas G. and GOLD, David. 1962. A mail-questionnaire adjunct to the interview. *Public Opinion Quarterly*, vol. 26, no. 1, pp. 111-114.

1348. **MAHALANOBIS**, P. C. 1949. Cost and accuracy of results in sampling and complete enumeration. *Bulletin of the International Statistical Institute*, vol. 32, part 2, pp. 210-213.

1349. **MAHALANOBIS**, P. C. 1952. Some aspects of the design of sample surveys. *Sankhya*, vol. 12, parts 1 and 2, pp. 1-7.

1350. **MAHALANOBIS**, P. C. and LAHIRI, D. B. 1961. Analysis of errors in censuses and surveys with special reference to experience in India. *Bulletin of the International Statistical Institute*, vol. 38, no. 2, pp. 401-433.

1351. **MAHER**, Brendan A., WATT, Norman and CAMPBELL, Donald T. 1960. Comparative validity of two projective and two structured attitude tests in a prison population. *Journal of Applied Psychology*, vol. 44, no. 4, pp. 284-288.

MAHER, Howard. 1962. *See* BECKNELL, James C. *Jr.*, and MAHER, Howard 1962.

MAHER, John R. 1967. *See* KLEIN, Stuart M., MAHER, John R. and DUNNINGTON, Richard A. 1967.

1352. **MAISEL**, Richard, *chairman*. 1957. Shortcuts in the everyday life of a survey statistician. *Public Opinion Quarterly*, vol. 21, no. 3, pp. 444-445.

1353. **MALLER**, Julius B. 1930. The effect of signing one's name. *School and Society*, vol. 31, no. 809, pp. 882-884.

MALLOWS, C. L. 1969. *See* WILLIAMS, W. H. and MALLOWS, C. L. 1969.

MALLOWS, C. L. 1970. *See* WILLIAMS, W. H. and MALLOWS, C. L. 1970.

1354. **MALMSTROM**, Edward J. and FRENCH, Gilbert M. 1963. Scale-symmetry and the semantic differential. *American Journal of Psychology*, vol. 76, no. 3, pp. 446-451.

1355. **MALONEY**, John C. 1961. Portfolio tests — are they here to stay? *Journal of Marketing*, vol. 25, no. 5, pp. 32-37.

1356. **MALONEY**, John C. 1962. More 'why' about portfolio tests. *Journal of Marketing*, vol. 26, no. 3, pp. 76.

1357. **MALONEY**, Paul W. 1954. Comparability of personal attitude scale administration with mail administration with and without incentive. *Journal of Applied Psychology*, vol. 38, no. 4, pp. 238-239.

1358. **MANDEVILLE**, John P. 1946. Improvements in methods of census and survey analysis. *Journal of the Royal Statistical Society*, vol. 109, part 2, pp. 111-120. *Discussion on Mr. Mandeville's paper*, pp. 120-129.

1359. **MANFIELD**, Manuel N. 1948. A pattern of response to mail surveys. *Public Opinion Quarterly*, vol. 12, no. 3, pp. 493-495.

MANFIELD, Manuel N. 1957. *See* GREENBERG, Allan and MANFIELD, Manuel N. 1957.

1360. **MANGUS**, A. Raymond. 1934. Sampling in the field of rural relief. *Journal of the American Statistical Association*, vol. 29, no. 188, pp. 410-415.

1361. **MANHEIMER**, Dean and HYMAN, Herbert. 1949. Interviewer performance in area sampling. *Public Opinion Quarterly*, vol. 13, no. 1, pp. 83-92.

MANN, Floyd. 1952. *See* METZNER, Helen and MANN, Floyd. 1952.

MANN, Floyd. 1953. *See* METZNER, Helen and MANN, Floyd. 1953.

MANN, Leon. 1965. *See* MILGRAM, Stanley, MANN, Leon and HARTER, Susan. 1965.

1362. **MANNICHE**, Erik and HAYES, Donald P. 1957. Respondent anonymity and data-matching. *Public Opinion Quarterly*, vol. 21, no. 3, pp. 384-388.

1363. **MANNING**, Peter K. 1967. Problems in interpreting interview data. *Sociology and Sociological Research*, vol. 51, no. 3, pp. 302-316.

1364. **MANVILLE**, Richard. 1968. A new advertising measurement. *Admap*, vol. 4, no. 6, pp. 272-273.

MARCIA, James E. 1967. *See* MARWIT, Samuel J. and MARCIA, James E. 1967.

MARCUSE, F. L. 1958. *See* MARTIN, R. M. and MARCUSE, F. L. 1958.

1365. **MARDER**, Eric. 1952. Linear segments: a technique for scalogram analysis. *Public Opinion Quarterly*, vol. 16, no. 3, pp. 417-431.

1366. **MARDER**, Eric and DAVID, Mort. 1961. Recognition of ad elements: recall or projection? *Journal of Advertising Research*, vol. 1, no. 6, pp. 23-25.

1367. **MARDER**, Eric. 1967. How good is the editorial-interest method of measuring magazine audiences? *Journal of Advertising Research*, vol. 7, no. 1, pp. 2-6.

1368. MARKET RESEARCH SOCIETY. Technical Committee. 1969. Road traffic studies: Technical Committee's working party report. *Commentary*, vol. 11, no. 2, pp. 152-173.

1369. MARKET RESEARCH SOCIETY. Working Party on Interviewing Methods. 1968. Fieldwork methods in general use: Working Party on Interviewing Methods first report, 1968. London: Market Research Society, 1968. 1v. (various pagings).

1370. MARKS, Eli S. 1947. Selective sampling in psychological research. *Psychological Bulletin*, vol. 44, no. 5, pp. 267-275.

1371. MARKS, Eli S. and MAULDIN, W. Parker. 1950. Response errors in census research. *Journal of the American Statistical Association*, vol. 45, no. 251, pp. 424-438.

MARKS, Eli S. 1950. *See* MAULDIN, W. Parker and MARKS, Eli S. 1950.

1372. MARKS, Eli S. 1951. Some sampling problems in educational research. *Journal of Educational Psychology*, vol. 42, no. 2, pp. 85-96.

1373. MARKS, Eli S., MAULDIN, W. Parker and NISSELSON, Harold. 1953. The post-enumeration survey of the 1950 census: a case history in survey design. *Journal of the American Statistical Association*, vol. 48, no. 262, pp. 220-243.

MARKS, Eli S. 1958. *See* HANSON, Robert H. and MARKS, Eli S. 1958.

1374. MARKS, Eli S. 1962. The fetish of sample size. *Public Opinion Quarterly*, vol. 26, no. 1, pp. 92-97.

1375. MARKS, Eli S. 1963. You can do it on a computer, but should you? *Public Opinion Quarterly*, vol. 27, no. 3, pp. 481-485.

1376. MARKS, Melvin R. and TAYLOR, Wilson L. 1965. A methodological study of the effects of propaganda. *Journal of Social Psychology*, vol. 65, no. 2, pp. 269-277.

MARQUIS, Kent H. 1966. *See* CANNELL, Charles F. and MARQUIS, Kent H. 1966.

MARQUIS, Kent H. 1967. *See* CANNELL, Charles F. and MARQUIS, Kent H. 1967.

1377. MARQUIS, Kent H. 1969. An experimental study of the effects of reinforcement, question length, and reinterviews on reporting selected chronic conditions in household interviews. Ann Arbor, Michigan: University of Michigan, Survey Research Center, 1969. 110pp.

1378. **MARQUIS**, Kent H. 1969. Interviewer-respondent interaction in a household interview. *AMERICAN STATISTICAL ASSOCIATION. Proceedings of the Social Statistics Section*, 1969. pp. 24-30.

1379. **MARQUIS**, Kent H. 1970. Effects of social reinforcement on health reporting in the household interview. *Sociometry*, vol. 33, no. 2, pp. 203-215.

1380. **MARRIOTT**, R. 1953. Some problems in attitude survey methodology. *Occupational Psychology*, vol. 27, no. 3, pp. 117-127.

1381. **MARRIOTT**, R. and DENERLEY, R. A. 1955. A method of interviewing used in studies of workers' attitudes, I: effectiveness of the questions and of interviewer control. *Occupational Psychology*, vol. 29, no. 1, pp. 1-14.

1382. **MARRIOTT**, R. and DENERLEY, R. A. 1955. A method of interviewing used in studies of workers' attitudes, II: validity of the method and discussion of the results. *Occupational Psychology*, vol. 29, no. 2, pp. 69-81.

1383. **MARSDEN**, Gerald. 1965. Content-analysis studies of therapeutic interviews: 1954 to 1964. *Psychological Bulletin*, vol. 63, no. 5, pp. 298-321.

MARSHALL, Helen. 1939. *See* CHAMPNEY, Horace and MARSHALL, Helen. 1939.

1384. **MARTIN**, J. David and GRAY, Louis N. 1969. Two comments on Guttman scaling: II. *American Journal of Sociology*, vol. 75, no. 2, pp. 279-280.

1385. **MARTIN**, John. 1964. Acquiescence – measurement and theory. *British Journal of Social and Clinical Psychology*, vol. 3, part 3, pp. 216-225.

1386. **MARTIN**, R. M. and MARCUSE, F. L. 1958. Characteristics of volunteers and nonvolunteers in psychological experimentation. *Journal of Consulting Psychology*, vol. 22, no. 6, pp. 475-479.

1387. **MARTINEAU**, Pierre, *chairman*. 1956. Techniques of presentation for research results. *Public Opinion Quarterly*, vol. 20, no. 4, pp. 755-757.

1388. **MARWIT**, Samuel J. and MARCIA, James E. 1967. Tester bias and response to projective instruments. *Journal of Consulting Psychology*, vol. 31, no. 3, pp. 253-258.

1389. **MASLOW**, A. H. and SAKODA, James M. 1952. Volunteer-error in the Kinsey study. *Journal of Abnormal and Social Psychology*, vol. 47, no. 2, pp. 259-262.

1390. **MASON**, J. W. 1954. Validity of readership studies. *Journal of Marketing*, vol. 18, no. 4, pp. 394.

1391. **MASON**, Ward S., DRESSEL, Robert J. and BAIN, Robert K. 1961. An experimental study of factors affecting response to a mail survey of beginning teachers. *Public Opinion Quarterly*, vol. 25, no. 2, pp. 296-299.

MASON, Ward S. 1953. *See* GROSS, Neal and MASON, Ward S. 1953.

MASON, William M. 1964. *See* BRADBURN, Norman M. and MASON, William M. 1964.

MASSON, Peter. 1969. *See* BROADBENT, Simon and MASSON, Peter. 1969.

MASSON, Peter. 1969. *See* BROADBENT, Simon and MASSON, Peter. 1969.

MASSY, William F. 1965. *See* FRANK, Ronald E., MASSY, William F. and MORRISON, Donald G. 1965.

MASSY, William F. 1966. *See* MORRISON, Donald G., FRANK, Ronald E. and MASSY, William F. 1966.

1392. **MATARAZZO**, Joseph D., SASLOW, George and GUZE, Samuel B. 1956. Stability of interaction patterns during interviews: a replication. *Journal of Consulting Psychology*, vol. 20, no. 4, pp. 267-274.

1393. **MATARAZZO**, Joseph D., SASLOW, George and MATARAZZO, Ruth G. 1956. The interaction chronograph as an instrument for objective measurement of interaction patterns during interviews. *Journal of Psychology*, vol. 41, no. 2, pp. 347-367.

1394. **MATARAZZO**, Joseph D., *et al.* 1963. Interviewer influence on durations of interviewee speech. *Journal of Verbal Learning and Verbal Behavior*, vol. 1, no. 5, pp. 451-458.

1395. **MATARAZZO**, Joseph D., *et al.* 1964. Interviewer mm-hmm and interviewee speech durations. *Psychotherapy, Theory, Research and Practice*, vol. 1, no. 3, pp. 109-114.

MATARAZZO, Joseph D. 1965. *See* WIENS, Arthur N., MATARAZZO, Joseph D. and SASLOW, George. 1965.

MATARAZZO, Joseph D. 1966. *See* WIENS, Arthur N., SASLOW, George and MATARAZZO, Joseph D. 1966.

1396. **MATARAZZO**, Joseph D., HOLMAN, David C. and WIENS, Arthur N. 1967. A simple measure of interviewer and interviewee speech durations. *Journal of Psychology*, vol. 66, no. 1, pp. 7-14.

MATARAZZO, Ruth G. 1956. *See* MATARAZZO, Joseph D., SASLOW, George and MATARAZZO, Ruth G. 1956.

MATTHEWS, Donald R. 1962. *See* AXELROD, Morris, MATTHEWS, Donald R. and PROTHRO, James W. 1962.

1397. **MAULDIN**, W. Parker and MARKS, Eli S. 1950. Problems of response in enumerative surveys. *American Sociological Review*, vol. 15, no. 5, pp. 649-657.

MAULDIN, W. Parker. 1950. *See* MARKS, Eli S. and MAULDIN, W. Parker. 1950.

MAULDIN, W. Parker. 1953. *See* MARKS, Eli S., MAULDIN, W. Parker and NISSELSON, Harold. 1953.

1398. **MAXWELL**, A. E. 1959. A statistical approach to scalogram analysis. *Educational and Psychological Measurement*, vol. 19, no. 3, pp. 337-349.

1399. **MAYER**, Charles S. 1964. Pretesting field interviewing costs through simulation. *Journal of Marketing*, vol. 28, no. 2, pp. 47-50.

1400. **MAYER**, Charles S. 1964. The interviewer and his environment. *Journal of Marketing Research*, vol. 1, no. 4, pp. 24-31.

1401. **MAYER**, Charles S. and PRATT, Robert W., *Jr.* 1966. A note on nonresponse in a mail survey. *Public Opinion Quarterly*, vol. 30, no. 4, pp. 637-646.

1402. **MAYER**, Charles S. 1968. A computer system for controlling interviewer costs. *Journal of Marketing Research*, vol. 5, no. 3, pp. 312-318.

1403. **MAYER**, Charles S. 1968. Subjectivity in research design. *Commentary*, vol. 10, no. 4, pp. 279-292.

1404. **MAYNES**, E. Scott. 1965. The anatomy of response errors: consumer saving. *Journal of Marketing Research*, vol. 2, no. 4, pp. 378-387.

MAYNES, E. Scott. 1965. *See* NETER, John, MAYNES, E. Scott and RAMANATHAN, R. 1965.

1405. **MAYNES**, E. Scott. 1968. Minimizing response errors in financial data: the possibilities. *Journal of the American Statistical Association*, vol. 63, no. 321, pp. 214-227.

MAYNES, E. Scott. 1968. *See* NETER, John, MAYNES, E. Scott and RAMANATHAN, R. 1968.

MEANS, Edgar R. 1918. *See* WEMBRIDGE, Eleanor Rowland and MEANS, Edgar R. 1918.

MEDICAL RESEARCH COUNCIL. Industrial Health Research Board. *See* INDUSTRIAL HEALTH RESEARCH BOARD.

MEEHL, Paul E. 1955. *See* CRONBACH, Lee J. and MEEHL, Pau E. 1955.

1406. MEHLING, Reuben. 1959. A simple test for measuring intensity of attitudes. *Public Opinion Quarterly*, vol. 23, no. 4, pp. 576-578.

MEIER, Norman C. 1939. *See* CAHALAN, Don and MEIER, Norman C. 1939.

1407. MEIER, Norman C. and BURKE, Cletus J. 1947. Laboratory tests of sampling techniques. *Public Opinion Quarterly*, vol. 11, no. 4, pp. 586-593.

MEIER, Norman C. 1951. *See* HANER, Charles F. and MEIER, Norman C. 1951.

MEIGH, Charles. 1952. *See* DVORAK, Beatrice, FOX, Frances C. and MEIGH, Charles. 1952.

MEISSNER, Frank. 1963. *See* BAUER, Rainald K. and MEISSNER, Frank. 1963.

1408. MELBIN, Murray. 1954. An interaction recording device for participant observers. *Human Organization*, vol. 13, no. 2, pp. 29-33.

1409. MELTZER, Leo. 1961. Using the IBM accounting machine to obtain frequencies, sums, and sums of squares, ignoring incomplete data. *Educational and Psychological Measurement*, vol. 21, no. 1, pp. 145-147.

1410. MENDELSOHN, Harold. 1962. Measuring the process of communications effect. *Public Opinion Quarterly*, vol. 26, no. 3, pp. 411-416.

MENDENHALL, John H. 1958. *See* ENGEL, Gerald, O'SHEA, Harriet E. and MENDENHALL, John H. 1958.

1411. MENEFEE, Selden C. 1936. The effect of stereotyped words on political judgments. *American Sociological Review*, vol. 1, no. 4, pp. 614-621.

1412. MENEFEE, Selden. 1944. Recruiting an opinion field staff. *Public Opinion Quarterly*, vol. 8, no. 2, pp. 262-269.

1413. **MENZEL**, Herbert. 1953. A new coefficient for scalogram analysis. *Public Opinion Quarterly*, vol. 17, no. 2, pp. 268-280.

1414. **MERCER**, Jane R. and BUTLER, Edgar W. 1965. Disengagement of the aged population and response differentials in survey research. *Social Forces*, vol. 46, no. 1, pp. 89-96.

1415. **MERTON**, Robert K. 1940. Fact and factitiousness in ethnic opinionnaires. *American Sociological Review*, vol. 5, no. 1, pp. 13-28.

1416. **MERTON**, Robert K. and KENDALL, Patricia L. 1946. The focused interview. *American Journal of Sociology*, vol. 51, no. 6, pp. 541-557.

1417. **MERTON**, Robert K. 1947. Selected problems of field work in the planned community. *American Sociological Review*, vol. 12, no. 3, pp. 304-312.

1418. **MESSICK**, Samuel J. 1957. Metric properties of the semantic differential. *Educational and Psychological Measurement*, vol. 17, no. 2. pp. 200-206.

1419. **MESSING**, Simon D. 1965. Application of health questionnaires to pre-urban communities in a developed country. *Human Organization*, vol. 24, no. 4, pp. 365-372.

1420. **METZNER**, Charles A. 1949/50. Three tests for errors of report in a sample interview survey. *International Journal of Opinion and Attitude Research*, vol. 3, no. 5, pp. 547-554.

1421. **METZNER**, Charles A. 1950. An application of scaling to questionnaire construction. *Journal of the American Statistical Association*, vol. 45, no. 249, pp. 112-118.

1422. **METZNER**, Gale D., GLASSER, Gerald J. and ELIASBERG, Jay. 1969. An experiment in ratings research methodology: the CONTAM committee. *ADVERTISING RESEARCH FOUNDATION. Annual Conference, 15th, New York City, 1969. Proceedings* . . . New York: Advertising Research Foundation, 1967. pp. 24-31.

1423. **METZNER**, Helen and MANN, Floyd. 1952. A limited comparison of two methods of data collection: the fixed alternative questionnaire and the open-ended interview. *American Sociological Review*, vol. 17, no. 4, pp. 486-491.

1424. **METZNER**, Helen and MANN, Floyd. 1953. Effects of grouping related questions in questionnaires. *Public Opinion Quarterly*, vol. 17, no. 1, pp. 136-141.

MEYER, Mary Alice. 1966. NICHOLS, Robert C. and MEYER, Mary Alice. 1966.

MIDDLETON, Warren C. 1941. *See* FAY, Paul J. and MIDDLETON, Warren C. 1941.

1425. MIDZUNO, H. 1961. On the post enumeration survey. *Bulletin of the International Statistical Institute,* vol. 38, no. 2, pp. 435-441.

1426. MILGRAM, Stanley, MANN, Leon and HARTER, Susan. 1965. The lost letter technique: a tool of social research. *Public Opinion Quarterly,* vol. 29, no. 3, pp. 437-438.

1427. MILGRIM, Stanley. 1969. Comment on 'A failure to validate the lost letter technique'. *Public Opinion Quarterly*, vol. 33, no. 2, pp. 263-264.

MILLER, C. Dean. 1969. *See* STEINHORST, R. Kirk and MILLER, C. Dean. 1969

MILLER, Herman P. 1969. *See* ONO, Mitsuo and MILLER, Herman P. 1969.

MILLER, James R. 1969. *See* EVAN, William M. and MILLER, James R. 1969.

1428. MILLER, S. M. 1952. The participant observer and 'over-rapport'. *American Sociological Review*, vol. 17, no. 1, pp. 97-99.

MILLERSON, G. L. 1968. *See* BELSON, W[illiam] [A.], MILLERSON, G. L. and DIDCOTT, P[eter] J. 1968.

1429. MINDAK, William A. 1961. Fitting the semantic differential to the marketing problem. *Journal of Marketing,* vol. 25, no. 4, pp. 28-33.

1430. MINER, Robert B. 1956. A critique of the cumulative frequency method for testing adequacy of sample size. *Journal of Marketing,* vol. 21, no. 1, pp. 76-77.

MINTON, George. 1964. *See* FASTEAU, Herman H., INGRAM, J. Jack and MINTON, George. 1964.

1431. MIRON, Murray S. 1961. The influence of instruction modification upon test-retest reliabilities of the semantic differential. *Educational and Psychological Measurement*, vol. 21, no. 4, pp. 883-893.

1432. MITCHELL, Claude. 1941. Do scales for measuring attitudes have any significance? *Journal of Educational Research*, vol. 34, no. 6, pp. 444-452.

1433. MITCHELL, Robert Edward. 1967. The use of content analysis for explanatory studies. *Public Opinion Quarterly,* vol. 31, no. 2, pp. 230-241.

1434. **MITCHELL**, Walter, *Jr.* 1939. Factors affecting the rate of return on mailed questionnaires. *Journal of the American Statistical Association*, vol. 34, no. 208, pp. 683-692.

1435. **MITSOS**, Spiro B. 1961. Personal constructs and the semantic differential. *Journal of Abnormal and Social Psychology*, vol. 62, no. 2, pp. 433-434.

MOE, Edward O. 1966. *See* SESSIONS, Frank Q., EPLEY, Robert J. and MOE, Edward O. 1966.

MOHR, Phillip J. 1950. *See* CAMPBELL, Donald T. and MOHR, Phillip J. 1950.

1436. **MONK**, D. M. and EHRENBERG, A. S. C. 1961. Aided recall in television research. *EUROPEAN SOCIETY FOR OPINION AND MARKETING RESEARCH/WORLD ASSOCIATION FOR PUBLIC OPINION RESEARCH. Congress, VII, Baden-Baden, 1961. Marketing and sociological research in the future: needs and prospects.* 5pp. Mimeo.

1437. **MONK**, D[onald] M. 1963. Some aspects of advertising research. *The Statistician*, vol. 13, no. 2, pp. 117-126.

1438. **MONK**, D[onald] M. 1963. Testing television commercials. *MARKET RESEARCH SOCIETY. Research in advertising.* London: Market Research Society with the Oakwood Press, 1963. pp. 62-69.

1439. **MONK**, Donald [H.] and COLLINS, Martin. 1968. The single interview as a source of media-product data. *Admap*, vol. 4, no. 3, pp. 147-149.

MONTGOMERY, Caroline. 1969. *See* COLLINS, Leslie and MONTGOMERY, Caroline. 1969.

MONTGOMERY, Caroline. 1970. *See* COLLINS, Leslie and MONTGOMERY, Caroline. 1970.

MOONEY, Peter. 1968. *See* BROADBENT, Simon and MOONEY, Peter. 1968.

1440. **MOORE**, Henry T. 1921. The comparative influence of majority and expert opinion. *American Journal of Psychology*, vol. 32, no. 1, pp. 16-20.

1441. **MORAN**, William T. 1951. A reply to Heller's note. *Journal of Applied Psychology*, vol. 35, no. 2, pp. 78-79.

1442. **MORAN**, William T. 1951. Measuring exposure to advertisements. *Journal of Applied Psychology*, vol. 35, no. 1, pp. 72-77.

MORE, Douglas M. 1956. *See* WINCH, Robert F. and MORE, Douglas M. 1956.

1443. MORGAN, Elizabeth Gregory. 1951. The right interviewer for the job. *Journal of Marketing,* vol. 16, no. 2, pp. 201-202.

MORGAN, J[ames] N. 1951. *See* KLEIN, L. R. and MORGAN, J[ames] N. 1951.

MORGAN, James [N.] 1960. *See* BARLOW, Robin, MORGAN, James [N.] and WIRICK, Grover. 1960.

1444. MORGAN, James N. and SONQUIST, John A. 1963. Problems in the analysis of survey data, and a proposal. *Journal of the American Statistical Association,* vol. 58, no. 302, pp. 415-434.

MORGAN, James N. 1964. *See* SONQUIST, John A. and MORGAN, James N. 1964.

MORGAN, James N. 1969. *See* ANDREWS, Frank M., MORGAN, James N. and SONQUIST, John A. 1969.

MORGAN, James N. 1971. *See* SONQUIST, John A., BAKER, Elizabeth Lauh and MORGAN, James N. 1971.

1445. MORGAN, Roy. 1947/48. Interviewer introspection on 'bias'. *Public Opinion Quarterly,* vol. 11, no. 4, pp. 615-616.

1446. MORGAN, Roy. 1948. A note on question wording. *Public Opinion Quarterly,* vol. 12, no. 2, pp. 328.

1447. MORGAN, Roy. 1948. Comments. *International Journal of Opinion and Attitude Research,* vol. 2, no. 1, pp. 100.

1448. MORGAN, Roy. 1949. Follow-up letters disclose trends following opinion surveys. *Public Opinion Quarterly,* vol. 13, no. 4, pp. 686-688.

1449. MORRISON, Denton E. 1958. A boxing system for interview schedules. *American Sociological Review*, vol. 23, no. 1, pp. 83-84.

1450. MORRISON, Denton E. and HENKEL, Ramon E. 1969. Significance tests reconsidered. *American Sociologist,* vol. 4, no. 2, pp. 131-140.

MORRISON, Donald G. 1965. *See* FRANK, Ronald E., MASSY, William F. and MORRISON, Donald G. 1965.

1451. MORRISON, Donald G., FRANK, Ronald E. and MASSY, William F. 1966. A note on panel bias. *Journal of Marketing Research,* vol. 3, no. 1, pp. 85-88.

1452. **MORRISON**, Donald G. 1969. On the interpretation of discriminant analysis. *Journal of Marketing Research,* vol. 6, no. 2, pp. 156-163.

1453. **MORTON-WILLIAMS**, Jean. 1955. The selection of interviewers for short term surveys. 53pp. Typescript. Dissertation for Diploma in Psychology, Birkbeck College, University of London.

1454. **MOSER**, C. A. 1949. The use of sampling in Great Britain. *Journal of the American Statistical Association,* vol. 44, no. 246, pp. 231-259.

1455. **MOSER**, C. A. 1950. Social research: the diary method. *Social Services,* vol. 24, no. 2, pp. 80-84.

1456. **MOSER**, C. A. 1951. Interview bias. *Review of the International Statistical Institute.* vol. 19, no. 1, pp. 28-40.

1457. **MOSER**, C. A. 1951. Remarks on the sampling aspects of family expenditure surveys. *Bulletin of the International Statistical Institute.* vol. 33, part 3, pp. 189-196.

1458. **MOSER**, C. A. 1952. Quota sampling. *Journal of the Royal Statistical Society, series A*, vol. 115, part 3, pp. 411-423.

1459. **MOSER**, C. A. and STUART, A. [Ian]. 1953. An experimental study of quota sampling. *Journal of the Royal Statistical Society, series A,* vol. 116, part 4, pp. 349-394. Discussion on the paper by C. A. Moser and A. Stuart, pp. 394-405.

MOSER, C. A. 1954. *See* HALL, J. and MOSER, C. A. 1954.

1460. **MOSER**, C. A. 1955. Recent developments in the sampling of human populations in Great Britain. *Journal of the American Statistical Association,* vol. 50, no. 272, pp. 1195-1214.

1461. **MOSHMAN**, Jack. 1964. Sequential estimation as a tool in marketing research. *Journal of Marketing Research,* vol. 1, no. 4, pp. 62-65.

MOSS, Abigail J. 1969. *See* CASH, William S. and MOSS, Abigail J. 1969.

1462. **MOSS**, Louis. 1955. The scope of sample surveys. *The Incorporated Statistician*, vol. 5, no. 4, pp. 1-15.

1463. **MOSTELLER**, Frederick and McCARTHY, Philip J. 1942. Estimating population proportions. *Public Opinion Quarterly,* vol. 6, no. 3, pp. 452-458.

1464. **MOSTELLER**, Frederick. 1944. Correcting for interviewer bias. *CANTRIL, Hadley, et al. Gauging public opinion.* Princeton:

Princeton University Press; London: H. Milford, Oxford University Press, 1944. pp. 286-288.

1465. **MOSTELLER**, Frederick. 1944. The reliability of interviewers' ratings. *CANTRIL, Hadley, et al. Gauging public opinion.* Princeton: Princeton University Press; London: H. Milford, Oxford University Press, 1944. pp. 98-106.

1466. **MOSTELLER**, Frederick and **CANTRIL**, Hadley, 1944. The use and value of a battery of questions. *CANTRIL, Hadley, et al. Gauging public opinion.* Princeton: Princeton University Press; London: H. Milford, Oxford University Press, 1944. pp. 66-73.

MOSTELLER, Frederick. 1953. *See* COCHRAN, William G., MOSTELLER, Frederick and TUKEY, John W. 1953.

MULLEN, James J. 1968. *See* DANIELSON, Wayne A. and MULLEN, James J. 1965.

MULLER, Mervin E. 1962. *See* FAN, C. T., MULLER, Mervin E. and REZUCHA, Ivan 1962.

1467. **MULLER-GROTE**, Peer. 1968. Experience gained in a multi-stage verbal panel survey. *EUROPEAN SOCIETY FOR OPINION AND MARKETING RESEARCH. Congress, XXI, Opatija, 1968. Papers...* Brussels: ESOMAR. 1968. pp. 635-650.

MURPHY, Gardner. 1934. *See* LIKERT, Rensis, ROSLOW, Sydney and MURPHY, Gardner. 1943.

MURPHY, Gardner. 1943. *See* LEVINE, Jerome M. and MURPHY, Gardner. 1943.

MURPHY, M. J. 1939. *See* LUCAS, D. B. and MURPHY, M. J. 1939.

1468. **MURTHY**, M. N. 1963. Assessment and control of non-sampling errors in censuses and surveys. *Sankhya, series B,* vol. 25, part 3, pp. 263-282.

1469. **MURTHY**, M. N. 1964. The work of the United States Bureau of the Census with emphasis on sample designs and control of errors in censuses and surveys. *Sankhya, series B,* vol. 26, part 3, pp. 257-300.

1470. **MUSCIO**, Bernard. 1916. The influence of the form of a question. *British Journal of Psychology,* vol. 8, no. 3, pp. 351-389.

MUSSEN, Paul H. 1957. *See* RYCHLAK, Joseph K., MUSSEN, Paul H. and BENNETT, John W. 1957.

1471. **MYERS**, George C. 1969. The elusive male: some methodological notes on survey research design. *Public Opinion Quarterly*, vol. 33, no. 2, pp. 255-259.

1472. **MYERS**, James H. and WARNER, W. Gregory. 1968. Semantic properties of selected evaluation adjectives. *Journal of Marketing Research*, vol. 5, no. 4, pp. 409-412.

1473. **MYERS**, James H. and HAUG, Arne F. 1969. How a preliminary letter affects mail survey returns and costs. *Journal of Advertising Research*, vol. 9, no. 3, pp. 37-39.

1474. **MYERS**, Robert Cobb. 1949. Social control of opinion survey agencies. *American Psychologist*, vol. 4, no. 1, pp. 18-20.

1475. **MYERS**, Robert J. 1954. Accuracy of age reporting in the 1950 United States census. *Journal of the American Statistical Association*, vol. 49, no. 268, pp. 826-831.

MYERS, Roger A. 1966. *See* HELLER, Kenneth, DAVIS, John D. and MYERS, Roger A. 1966.

1476. **NAFZIGER**, Ralph O. 1945. Problems in reader-interest surveys. *Journal of Marketing*, vol. 9, no. 4, pp. 359-363.

1477. **NAKAMURA**, Charles Y. 1959. Salience of norms and order of questionnaire items: their effect on responses to the items. *Journal of Abnormal and Social Psychology*, vol. 59, no. 1, pp. 139-142.

NAKANISHI, Masao. 1967. *See* KASSARJIAN, Harold H. and NAKANISHI, Masao. 1967.

1478. **NAMIAS**, Jean. 1962. A rapid method to detect differences in interviewer performance. *Journal of Marketing*, vol. 26, no. 2, pp. 68-72.

1479. **NATHAN**, Peter E. and WALLACE, Wallace H. 1965. An operant behavioral measure of TV commercial effectiveness. *Journal of Advertising Research*, vol. 5, no. 4, pp. 13-20.

1480. **NATIONAL CENTER FOR HEALTH STATISTICS.** Vital and Health Statistics. 1965. Comparison of hospitalization reporting in three survey procedures ... Washington, D.C.: U.S. Department of Health, Education, and Welfare, Public Health Service, 1965. i,48pp. (*Public Health Service Publication no. 1000-series 2-no. 8*).

NATIONAL CENTER FOR HEALTH STATISTICS. Vital and Health Statistics. 1966. *See* McCARTHY, Philip J. 1966.

1481. **NATIONAL CENTER FOR HEALTH STATISTICS.** Vital and Health Statistics. 1968. The influence of interviewer and respondent psychological and behavioral variables on the reporting in household interviews ... Washington, D.C.: U.S. Department of Health, Education, and Welfare, Public Health Service, 1968. viii,65pp. (*Public Health Service Publication no. 1000-series 2-no. 26*).

1482. **NEFF**, Walter S. and COHEN, Jacob. 1967. A method for the analysis of the structure and internal consistency of Q-sort arrays. *Psychological Bulletin,* vol. 68, no. 5, pp. 361-368.

NELSON, B. 1966. *See* COLLINS, J. and NELSON, B. 1966.

1483. **NELSON**, Harold L. 1960. A comparison of scales for degrees of opinion. *Journalism Quarterly,* vol. 37, no. 2, pp. 280-283.

1484. **NELSON**, Thomas M., BARTLEY, S. Howard and DeHARDT, Doris. 1960. A comparison of variability of three sorts of observers in a sensory experiment. *Journal of Psychology,* vol. 49, no. 1, pp. 3-11.

1485. **NETER**, John and WAKSBERG, Joseph. 1961. Measurement of nonsampling errors in a survey of homeowners' expenditures for alterations and repairs. *AMERICAN STATISTICAL ASSOCIATION. Proceedings of the Social Statistics Section.* 1961. pp. 201-210.

1486. **NETER**, John and WAKSBERG, Joseph. 1963. Effects of interviewing designated respondents in a household survey of home owners' expenditures on alterations and repairs. *Applied Statistics,* vol. 12, no. 1, pp. 46-60.

1487. **NETER**, John, MAYNES, E. Scott and RAMANATHAN, R. 1965. The effect of mismatching on the measurement of response errors. *Journal of the American Statistical Association,* vol. 60, no. 312, pp. 1005-1027.

1488. **NETER**, John, MAYNES, E. Scott and RAMANATHAN, R. 1968. The effect of mismatching on the measurement of response errors. *AMERICAN STATISTICAL ASSOCIATION. Proceedings of the Social Statistics Section,* 1968. pp. 2-8.

1489. **NEU**, D. Morgan. 1961. Measuring advertisement recognition. *Journal of Advertising Research*, vol. 1, no. 6, pp. 17-22.

1490. **NEW**, Peter Kong-Ming. 1956. The personal identification of the interviewer. *American Journal of Sociology,* vol. 62, no. 2, pp. 213-214.

1491. **NEW** study shows management the most fruitful way to question consumers. 1958. *Printer's Ink*, vol. 265, no. 9, pp. 23-26, 29.

1492. NEWHALL, Sidney M. 1930. The reliability of order of merit evaluations of advertisements. *Journal of Applied Psychology*, vol. 14, no. 6, pp. 532-548.

NEWMAN, Dianne Z. 1969. *See* WOLF, Abraham, NEWMAN, Dianne Z. and WINTERS, Lewis C. 1969.

1493. NEWMAN, Sheldon W. 1962. Differences between early and late respondents to a mailed survey. *Journal of Advertising Research*, vol. 2, no. 2, pp. 37-39.

1494. NICHOLS, Robert C. and MEYER, Mary Alice. 1966. Timing postcard follow-ups in mail-questionnaire surveys. *Public Opinion Quarterly*, vol. 30, no. 2, pp. 306-307.

NIDORF, Louis J. 1967. *See* CROCKETT, Walter H. and NIDORF, Louis J. 1967.

NILES, Patricia. 1964. *See* LEVENTHAL, Howard and NILES, Patricia. 1964.

NISSELSON, Harold. 1953. *See* MARKS, Eli S., MAULDIN, W. Parker and NISSELSON, Harold. 1953.

1495. NISSELSON, Harold and WOOLSEY, Theodore D. 1959. Some problems of the household interview design for the National Health Survey. *Journal of the American Statistical Association*, vol. 54, no. 285, pp. 69-87.

1496. NIVEN, Jarold R. 1953. A comparison of two attitude scaling techniques. *Educational and Psychological Measurement*, vol. 13, no. 1, pp. 65-76.

1497. NIXON, H. K. 1936. Notes on the measurement of consumers' attitudes. *Journal of Marketing*, vol. 1, no. 1, pp. 13-19.

1498. NIXON, H. K. 1946. Internal evidence of validity of a rating scale. *Journal of Psychology*, vol. 22, no. 2, pp. 97-115.

1499. NIXON, J. W. 1961. Classification of the population by economic activities. *Journal of the Royal Statistical Society, series A*, vol. 124, part 4, pp. 526-542.

1500. NOELLE-NEUMANN, Elisabeth. 1955. Some observations on the problem of consistency. Paper given at the VIII ESOMAR Congress, Konstanz, 1955. 19pp. Mimeo.

1501. NORDBOTTEN, Svein. 1955. Measuring the error of editing the questionnaires in a census. *Journal of the American Statistical Association*, vol. 50, no. 270, pp. 364-369.

1502. **NORMAN**, Michael. 1968. The University of Bradford consumer panel: a study of panel methodology. Bradford: University of Bradford, Management Centre, 1968. 99ff. (*Research project series in marketing, no. 5*).

NORMAN, Ralph D. 1947. *See* EDGERTON, Harold A., BRITT, Steuart Henderson and NORMAN, Ralph D. 1947.

1503. **NORMAN**, Ralph D. 1948. A review of some problems related to the mail questionnaire technique. *Educational and Psychological Measurement*, vol. 8, no. 4, pp. 235-247.

1504. **NORTH**, Willard E. 1957. An analysis of J-47 jet mechanic checklist responses for response set and consistency. *Journal of Applied Psychology,* vol. 41, no. 2, pp. 114-120.

1505. **NOSANCHUK**, T. A. 1970. Pretesting effects: an inductive model. *Sociometry*, vol. 33, no. 1, pp. 12–19.

1506. **NUCKOLS**, Robert C. 1949/50. Verbi! *International Journal of Opinion and Attitude Research,* vol. 3, no. 4, pp. 575-586.

1507. **NUCKOLS**, Robert C. 1953. A note on pre-testing public opinion questions. *Journal of Applied Psychology,* vol. 37, no. 2, pp. 119-120.

1508. **NUCKOLS**, Robert C. 1953. A study of respondent forewarning in public opinion polls. *Journal of Applied Psychology,* vol. 37, no. 2, pp. 121-125.

1509. **NUCKOLS**, Robert C. 1964. The validity and comparability of mail and personal interview surveys. *Journal of Marketing Research,* vol. 1, no. 1, pp. 11-16.

1510. **NUNNALLY**, Jum. 1962. The analysis of profile data. *Psychological Bulletin,* vol. 59, no. 4, pp. 311-319.

1511. **NUTTALL**, C. G. F. 1963. How many programme viewers watch the commercials? *MARKET RESEARCH SOCIETY. Research in advertising.* London: Market Research Society with The Oakwood Press, 1963. pp. 1-16.

1512. **NYMAN**, Carl R. 1944. Visual analysis – a new method in market research. *Journal of Marketing,* vol. 8, no. 4, pp. 249-252.

1513. **OAKES**, Ralph H. 1954. Differences in responsiveness in telephone versus personal interviews. *Journal of Marketing,* vol. 19, no. 2, pp. 169.

ODBERT, H. S. 1939. *See* OSGOOD, C. E., ALLEN, C. N. and ODBERT, H. S. 1939.

O'DELL, William F. 1950. *See* PETERSON, Peter G. and O'DELL, William F. 1950.

1514. O'DELL, William F. 1962. Personal interviews or mail panels? *Journal of Marketing,* vol. 26, no. 4, pp. 34-39.

1515. ODESKY, Stanford H. 1967. Handling the neutral vote in paired comparison product testing. *Journal of Marketing Research,* vol. 4, no. 2, pp. 199-201.

1516. OEHLER, C. M. 1948/49. Qualitative evaluation of opinions. *Public Opinion Quarterly,* vol. 12, no. 4, pp. 659-668.

1517. OETTING, E. R. 1967. The effect of forcing response on the semantic differential. *Educational and Psychological Measurement,* vol. 27, no. 3, pp. 699-702.

OLDHAM, P. D. 1951. *See* COCHRANE, A. L., CHAPMAN, P. J. and OLDHAM, P. D. 1951.

OLESON, Virginia. 1963. *See* ELLIS, Robert A., LANE, W. Clayton and OLESON, Virginia. 1963.

OLIVER, James E. 1952. *See* KEPHART, N. C. and OLIVER, James E. 1952.

1518. OLLRY, Francis and SMITH, Elias. 1939. An index of 'radio-mindedness' and some applications. *Journal of Applied Psychology,* vol. 23, no. 1, pp. 8-18.

1519. OLMSTED, Donald W. 1962. The accuracy of the impressions of survey interviewers. *Public Opinion Quarterly,* vol. 26, no. 4, pp. 635-647.

1520. OLSON, Willard C. 1936. The waiver of signature in personal reports. *Journal of Applied Psychology,* vol. 20, no. 4, pp. 442-450.

1521. O'NEILL, Harry W. 1963. Pretesting advertising with the differential attitude technique. *Journal of Marketing,* vol. 27, no. 1, pp. 20-24.

1522. O'NEILL, Harry W. 1967. Response style influence in public opinion surveys. *Public Opinion Quarterly,* vol. 31, no. 1, pp. 95-102.

1523. ONO, Mitsuo and MILLER, Herman P. 1969. Income nonresponses in the Current Population Survey. *AMERICAN STATISTICAL ASSOCIATION. Proceedings of the Social Statistics Section,* 1969. pp. 277-288.

O'REGAN, William. 1957. *See* PILTZ, Albert and O'REGAN, William. 1957.

1524. **ORR**, David B. 1964. The importance of weighting: an illustrative example. *Educational and Psychological Measurement,* vol. 24, no. 1, pp. 91-93.

1525. **ORTENGREN**, John. 1957. When don't research panels wear out? *Journal of Marketing,* vol. 21, no. 4, pp. 442.

1526. **OSGOOD**, C. E., ALLEN, C. N. and ODBERT, H. S. 1939. The separation of appeal and brand-name in testing spot advertising. *Journal of Applied Psychology,* vol. 23, no. 1, pp. 60-75.

O'SHEA, Harriet E. 1958. *See* ENGEL, Gerald, O'SHEA, Harriet E. and MENDENHALL, John H. 1958.

1527. **OSTBERG**, Henry D. 1967. The measurement of non-verbal communication in copy testing. *ADVERTISING RESEARCH FOUNDATION. Annual Conference, 13th, New York City, 1967. Proceedings . . .* New York: Advertising Research Foundation, 1967. pp. 27-30.

1528. **PACE**, C. Robert. 1939. Factors influencing questionnaire returns from former university students. *Journal of Applied Psychology,* vol. 23, no. 3, pp. 388-397.

1529. **PACE**, C. Robert. 1950. Opinion and action: a study in validity of attitude measurement. *Educational and Psychological Measurement,* vol. 10, no. 3, pp. 411-419.

1530. **PAISLEY**, William J. and PARKER, Edwin B. 1965. A computer-generated sampling table for selecting respondents within households. *Public Opinion Quarterly,* vol. 29, no. 3, pp. 431-436.

1531. **PALMER**, Gladys L. 1943. Factors in the variability of response in enumerative studies. *Journal of the American Statistical Association,* vol. 38, no. 222, pp. 143-152.

1532. **PALMER**, Susan, 1967. On the character and influence of nonresponse in the Current Population Survey. *AMERICAN STATISTICAL ASSOCIATION. Proceedings of the Social Statistics Section,* 1967. pp. 73-80.

1533. **PAN**, Ju-shu. 1950. Social characteristics of respondents and nonrespondents in a questionnaire study of the aged. *American Sociological Review,* vol. 15, no. 6, pp. 780-781.

1534. **PAN**, Ju-Shun. 1951. Social characteristics of respondents and non-respondents in a questionnaire study of later maturity. *Journal of Applied Psychology,* vol. 35, no. 2, pp. 120-121.

PAPPI, Franz Urban. 1968. *See* KLINGEMANN, Hans Dieter and PAPPI, Franz Urban. 1968.

1535. **PARADISE**, L. M. and BLANKENSHIP, A[lbert] B. 1951. Depth questioning. *Journal of Marketing*, vol. 15, no. 3, pp. 274-288.

1536. **PARFITT**, John H. 1967. A comparison of purchase recall with diary panel records. *Journal of Advertising Research*, vol. 7, no. 3, pp. 16-31.

1537. **PARFITT**, John [H.] 1967. How accurately can product purchasing behaviour be measured by recall at single interview? *EUROPEAN SOCIETY FOR OPINION AND MARKETING RESEARCH/ WORLD ASSOCIATION FOR PUBLIC OPINION RESEARCH. Congress, XX, Vienna, 1967. ESOMAR WAPOR Congress 1967.* Brussels: ESOMAR, 1967, pp. 507-545.

1538. **PARFITT**, J[ohn] H. 1967. The use of panels for the collection of readership and other media data. *The Roy Thomson medals and awards for media research 1966.* London: The Thomson Organisation, 1967. pp. 71-109.

1539. **PARFITT**, John [H.] 1968. Inconsistent exaggerations of purchasing behaviour: the single call interview. *Admap*, vol. 4, no. 2, pp. 52-57.

1540. **PARFITT**, J[ohn] H. and COLLINS, B. J. K. 1968. Use of consumer panels for brand-share prediction. *Journal of Marketing Research*, vol. 5, no. 2, pp. 131-145.

1541. **PARFITT**, John [H.] and McGLOUGHLIN, Ivor. 1968. The use of consumer panels in the evaluation of promotional and advertising expenditures. *Admap*, vol. 4, no. 11, pp. 524, 526, 528, 530-534, 536.

1542. **PARK**, G. T. 1959. Note on the round-robin or fully balanced paired comparison design in household consumer research product testing. *Commentary*, no. 1, Summer, pp. 14-19.

PARKER, Edwin B. 1962 *See* DAVENPORT, John Scott, PARKER, Edwin B. and SMITH, Stewart A. 1962.

1543. **PARKER**, Edwin B. 1963. The effects of television and newspaper reading: a problem in methodology. *Public Opinion Quarterly*, vol. 27, no. 2, pp. 315-320.

1544. **PARKER**, Edwin B., SMITH, Stewart A. and DAVENPORT, John Scott, 1963. Advertising theory and measures of perception. *Journal of Advertising Research*, vol. 3, no. 4, pp. 40-43.

PARKER, Edwin B. 1965. *See* PAISLEY, William J. and PARKER, Edwin B. 1965.

PARKER Edwin B. 1968. *See* FUNKHOUSER, G. Ray and PARKER, Edwin B. 1968.

PARKER, Katherine G. 1948. *See* REED, Vergil D., PARKER, Katherine G. and VITROL, Herbert A. 1948.

1545. **PARKER**, S. R. 1968. The effect of interviewers' attitudes on answers obtained and recorded to attitude questions. London: Office of Population Censuses and Surveys, Social Survey Division, 1968. 3pp. (*Methodological series, M140*).

1546. **PARKER**, S. R. and BYNNER, J. M. 1968. Correlational analysis of data obtained from a survey of shop stewards: a comparison of McQuitty cluster analysis, factor analysis and principal component analysis. London: Office of Population Censuses and Surveys, Social Survey Division, 1968. 14pp. (*Methodological series, M137*).

PARRA, A. Aquileo. 1968. *See* LAURENT, Charles K. and PARRA, A. Aquileo. 1968.

1547. **PARRY**, Hugh J. and CROSSLEY, Helen M. 1950. Validity of responses to survey questions. *Public Opinion Quarterly*, vol. 14, no. 1, pp. 61-80.

PATERSON, Donald G. 1949. *See* HENEMAN, Herbert G., Jr. and PATERSON, Donald G. 1949.

PATERSON, Donald G. 1950. *See* KEATING, Elizabeth, PATERSON, Donald G. and STONE, C. Harold. 1950.

1548. **PATON**, Mary R. 1942. Selection of tabulation method, machine or manual. *Journal of Marketing*, vol. 6, no. 3, pp. 229-235.

1549. **PAYNE**, Donald E. 1966. Jet set, pseudo-store, and new product testing. *Journal of Marketing Research*, vol. 3, no. 4, pp. 372-376.

PAYNE, Stanley L. 1944. *See* HILGARD, Ernest R. and PAYNE, Stanley L. 1944.

1550. **PAYNE**. Stanley L. 1946. Some opinion research principles developed through studies of social medicine. *Public Opinion Quarterly*, vol. 10, no. 1, pp. 93-98.

1551. **PAYNE**, Stanley L. and RUGG, W. Donald. 1948. A sampling plan for verifying punching work. *Public Opinion Quarterly*, vol. 12, no. 2, pp. 328-330.

1552. **PAYNE**, Stanley L. 1949. Interviewer memory faults. *Public Opinion Quarterly*, vol. 13, no. 4, pp. 684-685.

1553. **PAYNE**, Stanley L. 1950. Respondents or contestants by mail. *Public Opinion Quarterly,* vol. 14, no. 3, pp. 550-551.

1554. **PAYNE**, Stanley L. 1950/51. Thoughts about meaningless questions. *Public Opinion Quarterly,* vol. 14, no. 4, pp. 687-696.

PAYNE, Stanley L. 1951. *See* CHOKEL, Frank J. and PAYNE, Stanley L. 1951.

1555. **PAYNE**, Stanley L. 1956. Some advantages of telephone surveys. *Journal of Marketing,* vol. 20, no. 3, pp. 278-281.

1556. **PAYNE**, Stanley L. 1960. Simple surveys for legal evidence. *Journal of Marketing,* vol. 24, no. 3, pp. 74-76.

1557. **PAYNE**, Stanley L. 1964. Combination of survey methods. *Journal of Marketing Research,* vol. 1, no. 2, pp. 61-62.

1558. **PAYNE**, Stanley L. 1965. Are open-ended questions worth the effort? *Journal of Marketing Research,* vol. 2, no. 4, pp. 417-419.

1559. **PEARLIN**, Leonard I. 1961. The appeals of anonymity in questionnaire response. *Public Opinion Quarterly,* vol. 25, no. 4, pp. 640-647.

PEARSON, Norman. 1939. *See* GOSNELL, Harold F. and PEARSON, Norman. 1939.

1560. **PEARSON**, Richard G. 1957. Plus percentage ratio and the co-efficient of scalability. *Public Opinion Quarterly,* vol. 21, no. 3, pp. 379-380.

PEATE, John L. 1966. *See* JOHNSON, Douglas J. and PEATE, John L. 1966.

PEATE, John [L]. 1968. *See* JOHNSON, Doug[las] [J.] and PEATE, John [L.] 1968.

PEATE, John [L.] 1968. *See* VOS, A. B. de and PEATE, John [L.] 1968.

PEATMAN, John G[ray]. 1945. *See* ZUBIN, Joseph and PEATMAN, John G[ray]. 1945.

1561. **PEATMAN**, John Gray and HALLONQUIST, Tore. 1950. Geographical sampling in testing the appeal of radio broadcasts. *Journal of Applied Psychology,* vol. 34, no. 4, pp. 270-279.

1562. **PEEL**, J. and SKIPWORTH, G. E. 1970. Sequential sampling as a technique in sociological surveys. *Applied Statistics,* vol. 19, no. 1, pp. 27-33.

1563. **PELZ**, Donald C. 1959. The influence of anonymity on expressed attitudes. *Human Organization*, vol. 18, no. 2, pp. 88-91.

1564. **PELZ**, Donald C. and ANDREWS, Frank M. 1964. Detecting causal priorities in panel study data. *American Sociological Review*, vol. 29, no. 6, pp. 836-848.

1565. **PENNINGTON**, Allan L. and PETERSON, Robert A. 1969. Interest patterns and product preferences: an exploratory analysis. *Journal of Marketing Research*, vol. 6, no. 3, pp. 284-290.

PENNOCK, Jean L. 1961. *See* JAEGER, Carol M. and PENNOCK, Jean L. 1961.

1566. **PERLMUTTER**, Howard V. 1953. Group memory of meaningful material. *Journal of Psychology*, vol. 35, no. 2, pp. 361-370.

1567. **PERLOFF**, Evelyn. 1948. Prediction of male readership of magazine articles. *Journal of Applied Psychology*, vol. 32, no. 6, pp. 663-674.

1568. **PERLOFF**, Evelyn. 1949. Prediction of female readership of magazine articles. *Journal of Applied Psychology*, vol. 33, no. 2, pp. 175-180.

PERLOFF, Robert. 1965. *See* BYHAM, William C. and PERLOFF, Robert. 1965.

PERRY, Josef. 1967. *See* ALEXANDER, C. Norman, *Jr.*, and PERRY, Josef. 1967.

1569. **PERRY**, Michael. 1969. Discriminant analysis of relations between consumers' attitudes, behavior, and intentions. *Journal of Advertising Research*, vol. 9, no. 2, pp. 34-39.

1570. **PERRY**, Paul. 1960. Election survey procedures of the Gallup Poll. *Public Opinion Quarterly*, vol. 24, no. 3, pp. 531-542.

1571. **PERRY**, Paul. 1962. Gallup poll election survey experience, 1950 to 1960. *Public Opinion Quarterly*, vol. 26, no. 2, pp. 272-279.

1572. **PERYAM**, David R. and HAYNES, John G. 1957. Prediction of soldiers' food preferences by laboratory methods. *Journal of Applied Psychology*, vol. 41, no. 1, pp. 2-6.

1573. **PESSEMIER**, Edgar A., BURGER, Philip C. and TIGERT, Douglas J. 1967. Can new product buyers be identified? *Journal of Marketing Research*, vol. 4, pp. 349-354.

1574. **PETERMAN**, Jack N. 1940. The 'program analyzer': a new technique in studying liked and disliked items in radio programs. *Journal of Applied Psychology*, vol. 24, no. 6, pp. 728-741.

PETERMAN, Jack N. 1947. *See* CIRLIN, Bernard D. and PETERMAN, Jack N. 1947.

1575. **PETERS**, William S. 1961. Selective response factors in tourist surveys. *Journal of Marketing*, vol. 25, no. 3, pp. 68-71.

1576. **PETERSON**, Peter G. and O'DELL, William F. 1950. Selecting sampling methods in commercial research. *Journal of Marketing*, vol. 15, no. 2, pp. 182-189.

1577. **PETERSON**, Richard A. 1961. A technique for the detection of blind checking in questionnaire research. *Educational and Psychological Measurement*, vol. 21, no. 2, pp. 361-362.

PETERSON, Robert A. 1969. *See* PENNINGTON, Allan L. and PETERSON, Robert A. 1969.

1578. **PHELPS**, Katherine. 1939. A flexible method of hand tabulation. *Journal of Marketing*, vol. 3, no. 3, pp. 265-268.

1579. **PHILIP**, B. R. 1945. A method for investigating color preferences in fashions. *Journal of Applied Psychology*, vol. 29, no. 2, pp. 108-114.

PHILLIPS, Bernard S. 1958. *See* SUCHMAN, Edward A., PHILLIPS, Bernard S. and STREIB, Gordon F. 1958.

1580. **PHILLIPS**, David H. 1970. Current developments in the measurement of exposure to print and television advertisements. *MARKET RESEARCH SOCIETY. Annual Conference, Brighton, March 15th-17th, 1970. Conference papers.* [London: Market Research Society], 1970. pp. 13-32.

1581. **PHILLIPS**, Derek L. and CLANCY, Kevin J. 1970. Response biases in field studies of mental illness. *American Sociological Review*, vol. 35, no. 3, pp. 503-515.

1582. **PHILLIPS**, William M., Jr. 1951. Weaknesses of the mail questionnaire: a methodological study. *Sociology and Social Research*, vol. 35, no. 4, pp. 260-267.

1583. **PILGRIM**, Francis J. and KAMEN, Joseph M. 1959. Patterns of food preferences through factor analysis. *Journal of Marketing*, vol. 24, no. 2, pp. 68-72.

PILKINGTON, G. W. 1963. *See* POPPLETON, Pamela K. and PILKINGTON, G. W. 1963.

1584. **PILTZ**, Albert and O'REGAN, William. 1957. Non-response and non-quantifiable data in sample surveys. *Journal of Educational Research*, vol. 51, no. 2, pp. 143-147.

1585. **PINTNER**, R. and FORLANO, G. 1937. The influence of attitude upon scaling of attitude items. *Journal of Social Psychology*, vol. 8, no. 1, pp. 39-45.

PINTO, Leonard. 1965. *See* SUDMAN, Seymour, GREELEY, Andrew and PINTO, Leonard. 1965.

PIPER, G. W. 1951. *See* HASTORF, A[lbert] H. and PIPER, G. W. 1951.

1586. **PIPPETTE**, G. L. 1940. An experiment with college questionnaires. *Journal of Marketing*, vol. 5, no. 2, pp. 122-124.

1587. **PLATTEN**, John H., Jr. 1958. Weighting procedures in probability-type samples. *Journal of Marketing*, vol. 23, no. 1, pp. 47-52.

1588. **PLOG**, Stanley C. 1963. Explanations for a high return rate on a mail questionnaire. *Public Opinion Quarterly*, vol. 27, no. 2, pp. 297-298.

1589. **PODELL**, Lawrence. 1955. The structured interview as a social relationship. *Social Forces*, vol. 34, no. 2, pp. 150-155.

1590. **PODELL**, Lawrence. 1956. An interviewing problem in values research. *Sociology and Social Research*, vol. 41, no. 2, pp. 121-126.

POLITZ, Alfred. 1942. *See* FRANZEN, Raymond and POLITZ, Alfred. 1942.

1591. **POLITZ**, Alfred. 1943. Family versus individual in measurement of audiences. *Journal of the American Statistical Association*, vol. 38, no. 222, pp. 233-237.

1592. **POLITZ**, Alfred and SIMMONS, Willard. 1949. An attempt to get the 'not at homes' into the sample without callbacks. *Journal of the American Statistical Association*, vol. 44, no. 245, pp. 9-31.

1593. **POLITZ**, Alfred and SIMMONS, Willard. 1950. Note on 'An attempt to get the not-at-homes into the sample without callbacks'. *Journal of the American Statistical Association*, vol. 45, no. 249, pp. 136-137.

1594. **POLITZ**, Alfred. 1953. Questionnaire validity through the opinion-forming question. *Journal of Psychology*, vol. 36, no. 1, pp. 11-15.

1595. **POLITZ**, Alfred. 1956/57. 'Motivation research' from a research viewpoint. *Public Opinion Quarterly*, vol. 20, no. 4, pp. 663-673.

1596. **POLK**, Kenneth. 1962. A note on asymmetric causal models. *American Sociological Review*, vol. 27, no. 4, pp. 539-542.

1597. **POLLACK**, Irwin. 1965. Iterative techniques for unbiased rating scales. *Quarterly Journal of Experimental Psychology*, vol. 17, part 2, pp. 139-148.

1598. **POLLAY**, Richard W. 1968. Customer impulse purchasing behavior: a reexamination. *Journal of Marketing Research*, vol. 5, no. 3, pp. 323-325.

1599. **POMEROY**, Wardell B. 1963. The reluctant respondent. *Public Opinion Quarterly*, vol. 27, no. 2, pp. 287-293.

1600. **POPE**, Benjamin and SIEGMAN, Aron W. 1968. Interviewer warmth in relation to interviewee verbal behavior. *Journal of Consulting and Clinical Psychology*, vol. 32, no. 5, pp. 588-595.

POPE, Hallowell. 1967. See KNUDSEN, Dean D., POPE, Hallowell and IRISH, Donald P. 1967.

1601. **POPPLETON**, Pamela K. and PILKINGTON, G. W. 1963. A comparison of four methods of scoring an attitude scale in relation to its reliability and validity. *British Journal of Social and Clinical Psychology*, vol. 2, no. 1, pp. 36-39.

POSTMAN, Dorothy L. 1948. See POSTMAN, Leo, JENKINS, William O. and POSTMAN, Dorothy L. 1948.

1602. **POSTMAN**, Leo, JENKINS, William O. and POSTMAN, Dorothy L. 1948. An experimental comparison of active recall and recognition. *American Journal of Psychology*, vol. 61, no. 4, pp. 511-519.

1603. **POTTER**, Jack. 1968. Polygraph: a new research development. *Admap*, vol. 4, no. 6, pp. 264, 266-267.

POTTER, Robert G., *Jr*. 1961/62. See WESTOFF, Charles F., POTTER, Robert G., *Jr*. and SAGI, Philip C. 1961/62.

1604. **POULTON**, E. C. 1957. Previous knowledge and memory. *British Journal of Psychology*, vol. 48, no. 4, pp. 259-270.

1605. **POULTON**, E. C. and FREEMAN, P. R. 1966. Unwanted asymmetrical transfer effects with balanced experimental designs. *Psychological Bulletin*, vol. 66, no. 1, pp. 1-8.

1606. **POWELL**, Barbara A. 1966. Recent research in reinterview procedures. *AMERICAN STATISTICAL ASSOCIATION. Proceedings of the Social Statistics Section*, 1966. pp. 420-433.

1607. **POWELL**, W. J., *Jr*. 1968. Differential effectiveness of interviewer interventions in an experimental interview. *Journal of Consulting and Clinical Psychology*, vol. 32, no. 2, pp. 210-215.

1608. **POWERS**, Richard D. and ROSS, J. E. 1959. New diagrams for calculating readability scores rapidly. *Journalism Quarterly*, vol. 36, Spring, pp. 177-182.

1609. **POWERS**, Richard D. and KEARL, Bryant E. 1968. Readability and display as readership predictors. *Journalism Quarterly*, vol. 45, no. 2, pp. 117-118.

PRATT, Robert W., *Jr.* 1966. *See* MAYER, Charles S. and PRATT, Robert W., *Jr.* 1966.

1610. **PRESTON**, Ivan L. 1967. Choosing the level of significance in communication research. *Public Opinion Research*, vol. 31, no. 1, pp. 80-86.

1611. **PRE-TESTING**: the insurance against weak ads. 1958. *Printer's Ink*, vol. 262, no. 12, pp. 70-73.

1612. **PRICE**, D[aniel] O. 1950. On the use of stamped return envelopes with mail questionnaires. *American Sociological Review*, vol. 15, no. 5, pp. 672-673.

1613. **PRICE**, Daniel O. and SEARLES, Ruth. 1961. Some effects of interviewer-respondent interaction on responses in a survey situation. *AMERICAN STATISTICAL ASSOCIATION. Proceedings of the Social Statistics Section*, 1961. pp. 211-221.

1614. **PRICE**, Orville O. and McKEON, Alfred J. 1953. A comparison of serial number digit sampling with systematic and random sampling. *Applied Statistics*, vol. 2, no. 1, pp. 39-43.

PRICHARD, Samuel V. O. 1967. *See* McCROSKEY, James C., PRICHARD, Samuel V. O. and ARNOLD, William E. 1967.

1615. **PRIDMORE**, W. A. 1968. The organization of a sensory testing panel. *The Statistician*, vol. 18, no. 1, pp. 1-10.

1616. **PRIEN**, Erich P., *et al.* 1964. Comparison of methods of measurement of job attitudes. *Journal of Industrial Psychology*, vol. 2, no. 4, pp. 87-97.

PRIEN, Erich P. 1967. *See* BARRETT, Gerald V., SVETLIK, Byron and PRIEN, Erich P. 1967.

PRITZKER, Leon. 1951. *See* ACKOFF, Russell L. and PRITZKER, Leon. 1951.

PRITZKER, Leon. 1951. *See* ECKLER, A. Ross and PRITZKER, Leon. 1951.

PRITZKER, Leon. 1953. *See* HANSEN, Morris H., HURWITZ, William N. and PRITZKER, Leon. 1953.

1617. **PRITZKER**, Leon, OGUS, Jack and HANSEN, Morris H. 1966. Computer editing methods — some applications and results. *Bulletin of the International Statistical Institute*, vol. 41, part 1, pp. 442-473.

1618. **PROCTOR**, Charles H. 1965. Variations in response errors induced by changing instructions to enumerators. *AMERICAN STATISTICAL ASSOCIATION. Proceedings of the Social Statistics Section*, 1965. pp. 51-55.

1619. **PROSHANSKY**, Harold M. 1943. A projective method for the study of attitudes. *Journal of Abnormal and Social Psychology*, vol. 38, no. 3, pp. 393-395.

1620. **PROTHRO**, E. Terry. 1955. The effect of strong negative attitudes on the placement of items in a Thurstone scale. *Journal of Social Psychology*, vol. 41, no. 1, pp. 11-17.

PROTHRO, James W. 1962. *See* AXELROD, Morris, MATTHEWS, Donald R. and PROTHRO, James W. 1962.

1621. **PRZEWORSKI**, Adam and TEUNE, Henry. 1966. Equivalence in cross-national research. *Public Opinion Quarterly*, vol. 30, no. 4, pp. 551-568.

1622. **PURVIS**, L. E. and GREENE, W. F. 1961. A technique to measure purchase influences. *Journal of Marketing*, vol. 25, no. 5, pp. 38-43.

1623. **QUALITY** control in survey research: interviewers are gaining recognition. 1958. *Printer's Ink*, vol. 263, no. 6, pp. 71-72.

QUARANTELLI, E. L. 1956. *See* BUCHER, Rue, FRITZ, Charles E. and QUARANTELLI, E. L. 1956.

QUARANTELLI, E. L. 1956. *See*, BUCHER, Rue., FRITZ, Charles E. and QUARANTELLI, E. L. 1956.

QUAY, Lorene Childs. 1960. *See* BARTLETT, Claude J., QUAY, Lorene Childs and WRIGHTSMAN, Lawrence S., *Jr.* 1960.

QUESADA, Carmencita C. 1967. *See* SCHUH, Allen J. and QUESADA, Carmencita C. 1967.

1624. **QUINN**, Susan B. and BELSON, William A. 1969. The effects of reversing the order of presentation of verbal rating scales in survey interviews. London: London School of Economics, Survey Research Centre, 1969. vi, 64pp.

QUINN, Susan B. 1969. *See* BELSON, William A. and QUINN, Susan B. 1969.

1625. QUINN, Susan B. and BELSON, William A. 1970. Thought processes and accuracy in the recall of purchases: petrol buying. London: London School of Economics, Survey Research Centre, 1970. xii, 118pp.

RADHAKRISHNAN, Belur K. 1967. *See* LORR, Maurice and RADHAKRISHNAN, Belur K. 1967.

1626. RADVANYI, Laszlo. 1947. Problems of international opinion surveys. *International Journal of Opinion and Attitude Research*, vol. 1, no. 2, pp. 30-51.

1627. RADVANYI, Laszlo. 1951/52. Ten years of sample surveying in Mexico. *International Journal of Opinion and Attitude Research*, vol. 5, no. 4, pp. 491-510.

1628. RAGNITZ, Klaus. 1969. Use of factor analysis and cluster analysis in market segmentation and consumer typology. *EUROPEAN SOCIETY FOR OPINION AND MARKETING RESEARCH. Congress, XXII, Amsterdam. 1969. Papers* . . . Brussels: ESOMAR, 1969. pp. 67-79.

RAHMEL, Henry A. 1962. *See* CORDELL, Warren N. and RAHMEL, Henry A. 1962.

1629. RAJU, Nambury S. and GUTTMAN, Isaiah. 1965. A new working formula for the split-half reliability model. *Educational and Psychological Measurement*, vol. 25, no. 4, pp. 963-967.

1630. RALIS, Max, SUCHMAN, Edward A. and GOLDSEN, Rose K. 1958. Applicability of survey techniques in Northern India. *Public Opinion Quarterly*, vol. 22, no. 3, pp. 245-250.

RAMANATHAN, R. 1965. *See* NETER, John, MAYNES, E. Scott and RAMANATHAN, R. 1965.

RAMANATHAN, R. 1968. *See* NETER, John, MAYNES, E. Scott and RAMANATHAN, R. 1968.

1631. RAMBO, William W. 1963. The distribution of successive interval judgments of attitude statements: a note. *Journal of Social Psychology*, vol. 60, no. 2, pp. 251-254.

RAMPLEY, B. 1968. *See* LOVELL, M. R. C., JOHNS, S. and RAMPLEY, B. 1968.

RAO, Vithala R. 1970. *See* GREEN, Paul E. and RAO, Vithala R. 1970.

RAPAPORT, Gerald M. 1954. *See* BERG, Irwin A. and RAPAPORT, Gerald M. 1954.

RAPHAEL, Winifred. 1949. *See* STRINGFELLOW, Cyril D. and RAPHAEL, Winifred. 1949.

RAVEN, Bertram H. 1962. *See* FISHBEIN, Martin and RAVEN, Bertram H. 1962.

1632. **RAVEN**, J. and RITCHIE, J. 1966. A comparison of 5 techniques of data analysis. London: Office of Population Censuses and Surveys, Social Survey Division, 1966. 23pp. *(Methodological series, M134).*

1633. **REECE**, Michael M. and WHITMAN, Robert N. 1962. Expressive movements, warmth, and verbal reinforcement. *Journal of Abnormal and Social Psychology*, vol. 64, no. 3, pp. 234-236.

1634. **REED**, Vergil D., CAPT, Katherine G. and VITRIOL, Herbert A. 1948. Selection, training, and supervision of field interviewers in marketing research. *American Statistician*, vol. 2, no. 3, pp. 15-20.

1635. **REED**, Vergil D., PARKER, Katherine G. and VITRIOL, Herbert A. 1948. Selection, training, and supervision of field interviewers in marketing research. *Journal of Marketing*, vol. 12, no. 3, pp. 365-378.

REES, Matilda B. 1967. *See* CAMPBELL, Donald T., SIEGMAN, Carole R. and REES, Matilda B. 1967.

1636. **REGAN**, Mary C. 1965. Development and classification of models for multivariate analysis. *Educational and Psychological Measurement*, vol. 25, no. 4, pp. 997-1010.

1637. **REID**, Seerley. 1942. Respondents and non-respondents to mail questionnaires. *Educational Research Bulletin*, vol. 21, no. 4, pp. 87-96.

REIF, Hans G. 1952. *See* HAMEL, La Verne and REIF, Hans G. 1952.

REISS, William J. 1959/60. *See* TALLENT, Norman and REISS, William J. 1959/60.

REMMERS, H. H. 1948. *See* GAGE, N. L. and REMMERS, H. H. 1948.

REMMERS, H. H. 1949. *See* WILLIAMSON, Marjorie and REMMERS, H. H. 1949.

1638. **RESULTS** of communiscope test convince research director it's a useful tool. 1958. *Printer's Ink*, vol. 262, no. 3, pp. 59.

1639. REUSS, Carl F. 1943. Differences between persons responding and not responding to a mailed questionnaire. *American Sociological Review*, vol. 8, no. 4, pp. 433-438.

REYNOLDS, William A. 1951. *See* VAUGHN, Charles L. and REYNOLDS, William A. 1951.

1640. REYNOLDS, William H. 1966. Some empirical observations on a ten-point poor-to-excellent scale. *Journal of Marketing Research*, vol. 3, no. 4, pp. 388-390.

REZUCHA, Ivan. 1962. *See* FAN, C. T., MULLER, Mervin E. and REZUCHA, Ivan. 1962.

1641. RICE, Stuart A. 1929. Contagious bias in the interview. *American Journal of Sociology*, vol. 35, no. 3, pp. 420-423.

1642. RICE, Stuart A. 1938. Quantitative methods in politics. *Journal of the American Statistical Association*, vol. 33, no. 201, pp. 126-130.

1643. RICHARDS, Elizabeth A. 1957. A commercial application of Guttman attitude scaling techniques. *Journal of Marketing*, vol. 22, no. 2, pp. 166-173.

1644. RICHARDSON, Marion W. 1951. Note on Travers' critical review of the forced-choice technique. *Psychological Bulletin*, vol. 48, no. 5, pp. 435-437.

1645. RICHARDSON, Stephen A. 1952. Training in field relations skills. *Journal of Social Issues*, vol. 8, no. 3, pp. 43-50.

1646. RICHARDSON, Stephen A. 1953. A framework for reporting field relations experiences. *Human Organization*, vol. 12, no. 3, pp. 31-37.

RICHARDSON, Stephen A. 1956. *See* DOHRENWEND, Barbara S[nell] and RICHARDSON, Stephen A. 1956.

1647. RICHARDSON, Stephen A. 1960. The use of leading questions in non-schedule interviews. *Human Organization*, vol. 19, no. 2, pp. 86-89.

RICHARDSON, Stephen A. 1963. *See* DOHRENWEND, Barbara Snell and RICHARDSON, Stephen A. 1963.

1648. RIDDLE, George W. N. 1953. Validity of readership studies. *Journal of Marketing*, vol. 18, no. 1, pp. 26-32.

1649. RIDDLE, George W. N. 1954. Rejoinder. *Journal of Marketing*, vol. 18, no. 4, pp. 395-396.

1650. **RIECKEN**, Henry W. 1956. The unidentified interviewer. *American Journal of Sociology*, vol. 62, no. 2, pp. 210-212.

1651. **RIESMAN**, David and GLAZER, Nathan. 1948. The meaning of opinion. *Public Opinion Quarterly*, vol. 12, no. 4, pp. 633-648.

1652. **RIESMAN**, David and GLAZER, Nathan. 1950/51. One from the gallery: an experiment in the interpretation of an interview. *International Journal of Opinion and Attitude Research*, vol. 4, no. 4, pp. 515-540.

1653. **RIESMAN**, David and GLAZER, Nathan, 1951. One from the gallery: an experiment in the interpretation of an interview. *International Journal of Opinion and Attitude Research*, vol. 5, no. 1, pp. 53-78.

RIESMAN, David. 1956. *See* BENNEY, Mark, RIESMAN, David and STAR, Shirley A. 1956.

RIESMAN, David. 1956. *See* EHRLICH, June Sachar and RIESMAN, David. 1961.

1654. **RIGGS**, Margaret M. and KAESS, Walter. 1955. Personality differences between volunteers and nonvolunteers. *Journal of Psychology*, vol. 40, no. 2, pp. 229-245.

1655. **RIKER**, Britten L. 1944. A comparison of methods used in attitude research. *Journal of Abnormal and Social Psychology*, vol. 39, no. 1, pp. 24-42.

1656. **RIKER**, Britten L. 1945. Comparison of attitude scales – a correction. *Journal of Abnormal and Social Psychology*, vol. 40, no. 1, pp. 102-103.

1657. **RILEY**, John W., *Jr.* 1962. Reflections on data sources in opinion research. *Public Opinion Quarterly*, vol. 26, no. 3, pp. 313-322.

1658. **RILEY**, Matilda White and TOBY, Jackson. 1952. Subject and object scales: a sociological application. *American Sociological Review*, vol. 17, no. 3, pp. 287-296.

RITCHIE, J. 1966. *See* RAVEN, J. and RITCHIE, J. 1966.

1659. **ROBIN**, Stanley S. 1965. A procedure for securing returns to mail questionnaires. *Sociology and Social Research*, vol. 50, no. 1, pp. 24-35.

1660. **ROBINS**, Lee N. 1963. The reluctant respondent. *Public Opinion Quarterly*, vol. 27, no. 2, pp. 276-286.

1661. **ROBINSON**, Duane and ROHDE, Sylvia. 1946. Two experiments with an anti-semitism poll. *Journal of Abnormal and Social Psychology*, vol. 41, no. 2, pp. 136-144.

1662. **ROBINSON**, James A. 1960. Survey interviewing among members of Congress. *Public Opinion Quarterly*, vol. 24, no. 1, pp. 127-138.

1663. **ROBINSON**, R. A. 1947. Use of the panel in opinion and attitude research. *International Journal of Opinion and Attitude Research*, vol. 1, no. 1, pp. 83-86.

1664. **ROBINSON**, R. A. and AGISM, Philip. 1951. Making mail surveys more reliable. *Journal of Marketing*, vol. 15, no. 4, pp. 415-424.

1665. **ROBINSON**, R. A. 1952. How to boost returns from mail surveys. *Printer's Ink*, vol. 239, no. 10, pp. 35-37.

1666. **ROBINSON**, Ray. 1946. Five features helped this mail questionnaire pull from 60 to 70%. *Printer's Ink*, vol. 214, no. 8, pp. 25-26.

1667. **ROBINSON**, W. S. 1947. Radio audience measurement: and its limitations. *Journal of Social Issues*, vol. 3, no. 3, pp. 42-50.

1668. **ROBINSON**, W. S. 1962. Asymmetric causal models: comments on Polk and Blalock. *American Sociological Review*, vol. 27, no. 4, pp. 545-548.

1669. **ROEHER**, G. Allan. 1963. Effective techniques in increasing response to mailed questionnaires. *Public Opinion Quarterly*, vol. 27, no. 2, pp. 299-302.

1670. **ROGERS**, Carl R. 1945. The nondirective method as a technique for social research. *American Journal of Sociology*, vol. 50, no. 4, pp. 279-283.

1671. **ROGERS**, Everett M. and BEAL, George M. 1958. Projective techniques in interviewing farmers. *Journal of Marketing*, vol. 23, no. 2, pp. 177-179.

ROHDE, Sylvia. 1946. *See* ROBINSON, Duane and ROHDE, Sylvia. 1946.

1672. **ROHLOFF**, Albert C. 1966. Quantitative analyses of the effectiveness of TV commercials. *Journal of Marketing Research*, vol. 3, no. 3, pp. 239-245.

1673. **ROLLINS**, Malcolm. 1940. The practical use of repeated questionnaire waves. *Journal of Applied Psychology*, vol. 24, no. 6, pp. 770-772.

1674. **ROMAN**, Hope S. 1969. Semantic generalization in formation of consumer attitudes. *Journal of Marketing Research*, vol. 6, no. 3, pp. 369-373.

1675. **ROOS**, F. J. and HEIL, L. M. 1939. Measuring the listener's attitude toward a radio art appreciation course. *Journal of Applied Psychology*, vol. 23, no. 1, pp. 75-85.

1676. **ROOS**, Leslie L. and ROOS, Noralou P. 1967. Secondary analysis in the developing areas. *Public Opinion Quarterly*, vol. 31, no. 2, pp. 272-278.

ROOS, Noralou P. 1967. *See* ROOS, Leslie L. and ROOS, Noralou P. 1967.

1677. **ROOT**, Alfred R. and WELCH, Alfred C. 1942. The continuing consumer study: a basic method for the engineering of advertising. *Journal of Marketing*, vol. 7, no. 1, pp. 3-21.

1678. **ROPER**, Burns W. 1969. Sensitivity, reliability, and consumer taste testing: some 'rights' and 'wrongs'. *Journal of Marketing Research*, vol. 6, no. 1, pp. 102-106.

1679. **ROPER**, Elmo. 1940. Classifying respondents by economic status. *Public Opinion Quarterly*, vol. 4, no. 2, pp. 270-272.

1680. **ROPER**, Elmo. 1940. Sampling public opinion. *Journal of the American Statistical Association*, vol. 35, no. 210, pp. 325-334.

1681. **ROPER**, Elmo. 1940. Wording questions for the polls. *Public Opinion Quarterly*, vol. 4, no. 1, pp. 129-130.

1682. **ROPER**, Elmo. 1941. Checks to increase polling accuracy. *Public Opinion Quarterly*, vol. 5, no. 1, pp. 87-90.

1683. **RORER**, Leonard G. 1965. The great response-style myth. *Psychological Bulletin*, vol. 63, no. 3, pp. 129-156.

1684. **ROSANDER**, A. C. 1936. The Spearman-Brown formula in attitude scale construction. *Journal of Experimental Psychology*, vol. 19, no. 4, pp. 486-495.

1685. **ROSE**, Alvin W. 1949. Projective techniques in sociological research. *Social Forces*, vol. 28, no. 2, pp. 175-183.

1686. **ROSE**, Arnold M. 1945. A research note on experimentation in interviewing. *American Journal of Sociology*, vol. 51, no. 2, pp. 143-144.

1687. **ROSE**, Arnold M. 1947. Interviewing to test for validity and reliability. *International Journal of Opinion and Attitude Research*, vol. 1, no. 1, pp. 100-101.

1688. **ROSE**, Arnold M. 1950. Public opinion research techniques suggested by sociological theory. *Public Opinion Quarterly*, vol. 14, no. 2, pp. 205-214.

1689. **ROSEN**, Ephraim. 1951. Differences between volunteers and non-volunteers for psychological studies. *Journal of Applied Psychology*, vol. 35, no. 3, pp. 185-193.

1690. **ROSEN**, Hjalmar and ROSEN, R. A. Hudson. 1955. The validity of 'undecided' answers in questionnaire responses. *Journal of Applied Psychology*, vol. 39, no. 3, pp. 178-181.

1691. **ROSEN**, Ned A. 1960. Anonymity and attitude measurement. *Public Opinion Quarterly*, vol. 24, no. 4, pp. 675-679.

ROSEN, R. A. Hudson. 1955. *See* ROSEN, Hjalmar and ROSEN, R. A. Hudson. 1955.

1692. **ROSENAU**, James N. 1964. Meticulousness as a factor in the response to mail questionnaires. *Public Opinion Quarterly*, vol. 28, no. 2, pp. 312-314.

1693. **ROSENBAUM**, Milton E. 1956. The effect of stimulus and background factors on the volunteering response. *Journal of Abnormal and Social Psychology*, vol. 53, no. 1, pp. 118-121.

ROSENBERG, Milton J. 1966. *See* BUCKHOUT, Robert and ROSENBERG, Milton J. 1966.

ROSENBLUM, A. Leon. 1965. *See* McDONAGH, Edward C. and ROSENBLUM, A. Leon. 1965.

ROSENSTOCK, Irwin M. 1952. *See* SANFORD, Fillmore H. and ROSENSTOCK, Irwin M. 1952.

1694. **ROSENTHAL**, Robert, *et al.* 1963. The role of the research assistant in the mediation of experimenter bias. *Journal of Personality*, vol. 31, no. 3, pp. 313-335.

1695. **ROSENTHAL**, Robert. 1965. The volunteer subject. *Human Relations*, vol. 18, part 4, pp. 389-406.

1696. **ROSENTHAL**, Robert. 1967. Covert communication in the psychological experiment. *Psychological Bulletin*, vol. 67, no. 5, pp. 356-367.

1697. **ROSENTHAL**, Robert. 1968. Experimenter expectancy and the reassuring nature of the null hypothesis decision procedure. *Psychological Bulletin*, vol. 70, no. 6, part 2, pp. 30-47.

1698. **ROSHWALB**, Irving. 1953. Effect of weighting by card-duplication on the efficiency of survey results. *Journal of the American Statistical Association*, vol. 48, no. 264, pp. 773-777.

1699. **ROSLOW**, Laurence and ROSLOW, Sydney. 1963. A low-cost method for identifying TV audiences. *Journal of Marketing*, vol. 27, no. 2, pp. 13-16.

ROSLOW, Sydney. 1934. *See* LIKERT, Rensis, ROSLOW, Sydney and MURPHY, Gardner. 1934.

1700. ROSLOW, Sydney. 1938. Apparatus to facilitate the scoring of the Thurstone attitude scales. *Journal of Social Psychology*, vol. 9, no. 1, pp. 103-105.

1701. ROSLOW, Sydney and BLANKENSHIP, Albert B. 1939. Phrasing the question in consumer research. *Journal of Applied Psychology*, vol. 23, no. 5, pp. 612-622.

1702. ROSLOW, Sydney, WULFECK, Wallace H. and CORBY, Philip G. 1940. Consumer and opinion research: experimental studies on the form of the question. *Journal of Applied Psychology*, vol. 24, no. 3, pp. 334-346.

1703. ROSLOW, Sydney. 1943. Measuring the radio audience by the personal interview roster method. *Journal of Applied Psychology*, vol. 27, no. 6, pp. 526-534.

ROSLOW, Sydney. 1963. *See* ROSLOW, Laurence and ROSLOW, Sydney. 1963.

1704. ROSOW, Irving. 1957. Interviewing British psychiatrists. *Public Opinion Quarterly*, vol. 21, no. 2, pp. 279-287.

1705. ROSS, H. Laurence. 1963. The inaccessible respondent: a note on privacy in city and country. *Public Opinion Quarterly*, vol. 27, no. 2, pp. 269-275.

1706. ROSS, Ivan. 1969. Handling the neutral vote in product testing. *Journal of Marketing Research*, vol. 6, no. 2, pp. 221-222.

ROSS, J. E. 1959. *See* POWERS, Richard D. and ROSS, J. E. 1959.

1707. ROSS, Robert T. 1934. Optimum orders for the presentation of pairs in the method of paired comparisons. *Journal of Educational Psychology*, vol. 25, no. 5, pp. 375-382.

ROSSI, P[eter] H. 1956. *See* INKELES, A[lex] and ROSSI, P[eter] H. 1956.

1708. ROSSI, Peter H. and INKELES, Alex. 1957. Multidimensional ratings of occupations. *Sociometry*, vol. 20, no. 3, pp. 234-251.

1709. ROTHMAN, James. 1968. Some considerations affecting the use of factor analysis in market research. *Commentary*, vol. 10, no. 3, pp. 208-219.

1710. **ROTHWELL**, N[aomi] D. 1955. Motivational research revisited. *Journal of Marketing*, vol. 20, no. 2, pp. 150-154.

1711. **ROTHWELL**, N[aomi] D. 1956. Rejoinder. *Journal of Marketing*, vol. 21, no. 2, pp. 198-199.

ROTHWELL, Naomi D. 1970. *See* JABINE, Thomas B. and ROTHWELL, Naomi D. 1970.

1712. **ROY**, Donald F. 1965. The role of the researcher in the study of social conflict: a theory of protective distortion of response. *Human Organization*, vol. 24, no. 3, pp. 262-271.

1713. **RUCKMICK**, Christian A. 1930. The uses and abuses of the questionnaire procedure. *Journal of Applied Psychology*, vol. 14, no. 1, pp. 32-41.

1714. **RUDERMAN**, Armand Peter. 1950. Sequential analysis in marketing sampling. *Journal of Marketing*, vol. 15, no. 4, pp. 470-476.

1715. **RUDOLPH**, Lloyd and RUDOLPH, Susanne H. 1958. Surveys in India: field experience in Madras State. *Public Opinion Quarterly*, vol. 22, no. 3, pp. 235-244.

RUDOLPH, Susanne H. 1958. *See* RUDOLPH, Lloyd and RUDOLPH, Susanne H. 1958.

RUGG, Donald. 1940. *See* CRESPI, Leo [P.] and RUGG, Donald. 1940

1716. **RUGG**, Donald. 1941. Experiments in wording questions: II. *Public Opinion Quarterly*, vol. 5, no. 1, pp. 91-92.

1717. **RUGG**, Donald. 1944. How representative are 'representative samples'. *CANTRIL, Hadley, et al., Gauging public opinion*. Princeton: Princeton University Press; London: H. Milford, Oxford University Press, 1944. pp. 143-149.

1718. **RUGG**, Donald. 1944. 'Trained' vs. 'untrained' interviewers. *CANTRIL, Hadley, et al. Gauging public opinion.* Princeton: Princeton University Press; London: H. Milford, Oxford University Press, 1944. pp. 83-97.

1719. **RUGG**, Donald and CANTRIL, Hadley. 1944. The wording of questions. *CANTRIL, Hadley, et al. Gauging public opinion.* Princeton: Princeton University Press; London: H. Milford, Oxford University Press, 1944. pp. 23-50.

RUGG, W. Donald. 1948. *See* PAYNE, Stanley L. and RUGG, W. Donald. 1948.

1720. **RUNDQUIST**, Edward A. 1950. Response sets: a note on consistency in taking extreme positions. *Educational and Psychological Measurement*, vol. 10, no. 1, pp. 97-99.

1721. **RUNDQUIST**, Edward A. 1966. Item and response characteristics in attitude and personality measurement: a reaction to L. G. Rorer's 'The great response style myth'. *Psychological Bulletin*, vol. 66, no. 3, pp. 166-177.

RUTTIGER, Katherine Ford. 1944. *See* HANAWALT, Nelson G. and RUTTIGER, Katherine Ford. 1944.

1722. **RYAN**, Michael. 1966. Can reading and noting be applied to industrial media. *Admap*, July/August, pp. 376-379.

1723. **RYCHLAK**, Joseph F., MUSSEN, Paul H. and BENNETT, John W. 1957. An example of the use of the incomplete sentence test in applied anthropological research. *Human Organization*, vol. 16, no. 1, pp. 25-29.

1724. **SAADI**, Mitchel and FARNSWORTH, Paul R. 1934. The degrees of acceptance of dogmatic statements and preferences for their supposed makers. *Journal of Abnormal and Social Psychology*, vol. 29, no. 2, pp. 143-150.

SAAVEDRA, Antonio. 1967. *See* LANDSBERGER, Henry A. and SAAVEDRA, Antonio. 1967.

SABAGH, Georges. 1965. *See* SIMPSON, Jon E., VAN ARSDOL, Maurice D., *Jr.* and SABAGH, Georges. 1965.

1725. **SABAGH**, Georges and SCOTT, Christopher. 1967. A comparison of different survey techniques for obtaining vital data in a developing country. *Demography*, vol. 4, no. 2, pp. 759-772.

1726. **SAGEN**, O. K., DUNHAM, Ruth E. and SIMMONS, Walt R. 1959. Health statistics from record sources and household interviews compared. *AMERICAN STATISTICAL ASSOCIATION. Proceedings of the Social Statistics Section*, 1959. pp. 6-14.

SAGI, Philip C. 1961/62. *See* WESTOFF, Charles F., POTTER, Robert G., *Jr.* and SAGI, Philip C. 1961/62.

SAKODA, James M. 1952. *See* MASLOW, A. H. and SAKODA, James M. 1952.

1727. **SALSTROM**, William, *et al.* 1944. Interviewer bias and rapport. *CANTRIL, Hadley, et al. Gauging public opinion.* Princeton: Princeton University Press; London: H. Milford, Oxford University Press, 1944. pp. 107-118.

1728. **SAMPSON**, Peter M. J. 1967. Commonsense in qualitative research. *Commentary*, vol. 9, no. 1, pp. 30-38.

1729. **SAMPSON**, Peter [M. J.] 1969. Exploration – an examination of exploratory research techniques. *EUROPEAN SOCIETY FOR OPINION AND MARKETING RESEARCH. Congress, XXII, Amsterdam, 1969. Papers*... Brussels: ESOMAR, 1969. pp. 1-18.

1730. **SAMPSON**, Peter [M. J.] and HARRIS, Paul. 1970. A user's guide to 'Fishbein'. *MARKET RESEARCH SOCIETY. Annual Conference, Brighton, March 15th-17th. 1970. Conference papers*. Southampton: Hobbs, 1970. pp. 197-221.

1731. **SANDAGE**, C. H. 1956. Do research panels wear out? *Journal of Marketing*, vol. 20, no. 4, pp. 397-401.

1732. **SANDLER**, Jack. 1962. The effect of negative verbal cues upon verbal behavior. *Journal of Abnormal and Social Psychology*, vol. 64, no. 4, pp. 312-316.

1733. **SANFORD**, Fillmore H. 1950/51. The use of a projective device in attitude surveying. *Public Opinion Quarterly*, vol. 14, no. 4, pp. 697-709.

1734. **SANFORD**, Fillmore H. and ROSENSTOCK, Irwin M. 1952. Projective techniques on the doorstep. *Journal of Abnormal and Social Psychology*, vol. 47, no. 1, pp. 3-16.

SASLOW, George. 1956. *See* MATARAZZO, Joseph D., SASLOW, George and GUZE, Samuel B. 1956.

SASLOW, George. 1956. *See* MATARAZZO, Joseph D., SASLOW, George and MATARAZZO, Ruth G. 1956.

1735. **SASLOW**, George, *et al.* 1957. Test-retest stability of interaction patterns during interviews conducted one week apart. *Journal of Abnormal and Social Psychology*, vol. 57, no. 3, pp. 295-302.

SASLOW, George. 1965. *See* WIENS, Arthur N., MATARAZZO, Joseph D. and SASLOW, George. 1965.

SASLOW, George. 1966. *See* WIENS, Arthur N., SASLOW, George and MATARAZZO, Joseph D. 1966.

1736. **SATTLER**, Jerome M. 1970. Racial 'experimenter effects' in experimentation, testing, interviewing, and psychotherapy. *Psychological Bulletin*, vol. 73, no. 2, pp. 137-160.

1737. **SAYLES**, Leonard R. 1954. Field use of projective methods: a case example. *Sociology and Social Research*, vol. 38, no. 3, pp. 168-173.

1738. **SAYRE**, Jeannette. 1939. A comparison of three indices of attitude toward radio advertising. *Journal of Applied Psychology*, vol. 23, no. 1, pp. 23-33.

1739. **SAYRE**, Jeanette. 1939. Progress in radio fan-mail analysis. *Public Opinion Quarterly*, vol. 3, no. 2, pp. 272-278.

SCATES, Alice Yeomans. 1952. *See* SCATES, Douglas E. and SCATES, Alice Yeomans. 1952.

1740. **SCATES**, Douglas E. and SCATES, Alice Yeomans. 1952. Developing a depth questionnaire to explore motivation and likelihood of action. *Educational and Psychological Measurement*, vol. 12, no. 4, pp. 620-631.

1741. **SCHAEFER**, Wolfgang. 1965. Scale measures of magazine reading. *Journal of Advertising Research*, vol. 5, no. 4, pp. 21-26.

SCHAFFER, Karl-August. 1964. *See* SZAMEITAT, Klause and SCHAFFER, Karl-August. 1964.

1742. **SCHAIE**, K. Warner. 1963. Scaling the scales: use of expert judgment in improving the validity of questionnaire scales. *Journal of Consulting Psychology*, vol. 27, no. 4, pp. 350-357.

1743. **SCHANCK**, R. L. and GOODMAN, Charles. 1939. Reactions to propaganda on both sides of a controversial issue. *Public Opinion Quarterly*, vol. 3, no. 1, pp. 107-112.

1744. **SCHATZMAN**, Leonard and STRAUSS, Anselm. 1955. Social class and modes of communication. *American Journal of Sociology*, vol. 60, no. 4, pp. 329-338.

SCHATZMAN, Leonard. 1955. *See* STRAUSS, Anselm and SCHATZMAN, Leonard. 1955.

SCHICK, Jane Holtzberg. 1945. *See* KAY, Lillian Wald and SCHICK, Jane Holtzberg. 1945.

1745. **SCHLINGER**, Mary Jane. 1969. Cues on Q-technique. *Journal of Advertising Research*, vol. 9, no. 3, pp. 53-60.

1746. **SCHLOSBERG**, Harold. 1941. A comparison of five shaving creams by the method of constant stimuli. *Journal of Applied Psychology*, vol. 25, no. 4, pp. 401-407.

1747. **SCHLOSBERG**, Harold. 1954. Selection and training of panels. PERYAM, D. R., et al., eds. *Food acceptance testing methodology: a symposium, Chicago, October, 1953.* Washington: Advisory Board on Quartermaster Research and Development, Committee on Food; National Academy of Sciences; National Research Council, 1954. pp. 45-54.

SCHMID, Robert C. 1941. *See* McCORMICK, Thomas C. and SCHMID, Robert C. 1941.

1748. **SCHMIEDESKAMP**, Jay W. 1962. Reinterviews by telephone. *Journal of Marketing*, vol. 26, no. 1, pp. 28-34.

1749. **SCHOLL**, J. C. and BURKHEAD, C. E. 1949. Interviewing non-respondents to a mail survey: an experiment in connection with April 1948 farm stocks report. *Agricultural Economics Research*, vol. 1, part 1, pp. 16-23.

SCHRAMM, Wilbur. 1949. *See* HARRELL, Thomas W., BROWN, Donald E. and SCHRAMM, Wilbur. 1949.

SCHRAMM, Wilbur. 1956. *See* KUMATA, Hideya and SCHRAMM, Wilbur. 1956.

1750. **SCHREIER**, Fred T. and WOOD, Albert J. 1948. Motivation analysis in market research. *Journal of Marketing*, vol. 13, no. 2, pp. 172-182.

1751. **SCHREIER**, Fred T. and WOOD, Albert J. 1949. Reply to criticism by Lazare Teper on 'Motivation analysis in market research'. *Journal of Marketing*, vol. 14, no. 3, pp. 453-456.

1752. **SCHUESSLER**, Karl F. 1952. Item selection in scale analysis. *American Sociological Review*, vol. 17, no. 2, pp. 183-192.

1753. **SCHUESSLER**, Karl F. 1966. A note on statistical significance of scalogram. *Sociometry*, vol. 29, no. 4, pp. 312-318.

1754. **SCHUH**, Allen J. and QUESADA, Carmencita C. 1967. Attitudes of Filipino and American college students assessed with the semantic differential. *Journal of Social Psychology*, vol. 72, no. 2, pp. 301-302.

1755. **SCHULMAN**, Gary I. and TITTLE, Charles R. 1968. Assimilation-contrast effects and item selection in Thurstone scaling. *Social Forces*, vol. 46, no. 4, pp. 484-491.

1756. **SCHUMAN**, Howard. 1966. The random probe: a technique for evaluating the validity of closed questions. *American Sociological Review*, vol. 31, no. 2, pp. 218-222.

SCHUNEMAN, R. Smith. 1963. *See* CARTER, Roy E., *Jr.*, TROLDAHL, Verling C. and SCHUNEMAN, R. Smith. 1963.

1757. **SCHUTZ**, Howard G. and KAMENETZKY, Joe. 1958. Response set in measurement of food preference. *Journal of Applied Psychology*, vol. 42, no. 3, pp. 175-177.

1758. **SCHUTZ**, William C. 1960. The Little Jiffy Correlator: a simple technique for a complex analysis of large numbers of measures on the same individuals. *Educational and Psychological Measurement*, vol.. 20, no. 1, pp. 111-118.

1759. SCHWARTZ, Alvin. 1963. The public relations of interviewing. *Journal of Marketing*, vol. 27, no. 3, pp. 34-37.

1760. SCHWARTZ, Alvin. 1964. Interviewing and the public. *Public Opinion Quarterly*, vol. 28, no. 1, pp. 135-142.

SCHWARTZ, Charlotte Green. 1955. *See* SCHWARTZ, Morris S. and SCHWARTZ, Charlotte Green. 1955.

SCHWARTZ, Michael. 1963. *See* GUSFIELD, Joseph R. and SCHWARTZ, Michael. 1963.

1761. SCHWARTZ, Morris S. and SCHWARTZ, Charlotte Green. 1955. Problems in participant observation. *American Journal of Sociology*, vol. 60, no. 4, pp. 343-353.

1762. SCHWERIN, Horace. 1940. An exploratory study of the reliability of the 'program analyzer'. *Journal of Applied Psychology*, vol. 24, no. 6, pp. 742-745.

1763. SCHWIRIAN, Kent P. and BLAINE, Harry R. 1966. Questionnaire-return bias in the study of blue-collar workers. *Public Opinion Quarterly*, vol. 30, no. 4, pp. 656-663.

1764. SCHYBERGER, Bo W:son. 1963. The accumulative and repeat audiences of Swedish weekly magazines. *Journal of Advertising Research*, vol. 3, no. 4, pp. 25-33.

1765. SCHYBERGER, Bo W:son. 1966. A case against direct questions on reading habits. *Journal of Advertising Research*, vol. 6, no. 4, pp. 25-29.

1766. SCHYBERGER, Bo W:son. 1967. A study of interviewer behaviour. *Journal of Marketing Research*, vol. 4, no. 1, pp. 32-35.

SCOBLE, Harry M. 1967. *See* BACHRACK, Stanley D. and SCOBLE, Harry M. 1967.

1767. SCOTT, C[hristopher]. 1959. A three-way check on memory for letters sent. *SCOTT, C. The postal services and the general public.* London: Office of Population Censuses and Surveys, 1959. (*CSS 286B, appendix B2, P77*). 8pp.

1768. SCOTT, Christopher and JACKSON, Stuart. 1960. The use of the telephone for making interview appointments. London: Office of Population Censuses and Surveys, Social Survey Division, 1960. 4pp. (*Methodological series, M92*).

1769. **SCOTT**, Christopher. 1961. Research on mail surveys. *Journal of the Royal Statistical Society, series A,* vol. 124, part 2, pp. 143-195. Discussion on Mr. Scott's paper. pp. 196-205.

SCOTT, Christopher. 1967. *See* SABAGH, Georges and SCOTT, Christopher. 1967.

1770. **SCOTT**, Frances Gillespie. 1957. Mail questionnaires used in a study of older women. *Sociology and Social Research,* vol. 41, no. 4, pp. 281-284.

1771. **SCOTT**, William A. 1955. Reliability of content analysis: the case of nominal scale coding. *Public Opinion Quarterly,* vol. 19, no. 3, pp. 321-325.

1772. **SCOVILLE**, J. G. 1965. Making occupational statistics more relevant. *AMERICAN STATISTICAL ASSOCIATION. Proceedings of the Business and Economics Section,* 1965. pp. 317-323.

SEAR, Alan M. 1969. *See* CHAMPION, Dean J. and SEAR, Alan M. 1969.

SEARLES, Ruth. 1961. *See* PRICE, Daniel O. and SEARLES, Ruth. 1961.

SEARS, Angela. 1963. *See* HARRIS, Amelia I., HUGHES, Gwenda and SEARS, Angela. 1963.

1773. **SEASHORE**, Robert H. and HEVNER, Kate. 1933. A time-saving device for the construction of attitude scales. *Journal of Social Psychology,* vol. 4, no. 3, pp. 366-372.

1774. **SEGNIT**, Susanna and BROADBENT, Simon. 1970. Area tests and consumer surveys to measure advertising effectiveness. *EUROPEAN SOCIETY FOR OPINION AND MARKETING RESEARCH. Congress, XXIII, Barcelona, 1970. Papers. . .* Amsterdam: ESOMAR, 1970. pp. 449-462.

1775. **SEITZ**, Richard M. 1944. How mail surveys may be made to pay. *Printer's Ink,* vol. 209, no. 9, pp. 17-19, 96, 98-102.

1776. **SELLERS**, Marie. 1942. Pre-testing of products by consumer juries. *Journal of Marketing,* vol. 6, no. 4, part 2, pp. 76-80.

1777. **SELLTIZ**, Claire. 1949. Some technical problems of a self-survey. *Journal of Social Issues,* vol. 5, no. 2, pp. 30-45.

SELLTIZ, Claire. 1964. *See* COOK, Stuart W. and SELLTIZ, Claire. 1964.

1778. SELVIN, Hanan C. 1957. A critique of tests of significance in survey research. *American Sociological Review*, vol. 22, no. 5, pp. 519-527.

1779. SELVIN, Hanan C. and STUART, Alan. 1966. Data-dredging procedures in survey analysis. *The American Statistician*, vol. 20, no. 3, pp. 20-23.

1780. SEMON, Thomas T., et al. 1959. Sampling in marketing research. *Journal of Marketing*, vol. 23, no. 3, pp. 263-273.

1781. SENG, You Poh. 1959/60. Errors in age reporting in statistically underdeveloped countries. *Population Studies*, vol. 13, no. 2, pp. 164-182.

1782. SENGUPTA, J. M. 1966. On the validity of fertility data collected through interviews. *Sankhya, series B*, vol. 28, part 3, pp. 259-268.

1783. SERMUL, Marilyn J. 1961. Comparison of panel and comparable group sampling results in before-and-after study. *Human Organization*, vol. 20, no. 3, pp. 149-150.

1784. SESSIONS, Frank Q., EPLEY, Robert J. and MOE, Edward O. 1966. The development, reliability, and validity of an all-purpose optical scanner questionnaire form. *Public Opinion Quarterly*, vol. 30, no. 3, pp. 423-428.

1785. SEWELL, William H. 1949. Field techniques in social psychological study in a rural community. *American Sociological Review*, vol. 14, no. 6, pp. 718-726.

1786. SHAFFER, James D. 1955. The reporting period for a consumer purchase panel. *Journal of Marketing*, vol. 19, no. 3, pp. 252-257.

SHAH, B. V. 1967. *See* HORVITZ, D[aniel] G., SHAH, B. V. and SIMMONS, Walt R. 1967.

SHAH, B. V. 1969. *See* GOULD, A. L., SHAH, B. V. and ABERNATHY, J[ames] R. 1969.

1787. SHANKLEMAN Eric. 1955. Measuring the readership of newspapers and magazines. *Applied Statistics*, vol. 4, no. 3, pp. 183-194.

1788. SHAPIRO, Emory P. 1952. The group interview as a tool of research. *Journal of Marketing*, vol. 16, no. 4, pp. 452-454.

1789. SHAPIRO, Jeffrey G. 1966. Agreement between channels of communication in interviews. *Journal of Consulting Psychology*, vol. 30, no. 6, pp. 535-538.

SHAPIRO, Leopold J. 1956. *See* WAX, Murray and SHAPIRO, Leopold J. 1956.

1790. **SHAPIRO**, Michael J. 1970. Discovering interviewer bias in open-ended survey responses. *Public Opinion Quarterly*, vol. 34, no. 3, pp. 412-415.

1791. **SHAPIRO**, Sam and EBERHART, John C. 1947. Interviewer differences in an intensive interview survey. *International Journal of Opinion and Attitude Research*, vol. 1, no. 2, pp. 1-17.

1792. **SHARP**, Harry. 1955. The mail questionnaire as a supplement to the personal interview. *American Sociological Review*, vol. 20, no. 6, pp. 718.

1793. **SHARP**, Harry and FELDT, Allan. 1959. Some factors in a probability sample survey of a metropolitan community. *American Sociological Review*, vol. 24, no. 5, pp. 650-661.

1794. **SHARP**, Peggie. 1967. Shopping centre surveys in Great Britain. *Commentary*, vol. 9, no. 4, pp. 191-202.

1795. **SHAUL**, J. R. H. 1952. Sampling surveys in central Africa. *Journal of the American Statistical Association*, vol. 47, no. 258, pp. 239-254.

1796. **SHEATSLEY**, Paul B. 1947/48. Some uses of interviewer-report forms. *Public Opinion Quarterly*, vol. 11, no. 4, pp. 601-611.

1797. **SHEATSLEY**, Paul B. 1948. Closed questions sometimes more valid than open. *Public Opinion Quarterly*, vol. 12, no. 1, pp. 127.

SHEATSLEY, Paul B. 1948. *See* HYMAN, Herbert H. and SHEATSLEY, Paul B. 1948.

1798. **SHEATSLEY**, Paul B. 1949. The influence of sub-questions on interviewer performance. *Public Opinion Quarterly*, vol. 13, no. 2, pp. 310-313.

1799. **SHEATSLEY**, Paul B. 1950. An analysis of interviewer characteristics and their relationship to performance. *International Journal of Opinion and Attitude Research*, vol. 4, no. 4, pp. 473-498.

1800. **SHEATSLEY**, Paul B. 1951. An analysis of interviewer characteristics and their relationship to performance: part II. *International Journal of Opinion and Attitude Research*, vol. 5, no. 1, pp. 79-94.

1801. **SHEATSLEY**, Paul B. 1951. An analysis of interviewer characteristics and their relationship to performance: part III. *International Journal of Opinion and Attitude Research,* vol. 5, no. 2, pp. 191-220.

1802. **SHEATSLEY**, Paul B. 1953. The art of interviewing and a guide to interviewer selection and training. *JAHODA, M., DEUTSCH, M.*

and COOK, S., eds. *Research methods in social relations.* New York: Dryden Press, 1953. pp. 464-492.

SHEINBERG, Jill. 1966. *See* HABERMAN, Paul W. and SHEINBERG, Jill. 1966.

1803. **SHELDON**, Richard C. and DUTKOWSKI, John. 1952/53. Are Soviet satellite refugee interviews projectable? *Public Opinion Quarterly*, vol. 16, no. 4, pp. 579-594.

1804. **SHEPARD**, T. Mills. 1942. The Starch application of the recognition technique. *Journal of Marketing*, vol. 6, no. 4, part 2, pp. 118-124.

1805. **SHEPPARD**, D. 1954. The adequacy of everyday quantitative expressions as measurements of qualities. *British Journal of Psychology*, vol. 45, no. 1, pp. 40-50.

1806. **SHEPPARD**, D. 1960. A comparison of methods for measuring intensity. London: Office of Population Censuses and Surveys, Social Survey Division, 1960. 9pp. (*Methodological series, M88*).

1807. **SHEPPARD**, D. 1960. Respondents who have heard that a survey is being carried out. London: Office of Population Censuses and Surveys, Social Survey Division, 1960. 11pp. (*Methodological series, M90*).

1808. **SHEPPARD**, D. 1960. The use of photographs in a survey on an architectural topic. London: Office of Population Censuses and Surveys, Social Survey Division, 1960. 2pp. (*Methodological series, M91*).

1809. **SHEPPARD**, D. 1961. More on schedule layout. London: Office of Population Censuses and Surveys, Social Survey Division, 1961. 3pp. (*Methodological series, M97*).

1810. **SHEPPARD**, D. 1961. Should the respondent be interviewed alone? London: Office of Population Censuses and Surveys, Social Survey Division, 1961. 5pp. (*Methodological series, M101*).

1811. **SHEPPARD**, D. 1963. Developing a method for testing the effectiveness of a campaign. London: Office of Population Censuses and Surveys, Social Survey Division, 1963. 19pp. (*Methodological series, M107*).

SHEWAN, J. M. 1960. *See* EHRENBERG, A. S. C. and SHEWAN, J. M. 1960.

1812. **SHUTTLEWORTH**, Frank K. 1931. A study of questionnaire technique. *Journal of Educational Psychology*, vol. 22, no. 9, pp. 652-658.

1813. **SHUTTLEWORTH**, Frank K. 1941. Sampling errors involved in incomplete returns to mail questionnaires. *Journal of Applied Psychology*, vol. 25, no. 5, pp. 588-591.

1814. **SICHER**, Frederic. 1963. An evaluation of Lindsley's new measure of TV viewing behavior. *Journal of Advertising Research*, vol. 3, no. 1, pp. 44-47.

SIEGEL, Paul M. 1966. *See* HODGE, Robert W. and SIEGEL, Paul M. 1966.

1815. **SIEGMAN**, Aron W. 1956. Responses to a personality questionnaire by volunteers and nonvolunteers to a Kinsey interview, *Journal of Abnormal and Social Psychology*, vol. 52, no. 2, pp. 280-281.

SIEGMAN, Aron W. 1968. *See* POPE, Benjamin and SIEGMAN, Aron W. 1968.

SIEGMAN, Carole R. 1967. *See* CAMPBELL, Donald T., SIEGMAN, Carole R. and REES, Matilda B. 1967.

1816. **SIGBAND**, Norman Bruce. 1953. The cover letter. *Journal of Marketing*, vol. 17, no. 4, pp. 424-428.

SILVER, Maurice J. 1968. *See* BARBER, Theodore Xenophon and SILVER, Maurice J. 1968.

SILVER, Maurice J. 1968. *See* BARBER, Theodore Xenophon and SILVER, Maurice J. 1968.

1817. **SILVEY**, R[obert] J. E. 1944. Methods of listener research employed by the British Broadcasting Corporation. *Journal of the Royal Statistical Society*, vol. 107, parts 3-4, pp. 190-220. Discussion on Mr. Silvey's paper, pp. 220-230.

1818. **SILVEY**, Robert, [J. E.], *et al.* 1950. Methodological problems in polling listeners and consumers. *International Journal of Opinion and Attitude Research*, vol. 4, no. 4, pp. 605-618.

1819. **SILVEY**, Robert [J. E.] 1951. Methods of viewer research employed by the British Broadcasting Corporation. *Public Opinion Quarterly*, vol. 15, no. 1, pp. 89-104.

SIMMONS, J. L. 1966. *See* McCALL, George J. and SIMMONS, J. L. 1966.

SIMMONS, Martin. 1968. *See* DURANT, Henry and SIMMONS, Martin. 1968.

SIMMONS, Walt R. 1959. *See* SAGEN, O. K., DUNHAM, Ruth E. and SIMMONS, Walt R. 1959.

1820. **SIMMONS**, Walt R., LITTLE, Robert T. and MADIGAN, Eleanor L. 1961. Selected computer applications in processing data from a continuing health household interview survey. *AMERICAN STATISTICAL ASSOCIATION. Proceedings of the Social Statistics Section*, 1961. pp. 15-22.

SIMMONS, Walt R. 1967. *See* HORVITZ, D[aniel] G., SHAH, B. V. and SIMMONS, Walt R. 1967.

SIMMONS, Willard [R.] 1949. *See* POLITZ, Alfred and SIMMONS, Willard [R.] 1949.

SIMMONS, Willard [R.] 1950. *See* POLITZ, Alfred and SIMMONS, Willard [R.] 1950.

1821. **SIMMONS**, Willard R. 1953. Prelisting in market or media surveys. *Journal of Marketing*, vol. 18, no. 1, pp. 6-17.

1822. **SIMMONS**, Willard R. 1954. A plan to account for 'not-at-homes' by combining weighting and callbacks. *Journal of Marketing*, vol. 19, no. 1, pp. 42-53.

1823. **SIMMONS**, W[illard] R. 1962. Letter to the editor. *Commentary*, no. 7, pp. 42-43.

1824. **SIMON**, Raymond. 1967. Responses to personal and form letters in mail surveys. *Journal of Advertising Research*, vol. 7, no. 1, pp. 28-30.

1825. **SIMPSON**, H. R. 1961. The analysis of survey data on an electronic computer. *Journal of the Royal Statistical Society, series A*, vol. 124, part 2, pp. 219-226.

1826. **SIMPSON**, Jon E., VAN ARSDOL, Maurice D., *Jr.* and SABAGH, Georges. 1965. Records matching as a technique for social research: an illustrative case. *Sociology and Social Research*, vol. 50, no. 1, pp. 89-100.

SIRKEN, Monroe G. 1950. *See* BIRNBAUM, Z. W. and SIRKEN, Monroe G. 1950.

SIRKEN, Monroe G. 1950. *See* BIRNBAUM, Z. W. and SIRKEN, Monroe G. 1950.

1827. **SJOBERG**, Lennart. 1965. A study of four methods for scaling paired comparisons data. *Scandinavian Journal of Psychology*, vol. 6, no. 3, pp. 173-185.

1828. **SJOBERG**, Lennart. 1967. Successive intervals scaling of paired comparisons. *Psychometrika*, vol. 32, no. 3, pp. 297-308.

1829. **SKELLY**, Florence R. 1954. Interviewer-appearance stereotypes as a possible source of bias. *Journal of Marketing*, vol. 19, no. 1, pp. 74-75.

SKIPWORTH, G. E. 1970. *See* PEEL, J. and SKIPWORTH, G. E. 1970.

SLATER, Carol W. 1960. *See* KISH, Leslie and SLATER, Carol W. 1960.

1830. **SLETTO**, Raymond F. 1940. Pretesting of questionnaires. *American Sociological Review*, vol. 5, no. 2, pp. 193-200.

1831. **SLOCUM**, W. L., EMPEY, L. T. and SWANSON, H. S. 1956. Increasing response to questionnaires and structured interviews. *American Sociological Review*, vol. 21, no. 2, pp. 221-225.

1832. **SLONIM**, Morris James. 1957. Sampling in a nutshell. *Journal of the American Statistical Association*, vol. 52, no. 278, pp. 143-161.

1833. **SMART**, Reginald G. 1964. A response to Sprott's 'Use of chi square'. *Journal of Abnormal and Social Psychology*, vol. 69, no. 1, pp. 103-105.

1834. **SMIGEL**, Irwin. 1952. A note on the use of the city directory for the selection of individual survey samples. *Human Organization*, vol. 11, no. 4, pp. 39-40.

1835. **SMITH**, B. Babington. 1950. An evaluation of factor analysis from the point of view of a psychologist. *Journal of the Royal Statistical Society, series B*, vol. 12, no. 1, pp. 73-85. Discussion on the papers by Professor Kendall and Mr. Smith, pp. 85-94.

1836. **SMITH**, David Horton. 1967. Correcting for social desirability response sets in opinion-attitude survey research. *Public Opinion Quarterly*, vol. 31, no. 1, pp. 87-94.

SMITH, Dilman M. K. 1948. *See* HOCHSTIM, Joseph R. and SMITH, Dilman M. K. 1948.

1837. **SMITH**, E. Dillon. 1939. Market sampling. *Journal of Marketing*, vol. 4, no. 1, pp. 45-50.

1838. **SMITH**, Edward W. L. and DIXON, Theodore R. 1968. Verbal conditioning as a function of race of the experimenter and prejudice of the subject. *Journal of Experimental Social Psychology*, vol. 4, no. 3, pp. 285-301.

1839. **SMITH**, Elias. 1939. A difficulty in the feature-analysis of a radio program. *Journal of Applied Psychology*, vol. 23, no. 1, pp. 57-60.

SMITH, Elias. 1939. *See* OLLRY, Francis and SMITH, Elias. 1939.

1840. SMITH, Francis F. 1935. Objectivity as a criterion for estimating the validity of questionnaire data. *Journal of Educational Psychology*, vol. 26, no. 7, pp. 481-496.

1841. SMITH, Francis F. 1936. The relation between objectivity and validity in the arrangement of items in rank order. *Journal of Applied Psychology*, vol. 20, no. 1, pp. 154-160.

SMITH, Georgianna. 1960. *See* WELLS, William D. and SMITH, Georgianna. 1960.

SMITH, H. 1967. *See* ISAACSON, H. L., KOENIGSBERG, A. and SMITH, H. 1967.

1842. SMITH, H. A. 1967. The use of panels for the collection of readership data. *The Roy Thomson medals and awards for media research 1966*. London: The Thomson Organisation, 1967. pp. 9-27.

1843. SMITH, Harry L. and HYMAN, Herbert. 1950. The biasing effect of interviewer expectations on survey results. *Public Opinion Quarterly*, vol. 14, no. 3, pp. 491-506.

SMITH, Joan Macfarlane. 1968. *See* THOMAS, R. E., SMITH, Joan Macfarlane and SPENCE, P. A. 1968.

1844. SMITH, Joan Macfarlane. 1969. Selection and training of interviewers. *EUROPEAN SOCIETY FOR OPINION AND MARKETING RESEARCH. Congress, XXII, Amsterdam, 1969.* Papers . . . Brussels: ESOMAR, 1969. pp. 19-35.

1845. SMITH, Joel. 1954. A method for the classification of areas on the basis of demographically homogeneous populations. *American Sociological Review*, vol. 19, no. 2, pp. 201-207.

SMITH, Joel. 1968. *See* TURK, Herman and SMITH, Joel. 1968.

1846. SMITH, John S. 1958. The 'G' technique of attitude scaling. *The Incorporated Statistician*, vol. 9, no. 1, pp. 9-16.

1847. SMITH, John S. 1960. The use of the Guttman scale in market research. *The Incorporated Statistician*, vol. 10, no. 1, pp. 15-28.

SMITH, Karl U. 1951. *See* WEDELL, Carl and SMITH, Karl U. 1951.

1848. SMITH, Mapheus. 1933. A note on stability in questionnaire response. *American Journal of Sociology*, vol. 38, no. 5, pp. 713-720.

SMITH, Marshall S. 1965. *See* DUNPHY, Dexter C., STONE, Philip J. and SMITH, Marshall S. 1965.

SMITH, Stewart A. 1962. *See* DAVENPORT, John Scott, PARKER, Edwin B. and SMITH, Stewart A. 1962.

SMITH, Stewart A. 1963. *See* PARKER, Edwin B., SMITH, Stewart A. and DAVENPORT, John Scott. 1963.

1849. SMITH, Virgil B. 1968. Adapting a machine-read response sheet for combined use as a semantic differential scale questionnaire. *Educational and Psychological Measurement*, vol. 28, no. 1, pp. 181-183.

1850. SNEAD, Roswell P. 1942. Problems of field interviewers. *Journal of Marketing*, vol. 7, no. 2, pp. 139-145.

1851. SNEDECOR, George W. 1948. On the design of sampling investigations. *American Statistician*, vol. 2, no. 6, pp. 6-9, 13.

1852. SOFTLEY, Paul. 1965. Guttman scaling on conventional data processing machinery. London: Office of Population Censuses and Surveys, Social Survey Division, 1965. 3pp. (*Methodological series, M119*).

1853. SOKAL, R. R. 1966. Numerical taxonomy. *Scientific American*, vol. 215, no. 6, pp. 106-116.

1854. SOMERS, Robert H. 1968. An approach to the multivariate analysis of ordinal data. *American Sociological Review*, vol. 33, no. 6, pp. 971-977.

SONQUIST, John A. 1963. *See* MORGAN, James N. and SONQUIST, John A. 1963.

1855. SONQUIST, John A. and MORGAN, James N. 1964. The detection of interaction effects: a report on a computer program for the selection of optimal combinations of explanatory variables. Ann Arbor, Michigan: University of Michigan, Survey Research Center, 1964. xi, 294pp.

1856. SONQUIST, John A. 1967. Simulating the research analyst. *Social Science Information*, vol. 6, no. 4, pp. 207-215.

SONQUIST, John A. 1969. *See* ANDREWS, Frank M., MORGAN, James N. and SONQUIST, John A. 1969.

1857. SONQUIST, John A., BAKER, Elizabeth Lauh and MORGAN, James N. 1971. Searching for structure, alias AID III: an approach to analysis of substantial bodies of micro-data and documentation for a computer program... Ann Arbor, Michigan: University of Michigan, Survey Research Center, 1971. vi, 287pp.

1858. SOUEIF, M. I. 1958. Extreme response sets as a measure of intolerance of ambiguity. *British Journal of Psychology*, vol. 49, part 4, pp. 329-333.

1859. SPEAK, Mary. 1964. Some characteristics of respondents, partial-respondents and non-respondents to questionnaires on job satisfaction. *Occupational Psychology*, vol. 38, no. 2, pp. 173-182.

1860. SPEAK, Mary. 1967. Communication failure in questioning: errors, misinterpretations and personal frames of reference. *Occupational Psychology*, vol. 41, no. 4, pp. 169-181.

SPENCE, P. A. 1968. *See* THOMAS, R. E., SMITH, Joan Macfarlane and SPENCE, P. A. 1968.

1861. SPIEGELMAN, Marvin, TERWILLIGER, Carl and FEARING, Franklin. 1953. The reliability of agreement in content analysis. *Journal of Social Psychology*, vol. 37, no. 2, pp. 175-187.

1862. SPIERS, Emmett F. and KNOTT, Joseph K. 1969. Computer method to process missing income and work experience information in the Current Population Survey. *AMERICAN STATISTICAL ASSOCIATION. Proceedings of the Social Statistics Section*, 1969. pp. 289-297.

1863. SPROTT, D. A. 1964. Use of chi square. *Journal of Abnormal and Social Psychology*, vol. 69, no. 1, pp. 101-103.

1864. SPROWLS, R. Clay. 1964. Sample sizes in chi-square tests for measuring advertising effectiveness. *Journal of Marketing Research*, vol. 1, no. 1, pp. 60-64.

1865. SPURR, John C. 1949. Measuring magazine readership. *International Journal of Opinion and Attitude Research*, vol. 3, no. 2, pp. 263-268.

1866. STAFFORD, James E. 1966. Influence of preliminary contact on mail returns. *Journal of Marketing Research*, vol. 3, no. 4, pp. 410-411.

1867. STAGNER, Ross. 1942. Grammer versus logic in public opinion polls: comment on Dr. Blankenship's paper. *Sociometry*, vol. 5, no. 1, pp. 102-103.

1868. STAMBLER, Howard V. 1969. Problems of analysis of Urban Employment Survey data. *AMERICAN STATISTICAL ASSOCIATION. Proceedings of the Social Statistics Section*, 1969. pp. 31-34.

1869. STANDARD breakdowns for population data. *Journal of Marketing*, vol. 15, no. 4, pp. 476-478.

1870. **STANTON**, Frank N. 1934. Memory for advertising copy presented visually vs. orally. *Journal of Applied Psychology*, vol. 18, no. 1, pp. 45-64.

1871. **STANTON**, Frank [N.] 1939. Notes on the validity of mail questionnaire returns. *Journal of Applied Psychology*, vol. 23, no. 1, pp. 95-104.

1872. **STANTON**, Frank [N.] and BAKER, Kenneth H. 1942. Interviewer-bias and the recall of incompletely learned materials. *Sociometry*, vol. 5, no. 2 pp. 123-134.

1873 **STANTON**, Howard, BACK, Kurt W. and LITWAK, Eugene. 1956. Role-playing in survey research. *American Journal of Sociology*, vol. 62, no. 2, pp. 172-176.

1874. **STAPEL**, Jan. 1947/48. The convivial respondent. *Public Opinion Quarterly*, vol. 11, no. 4, pp. 524-529.

STAPEL, J[an]. 1968. *See* JONGE, W. J. de, and STAPEL, J[an]. 1968.

1875. **STAR**, Shirley A. 1953. Obtaining household opinions from a single respondent. *Public Opinion Quarterly*, vol. 17, no. 3, pp. 386-391.

STAR, Shirley A. 1956. *See* BENNEY, Mark, RIESMAN, David and STAR, Shirley A. 1956.

1876. **STEELE**, Howard L. 1964. On the validity of projective questions. *Journal of Marketing Research*, vol. 1, no. 3, pp. 46-49.

STEINBERG, Joseph. 1956. *See* HANSEN, Morris H. and STEINBERG, Joseph. 1956.

STEINER, Gary A. 1961. *See* LAVIDGE, Robert J. and STEINER, Gary A. 1961.

1877. **STEINER**, Gary A. 1966. 'Feedback' – a progress report. *Public Opinion Quarterly*, vol. 30, no. 2, pp. 262-270.

1878. **STEINER**, Ivan D. 1955/56. Scalogram analysis as a tool for selecting poll questions. *Public Opinion Quarterly*, vol. 19, no. 4, pp. 415-424.

1879. **STEINER**, Peter O. 1951. A source of bias in one of the samples of the 1950 census. *Journal of the American Statistical Association*, vol. 46, no. 253, pp. 110-113.

1880. **STEINHORST**, R. Kirk and MILLER, C. Dean. 1969. Disproportionality of cell frequencies in psychological and educational experiments involving multiple classification. *Educational and Psychological Measurement*, vol. 29, no. 4, pp. 799-811.

1881. **STEININGER**, Marion. 1965. Situational and individual determinants of attitude scale responses. *Educational and Psychological Measurement*, vol. 25, no. 3, pp. 757-765.

1882. **STEMBER**, Charles Herbert. 1956. The effect of field procedures on public opinion data. *Dissertation Abstracts*, vol. 16, no. 3, pp. 590-591.

1883. **STEMBER**, Herbert and HYMAN, Herbert. 1949/50. Interviewer effects in the classification of responses. *Public Opinion Quarterly*, vol. 13, no. 4, pp. 669-682.

1884. **STEMBER**, Herbert and HYMAN, Herbert. 1949/50. How interviewer effects operate through question form. *International Journal of Opinion and Attitude Research*, vol. 3, no. 4, pp. 493-511.

1885. **STEMBER**, Herbert and HYMAN, Herbert. 1949/50. Interviewer effects in the classification of responses. *Public Opinion Quarterly*, vol. 13, no. 4, pp. 669-682.

1886. **STEMBER**, Herbert. 1951. Which respondents are reliable? *International Journal of Opinion and Attitude Research*, vol. 5, no. 4, pp. 475-479.

STEMBER, Herbert. 1951. *See* BELDEN, Joe, STEMBER, Herbert and HOCHSTIM, Joseph [R.] 1951.

1887. **STEMPEL**, Guido H. 1955. Increasing reliability in content analysis. *Journalism Quarterly*, vol. 32, Fall, pp. 449-455.

1888. **STEPHAN**, Frederick F. 1936. Practical problems of sampling procedure. *American Sociological Review*, vol. 1, no. 4, pp. 569-580.

1889. **STEPHAN**, Frederick F. 1939. Representative sampling in large-scale surveys. *Journal of the American Statistical Association*, vol. 34, no. 206, pp. 343-352.

1890. **STEPHAN**, Frederick F. 1941. Stratification in representative sampling. *Journal of Marketing*, vol. 6, no. 1, pp. 38-46.

1891. **STEPHAN**, Frederick F. 1950. Sampling. *American Journal of Sociology*, vol. 55, no. 4, pp. 371-375.

STEPHAN, Frederick F. 1951. *See* McCARTHY, Philip J. and STEPHAN, Frederick F. 1951.

STEPHAN, F[rederick] F. 1955. *See* EL-BADRY, M. A. and STEPHAN, F[rederick] F. 1955.

1892. **STEPHAN**, Frederick F. 1957. Advances in survey methods and measurement techniques. *Public Opinion Quarterly*, vol. 21, no. 1, pp. 79-90.

1893. **STEPHAN**, Frederick F., *chairman*. 1957. The machine revolution in the processing of data. *Public Opinion Quarterly*, vol. 21, no. 3, pp. 410-413.

STEPHAN, Frederick F. 1962. *See* COALE, Ansley J. and STEPHAN, Frederick F. 1962.

STEPHENSON, Ronald. 1967. *See* KELLY, Robert F. and STEPHENSON, Ronald. 1967.

1894. **STEPHENSON**, William. 1952. Q-methodology and the projective techniques. *Journal of Clinical Psychology*, vol. 8, no. 3, pp. 219-229.

1895. **STEPHENSON**, William. 1952. Some observations on Q technique. *Psychological Bulletin*, vol. 49, no. 5, pp. 483-498.

1896. **STEVENS**, Bill and AXELROD, Joel. 1961. Three ways to improve ad pre-tests. *Journal of Advertising Research*, vol. 1, no. 6, pp. 33-36.

1897. **STEWART**, Frank A. 1948. Some sampling problems in sociometric surveys. *Sociometry*, vol. 11, no. 4, pp. 301-307.

1898. **STEWART**, Isabel A. 1948. An interviewer's report on adult sociometric study. *Sociometry*, vol. 11, no. 4, pp. 308-319.

1899. **STEWART**, Naomi and FLOWERMAN, Samuel H. 1950. An investigation of two different methods for evaluation of interviewer job performance. *American Psychologist*, vol. 5, no. 7, p. 314.

1900. **STEWART**, Roger G. 1959. An IBM procedure for cumulative pattern analysis. *Educational and Psychological Measurement*, vol. 19, no. 1, pp. 77-80.

1901. **STOCK**, J. Stevens. 1944. Some general principles of sampling. *CANTRIL, Hadley, et al. Gauging public opinion.* Princeton: Princeton University Press; London: H. Milford, Oxford University Press, 1944. pp. 127-142.

1902. **STOCK**, J. Stevens, *chairman*. 1948. Experiences with probability sampling in private agencies: II. *Public Opinion Quarterly*, vol. 12, no. 4, pp. 799-803.

1903. **STOCK**, J. Stevens and HOCHSTIM, Joseph R. 1951. A method of measuring interviewer variability. *Public Opinion Quarterly*, vol. 15, no. 2, pp. 322-334.

1904. STOCK, J. Stevens, *chairman*. 1957. Measurement of advertising effectiveness. *Public Opinion Quarterly*, vol. 21, no. 3, pp. 434-436.

1905. STOCK, J. Stevens. 1961. A comparison of eight audience estimates. *Journal of Advertising Research*, vol. 1, no. 5, pp. 9-15.

1906. STOCK, J. Stevens. 1962. How to improve samples based on telephone listings. *Journal of Advertising Research*, vol. 2, no. 3, pp. 50-51.

1907. STOCK, J. Stevens and AUERBACH, Barbara K. 1963. How not to do consumer research. *Journal of Marketing*, vol. 27, no. 3, pp. 20-25.

STOCK, J. Stevens. 1966. *See* GREENE, Jerome D. and STOCK, J. Stevens. 1966.

1908. STOCKS, J. M. B. 1965. Validating television advertisement tests. *Commentary*, vol. 7, no. 3, pp. 159-165.

1909. STOKES, Judy. 1968. Two methods of cluster analysis used on the results of the 'deterrents survey'. London: Office of Population Censuses and Surveys, Social Survey Division, 1968. 12pp. (*Methodological series, M135*).

1910. STONBOROUGH, Thomas H. W. 1942. Fixed panels in consumer research. *Journal of Marketing*, vol. 7, no. 2, pp. 129-138.

1911. STONBOROUGH, Thomas H. W. 1942. The continuous consumer panel: a new sampling device in consumer research. *Applied Anthropology*, vol. 1, no. 2, pp. 37-41.

STONE, C. Harold. 1950. *See* KEATING, Elizabeth, PATERSON, Donald G. and STONE, C. Harold. 1950.

STONE, Philip J. 1965. *See* DUNPHY, Dexter C., STONE, Philip J. and SMITH, Marshall S. 1965.

STONE, Sarah. 1935. *See* KIRKPATRICK, Clifford and STONE, Sarah. 1935.

1912. STOTT, M. B. 1935. The limitations of the postal questionnaire in occupation analysis. *Human Factor*, vol. 9, no. 10, pp. 350-357.

1913. STOUFFER, Samuel A. 1933. A technique for analyzing sociological data classified in non-quantitative groups. *American Journal of Sociology*, vol. 39, no. 2, pp. 180-193.

1914. STOUFFER, Samuel A. 1950. Some observations on study design. *American Journal of Sociology*, vol. 55, no. 4, pp. 355-361.

1915. STOUFFER, Samuel A., *et al.* 1952. A technique for improving cumulative scales. *Public Opinion Quarterly*, vol. 16, no. 2, pp. 273-291.

1916. **STRAUSS**, Anselm and SCHATZMAN, Leonard. 1955. Cross-class interviewing: an analysis of interaction and communicative styles. *Human Organization*, vol. 14, no. 2, pp. 28-31.

STRAUSS, Anselm. 1955. *See* SCHATZMAN, Leonard and STRAUSS, Anselm. 1955.

STREIB, Gordon F. 1958. *See* SUCHMAN, Edward A., PHILLIPS, Bernard S. and STREIB, Gordon F. 1958.

1917. **STRICKER**, George. 1963. The use of the semantic differential to predict voting behavior. *Journal of Social Psychology*, vol. 59, no. 1, pp. 159-167.

1918. **STRICKER**, Lawrence J. 1967. The true deceiver. *Psychological Bulletin*, vol. 68, no. 1, pp. 13-20.

1919. **STRICKLAND**, Lloyd H. and COWAN, Frederic J., *Jr*. 1966. Optional anonymity and political balloting. *Psychological Reports*, vol. 18, no. 1, pp. 115-120.

1920. **STRINGFELLOW**, Cyril D. and RAPHAEL, Winifred. 1949. The confidential interview method in attitude surveys. *International Journal of Opinion and Attitude Research*, vol. 3, no. 1, pp. 87-94.

1921. **STROTHMANN**, Karl-Heinz. 1966. The attitude to interviews of industrial staff. *Commentary*, vol. 8, no. 1, pp. 26-34.

STUART, A[lan]. 1951. *See* DURBIN, J. and STUART, A[lan]. 1951.

STUART, A[lan]. 1954. *See* DURBIN, J. and STUART, A[lan]. 1954.

STUART, A[lan]. 1954. *See* DURBIN, J. and STUART, A[lan]. 1954.

1922. **STUART**, Alan. 1966. Stratification problems summary. *Commentary*, vol. 8, no. 2, pp. 113-115.

STUART, Alan. 1966. *See* SELVIN, Hanan C. and STUART, Alan. 1966.

1923. **STUART**, Walter J. 1966. Computer editing of survey data – five years of experience in BLS manpower surveys. *Journal of the American Statistical Association*, vol. 61, no. 314, part 1, pp. 375-383.

1924. **STYCOS**, J. Mayone. 1952. Interviewer training in another culture. *Public Opinion Quarterly*, vol. 16, no. 2, pp. 236-246.

1925. **STYCOS**, J. Mayone. 1955. Further observations on the recruitment and training of interviewers in other cultures. *Public Opinion Quarterly*, vol. 19, no. 1, pp. 68-78.

1926. **SUCHMAN**, Edward A. and McCANDLESS, Boyd. 1940. Who answers questionnaires? *Journal of Applied Psychology*, vol. 24, no. 6, pp. 758-769.

1927. **SUCHMAN**, Edward A. and GUTTMAN, Louis. 1947. A solution to the problem of question 'bias'. *Public Opinion Quarterly*, vol. 11, no. 3, pp. 445-455.

SUCHMAN, Edward A. 1947. *See* GUTTMAN, Louis and SUCHMAN, Edward A. 1947.

SUCHMAN, Edward A. 1949/50. *See* KAHN, Lessing A. and SUCHMAN, Edward A. 1949/50.

1928. **SUCHMAN**, Edward A. 1950. The logic of scale construction. *Educational and Psychological Measurement*, vol. 10, no. 1, pp. 79-93.

1929. **SUCHMAN**, Edward A., PHILLIPS, Bernard S. and STREIB, Gordon F. 1958. An analysis of the validity of health questionnaires. *Social Forces*, vol. 36, no. 3, pp. 223-232.

SUCHMAN, Edward A. 1958. *See* RALIS, Max, SUCHMAN, Edward A. and GOLDSEN, Rose K. 1958.

1930. **SUCHMAN**, Edward A. 1962. An analysis of 'bias' in survey research. *Public Opinion Quarterly*, vol. 26, no. 1, pp. 102-111.

1931. **SUDMAN**, Seymour. 1964. On the accuracy of recording of consumer panels: I. *Journal of Marketing Research*, vol. 1, no. 2, pp. 14-20.

1932. **SUDMAN**, Seymour. 1964. On the accuracy of recording of consumer panels: II. *Journal of Marketing Research*, vol. 1, no. 3, pp. 69-80.

1933. **SUDMAN**, Seymour. 1965. Time allocation in survey interviewing and in other field occupations. *Public Opinion Quarterly*, vol. 29, no. 4, pp. 638-648.

1934. **SUDMAN**, Seymour. 1965. What makes a good interviewer? Chicago: University of Chicago, National Opinion Research Center, 1965. 27ff.

1935. **SUDMAN**, Seymour, GREELEY, Andrew and PINTO, Leonard. 1965. The effectiveness of self-administered questionnaires. *Journal of Marketing Research*, vol. 2, no. 3, pp. 293-297.

1936. **SUDMAN**, Seymour. 1966. New approaches to control of interviewing costs. *Journal of Marketing Research*, vol. 3, no. 1, pp. 56-61.

1937. **SUDMAN**, Seymour. 1966. New uses of telephone methods in survey research. *Journal of Marketing Research*, vol. 3, no. 2, pp. 163-167.

1938. **SUDMAN**, Seymour. 1966. Quantifying interviewer quality. *Public Opinion Quarterly*, vol. 30, no. 4, pp. 664-667.

1939. **SUDMAN**, Seymour. 1967. The use of computers to code free response answers in survey research. *SUDMAN, Seymour. Reducing the cost of surveys*. Chicago: Aldine, 1967. pp. 154-183.

1940. **SUDMAN**, Seymour. 1967. The use of optical scanners to code survey results. *SUDMAN, Seymour. Reducing the cost of surveys*. Chicago: Aldine, 1967. pp. 184-189.

SUDMAN, Seymour. 1968. *See* FRISBIE, Bruce and SUDMAN, Seymour. 1968.

1941. **SUKHATME**, P. V. 1952. Measurement of observational errors in surveys. *Review of the International Statistical Institute*, vol. 20, nos. 2-3, pp. 121-133.

1942. **SURVEY** on problems of interviewer cheating. 1947. *International Journal of Opinion and Attitude Research*, vol. 1, no. 3, pp. 93-106.

SURVEY RESEARCH CENTRE. *See* LONDON SCHOOL OF ECONOMICS. Survey Research Centre.

SURVEY RESEARCH UNIT. *See* LONDON SCHOOL OF ECONOMICS. Survey Research Unit.

SVETLIK, Byron. 1967. *See* BARRETT, Gerald V., SVETLIK, Byron and PRIEN, Erich P. 1967.

SWANSON, H. S. 1956. *See* SLOCUM, W. L., EMPEY, L. T. and SWANSON, H. S. 1956.

1943. **SWEETLAND**, Anders and DREGER, Ralph Mason. 1954. A mechanical short-cut for computing tetrachoric correlations. *Journal of Clinical Psychology*, vol. 10, no. 1, pp. 82-84.

1944. **SYMONDS**, Percival M. 1939. Research on the interviewing process. *Journal of Educational Psychology*, vol. 30, no. 4, pp. 346-353.

1945. **SYMONDS**, Percival M. and DIETRICH, Donald H. 1941. The effect of variations in the time interval between an interview and its recording. *Journal of Abnormal and Social Psychology*, vol. 36, no. 4, pp. 593-598.

1946. SZAMEITAT, Klaus and SCHAFFER, Karl-August. 1964. Imperfect frames in statistics and the consequences for their use in sampling. *Bulletin of the International Statistical Institute*, vol. 40, part 1, pp. 517-544.

1947. TAFT, Ronald. 1955. The ability to judge people. *Psychological Bulletin*, vol. 52, no. 1, pp. 1-23.

TAKAHASHI, Shiego. 1967. *See* ZAX, Melvin and TAKAHASHI, Shigeo. 1967.

1948. TALLENT, Norman and REISS, William J. 1959/60. A note on an unusually high rate of returns for a mail questionnaire. *Public Opinion Quarterly*, vol. 23, no. 4, pp. 579-581.

TAMULONIS, Valerie. 1947. *See* CAHALAN, Don, TAMULONIS, Valerie and VERNER, Helen W. 1947.

1949. TANNENBAUM, Arnold S., *chairman*. 1957. Application of survey techniques to the study of organizational structure and functioning. *Public Opinion Quarterly*, vol. 21, no. 3, pp. 439-442.

1950. TANNENBAUM, Percy H. 1954. Effect of serial position on recall of radio news stories. *Journalism Quarterly*, vol. 31, Summer, pp. 319-323.

1951. TATARCZUK, Theodore. 1968. Infrastructure for the collection of data without coding (IPSISCO). *EUROPEAN SOCIETY FOR OPINION AND MARKETING RESEARCH. Congress, XXI, Opatija, 1968. Papers*... Brussels: ESOMAR, 1968. pp. 401-414.

1952. TAVES, Marvin J. 1952. The application of analysis of covariance in social science research. *American Sociological Review*, vol. 15, no. 3, pp. 373-381.

1953. TAVES, Marvin J. 1953. An experimental design to preserve randomization in social experiments. *American Sociological Review*, vol. 18, no. 1, pp. 90-96.

TAYLOR, Erwin K. 1950. *See* BROGDEN, Hubert E. and TAYLOR, Erwin K. 1950.

1954. TAYLOR, J. 1968. The influence of statistical principles on the design and conduct of sensory tests of foodstuffs. *The Statistician*, vol. 18, no. 1, pp. 19-23.

1955. TAYLOR, James Bentley. 1961. What do attitude scales measure:

the problem of social desirability. *Journal of Abnormal and Social Psychology*, vol. 62, no. 2, pp. 386-390.

TAYLOR, Wilson L. 1965. *See* MARKS, Melvin R. and TAYLOR, Wilson L. 1965.

1956. **TELLEGEN**, Auke. 1965. Direction of measurement: a source of misinterpretation. *Psychological Bulletin*, vol. 63, no. 4, pp. 233-243.

1957. **TenHOUTEN**, Warren D. 1969. Scale gradient analysis: a statistical method for constructing and evaluating Guttman scales. *Sociometry*, vol. 32, no. 1, pp. 80-98.

1958. **TEPER**, Lazare. 1949. 'Motivation analysis in market research' – a criticism. *Journal of Marketing*, vol. 13, no. 4, pp. 524-527.

TEPPING, Benjamin J. 1942. *See* DEMING, W. Edwards, TEPPING, Benjamin J. and GEOFFREY, Leon. 1942.

1959. **TEPPING**, Benjamin J. and WITTREICH, Warren J. 1960. Sample surveys for legal evidence. *Journal of Marketing*, vol. 25, no. 2, pp. 57-59.

TEPPING, Benjamin J. 1969. *See* BERSHAD, Max A. and TEPPING, Benjamin J. 1969.

1960. **TERMAN**, Lewis M. 1948. Kinsey's 'Sexual behaviour in the human male': some comments and criticisms. *Psychological Bulletin*, vol. 45, no. 5, pp. 443-459.

1961. **TERRIS**, Fay. 1949. Are poll questions too difficult? *Public Opinion Quarterly*, vol. 13, no. 2, pp. 314-319.

1962. **TERRY**, M. E. 1964. The principles of statistical analysis using large electronic computers. *Bulletin of the International Statistical Institute* vol. 40, no. 1, pp. 547-552.

TERWILLIGER, Carl. 1953. *See* SPIEGELMAN, Marvin, TERWILLIGER, Carl and FEARING, Franklin. 1953.

TEUNE, Henry. 1966. *See* PRIZEWORSKI, Adam and TEUNE, Henry. 1966.

THAYER, Paul W. 1954. *See* WISPE, Lauren G. and THAYER, Paul W. 1954.

1963. **THISTLETHWAITE**, Donald L. and CAMPBELL, Donald T. 1960. Regression discontinuity analysis: an alternative to the ex post facto experiment. *Journal of Educational Psychology*, vol. 51, no. 6, pp. 309-317.

THOMAS, Geoffrey. 1944. *See* BOX, Kathleen and THOMAS, Geoffrey. 1944.

1964. THOMAS, R. E., SMITH, Joan Macfarlane and SPENCE, P. A. 1968. Wheeling and dealing — a new approach to the collection of attitude and motivational data by the use of semantic differential scales. *Commentary*, vol. 10, no. 2, pp. 78-86.

THOMAS, R. K. [196–]. *See* McKENNELL, A. C. and THOMAS, R. K. [196–].

1965. THOMAS, R. K. and McKENNELL, A. C. 1968. Some uses of multicoded computer items in survey analysis. London: Office of Population Censuses and Surveys, Social Survey Division, 1968. 11pp. (*Methodological series, M142*).

THOMAS, R. K. 1968. *See* McKENNELL, A. C. and THOMAS, R. K. 1968.

1966. THOMPSON, John W. 1962. Meaningful and unmeaningful rotation of factors. *Psychological Bulletin*, vol. 59, no. 3, pp. 211-223.

1967. THOMPSON, John W. 1963. Bi-polar and unidirectional scales. *British Journal of Psychology*, vol. 54, no. 1, pp. 15-24.

THORNDIKE, Robert L. 1951. *See* KEMPER, Raymond A. and THORNDIKE, Robert L. 1951.

THORNTON, Crossley. 1968. *See* CLEMENS, John and THORNTON, Crossley. 1968.

1968. THRIFT, H. J. 1959. The Newspaper Society regional readership survey. *The Incorporated Statistician*, vol. 9, no. 4, pp. 115-137.

THRIFT, H. J. 1966. *See* HEADS, J. and THRIFT, H. J. 1966.

1969. THUMIN, Frederick J. 1962. Watch for those unseen variables. *Journal of Marketing*, vol. 26, no. 3, pp. 58-60.

1970. THURSTONE, L. L. 1940. Current issues in factor analysis. *Psychological Bulletin*, vol. 37, no. 4, pp. 189-236.

1971. THURSTONE, L. L. 1948. The edge-marking method of analyzing data. *Journal of the American Statistical Association*, vol. 43, no. 243, pp. 451-462.

1972. THURSTONE, L. L. 1951. Experimental methods in food tasting. *Journal of Applied Psychology*, vol. 35, no. 3, pp. 141-145.

1973. THURSTONE, L. L. and JONES, Lyle V. 1957. The rational origin for measuring subjective values. *Journal of the American Statistical Association*, vol. 52, no. 280, pp. 458-471.

TIERNEY, David E. 1969. *See* DRAPER, Norman R., HUNTER, William G. and TIERNEY, David E. 1969.

1974. **TIFFANY**, Donald W., COWAN, James R. and BLINN, Elaine. 1970. Sample and personality biases of volunteer subjects. *Journal of Consulting and Clinical Psychology*, vol. 35, no. 1, pp. 38-43.

1975. **TIFFIN**, Joseph and WINICK, Darvin M. 1954. A comparison of two methods of measuring the attention-drawing power of magazine advertisements. *Journal of Applied Psychology*, vol. 38, no. 4, pp. 272-275.

TIFFT, Larry L. 1966. *See* CLARK, John P. and TIFFT, Larry L. 1966.

TIGERT, Douglas J. 1967. *See* PESSEMIER, Edgar A., BURGER, Philip C. and TIGERT, Douglas J. 1967.

1976. **TITTLE**, Charles R. and HILL, Richard J. 1967. The accuracy of self-reported data and prediction of political activity. *Public Opinion Quarterly*, vol. 31, no. 1, pp. 103-106.

TITTLE, Charles R. 1968. *See* SCHULMAN, Gary I. and TITTLE, Charles R. 1968.

TOBY, Jackson. 1952. *See* RILEY, Matilda White and TOBY, Jackson. 1952.

1977. **TOMAN**, Walter. 1953. Pause analysis as a short interviewing technique. *Journal of Consulting Psychology*, vol. 17, no. 1, pp. 1-7.

1978. **TOOPS**, Herbert A. 1923. Validating the questionnaire method. *Journal of Personnel Research*, vol. 2, nos. 4 & 5, pp. 153-169.

1979. **TOOPS**, Herbert A. 1926. The returns from follow-up letters to questionnaires. *Journal of Applied Psychology*, vol. 10, no. 1, pp. 92-101.

1980. **TOOPS**, Herbert A. 1937. The factor of mechanical arrangement and typography in questionnaires. *Journal of Applied Psychology*, vol. 21, no. 2, pp. 225-229.

1981. **TORTOLANI**, Ray. 1965. Introducing bias intentionally into survey techniques. *Journal of Marketing Research*, vol. 2, no. 1, pp. 51-55.

1982. **TOWERS**, Irwin M., GOODMAN, Leo A. and ZEISEL, Hans. 1963. What could nonexposure tell the TV advertiser? *Journal of Marketing*, vol. 27, no. 3, pp. 52-56.

1983. **TRAVERS**, R[obert] M. W. 1941. A study in judging the opinions of groups. *Archives of Psychology*, vol. 266, pp. 1-73.

1984. **TRAVERS**, R[obert] M. W. 1942. Who are the best judges of the public? *Public Opinion Quarterly*, vol. 6, no. 4, pp. 628-633.

1985. **TRAVERS**, Robert M. W. 1951. A critical review of the validity and rationale of the forced-choice technique. *Psychological Bulletin*, vol. 48, no. 1, pp. 62-70.

TROLDAHL, Verling C. 1962. *See* CARTER, Roy E., Jr. and TROLDAHL, Verling C. 1962.

TROLDAHL, Verling C. 1963. *See* CARTER, Roy E., Jr., TROLDAHL, Verling C. and SCHUNEMAN, R. Smith. 1963.

1986. **TROLDAHL**, Verling C. and CARTER, Roy E., Jr. 1964. Random selection of respondents within households in phone surveys. *Journal of Marketing*, vol. 1, no. 2, pp. 71-76.

1987. **TROW**, Martin. 1957. Comment on 'Participant observation and interviewing: a comparison'. *Human Organization*, vol. 16, no. 3, pp. 33-35.

1988. **TRUESDELL**, Leon E. 1935. The mechanics of the tabulation of the population census. *Journal of the American Statistical Association*, vol. 30, no. 189, pp. 89-94.

TUCKER, Wyn. 1967. *See* CARTWRIGHT, Ann and TUCKER, Wyn. 1967.

TUKEY, John W. 1953. *See* COCHRAN, William G., MOSTELLER, Frederick and TUKEY, John W. 1953.

1989. **TULDER**, Johan J. M. van. 1969. Pre-testing bias in product testing, resulting from respondents' expectations. *EUROPEAN SOCIETY FOR OPINION AND MARKETING RESEARCH. Congress, XXII, Amsterdam, 1969. Papers* . . . Brussels: ESOMAR, 1969. pp. 501-513.

1990. **TUNE**, G. S. 1968. A note on differences between cooperative and non-cooperative volunteer subjects. *British Journal of Social and Clinical Psychology*, vol. 7, part 3, pp. 229-230.

1991. **TURK**, Herman and SMITH, Joel. 1968. Random sampling from an unenumerated population. *Sociology and Social Research*, vol. 53, no. 1, pp. 78-87.

1992. **TURNBULL**, William 1944. Secret vs. non-secret ballots. *CANTRIL, Hadley, et al. Gauging public opinion.* Princeton: Princeton University Press; London: H. Milford, Oxford University Press, 1944. pp. 77-82.

1993. **TURNER**, Robert. 1961. Inter-week variations in expenditure recorded during a two-week survey of family expenditure. *Applied Statistics*, vol. 10, no. 3, pp. 136-146.

1994. **TWEDT**, Dik Warren. 1952. A multiple factor analysis of advertising readership. *Journal of Applied Psychology*, vol. 36, no. 3, pp. 207-215.

1995. **TWEDT**, Dik Warren. 1954. A convenient recording matrix for planning the tabulation schedule. *Journal of Marketing*, vol. 19, no. 1, pp. 75-76.

1996. **TWEDT**, Dik Warren. 1966. What about other sources of sampling error? *Journal of Marketing*, vol. 30, no. 4, pp. 62-63.

1997. **TWERY**, Raymond J. 1958. Detecting patterns of magazine reading. *Journal of Marketing*, vol. 22, no. 3, pp. 290-294.

1998. **TWIGG**, Jacqueline. 1969. What is interviewer bias? *EUROPEAN SOCIETY FOR OPINION AND MARKETING RESEARCH. Congress, XXII, Amsterdam, 1969. Papers* . . . Brussels: ESOMAR, 1969. pp. 37-52.

TWYMAN, W. A. 1967. *See* EHRENBERG, A. S. C. and TWYMAN, W. A. 1967.

1999. **TWYMAN**, W. A. 1969. Research into methods of measuring television audiences and data requirements for the British television advertising industry. *EUROPEAN SOCIETY FOR OPINION AND MARKETING RESEARCH. Congress, XXII, Amsterdam, 1969. Papers* . . . Brussels: ESOMAR, 1969. pp. 555-579.

2000. **TWYMAN**, W. A. 1969. Techniques for measuring program vs. commercial audiences. *ADVERTISING RESEARCH FOUNDATION. Annual Conference, 15th, New York City, 1969. Proceedings* . . . New York: Advertising Research Foundation, 1969. pp. 32-37.

TYLER, Bonnie B. 1957. *See* CAMPBELL, Donald T. and TYLER, Bonnie B. 1957.

2001. **TYLER**, Vernon O., *Jr.*, and KELLY, Robert F. 1964. A method for rapid rating of many people on many dimensions by many raters using electronic data processing equipment. *Educational and Psychological Measurement*, vol. 24, no. 1, pp. 129-135.

2002. **UDOW**, Alfred B. 1942. The 'interviewer-effect' in public opinion and market research surveys. *Archives of Psychology*, vol. 39, no. 277, pp. 1-36.

2003. **UNDERWOOD**, Benton J. 1957. Interference and forgetting. *Psychological Review*, vol. 64, no. 1, pp. 49-60.

2004. **UNITED NATIONS.** Statistical Office. 1950. The preparation of sampling survey reports. *American Statistician*, vol. 4, no. 3, pp. 6-10, 12.

2005. **UNIVERSITY OF MICHIGAN.** Survey Research Center. 1969. Interviewer's manual. Ann Arbor, Michigan: University of Michigan, Survey Research Center, 1969. lv. (various pagings).

UPHOFF, Walter H. 1955. *See* KIRCHNER, Wayne K. and UPHOFF, Walter H. 1955.

UPHOFF, Walter [H.] 1956. *See* DUNNETTE, Marvin D., UPHOFF, Walter [H.] and AYLWARD, Merriam. 1956.

U.S. DEPARTMENT OF HEALTH, EDUCATION, AND WELFARE. Public Health Service. *National Center for Health Statistics See* NATIONAL CENTER FOR HEALTH STATISTICS.

U.S. PUBLIC HEALTH SERVICE. National Center for Health Statistics. *See* NATIONAL CENTER FOR HEALTH STATISTICS.

UTTING, J. E. G. 1956. *See* COLE, Dorothy and UTTING, J. E. G. 1956.

VAN ARSDOL, Maurice D., *Jr.* 1965. *See* SIMPSON, Jon E., VAN ARSDOL, Maurice D., *Jr.* and SABAGH, Georges. 1965.

VAN DUSEN, A. C. 1951. *See* CAREY, James F., *Jr.*, BERG, Irwin A. and VAN DUSEN, A. C. 1951.

VAUGHN, Charles L. 1946. *See* FREIBERG, Albert D., VAUGHN, Charles L. and EVANS, Mary C. 1946.

2006. **VAUGHN**, Charles L. and REYNOLDS, William A. 1951. Reliability of personal interview data. *Journal of Applied Psychology*, vol. 35, no. 1, pp. 61-63.

2007. **VAUGHN**, Charles L. 1958. A scale for assessing socio-economic status in survey research. *Public Opinion Quarterly*, vol. 22, no. 1, pp. 19-34.

2008. **VENKATESAN**, M. 1967. Laboratory experiments in marketing: the experimenter effect. *Journal of Marketing Research*, vol. 4, no. 2, pp. 142-146.

VERNER, Helen W. 1947. *See* CAHALAN, Don, TAMULONIS, Valerie and VERNER, Helen W. 1947.

2009. **VERNON**, P. E. 1938. The assessment of psychological qualities by verbal methods... London: H.M.S.O., 1938. vi, 132pp. (*Industrial Health Research Board, report no. 83*).

2010. **VERNON**, P. E. 1939. Questionnaire, attitude tests and rating scales. *BARTLETT, F. C., et al., eds. The study of society.* London: Kegan Paul, 1939. pp. 199-229.

2011. **VERNON**, Raymond. 1937. Predetermining the necessary size of a sample in marketing studies. *Journal of Marketing*, vol. 2, no. 1, pp. 9-12.

2012. **VICARY**, James M. 1948. Word association and opinion research: 'advertising' — an illustrative example. *Public Opinion Quarterly*, vol. 12, no. 1, pp. 81-98.

2013. **VICARY**, James M. 1950. Gestalt theory and paired comparisons. *Public Opinion Quarterly*, vol. 14, no. 1, pp. 139-141.

2014. **VICARY**, James M. 1955. The circular test of bias in personal interview surveys. *Public Opinion Quarterly*, vol. 19, no. 2, pp. 215-218.

2015. **VICKERY**, C. W. 1938. Punched card technique for the correction of bias in sampling. *Journal of the American Statistical Association*, vol. 33, no. 203, pp. 552-556.

2016. **VIDICH**, A. and BENSMAN, J. 1954. The validity of field data. *Human Organization*, vol. 13, no. 1, pp. 20-27.

2017. **VIDICH**, Arthur J. 1955. Participant observation and the collection and interpretation of data. *American Journal of Sociology*, vol. 60, no. 4, pp. 354-360.

2018. **VINCENT**, Clark E. 1954. The unwed mother and sampling bias. *American Sociological Review*, vol. 19, no. 5, pp. 562-567.

2019. **VINCENT**, Clark E. 1964. Socioeconomic status and familial variables in mail questionnaire responses. *American Journal of Sociology*, vol. 69, no. 6, pp. 647-653.

2020. **VINCENT**, Douglas F. 1953. The origin and development of factor analysis. *Applied Statistics*, vol. 2, no. 2, pp. 107-117.

VITAL AND HEALTH STATISTICS. *See* NATIONAL CENTER FOR HEALTH STATISTICS. Vital and Health Statistics.

VITRIOL, Herbert A. 1948. *See* REED, Vergil D., CAPT, Katherine G. and VITRIOL, Herbert A. 1948.

VITRIOL, Herbert A. 1948. *See* REED, Vergil D., PARKER, Katherine G. and VITRIOL, Herbert A. 1948.

2021. **VOGT**, Evon Z. 1956. Interviewing water-dowsers. *American Journal of Sociology*, vol. 62, no. 2, pp. 198.

2022. **VOIGHT**, Robert B. and KRIESBERG, Martin. 1952. Some principles of processing census and survey data. *Journal of the American Statistical Association*, vol. 47, no. 258, pp. 222-231.

2023. **VOS**, A. B. de and PEATE, John [L.] 1968. Evaluation of a method of pre-testing advertising. *Admap*, vol. 4, no. 10, pp. 483-483, 486, 488, 490-491.

2024. **WADSWORTH**, Robert N. 1952. The experience of a user of a consumer panel. *Applied Statistics*, vol. 1, no. 3, pp. 169-178.

2025. **WAGNER**, Isabelle F. 1939. Articulate and inarticulate replies to questionnaires. *Journal of Applied Psychology*, vol. 23, no. 1, pp. 104-115.

2026. **WAGNER**, Nathaniel N. 1968. Birth order of volunteers: cross-cultural data. *Journal of Social Psychology*, vol. 74, no. 1, pp. 133-134.

WAHIKE, John C. 1964. *See* HUNT, William H., CRANE, Wilder W. and WAHIKE, John C. 1964.

2027. **WAISANEN**, F. B. 1954. A note on the response to a mailed questionnaire. *Public Opinion Quarterly*, vol. 18, no. 2, pp. 210-212.

WAKSBERG, Joseph. 1961. *See* NETER, John and WAKSBERG, Joseph. 1961.

WAKSBERG, Joseph. 1963. *See* NETER, John and WAKSBERG, Joseph. 1963.

WAKSBERG, Joseph. 1964. *See* NETER, John and WAKSBERG, Joseph. 1964.

WALDO, Leslie C. 1964. *See* WALLIN, Paul and WALDO, Leslie C. 1964.

WALES, Hugh G. 1952. *See* FERBER, Robert and WALES, Hugh G. 1952.

WALES, Hugh G. 1962. *See* ENGEL, James F. and WALES, Hugh G. 1962.

WALES, Hugh G. 1963. *See* ENGEL, James F. and WALES, Hugh G. 1963.

WALES, Hugh G. 1963. *See* FERBER, Robert and WALES, Hugh G. 1963.

2028. **WALKER**, Kirby P. 1937. Examining personal information items of a questionnaire study. *Journal of Educational Research*, vol. 31, no. 4, pp. 281-282.

2029. **WALLACE**, David. 1947. Mail questionnaires can produce good samples of homogeneous groups. *Journal of Marketing*, vol. 12, no. 1, pp. 53-60.

2030. **WALLACE**, David. 1954. A case for — and against — mail questionnaires. *Public Opinion Quarterly*, vol. 18, no. 1, pp. 40-52.

WALLACE, Wallace H. 1965. *See* NATHAN, Peter E. and WALLACE, Wallace H. 1965.

2031. **WALLERSTEIN**, Edward. 1967. Measuring commercials on CATV. *Journal of Advertising Research*, vol. 7, no. 2, pp. 15-19.

2032. **WALLIN**, Paul. 1949. An appraisal of some methodological aspects of the Kinsey report. *American Sociological Review*, vol. 14, no. 2, pp. 197-210.

2033. **WALLIN**, Paul. 1949. Volunteer subjects as a source of sampling bias. *American Journal of Sociology*, vol. 54, no. 6, pp. 539-544.

WALLIN, Paul. 1955. *See* CLARK, Alexander L. and WALLIN, Paul. 1955.

2034. **WALLIN**, Paul and WALDO, Leslie C. 1964. Indeterminacies in ranking of fathers' occupations. *Public Opinion Quarterly*, vol. 28, no. 2, pp. 287-292.

WALSH, H. Robert. 1952. *See* WEILBACHER, William M. and WALSH, H. Robert. 1952.

WALSH, J. J. 1958. *See* GETZELS, J. W. and WALSH, J. J. 1958.

2035. **WALTERS**, J. Hart, Jr. 1961. Structured or unstructured techniques? *Journal of Marketing*, vol. 25, no. 4, pp. 58-62.

WALTERS, S. George. 1958. *See* JACOBI, John E. and WALTERS, S. George. 1958.

2036. **WARD**, Charles D. 1964. A further examination of birth order as a selective factor among volunteer subjects. *Journal of Abnormal and Social Psychology*, vol. 69, no. 3, pp. 311-313.

2037. **WARD**, Denis H. 1959. The use of edge-punched cards in statistical computation. *Applied Statistics*, vol. 8, no. 2, pp. 104-113.

WARD, Joseph. 1955. *See* WINDLE, Charles, McFANN, Howard and WARD, Joseph. 1955.

2038. **WARNER**, Lucien. 1939. The reliability of public opinion surveys. *Public Opinion Quarterly*, vol. 3, no. 3, pp. 376-390.

2039. **WARNER**, Stanley L. 1965. Randomized response: a survey technique for eliminating evasive answer bias. *Journal of the American Statistical Association*, vol. 60, no. 309, pp. 63-69.

WARNER, W. Gregory. 1968. *See* MYERS, James H. and WARNER, W. Gregory. 1968.

WATSON, Alfred N. 1940. *See* LOCKLEY, Lawrence C. and WATSON, Alfred N. 1940.

2040. WATSON, Alfred N. 1950. Note on 'probability' sampling in the field: a case study. *Public Opinion Quarterly*, vol. 14, no. 3, pp. 610-611.

2041. WATSON, John J. 1965. Improving the response rate in mail research. *Journal of Advertising Research*, vol. 5, no. 2, pp. 48-50.

WATT, Norman. 1960. *See* MAHER, Brendan A., WATT, Norman and CAMPBELL, Donald T. 1960.

2042. WAX, Murray and SHAPIRO, Leopold J. 1956. Repeated interviewing. *American Journal of Sociology*, vol. 62, no. 2, pp. 215-217.

2043. WAX, Rosalie Hankey. 1952. Reciprocity as a field technique. *Human Organization*, vol. 11, no. 3, pp. 34-37.

2044. WEBB, James T. and BRISTER, David M. 1967. The relation of verbal rate to syllable length of verbal action in two interview situations. *British Journal of Psychology*, vol. 58, parts 3 & 4, pp. 283-289.

2045. WEBB, John N. 1939. Concepts used in unemployment surveys. *Journal of the American Statistical Association*, vol. 34, no. 205, pp. 49-59. Discussion, pp. 59-61.

2046. WEBB, N[orman] L. 1965. Validation in television research. *Commentary*, vol. 7, no. 3, pp. 142-149.

2047. WEBB, Norman [L.] 1966. Measurement of overlap viewing. *Admap.*, vol. 2, November, pp. 510-512.

2048. WEBB, Norman [L.] 1968. The hardware of audience research. *Admap*, vol. 4, no. 8, pp. 370-372, 375.

2049. WEBB, Sam C. 1955. Scaling of attitudes by the method of equal-appearing intervals: a review. *Journal of Social Psychology*, vol. 42, no. 2, pp. 215-239.

2050. WEBB, Sam C. 1955. Studies of scale and ambiguity values obtained by the method of equal-appearing intervals. *Psychological Monographs*, vol. 69, no. 3, pp. 1-20.

2051. WEBB, Wilse B. and HOLLANDER, E. P. 1956. Comparison of three morale measures: a survey, pooled group judgments, and self evaluations. *Journal of Applied Psychology*, vol. 40, no. 1, pp. 17-20.

2052. **WEBBER**, Harold H. 1944. The consumer panel: a method of media evaluation. *Journal of Marketing*, vol. 9, no. 2, pp. 137-140.

2053. **WEBSTER**, Lucy L. 1966. Comparability in multi-country surveys. *Journal of Advertising Research*, vol. 6, no. 4, pp. 14-18.

2054. **WECHSLER**, James. 1940. Interviews and interviewers. *Public Opinion Quarterly*, vol. 4, no. 2, pp. 258-260.

2055. **WEDELL**, Carl and SMITH, Karl U. 1951. Consistency of interview methods in appraisal of attitudes. *Journal of Applied Psychology*, vol. 35, no. 6, pp. 392-396.

2056. **WEGROCKI**, Henry J. 1934. The effect of prestige suggestibility on emotional attitudes. *Journal of Social Psychology*, vol. 5, no. 3, pp. 384-394.

2057. **WEIGLE**, Clifford F. 1941. Two techniques for surveying newspaper readership compared. *Journalism Quarterly*, vol. 18, June, pp. 153-157.

2058. **WEILBACHER**, William M. and WALSH, H. Robert. 1952. Mail questionnaires and the personalized letter of transmittal. *Journal of Marketing*, vol. 16, no. 3, pp. 331-336.

2059. **WEINLAND**, James D. 1930. An objective method for the measurement of attitudes. *Journal of Applied Psychology*, vol. 14, no. 5, pp. 427-436.

2060. **WEISS**, Carol H. 1968. Validity of welfare mothers' interview responses. *Public Opinion Quarterly*, vol. 32, no. 4, pp. 622-633.

WEISS, Carol H. 1969. *See* DOHRENWEND, Barbara Snell, WILLIAMS, J. Allen, *Jr.* and WEISS, Carol H. 1969.

2061. **WEISS**, David J. and DAWIS, Rene V. 1960. An objective validation of factual interview data. *Journal of Applied Psychology*, vol. 44, no. 6, pp. 381-385.

WEISS, David J. 1968. *See* FISHER, Stephen T., WEISS, David J. and DAWIS, Rene V. 1968.

2062. **WEISS**, Robert S. 1966. Alternative approaches in the study of complex situations. *Human Organization*, vol. 25, no. 3, pp. 198-206.

2063. **WEITZ**, Joseph. 1950. Verbal and pictorial questionnaires in market research. *Journal of Applied Psychology*, vol. 34, no. 5, pp. 363-366.

WELCH, A[lfred] C. 1934. *See* HATHAWAY, S. R. and WELCH, A[lfred] C. 1934.

WELCH, Alfred C. 1940. *See* COOK, Stuart W. and WELCH, Alfred C. 1940.

2064. WELCH, Alfred C. 1941. An analytic system of testing competitive advertising. *Journal of Applied Psychology*, vol. 25, no. 2, pp. 176-190.

WELCH, Alfred C. 1942. *See* ROOT, Alfred R. and WELCH, Alfred C. 1942.

WELCH, Emmett H. 1946. *See* BANCROFT, Gertrude and WELCH, Emmett H. 1946.

2065. WELDON, Peter. 1969. Two comments on Guttman scaling: I. *American Journal of Sociology*, vol. 75, no. 2, pp. 278-279.

2066. WELLS, William D. 1956. Is motivation research really an instrument of the Devil. *Journal of Marketing*, vol. 21, no. 2, pp. 196-198.

2067. WELLS, William D. and SMITH, Georgianna. 1960. Four semantic rating scales compared. *Journal of Applied Psychology*, vol. 44, no. 6, pp. 393-397.

2068. WELLS, William D. 1961. The influence of yeasaying response style. *Journal of Advertising Research*, vol. 1, no. 4, pp. 1-12.

2069. WELLS, William D. and DAMES, Joel. 1962. Hidden errors in survey data. *Journal of Marketing*, vol. 26, no. 4, pp. 50-54.

2070. WELLS, William D. 1963. How chronic overclaimers distort survey findings. *Journal of Advertising Research*, vol. 3, no. 2, pp. 8-18.

2071. WELLS, William D. 1964. EQ, son of EQ, and the reaction profile. *Journal of Marketing*, vol. 28, no. 4, pp. 45-52.

2072. WELLS, William D. 1964. Recognition, recall, and rating scales. *Journal of Advertising Research*, vol. 4, no. 3, pp. 2-8.

2073. WELLS, William D. 1965. Communicating with children. *Journal of Advertising Research*, vol. 5, no. 2, pp. 2-14.

2074. WELLS, William D. and LO SCIUTO, Leonard A. 1966. Direct observation of purchasing behavior. *Journal of Marketing Research*, vol. 3, no. 3, pp. 227-233.

2075. WELLS, William D. and LO SCIUTO, Leonard A. 1967. A reply. *Journal of Marketing Research*, vol. 4, no. 4, pp. 404.

WELSCH, Delane E. 1968. *See* CONNER, James R. and WELSCH, Delane E. 1968.

2076. **WEMBRIDGE**, Eleanor Rowland and MEANS, Edgar R. 1918. Obscurities in voting upon measures due to double-negative. *Journal of Applied Psychology*, vol. 2, no. 2, pp. 156-163.

2077. **WENDEROTH**, Peter M. 1963. Comment on 'Spoken versus pictured questions on taboo topics'. *Journal of Advertising Research*, vol. 3, no. 1, pp. 42-43.

WERNER, Emmy E. 1957. *See* BEILIN, Harry and WERNER, Emmy E. 1957.

2078. **WERTS**, Charles E. and LINN, Robert L. 1970. Cautions in applying various procedures for determining the reliability and validity of multiple-item scales. *American Sociological Review*, vol. 35, no. 4, pp. 757-759.

2079. **WESCHLER**, Irving R. and BERNBERG, Raymond E. 1950. Indirect methods of attitude measurement. *International Journal of Opinion and Attitude Research*, vol. 4, no. 2, pp. 209-228.

2080. **WESCHLER**, Irving R. 1951. Problems in the use of indirect methods of attitude measurements. *Public Opinion Quarterly*, vol. 15, no. 1, pp. 133-138.

WEST, M. J. 1968. *See* BUCK, S. F. and WEST, M. J. 1968.

2081. **WESTEFELD**, Albert. 1953. A problem of interpretation in survey results. *Journal of Marketing*, vol. 17, no. 3, pp. 295-297.

WESTFALL, Ralph. 1955. *See* BOYD, Harper W., *Jr.* and WESTFALL, Ralph. 1955.

2082. **WESTFALL**, Ralph L., BOYD, Harper W., *Jr.* and CAMPBELL, Donald T. 1957. The use of structured techniques in motivation research. *Journal of Marketing*, vol. 22, no. 2, pp. 134-139.

WESTFALL, Ralph. 1965. *See* BOYD, Harper W., *Jr.* and WESTFALL, Ralph. 1965.

2083. **WESTOFF**, Charles F., POTTER, Robert G., *Jr.* and SAGI, Philip C. 1961/62. Some estimates of the reliability of survey data on family planning. *Population Studies*, vol. 15, no. 1, pp. 52-69.

2084. **WHERRY**, Robert J. 1938. Orders for the presentation of pairs in the method of paired comparison. *Journal of Experimental Psychology*, vol. 23, no. 6, pp. 651-660.

WHITE, Alice M. 1956. *See* AULD, Frank, *Jr.*, and WHITE, Alice M. 1956.

2085. WHITE, Ralph K. 1944. Value analysis: a quantitative method for describing qualitative data. *Journal of Social Psychology*, vol. 19, no. 2, pp. 351-358.

2086. WHITFIELD, J. W. 1950. The imaginary questionnaire. *Quarterly Journal of Experimental Psychology*, vol. 2, part 2, pp. 76-87.

WHITMAN, Robert N. 1962. *See* REECE, Michael N. and WHITMAN, Robert N. 1962.

2087. WHYTE, William F[oote]. 1953. Interviewing for organizational research. *Human Organization*, vol. 12, no. 2, pp. 15-22.

2088. WHYTE, William F[oote]. 1957. On asking indirect questions. *Human Organization*, vol. 15, no. 4, pp. 21-23.

WHYTE, William Foote. 1958. *See* DEAN, John P. and WHYTE, William Foote. 1958.

2089. WICKER, Allan W. 1969. A failure to validate the lost-letter technique. *Public Opinion Quarterly*, vol. 33, no. 2, pp. 260-262.

2090. WIEBE, Gerhart D., *chairman*. 1955. Motivation research, II: the impact of motivational research on market research. *Public Opinion Quarterly*, vol. 19, no. 4, pp. 433-435.

2091. WIEBE, Gerhart D., *chairman*. 1956. Four independent analyses of twenty qualitative interviews. *Public Opinion Quarterly*, vol. 20, no. 4, pp. 744-748.

2092. WIEBE, G[erhart] D. 1958. Is it true what Williams says about motivation research? *Journal of Marketing*, vol. 22, no. 4, pp. 408-411.

2093. WIEBE, Gerhart D. 1958. Sampling-motivation research merger: how will it aid ad men? *Printer's Ink*, vol. 265, no. 9, pp. 23-26, 29.

2094. WIELAND, George F. 1966. To judge items or people: a note on instructions to Thurstone-item judges. *Public Opinion Quarterly*, vol. 30, no. 3, pp. 429-432.

2095. WIENS, Arthur N., MATARAZZO, Joseph D. and SASLOW, George. 1965. The interaction recorder: an electronic punched paper tape unit for recording speech behavior during interviews. *Journal of Clinical Psychology*, vol. 21, no. 2, pp. 142-145.

2096. WIENS, Arthur N., *et al.* 1966. Can interview interaction measures be taken from tape recordings? *Journal of Psychology*, vol. 63, no. 2, pp. 249-260.

2097. **WIENS**, Arthur N., SASLOW, George and MATARAZZO, Joseph D. 1966. Speech interruption behavior during interviews. *Psychotherapy: Theory, Research and Practice*, vol. 3, no. 4, pp. 153-158.

WIENS, Arthur N. 1967. *See* MATARAZZO, Joseph D., HOLMAN, David C. and WIENS, Arthur N. 1967.

2098. **WIGGLESWORTH**, F. G. 1963. A combinative scale. *MARKET RESEARCH SOCIETY. New developments in research.* London: Market Research Society with The Oakwood Press, 1963. pp. 118-120.

2099. **WILBER**, George L. 1967. Causal models and probability. *Social Forces*, vol. 46, no. 1, pp. 81-89.

2100. **WILCOX**, Roger C. 1966. Effects of context on semantic differential ratings. *Psychological Reports*, vol. 18, no. 3, pp. 873-874.

2101. **WILEY**, David E. and WILEY, James A. 1970. The estimation of measurement error in panel data. *American Sociological Review*, vol. 35, no. 1, pp. 112-117.

WILEY, James A. 1970. *See* WILEY, David E. and WILEY, James A. 1970.

WILKE, Walter H. 1942. *See* BRYAN, Alice I. and WILKE, H. 1942.

2102. **WILKINS**, Leslie T. [195–]. Constructing criminological prediction tables. London: Office of Population Censuses and Surveys, Social Survey Division, [195–]. 9pp. (*Methodological series, M70*).

2103. **WILKINS**, Leslie T. 1952. Estimating the social class of towns. *Applied Statistics*, vol. 1, no. 1, pp. 27-33.

WILKINS, Leslie T. 1952. *See* LAMBERTH, Denis L. and WILKINS, Leslie T. 1952.

WILKINS, L[eslie] T. 1953. *See* FOTHERGILL, J. E. and WILKINS, L[eslie] T. 1953.

WILKINS, L[eslie] T. 1953. *See* HARRIS, A[melia] [I.] and WILKINS, L[eslie] T. 1953.

WILKINS, L[eslie] T. 1955. *See* FOTHERGILL, J. E. and WILKINS, L[eslie] T. 1955.

2104. **WILKS**, S. S. 1940. Representative sampling and poll reliability. *Public Opinion Quarterly*, vol. 4, no. 3, pp. 261-269.

2105. **WILLCOCK**, H. D. 1951. Research on interviewing. London: Office of Population Censuses and Surveys, Social Survey Division, 1951. 8pp. (*Methodological series, M36*).

2106. **WILLCOCK**, H. D. 1951. The effect of interviewers' own opinions about minorities and foreigners on the opinions about negroes which they obtain or record from informants. London: Office of Population Censuses and Surveys, Social Survey Division, 1951. 5pp. (*Methodological series, M45*).

2107. **WILLCOCK**, H. D. and HOY, K. E. 1951. Hindsight on interviewer X. London: Office of Population Censuses and Surveys, Social Survey Division, 1951. 4pp. (*Methodological series, M43*).

2108. **WILLCOCK**, H. D. 1952. Interviewer research, paper II: description of work in progress. London: Office of Population Censuses and Surveys, Social Survey Division, 1952. 9pp. (*Methodological series, M48*).

2109. **WILLCOCK**, H. D. 1952. Interviewer research, paper III: some data relating to refusals and refusal-prone interviewers, based on performance on routine inquiries. London: Office of Population Censuses and Surveys, Social Survey Division, 1952. 9pp. (*Methodological series, M49*).

2110. **WILLCOCK**, H. D. 1952. Interviewer research, paper IV: some characteristics of interviewers: (i) job background. London: Office of Population Censuses and Surveys, Social Survey Division, 1952. 3pp. (*Methodological series, M50*).

2111. **WILLCOCK**, H. D. 1952. Interviewer research, paper V: interviewer efficiency as assessed by test and by regional organisers. London: Office of Population Censuses and Surveys, Social Survey Division, 1952. 2pp. (*Methodological series, M51*).

2112. **WILLCOCK**, H. D. 1952. Interviewer research, paper VII: field observation: progress note. London: Office of Population Censuses and Surveys, Social Survey Division, 1952. 4pp. (*Methodological series, M53*).

WILLCOCK, H. D., *ed*. 1952. *See* INGLEDEW, Gwen E. 1952.

WILLCOCK, H. D. 1953. *See* FOTHERGILL, J. E. and WILLCOCK, H. D. 1953.

WILLCOCK, H. D. 1955. *See* FOTHERGILL, J. E. and WILLCOCK, H. D. 1955.

WILLCOCK, H. D. 1956. *See* FOTHERGILL, J. E. and WILLCOCK, H. D. 1956.

2113. **WILLIAMS**, Douglas. 1942. Basic instructions for interviewers. *Public Opinion Quarterly*, vol. 6, no. 4, pp. 634-641.

2114. **WILLIAMS**, Faith M. 1937. Methods of measuring variation in family expenditures. *Journal of the American Statistical Association*, vol. 32, no. 197, pp. 40-46. Discussion, pp. 47-49.

2115. **WILLIAMS**, Frederick and CANTRIL, Hadley. 1945. The use of interviewer rapport as a method of detecting differences between 'public' and 'private' opinion. *Journal of Social Psychology*, vol. 22, no. 2, pp. 171-175.

2116. **WILLIAMS**, J. Allen, *Jr.* 1964. Interviewer-respondent interaction: a study of bias in the information interview. *Sociometry*, vol. 27, no. 3, pp. 338-352.

2117. **WILLIAMS**, J. Allen, *Jr.* 1968. Interviewer role performance: a further note on bias in the information interview. *Public Opinion Quarterly*, vol. 32, no. 2, pp. 287-294.

WILLIAMS, J. Allen, *Jr.* 1969. *See* DOHRENWEND, Barbara Snell, WILLIAMS, J. Allen, *Jr.* and WEISS, Carol H. 1969.

2118. **WILLIAMS**, Robert. 1950. Probability sampling in the field: a case history. *Public Opinion Quarterly*, vol. 14, no. 2, pp. 316-330.

2119. **WILLIAMS**, Robert. 1950. A rejoinder. *Public Opinion Quarterly*, vol. 14, no. 3, pp. 611.

WILLIAMS, Robert. 1956. *See* FRANZEN, Raymond and WILLIAMS, Robert. 1956.

2120. **WILLIAMS**, Robert J. 1957. Is it true what they say about motivation research? *Journal of Marketing*, vol. 22, no. 2, pp. 125-133.

2121. **WILLIAMS**, Robert, *chairman*. 1957. Techniques of presentation for research results. *Public Opinion Quarterly*, vol. 21, no. 3, pp. 448-449.

2122. **WILLIAMS**, Thomas Rhys. 1959. A critique of some assumptions of social survey research. *Public Opinion Quarterly*, vol. 23, no. 1, pp. 55-62.

2123. **WILLIAMS**, W. H. 1968. The systematic bias effects of incomplete responses. *AMERICAN STATISTICAL ASSOCIATION, Proceedings of the Social Statistics Section*, 1968. pp. 308-312.

2124. **WILLIAMS**, W. H. and MALLOWS, C. L. 1969. The potential systematic behaviour of some panel survey estimates. *AMERICAN*

STATISTICAL ASSOCIATION. *Proceedings of the Social Statistics Section*, 1969. pp. 44-54.

2125. **WILLIAMS**, W. H. and **MALLOWS**, C. L. 1970. Systematic biases in panel surveys due to differential nonresponse. *Journal of the American Statistical Association*, vol. 65, no. 331, pp. 1338-1349.

2126. **WILLIAMSON**, Marjorie and **REMMERS**, H. H. 1949. A comparison of the paper-and-pencil method and the radio method of polling public opinion. *International Journal of Opinion and Attitude Research*, vol. 3, no. 3, pp. 421-434.

2127. **WILLIS**, Richard. 1954. Estimating the scalability of a series of items – an application of information theory. *Psychological Bulletin*, vol. 51, no. 5, pp. 511-516.

2128. **WILLIS**, Richard H. 1960. Manipulation of item marginal frequencies by means of multiple-response items. *Psychological Review*, vol. 67, no. 1, pp. 32-50.

WILSON, E[lmo] C. 1940. *See* GAUDET, Hazel and WILSON, E[lmo] C. 1940.

2129. **WILSON**, Elmo C. 1950. Adapting probability sampling to Western Europe. *Public Opinion Quarterly*, vol. 14, no. 2, pp. 215-223.

2130. **WILSON**, Elmo C. 1954. New light on old problems through panel research. *ESOMAR Journal*, no. 1, pp. 87-92.

2131. **WILSON**, Elmo C. 1958. Problems of survey research in modernizing areas. *Public Opinion Quarterly*, vol. 22, no. 3, pp. 230-234.

2132. **WILSON**, Robert C. and **COMREY**, Andrew L. 1954. A short method of factor analysis. *Journal of Applied Psychology*, vol. 38, no. 3, pp. 181-184.

2133. **WINCH**, Robert F. 1952. Rejoinder: a plea for sweet reasonableness. *American Sociological Review*, vol. 17, no. 3, pp. 362-364.

2134. **WINCH**, Robert F. and **MORE**, Douglas M. 1956. Quantitative analysis of qualitative data in the assessment of motivation: reliability, congruence, and validity. *American Journal of Sociology*, vol. 61, no. 5, pp. 445-452.

2135. **WINCH**, Robert F. and **CAMPBELL**, Donald T. 1969. Proof? No. Evidence? Yes. The significance of tests of significance. *American Sociologist*, vol. 4, no. 2, pp. 140-143.

2136. **WINDLE**, Charles, **McFANN**, Howard and **WARD**, Joseph. 1955. The effect of various interview techniques in evoking fear responses. *Journal of Clinical Psychology*, vol. 11, no. 2, pp. 171-173.

2137. **WINDLE**, Charles D. and DINGMAN, Harvey F. 1960. Interrater agreement and predictive validity. *Journal of Applied Psychology*, vol. 44, no. 3, pp. 203-204.

WINICK, Darvin M. 1954. *See* TIFFIN, Joseph and WINICK, Darvin M. 1954.

WINTERS, Lewis C. 1969. *See* WOLF, Abraham, NEWMAN, Dianne Z. and WINTERS, Lewis C. 1969.

WIRICK, Grover. 1960. *See* BARLOW, Robin, MORGAN, James [N.] and WIRICK, Grover. 1960.

WIRT, Robert D. 1958. *See* BROEN, William E., *Jr.* and WIRT, Robert D. 1958.

WIRT, Robert D. 1961. *See* BRIGGS, Peter F., WIRT, Robert D. and JOHNSON, Rochelle. 1961.

2138. **WISHART**, David. 1969. An algorithm for hierarchical classifications. *Biometrics*, vol. 25, no. 1, pp. 165-170.

2139. **WISHART**, John. 1955. Multivariate analysis. *Applied Statistics*, vol. 4, no. 2, pp. 103-116.

2140. **WISPE**, Lauren G. and THAYER, Paul W. 1954. Some methodological problems in the analysis of the unstructured interview. *Public Opinion Quarterly*, vol. 18, no. 2, pp. 223-227.

2141. **WITHEY**, Stephen B. 1954. Reliability of recall of income. *Public Opinion Quarterly*, vol. 18, no. 2, pp. 197-204.

2142. **WITRYOL**, Sam L. 1954. Scaling procedures based on the method of paired comparisons. *Journal of Applied Psychology*, vol. 38, no. 1, pp. 31-37.

2143. **WITT**, Edith. 1949. The San Francisco program for improving standards. *International Journal of Opinion and Attitude Research*, vol. 3, no. 3, pp. 435-446.

WITTREICH, Warren J. 1960. *See* TEPPING, Benjamin J. and WITTREICH, Warren J. 1960.

2144. **WOLF**, Abraham, NEWMAN, Dianne Z. and WINTERS, Lewis C. 1969. Operant measures of interest as related to ad lib readership. *Journal of Advertising Research*, vol. 9, no. 2, pp. 40-45.

2145. **WOLFE**, David F. 1956. A new questionnaire design. *Journal of Marketing*, vol. 21, no. 2, pp. 186-190.

2146. **WOLFE**, Harry Deane. 1942. Techniques of appraising brand preference and brand consciousness by consumer interviewing. *Journal of Marketing*, vol. 6, no. 4, part 2, pp. 81-87.

WOLFSON, William 1964. *See* YAGODA, Gerald and WOLFSON, William. 1964.

2147. **WOMER**, Stanley. 1944. Some applications of the continuous consumer panel. *Journal of Marketing*, vol. 9, no. 2, pp. 132-136.

2148. **WOMER**, Stanley and BOYD, Harper. 1951. The use of a voice recorder in the selection and training of field workers. *Public Opinion Quarterly*, vol. 15, no. 2, pp. 358-363.

WOOD, Albert J. 1948. *See* SCHREIER, Fred T. and WOOD, Albert J. 1948.

WOOD, Albert J. 1949. *See* SCHREIER, Fred T. and WOOD, Albert J. 1949.

2149. **WOOD**, J. F. 1967. Pre-testing of product name and pack. *Admap*, vol. 3, no. 6, pp. 224-228, 272-274.

2150. **WOODSIDE**, Moya. 1945. The research interview. *Sociological Review*, vol. 37, nos. 1-4, pp. 28-36.

2151. **WOODWARD**, Julian L. and FRANZEN, Raymond. 1948. A study of coding reliability. *Public Opinion Quarterly*, vol. 12, no. 2, pp. 253-257.

2152. **WOODWARD**, Julian L. 1950. Polling methodology: present state and future prospects. *International Journal of Opinion and Attitude Research*, vol. 4, no. 1, pp. 1-15.

2153. **WOODWARD**, Julian L., *chairman*. 1950. Depth interviewing. *Journal of Marketing*, vol. 14, no. 5, pp. 721-724.

2154. **WOODWARD**, Julian L. and DeLOTT, Jack. 1952. Field coding versus office coding. *Public Opinion Quarterly*, vol. 16, no. 3, pp. 432-436.

2155. **WOODYATT**, Philip C. 1942. A test comparison of two techniques in readership research. *Journalism Quarterly*, vol. 19, June, pp. 185-192.

2156. **WOOFTER**, T. J. 1933. Common errors in sampling. *Social Forces*, vol. 11, no. 4, pp. 521-525.

WOOLSEY, Theodore D. 1959. *See* NISSELSON, Harold and WOOLSEY, Theodore D. 1959.

2157. **WORTHY**, Morgan. 1969. Note on scoring midpoint responses in extreme response-style scores. *Psychological Reports*, vol. 24, no. 1, pp. 189-190.

2158. **WOTRUBA**, Thomas R. 1966. Monetary inducements and mail questionnaire response. *Journal of Marketing Research*, vol. 3, no. 4, pp. 398-400.

2159. **WRIGHT**, Benjamin and EVITTS, Mary Sue. 1961. [Q technique and] Direct factor analysis in sociometry. *Sociometry*, vol. 24, no. 1, pp. 82-98.

2160. **WRIGHT**, Charles R. 1964. Access to social science data in commercial communications reports. *Public Opinion Quarterly*, vol. 28, no. 4, pp. 573-583.

WRIGHT, Charles R. 1967. *See* HYMAN, Herbert H., LEVINE, Gene N. and WRIGHT, Charles R. 1967.

WRIGHTSMAN, Lawrence S., Jr. 1960. *See* BARTLETT, Claude J., QUAY, Lorene Childs and WRIGHTSMAN, Lawrence S., *Jr.* 1960.

WULFECK, Wallace H. 1940. *See* ROSLOW, Sydney, WULFECK, Wallace H. and CORBY, Philip G. 1940.

2161. **WYATT**, Dale F. and CAMPBELL, Donald T. 1950. A study of interviewer bias as related to interviewers' expectations and own opinions. *International Journal of Opinion and Attitude Research*, vol. 4, no. 1, pp. 77-83.

2162. **YAGODA**, Gerald and WOLFSON, William. 1964. Examiner influence on projective test responses. *Journal of Clinical Psychology*, vol. 20, no. 3, pp. 389.

2163. **YATES**, F. 1946. A review of recent statistical developments in sampling and sampling surveys. *Journal of the Royal Statistical Society*, vol. 109, part 1, pp. 12-30. Discussion on Dr. Yate's paper, pp. 31-42.

2164. **YATES**, F. and HEALY, M. J. R. 1962. Electronic computation and data processing for research statistics. *Bulletin of the International Statistical Institute*, vol. 39, part 4, pp. 305-317.

2165. **YAUKEY**, David. 1955. A metric measurement of occupational status. *Sociology and Social Research*, vol. 39, no. 5, pp. 317-323.

2166. **YINGER**, J. Milton, IKEDA, Kiyoshi and LAYCOCK, Frank. 1967. Treating matching as a variable in a sociological experiment. *American Sociological Review*, vol. 32, no. 5, pp. 801-812.

YULE, V. R. 1969. *See* BELSON, William A. and YULE, V. R. 1969.

2167. **ZARATE**, Alvan O. 1967. A note on the accuracy of male responses to questions on fertility. *Demography*, vol. 4, no. 2, pp. 846-849.

2168. **ZARKOVICH**, Slobodan S. 1960. Some problems of sampling work in underdeveloped countries. *Bulletin of the International Statistical Institute*, vol. 37, part 2, pp. 249-262.

2169. **ZAVALA**, Albert. 1965. Development of the forced-choice rating scale technique. *Psychological Bulletin*, vol. 63, no. 2, pp. 117-124.

2170. **ZAX**, Melvin and **TAKAHASHI**, Shigeo. 1967. Cultural influences on response style: comparisons of Japanese and American college students. *Journal of Social Psychology*, vol. 71, no. 1, pp. 3-10.

ZEE, H. van der. 1969. *See* HART, H. 't., CORMAN, T. and ZEE, H. van der. 1969.

ZEISEL, Hans. 1949. *See* FORD, Robert N. and ZEISEL, Hans. 1949.

ZEISEL, Hans. 1950. *See* FORD, Robert N. and ZEISEL, Hans. 1950.

ZEISEL, Hans. 1963. *See* TOWERS, Irwin M., GOODMAN, Leo A. and ZEISEL, Hans. 1963.

2171. **ZELDITCH**, Morris, *Jr*. 1962. Some methodological problems of field studies. *American Journal of Sociology*, vol. 67, no. 5, pp. 566-576.

2172. **ZIELSKE**, Hugh. 1949. Tabulation planning. *Journal of Marketing*, vol. 14, no. 3, pp. 458-459.

2173. **ZIFF**, Ruth. 1963. How to locate purchasers of a product. *Journal of Advertising Research*, vol. 3, no. 3, pp. 32-34.

2174. **ZILLER**, Robert C. and **LONG**, Barbara H. 1965. Some correlates of the don't-know response in opinion questionnaires. *Journal of Social Psychology*, vol. 67, no. 1, pp. 139-147.

2175. **ZIMMER**, Herbert. 1956. Validity of extrapolating nonresponse bias from mail questionnaire follow-ups. *Journal of Applied Psychology*, vol. 40, no. 2, pp. 117-121.

2176. **ZIMMERMAN**, Claire and **BAUER**, Raymond A. 1956. The effect of an audience upon what is remembered. *Public Opinion Quarterly*, vol. 20, no. 1, pp. 238-248.

ZIMMERMAN, Wayne S. 1963. *See* GUILFORD, J. P. and ZIMMERMAN, Wayne S. 1963.

2177. ZOBER, Martin. 1956. Some projective techniques applied to marketing research. *Journal of Marketing*, vol. 20, no. 3, pp. 262-268.

ZUBIN, Joseph. 1942. *See* FULCHER, John S. and ZUBIN, Joseph. 1942.

ZUBIN, Joseph. 1943. *See* GARRETT, Henry E. and ZUBIN, Joseph. 1943.

2178. ZUBIN, Joseph and PEATMAN, John G[ray]. 1945. Testing the pulling power of advertisements by the split-run copy method. *Journal of Applied Psychology*, vol. 29, no. 1, pp. 40-57.

ZUCKERMAN, Marvin. 1962. *See* LUBIN, Bernard, LEVITT, Eugene E. and ZUCKERMAN, Marvin. 1962.

ZWICK, Charles J. 1958. *See* ALLISON, Harry E., ZWICK, Charles J. and BRINSER, Ayres. 1958.

INDEX TO SUBJECTS

ACCESSIBILITY, of respondents
See AVAILABILITY, of respondents

ACCURACY *See* ERROR

ACTIVITY SAMPLING, 1104

ADVERTISING RESEARCH TECHNIQUES
    advertisement testing techniques, 8, 11, 18, 107, 135, 295, 325, 357, 714, 772, 852, 877, 1007, 1061, 1078, 1122, 1180, 1181, 1253, 1254, 1257, 1278, 1279, 1283, 1342, 1355, 1356, 1437, 1438, 1489, 1492, 1521, 1526, 1527, 1603, 1611, 1804, 1814, 1870, 1908, 1975, 2023, 2031, 2071, 2178
    aided recall, 97, 513, 600, 956, 1122, 1257, 1282, 1283, 1284, 1285, 1286, 1355, 1366, 1441, 1442, 1489, 1511, 1544, 1638, 1804, 1870, 2072
    area tests, 1061, 1774
    association testing, 325
    at-home testing, 11, 1257, 1611, 1774
    attention measures, 877, 1078, 1283, 1511, 1975
    booklets, 1284
    concept testing, 68, 2073
    copy testing, 8, 18, 325, 511, 732, 740, 852, 1007, 1284, 1492, 1527, 1611, 1896, 1975, 2064, 2178
    eye camera, 714, 877, 1078, 1975
    for brand share prediction, 1540, 1541
    for mail-advertising, 406
    for measuring advertising effectiveness 18, 47, 111, 112, 348, 406, 436, 466, for measuring advertising effectiveness *(contd.)* 591, 596, 600, 609, 713, 731, 772, 837, 852, 942, 997, 998, 1048, 1061, 1182, 1206, 1245, 1257, 1276, 1279, 1342, 1364, 1437, 1479, 1521, 1541, 1622, 1638, 1672, 1677, 1774, 1811, 1864, 1904, 1908, 1982, 2072, 2146, 2178
    for press advertisements, 18, 107, 112, 295, 600, 740, 837, 877, 1008, 1078, 1122, 1278, 1283, 1284, 1328, 1355, 1356, 1366, 1437, 1489, 1492, 1580, 1611, 1638, 1975, 2178
    for radio commercials, 713, 772, 1245, 1526, 1738
    for TV commercials, 11, 18, 357, 436, 842, 1007, 1061, 1181, 1253, 1254, 1437, 1438, 1479, 1511, 1580, 1672, 1814, 1908, 1975, 1982, 2031, 2178
    group discussion, 1818
    group testing, 1818
    mail survey, 852, 1008
    on-air testing, 11
    operant behavioural measures, 1253, 1254, 1479, 1814
    panels, 609, 1540, 1541
    portfolio tests, 107, 1355, 1356, 1366, 1437
    post-testing, 732, 1061
    poster research techniques, 206, 457, 466, 467
    pretesting, 107, 135, 159, 295, 357, 732, 842, 1061, 1181, 1253, 1254, 1278, 1279, 1355, 1356, 1437, 1438, 1521, 1527, 1611, 1814, 1896, 2023
    psychogalvanometer, 325, 596, 1603

pupil size measurement, 1180,
    1181, 1603
rating scales, 2071, 2072
recall, 97, 107, 539, 600, 631,
    799, 956, 1122, 1257,
    1279, 1282, 1283, 1284,
    1285, 1328, 1355, 1356,
    1366, 1436, 1441, 1442,
    1489, 1544, 1638, 1804,
    1870, 2072
semantic differential, 1429
tachistoscope, 325, 877, 1975
time tests, 1061
unaided recall, 1355, 1870
value of measurement
    techniques, 88
See also: AUDIENCE
RESEARCH TECHNIQUES;
READERSHIP RESEARCH
TECHNIQUES

AIDED RECALL
    comparison with unaided recall,
        1319, 1602, 1604, 1870
    in advertising research, 97,
        513, 600, 956, 1122, 1257,
        1282, 1283, 1284, 1285,
        1286, 1355, 1366, 1441,
        1442, 1489, 1511, 1544,
        1638, 1804, 1870, 2072
    in audience research, 402, 613,
        615, 617, 837, 956, 1077,
        1284, 1319, 1436, 1441,
        1442, 1511, 1699, 1703
    in readership research, 6, 97,
        376, 476, 513, 841, 956,
        1011, 1122, 1282, 1283,
        1284, 1285, 1286, 1287,
        1318, 1319, 1366, 1367,
        1441, 1442, 1476, 1489,
        1804, 1905

ANALYSIS, of data *See* DATA
PROCESSING; STATISTICAL
ANALYSIS OF DATA

ANALYTICAL SURVEYS
    comparison with enumerative
        surveys, 532
    statistical analysis of data, 443,
        532
    used in decision making, 924

ANONYMITY, of respondent
    and bias, 702, 983, 1157,
        1163, 1185, 1353, 1520,
        1559, 1563, 1691, 1919
    effect on response rate, 271,
        1391, 1769
    effect on responses to
        questions, 34, 59, 351, 470,
        546, 577, 628, 632, 633
        702, 886, 982, 983, 1157,
        1163, 1185, 1186, 1317,
        1353, 1520, 1559, 1563,
        1691, 1919
    techniques for preserving, 1362

AREA SAMPLING
    choice of sampling units, 381,
        1300, 1345, 1780
    comparison with quota
        sampling, 17, 291, 893,
        896, 930, 945, 985, 1407
    criteria for usage, 945, 1302
    in international surveys, 1626
    in public opinion polling, 893,
        1407, 1626
    in sociometric surveys, 1897
    interviewer bias in, 1361
    non-coverage of sampling units,
        1148
    principles of sample design,
        381, 896, 906, 945, 1145,
        1300, 1346, 1780

AREA TESTS, 1061, 1774

**ASSOCIATION REACTION
METHOD,** 316

ATTITUDE QUESTIONNAIRES
    and respondent anonymity, 59,
        470, 577
    description of various
        constructions, 573, 2010
    for measuring intergroup
        attitudes, 536
    for measuring leadership
        attitudes, 712
    percentage analysis of, 1310
    responses to questions in, 578
    self-completion, 1318

ATTITUDE RESEARCH TECHNIQUES
analysing generalised attitudes, 1516
and response sets, 141, 494, 1385, 1683, 1721, 1836, 1955, 2068
association reaction method, 316
attitude change measures, 4, 276, 311, 346, 448, 460, 540, 544, 701, 788, 789, 837, 873, 980, 1195, 1196, 1230, 1231, 1250, 1275, 1331, 1332, 1364, 1521, 1748, 1783
attitude intensity measures, 125, 364, 872, 873, 1022, 1312, 1406, 1655, 1656
attitude measures, 69, 316, 386, 387, 461, 526, 712, 1081, 1310, 1331, 1332, 1655, 1656, 2009, 2010, 2059
attitude questionnaires, 59, 470, 536, 573, 577, 578, 712, 1310, 1318, 2009, 2010
attitude scaling, 16, 32, 36, 43, 57, 64, 82, 118, 154, 246, 257, 258, 259, 278, 286, 324, 345, 346, 365, 382, 412, 416, 442, 448, 455, 485, 493, 510, 515, 519, 542, 549, 550, 572, 573, 602, 603, 604, 605, 606, 621, 655, 685, 686, 687, 690, 699, 705, 716, 724, 752, 753, 786, 822, 866, 869, 870, 871, 873, 874, 888, 891, 919, 930, 951, 960, 961, 970, 975, 980, 981, 1002, 1016, 1020, 1056, 1060, 1072, 1073, 1079, 1081, 1097, 1103, 1105, 1121, 1140, 1141, 1243, 1244, 1265, 1288, 1291, 1295, 1312, 1315, 1318, 1322, 1325, 1331, 1332, 1351, 1354, 1357,
attitude scaling (*contd.*) 1365, 1369, 1381, 1384, 1398, 1406, 1413, 1415, 1421, 1431, 1432, 1483, 1496, 1517, 1560, 1585, 1620, 1631, 1643, 1644, 1655, 1656, 1674, 1684, 1699, 1700, 1742, 1752, 1753, 1754, 1755, 1773, 1827, 1846, 1847, 1852, 1927, 1928, 1954, 1957, 1959, 1964, 1967, 1973, 1985, 2009, 2010, 2049, 2050, 2055, 2065, 2078, 2094, 2100, 2127, 2128, 2142, 2157, 2169
attitude surveys, 347, 577, 628, 1157, 1920
bibliography of reviews of, 518
card sorting, 383
chain interviewing, 1294
circular test of bias, 1294, 2014
depth interview, 2082
ethical considerations, 2080
group feedback analysis, 954
in communications research, 1296
in consumer attitude research, 69, 134, 292, 430, 823, 999, 1034, 1038, 1105, 1291, 1569, 1628, 1674, 1730, 1964, 2082
in social psychological research, 1081
indirect, 196, 338, 461, 888, 1184, 1309, 1491, 1497, 2079, 2080, 2088
motivational, 386, 387, 450, 451, 1297, 2082
objective, 384, 386, 387
observational, 461, 536
panels, 540, 788, 789, 1663, 1711, 1783
physiological, 461
projective, 317, 338, 432, 451, 461, 536, 770, 781, 809, 831, 880, 1097, 1250, 1294, 1297, 1351, 1619,

projective (*contd.*)
1671, 1733, 1737, 1876, 2014, 2079, 2082
ranking methods, 448, 573, 1079, 2009
reliability, 384, 526, 701, 1079, 1141, 1331, 1332, 1432
self-reports, 461
to measure employee attitudes, 80, 347, 577, 886, 1015, 1380, 1616, 1737, 1920
used in multilingual communities, 497
validity, 316, 384, 455, 701, 873, 1022, 1027, 1079, 1141, 1184, 1331, 1332, 1351, 1529, 2009, 2010

ATTITUDE SCALES *See* ATTITUDE SCALING TECHNIQUES

ATTITUDE SCALING TECHNIQUES
administration of scales, 1357
attitude statements, 369, 519, 573, 1351
bi-polar scales, 621, 1967
bias, 57, 118, 1016, 1121, 1315, 1927, 1954
comparison with other methods, 1331, 1332
contextual effects, 699
correlational scaling, 1827
cumulative scales, 36, 259, 510, 606, 961, 1915
direction-of-perception technique, 196, 572
equal appearing intervals, 365, 448, 573, 602, 603, 2049, 2050
error-choice technique, 246, 888
Fishbein, 1730
forced-choice technique, 82, 118, 801, 1016, 1517, 1644, 1985, 2169
functions of, 1081
graphic scales, 573, 1655, 1656
Guildford Short Cut scaling, 2142
Guttman scaling, 32, 36, 257, 258, 259, 345, 346, 416, 442, 510, 549, 550, 604, 690, 716, 724, 800, 864, 869, 870, 871, 874, 919, 930, 951, 960, 970, 1072, 1073, 1172, 1265, 1318, 1322, 1331, 1332, 1365, 1384, 1398, 1413, 1496, 1560, 1636, 1643, 1752, 1753, 1846, 1847, 1852, 1951, 1957, 1959, 1960, 1967, 2065, 2127
item analysis, 753, 1020, 1172, 1288, 1752, 2128
Likert techniques, 118, 448, 550, 572, 603, 705, 1079, 1165, 1243, 1331
limitations of, 2009, 2010
method of controlled marginals, 2128
method of graded dichotomies, 64
method of reciprocal averages, 1002, 1496
method of summated ratings, 603
multidimensional, 705, 822, 974, 1183
objectivity, 16
paired comparisons technique, 448, 573, 705, 827, 866, 975, 1079, 1103, 1827, 2142
pictorial techniques, 1097
presentation of scales, 1964
reliability of, 16, 118, 324, 365, 455, 515, 687, 980, 1079, 1141, 1166, 1325, 1331, 1332, 1431, 1432, 1684, 2065, 2078, 2127
repertory grid, 408, 752, 1291, 1729
reproducibility, 36, 416, 606, 951, 1413, 1753, 2127
scale construction techniques, 64, 278, 382, 605, 655, 685, 686, 687, 891, 982, 1140, 1288, 1684, 1742, 1773, 1928, 1957, 2009, 2010

scale discrimination techniques, 605
scale product techniques, 655
scalogram analysis, 36, 257, 258, 416, 604, 690, 715, 716, 870, 871, 951, 960, 1072, 1073, 1172, 1318, 1322, 1365, 1384, 1398, 1413, 1560, 1753, 1878
scoring methods, 510, 519, 724, 1244, 1700, 1967, 2157
Seashore-Hevner scales, 1773
self-assessment ratings, 573, 1381, 2055
semantic differential, 43, 57, 278, 412, 485, 493, 542, 752, 786, 1105, 1121, 1154, 1291, 1295, 1312, 1354, 1406, 1431, 1435, 1517, 1674, 1754, 1964, 2100, 2157
Stapel scales, 485, 1483
Thurstone scaling, 365, 448, 573, 602, 603, 685, 980, 981, 982, 1002, 1056, 1103, 1140, 1243, 1244, 1331, 1332, 1415, 1421, 1585, 1620, 1631, 1655, 1656, 1700, 1755, 1827, 1973, 2009, 2010, 2049, 2050, 2094, 2142
uni-dimensionality, 455, 549, 690, 1288, 1331, 1332, 1928, 1967
validity, 16, 118, 286, 324, 416, 515, 685, 687, 866, 870, 873, 981, 982, 1060, 1079, 1141, 1331, 1332, 1415, 1742, 2078, 2169
weighting, 891
zero-point, 346, 872, 873, 970

ATTITUDE STATEMENTS
comparison with projective techniques, 1351
end effect, 519
intervening responses to 369
sorting of, 519
weighting, 891
wording of, 519

ATTITUDE SURVEYS
and respondent anonymity, 577, 628, 1157
to measure employee attitudes, 347, 1157

AUDIENCE RESEARCH TECHNIQUES
aided recall, 402, 613, 615, 617, 837, 956, 1077, 1284, 1319, 1436, 1441, 1442, 1511, 1699, 1703
audience for advertising, 24, 25, 101, 423, 457, 467, 517, 956, 1005, 1071, 1188, 1285, 1441, 1442, 1580, 1591, 1603, 1738, 1982, 1999, 2000
audience reaction measurement, 101, 303, 410, 662, 708, 709, 837, 882, 1253, 1254, 1574, 1603, 1675, 1738, 1739, 1762, 1814, 1817, 1819
audience size measurement, 24, 25, 31, 373, 411, 423, 467, 517, 617, 741, 956, 1005, 1071, 1188, 1284, 1319, 1422, 1441, 1442, 1580, 1591, 1699, 1739, 1764, 1817, 1905, 1999, 2000
bias related to, 456, 469, 733, 937
button-pressing methods, 410, 709, 1253, 1254, 1561, 1574, 1762, 1814
cinema audience research techniques, 410, 411, 707, 708, 709
diaries, 201, 456, 459, 469, 617, 733, 1065, 1580, 1999, 2000
effects measurement, 143, 144, 145, 152, 154, 164, 637, 1543, 1982
exposure-probability index, 1199
group discussions, 148
group testing, 145, 1560, 1561, 1999

magazine audiences, 25, 741, 1071, 1284, 1319, 1367, 1764, 1905
panels, 310, 456, 459, 617, 618, 733, 837, 908, 937, 1065, 1817, 1818, 1819, 1877
pilot programme testing, 1272
planning studies, 145, 148
pretesting, 837, 1253, 1254, 1611, 1814, 1830, 2023
psycho-galvanic reflex recording, 1603
radio audience research techniques, 200, 201, 402, 481, 662, 773, 1077, 1272, 1518, 1561, 1574, 1667, 1675, 1703, 1738, 1739, 1762, 1817, 1839, 1950
rating indices, 574
recording meters, 617, 618, 937, 1077, 1999, 2047, 2048
sampling for, 837
statistical analysis, 143, 144, 145, 152, 154, 881, 1543
telephone methods, 200, 373, 469, 1077, 1422
television audience research techniques, 31, 143, 144, 152, 154, 164, 310, 373, 456, 459, 469, 613, 615, 617, 618, 626, 637, 733, 881, 882, 937, 1049, 1065, 1199, 1253, 1254, 1422, 1436, 1511, 1543, 1580, 1699, 1709, 1814, 1818, 1819, 1877, 1982, 1999, 2000, 2046, 2047, 2048
theatre audience research techniques, 1221
unaided recall, 200, 373, 1077, 1319, 1950
used by **BBC**, 1817, 1818, 1819
used by **ITA**, 613, 1580
used on captive audiences, 1253, 1254, 1814

See also: ADVERTISING RESEARCH TECHNIQUES; READERSHIP RESEARCH TECHNIQUES

AUDIMETER, 2048

AVAILABILITY, of respondents
characteristics of those available, 136, 501, 774, 1793
characteristics of those not available, 774, 973, 1290, 1471, 1705, 1793
in household surveys, 1471
of male respondents, 1471

BIAS
and audience research techniques, 456, 469, 733, 937
and response set, 141, 193, 494, 786, 892, 914, 1161, 1173, 1200, 1385, 1440, 1504, 1581, 1683, 1720, 1721, 1836, 2068, 2069, 2070, 2170
and response style, 786, 1522, 1581, 1683, 1721, 2068, 2069, 2070, 2170
'big name' effect, 230, 359, 1293, 1719
correction for, 189, 1464
detection of, 337, 667, 670, 671, 674, 723, 725, 1171, 1790, 2014
due to anonymity, 702, 983, 1157, 1163, 1185, 1353, 1520, 1559, 1563, 1691, 1919
due to expectation, 105, 106, 934, 1102, 1519, 1598, 1981, 1989
due to interviewer, 62, 106, 137, 231, 239, 254, 266, 267, 304, 328, 332, 355, 374, 440, 452, 529, 558, 560, 620, 664, 674, 704, 746, 750, 856, 857, 907, 930, 933, 934, 963, 972, 1028, 1029, 1084, 1085, 1151, 1225, 1255, 1289, 1361, 1379, 1394, 1395, 1445, 1456, 1464, 1481, 1519, 1545, 1613, 1633, 1641, 1727, 1732, 1736,

due to interviewer (*contd.*) 1790, 1791, 1798, 1802, 1829, 1838, 1843, 1872, 1883, 1884, 1885, 1998, 2000, 2002, 2006, 2014, 2054, 2055, 2060, 2106, 2115, 2116, 2117, 2161

due to interviewer-respondent rapport, 1428, 1727

due to late returns, 529

due to non-availability of respondents, 117, 211, 501, 973, 1587, 1822

due to non-coverage, 1148

due to non-response, 72, 117, 123, 212, 267, 299, 314, 330, 337, 422, 501, 529, 531, 564, 583, 612, 624, 650, 667, 670, 671, 672, 681, 682, 683, 723, 725, 733, 818, 897, 910, 937, 958, 971, 973, 987, 1041, 1203, 1314, 1401, 1414, 1587, 1592, 1637, 1664, 1749, 1763, 1769, 1780, 1793, 1813, 1822, 1871, 1926, 2124, 2125, 2175

due to prestige-seeking, 565, 1024, 1388, 1724, 1992

due to refusals, 910, 937, 959, 1414

due to respondent, 10, 39, 57, 58, 78, 304, 332, 355, 565, 577, 639, 677, 678, 702, 777, 796, 836, 875, 914, 1004, 1024, 1036, 1147, 1157, 1163, 1172, 1229, 1293, 1353, 1414, 1440, 1520, 1559, 1563, 1661, 1724, 1732, 1807, 1886, 1919, 2039, 2068, 2069, 2070, 2115, 2141

due to survey sponsor, 492, 529, 1704

due to timing of survey, 529

due to unrepresentativeness of respondents, 499, 529, 538, 789, 906, 973, 1114, 1143, 1203, 1314, 1361, 1803, 1976, 2018, 2030, 2032

experimenter, 103, 104, 105, 106, 1102, 1138, 1236, 1320, 1388, 1597, 1694, 1696, 1697, 1736, 1838, 2008

in attitude scaling techniques, 57, 118, 1016, 1121, 1315, 1927, 1954, 2068

in cluster sampling, 407

in diaries, 456, 469, 733, 1932

in estimation, 1404

in group testing, 150, 1693

in interviewing, 78, 355, 490, 930, 933, 1030, 1456

in mail surveys, 123, 337, 422, 439, 564, 667, 670, 671, 672, 673, 723, 725, 897, 958, 1203, 1314, 1401, 1637, 1749, 1763, 1769, 1813, 1871, 1926, 2030, 2175

in observation, 56, 1102, 1135

in public opinion polling, 229, 236, 490, 492, 498, 499, 502, 678, 704, 806, 856, 973, 1024, 1029, 1089, 1090, 1161, 1168, 1247, 1411, 1445, 1522, 1719, 1790, 1886, 1992, 2030, 2054, 2115, 2161

in questions, 17, 227, 229, 236, 269, 315, 328, 359, 361, 453, 490, 571, 764, 783, 858, 930, 941, 950, 1009, 1131, 1256, 1263, 1293, 1411, 1421, 1424, 1446, 1470, 1647, 1702, 1716, 1719, 1881, 1886, 1927

in quota sampling, 239, 374, 900, 945, 1458

in rating scales, 887, 1597

in responses to questions, 10, 17, 58, 62, 73, 193, 229, 269, 304, 328, 332, 393, 415, 439, 453, 480, 494, 558, 560, 565, 571, 577, 652, 677, 682, 702, 750, 777, 786, 796, 807, 836, 875, 892, 914, 941, 950,

in response to questions (*contd.*)
966, 983, 1004, 1009, 1024, 1084, 1085, 1131, 1157, 1161, 1163, 1171, 1173, 1200, 1293, 1346, 1353, 1385, 1394, 1395, 1411, 1440, 1446, 1477, 1504, 1519, 1520, 1522, 1550, 1559, 1563, 1581, 1598, 1607, 1613, 1633, 1661, 1663, 1683, 1691, 1702, 1716, 1719, 1720, 1721, 1724, 1727, 1732, 1810, 1836, 1838, 1881, 1884, 1886, 1919, 1927, 1969, 1992, 2032, 2039, 2060, 2068, 2069, 2070, 2081, 2115, 2116, 2123, 2124, 2141, 2161, 2170
in sampling frames, 499, 502, 906, 1901
in selection of respondents, 374, 674, 1693
in semantic differential scaling, 57, 786, 1121
in triad comparisons procedure, 843
incentive, 649
of purchase recall, 571, 610, 675, 677, 1932
panel, 309, 375, 395, 456, 610, 675, 733, 789, 937, 977, 1124, 1451, 1525, 1731, 1910, 2124, 2125
reduction of, 10, 117, 141, 189, 211, 422, 652, 674, 807, 836, 885, 1004, 1131, 1346, 1421, 1587, 1597, 1694, 1822, 1927, 2039, 2117
sample, 117, 188, 211, 299, 367, 433, 478, 499, 502, 505, 557, 906, 910, 973, 1019, 1026, 1067, 1127, 1280, 1524, 1575, 1698, 1717, 1780, 1803, 1960, 1974, 2018, 2026, 2032, 2033, 2036
sampling, 239, 266, 267, 374,

sampling (*contd.*)
529, 530, 900, 906, 945, 1148, 1150, 1280, 1361, 1458, 2015
significance of, 1930
sources of, 452, 529, 674, 933, 1229, 1247, 1969
volunteer, 139, 140, 145, 150, 156, 188, 284, 290, 367, 505, 557, 978, 1026, 1229, 1389, 1654, 1693, 1695, 1815, 1974, 2026, 2032, 2033, 2036

BIAS, due to interviewer *See* INTERVIEWER BIAS

BIAS, due to non-response *See* NON-RESPONSE BIAS; BIAS, in response to questions

BIAS, due to respondent *See* RESPONDENT BIAS

BIAS, in question *See* QUESTION BIAS

BIAS, in responses to questions
and interviewer-respondent rapport, 560, 1727, 2060
and perceptual defense, 332, 796, 1157
and presence of 'other persons' during interview, 1810
and respondent anonymity, 983, 1157, 1163, 1353, 1520, 1559, 1563, 1691, 1919
and response set, 193, 480, 494, 786, 892, 914, 1161, 1173, 1200, 1385, 1440, 1504, 1581, 1683, 1720, 1721, 1836, 2068, 2070
and response style, 786, 1522, 1581, 1683, 1721, 2068, 2069, 2070, 2170
and social distance between interviewer and respondent, 332, 560, 1613, 1727, 2060, 2116
and social status of interviewer, 1084, 1085, 1613, 1727, 2116

and type of questionnaire administration, 652, 983
detection of, 875, 1346
due to anticipation of retest, 1598
due to changing response probability, 2123, 2124
due to interviewer conditioning of respondent's verbal behaviour, 393, 1394, 1395, 1607, 1633, 1732, 1838
due to interviewer expectations, 750, 2161
due to loaded response alternatives, 17, 1702, 1719
due to prestige-seeking, 58, 332, 453, 565, 941, 1024, 1293, 1440, 1702, 1724, 1992
due to question form, 328, 1702, 1719, 1884, 2081
due to question order, 269
due to question wording, 17, 58, 73, 229, 315, 328, 359, 361, 453, 571, 764, 941, 950, 966, 1009, 1293, 1411, 1421, 1446, 1550, 1702, 1716, 1719, 1881, 1886, 1926, 1969, 2081
due to race of interviewer, 62, 304, 1613, 1661, 1838, 2115, 2116
due to respondent guessing, 777
due to respondent's interpretation of question, 439
due to sex of interviewer, 1969
due to topic of question, 304, 652, 682, 875, 1024, 1163, 1477, 1550, 1719, 1886, 2032, 2081, 2115, 2141
due to use of buffer questions, 1969
due to use of stereotypes, 453, 1411, 1719
techniques for eliminating, 10, 807, 836, 1004, 1131, 2039

'BIG NAME' EFFECT, 230, 359, 1293, 1719

BIOGRAMS *See* LIFE HISTORIES

BI-POLAR SCALES, 621, 1967, 2098

BRAND IMAGE MEASUREMENT, 1034, 1062, 1121, 1674, 2149

'CAFETARIA' QUESTION *See* MULTIPLE-CHOICE QUESTION

CALL-BACKS
and advance letter, 378
and the 'hard to reach' respondent, 501, 591, 973, 1471
alternative procedures to 72, 586, 588, 612, 1123, 1592, 1593, 1823
combined with weighting for non-response, 1822
cost of, 586
in sociometric surveys, 1897
number required, 212, 501, 531, 1400
reduction of, 72, 212, 378, 1822

CARD SORTING TECHNIQUES, 383

CAUSALITY, 218, 219, 220, 221, 222, 224, 225, 243, 263, 268, 434, 507, 1564, 1596, 1668, 2099

CHEATING, in interviewers
and characteristics of cheaters, 653, 932, 1942, 2107
and interviewer morale, 488
causes, 237, 487, 580, 932, 1369, 1942
detection, 51, 237, 487, 580, 627, 653, 1942, 2107

different forms of, 266, 653, 932, 1369, 1456, 1942
extent of, 237, 1456, 1942
in public opinion polling, 487, 1942, 1919
prevention, 50, 51, 179, 180, 237, 420, 487, 580, 1447, 1942, 2107

CHECKLIST QUESTION
comparison with open question, 153
effect on responses, 1256, 1701, 1702
in public opinion polling, 1256
order effects, 339

CINEMA AUDIENCE RESEARCH TECHNIQUES
audience composition measurement, 707
audience reaction measurement, 410, 708, 709
button-pressing methods, 410, 709
focused interviews, 709
foyer interviews, 411

CIRCULAR TEST OF BIAS, 1294, 2014

CLASSIFICATION, of respondents
and segmentation techniques, 27, 158, 282, 283, 1063
by age, 1869
by interviewer, 1289, 1465, 1874, 2006
by level of consumption, 935
by personality, 1874
by socio-economic status, 38, 120, 274, 388, 568, 634, 761, 814, 838, 846, 867, 883, 943, 984, 988, 994, 1035, 1211, 1239, 1289, 1341, 1465, 1499, 1679, 1708, 1772, 1869, 2006, 2007, 2034, 2103, 2165
compared with measurement, 761

clustering techniques, 1063
criteria for, 29, 158, 282, 283, 388, 994, 1679, 1869
cross classification, 1063
for matching purposes, 158, 1063
in consumer product surveys, 120, 282, 283
in employment surveys, 95
in media surveys, 27, 29, 158, 282, 283
in public opinion polling, 360, 1874
of families, 388, 994
questions for, 95, 1219, 2141
reliability, 1341, 1465, 2006

CLASSIFICATION, of responses
and interviewer-respondent rapport, 976
interviewer bias in, 1255, 1791, 1798, 1872, 1883, 1884, 1885, 2055

CLASSIFICATION QUESTIONS, 95, 1219, 2141

CLINICAL INTERVIEW, 9, 979, 1728

CLOSED QUESTIONS
clarifying meaning of responses to, 1756
comparison with open, 335, 556, 1256, 1423, 1558, 1616, 1719, 1797, 1806
in intensity measurement, 1806
influence on responses, 556, 1719
validity, 1756, 1797
when to use, 349

CLUSTER ANALYSIS
B-coefficient, 1909
coefficient alpha, 1325, 1327
comparison of methods, 808, 823, 1277
comparison with other methods of analysis, 1546, 1632
complete analysis, 999

description of methods, 776, 808, 931, 1051, 1055, 1063, 1277, 1546, 1909, 2138
linkage analysis, 1063, 1339, 1632, 1909
McQuitty type, 1546, 1909
subgroup detection, 776, 1063
subgroup specification, 776, 1063
use in consumer attitude research, 828
use in market research, 408, 1034, 1628

CLUSTER SAMPLING
and statistical analysis of data, 1147
bias in, 407
choice of sampling units, 552, 894
cluster size, 1780
comparison with other sampling methods, 1780
cost of, 588
effect of homogeneity within sample, 894
precision of, 407, 588, 1906
techniques of, 552, 1780

See also: AREA SAMPLING

CODERS *See* CODING

CODING
aids in, 569
by computer, 751
checking for accuracy, 661, 754, 918, 920
errors in, 175, 587, 625, 754, 1469
field, 625, 918, 2154
frames, 569, 858, 918, 920
function of, 569, 918
group, 46
multi-coding, 1965
of establishment question, 826
of occupations, 984, 1341
of open response material, 751, 859, 918, 920, 2151, 2154
of qualitative material, 859, 920, 1108, 2140
office, 661, 918, 920, 2151, 2154
on punched cards, 195
precoding, 46, 569, 647, 918, 920, 1058, 1193, 1423, 1882, 2145
reliability of, 587, 754, 859, 1231, 1341, 1887, 2151
spot, 46
supervision of coders, 661, 918, 920
variation between coders, 587, 754

CODING ERROR, 175, 587, 625, 1469

CODING FRAMES
design of, 569, 858, 859, 918, 920

COEFFICIENT ALPHA, 1325, 1327

COEFFICIENT OF REPRODUCIBILITY *See* REPRODUCIBILITY

COMMUNITY RESEARCH TECHNIQUES
community background studies, 1025
community study method, 636
control group technique, 399
depth interviews, 1098
intensive interviews, 567
life histories, 561
participant observation, 131, 132, 133, 245, 989, 1159, 1276, 1417, 1490, 1650, 1761, 1987, 2017, 2171

COMPARABILITY
of aided and unaided recall, 1602, 1870
of attitude scaling techniques, 572, 1079
of diary and personal interview responses, 281, 1112, 1536, 1537, 1932
of factor analysis and Guttman scale analysis, 864, 1636

of international surveys, 787, 1021, 1626, 2053
of interviewer's classification of respondents, 568
of mail survey and group testing, 983
of methods of consumer purchase measurement, 1514, 1537, 1932
of open and closed questions, 335, 1256, 1423, 1616, 1719, 1797, 1806
of panel and personal interview responses, 5, 1514, 1537, 1932
of personal interview and mail survey responses, 5, 127, 669, 742, 829, 986, 1314, 1357, 2057, 2155
of personal interview and secret ballot responses, 1107, 1992
of personal interview and self-completion questionnaire responses, 33, 37, 351, 1163, 1318, 1423, 1480, 1935, 2055
of polygraph and self-completion questionnaire responses, 415
of public opinion polls, 238, 363, 498, 499, 502, 645, 1082, 1090, 1175
of questions, 153, 651, 782, 851, 1175, 1719
of quota and area sampling, 291, 893, 896, 930, 945, 985, 1407
of quota and probability sampling, 893, 900
of quota and random sampling, 291, 581, 608, 1458, 1459
of responses to free-answer and pre-coded questions, 1423, 1882
of responses to open and checklist questions, 153
of socio-economic and classification methods, 568
of stratified and systematic space sampling, 1344
of survey and observational techniques, 132, 133, 1987

COMPLETION RATES, of interviewers
and interviewer experience, 585
and payment of interviewer, 944, 1194
and use of advance letter, 378
factors affecting, 301, 440, 581, 585, 1400, 1793
in financial surveys, 440
techniques for increasing, 543, 1831

COMPONENT ANALYSIS 692, 1034, 1116, 1546, 1632, 1636, 1709

COMPUTER
administration of questionnaire, 652
and incomplete information in surveys, 1862
and life history data, 89
and longitudinal studies, 793, 794
and sociometric data, 444
automation of readability formulas, 511
programs for statistical data analysis, 13, 89, 307, 444, 462, 758, 794, 800, 822, 931, 1020, 1034, 1240, 1825, 1855, 1856, 1857, 1962, 2138, 2164
simulation of interviewing costs, 1399, 1402
use in data processing, 13, 89, 173, 307, 444, 747, 748, 751, 758, 794, 800, 1020, 1375, 1617, 1820, 1825, 1893, 1923, 1939, 1951, 1962, 1965, 2164
use in sampling, 658, 1530

CONSISTENCY *See* **RELIABILITY**

CONSUMER PANELS *See* PANELS

CONSUMER RESEARCH TECHNIQUES *See* PANELS; DIARIES; CONSUMER SURVEYS

CONSUMER SURVEYS
  classification of respondents, 120, 282, 283
  consumer product surveys, 121, 282, 283, 392, 591, 840, 1439, 1467, 1677, 1774, 2146
  for measuring purchase intentions, 1070
  for measuring purchase probability, 1070
  in advertising effectiveness measurement, 731, 1677, 1774, 2146
  payment of interviewers, 944
  projective techniques, 717, 770, 880, 1876, 2177
  question form, 1702
  question wording, 571, 785, 1701, 1702

CONTENT ANALYSIS
  by computer, 576, 1939
  in communications research, 312, 318, 319, 372, 512, 707, 757, 1044, 1045, 1092, 1170, 1433, 1861
  of open-response material, 66, 1771, 1887, 1939
  verbal interaction analysis, 90, 1378, 1392, 1393, 1396, 1735, 2095, 2096

CONTENT ANALYSIS, of open-response material
  by computer, 1939
  effect of punctuation on, 66
  reliability of, 66, 1771, 1887
  rules for, 66

CONTINUING PANELS *See* PANELS

CONTINUING SURVEYS
  administration, 309
  bias due to non-response, 2123
  memory factor, 309
  panels vs. independent samples, 309, 609, 1783
  sample design, 309, 1150, 1469
  successive partial replacement of sample, 309

See also: PANELS

CONTINUOUS SAMPLING, 309, 1151

CONVERSATIONAL INTERVIEW, 245, 1920, 2087

COPY TESTING TECHNIQUES, 8, 18, 325, 511, 732, 740, 852, 1007, 1284, 1492, 1527, 1611, 1896, 1975, 2064, 2178

COSTS
  computer simulation of, 1399, 1402
  in financial surveys, 440
  interviewer, 355, 440, 930, 944, 1194, 1399, 1402, 1766, 1802, 1933, 1936, 2143
  methods of reducing, 72, 1348, 1935, 1936, 1937
  of advance letters, 1473
  of call-backs, 586
  of conducting surveys, 1348
  of data processing, 1375, 1548
  of editing questionnaires, 1501
  of fieldwork, 72, 440, 1399, 1933, 1936
  of follow-ups 818
  of sampling, 581, 588, 893, 900, 930, 1348, 1902, 2118
  of self-completion survey, 1935

COUNTER – SORTER
  use in data processing, 46, 1108, 1358, 1988
  use in Guttman scaling, 259, 510, 1852

CRITICAL INCIDENT TECHNIQUE, 468, 710

CROSS-CULTURAL RESEARCH METHODS
    and illiterate respondents, 566
    international surveys, 344, 787, 1021, 1621
    methodological problems, 409, 497, 787, 1012, 1021, 1186, 1621
    projective techniques, 566, 1723

CUMULATIVE FREQUENCY METHOD
    to test adequacy of sample size, 1430

CUMULATIVE SCALES
    H-technique used with, 961, 1915
    techniques for increasing precision, 36, 606, 961, 1915
    use of counter-sorter, 259, 510

DATA ANALYSIS *See* DATA PROCESSING; STATISTICAL ANALYSIS OF DATA

DATA, editing of
    by computer, 173, 747, 748, 1923, 2164
    consistency runs, 747, 748, 1923
    in longitudinal studies, 794
    logical checks, 1617
    matched sample criteria, 1923
    range checks, 1617

DATA PROCESSING
    coding, 46, 175, 195, 569, 587, 647, 661, 751, 754, 826, 859, 918, 920, 984, 1010, 1108, 1887, 1939, 1965, 2140, 2151, 2154
    computers in, 13, 89, 173, 307, 444, 579, 747, 748, 751, 758, 794, 800, 1020, 1240, 1375, 1617, 1820, 1825, 1856, 1857, 1893, 1923, 1939, 1951, 1962, 1965, 2164
    content analysis, 66, 579, 1771, 1887, 1939
    cost, 1375, 1548
    counter-sorter used in, 46, 1108, 1358, 1988
    editing, 46, 569, 747, 748, 794, 1501, 1617, 1923, 1951, 2164
    errors in, 175, 431, 527, 528, 529, 587, 754, 1220, 1551, 1617
    hand counters, 46
    in censuses, 173, 527, 661, 820, 1358, 1452, 1469, 1501, 1617, 1988, 2022
    in longitudinal studies, 793, 794, 1676
    in surveys, 46, 195, 262, 307, 726, 728, 747, 748, 758, 1174, 1358, 1469, 1676, 1820, 1825, 1965, 1995, 2022, 2164,
    Keysort, 46
    manual analysis, 46, 1548, 1578, 1971
    mark-sensing, 525, 759, 1058, 1174, 1358, 1784, 1849, 1940
    mechanical, 46, 174, 199, 700, 726, 728, 1001, 1094, 1108, 1119, 1220, 1358, 1409, 1548, 1758, 1900, 1943, 1988
    merging data from surveys, 262, 1158, 1676
    of clinical interview material, 9
    of guided interview material, 9
    of life-history data, 89
    of paired comparisons data, 1119
    of qualitative data, 2091, 2140
    of sociometric data, 35, 199, 444, 1094
    Pegboard, 46
    photo-electric sensing, 1358
    pre-planning for 46, 1174, 1995
    punched cards, 35, 46, 174, 195, 528, 759, 1094, 1108, 1119, 1220, 1228, 1240, 1358, 1512, 1988, 2037
    reproducer used in 1108

tabulation, 46, 199, 647, 700, 1001, 1174, 1578, 1988, 1995, 2164
tabulator used in 647, 700, 1094
transcribing 305, 306
visual analysis 1512

See also: STATISTICAL ANALYSIS OF DATA

DEPTH INTERVIEW
applications, 1535
definition, 1729, 2153
for public opinion polling, 1260
interviewing techniques, 256, 790, 802, 1260, 1535, 1590
group, 790
structured, 1535, 1590, 2082
training interviewers for, 1098
unstructured, 1535
used in readership research, 53
validity, 790, 1215, 1260

DETAILED INTERVIEW, 1209, 1215

DIAGNOSTIC INTERVIEW, 979

DIARIES
bias in, 456, 469, 733, 1932
comparison with personal interview, 281, 1112, 1204, 1536, 1537, 1932
error related to, 121, 469, 977, 1536, 1931, 1993
for recording behaviour, 201, 456, 617, 1455, 1580, 1999, 2000
for recording family expenditure, 1110, 1112, 1113
for recording product purchases, 121, 281, 289, 610, 977, 1238, 1502, 1536, 1537, 1910, 1931, 1932, 1993
layout, 1932
length of, 121, 1993
running-in period, 456, 459
use in audience research, 201, 456, 459, 469, 617, 733, 1065, 1580, 1999, 2000
use in consumer research, 121, 281, 289, 977, 1502, 1536, 1537, 1910, 1931, 1932
use in health surveys, 1204
use in readership research, 1065

DIARIES, used in audience research
conditioning effect, 469
for measuring audience size, 459, 469, 617, 1580, 1999, 2000
meter-controlled, 469, 617
non-cooperation, 733
programme/break diaries, 2000
used in radio audience research, 201
used in television audience research, 456, 459, 469, 617, 618, 733, 1065, 1580, 1999, 2000

DIARY STUDIES *See* DIARIES

DICHOTOMOUS QUESTIONS
and question bias, 777, 858, 930, 1719
comparison with multiple-choice, 782, 858, 1175, 1719
comparison with open, 645, 1719
in public opinion polling, 645, 765, 782, 1175

DIRECTIVE INTERVIEW, 321, 554

DIRECTION-OF-PERCEPTION TECHNIQUE, 196, 572

DISCRIMINATORY ANALYSIS
discriminant functions, 761, 2139
interpretation of, 1452
multiple discriminant analysis, 308, 736
use in market research, 430

223

EDGE-PUNCHED CARDS, 1228, 1512, 1971, 2037

EDITING
cost, 1501
data, 173, 747, 748, 1617, 1923, 2164
error in, 1501
questionnaires, 569, 1501, 1951

EDITING DATA *See* DATA, editing of

EDITING QUESTIONNAIRES *See* QUESTIONNAIRES editing of

EDUCATIONAL RESEARCH TECHNIQUES
critical incident technique, 468
sampling, 552, 1252, 1372
standard error analysis, 1252

EFFECTS MEASUREMENT
active response scale, 1410
before and after studies, 545, 609
in advertising research, 251, 436, 609, 1672, 1774, 1811
in audience research, 143, 145, 152, 154, 164, 637, 1543, 1982
in communications research, 544
in television audience research, 143, 144, 152, 154, 164, 637, 1543, 1982
measuring effect of public opinion polling, 460
panels used in, 609, 1212
propaganda effects measurement, 251, 358, 369, 544, 545, 1195, 1196, 1212, 1230, 1376, 1743, 1811, 2056

ENUMERATIVE SURVEYS
comparison with analytical surveys, 532
comparison with sample surveys, 623, 1348

consistency of responses, 1531
cost, 1348
error in responses, 253, 1371, 1397, 1618
in absence of sample frame, 608
interview vs. self enumeration, 253, 1371
situations when used, 924
statistical analysis of data, 532
used in decision making, 924

EQUAL APPEARING INTERVALS *See* THURSTONE SCALING TECHNIQUES

ERROR
and memory, 677, 813, 816, 876, 1172, 1328, 1552, 1602, 1767, 1781, 1782
coding, 175, 587, 625, 754, 1469
deliberate, 1172, 1577
deduction of, 665, 666, 804
detection of, 40, 83, 94, 142, 159, 593, 720, 903, 907, 917, 929, 1125, 1219, 1396, 1420, 1425, 1469, 1485, 1488, 1552, 1606, 1617, 1726, 2148
due to faulty rapport, 1718
due to interviewers, 165, 254, 266, 267, 352, 368, 414, 435, 440, 452, 482, 625, 653, 655, 704, 727, 729, 762, 817, 853, 856, 857, 903, 907, 917, 929, 930, 932, 934, 1113, 1151, 1152, 1242, 1305, 1307, 1397, 1465, 1469, 1478, 1552, 1718, 1766, 1791, 1843, 1903, 1945, 2006, 2112, 2148
due to method of data collection, 529
due to question form, 236, 1702
due to question order, 269
due to question wording, 236, 1702

due to questionnaire design, 529, 1131
due to respondents, 19, 37, 40, 94, 95, 113, 155, 159, 162, 194, 322, 332, 334, 351, 352, 353, 361, 377, 413, 415, 421, 439, 440, 503, 513, 659, 677, 735, 777, 801, 804, 816, 875, 878, 879, 903, 909, 942, 1024, 1046, 1047, 1124, 1142, 1146, 1219, 1269, 1273, 1282, 1307, 1328, 1366, 1367, 1397, 1404, 1405, 1420, 1480, 1485, 1536, 1539, 1550, 1577, 1625, 1648, 1765, 1767, 1781, 1782, 1860, 1976, 2016, 2032, 2141
due to tabulation design, 529
in censuses, 83, 172, 173, 253, 405, 431, 527, 593, 594, 595, 625, 665, 902, 904, 905, 1125, 1343, 1350, 1371, 1425, 1468, 1469, 1475, 1501, 1617, 1781, 1879
in data processing, 175, 431, 527, 528, 529, 587, 754, 1220, 1551, 1617
in diary studies, 121, 469, 977, 1536, 1931, 1993
in editing, 1501
in enumerative surveys, 253, 1371, 1397, 1618
in financial surveys, 260, 261, 681, 683, 798, 875, 909, 1114, 1124, 1404, 1405, 1485, 1993
in household surveys, 198, 253, 1043, 1114, 1124, 1481, 1485, 1495, 1993
in interpretation of data, 529, 899, 1450, 1778, 1907, 1960
in mail surveys, 439, 1076, 1769
in observational techniques, 56, 1484
in panel data, 121, 1124, 1306, 1931, 1932, 2101

in personal interview surveys, 1469
in presentation of data, 529, 1475, 1907
in public opinion research, 236, 238, 329, 453, 854, 856, 1089, 1090, 1247, 1306
in recording of responses, 435, 440, 625, 704, 801, 1397, 1552, 1843, 1931, 1945
in responses to questions, 37, 40, 84, 94, 172, 260, 261, 332, 352, 377, 421, 439, 504, 529, 665, 666, 671, 681, 683, 777, 801, 816, 875, 876, 879, 904, 942, 1024, 1042, 1142, 1143, 1146, 1219, 1220, 1307, 1346, 1371, 1397, 1404, 1405, 1420, 1481, 1485, 1487, 1488, 1514, 1536, 1537, 1550, 1577, 1618, 1625, 2061, 2141
in self completion surveys, 351
in surveys, 159, 535, 593, 595, 903, 904, 905, 992, 1350, 1397, 1468, 1469
in television audience research, 469, 618
margins of, 1610
mathematical models of, 84, 666, 901, 904, 1346, 1468, 1618, 1941, 1946, 2101
measurement, 222, 225, 593, 904, 905, 1151, 1306, 2101
non-sampling, 593, 654, 1403, 1468, 1469, 1485, 1941
randomization of, 1131
recall, 322, 513, 571, 677, 816, 851, 876, 977, 1043, 1046, 1047, 1124, 1269, 1282, 1328, 1366, 1397, 1485, 1536, 1537, 1602, 1625, 1767, 1782, 1932, 2032, 2141
reduction of, 159, 735, 857, 1148, 1346, 1397, 1468, 1507, 1718, 2148
reporting, 113, 155, 159, 260, 261, 332, 351, 352, 353,

reporting (*contd.*)
354, 377, 413, 415, 421,
435, 439, 529, 571, 677,
681, 683, 851, 875, 876,
879, 909, 1046, 1047,
1124, 1142, 1204, 1269,
1274, 1367, 1377, 1404,
1405, 1420, 1480, 1481,
1485, 1536, 1537, 1539,
1552, 1648, 1723, 1791,
1976
sampling, 176, 475, 477, 529,
534, 798, 896, 1114, 1469,
1780, 1890, 1922, 1946,
2156
sources of, 238, 253, 332, 529,
535, 854, 1308, 1420,
1469, 1713
total survey, 298, 1308

ERROR, deduction of
from Guttman scaling
technique, 930
from patterns of error, 665,
666

ERROR, detection of
by post-testing, 1469
by record checks, 94, 142,
1488, 1726
by re-interviews, 83, 720, 804,
1125, 1397, 1469, 1606
by running analysis, 1219
by tape-recording, 2148
in censuses, 83, 593, 1125,
1425, 1606, 1617

ERROR, due to interviewer *See*
INTERVIEWER ERROR

ERROR due to respondent
and characteristics of
respondent, 332
classification errors, 1219,
1976
detection, 40, 94, 159, 903,
1219, 1307, 1420, 1577
embarrassment, 351, 2032
evasion, 334
failure to follow instructions,
801, 1577
fatigue, 878

guessing, 40, 735, 777, 942,
1307
in estimation, 440, 1146,
1269, 1404, 1405, 1485,
1625
lying, 37, 421, 440, 659, 903,
1024, 1781, 1976, 2016
memory, 677, 816, 1328,
1781, 1782
misinterpreting question, 19,
95, 159, 334, 361, 503,
804, 1397, 1860
misunderstanding question,
19, 162, 334, 361, 503,
804, 1397, 1860
motivation, 351, 1404, 2016
over-reporting, 332, 421, 879,
1124, 1142, 1269, 1404,
1405, 1485, 1536, 1539,
1648, 1765, 1976
recall, 322, 513, 677, 816,
1047, 1124, 1269, 1282,
1328, 1366, 1397, 1485,
1536, 1625, 1767, 1782,
2032, 2141
self-protection, 332, 2016
under-reporting, 113, 159,
351, 352, 353, 377, 413,
415, 677, 875, 909, 1142,
1143, 1269, 1273, 1367,
1404, 1405, 1480, 1648

ERROR, in data processing
detection, 1551, 1617
in card punching, 431, 1528,
1551
in coding responses, 175, 587,
625, 754

ERROR, reduction of
through control of
interviewers, 930
through interviewer training,
930, 1718, 2148
through piloting, 159
through pretesting, 159,
1507
through selection of
interviewers, 2148
in enumerative surveys,
1397

ERROR-CHOICE TECHNIQUE
   in attitude research, 246, 888, 1184
   validity, 246, 888, 1184

ETHICS
   ethical codes, 241, 946
   ethical standards, 241, 548, 946, 1223
   in attitude research, 2080
   in public opinion research, 252, 329, 946, 1223
   in survey research, 241
   of tape recording interviews, 204
   unethical practices, 55, 126, 205, 1106, 1362, 1474, 1650, 1918

EXPERIMENTAL RESEARCH DESIGNS
   and repeated measurement, 760
   and validity of social science experiments, 341, 889, 1914
   artificiality of, 839, 889
   counter balancing, 760, 1605
   for discrimination testing, 839
   for measuring message diffusion, 551
   for preference testing, 326, 843, 1954
   for taste-testing, 843, 1954
   in human relations research, 356
   in marketing research, 300
   in public opinion research, 400
   Latin square, 99, 313, 1333
   pre-experimental, 98, 341
   projective, 400
   quasi-experimental, 98
   randomised experiments, 616, 1953
   sources of invalidity in, 341, 399, 889
   true experimental, 98, 341, 356

EXPERIMENTER BIAS
   and experience of experimenter, 1138, 1696
   and opinions of experimenter, 1138, 1696
   and personality of experimenter, 1138
   and race of experimenter, 1736, 1838
   and sex of experimenter, 1138
   due to expectation, 103, 104, 105, 106, 1102, 1138, 1388, 1694, 1696, 1697, 2008
   reduction of, 1320, 1694, 2008
   replication of, 103, 104, 1236, 1697
   sources of, 2008
   stimulas bias, 1597

EXPLORATORY RESEARCH TECHNIQUES
   content analysis, 1433
   group discussion, 1729
   interviewing, 2, 727, 1729
   projective techniques, 2, 451
   repertory grid, 1729

FACTOR ANALYSIS
   basic factor analytic designs, 385, 1116, 1329
   centroid method, 447, 1116, 2132
   comparison with cluster analysis, 1546
   comparison with component analysis, 1546
   comparison with correlation analysis, 1546
   comparison with Guttman scaling, 864, 1636
   comparison with homogeneous tests, 1265
   component analysis, 923
   criticism of usage, 656, 755, 860
   diagonal method, 2132
   general factors, 1970
   group factors, 656
   historical development of, 1835, 2020

image analysis, 923
interpretation of factors, 1970
invariance of factors, 1970
limitations, 638, 1970
multiple, 923, 1994
of sociometric data, 1340
principal axes method, 447, 1329
Q-technique, 968, 1040, 1063, 1482, 1745, 1835, 1894, 1895, 2159
rotation of factors, 861, 1546, 1966
scale free, 923
three-mode, 1232
use of coefficient alpha, 1325, 1327
use in consumer attitude research, 134, 1291, 1745
use in preference testing, 1583
use in image research, 134
use in market research, 430, 447, 1034, 1291, 1628, 1709
use in readability measurement, 277
use in readership research, 1994, 1997
use in social survey research, 323, 1321
use in television audience research, 1709

FIELD WORK
administration, 63, 995, 1013, 1242, 1369, 1850
control of, 419, 1013, 1242, 1336
cost, 72, 73, 440, 1399, 1933, 1936
in sociological research, 1417, 1645, 1646, 2043, 2171
strategy, 54, 543, 694, 1013, 1017, 1646, 2171
tape-recording used in, 305, 306, 640
training for, 1645

FILTER
questions, 765, 1193
systems on questionnaires, 1193, 1449

FINANCIAL SURVEYS
completion rate of interviews, 440
cost of fieldwork, 440
dealing with incomplete information in, 1201
error, 260, 261, 681, 683, 798, 875, 909, 1114, 1124, 1404, 1405, 1485, 1993
family budget surveys, 441, 1109, 1110, 1111, 1112, 1113, 1114, 1457, 1485, 1486, 1993, 2114
interviewing incomplete families, 1201
misleading information, 440
non coverage of sample dwellings, 1201
non-response, 440, 681, 683, 1202, 1457
of earnings information, 260, 261
panels used in, 680, 681, 683, 1112, 1124
problems of conducting interviews in, 440, 1304
questionnaire design for, 261, 1304
refusals in 440
response rate, 440
sampling for, 1114, 1457, 1460
use of incompleted interviews, 1201
validity of, 868, 1080

FOCUSED INTERVIEW, 75, 709, 1416, 1728

FOLLOW-UP, of non-respondents
alternative procedures to, 586, 1822
by interview, 987, 1290, 1314, 1749
by mail, 738, 739, 865, 938, 1076, 1120, 1235, 1290,

by mail (*contd.*)
    1494, 1637, 1659, 1673, 1769, 1770, 1978, 1979
by visit, 586, 1749
in mail surveys, 271, 484, 564, 624, 689, 734, 738, 739, 787, 792, 865, 938, 987, 1076, 1120, 1235, 1314, 1494, 1503, 1637, 1659, 1673, 1749, 1769, 1770, 1978, 1979
'not-at-homes', 586, 1290, 1822
timing of, 1494

FORCED-CHOICE TECHNIQUE
acceptability to raters, 2169
bias, 118, 1016, 2169
comparison with Likert technique, 118
reliability, 118
respondents' failure to follow instructions on, 801
validity, 82, 118, 1016, 1644, 1985, 2169

FOYER INTERVIEW
in cinema audience research, 411

FREE-ANSWER QUESTION, 334, 335, 1423, 1702, 1719, 1882

GAP ANALYSIS, 426

GRAPHIC SCALES, 573, 1655, 1656, 1806

GROUP DISCUSSION TECHNIQUE
application in various research fields, 398, 599, 913
as an adjunct to personal interviews, 96, 398
as an adjunct to self-completion questionnaires, 954
comparison with repertory grid technique, 1729
group size, 599
in advertising research, 1818
in audience research, 148
in exploratory research, 1729
in motivational research, 75
in qualitative research, 1728
problem of representativeness, 599
selection of group members, 599
validity of opinions expressed in, 96, 1317

GROUP FEEDBACK ANALYSIS, 954

GROUP INTERVIEW *See* GROUP DISCUSSION TECHNIQUE

GROUP TESTING TECHNIQUE
and volunteer bias, 145, 150, 156, 367, 505, 978, 1693
as an adjunct to personal interviews, 1788
comparison with mail survey, 983
in advertising research, 1818
in audience research, 145, 1561
in market research, 156
in public opinion research, 2126
'paper and pencil' method, 2126
problem of representativeness, 1693
questionnaire administered by radio broadcast, 2126
recruitment of group members, 145, 1693
test-room procedures, 145, 156

GUIDED INTERVIEW
analysis of interview material, 9
clinical, 9
comparison with projective techniques, 1685

GUILDFORD SHORT CUT SCALING
of paired comparisons data, 2142

GUTTMAN SCALING
  and information theory, 2127
  comparison with factor analysis, 864, 1636
  comparison with homogeneous tests, 1265
  comparison with method of reciprocal averages, 1496
  computer programs for, 800
  Cornell technique, 690, 800, 871, 919, 1172
  'G' technique, 1846
  mechanised techniques for, 32, 259, 510, 724, 951, 1073, 1852
  multidimensional scale analysis, 442
  of qualitative data, 690, 869
  reproducibility index, 416, 951, 1413, 1957
  scale gradient analysis, 1957
  scalogram analysis, 258, 416, 690, 716, 951, 960, 1072, 1073, 1172, 1318, 1365, 1384, 1398, 1413, 1560, 1753
  scalogram board, 1072, 1365
  techniques for placement of non-response patterns in, 36, 257, 604, 1960
  unidimensionality, 549, 690, 1967
  utility of, 345, 550, 604, 874, 930, 1847
  validity, 416, 1331, 1332, 1384, 1643, 1753, 2065
  zero-point, 970

H-TECHNIQUE
  and cumulative scale precision, 961, 1915

'HALO' EFFECT
  and rating scales, 1315
  in product testing, 189
  in radio programme feature analysis, 1839

HEALTH SURVEYS, 113, 142, 353, 354, 377, 435, 496, 1204, 1242, 1469, 1480, 1820

HOLLERITH CARDS *See* PUNCHED CARDS

HOMOGENEOUS TESTS
  comparison with factor analysis, 1265
  comparison with Guttman scale analysis, 1265

HOUSEHOLD SURVEY
  availability of respondents, 1471
  comparison of methods of data collection for, 986
  classification of households, 388, 994
  development of, as method of data collection, 198
  error related to, 198, 253, 1043, 1114, 1124, 1481, 1485, 1495, 1993
  for recording family expenditure, 1109, 1111, 1112, 1113, 1114, 1124, 1457, 1485, 1486, 1993, 2114
  in urban poverty neighbourhoods, 780
  obtaining information from single respondent, 93, 1420, 1495, 1875
  selection of respondent within household, 1124, 1144, 1485, 1486, 1530, 1986

HOUSEWIFE PANELS *See* PANELS

HYPOTHESIS TESTING, 598, 1054, 1610, 1779

IMAGE STUDIES, 2035

INCENTIVES
  bias due to, 649
  effect on response rate, 203, 273, 396, 649, 738, 739, 938, 949, 977, 1037, 1120, 1128, 1162, 1235, 1493, 1503, 1664, 1812, 2158
  in mail surveys, 203, 273, 396, 649, 738, 739, 938, 949, 1037, 1076, 1128, 1162, 1235, 1357, 1493, 1503, 1664, 1812, 2158
  used with panels, 121, 977, 1112, 1210, 1910, 1911

INCOMPLETE SENTENCE TEST
See SENTENCE COMPLETION TEST

INDUSTRIAL MARKET RESEARCH TECHNIQUES
and non-response bias, 1041
desk research, 333
interviewing, 21, 22, 1132, 1921
mail surveys, 21, 333, 403, 439
personal interviews, 23, 333
sampling, 20, 22, 1167
sampling frames, 20, 22, 333, 1167
telephone, 21, 22, 333

INFORMANT
international survey of, 787, 1031
motivation, 77
qualities required of, 77
selection of, 77, 1017, 1031
used in public opinion research, 1169
used in studies of morale, 340
validity of data obtained from, 340, 524, 1101, 1420, 1947, 1983, 1984, 2016, 2043, 2171

INTENSITY ANALYSIS
in public opinion research, 715
in sociometric research, 716

INTENSIVE INTERVIEW
functions of, 159
in community research, 567
in readership research, 155, 159, 424, 476, 965
interpretation of, 1652, 1653

INTERACTION
and theory building, 223
between interviewer and respondent, 78
between variables, 507, 1156, 1444, 1855, 1856, 1857
during the interview, 78
interpersonal, 78, 355, 1613
social, 1379

INTERNATIONAL SURVEY
area sampling for, 1626
as a cross-cultural research method, 344
comparability of data, 1021, 1621, 2053
comparability of questions, 14, 651, 1621, 1626
comparability of survey procedures, 2053
international public opinion surveys, 14, 344, 1031, 1621, 1626
interviewers, 1626
interviewing, 1626
language problems, 651, 1626
mail surveys, 787
meaning of question to respondents, 651, 1621, 1626
of informants, 787, 1031
problems of conducting, 1021, 1031, 1621
question wording for, 14, 1621, 1626
quota sampling for, 1626
respondents, 1621
sample controls, 1626

INTERPRETATION, of research results, 529, 726, 728, 899, 1118, 1156, 1450, 1610, 1778, 1907, 1960

INTERVIEW
as a source of bias, 490, 930, 933, 1641, 1704
as interpersonal interaction, 78, 355, 1613
as social interaction, 181, 250, 1241, 1379, 1589, 1613
clinical, 9, 979, 1728
comparison with other means of data collection, 5, 33, 37, 127, 132, 133, 240, 253, 281, 351, 632, 633, 669, 742, 829, 986, 1107, 1112, 1163, 1202, 1204, 1213, 1305, 1314, 1318, 1357, 1403, 1423, 1480, 1514, 1536, 1537, 1932, 1935, 1987, 1992, 2055, 2057, 2155
completion rates, 301, 378,

completion rates (contd.)
440, 543, 581, 585, 944,
1014, 1194, 1400, 1793,
1831
conditions, 353, 389, 1017, 1920
conversational, 245, 1920, 2087
counselling, 321, 979
depth, 256, 790, 802, 1098, 1209, 1215, 1260, 1535, 1590, 1728, 1729, 2082, 2153
design, 554
detailed, 1209, 1215
diagnostic, 979
directive, 321, 554
extended, 245, 848, 1728
field, 1017
focused, 709, 1416, 1728
foyer, 411
free, 979, 1313, 1728
guide, 1416
guided, 9, 1685
house, 1471
industrial, 21, 22, 23, 333, 1132
informal, 1260, 1920
intensive, 155, 159, 424, 476, 567, 930, 965, 1209, 1215, 1652, 1653, 1728, 1791, 2042
interviewer-respondent speech interaction behaviour in, 1378, 1392, 1393, 1396, 1735, 2095, 2096, 2097
length of, 848
limitations as a method of data collection, 349, 632, 633, 1363
methods of securing, 63, 543, 1052, 1132, 1471, 1662, 1704
non-directive, 167, 321, 554, 930, 1248, 1670, 1710, 1728, 2087
non-schedule, 1647
nonverbal communication in 622, 1789
payment for, 930, 1932
personal, 23, 333, 1202, 1513

'phony', 205
place of, 389, 1017
psychology of the, 349
refusals, 191, 267, 301, 378, 440, 559, 563, 585, 774, 910, 937, 944, 959, 1014, 1414, 1660, 1712, 1831, 2109
re-interviews, 83, 429, 463, 720, 778, 804, 1125, 1212, 1214, 1377, 1397, 1469, 1471, 1606, 1748, 2042
reports on the, 350, 414, 706, 930, 1796, 1898
role relationships in the, 1305
single call, 1539
sources of bias in the, 1456
standardised, 955, 1305
structured, 9, 63, 240, 1313, 1491, 1535, 1589, 1590, 1728, 2035, 2082
supplemented by use of mail survey, 815, 1347, 1792
tandem, 1132, 1133
tape-recording of, 157, 161, 204, 305, 306, 640, 821, 853, 2096, 2148
telephone, 21, 22, 60, 200, 240, 333, 373, 463, 469, 592, 821, 972, 986, 1003, 1077, 1126, 1202, 1335, 1422, 1499, 1513, 1555, 1667, 1748, 1937, 1986
therapeutic, 979, 1383
timing of, 581, 1096
types used in qualitative research, 1728
unstructured, 1305, 1491, 1535, 1728, 2035, 2140
use in various research fields, 116, 333, 1248, 1471
used in prediction of job performance, 116
usefulness of incomplete, 1201
validity as a means of data collection, 116, 281, 351, 355, 414, 632, 633, 1030, 1202, 1249, 1305, 1363, 1382, 1439, 1514, 1537, 1944, 2061

See also: INTERVIEWING; GROUP DISCUSSION

INTERVIEW, length of
and fatigue of respondent, 848
and interest of respondent, 848
and rapport with respondent, 848
methodological problems of, 848

INTERVIEW SCHEDULE *See* QUESTIONNAIRE

INTERVIEW SURVEY *See* INTERVIEW

INTERVIEW, tape recording of *See* TAPE-RECORDING, of interview

INTERVIEWER
accuracy of recording responses, 435, 452, 704, 853, 907, 1242, 1552, 1791, 1798, 1945
age of, 182, 585, 620, 730, 1453
and failure to contact respondent, 585, 1361, 1471
and interview completion rate, 301, 378, 440, 543, 581, 585, 944, 1194, 1400, 1793, 1831
and interview refusals, 191, 267, 440, 559, 585, 922, 959, 1712, 2109
and response rate, 440, 585, 922, 1712, 1766
as a source of bias, 62, 106, 137, 231, 239, 266, 267, 304, 328, 332, 355, 374, 440, 452, 529, 558, 560, 620, 664, 674, 704, 746, 750, 856, 857, 907, 930, 933, 934, 963, 972, 1028, 1029, 1084, 1151, 1225, 1255, 1289, 1361, 1379, 1394, 1395, 1445, 1456, 1464, 1481, 1519, 1545,
as a source of bias (*contd.*) 1613, 1633, 1641, 1717, 1727, 1732, 1736, 1790, 1791, 1798, 1802, 1829, 1838, 1843, 1872, 1883, 1884, 1885, 1998, 2000, 2002, 2006, 2014, 2054, 2055, 2060, 2106, 2115, 2116, 2117, 2161
behaviour during interview, 366, 553, 696, 698, 955, 972, 1378, 1481, 1589, 1766
briefing of, 1369, 1635
cheating by, 50, 51, 179, 180, 237, 266, 420, 487, 488, 580, 627, 653, 932, 1369, 1447, 1456, 1942, 2107
classification of respondent, 568, 1289, 1465, 1874, 2006
competence, criteria for, 70, 110, 420, 589, 730, 853, 1453, 1635, 1802, 1899, 1938
control of performance, 267, 419, 553, 592, 727, 730, 1003, 1242, 1623
costs, 355, 440, 930, 944, 1194, 1399, 1402, 1766, 1802, 1933, 1936, 2143
deviation from instructions, 907, 1361, 1766
error, 165, 254, 266, 267, 328, 352, 368, 414, 435, 440, 452, 482, 625, 653, 655, 704, 727, 729, 762, 817, 853, 856, 857, 903, 907, 917, 929, 930, 932, 934, 1113, 1151, 1152, 1242, 1305, 1307, 1397, 1465, 1469, 1478, 1552, 1718, 1766, 1791, 1843, 1903, 1945, 2006, 2112, 2148
evaluation of, 48, 110, 190, 293, 553, 589, 727, 729, 730, 853, 927, 929, 1369, 1453, 1623, 1718, 1799, 1899, 1938, 2107, 2111, 2148

expectation, 730, 750, 934, 1843, 2161
experience, 254, 368, 585, 730, 780, 930, 1453, 1766, 1801
fatigue, 1003
function of, 253
in international surveys, 1626
in multilingual communities, 226, 1013
in other cultures, 1630, 1924, 1925, 2131
in public opinion research, 202, 293, 856, 1029, 1084, 1085, 1160, 1412, 1445, 1626, 1884, 2054
in social psychological research, 1785
incentives, 48, 1194
influence on interview data, 182, 267, 352, 664, 955, 972, 1084, 1085, 1378
influence on self-completion questionnaire responses, 352
memory, 1552, 1945
morale, 420, 488, 580, 930, 932, 1785, 1850, 1925
motivation, 1802, 1925
neutrality during interview, 366, 541, 1589, 1686, 2021
part-time, 178, 180, 729, 1369, 1453
payment of, 48, 930, 944, 1194, 1369, 1766, 1850, 1933, 1936, 2143
perception of interview, 1481
personal characteristics of, 52, 110, 178, 440, 585, 589, 727, 730, 907, 1225, 1412, 1453, 1623, 1635, 1799, 1934,
predicting success of, 70, 110, 589, 730, 1453, 1934, 2110
prescription of respondent's verbal behaviour, 393, 1233, 1379, 1394, 1395, 1607, 1732
previous employment of, 2110

problems encountered by, 226, 780, 930, 1017, 1160, 1400, 1704, 1710, 1850
qualities required of, 52, 110, 256, 389, 419, 589, 727, 1033, 1369, 1412, 1443, 1453, 1623, 1635, 1799, 1801, 1802, 1934, 2110
race of, 62, 71, 304, 889, 1613, 1661, 1736, 1838, 2115, 2116, 2117
rapport with respondent, 696, 848, 976, 1029, 1378, 1428, 1589, 1727, 1785, 2005, 2060, 2073, 2115, 2117
recruitment, 71, 202, 440, 464, 589, 727, 930, 1242, 1369, 1412, 1453, 1635, 1799, 1802, 2110
relationship with respondent, 250, 293, 440, 696, 1225, 1305, 1378, 1481, 1589, 1686, 1727, 1744, 2005
reports on the interview, 706, 930, 1796, 1898
representativeness of, 889
research on, 927, 928, 929, 1028, 1033, 2105, 2106, 2107, 2108, 2109, 2110, 2111, 2112
respondent perception of, 182, 350, 366, 620, 1029, 1225, 1443, 1481, 1589, 1727, 1829
respondent speech interaction behaviour, 1378, 1392, 1393, 1396, 1735, 2095, 2096, 2097
role in interview situation, 848, 1305
selection of, 71, 110, 202, 256, 267, 355, 419, 420, 440, 464, 589, 729, 730, 930, 1242, 1369, 1412, 1453, 1623, 1634, 1635, 1785, 1799, 1802, 1844, 2131, 2148
sex, 182, 585, 1969
students as, 585, 1453, 1635

supervision of, 48, 63, 202, 419, 420, 930, 1242, 1369, 1412, 1623, 1634, 1635, 1796

training of, 48, 63, 71, 79, 102, 110, 202, 267, 355, 419, 464, 727, 729, 730, 853, 857, 930, 1098, 1242, 1369, 1412, 1623, 1634, 1635, 1645, 1728, 1766, 1785, 1802, 1844, 1924, 1925, 2131, 2148

turnover of, 730, 780, 927, 928, 1800

variability between interviewers, 115, 137, 254, 368, 414, 435, 568, 664, 743, 746, 762, 817, 857, 907, 922, 1068, 1111, 1113, 1152, 1469, 1478, 1791, 1903

variability of interviewer, 762, 817, 1152, 1903

verbal behaviour of, 1233, 1394, 1395, 1607, 1633, 1732, 2097

warmth toward respondent, 39, 560, 693, 1029, 1378, 1589, 1600, 1633, 1727

INTERVIEWER BIAS

and area sampling, 1361

and interviewer appearance-stereotypes, 1829

and card questions, 328, 1872

and dichotomous questions, 328, 930, 1872

and interviewer's attitudes, 266, 440, 560, 704, 907, 1456, 1481, 1545, 1641, 1727, 1829, 1885, 1998, 2002

and interviewer's expectations, 137, 750, 907, 934, 1456, 1519, 1843, 1885, 2161

and interviewer's experience, 254, 704, 930, 1727, 1872, 1885, 2055

and interviewer's opinions, 231, 266, 704, 934, 1456,

and interviewer's opinions (*contd.*)
1727, 1884, 2002, 2106, 2161

and interviewer's race, 62, 304, 1613, 1727, 1736, 1838, 2115, 2116, 2117

and interviewer's training, 857

and memory dependent questions, 1872

and open-ended questions, 328, 664, 704, 1727, 1790, 1791

and polling questions, 328, 704, 1084, 1085, 1790, 1884, 2054, 2115

and question form, 328, 664, 1790, 1884

and question wording, 328, 907

and quota sampling, 239, 266, 374, 930

and rapport with respondent, 1029, 1727, 2060, 2117

and social distance between interviewer and respondent, 332, 355, 440, 560, 620, 934, 1084, 1085, 1225, 1613, 1727, 2060, 2116, 2117

and socio-economic status of respondent, 355, 440, 1225, 1289, 1727, 2116, 2117

and socio-economic status of interviewer, 355, 440, 1225, 1456, 1613, 1727, 2116, 2117

and verbal reinforcement, 972, 1379, 1395, 1633, 1732

answer bias, 674, 1545

correction of, 674, 857, 963, 1727

detection of, 452, 674, 704, 1790, 1791, 2014

in classifying respondent, 239, 664, 1289, 2006

in classifying responses, 1255, 1791, 1798, 1872, 1883, 1884, 1885, 2055

in public opinion polling, 231,
328, 704, 856, 1029, 1084,
1085, 1445, 1717, 1727,
1790, 1884, 2054, 2115,
2161
in recording responses, 266,
452, 704, 856, 907, 1255,
1791, 1798, 1872, 2054,
2115
interviewer's comments on,
1445
measurement of, 1028, 1151,
1790
reduction of, 746, 963, 2117
selection bias, 266, 374, 674
sources of, 137, 266, 267, 355,
704, 856, 933, 934, 963,
1028, 1029, 1456, 1727,
1791, 1798, 1802, 2115

INTERVIEWER CHEATING *See*
CHEATING, by interviewers

INTERVIEWER ERRORS
detection of, 903, 917, 929,
1552, 1766, 2112, 2148
due to cheating, 266, 653, 932
due to deviation from
instructions, 165, 440, 907,
1766
due to incompetence, 440, 853
due to inexperience, 254, 368,
930, 1242, 1766
due to interviewer bias, 266,
328, 674, 704, 853, 856,
907, 934, 1151, 1843
due to interviewer expectation,
266, 907, 934, 1843
due to lack of probing, 929
due to lack of training, 857,
930, 1718, 1766
due to variability between
interviewers, 368, 414, 435,
762, 817, 907, 1113, 1152,
1478, 1791, 1903
due to variability of single
interviewer, 762, 1152
in classifying respondent,
1465, 2006
in delivery of questions, 266,
440, 853, 907

in probability sampling, 266,
267, 1902
in recording responses, 266,
435, 440, 482, 625, 704,
853, 907, 1397, 1552,
1843, 1945
reduction of, 267, 857, 930,
2112
selective reporting, 452, 853,
1791
sources of, 266, 267, 440, 727,
929, 934, 1242, 1305, 1791,
2112

INTERVIEWER REPORTS, on
the interview
use in maintaining interviewer
morale, 1796
use in supervision of
interviewers, 1796

INTERVIEWER VARIABILITY
and question form, 664, 1113
and response rate, 922, 1111
and responses to opinion
questions, 115, 817, 1152,
1791
and responses to factual
questions, 817, 1113, 1791
between interviewers, 115,
137, 254, 368, 414, 435,
568, 664, 743, 746, 762,
817, 857, 907, 922, 1068,
1111, 1113, 1152, 1469,
1478, 1791, 1903
cancelling out, 746
detection of, 137, 1113, 1478
factors contributing towards, 254,
414, 762, 817, 857, 1791
in classification of respondents,
568, 664
in single interviewer, 762, 817,
1152, 1903
measurement of, 137, 743,
762, 817, 907, 1068, 1111,
1152, 1478, 1903
reduction of, 137, 1113, 1903

INTERVIEWING
bias in, 78, 355, 490, 930, 933,
1030, 1456

by telephone, 22, 240, 463, 592, 821, 1003, 1555, 1748, 1986
checks on quality of, 420, 553, 729, 853, 1369, 1552, 1938, 2148
commencing the interview, 63, 250, 349, 916, 995, 1304, 1704, 2005
comparison with secret ballot, 184, 1992
cost of, 930, 944, 1399, 1402, 1933, 1935, 1936
effect on subsequent self-completion questionnaire responses, 34
effect on reinterview responses, 490
ethical considerations in, 55, 1704
followed by group discussions, 96, 398
historical development of, 727, 729, 730, 1305
in multilingual communities, 226, 497, 1013
in presence of 'other persons', 1810
in schools, 629
in underdeveloped countries, 1630, 2131
in various research fields, 21, 22, 116, 214, 389, 398, 450, 463, 567, 577, 629, 1026, 1038, 1098, 1132, 1133, 1241, 1304, 1363, 1380, 1381, 1382, 1471, 1599, 1626, 1670, 1728, 1898, 1921, 2032, 2087, 2150
instructions for, 63, 979, 995, 1618, 2113
job analysis of, 553, 729, 730, 1453, 1933, 1944
neutrality of interviewer, 541, 1686, 2021
non-verbal communication in, 209, 1789
on delicate issues, 182, 433, 641, 642, 1026, 1241,
on delicate issues (*contd.*) 1599, 1712, 2032, 2077, 2136, 2150
principles of, 240, 366, 553, 995, 1095, 1802, 1944, 2005
public relations of, 63, 953, 1759, 1760
qualitative, 240, 920, 1728, 1924, 2091
quality of, 482, 930, 1623, 1802
role-playing, 835, 1873
role rehearsal technique, 2
sources of failure, 729, 930, 1712
special categories of respondent, 130, 414, 449, 577, 629, 779, 845, 875, 913, 921, 1018, 1021, 1036, 1052, 1132, 1227, 1241, 1305, 1414, 1613, 1662, 1671, 1704, 1921, 2021, 2073, 2150
strategy, 129, 553, 727, 1017, 1304, 1704
techniques of, 2, 63, 129, 163, 167, 214, 240, 256, 321, 349, 353, 354, 355, 383, 389, 553, 567, 629, 693, 696, 697, 698, 770, 797, 995, 1017, 1133, 1227, 1305, 1480, 1590, 1599, 1618, 1671, 1686, 1704, 1728, 1802, 1916, 2005, 2087, 2136
to obtain 'household' information, 377, 835
to obtain product purchase data, 1059, 1537, 1539
visual aids, 353, 1808
with tape recorder, 204, 640, 821, 853, 1552

See also: INTERVIEW

INTERVIEWING, in various research fields
    in child development research, 629

in community research, 567,
    1098
in employee-attitude research,
    116, 398, 577, 1380, 1381,
    1382
in exploratory research, 2, 727
in financial surveys, 1304
in human relations research,
    2087
in industrial market research,
    21, 22, 1132, 1921
in international public-opinion
    research, 1626
in life-history studies, 389
in longitudinal studies, 463
in motivational research, 75,
    1248, 1710, 2120
in organisational research, 398,
    2087
in qualitative research, 240,
    920, 1133, 1728, 1924,
    2091
in sexual behaviour research,
    1026, 1241, 1599, 2032,
    2150
in social psychological research,
    214, 1133, 1363, 1471
in social research, 1471, 1670,
    2150
in sociometric research, 1898

INTERVIEWING, of special
categories of respondent
    aged respondents, 779, 875,
        921, 1036, 1414
    business executives, 1018,
        1132, 1921
    children, 629, 1305, 2073
    elites, 845, 1021, 1052, 1132
    employees, 577
    farmers, 1671
    Frenchmen, 1227,
    homosexuals, 1241
    married couples, 449, 2150
    medical students, 130
    Members of Congress, 1662
    Negroes, 1613
    psychiatrists, 1704
    students, 414, 913
    Water-Dowsers, 2021

INTOMETER
    used in television audience
        research, 2048

**KELLEY'S REPERTORY GRID
TECHNIQUE** *See* REPERTORY
GRID TECHNIQUE

LATENT DISTANCE ANALYSIS
    and non-scale response
        patterns, 257

**LATENT STRUCTURE
ANALYSIS,** 550, 1632

LEADING QUESTIONS
    and question bias, 315, 783,
        1009, 1470, 1647, 1719
    in non-schedule interviews,
        1647
    in public opinion polling, 229,
        783, 1594
    leading probes, 1647
    valid use of, 555, 1594

LIFE-HISTORIES
    biograms, 1
    computer analysis of, 89
    computer processing of, 89
    in community research, 561
    interviewing for, 389
    methods of analysis, 89, 389
    pause analysis, 1977
    recording of, 389, 1977

LIKERT SCALES *See* LIKERT
SCALING

LIKERT SCALING
    bias, 118
    comparison with
        direction-of-perception
        technique, 572
    comparison with forced-choice
        technique, 118
    comparison with open-choice
        technique, 1079
    comparison with paired
        comparisons technique,
        705, 1079
    comparison with ranking, 1079
    comparison with Thurstone
        scaling, 603, 1243

description of, 448, 1243
determination of neutral point, 1165
in multivariate attitude scaling, 705
in preference testing, 1079
reliability, 118, 550, 1079, 1243
summation technique, 603
validity, 118, 1079, 1243

LINEAR SEGMENTS TECHNIQUE
use in scalogram analysis, 1365

LISTENER RESEARCH *See* RADIO AUDIENCE RESEARCH

LISTENING PANELS *See* PANELS

LOADED QUESTIONS
and prestige, 1702
and question bias, 229, 1009, 1702, 1719
in public opinion polling, 229

LONGITUDINAL STUDIES
data processing, 793, 794, 1676
reinterviews, 463
research design, 793
sampling, 793
secondary data analysis in, 1676
statistical analysis of data, 793, 794, 1676
use of telephone interview, 463

'LOST-LETTER' TECHNIQUE
in public opinion research, 1426, 1427, 2089
validity of, 1427, 2089

LURIA TECHNIQUE, 316

MAIL-BALLOT POLLING
representativeness of respondents, 327, 499
representativeness of response, 185
to measure opinion change, 1448
to predict election results, 185
validity, 185, 327, 1919

MAIL PANELS *See* PANELS

MAIL QUESTIONNAIRES
completion of questions, 682
design, 124, 240, 422, 719, 734, 1000, 1099, 1274, 1769, 1774
layout, 1503
long vs. short, 296, 396, 583, 734, 1391, 1503
multiphasic type, 422
order effects, 673
postcard used as a, 249, 296, 583, 1000, 1099
pretesting of, 1274
structure, 124, 240

See also: MAIL SURVEYS

MAIL SURVEYS
advance letter used in, 718, 952, 1076, 1120, 1235, 1473, 1659, 1769, 1770, 1866
advance telephone call used in, 1866, 2027
advantages of, 240, 742, 1076, 1769
characteristics of non-respondents, 123, 280, 422, 537, 564, 583, 597, 682, 987, 1076, 1281, 1314, 1401, 1503, 1534, 1639, 1669, 1749, 1769, 1926
characteristics of respondents, 337, 396, 422, 564, 583, 597, 670, 742, 1099, 1281, 1503, 1639, 1669, 1692, 1770, 1926, 2019, 2029, 2030
comparison with group testing, 983
comparison with personal interview method, 5, 127, 240, 632, 633, 669, 720, 742, 818, 829, 986, 1213, 1357, 1509, 1514, 2057, 2155
costs, 1473
cover letter, 734, 744, 1037, 1076, 1262, 1274, 1588,

cover letter (*contd.*)
  1659, 1664, 1769, 1816, 1824, 2058
differences between respondents and non-respondents, 114, 123, 422, 564, 583, 597, 740, 742, 818, 987, 1203, 1281, 1314, 1503, 1637, 1639, 1749, 1769, 1871, 1926, 2019, 2029
differences between early and late respondents, 123, 337, 422, 564, 583, 670, 818, 1203, 1493, 1528, 1637, 1673, 1769, 1813, 1871
disadvantages of, 240, 742, 1076
error related to, 439, 1076, 1769
follow-ups, 271, 484, 564, 624, 689, 734, 738, 739, 787, 792, 818, 863, 865, 938, 987, 1120, 1235, 1494, 1503, 1637, 1659, 1673, 1749, 1769, 1770, 1978, 1979
forecasting response, 1664
in industrial market research, 21, 333, 403, 439
in underdeveloped countries, 1205
incentives, 203, 273, 396, 649, 738, 739, 938, 949, 1037, 1076, 1128, 1162, 1235, 1357, 1493, 1503, 1664, 1812, 2158
international, 787
motivation of non-respondents, 422, 537, 564, 597, 1503, 1926
motivation of respondents, 422, 564, 597, 1099, 1207, 1503, 1926
multi-wave, 1120
non-response bias, 114, 123, 337, 422, 564, 583, 624, 667, 670, 671, 672, 682, 723, 725, 818, 897, 958, 987, 1076, 1203, 1314,

non-response bias (*contd.*)
  1401, 1637, 1664, 1749, 1763, 1769, 1813, 1871, 1926, 2175
of special groups of respondents, 439, 537, 1120, 1235, 1770, 1948
patterns of response, 484, 1120, 1159, 1769, 1770, 1978
representativeness of respondents, 271, 327, 330, 422, 499, 538, 564, 583, 742, 1203, 1503, 1582, 1583, 1871, 2029, 2030
representativeness of response, 123, 271, 296, 422, 538, 564, 1203, 1582, 2029
response rate, 76, 123, 203, 271, 273, 280, 296, 330, 396, 403, 422, 442, 484, 537, 564, 583, 624, 648, 649, 689, 718, 719, 734, 738, 739, 744, 792, 818, 863, 865, 938, 949, 950, 952, 987, 1000, 1037, 1076, 1099, 1120, 1128, 1162, 1163, 1203, 1207, 1235, 1262, 1274, 1275, 1391, 1434, 1473, 1493, 1494, 1503, 1588, 1612, 1659, 1664, 1665, 1666, 1669, 1692, 1769, 1770, 1775, 1812, 1816, 1824, 1831, 1866, 1871, 1926, 1948, 1978, 1979, 2027, 2041, 2058, 2158
responses to questions in, 5, 439, 484, 537, 632, 633, 669, 682, 718, 720, 742, 829, 950, 983, 1210, 1314, 1357, 1509, 1514, 1769
sampling procedures for, 624, 1076
speed of questionnaire returns, 422, 484, 564, 583, 718, 1978
types of mailing used in, 422, 792, 863, 865, 1235, 1664, 1769

use of participant reply card, 271, 330
used as a supplement to personal interviews, 815, 818, 1347, 1792
used in advertising research, 852, 1008
used in preference testing, 684, 1213, 1586
used in product testing, 5
used in readership research, 127, 679, 1273, 1390, 1648, 1649, 1865, 1905, 2057, 2155
validity as a method of data collection, 632, 633, 1076 1205, 1213, 1314, 1553, 1769, 1871, 1912, 1978
versus telephone surveys, 22, 240, 986

See also: MAIL QUESTIONNAIRES; MAIL-BALLOT POLLING

MANUAL DATA ANALYSIS
edge-marking, 1971
frequency counts, 1548, 1578
hand counts, 46, 1548, 1578
keysorting, 46
posting, 46
preparation of inventory sheets, 46
sorting questionnaires, 46
tallying, 46
verifying, 46

MARK-SENSING
in data processing, 525, 759, 1058, 1174, 1358, 1784, 1849, 1940
mark-sense cards, 525, 759, 1058, 1174, 1784
optical mark-sensing, 1849, 1940

MARKET SEGMENTATION
application of personality measure to, 643
segmentation techniques, 27, 147, 151, 158, 308, 408, 430, 637, 638, 1291, 1444, 1628, 1855, 1856, 1857

MATCHING
and analysis of covariance, 1952
and biological classification, 27, 147, 151
in ex post facto studies, 745
in observational studies, 434
incomplete matching, 745
matched pairs, 208, 644, 2166
significance of difference between matched groups, 61, 657, 1075
Stable Correlates, 143, 144, 146, 149, 152, 154, 616, 637, 1543
standardization, 1075
to obtain equivalent groups, 644
weighting for, 27
with randomization, 2166

MEASUREMENT ERROR
analysis of, 904, 905
casual approach to, 222, 225
due to interviewer variance, 1151
estimation of, 904, 905, 1151, 2101
in censuses, 593, 905
in enumerative surveys, 593
in panel data, 2101
in public opinion polling 1306
in sample surveys, 905

MEDIA SURVEYS
classification of respondents in, 27, 29, 158, 282, 283

See also: READERSHIP SURVEYS; AUDIENCE RESEARCH TECHNIQUES; POSTER RESEARCH TECHNIQUES

MEDICAL SURVEYS
See: HEALTH SURVEYS

MEMOMOTION STUDIES, 969

MEMORY
and error, 677, 813, 816, 876, 1172, 1328, 1552, 1602, 1767, 1781, 1782

and open questions, 1702
dependent questions, 701, 816, 830, 1872
effect of presence of an audience on, 890, 2176
elimination of reliance on, 584
group, 1566
of advertisements, 539, 630, 631, 799
of behaviour, 506, 584, 799, 915
of interviewer, 1552, 1945
of product purchases, 584, 677
of respondent, 44, 353, 506, 539, 630, 631, 701, 756, 767, 799, 816, 830, 876, 915, 1032, 1566, 1602, 1604, 1702, 1767, 1960, 2003, 2073, 2176
reduction of reliance on, 584
retroactive inhibition, 1328, 2003
selective, 44
stimulation of, 353, 584, 631
tests, 631, 830, 1602, 1604
time duration, 677, 799, 813, 830, 876, 1234, 1604, 1767, 1782, 1945

See also: RECALL

METERS *See* RECORDING METERS

METHOD OF RECIPROCAL AVERAGES
comparison with Guttman scaling, 1496
comparison with Thurstone scaling, 1002

METHODOLOGY
of attitude research, 455, 489, 1331, 1332
of field studies, 2171
of observational studies, 434
of public opinion research, 455, 489, 766, 1222, 1331, 1332, 1688, 2152
of prison research, 660
of survey research, 12, 766, 1026, 1246, 1247, 2062

MONADIC TESTS
comparison with paired comparison technique, 171, 833, 884
for preference testing, 427, 833, 1706
for product testing, 171, 427, 522, 833, 884, 1706

MOTIVATION
of interviewers, 1802, 1925
of non-respondents, 422, 537, 564, 597, 1503, 1926
of respondents, 349, 351, 366, 422, 564, 567, 597, 1207, 1503, 1926
of volunteers, 67, 217, 290, 1695
research techniques, 75, 215, 279, 450, 451, 1177, 1248, 1297, 1575, 1595, 1710, 1711, 1740, 1750, 1751, 1958, 2035, 2066, 2082, 2090, 2092, 2120

MOTIVATION RESEARCH TECHNIQUES
associative interview, 75
focused group interview, 75
historical development of, 450, 1177
in market research, 1750, 1751
limitations of, 215, 279, 451, 1710, 1711, 1958, 2066, 2092
non-directive interviewing, 1248, 1710, 2120
reliability, 279
self-completion questionnaire, 1740
use of projective techniques, 75, 450, 1297, 1595, 1710, 1711, 2066, 2082, 2090, 2120
use of structured techniques, 451, 2035, 2082
validity, 279
value of, 215, 451, 1595, 1710, 1711, 2066, 2090, 2093, 2120

MULTI-COUNTRY SURVEY *See* INTERNATIONAL SURVEY

MULTIDIMENSIONAL SCALING
nonmetric unfolding analysis techniques, 705, 822, 974, 1183

MULTIPLE-CHOICE QUESTION
and guessing by respondent, 30
and question bias, 1719
comparison with dichotomous questions, 782, 858, 1175, 1719
elimination of bias in responses to, 1131
in public opinion polling, 764, 782, 1175, 1719
randomizing error in responses to, 1131

MULTIPLE REGRESSION ANALYSIS
computational procedure, 430, 446, 803, 1198

MULTIVARIATE STATISTICAL ANALYSIS *See* STATISTICAL ANALYSIS OF DATA

NON-COVERAGE
bias due to, 1148
estimation of, 1148

NON-DIRECTIVE INTERVIEW
in human relations research, 2087,
in motivational research, 1248, 1710, 2120
in organisational research, 2087
in qualitative interviewing, 1728
in social research, 321, 1670
interviewing techniques, 167, 321

NON-PROPORTIONAL SAMPLING
comparison with quota sampling, 291
comparison with random sampling, 291
overcoming limitations of, 291

NONRANDOM SAMPLE
in experimental psychology, 598
testing statistical hypotheses with, 598

NON-RESPONDENTS
among volunteers, 1693, 1990
characteristics, 123, 280, 314, 422, 501, 537, 564, 583, 597, 682, 749, 987, 1076, 1281, 1290, 1314, 1401, 1414, 1503, 1523, 1533, 1534, 1639, 1669, 1704, 1749, 1763, 1769, 1793, 1859, 1926
comparison with respondents, 114, 123, 422, 501, 564, 583, 597, 740, 742, 774, 818, 987, 1203, 1281, 1314, 1503, 1533, 1534, 1637, 1639, 1749, 1769, 1871, 1926, 2019, 2029
follow-up of, 114, 501, 564, 586, 624, 738, 739, 865, 938, 987, 1076, 1120, 1235, 1290, 1314, 1637, 1769, 1822, 1978, 1979
in mail surveys, 114, 123, 280, 330, 422, 537, 564, 583, 597, 624, 667, 682, 738, 739, 740, 742, 818, 865, 938, 987, 1076, 1203, 1281, 1314, 1401, 1503, 1534, 1637, 1639, 1669, 1749, 1769, 1871, 1926, 1978, 1979, 2019, 2029
in public opinion polling, 973
motivation, 422, 537, 564, 597, 1503, 1926
'not-at-homes', 117, 267, 601, 612, 973, 1123, 1290, 1587, 1592, 1593, 1705, 1822, 1823
privacy-maintaining mechanisms used by, 1704
techniques for securing interviews with, 191, 501, 1704
to self-completion questionnaires, 314

NON-RESPONDENTS, in mail surveys
- characteristics of, 123, 280, 422, 537, 564, 583, 597, 682, 987, 1076, 1281, 1314, 1401, 1503, 1534, 1639, 1669, 1749, 1769, 1926
- comparison with respondents, 114, 123, 422, 564, 583, 597, 740, 742, 818, 987, 1203, 1281, 1314, 1503, 1534, 1637, 1639, 1749, 1769, 1871, 1926, 2019, 2029
- follow-up of, 114, 564, 624, 738, 739, 938, 987, 1314, 1637, 1769, 1978, 1979
- motivation, 422, 537, 564, 1503, 1926
- sampling of, 114, 624, 738, 739, 938, 1314, 1637
- securing response from, 422, 624, 865, 987, 1769, 1978, 1979

NON-RESPONSE
- and rapport, 976
- bias due to, 72, 114, 117, 123, 212, 267, 299, 314, 330, 337, 422, 501, 529, 531, 564, 583, 612, 624, 650, 667, 670, 671, 672, 681, 682, 683, 723, 725, 733, 818, 897, 910, 937, 958, 971, 973, 987, 1041, 1149, 1203, 1314, 1401, 1414, 1587, 1592, 1637, 1664, 1749, 1763, 1769, 1780, 1793, 1813, 1822, 1871, 1926, 2124, 2125, 2175
- causes, 267, 440, 501, 537, 564, 682, 922, 1290, 1532, 1712, 1793
- effect on survey results, 299, 473, 508, 682, 973
- extent of, 682, 922, 1532
- in financial surveys, 440, 681, 683, 1202, 1457
- in mail surveys, 76, 280, 330, 337, 422, 537, 564, 583, 624, 667, 670, 671, 672, 682, 718, 723, 818, 897, 958, 987, 1203, 1314, 1401, 1637, 1763, 1813, 1831, 1871, 1926, 1978, 1979, 2158
- interviewers as cause of, 440, 1712, 1766, 2109
- methods of allowing for, 508, 588, 612, 650, 958, 1041, 1123, 1584, 1587, 1592, 1593, 1822, 1823
- reduction of, 76, 330, 422, 473, 501, 508, 543, 586, 624, 650, 1041, 1457, 1523, 1822, 1831, 1978, 1979, 2158
- to questions, 682, 718, 976, 1523
- to self-completion questionnaires, 971
- weighting for, 422, 501, 508, 586, 588, 612, 1123, 1201, 1587, 1592, 1593, 1822, 1823

NON-RESPONSE BIAS
- analysis of, 299, 422, 958, 1041, 1414, 1763, 1769, 1793, 1813, 2175
- and recording meters, 733, 937
- control, 1041, 1587, 1822
- detection of, 337, 667, 670, 671, 672, 723, 725, 958, 1041, 1763, 2175
- in continuing panels, 733, 2124, 2125
- in industrial market research, 1041
- in mail surveys, 114, 123, 330, 337, 422, 564, 583, 624, 667, 670, 671, 672, 682, 723, 725, 818, 897, 958, 987, 1076, 1203, 1314, 1401, 1637, 1664, 1749,

in mail surveys (*contd.*)
1763, 1769, 1813, 1871, 1926, 2175
in public opinion polling, 910, 973
in self-completion surveys, 314, 971
reduction, 72, 330, 422, 501, 531, 624, 897, 1041, 1149, 1587, 1592, 1664, 1780, 1822
techniques for estimating, 114, 117, 212, 337, 612, 667, 670, 671, 672, 681, 683, 723, 725, 958, 1203, 1314, 1587, 1592, 1637

NON-RESPONSE BIAS, in mail surveys
analysis of, 422, 958, 1763, 1769, 2175
and characteristics of non-respondents, 123, 422, 564, 583, 682, 1076, 1314, 1401, 1749, 1763, 1769, 1926
and response rate, 330, 422, 564, 583, 818, 987, 1203, 1637, 1664, 1769
detection of, 337, 667, 670, 672, 725, 958, 1763, 2175
early vs. late, 123, 337, 422, 564, 583, 667, 670, 671, 672, 723, 725, 818, 1203, 1401, 1769, 1813, 1871, 2175
estimated by interview follow-up, 818, 1314, 1749
reduction, 422, 624, 897, 1664
techniques for estimating, 114, 337, 667, 670, 672, 725, 958, 1203, 1637

NON-RESPONSE BIAS, in self-completion surveys
and characteristics of non-respondents, 314
and validity of brand market share measurement, 971

NON-SCHEDULE INTERVIEW
use of leading questions in, 1647

NON-STANDARDISED INTERVIEW *See* UNSTRUCTURED INTERVIEW

'NOT-AT-HOME' RESPONDENTS
and public opinion polling, 1290
bias due to, 117, 267, 973, 1587
characteristics of, 973
follow-up of, 586, 1290, 1822
'nights-at-home' formula, 612, 1123, 1592, 1593, 1823
securing response from, 267, 601, 1705

NUMERICAL TAXONOMY, 27, 147, 151, 737, 999, 1063, 1291, 1444, 1853, 1855, 1856, 1857

OBSERVATIONAL TECHNIQUES
activity sampling, 288, 1104
community study method, 636
comparison with survey method, 636
critical incident technique, 468, 710
data form, 240
errors in, 56, 1484
in attitude research, 461, 536
in product testing, 885, 969, 2074, 2075
in sociological research, 636, 2043, 2171
in studies of purchasing behaviour, 969, 2074, 2075
memomotion studies, 969
principles of data collection by, 240, 2043
reliability, 56, 514, 1135, 1484, 1987

See also: PARTICIPANT OBSERVATION

OBSERVER
bias due to, 56, 1102, 1135
reliability, 1484
training of, 56, 1645

OBSERVER BIAS, 56, 1102, 1135

OPEN QUESTIONS
and interviewer bias, 328, 664, 704, 1727, 1790, 1791
comparison with checklist, 153
comparison with closed question, 335, 556, 1256, 1423, 1558, 1616, 1719, 1797, 1806
comparison with dichotomous question, 645, 1719
in intensity measurement, 1806
in public opinion polling, 334, 335, 645, 693, 765, 1701, 1719, 1790
influence on responses, 556, 1719
validity, 1558, 1797
when to use, 349, 1558

OPEN RESPONSES
accuracy of, 1702
coding of, 751, 859, 918, 920, 2151, 2154
content analysis of, 66, 1771, 1887, 1939
fullness of, 693, 1558, 2025

OPINION QUESTIONS
biased, 490
commitment bias, 490
oversimplification, 490
preamble bias, 490
responses to, 115, 227, 453, 490, 779, 817, 1152, 1550, 1594, 1791
salience bias, 490, 1477, 1550
topical bias, 490, 1550

See also: POLLING QUESTIONS

ORDER EFFECTS
and recall, 1950
and the semantic differential, 428, 1270
in check lists, 338, 673, 1131

in Guttman scales, 948
in paired comparisons, 523, 1707, 2084
in public opinion polling, 1719
in rating scales, 160, 576, 1271, 1381, 1624
in taste tests, 192
in the National Readership Survey, 6, 155, 476, 965, 1787
on interview schedules, 269
on mail questionnaires, 673
on self-completion questionnaires, 1477
rotation to reduce, 6, 155, 1131, 1787

OVER-CLAIMING *See* OVER-REPORTING

OVER-REPORTING
error due to, 332, 421, 879, 1124, 1142, 1143, 1269, 1404, 1405, 1485, 1536, 1539, 1648, 1965, 1976
of product purchases, 571, 1269, 1536, 1539
over-claiming by respondent, 155, 332, 421, 571, 879, 1142, 1269, 1404, 1405, 1485, 1536, 1648, 1765, 1976

PAIRED COMPARISONS TECHNIQUE
and Gestalt theory, 2013
and Guilford Short Cut scaling, 2142
and response styles, 2068
and Thurstone scaling, 2142
as an attitude research method, 448, 573, 705, 827, 866, 975, 1079, 1103, 1827, 2142
coefficient of agreement used with, 91
comparison with correlational scaling, 1827
comparison with Likert technique, 705, 1079

comparison with monadic
tests, 171, 833, 884
comparison with open-choice
technique, 1079
comparison with ranking, 1079
comparison with successive
intervals technique, 1827,
1828
data processing, 1119
fatigue effects, 2084
for ranked data, 438, 448,
1854
in multivariate attitude scaling,
705
in preference testing, 91, 242,
427, 520, 521, 522, 523,
570, 684, 692, 833, 834,
1079, 1515, 1678, 1706,
1981, 1989
in product testing, 91, 171,
242, 418, 427, 448, 520,
521, 522, 523, 570, 833,
834, 884, 1542, 1678,
1706, 1981, 1989
in taste-testing, 427, 684, 833,
834, 1678
limitations of, 242, 1981
matrices, 438
neutral responses, 570, 1515,
1706
order effects, 523, 1707, 2084
preference distribution
analysis, 521
reliability, 975, 1079
round-robin design, 1542
'side-by-side', 573
used in interviewer
performance evaluation, 190

PANEL BIAS
and length of membership,
610, 675, 1210, 1211,
1451, 1525, 1731
and number of items recorded,
610
due to exaggeration in
purchase recall, 610, 675,
1124
due to increased accuracy of
recall, 675
due to increased respondent
interest, 395
due to non-response, 733, 937,
2124, 2125
due to preparation for
anticipated retest, 395
due to unrepresentativeness of
panel members, 789, 977
due to respondent
conditioning, 789, 977,
1124, 1525
due to selective mortality,
675
due to volunteering, 1210,
1211
in continuing panels, 309, 675,
1731, 2124
running-in effect, 456

PANELS
and accuracy of purchase
recall, 610, 668, 675, 977,
1124
and accuracy of purchase
recording, 392, 977, 1238,
1536, 1931, 1932
B.B.C., 1817, 1818, 1819
bias, 309, 375, 395, 456,
610, 675, 733, 789, 937,
977, 1124, 1210, 1211,
1451, 1525, 1731, 1910,
2124, 2125
comparison with independent
matched samples, 309, 609,
1783
comparison with other
methods of consumer
purchase measurement, 60,
121, 1514, 1536, 1537,
1910
comparison with personal
interview, 5, 1210, 1509,
1514, 1537, 1932
comparison with successive
samples, 795
consumer, 42, 60, 310, 392,
516, 610, 668, 675, 681,
683, 711, 768, 977, 1124,
1218, 1238, 1451, 1467,
1502, 1514, 1525, 1540,

consumer (*contd.*)
  1541, 1677, 1776, 1786, 1910, 1911, 1931, 1932, 2024, 2052, 2147
continuing, 309, 391, 392, 456, 610, 668, 675, 680, 733, 769, 1218, 1502, 1525, 1663, 1677, 1731, 1786, 1910, 1911, 1931, 1932, 2024, 2124, 2125, 2130, 2147
controls, 977, 1210
errors in data from, 121, 1124, 1306, 1931, 1932, 2101
housewife, 392, 1536, 1776, 2147
length of membership, 121, 610, 675, 1210, 1211, 1218, 1451, 1467, 1525, 1731
length of reporting period, 310, 392, 668, 1112, 1124, 1238, 1786
listener, 1817
mail, 5, 392, 837, 1099, 1112, 1509, 1514, 1731, 1910, 1911
mortality, 289, 675, 908, 977, 1210, 1910, 1911
obtaining cooperation of, 42, 516, 977, 1210, 1218, 1819, 2024
operating, 42, 309, 516, 977, 1210, 1218, 1467, 1502, 1615, 1776, 2024
payment, 1502, 1932
product testing, 5, 611, 711, 837, 1615, 1747, 1776
reliability of data from, 610, 611, 617, 619, 668, 675, 680, 681, 683, 977, 1210, 1306, 1509, 1783, 1910, 1932, 2130
representativeness of, 309, 733, 789, 937, 977, 1210, 1819
rotation of membership, 1818
running-in period, 459
selection of, 42, 121, 392, 1210, 1218, 1467, 1502, 1747, 1819

self-completion questionnaire used by, 1210
sensory, 611, 839, 1615, 1747, 1776
short-term, 121, 1514
size, 1210
successive partial replacement of, 309
training of, 42, 1747, 1932
use of incentives to respond, 121, 977, 1112, 1210, 1910, 1911
used in advertising effectiveness measurement, 540, 1212, 1541
used in attitude research, 540, 788, 789, 1663, 1783
used in audience research, 310, 456, 459, 617, 618, 733, 837, 908, 937, 1065, 1817, 1818, 1819, 1877, 1999
used in before-and-after studies, 609, 1783
used in brand share prediction, 108, 1540, 1541, 1932, 2147
used in consumer research, 42, 121, 289, 309, 392, 516, 680, 768, 1124, 1218, 1451, 1467, 1502, 1514, 1525, 1537, 1677, 1776, 1786, 1910, 1911, 1931, 1932, 2024, 2147
used in effects measurement, 609, 1212
used in financial surveys, 680, 681, 683, 1112, 1124
used in measuring purchasing consistency, 289, 310, 1124 1238, 1451, 1467, 1786
used in measuring TV viewing, 310, 456, 733, 1065, 1819
used in public opinion research, 788, 789, 795, 967, 1210, 1212, 1216, 1306, 1663, 1877
used in readership research, 28, 619, 908, 1065, 1066, 1538, 1842
used in sociological research, 789, 1216

validity of use, 619, 937, 977, 1212, 1216, 1509, 1514, 2130
viewer, 310, 459, 617, 618, 733, 937, 1818, 1819, 1999

PARTICIPANT OBSERVATION TECHNIQUE
analysis of material from, 131
comparison with interview, 132, 133, 1987
formalization of procedures in, 131, 1761
in action research, 245
in community studies, 989, 1159, 1417
interview-conversation, 245
language problems, 132
recording of data, 1408
reliability, 1987
role of participant observer, 1276, 1490, 1650, 1761, 2017
validity, 1159, 1490, 2017, 2171

PAYMENT
bonuses, 1194, 1369
of interviewer, 48, 930, 944, 1194, 1369, 1766, 1850, 1933, 1936, 2143
of panel members, 1502, 1932
of respondent, 930, 1112, 1932

PAUSE ANALYSIS
of life histories, 1977

PERSONAL INTERVIEW RESPONSES
and scalogram analysis, 1318
comparison with diaries, 281, 1112, 1204, 1536, 1537, 1932
comparison with mail survey responses, 5, 127, 669, 720, 742, 829, 1509, 1514, 2057, 2155
comparison with panel responses, 5, 1509, 1537, 1932
comparison with secret ballot responses, 1107, 1992
comparison with self-completion questionnaire responses, 33, 1163, 1318, 1423, 1480, 1935, 2055
comparison with telephone interview responses, 1202, 1513
reliability, 92, 390, 677, 1420, 1509, 1531, 2006, 2083, 2167
validity, 92, 1101, 1231, 1547

PERSONAL INTERVIEW ROSTER METHOD See AIDED RECALL

'PHONY' INTERVIEW, 205

PILOTING
and reduction of error, 159
functions of, 233
methods of, 1313
of questionnaires, 159, 233

PLANNING STUDIES, for audience research
for policy development, 145, 148
for programme development, 145, 148

POLLING See PUBLIC OPINION POLLING

POLLING QUESTIONS
and interviewer bias, 328, 704, 1084, 1085, 1790, 1884, 2054, 2115
and prediction of poll results, 232, 234, 1867
bandwagon effects, 460
battery of, 1466
biased, 229, 236, 328, 359, 490, 764, 1411, 1446, 1886, 1927
'big name' effect, 230, 359
checklist, 1256
commitment bias, 490
dichotomous vs. multiple-choice, 645, 1175

'end' effect, 1446
form of, 232, 236, 328, 335, 361, 645, 764, 1256, 1446, 1702, 1867, 1884
free-answer, 334, 335
in personal interviews, 184
in secret ballot, 184, 1992
leading, 229, 783, 1594
loaded, 229
open vs. closed response, 335, 1256
oversimplification, 490
'personalization' of questions, 229, 1550
prestige effects, 453, 764, 1024, 1992
pretesting, 1155, 1507, 1878
reality of topic to respondent, 962
respondent interpretation of, 183, 361, 503, 990, 991
respondent understanding of, 183, 361, 503, 990, 991, 1506, 1554, 1961
responses to, 184, 227, 229, 231, 232, 234, 334, 335, 453, 490, 500, 693, 704, 782, 990, 991, 1024, 1084, 1085, 1256, 1446, 1466, 1506, 1550, 1716, 1719, 1867, 1884, 1886, 1919, 1927, 2076, 2115, 2161, 2174
structure of, 234
topical bias, 490
using 'stereotypes', 453, 764, 1411
validity of 236, 453, 990, 991, 1083
wording of, 14, 183, 227, 228, 229, 230, 232, 234, 236, 328, 335, 359, 361, 453, 764, 783, 1155, 1411, 1446, 1506, 1554, 1594, 1626, 1680, 1681, 1702, 1716, 1867, 1886, 1927, 1961, 2076

See also: OPINION QUESTIONS

POLLS *See* PUBLIC OPINION POLLING

POSTAL QUESTIONNAIRES *See* MAIL QUESTIONNAIRES

POSTAL SURVEYS *See* MAIL SURVEYS

POSTER RESEARCH TECHNIQUES, 206, 457, 466, 467

POST-TESTING
of advertisements, 732, 1061

PRECODING
effect on responses, 1882
of questionnaires, 46, 647, 920, 1058, 1193, 1423, 2145
of questions, 46, 569, 920, 1193, 1423, 1882

PREDICTION TECHNIQUES
constructing criminological prediction tables, 275, 2102
design of prediction surveys, 1070, 1192
for brand share prediction, 108, 1540, 1541
for predicting consumer behaviour, 4, 69, 1038, 1070, 1569, 1730
for predicting interviewer success, 70
for predicting job performance, 116
for predicting opinions, 549, 1192
for predicting product preferences, 326, 1565, 1572
statistical analysis techniques, 3, 146, 147, 151, 308, 430, 862, 1444, 1730, 1900, 2102

PREFERENCE TESTING TECHNIQUES
comparison of various techniques, 380, 1079
components analysis, 692
experimental design, 326, 843, 1954
factor analysis, 1583

for radio program preferences, 590, 773
for taste preference, 91, 192, 684, 711, 833, 834, 843, 844, 1583, 1678, 1747, 1757, 1954
in-theatre testing, 306
Likert scaling, 1079
mail survey, 684, 1213, 1586
marginal preference model, 186, 187
memomotion studies, 969
monadic testing, 427, 833, 1706
no preference responses, 570, 1515, 1706
nonmetric unfolding analysis, 822, 974
open-choice techniques, 1079
paired comparisons, 91, 242, 427, 520, 521, 522, 523, 570, 684, 692, 833, 834, 1079, 1515, 1678, 1706, 1981, 1989
panels, 711, 1747
prediction techniques, 326, 1565, 1572
ranking methods, 590, 692, 1079, 1179, 1579
rating scales, 169, 692, 1079, 1640, 1706, 1746, 1805
reliability, 1079
repeated exposure, 1179
response set, 1757
validity, 1079
verbal vs. pictorial techniques, 2063

PRE-EXPERIMENTAL RESEARCH DESIGNS
one-group pretest-post-test design, 98, 341
one-shot case study, 98, 341
sources of invalidity in, 341
static group comparison, 98, 341

PRESENTATION, of research results, 1387, 2004, 2121

PRESTIGE
and loaded questions, 1702
bias, 58, 453, 764, 1024, 1293, 1440, 1702, 1719, 1724, 1992
rating of occupations, 867
-seeking by respondent, 58, 332, 453, 565, 1024, 1171, 1293, 1440, 1724

PRE TESTING
and reduction of bias, 1421
and reduction of error, 159, 1507
in audience research, 837, 1253, 1254, 1814
in communications research, 372
in public opinion polling, 228, 1155, 1507, 1878
methods of, 1061, 1155, 1253, 1254, 1611, 1814, 1830, 2023
of advertisements, 107, 135, 159, 295, 357, 732, 842, 1061, 1181, 1253, 1254, 1278, 1279, 1355, 1356, 1437, 1438, 1521, 1527, 1611, 1814, 1896, 2023
of questionnaires, 228, 349, 1039, 1274, 1371, 1830
of questions, 228, 1136, 1155, 1421, 1507, 1878
pretest sensitization, 395, 885, 1195, 1196, 1505, 1598
reasons for, 349, 1611, 1687

PRICE STUDIES
shopping techniques, 1069

PRINCIPAL COMPONENTS ANALYSIS *See* **COMPONENTS ANALYSIS**

PROBABILITY SAMPLING
advantages, 900, 1780, 1902
comparison with judgment sampling, 530
comparison with quota sampling, 893, 900
cost, 893, 900, 1902, 2118
effect of failure to make call-backs, 501, 2118
effects of substitutions, 893, 1902, 2040

in public opinion polling, 893, 1280, 2118, 2129
interviewer errors in, 266, 267, 1902
limitations, 893, 1229, 1780, 1902
sources of bias in, 1280, 1793, 2118
weighting for non-response, 501, 1587

PROBING
clarifying probes, 63, 349, 1756
direction of, 993
exploratory probes, 63
leading, 1647
non-leading, 349, 1647, 1756
techniques, 2136

PRODUCT PURCHASE MEASUREMENT
consumer surveys, 591, 1677
diaries, 1536
direct observation, 969, 2074, 2075
locating product purchases, 1573, 2173
measuring brand last bought, 591, 1046, 1047, 1142
measuring impulse buying, 1598
measuring purchase consistency, 289, 310, 1070, 1124, 1142, 1238, 1451, 1467, 1536, 1786
measuring purchase intentions, 69, 784, 1038, 1569
measuring purchase probability, 784, 1038, 1070
panels, 289, 310, 392, 1467, 1502, 1536, 1537, 1677, 1931, 1932
personal interview, 1059, 1537, 1539
recall, 222, 571, 610, 675, 677, 784, 851, 977, 1043, 1046, 1047, 1124, 1269, 1536, 1625, 1932
reporting error, 281, 571, 677,

reporting error (*contd.*) 851, 1046, 1047, 1124, 1142, 1269, 1536, 1539, 1625, 1931, 1932

PRODUCT TESTING PANELS
See PANELS

PRODUCT TESTING TECHNIQUES
and 'halo' effect, 189
blind testing, 522, 1981, 2149
buying-interest measurement, 437, 784, 847, 1549
combination of data collection methods, 1557
discrimination testing, 839, 1747
effect of variability of product, 1996
home placement, 418, 1557, 1981
mail surveys, 5
monadic tests, 171, 427, 522, 833, 884, 1706
observational techniques, 885
open testing, 2149
paired comparisons technique, 91, 171, 242, 418, 427, 448, 520, 521, 522, 523, 570, 833, 834, 884, 1542, 1678, 1706, 1981, 1989
panels, 5, 611, 711, 837, 1615, 1747, 1776
preference testing, 91, 192, 326, 427, 520, 521, 570, 590, 692, 711, 833, 834, 1565, 1579, 1583, 1678, 1706, 1746, 1747, 1757, 1805, 1954, 1972, 1981, 1989, 2063
projective techniques, 717
pseudo store, 1549
rating scales, 5, 297, 448, 522, 611, 1583, 1706, 1746, 1805
repertory grid technique, 752
semantic differential scaling, 522, 752, 1674, 2098
single placement test, 418
staggered test, 522

taste-testing, 91, 192, 427, 590, 611, 684, 711, 833, 834, 839, 843, 844, 849, 850, 1583, 1615, 1678, 1747, 1757, 1776, 1954, 1972
triadic tests, 522, 843, 849, 850, 1678
used by consumer associations, 287

PROFILE ANALYSIS
absolute profiles in, 775
and nosological groups, 775
characteristic permutation, 775
classification of individuals 775, 1510
ordinal profiles in, 775

PROJECTIVE TECHNIQUES
and illiterate respondents, 566
cartoon techniques, 641, 642, 1097, 1294, 1733, 1734, 2077, 2177
comparison with guided interview, 1685
free association techniques, 717
in attitude research, 317, 338, 432, 451, 461, 536, 770, 781, 809, 831, 880, 1097, 1250, 1294, 1297, 1351, 1619, 1671, 1711, 1733, 1737, 1876, 2014, 2079, 2082
in consumer surveys, 717, 770, 880, 1876, 2177
in cross-cultural research, 566, 1723
in exploratory research, 2, 451
in motivational research, 75, 450, 1297, 1595, 1710, 1711, 2066, 2082, 2090, 2120
in product testing, 717
in public opinion research, 432, 2012
in sociological research, 1685
picture frustration, 2177
reliability, 1733, 1734
play techniques, 770, 2079
role rehearsal technique, 2

role-playing, 835, 880, 1873, 2079
Rorschach ink blot test, 1388, 1685
sentence completion, 317, 781, 1250, 1351, 1723
shopping list test, 880
stimulus pictures, 809, 1619, 1671, 1733, 1876
Thematic Apperception Test, 1619, 1685, 2177
validity, 566, 1351, 1595, 1671, 1685, 1733, 1734, 1872, 1873, 1876, 2162
verbal, 831, 2079
visual, 641, 642, 809, 831, 1178, 1297, 1619, 1671, 1733, 1734, 1876, 2077, 2079
weaknesses of, 1685
word association test, 1294, 2012

PROMPTING
and aided recall cards, 63, 328, 353, 841, 1808

PUBLIC OPINION POLLING
and interviewer bias, 231, 328, 704, 856, 1029, 1084, 1085, 1445, 1727, 1884, 2054, 2115, 2161
and interviewer cheating, 487, 1919, 1942
bandwagon effect, 460, 783, 1082
by international surveys, 14, 1621, 1626
by mail-ballot, 185, 327, 499, 1448, 1919
by self-completion questionnaire, 1226, 2126
by telephone interviews, 821
classification of respondents, 360, 1874
comparison of various polls, 238, 363, 498, 499, 502, 645, 1082, 1090, 1175
dichotomous vs. open question, 645, 765, 782, 1175

effect of advance letter on, 1508
effect of previous interview on re-interview responses, 490, 1212
ethics of, 252, 1264, 1474
form of question, 232, 234, 236, 328, 334, 335, 361, 645, 693, 764, 765, 1256, 1446, 1701, 1702, 1719, 1790, 1867, 1884
in developing countries, 210, 1715
interpretation of polls, 417, 1083, 1888
of experts, 1169
predictive accuracy of, 232, 234, 329, 491, 498, 499, 500, 562, 691, 806, 828, 1082, 1089, 1090, 1247, 1570, 1680, 1682, 1867
pretesting of, 228, 1155, 1507, 1878
question design, 234, 236, 359, 361, 1463, 1466, 1719, 1886
questionnaire design, 582, 765, 1260, 1466, 1719, 1886
readability of question, 1155, 1506
reliability, 547, 691, 1082, 1089, 1226, 1259, 1306, 1331, 1332, 2038, 2104
sampling, 362, 893, 1280, 1407, 1626, 1680, 2038, 2104, 2118, 2129
secret ballot, 184, 479, 828, 1992
sources of bias in, 229, 236, 490, 492, 498, 499, 502, 678, 806, 856, 910, 973, 1024, 1029, 1089, 1090, 1168, 1247, 1411, 1445, 1522, 1661, 1717, 1719, 1790, 1886, 1992, 2030, 2054, 2115, 2161
sources of error in, 236, 238, 329, 453, 854, 856, 1089, 1090, 1247, 1306

to measure intensity of opinion, 1022, 1086, 1175, 1516
use of multiple-choice question, 229, 764, 782, 1175, 1719
use of open question, 334, 645, 693, 1719
use of battery of questions, 1463, 1466
validity, 229, 234, 236, 247, 327, 329, 486, 489, 491, 562, 688, 691, 783, 828, 1082, 1083, 1087, 1088, 1089, 1090, 1247, 1259, 1331, 1332, 1465, 1642, 1651, 1715, 2115
wording of questions, 14, 183, 227, 228, 229, 230, 232, 234, 236, 328, 335, 359, 361, 453, 490, 764, 783, 1155, 1411, 1446, 1506, 1554, 1594, 1626, 1680, 1681, 1702, 1716, 1719, 1867, 1886, 1927, 1961, 2076

PUBLIC OPINION POLLS *See* PUBLIC OPINION POLLING

PUBLIC OPINION RESEARCH TECHNIQUES
and qualitative evaluation of opinions, 940, 1516
commercial opinion polls, 582, 1261, 1570, 1571
community background studies, 1025
ethical standards for, 252, 329, 946, 1223
experimental research design, 400
for predicting election results, 185, 238, 327, 329, 421, 491, 500, 691, 828, 926, 1082, 1086, 1089, 1090, 1306, 1426, 1427, 1570, 1651, 1682, 1917, 2089
history of, 1261, 1892
intensity analysis, 715
'lost-letter' technique, 1426, 1427, 2089

opinion-change measurement, 1195, 1196, 1214, 1275, 1448, 1682
opinion-intensity measurement, 229, 429, 788, 795, 872, 1022, 1086, 1175, 1292, 1312, 1483, 1516
panels, 788, 789, 795, 967, 1210, 1212, 1216, 1306, 1663, 1877
projective techniques, 432, 2012
public opinion polling, 14, 183, 184, 185, 210, 227, 228, 229, 230, 231, 232, 234, 236, 238, 247, 252, 327, 328, 329, 334, 335, 359, 361, 362, 363, 417, 453, 460, 479, 486, 487, 489, 490, 491, 492, 498, 499, 500, 502, 547, 562, 582, 645, 678, 688, 691, 693, 704, 764, 765, 782, 783, 806, 821, 828, 854, 856, 893, 910, 1022, 1029, 1082, 1083, 1084, 1085, 1086, 1087, 1088, 1089, 1090, 1155, 1168, 1169, 1175, 1212, 1226, 1247, 1256, 1259, 1260, 1264, 1280, 1303, 1306, 1331, 1332, 1407, 1411, 1445, 1446, 1448, 1463, 1465, 1466, 1474, 1506, 1507, 1508, 1516, 1522, 1554, 1570, 1594, 1621, 1626, 1642, 1651, 1661, 1680, 1681, 1682, 1701, 1702, 1715, 1716, 1719, 1727, 1790, 1867, 1874, 1878, 1884, 1886, 1888, 1919, 1927, 1961, 1992, 2038, 2054, 2076, 2104, 2115, 2118, 2126, 2129, 2161
public opinion surveys, 14, 344, 645, 910, 940, 1031, 1554, 1621, 1626, 2038
questionnaires, 573, 765, 1226
reliability, 547, 691, 1082,

reliability (*contd.*) 1089, 1226, 1259, 1306, 1331, 1332, 2038, 2104
scale analysis, 715
secondary data analysis, 1657
successive-samples, 795
'survey-by-radio', 2126
'survey-by-television' technique, 1877
telephone interview, 821
validity, 229, 234, 236, 247, 327, 329, 421, 486, 489, 491, 562, 688, 691, 783, 828, 925, 940, 1082, 1083, 1087, 1088, 1089, 1090, 1247, 1259, 1331, 1332, 1465, 1642, 1651, 1715, 2089, 2115
voting behaviour studies, 38, 421, 805, 925, 1306, 1917

PUBLIC OPINION SURVEYS
comparability of questions, 645
international, 14, 344, 1031, 1621, 1626
interview refusals in, 910
non-response bias, 910
reliability, 2038
sources of bias in, 940
wording of questions, 1554

See also: PUBLIC OPINION POLLING

PUNCHED CARDS
and paired comparisons technique, 1119
and sampling bias correction, 2015
coding on, 195
detecting cards out of sequence, 1240
edge-punched, 1228, 1512, 1971, 2037
Hollerith, 1358
mark-sense, 525, 759, 1058, 1358
multi-punching, 174, 1094, 1108
punching of, 46, 431, 528, 1108, 1220, 1358, 1988

reproducing of, 1108, 1119
sorting of, 46, 1119, 1358
verifying of, 46, 527, 1220, 1551, 1988
written data on, 195

Q-TECHNIQUE, in factor analysis, 968, 1040, 1063, 1482, 1745, 1835, 1894, 1895, 2159

QUALITATIVE INTERVIEWING
advantages of, 240, 1728
analysis of material from, 920, 2091
coding of material from, 859, 920, 1108, 2140
comparison with other methods of data collection, 240
form of interview used, 1728
interview guide for, 240
limitations of, 240, 1728
techniques, 240, 1728
training interviews, 1728, 1924

QUASI-EXPERIMENTAL RESEARCH DESIGNS
equivalent materials design, 98
equivalent time sample design, 98
multiple time-series design, 98
non-equivalent control design space, 98
separate sample pretest-post-test, 98
sources of invalidity in, 98
time-series experiment, 98

QUESTION
actuality of, 962
ambiguous, 244, 361, 639, 804, 1095, 1263, 1719, 2076
attitude, 1357, 1381, 1545, 2055, 2068
battery, 1463, 1466
bias due to, 17, 227, 229, 236, 269, 315, 328, 359, 361, 453, 490, 571, 764, 783, 858, 930, 941, 950, 1009, 1131, 1256, 1263, 1293, 1411, 1421, 1424, 1446,

bias due to (*contd.*)
1470, 1647, 1702, 1716, 1719, 1881, 1886, 1927
card, 328
categorical, 328
checklist, 153, 339, 673, 1256, 1701, 1702
classification, 95, 1219, 2141
closed, 349, 556, 777, 1208, 1423, 1466, 1558, 1616, 1719, 1756, 1797, 1806
comprehensibility, 361, 729, 1554, 1961
design, 234, 235, 236, 240, 270, 349, 355, 359, 361, 743, 1009, 1095, 1136, 1208, 1305, 1421, 1463, 1466, 1701, 1719, 1886
dichotomous, 328, 645, 765, 777, 782, 858, 1175, 1719
factual, 729, 1701
filter, 765, 1193
fixed-alternative, 777, 1423, 1719
form of, 153, 232, 234, 236, 328, 334, 335, 361, 556, 645, 664, 729, 743, 764, 858, 1256, 1263, 1264, 1381, 1423, 1446, 1616, 1702, 1719, 1790, 1867, 1884, 2068, 2081
free-answer, 1423, 1702, 1719, 1882
grouping of related, 1139, 1193, 1424, 1719
idea-centred, 1136
in public opinion polling, 14, 228, 229, 232, 234, 236, 334, 335, 359, 361, 453, 503, 582, 645, 764, 765, 783, 1155, 1256, 1446, 1463, 1554, 1594, 1626, 1680, 1681, 1716, 1719, 1867, 1884, 1961, 2076
income, 1115
indirect, 2088
leading, 229, 315, 555, 783, 1009, 1470, 1594, 1647, 1719
length, 361, 1377, 1961

loaded, 229, 1009, 1702, 1719
meaningless, 361, 1554
memory dependent, 701, 816, 830, 1872
multiple-choice, 30, 328, 764, 782, 858, 1131, 1175, 1719
non-response to, 682, 718, 976, 1523
on racial issues, 62
on sensitive issues, 119, 182, 641, 642, 1026, 1163, 2077
open, 153, 328, 334, 335, 349, 556, 645, 664, 693, 704, 765, 1423, 1558, 1616, 1701, 1702, 1719, 1727, 1790, 1791, 1797, 1806, 2025
opinion, 227, 453, 490, 779, 817, 1477, 1550, 1594
opinion-forming, 1594, 1886
order, 235, 269, 349, 369, 673, 777, 847, 964, 1193, 1424, 1477, 1719
'phony', 40, 1307
polling, 14, 183, 184, 229, 230, 232, 234, 236, 328, 334, 335, 359, 361, 453, 460, 490, 500, 503, 645, 693, 704, 764, 783, 962, 990, 991, 1024, 1083, 1084, 1085, 1155, 1175, 1256, 1411, 1446, 1463, 1466, 1506, 1507, 1550, 1594, 1680, 1681, 1702, 1716, 1719, 1790, 1841, 1867, 1878, 1884, 1886, 1919, 1927, 1961, 1992, 2054, 2076, 2115, 2161, 2174
precoded, 46, 569, 920, 1193, 1423, 1882
pretesting, 228, 1136, 1155, 1421, 1507, 1878
probing, 1647
projective, 537, 1294, 1876
readability level of, 1155, 1506, 1961
reliability of, 232, 390, 830, 1136, 1867
retrospective, 701, 2081

respondent interpretation of, 19, 95, 159, 183, 226, 334, 361, 439, 503, 639, 676, 693, 804, 1507, 1701, 1719, 1860
respondent understanding of, 19, 162, 183, 226, 228, 230, 334, 335, 361, 390, 439, 503, 639, 651, 676, 693, 804, 875, 990, 991, 1155, 1186, 1267, 1268, 1397, 1421, 1506, 1550, 1554, 1621, 1626, 1701, 1719, 1860, 1961
responses to, 5, 10, 17, 33, 34, 37, 40, 59, 62, 66, 84, 85, 92, 93, 94, 113, 138, 142, 157, 161, 172, 184, 194, 227, 229, 231, 232, 234, 260, 261, 264, 266, 269, 285, 301, 304, 311, 332, 334, 335, 336, 339, 351, 352, 353, 354, 359, 361, 369, 377, 389, 390, 393, 415, 421, 422, 439, 452, 453, 470, 482, 490, 494, 496, 504, 531, 537, 546, 554, 556, 558, 560, 565, 570, 571, 577, 578, 620, 625, 632, 633, 642, 652, 666, 669, 674, 677, 678, 681, 682, 683, 693, 701, 702, 704, 709, 718, 720, 750, 751, 777, 778, 779, 782, 785, 786, 791, 801, 807, 816, 817, 829, 830, 836, 847, 851, 856, 858, 859, 876, 879, 886, 892, 904, 907, 914, 941, 942, 950, 966, 976, 983, 990, 991, 995, 1004, 1009, 1024, 1026, 1036, 1043, 1058, 1084, 1101, 1107, 1131, 1142, 1146, 1155, 1157, 1161, 1163, 1171, 1173, 1185, 1202, 1210, 1212, 1219, 1231, 1233, 1255, 1256, 1269, 1293, 1296, 1307, 1314, 1317, 1337, 1338, 1346, 1353, 1357,

responses to (*contd.*)
    1377, 1378, 1379, 1381,
    1385, 1392, 1393, 1394,
    1395, 1396, 1397, 1405,
    1420, 1423, 1440, 1446,
    1466, 1470, 1477, 1480,
    1481, 1485, 1487, 1488,
    1500, 1504, 1506, 1508,
    1509, 1513, 1514, 1515,
    1519, 1520, 1522, 1531,
    1536, 1537, 1547, 1550,
    1558, 1559, 1563, 1577,
    1594, 1600, 1607, 1617,
    1618, 1620, 1625, 1633,
    1661, 1690, 1691, 1701,
    1702, 1706, 1716, 1719,
    1727, 1732, 1735, 1744,
    1748, 1754, 1756, 1769,
    1782, 1798, 1806, 1815,
    1836, 1838, 1843, 1848,
    1867, 1872, 1881, 1882,
    1883, 1884, 1886, 1916,
    1919, 1929, 1931, 1932,
    1935, 1945, 1965, 1969,
    1992, 2005, 2006, 2028,
    2032, 2044, 2055, 2060,
    2061, 2068, 2069, 2070,
    2076, 2077, 2081, 2083,
    2086, 2095, 2096, 2106,
    2115, 2116, 2123, 2124,
    2133, 2141, 2151, 2154,
    2161, 2167, 2170, 2174
scaling, 676, 858, 1357, 1881
self-evaluation, 1381, 1929, 2055
self-report, 352, 415, 1185, 1929
suggestion in, 58, 315, 453, 1009, 1293, 1421, 1470, 1594, 1886
unanswerable, 1701
validity, 232, 234, 236, 264, 453, 701, 830, 990, 991, 1083, 1558, 1756, 1797, 1867, 1876, 2133
variable, 743, 1294
verbose, 1095
wording of, 14, 17, 19, 58, 73, 95, 119, 138, 183, 227, 228, 229, 230, 232, 234,

wording of (*contd.*)
    235, 236, 240, 244, 315,
    328, 335, 349, 359, 361,
    453, 470, 503, 571, 651,
    676, 743, 764, 783, 785,
    804, 816, 851, 907, 941,
    950, 966, 1000, 1009, 1095,
    1155, 1263, 1293, 1305,
    1381, 1411, 1421, 1446,
    1470, 1506, 1550, 1554,
    1594, 1621, 1626, 1680,
    1681, 1701, 1702, 1716,
    1719, 1867, 1881, 1886,
    1961, 1969, 2076, 2081

QUESTION BIAS
due to question order, 269, 1424, 1719
in dichotomous questions, 858, 930, 1719
in leading questions, 315, 783, 1009, 1470, 1647, 1719
in loaded questions, 229, 1009, 1702, 1719
in opinion questions, 453, 490
in polling questions, 227, 229, 236, 328, 359, 361, 453, 490, 783, 1411, 1446, 1702, 1716, 1719, 1886, 1927
in question form, 236, 328, 361, 764, 858, 1256, 1263, 1446, 1702, 1719,
in question wording, 17, 227, 229, 236, 315, 328, 359, 361, 453, 571, 764, 783, 941, 950, 1009, 1263, 1293, 1411, 1446, 1470, 1702, 1716, 1719, 1881, 1886, 1927
reduction of, 1131, 1421, 1927

QUESTION DESIGN
for product purchase interviewing, 1059
in public opinion polling, 234, 236, 359, 361, 1463, 1466, 1719, 1886
increasing accuracy of question, 1421.

increasing objectivity of
  question, 743, 1421
principles of, 235, 240, 270,
  349, 355, 1009, 1095,
  1136, 1208, 1305, 1701,
  1719
use of Thurstone scaling, 1421

QUESTION FORM
  and interviewer bias, 328, 664,
    1790, 1884
  and question bias, 236, 328,
    361, 764, 858, 1256, 1263,
    1446, 1702, 1719
  comparison of various types,
    153, 743, 858, 1381, 1616,
    1702, 1719
  experimental studies on, 1702
  in consumer surveys, 1702
  in public opinion polling, 232,
    234, 236, 328, 334, 335,
    361, 645, 693, 764, 765,
    1256, 1446, 1701, 1702,
    1719, 1790, 1867, 1884
  influence on responses, 153,
    232, 234, 335, 361, 556,
    645, 764, 858, 1256, 1423,
    1446, 1616, 1702, 1719,
    1867, 2081

QUESTION PHRASING *See*
QUESTION WORDING

QUESTION, in public opinion
polling *See* POLLING QUESTION

QUESTION RESPONSES *See*
RESPONSES, to questions

QUESTION WORDING
  allowing respondent means of
    expression, 361, 1381, 1701
  and establishment of rapport
    with respondent, 1701
  and interviewer bias, 328, 907
  and question bias, 17, 227,
    229, 236, 315, 328, 359,
    361, 453, 470, 571, 764,
    783, 941, 1009, 1263,
    1293, 1411, 1470, 1702,
    1716, 1719, 1881, 1886
  avoiding abstract questions,
    361, 1554, 1701

avoiding ambiguity, 244, 361,
  1095, 1701, 1719
avoiding emotive questions
  235, 1701
avoiding hidden implications,
  1701, 1719
avoiding over formal language,
  361
avoiding over technical
  language, 361
avoiding unfamiliar words,
  235, 361, 1554
avoiding wordy questions,
  1095
bias in, 17, 58, 73, 229, 315,
  328, 359, 361, 453, 571,
  764, 941, 950, 966, 1009,
  1293, 1411, 1421, 1446,
  1550, 1702, 1716, 1719,
  1881, 1886, 1926, 1969,
  2081
'big name effect', 230, 359,
  1293, 1719
context effects, 1550, 1719,
  1881
deviations from 'objective',
  743, 1009
direction-of-wording effect,
  966
effect of double negative,
  2076
effect of variations in, 14, 73,
  232, 234, 236, 359, 764,
  785, 851, 1000, 1009,
  1446, 1702, 1716, 1719,
  1867, 1881
effect on responses, 17, 73,
  138, 227, 232, 234, 244,
  335, 361, 439, 453, 571,
  764, 785, 851, 941, 950,
  1009, 1446, 1470, 1550,
  1594, 1701, 1702, 1716,
  1719, 1867, 1886, 1969,
  2076, 2081
'end' effect, 1446, 1719
familiarity to respondent, 361
in consumer research, 571,
  785, 1701, 1702
in international surveys, 651,
  1621, 1626

in public opinion polling
14, 183, 227, 228, 229,
230, 232, 234, 236, 328,
335, 359, 361, 453, 490,
764, 783, 1155, 1411,
1446, 1506, 1554, 1594,
1626, 1680, 1681, 1702,
1716, 1719, 1867, 1886,
1927, 1961, 2076
leading, 229, 230, 315, 783,
1009, 1470, 1594, 1719
loaded, 229, 230, 1009, 1702,
1719
of memory dependent
questions, 816
prestige effects, 58, 764, 941,
1293, 1702
personalization of question,
1701, 1719
principles of, 228, 235, 240,
349, 1009, 1305, 1681,
1701, 1719
relating question to
respondent's environment
14, 1701
relating question to respondent's
experience, 1701
respondent's interpretation of,
19, 95, 183, 361, 503, 676,
804, 1421, 1550, 1719
respondent's understanding of,
19, 183, 228, 230, 335,
349, 361, 503, 651, 804,
1155, 1421, 1554, 1621,
1626, 1701, 1719, 1961
'split-ballot' technique, 1155,
1719
suggestion in, 58, 227, 230,
315, 453, 941, 1009,
1293, 1421, 1470, 1594,
1886
use of stereotypes, 764, 1411,
1719

QUESTIONNAIRE
administration of, 652, 983,
1357
attitude, 59, 470, 573, 577,
578, 712, 1318, 2009,
2010
comparison with other
methods of data collection,
632, 633, 1163, 1318
design, 46, 177, 240, 261, 269,
349, 582, 647, 673, 765,
835, 863, 964, 1058, 1095,
1136, 1174, 1193, 1208,
1260, 1304, 1423, 1424,
1449, 1466, 1477, 1535,
1719, 1809, 1886, 1980,
2009, 2010, 2063, 2145
editing of, 569, 1501, 1951
health, 1929
in life history studies, 389
in multilingual interviews, 226
mail, 124, 240, 249, 296, 396,
422, 583, 597, 600, 673,
682, 719, 734, 1000, 1076,
1099, 1274, 1391, 1503,
1769
opinion, 573, 765, 1226
order effects on, 269, 339,
673, 847, 1477
piloting of, 159, 233
precoding of, 46, 647, 920,
1058, 1193, 1423, 2145
pretesting, 228, 349, 1039,
1274, 1371, 1830
reliability, 390, 504, 1226,
1713
self-completion, 7, 33, 34, 37,
314, 351, 352, 415, 496,
504, 546, 601, 702, 801,
879, 886, 954, 971, 1157,
1163, 1226, 1318, 1353,
1423, 1477, 1480, 1559,
1563, 1577, 1740, 1840,
1848, 1929, 1935, 2028,
2055, 2126
translation of, 226
validity, 264, 2133

QUESTIONNAIRE,
administration of
and bias in responses to
questions, 652, 983
by computer, 652
by mail, 983, 1357
comparison of methods, 983,
1357

group, 983
personal, 1357
place of, 983

QUESTIONNAIRE DESIGN
and maintenance of respondent's interest, 349, 835
and punching procedure requirements, 647, 964, 2145
and 'split-ballot' technique, 1719
and tabulation requirements, 46, 647, 1174, 2145
colour, 863
filter systems, 1193, 1449
for depth interview, 1260, 1535
for financial surveys, 261, 1304
for public opinion polling, 582, 765, 1260, 1466, 1719, 1886
for structured interview, 240
grouping of related questions, 1193, 1424
interviewer instructions, 1193, 1449
layout, 1193, 1449, 1809, 1980
pictorial questionnaire, 2063
precoding, 46, 647, 1058, 1193, 1423, 2145
principles of, 177, 240, 349, 964, 1095, 1136, 1208, 1719, 1809, 2009, 2010
question order, 235, 269, 349, 369, 673, 777, 847, 964, 1193, 1424, 1477, 1719
quintamensional plan, 765
size, 1193
structure, 1193
typography, 1980

See also: MAIL QUESTIONNAIRE

QUESTIONNAIRES, editing of
cost, 1501
error, 1501
office, 569

QUOTA SAMPLING
and interviewer classification of respondent, 226, 239, 568
and interviewer selection of respondent, 266, 374
and socio-economic classification, 568
comparison with area sampling, 17, 291, 893, 896, 930, 945, 985, 1407
comparison with non-proportional sampling, 291
comparison with probability sampling, 893, 900
comparison with random sampling, 291, 581, 608, 1458, 1459
control systems, 1458
cost, 581
in international public opinion surveys, 1626
in public opinion polling, 1407
sources of bias in, 239, 374, 900, 945, 1458
sources of error in, 900, 1458

RADIO AUDIENCE RESEARCH TECHNIQUES
aided recall, 402, 1703
audience composition measurement, 200, 1574
BBC Local Correspondents, 1817
button-pressing methods, 1561, 1574, 1762
diaries, 201
for audience reaction measurement, 481, 662, 1518, 1561, 1675, 1739, 1762, 1817, 1839
for audience size measurement, 1739
for programme preference measurement, 590, 773
listening panels, 1817
programme feature analysis, 1574, 1762
recording meters, 1077

telephone interview, 1667
unaided recall, 200, 1950

RANDOM SAMPLING
and stratification, 291, 811, 1344, 1890
comparison with non-proportional sampling, 291
comparison with quota sampling, 291, 581, 608, 1458, 1459
costs, 581
for social surveys, 122, 811
of unenumerated populations, 1991
random route, 65, 1467

RANDOM-SYSTEMATIC ERROR COEFFICIENT, 754

RANDOMIZED RESPONSE MODEL, 10, 807, 836, 1004, 2039

RANKING, 438, 590, 692, 1079, 1640, 1746

RAPPORT
and bias, 1029, 1428, 1727, 2060, 2117
and classification of responses, 976
and nonresponse to questions, 976
and validity of responses, 976
description, 1589
factors affecting, 1785
in extended interviews, 848
in social psychological research, 1785

RATIO ESTIMATES, 623

RATING SCALES
amount of verbal anchoring, 168
arrangement of items, 1271
bias in, 887, 1597
bi-polar, 621, 1967, 2098
construction of, 82, 887, 1472, 1644, 1805, 1985, 2169
for measuring attitude change, 4
for predicting consumer behaviour, 4
forced-choice technique, 82, 118, 801, 1016, 1644, 1985, 2169
generalised, 519
graphic, 397, 573, 1086, 1655, 1656
'halo' effect, 1315
history of usage, 635
methods for calculating factor/component scores, 887
non-verbal, 485
number of response categories, 168, 169, 170, 397, 546, 824, 858
numerical, 1483
order effects, 160, 576, 1271, 1381, 1624
predictive accuracy of, 4
rating-by-others, 573, 2009, 2010, 2055
reliability of, 15, 168, 169, 170, 397, 546, 611, 1166, 1325, 1483, 1640
scale symmetry, 1354
self-rating scales, 168, 358, 573, 1086, 1655, 1656, 1929, 2009, 2010, 2055
Stapel scale, 485, 1483
symmetrical vs. asymmetrical, 5
used in advertising research, 2071, 2072
used in preference testing, 169, 692, 1079, 1640, 1706, 1746, 1805
used in product testing, 5, 297, 448, 522, 611, 1583, 1706, 1746, 1805
used to evaluate interviewer-respondent relationship, 293
validity, 1498, 1805, 1929, 2137
verbal, 160, 297, 1271, 1483, 1498, 1624

See also: SCALES; SCALING

READABILITY
  formulas, 8, 371, 511, 1155, 1608, 1961
  measurement of, 8, 277, 1023, 1608, 1609
  of questions, 1155, 1506, 1961

READABILITY FORMULAS
  computer automation of, 511
  cross-cultural administration, 371
  Dale-Chall, 8, 1608, 1961
  Farr-Jenkins-Paterson, 511, 1608
  Flesch Energy Score, 371
  Flesch Human Interest Score, 8, 371
  Flesch-Reading Ease Score, 8, 371, 511, 1155, 1608, 1961
  Flesch Realism Score, 371
  Fog Index, 8
  Gunning, 8, 1608

READERSHIP RESEARCH TECHNIQUES
  aided recall, 6, 97, 376, 476, 513, 841, 956, 1011, 1122, 1282, 1283, 1284, 1285, 1286, 1287, 1318, 1319, 1366, 1367, 1441, 1442, 1476, 1489, 1804, 1905
  comparison of techniques, 53, 127, 216, 376, 476, 1058, 1285, 1287, 1319, 1787, 1905, 2057, 2155
  diaries, 53, 1065
  direct observation of reading behaviour, 216, 714, 877, 1064, 1286, 1580
  editorial-interest method, 216, 476, 1058, 1318, 2057
  exposure-probability index, 1199
  false indentification, 155, 206, 207, 956, 965, 1273, 1282, 1283, 1284, 1366, 1390, 1441, 1442, 1489, 1648, 1649
  fatigue effects, 6, 878, 1787, 1804
  intensive interview, 155, 159, 424, 476, 965
  laboratory techniques, 424, 877, 1064, 1078, 1122, 1286, 1580, 2144
  mail survey, 127, 679, 1273, 1390, 1648, 1649, 1865, 1905, 2057, 2155
  modified recent reading techniques, 476
  non-readers, 1100
  order effects, 6, 155, 476, 965, 1787
  panels, 28, 619, 908, 1065, 1066, 1538, 1842
  reader-interest measurement, 318, 375, 763, 938, 1287, 1476, 1609, 2144
  readership of advertising, 97, 206, 424, 513, 714, 877, 878, 956, 1078, 1122, 1282, 1283, 1284, 1285, 1441, 1442, 1489, 1580, 1722, 1804, 1994
  readership panels, 28, 619, 679, 1065, 1066, 1538, 1842
  readership prediction, 939, 1567, 1568, 1609, 1994, 1997
  readership surveys, 6, 23, 127, 155, 159, 161, 294, 425, 476, 908, 965, 1058, 1096, 1100, 1273, 1287, 1295, 1476, 1787, 1865, 1968, 2155
  reading-and-noting studies, 799, 1722
  reading intensity measures, 458, 1057
  scales, 26, 458, 483, 939, 1057, 1295, 1741, 1905
  self-completion survey, 679
  tape-recording of interviews, 161
  telephone interview, 331, 1905
  unaided recall, 476, 1319

usual reading frequency
measures, 26, 375, 476,
1319, 1741, 1765
validation, 155, 424, 1273,
1286, 1580

RECALL, by respondent
aided, 6, 97, 376, 476, 513,
600, 613, 841, 956, 1011,
1257, 1279, 1282, 1283,
1284, 1285, 1286, 1287,
1319, 1366, 1367, 1436,
1441, 1442, 1476, 1544,
1602, 1604, 1638, 1703,
1804, 1870, 1905, 2072
bias in, 610, 675, 2141
errors in, 322, 513, 571, 677,
816, 851, 876, 977, 1043,
1046, 1047, 1124, 1282,
1328, 1366, 1397, 1485,
1536, 1537, 1602, 1625,
1767, 1782, 1932, 2032,
2141
factors influencing, 379, 402,
816, 832, 1234, 1604
in advertising research, 97,
107, 539, 600, 631, 799,
956, 1122, 1257, 1279,
1282, 1283, 1284, 1285,
1328, 1355, 1356, 1366,
1436, 1441, 1442, 1489,
1544, 1638, 1804, 1870,
2072
in audience research, 956,
1436, 1441, 1442
in quasi-longitudinal studies,
322
in readership research, 6, 97,
376, 476, 513, 799, 841,
956, 1011, 1122, 1282,
1283, 1284, 1285, 1286,
1287, 1319, 1366, 1367,
1441, 1442, 1476, 1489,
1804, 1905
'level of consciousness'
technique, 437
methods of assisting, 890,
1011
of behaviour, 322, 506, 799,
816, 1767

of controversial material, 44,
1234
of family expenditure, 1485
of product purchases, 322,
571, 610, 675, 677, 784,
851, 977, 1043, 1046,
1047, 1124, 1269, 1536,
1625, 1932
of radio programmes, 402,
506, 1950
of TV viewing, 613
of visual vs. oral material, 539,
1870
order effects, 1950
reliability of, 322, 506, 677,
701, 830, 1040, 1043,
1046, 1047, 1134, 1604,
1767, 2167
retroactive inhibition, 1234,
1328
time duration, 322, 379, 402,
677, 799, 830, 832, 876,
1096, 1234, 1485, 1604,
1767, 1782
unaided, 200, 476, 1279,
1319, 1355, 1602, 1604,
1870, 1950

See also: MEMORY

RECORDING METERS, in
audience research
and non-response bias, 733,
937
button-pressing meters, 410,
709, 1253, 1254, 1561,
1574, 1762, 1814
in radio audience research, 1077
in television audience research,
617, 618, 733, 937, 1999,
2047, 2048

RECORDING METERS, in
television audience research
and measurement of overlap
viewing, 2047
Audimeter, 2048
comparison with other
methods of data collection,
617
Intometer, 2048

non-response bias, 733, 937
Recordimeter, 618
Setmeter, 1999, 2048
Tammeter, 618, 1999, 2048

RECORDS MATCHING
in delinquency research, 1826

REFUSALS, by respondent
and bias, 910, 937, 959, 1414
effect of advance letter on, 378, 563
effect of payment of interviewer on, 944
effect of prior telephone call on, 301, 563
effect on survey results, 191, 910, 1414, 1660
in financial surveys, 440
interviewers as cause of, 191, 267, 440, 559, 585, 922, 959, 1712, 2109
question topic as cause, 1712
reduction of, 191, 563, 959, 1014, 1660, 1831
respondents as cause of, 559, 774, 1414, 1660
seasonal variations in, 959

REGRESSION ANALYSIS
alternatives to, 638
as a predictive technique, 446, 862
multiple regression analysis, 430, 446, 803, 1198
stepwise regression, 430
stepwise rejection regression, 430

RE-INTERVIEWS
and intensive interviewing, 2042
by telephone, 463, 1748
in censuses, 83, 1125, 1469, 1606
in longitudinal studies, 463
timing of, 83, 778
to detect error, 83, 149, 720, 804, 1125, 1397, 1606
to increase validity of response, 1377

to measure opinion-change, 1214, 1748
to measure opinion-intensity, 429

RELIABILITY
of attitude research techniques, 384, 526, 701, 1079, 1141, 1331, 1332, 1432
of attitude scaling techniques, 16, 118, 324, 365, 455, 515, 687, 980, 1079, 1141, 1166, 1325, 1331, 1332, 1431, 1432, 1684, 2065, 2078, 2127
of classification of respondents, 1341, 1465, 2006
of coding, 587, 754, 859, 1231, 1341, 2151
of content analysis, 66, 1771, 1887
of forced-choice technique, 118
of Likert technique, 118, 550, 1079, 1243
of mail survey responses, 829, 1076, 1509, 1769
of motivation research techniques, 279
of observational techniques, 56, 514, 1135, 1484, 1987
of paired comparisons technique, 975, 1079
of panel data, 61, 610, 611, 617, 619, 668, 675, 680, 681, 683, 977, 1210, 1306, 1509, 1783, 1910, 1932, 2130
of personal interview responses, 92, 390, 677, 1420, 1509, 1531, 2006, 2083, 2167
of projective techniques, 1733, 1734
of preference testing techniques, 1079
of public opinion polling, 547, 691, 1082, 1226, 1259, 1306, 1331, 1332, 2038, 2104

of questions, 232, 390, 830,
    1136, 1867
of questionnaires, 390, 504,
    1226, 1713
of rating scales, 15, 168, 169,
    170, 397, 546, 611, 1166,
    1325, 1483, 1640
of respondent's recall, 322,
    506, 677, 830, 1040, 1043,
    1047, 1134, 1604, 1767,
    1782, 2167
of responses to polling
    questions, 1886
of self-completion
    questionnaire responses, 85,
    504, 1571, 1848, 2028
of taste-testing, 849, 850, 1678
split-half, 384, 1306, 1629,
    2078
techniques for assessing, 691,
    754, 1134, 1325, 1420,
    1465, 1629, 1687
test-retest, 1079, 1226, 1306,
    1431

REPERTORY GRID TECHNIQUE
application in exploratory
    research, 1729
applications in consumer
    attitude research, 1291
applications in market
    research, 752, 1291
comparison with group
    discussion, 1729
in product testing, 752
methods of analysis, 752
reliability, 752
used in development of
    semantic differential scales,
    752
used to identify target groups,
    408, 752

REPORTING ERROR
by interviewers, 435, 1552,
    1791
by respondents, 113, 155, 159,
    260, 261, 332, 351, 352,
    353, 354, 377, 413, 415,
    439, 677, 683, 851, 875,

by respondents (*contd.*)
    876, 879, 909, 1046, 1047,
    1124, 1142, 1204, 1269,
    1273, 1367, 1377, 1404,
    1405, 1420, 1480, 1481,
    1485, 1536, 1539, 1648,
    1765, 1781, 1976
causes of, 155, 851, 1204,
    1481, 1976
detection of, 1046, 1047,
    1420, 1485
over-reporting, 155, 332, 415,
    421, 571, 879, 1124, 1142,
    1269, 1404, 1405, 1485,
    1536, 1539, 1648, 1765,
    1976
under-reporting, 113, 155,
    159, 351, 352, 353, 354,
    377, 413, 415, 677, 875,
    909, 1142, 1204, 1268,
    1269, 1273, 1367, 1377,
    1404, 1405, 1480, 1481,
    1648

REPORTS
on the interview, 350, 414,
    706, 930, 1796, 1898
standards for preparation of,
    2004

REPRODUCER
use in data processing, 1108
use in Guttman scaling, 1852

REPRODUCIBILITY
coefficient of, 416, 1413, 1753
of cumulative scales, 36, 606,
    1753

RESEARCH DESIGN
choice of, 1403, 2062
experimental, 98, 341, 356,
    616, 889, 1914, 1954
for mass communication
    effects measurement, 145,
    152, 154, 164, 637, 1543
in holiday research, 1050
in longitudinal studies, 793
in product testing, 326, 1542,
    1954
in sexual behaviour research,
    1026, 2032

in social research, 1914
in survey research, 509, 1373, 1471, 1725
pre-experimental, 98, 341
quasi-experimental, 98
regression discontinuity analysis, 1963
sources of invalidity, 98, 889
time factor in, 509

RESPONDENT
aged, 280, 779, 875, 921, 1036, 1414, 1533, 1534, 1770
and interview refusals, 559, 563, 585, 774, 1014, 1414, 1660
anonymity, 59, 271, 470, 546, 577, 628, 632, 633, 702, 886, 982, 983, 1157, 1163, 1185, 1186, 1317, 1353, 1362, 1391, 1520, 1559, 1563, 1691, 1919
anxiety during interview, 1704
availability of, 136, 501, 774, 973, 1021, 1290, 1471, 1705, 1793
bias due to, 10, 39, 57, 58, 78, 304, 332, 355, 565, 577, 639, 677, 678, 702, 777, 796, 836, 875, 914, 1004, 1024, 1036, 1147, 1157, 1163, 1171, 1229, 1293, 1353, 1414, 1440, 1520, 1559, 1563, 1581, 1661, 1691, 1724, 1732, 1807, 1886, 1919, 2039, 2068, 2069, 2070, 2115, 2141
characteristics of, 182, 332, 501, 564, 583, 774, 973, 1281, 1481, 1533, 1534, 1639, 1692, 1858, 1859, 1874, 2068,
child as, 74, 125, 390, 629, 1305, 1353, 2073
classification of, 27, 29, 38, 95, 120, 158, 274, 282, 283, 360, 388, 568, 634, 761, 838, 846, 867, 883, 935, 943, 983, 988, 994,

classification of (*contd.*)
1035, 1063, 1211, 1239, 1289, 1341, 1465, 1499, 1679, 1708, 1772, 1869, 1874, 2006, 2007, 2013, 2034, 2165
comparison with non-respondents, 422, 501, 564, 583, 774, 1281, 1314, 1533, 1534, 1639
cooperation of, 54, 63, 543, 733, 774, 995, 1021, 1132, 1304, 1305, 1508, 1704, 1712
disengaged, 779, 1036, 1414
error, 19, 37, 40, 94, 95, 113, 155, 159, 162, 194, 322, 332, 334, 351, 352, 353, 361, 377, 413, 415, 421, 439, 440, 503, 513, 659, 677, 735, 777, 801, 804, 816, 875, 878, 879, 903, 909, 942, 1024, 1046, 1047, 1124, 1142, 1146, 1219, 1269, 1273, 1282, 1307, 1328, 1366, 1367, 1397, 1404, 1405, 1420, 1480, 1485, 1536, 1539, 1550, 1577, 1625, 1648, 1765, 1767, 1781, 1782, 1860, 1976, 2016, 2032, 2141
exaggeration of consumer product purchase, 1046, 1047, 1124, 1539
failure to contact, 585, 1471, 1705
fatigue, 848
'hard to reach', 501, 973, 1021, 1290, 1471, 1660, 1937
illiterate, 566, 2131
in international surveys, 1621
in mail surveys, 123, 271, 337, 396, 422, 564, 583, 597, 670, 740, 742, 818, 987, 1099, 1203, 1207, 1281, 1493, 1503, 1582, 1637, 1639, 1669, 1692, 1749, 1769, 1770, 1871, 1926, 2019, 2029, 2030

267

in multi-lingual communities, 226
interest, 706, 835, 848, 1816, 1848, 1926, 1948
interviewing special categories of, 130, 1021, 1036, 1132, 1227, 1662, 1671, 1704, 1921, 2021, 2150
making contacts with, 63, 501, 543, 995, 1021, 1132, 1471, 1662, 1704, 1705, 1768, 1937, 2173
memory, 44, 353, 506, 539, 630, 631, 701, 756, 767, 799, 816, 830, 876, 915, 1032, 1566, 1602, 1604, 1702, 1767, 1960, 2003, 2073, 2176
motivation, 349, 351, 366, 422, 564, 567, 597, 1207, 1503, 1926
non verbal behaviour during interview, 622
'not-at-home', 117, 267, 601, 612, 973, 1123, 1290, 1587, 1592, 1593, 1705, 1822, 1823
obtaining 'household' information from single, 93, 377, 677, 1420, 1485, 1495, 1875
over-reporting by, 155, 332, 421, 571, 879, 1142, 1269, 1404, 1405, 1485, 1536, 1648, 1765, 1976
payment of, 930, 1112, 1932
perception of interview, 350, 1481
perception of interviewer, 182, 350, 366, 620, 1029, 1225, 1443, 1481, 1589, 1727, 1829
perception of interviewer empathy, 39, 1589, 1600, 1663
prestige-seeking by, 58, 332, 453, 565, 1024, 1171, 1293, 1440, 1724
rapport with interviewer, 696, 848, 976, 1029, 1589, 1727, 1785, 2005, 2060, 2115, 2117

reaction to being interviewed, 350
recall, 44, 322, 379, 402, 506, 513, 539, 613, 677, 701, 799, 830, 832, 1046, 1047, 1124, 1234, 1269, 1282, 1397, 1485, 1604, 1625, 1767, 1782, 2032, 2141, 2167
relationship with interviewer, 250, 293, 440, 696, 1225, 1305, 1378, 1481, 1589, 1686, 1727, 1744, 2005
report on the interview, 350
representativeness of, 299, 327, 499, 538, 789, 973, 1717, 1803, 1960, 2018, 2030
responsiveness during interview, 54, 182, 693, 835, 1021, 1379, 1513
role in interview situation, 1305, 1378
under-reporting by, 113, 155, 159, 351, 352, 353, 354, 377, 413, 415, 677, 875, 909, 1142, 1204, 1269, 1273, 1367, 1377, 1480, 1481, 1648
understanding/interpretation of question, 19, 95, 159, 162, 183, 226, 228, 230, 334, 335, 349, 361, 390, 439, 503, 639, 651, 676, 693, 804, 875, 990, 991, 1155, 1186, 1267, 1268, 1397, 1421, 1506, 1507, 1550, 1554, 1621, 1626, 1701, 1719, 1860, 1961
verbal behaviour during interview, 353, 393, 622, 698, 791, 955, 1378, 1379, 1394, 1395, 1600, 1607, 1633, 1732, 1744, 2044, 2097
verbal interaction with interviewer, 1378, 1392, 1393, 1396, 1735, 2095, 2096, 2097

See also: NON-RESPONDENT

RESPONDENT BIAS
  and respondent anonymity,
    577, 702, 1157, 1163,
    1353, 1520, 1559, 1563,
    1691, 1919
  and semantic differential
    scaling, 57
  due to ingratiation, 78
  due to lack of information
    678
  due to prestige seeking, 58,
    332, 565, 1024, 1171,
    1293, 1440, 1724
  due to prior knowledge of
    survey, 1807
  in aged respondents, 1036,
    1414
  in children, 1353
  in responses to questions, 10,
    39, 332, 355, 577, 639,
    677, 678, 702, 777, 796,
    836, 875, 914, 1004, 1024,
    1157, 1163, 1171, 1559,
    1563, 1581, 1661, 1724,
    1732, 1886, 2039, 2068,
    2069, 2070, 2115, 2141

RESPONDENT ERROR *See*
ERROR, due to respondent

RESPONDENT, in mail surveys
  anonymity of, 271, 1769
  characteristics of, 422, 564,
    583, 597, 742, 1281, 1503,
    1639, 1692, 1769
  comparison with
    non-respondents, 123, 422,
    564, 583, 597, 740, 742,
    818, 987, 1203, 1281,
    1503, 1637, 1639, 1749,
    1769, 1871, 1926, 2019,
    2029
  differences between early and
    late, 123, 337, 422, 564,
    583, 670, 818, 1203, 1493,
    1528, 1637, 1673, 1769,
    1871
  motivation, 422, 564, 597,
    1099, 1207, 1503, 1769,
    1813, 1871, 1926

  representativeness of, 327,
    330, 422, 499, 538, 564,
    583, 742, 1203, 1503,
    1582, 1583, 1871, 2029,
    2030

RESPONSE BIAS *See*
NON-RESPONSE BIAS; BIAS, in
response to questions

RESPONSE RATE
  and advance letter, 378
    718, 952, 1120, 1235,
    1473, 1659, 1769, 1770,
    1866
  and interviewers, 440, 585,
    922, 1712, 1766
  factors influencing, 76, 271,
    273, 296, 330, 396, 422,
    484, 501, 564, 585, 648,
    649, 689, 734, 863, 922,
    949, 1076, 1391, 1434,
    1503, 1926, 1948
  in financial surveys, 440
  in mail surveys, 76, 123, 203,
    271, 273, 280, 330, 396,
    403, 422, 484, 537, 564,
    583, 689, 718, 719, 734,
    738, 739, 744, 792, 818,
    863, 865, 938, 949, 952,
    987, 1000, 1037, 1099,
    1120, 1128, 1162, 1203,
    1207, 1235, 1236, 1262,
    1274, 1391, 1434, 1473,
    1493, 1503, 1588, 1612,
    1659, 1664, 1665, 1666,
    1669, 1692, 1769, 1770,
    1775, 1812, 1816, 1824,
    1831, 1866, 1926, 1948,
    1978, 1979, 2027, 2041,
    2058, 2158
  in panels, 121, 1467
  techniques for increasing, 76,
    203, 271, 273, 330, 422,
    501, 543, 564, 1000, 1014,
    1831
  to self-completion
    questionnaires, 1935

See also: COMPLETION RATE

RESPONSE RATE, in mail surveys
    and age of respondents, 280
    and anonymity of respondents, 271, 1391, 1769
    and business reply envelopes, 863, 1120
    and colour of questionnaire, 792, 863, 1274
    and cover letter, 422, 734, 744, 1037, 1128, 1262, 1274, 1588, 1659, 1664, 1769, 1816, 1824, 1948, 2058
    and date of despatch of questionnaire, 484, 1588, 1769, 1978
    and follow-ups, 271, 396, 422, 484, 564, 689, 734, 792, 818, 865, 987, 1120, 1235, 1494, 1503, 1659, 1769, 1770, 1978, 1979
    and interest of respondent, 123, 422, 564, 583, 1099, 1926, 1948
    and layout of questionnaire, 296, 719, 1000, 1235, 1274, 1769
    and length of questionnaire, 396, 583, 719, 734, 1099, 1391
    and meticulousness of respondents, 1207, 1692
    and incentives, 203, 273, 396, 649, 738, 739, 938, 949, 977, 1037, 1120, 1128, 1162, 1235, 1493, 1503, 1664, 1812, 2158
    and motivation of respondents, 422, 537, 1099, 1207, 1831, 1926, 1948
    and non-response bias, 330, 422, 564, 583, 818, 987, 1203, 1637, 1664, 1769
    and postcard reminder, 689
    and sponsorship of survey 123, 1235, 1503, 1769
    and stamped addressed return envelopes, 330, 863, 1274, 1612, 1659, 1769, 1948
    and subject matter of inquiry, 271, 330, 422, 564, 734, 1831
    and type of mailing, 396, 792, 863, 865, 1120, 1128, 1235, 1274, 1664, 1769
    and use of advance letter, 718, 952, 1120, 1235, 1473, 1659, 1769, 1770, 1866
    and use of advance telephone calls, 1866, 2027
    and use of 'deadline' date, 689, 1816, 1948
    and use of participant reply card, 271
    factors influencing, 76, 273, 296, 330, 396, 403, 422, 484, 564, 648, 649, 689, 734, 863, 949, 1076, 1434, 1503, 1926, 1948
    techniques for increasing, 76, 273, 296, 330, 396, 403, 422, 484, 564, 689, 718, 719, 734, 744, 792, 863, 865, 949, 952, 1120, 1128, 1162, 1235, 1275, 1503, 1659, 1664, 1665, 1666, 1669, 1769, 1775, 1831, 2041, 2158

RESPONSE SET
    acquiescence, 141, 285, 480, 892, 914, 1161, 1200, 1316, 1385, 1581, 1683, 2068, 2070
    and bias in responses to questions, 141, 193, 480, 494, 786, 892, 914, 1161, 1173, 1200, 1385, 1440, 1504, 1581, 1683, 1720, 1721, 1836, 2068, 2069, 2070, 2170
    and educational level of respondent, 1200
    and item referent ambiguity, 1200
    and personality inventories, 480, 1161
    and personality of respondent, 480, 914, 1316, 1858, 2070

and race of respondent, 914
and response style, 786, 1316,
  1683, 1721, 2068
and test design, 494
and the semantic differential,
  786, 1173
extreme, 786, 1197, 1858,
  2068
generalization, 786
in developing countries, 1200
in preference testing, 1757
in taste-testing, 1757
in unstructured test situations,
  100, 193
social desirability, 1173, 1440,
  1836, 1955

RESPONSE STYLE
and bias in responses to
  questions, 786, 1522, 1581,
  1683, 1721, 2068, 2069,
  2070, 2170
and form of question, 2068
and response set, 786, 1316,
  1683, 1721, 2068
and the semantic differential,
  786, 2170
extreme, 786, 2170
in public opinion polling, 1522
social desirability, 1581
studies of, 1683, 2170

RESPONSES, to questions
accuracy of, 37, 142, 157, 161,
  172, 332, 351, 352, 377,
  415, 422, 439, 632, 633,
  677, 701, 778, 830, 876,
  879, 1024, 1146, 1269,
  1378, 1397, 1420, 1481,
  1487, 1509, 1536, 1537,
  1577, 1625, 1702, 1727,
  1782, 2028, 2141, 2167
and interview design, 353, 554
and interviewer bias, 231, 452,
  558, 560, 674, 704, 750,
  856, 1084, 1085, 1255,
  1727, 1798, 1843, 1872,
  1883, 1885, 2055, 2106,
  2115, 2116, 2161
and respondent's ethnic
  origins, 496, 1754, 2170
and respondent's lack of
  information of subject, 361,
  578, 678, 2174
bias in, 10, 17, 58, 62, 73, 193,
  229, 269, 304, 332, 393,
  415, 439, 453, 480, 494,
  558, 560, 565, 571, 577,
  652, 677, 682, 702, 750,
  777, 786, 796, 807, 836,
  875, 892, 914, 941, 950,
  966, 983, 1004, 1009,
  1024, 1084, 1085, 1131,
  1157, 1161, 1163, 1171,
  1173, 1200, 1293, 1346,
  1353, 1385, 1394, 1395,
  1411, 1440, 1446, 1477,
  1504, 1519, 1520, 1522,
  1550, 1559, 1563, 1581,
  1598, 1607, 1633, 1661,
  1663, 1683, 1691, 1702,
  1716, 1719, 1720, 1721,
  1724, 1732, 1810, 1836,
  1838, 1881, 1884, 1886,
  1919, 1927, 1969, 1992,
  2032, 2039, 2060, 2068,
  2069, 2070, 2081, 2115,
  2116, 2123, 2124, 2141,
  2161, 2170
clarifying meaning of, 1756
classification of, 976, 1255,
  1798, 1872, 1883, 1885,
  2055
coding of, 625, 751, 859, 918,
  920, 1231, 1965, 2151,
  2154
comparability, 93, 94, 351,
  1314, 1357, 1806
consistency of, 94, 172, 504,
  677, 701, 720, 778, 830,
  876, 1043, 1500, 1504,
  1520, 1531, 1848, 1886,
  2083
content analysis of, 66, 1378,
  1392, 1393, 1396, 1735,
  1771, 1887, 1939, 2095,
  2096
differences in, 677, 914, 1550,
  1744, 1882
'don't know', 184, 227, 578,
  693, 858, 990, 991, 1155,

'don't know' (*contd.*)
  1515, 1690, 1702, 1706, 2174
effect of advance letter on, 1508
effect of interviewer's age on, 182, 620
effect of interviewer's race on, 62, 1661, 1838, 2115, 2116
effect of interviewer's sex on, 182, 1969
effect of praising respondent, 693
effect of previous interviewing on, 34, 490, 1212
effect of previous responses on, 847, 2086
effect of question form on, 153, 232, 234, 335, 361, 556, 645, 858, 1256, 1423, 1446, 1616, 1702, 1867, 2081
effect of question length on, 1377
effect of question order on, 269, 369, 777, 847, 1514, 1719
effect of question readability, 1506
effect of question wording on, 17, 73, 138, 227, 232, 234, 244, 335, 361, 439, 453, 571, 764, 785, 851, 941, 950, 1009, 1446, 1470, 1550, 1594, 1701, 1702, 1716, 1719, 1867, 1886, 1969, 2076, 2081
effect of reinforcement on, 311, 353, 354, 393, 1377, 1379, 1395, 1633, 1732, 1838
effect of respondent's age on, 779, 1036
effect of respondent's anonymity on, 34, 59, 351, 470, 546, 577, 628, 632, 633, 702, 886, 982, 983, 1157, 1163, 1185, 1186, 1317, 1353, 1520, 1559, 1563, 1691, 1919
effect of respondent's educational level, 496

effect of respondent's personality on, 194, 914, 1881, 2068, 2069, 2070
effect of respondent's socio-economic status on, 1163, 1744, 1916, 2060, 2116
effect of tape-recording on, 161
errors in, 37, 40, 84, 94, 172, 260, 261, 332, 352, 377, 421, 422, 439, 504, 529, 666, 671, 677, 681, 683, 777, 801, 816, 875, 876, 879, 904, 942, 1024, 1042, 1142, 1143, 1146, 1219, 1220, 1307, 1346, 1371, 1397, 1404, 1405, 1420, 1481, 1485, 1487, 1488, 1514, 1536, 1537, 1550, 1577, 1618, 1625, 2061, 2141
from panels, 5, 681, 683, 1210, 1509, 1931, 1932
fullness of, 353, 693, 1233, 1379, 1395, 1558, 1600, 1607, 2025
in consumer product purchase interviews, 785, 851, 1142, 1536, 1537, 1932
in enumerative surveys, 1397
in financial surveys, 260, 261
in group tests, 983
in mail surveys, 5, 439, 484, 537, 632, 633, 669, 682, 718, 720, 742, 829, 950, 983, 1210, 1314, 1357, 1509, 1514, 1769
in personal interviews, 5, 33, 34, 37, 92, 127, 182, 184, 281, 351, 352, 669, 677, 720, 742, 829, 976, 1101, 1107, 1112, 1163, 1202, 1231, 1269, 1314, 1357, 1420, 1423, 1480, 1509, 1513, 1514, 1531, 1536, 1537, 1547, 1932, 1935, 1992, 2006, 2055, 2057, 2060, 2061, 2083, 2155
in secret ballots, 184, 1107, 1992

in self-completion
questionnaires, 33, 34, 37,
351, 352, 496, 504, 702,
801, 879, 886, 1157, 1163,
1353, 1423, 1477, 1480,
1559, 1563, 1577, 1929,
1935, 2028, 2055
in telephone interviews, 1142,
1202, 1513, 1748
indefinite, 1155, 1515, 1690,
1702, 1706
intervening responses, 369
interviewer prescription of
content, 1233, 1607, 1633,
1732
interviewer prescription of
duration, 1379, 1394, 1600,
1607, 1633
interviewer's classification of,
817, 1883, 1884
length of, 1231, 1379, 1394,
1395, 1600, 2044
'no opinion', 779
'no preference', 570, 1515,
1706
on racial attitudes, 59
on racial issues, 62, 2106, 2116
on sexual behaviour, 1026,
1163, 1815, 2032
on 'taboo' topics, 642, 2077
open, 66, 335, 751, 859, 918,
920, 1771, 1887, 1939,
2151, 2154
pattern of, 301, 777, 791,
1337, 1338, 1392
recording of, 157, 266, 389,
435, 440, 452, 482, 625,
704, 801, 853, 856, 907,
995, 1058, 1242, 1255,
1392, 1393, 1396, 1397,
1552, 1735, 1791, 1843,
1872, 1931, 1932, 1945,
2005, 2054, 2095, 2096,
2115
reliability of, 85, 92, 336, 504,
677, 829, 1377, 1420,
1509, 1531, 1577, 1625,
1769, 1848, 1886, 2006,
2095, 2096, 2167
response set, 285, 786, 892,
1161, 1173, 1385, 1440,

response set (*contd.*)
1504, 1836, 2068, 2070
response style, 786, 1522,
2068, 2069, 2070, 2170
to attitude statements, 369
to check list questions, 339,
1256, 1702
to classification questions,
1219, 2028
to closed questions, 556,
777, 1423, 1719, 1756,
1806
to dichotomous questions,
777, 782, 858, 1719
to free answer questions, 1423,
1702, 1719, 1882
to multiple-choice questions,
537, 782, 1131, 1719
to open questions, 334, 335,
556, 693, 751, 1423, 1558,
1702, 1719, 1806
to opinion questions, 115, 227,
453, 490, 779, 817, 1152,
1550, 1594, 1791
to polling questions, 184, 227,
229, 231, 232, 234, 334,
335, 453, 490, 500, 693,
704, 782, 990, 991, 1024,
1084, 1085, 1256, 1446,
1466, 1506, 1550, 1716,
1719, 1867, 1884, 1886,
1919, 2076, 2115, 2161,
2174
to pre-coded questions, 1423,
1882
to self-evaluation questions,
1381, 1929, 2055
to self-report questions, 37,
421, 1185, 1929
undecided, 184, 578, 1155,
1690, 1702, 1706
validity of, 33, 92, 113,
234, 264, 332, 351, 377,
415, 421, 422, 435, 439,
453, 554, 632, 633, 677,
879, 976, 1026, 1101,
1163, 1202, 1231, 1232,
1314, 1377, 1420, 1509,
1514, 1547, 1625, 1769,
1929, 2060, 2061, 2115,
2133

RESPONSE VARIANCE *See* ERROR

RETROSPECTIVE DATA
  objective method of collection, 87

  See also: LIFE-HISTORIES

RETURN RATE, of mail questionnaires *See* RESPONSE RATE, in mail surveys

ROLE REHEARSAL TECHNIQUE
  in exploratory research, 2

ROLE-PLAYING, 835, 880, 1172, 1873, 2079

SAMPLE
  accuracy of, 176, 502, 1148
  bias, 117, 188, 211, 299, 367, 433, 478, 499, 502, 505, 557, 906, 910, 973, 1019, 1026, 1067, 1127, 1280, 1524, 1575, 1698, 1717, 1780, 1803, 1879, 1960, 1974, 2018, 2026, 2032, 2033, 2036
  control of variables in small sample, 1189, 1524
  design, 45, 309, 381, 471, 472, 473, 474, 530, 534, 591, 811, 896, 900, 945, 1006, 1145, 1150, 1300, 1335, 1345, 1460, 1469, 1780, 1906
  efficiency of, 208
  enumeration, 65, 608, 1114, 1143, 1361, 2005, 2168
  estimates, 623, 1469
  matched, 309, 609, 644, 827, 1251, 1783
  nonrandom, 598
  size, 45, 212, 213, 1129, 1130, 1258, 1374, 1430, 1780, 1837, 1864, 1897, 2011, 2131, 2168
  surveys, 533, 568, 623, 729, 905, 1348, 1462, 1469, 1627, 1959, 2004

  See also: SAMPLING

SAMPLE BIAS
  and birth order of subjects, 367, 557, 2026, 2036
  and telephone surveys, 1067, 1127
  correction by weighting, 1019, 1524, 1698
  due to interviewers, 266, 267, 1717
  due to minimal call-back, 973
  due to non-availability, 117, 211, 267, 973, 1717
  due to unrepresentativeness, 299, 309, 499, 608, 906, 910, 973, 1575, 1717, 1803, 1879, 2018, 2032
  due to volunteering, 188, 367, 505, 557, 1026, 1389, 1654, 2026, 2032, 2033, 2036
  estimation of, 502, 973
  in public opinion polling, 499, 502, 1717
  sources of, 188, 478, 1280, 1717
  in studies of sexual behaviour, 188, 433, 1026, 1137, 1389, 1960, 2032
  in tourist surveys, 1575

SAMPLE DESIGN
  for area sampling, 381, 896, 945, 1145, 1300, 1345, 1780
  for probability sampling, 474, 900
  for telephone surveys, 591, 1335, 1906
  in continuing surveys, 309, 1150, 1469
  principles of, 45, 381, 473, 530, 534, 811, 900, 1006, 1145, 1851
  use of industrialization index, 1460
  use of jury qualification index, 471, 472, 1460

SAMPLE ENUMERATION
  bias in, 1114, 1143, 1361

in underdeveloped countries,
 2131, 2168
procedures for, 65, 608, 2005

SAMPLE SIZE
 adequacy of, 212, 1129, 1130,
  1258, 1430, 1864
 and sample efficiency, 213,
  1258, 1780
 in sociometric surveys, 1897
 in underdeveloped countries,
  2131, 2168
 techniques for calculating, 45,
  212, 213, 1258, 1562,
  1780, 1837, 1864, 2011

SAMPLE SURVEYS
 comparison with complete
  enumeration, 623, 1348
 cost of, 1348
 for legal evidence, 533, 1959
 measurement error in, 905
 preparation of reports on,
  2004

SAMPLING
 activity sampling, 288, 1104
 and electoral registers 176,
  248, 608, 811, 812, 819
 and non-response bias, 650,
  1149, 1780
 and the jury qualification, 471,
  472, 814
 area, 17, 291, 381, 893, 896,
  906, 930, 945, 985, 1145,
  1148, 1300, 1345, 1361,
  1407, 1626, 1780, 1897
 area space, 906
 bias, 239, 266, 267, 374, 529,
  530, 900, 906, 945, 1148,
  1150, 1280, 1361, 1458,
  2015
 cluster, 407, 552, 588, 894,
  1147, 1780, 1906
 comparison with complete
  enumeration, 1348
 comparison with various
  methods, 291, 530, 591,
  608, 900, 906, 945, 985,
  1006, 1117, 1344, 1576,
  1614, 1780, 1832, 1901

computers used in, 658,
 1530
continuous. 309, 1151
costs, 581, 588, 893, 900,
 930, 1348, 1902,
 2118
errors, 176, 475, 477, 529,
 534, 798, 896, 1114, 1469,
 1780, 1890, 1922, 1946,
 2156
for mail surveys, 624, 1076
frames, 20, 22, 176, 248, 333,
 454, 465, 499, 502, 591,
 608, 811, 812, 819, 906,
 996, 1148, 1562, 1780,
 1834, 1901, 1906, 1946,
 2168
general considerations, 381,
 473, 530, 811, 1117, 1330,
 1349, 1370, 1372, 1832,
 1888, 1889, 1891, 1901,
 2163
improving accuracy of,
 895, 906, 1114,
 1143, 1148, 1258,
 1946
in audience research, 837
in economic surveys, 41
in educational research, 552,
 1252, 1372
in financial surveys, 1114, 1457,
 1460
in industrial marketing
 research, 20, 22, 1167
in international surveys 1626
in large scale surveys, 1889
in longitudinal studies, 793
in psychological research,
 1330, 1370
in public opinion polling, 362,
 893, 1280, 1407, 1626,
 1680, 2038, 2104, 2118,
 2129
in social surveys, 811, 895,
 1114, 1360, 1454, 1460,
 1562, 1795
in sociometric surveys, 1897
in underdeveloped countries,
 1627, 1795, 2131,
 2168

275

multi-stage, 475, 477, 552, 811, 1114, 1145, 1467, 1780
non-probability, 1780
non-proportional, 291
of establishments, 474, 898, 1153, 1780
of non-respondents, 738, 739, 938
of scattered samples, 1217
prelisting, 1821
probability, 266, 267, 501, 530, 893, 900, 906, 1280, 1299, 1587, 1780, 1793, 1902, 2040, 2118, 2129
quota, 226, 239, 266, 291, 374, 381, 568, 581, 608, 893, 896, 900, 930, 945, 985, 1407, 1458, 1459, 1626
random, 122, 291, 381, 581, 608, 658, 811, 930, 1280, 1344, 1458, 1459, 1890, 1991
random route, 65, 1467
sequential, 213, 658, 1461, 1562, 1714
serial number digit, 1614
stratified 291, 381, 475, 658, 811, 996, 1344, 1890, 1922
sub-sampling, 738, 739, 938, 1901
systematic space, 900, 1344
time-sampling, 288, 1104
units, 255, 454, 894, 906, 957, 996, 1153, 1345, 1360, 1780, 1845
variance, 1922

See also: SAMPLE

SAMPLING BIAS
correction of, 530, 1148, 2015
in area sampling, 1361
in quota sampling, 239, 374, 900, 945, 1458
interviewer as cause of, 266, 1361
sources of, 1280

SAMPLING ERROR
calculation of, 475, 477, 534, 1946, 2156
control of, 1469
in area sampling, 896
in financial surveys, 798, 1114
in stratified sampling, 475, 1890, 1922

SAMPLING FRAMES
accuracy of, 248, 454, 906, 1562, 1946
adequacy of, 248, 454, 465, 608, 906, 996, 1946
bias in, 499, 502, 906, 1901
coverage of, 248, 465, 906, 996, 1148, 1834, 1946
from city directories, 1834
from electoral registers, 176, 248, 608, 811, 812, 819, 1562
from local authority areas, 996
from telephone directory, 22, 465, 591, 1901, 1906
from the National Register, 811
from the Valuation Lists, 248, 811
in industrial market research, 20, 22, 333, 1167
in underdeveloped countries, 2168
types, 248, 996

SCALES
and response sets, 162, 1161, 1173, 1200, 1385, 1683, 1720, 1721
and response styles, 1683, 1721
arrangement of items, 519, 576, 1139, 1381
cumulative, 36, 259, 510, 515, 969, 1915
direction-of-wording effects, 343
direction of measurement, 1956
for socio-economic classification, 2007

forced-choice, 118, 801, 1016, 2169
generalized, 519
graphic, 397, 573, 1086, 1655, 1656
interval, 81, 448
non-verbal, 458, 1057, 2067
number of scale items/intervals on, 170, 519, 546, 824, 858, 1166
objective, 15, 1658
of measurement, 15, 81, 448, 1134
ordinal, 448
rank order, 448, 1841
rating, 4, 5, 82, 118, 160, 168, 169, 170, 293, 297, 358, 397, 448, 485, 519, 546, 573, 621, 635, 801, 824, 858, 887, 1016, 1086, 1166, 1271, 1315, 1354, 1381, 1472, 1483, 1498, 1583, 1597, 1624, 1640, 1644, 1655, 1656, 1805, 1929, 1985, 2009, 2010, 2055, 2071, 2072, 2098, 2137, 2169
ratio, 448
reliability, 16, 515, 1166, 1601, 1684, 2078, 2127
reproducibility, 1413, 2127
response patterns, 36, 257, 515, 604, 960
scalogram, 1072
scoring midpoint responses on, 455
scoring neutral responses on, 324, 519, 602, 1312, 1517
Seashore-Hevner, 1773
semantic differential, 542, 1016, 1173, 1312, 1354, 1517, 1917, 1964, 2067, 2100
subjective, 15, 1658
unidimensional, 1288
used in product testing, 5, 297, 1583
used in readership research, 26, 458, 483, 939, 1507, 1295, 1741, 1905

validity of, 16, 118, 286, 324, 515, 1016, 1097, 1498, 1601, 1742, 1841, 2078
verbal, 297, 1271, 1498, 1624, 2067

See also: ATTITUDE SCALING TECHNIQUES; SCALING

SCALING
objectivity-subjectivity ratio, 15
of beliefs, 703
of opinion-intensity, 125, 872, 1086, 1175, 1806
of paired comparisons, 1828
of reading intensity, 458, 483, 1057
of social experience, 721, 722
of unordered attributes, 1311
qualitative material, 869
questions, 676

See also: SCALES; ATTITUDE SCALING TECHNIQUES

SCALOGRAM ANALYSIS
coefficient of reproducibility, 951, 1413, 1753
coefficient of scalability, 1072, 1413, 1560
comparison with item analysis, 1172
Cornell technique, 690, 871, 1172
critique of, 416, 690, 870, 1384, 1398
error ratio, 258
in public opinion research, 715
in sociometric research, 716
linear segments technique, 1365
non-scale response patterns, 36, 257, 604, 960
of interview vs. self-completion questionnaire responses, 1318
procedures for, 690, 1073, 1322, 1398
use in pretesting questions, 1878

277

SCALOGRAM BOARDS
  construction, 690, 1072, 1365
  linear segments, 1365
  operation, 690, 1072, 1365, 1967

SCHEDULE *See* QUESTIONNAIRE

SEASHORE-HEVNER SCALES, 1773

SECONDARY-DATA
  analysis of, 1657, 1676
  applicability of, 1676
  in developing countries, 1676
  in longitudinal studies, 1676

SECRET BALLOT
  and prestige-seeking, 1992
  comparison with personal interview, 184, 1107, 1992
  effect on undecided responses, 184
  in public opinion polling, 184, 479, 828, 1992
  pin-prick method, 479

SEGMENTATION TECHNIQUES
  and biological classification, 27, 147, 151, 308
  and respondent classification, 27, 158
  in consumer attitude research, 27, 1291
  in market research, 27, 1628
  sample splitting, 27, 147, 151, 308
  sequential dichotomisation, 27, 147, 151, 308, 408, 430, 637, 638, 1444, 1855, 1856, 1857

  See also: MATCHING

SELF-ADMINISTERED QUESTIONNAIRES *See* SELF-COMPLETION QUESTIONNAIRES

SELF-COMPLETION QUESTIONNAIRES
  and interviewer bias, 352
  comparison with personal interview, 33, 37, 351, 352, 1163, 1318, 1423, 1480, 1935, 2055
  comparison with polygraph examination, 415
  cost, 1935
  in public opinion research, 1226, 2126
  non-respondents to, 314
  non-response, 314, 971
  order effects, 1477
  reliability of, 504, 1577
  response rate to, 1935
  responses to questions in, 33, 34, 37, 351, 352, 415, 496, 702, 801, 879, 886, 1157, 1163, 1318, 1353, 1477, 1480, 1559, 1563, 1577, 1848, 1929, 1935, 2028, 2055
  supplemented by group discussion, 954
  use in motivational research, 1740
  used by panels, 611, 839, 1210, 1615, 1747, 1776
  used to measure brand market positions, 971
  used to measure effectiveness of educational training programmes, 546
  used to secure response from 'not-at-home' respondents, 601
  validity, 7, 351, 415, 971, 1163, 1230, 1840, 1929

SELF-COMPLETION SURVEY *See* SELF-COMPLETION QUESTIONNAIRES

SELF-ENUMERATIVE QUESTIONNAIRES *See* SELF-COMPLETION QUESTIONNAIRES

SELF-EVALUATION QUESTIONS, 1381, 1929, 2055

SELF-REPORT QUESTIONS, 352, 415, 1185, 1929

SELF-SURVEY, 404, 912, 1191, 1777

SEMANTIC DIFFERENTIAL
accuracy of, 57, 166, 1354
and personal constructs, 1435
and prediction of voting behaviour, 1917
and response set, 786, 1173
and response style, 786, 2170
application in advertising research, 1429
application in attitude research, 278, 542, 1105, 1154, 1291, 1406, 1435, 1674, 1754, 1964
application in brand attitude measurement, 100, 1121
application in market research, 425, 1291, 1429
application in readership research, 1295
bias in, 57, 786, 1121
comparison with Stapel scales, 485
context effects, 1186, 2100
D-scores, 428
effect of forcing responses, 1016, 1517
in product testing, 522, 752, 1674, 2098
individual-scale-interaction, 493
instructions for delivering, 165, 1431
language medium effects, 412, 1186
neutral responses, 1312, 1517, 2157
order effects, 428, 1270
presentation of scales, 165, 1964, 2067
questionnaire design for, 1849
reliability, 1431
repertory grid technique used in development of scales, 752
scale-symmetry, 1354, 1418
semantic generalization, 1674
using adverbs as multipliers, 43

SEMANTIC SPACE, 825
See also: SEMANTIC DIFFERENTIAL

SENTENCE COMPLETION TEST
used in attitude change measurement, 317, 1250
used in attitude measurement, 781, 1351
used in cross-cultural research, 1723

SEQUENTIAL DICHOTOMISATION TECHNIQUES
A.I.D., 430, 637, 638, 1444, 1855, 1856, 1857
biological classification method, 27, 147, 151, 308, 408, 430, 637, 638

SEQUENTIAL SAMPLING
advantages, 1714
and number of interviews required, 213
applications, 1461, 1562, 1714
sequential selection by computer, 658

SETMETER
used in television audience research, 1999, 2048

SHORT TERM PANELS *See* PANELS

SOCIO-ECONOMIC CLASSIFICATION
and quota sampling, 568
by discriminatory analysis, 761
by income, 568, 994, 1679, 1869, 2103
by interviewers, 1289, 1465, 1679, 2006, 2007
by occupation, 38, 568, 634, 838, 846, 867, 883, 943, 984, 988, 994, 1035, 1239, 1341, 1708, 1772, 1869, 2034, 2165
by social status, 38, 634, 883, 943, 1035, 1211
comparability, 761, 1035, 1211, 1239

for consumer product survey, 120
for voting behaviour studies, 38
in Britain, 274
in France, 274
international systems, 274, 1499
of families, 120, 388, 568, 994
of towns, 814, 2103
validity, 568, 1289, 2034
use of scales for, 1289, 2007

SOCIOMETRIC DATA
analysis, 394, 443, 444, 663, 1093, 1094, 1340, 1909
and mechanical tabulation, 199, 1094
processing of, 35, 199, 444, 1094

SOCIOMETRIC SURVEY
area sampling, 1897
call-backs, 1897
interviewing, 1898
sample size, 1897

SPECIALIST PANELS *See* **PANELS**

'SPLIT-BALLOT' TECHNIQUE *See* **SPLIT-SAMPLE TECHNIQUE**

SPLIT PANEL TESTS, 1039

SPLIT-SAMPLE TECHNIQUE, 1155, 1719

STABLE CORRELATES, 143, 144, 146, 149, 152, 154, 616, 637, 1543

STANDARDISED INTERVIEW, 955, 1305

STANDARDIZATION, 1075

STAPEL SCALES
comparison with semantic differential scaling, 485
for opinion-intensity measurement, 1483

STATISTICAL ANALYSIS OF DATA
analysis of covariance, 1074, 2139
analysis of variance, 445, 760, 771, 810, 1054, 1855, 1856, 1857, 1880, 1913, 2139
and cluster sampling, 1147
ANOVA procedures, 401, 760
association analysis, 430, 1324
canonical correlations, 638, 1636
chi-square, 401, 663, 855, 1129, 1130, 1237, 1833, 1863, 1864
clumping techniques, 638
clustering techniques, 430, 607, 638, 776, 808, 823, 882, 931, 999, 1034, 1051, 1055, 1063, 1277, 1325, 1327, 1339, 1510, 1546, 1628, 1632, 1909, 2138
component analysis, 692, 1034, 1116, 1546, 1632, 1636
computer programs, 13, 89, 307, 444, 462, 758, 794, 800, 822, 931, 1020, 1034, 1240, 1825, 1855, 1856, 1857, 1962, 2138, 2164
confidence intervals, 1190
correlation analysis, 446, 1074, 1323, 1546, 1636
discriminatory analysis, 430, 638, 761, 1452, 1569, 2139
extreme value theory, 401
factor analysis, 134, 323, 385, 430, 447, 638, 656, 755, 860, 861, 864, 923, 968, 1034, 1040, 1116, 1232, 1291, 1321, 1325, 1327, 1329, 1340, 1482, 1546, 1583, 1628, 1636, 1709, 1745, 1835, 1894, 1966, 1970, 2020, 2132, 2159
for audience research 143, 144, 145, 152, 154, 881, 1543

for analytical surveys, 443,
532
for consumer attitude research,
134, 430, 823, 999, 1034,
1291, 1628, 1730
for enumerative surveys, 532
for life-history data analysis,
89, 389
for longitudinal studies, 793,
794, 1676
for market research, 1063,
1352
for organisational research, 443
for sociometric data analysis,
394, 443, 444, 663, 1093,
1094, 1340, 1909
free analysis, 607
gap analysis, 426, 974
latent structure analysis, 550,
1632
linkage analysis, 1063, 1632,
1909
matching, 27, 61, 143, 144,
146, 147, 149, 151, 152,
154, 208, 434, 616, 637,
644, 657, 745, 1075, 1543,
2166
multidimensional scaling, 705,
822, 1183
multiple classification analysis,
49
multiple discriminant
techniques, 736, 1452
multiple regression and
correlation, 49, 268, 446,
803, 1198
of multi-coded data, 1965
pattern analysis, 507, 1337,
1338, 1900
pause analysis, 1977
prediction techniques, 3,
146, 147, 151, 308, 430,
862, 1444, 1730, 1900,
2102
profile analysis, 775, 823,
1510
regression analysis, 263, 430,
446, 638, 803, 862, 1198
segmentation techniques, 27,
147, 151, 158, 308, 408,

segmentation techniques (*contd.*)
430, 637, 638, 1291, 1444,
1628, 1855, 1856, 1857
significance tests, 61, 86, 855,
936, 1075, 1190, 1251,
1450, 1610, 1778, 2135,
2139
weighting, 27, 422, 501, 508,
586, 612, 1019, 1123,
1201, 1524, 1587, 1592,
1593, 1698, 1823, 2172

STRATIFIED SAMPLING
and sampling error, 475, 1890,
1922
comparison with systematic
space sampling, 1344
effect of stratification on
various methods of
sampling, 291, 1890
for social surveys, 811
sampling frames for, 811, 996

STRUCTURED INTERVIEW
advantages of, 240
as social relationship, 1589
clinical, 9
comparison with mail
questionnaire, 240
comparison with unstructured
interview, 1491, 2035
fully structured, 1491
in motivational research, 2035,
2082
limitations of, 240
questionnaire design for, 240
semi-structured, 1313, 1491
structured depth interview,
1535, 1590, 2082

SUBJECTS *See* RESPONDENTS

SUGGESTION
in question wording, 58, 227,
230, 315, 453, 1009, 1293,
1421, 1470, 1594, 1886
in specific wording, 1470
situational, 58, 565, 2056

SUMMATION METHODS, 603

SURVEY
- analytical, 443, 532, 924
- attitude, 347, 577, 628, 1157
- classifying respondents in, 95, 2007
- commercial, 2160
- conducted in Asia, 128, 1164, 1350, 1630, 1715
- conducted in Europe, 333
- consumer, 121, 282, 283, 392, 591, 731, 770, 785, 840, 880, 944, 1070, 1439, 1467, 1677, 1701, 1702, 1774, 1876, 2146, 2177
- continuing, 309, 391, 731, 1150, 1469, 1677, 1820, 2123
- cost of conducting, 1348
- data processing of, 46, 195, 262, 307, 726, 728, 747, 748, 758, 1174, 1358, 1469, 1676, 1820, 1825, 1965, 1995, 2022, 2164
- design, 12, 509, 1070, 1110, 1124, 1192, 1469, 1725
- economic, 41, (898), 1469, (2045)
- enumerative, 95, 253, 532, 593, 608, 924, 1348, 1371, 1397, 1469, 1531, 1618
- financial, 260, 261, 440, 441, 680, 681, 683, 798, 868, 875, 909, 1080, 1109, 1110, 1111, 1112, 1113, 1114, 1124, 1201, 1202, 1304, 1404, 1457, 1485, 1486, 1993, 2114
- for decision making, 370
- for legal evidence, 533, 1556, 1959
- health, 113, 142, 353, 354, 377, 435, 496, 1204, 1242, 1469, 1480, 1820
- household, 198, 253, 388, 986, 994, 1043, 1109, 1110, 1111, 1112, 1113, 1114, 1124, 1471, 1481, 1485, 1486, 1495, 1875, 1986, 1993, 2114
- in occupied countries, 1224
- in underdeveloped countries, 128, 210, 1205, 1350, 1419, 1626, 1630, 1676, 1715, 1725, 1781, 1795, 2131
- incomplete information in, 307, 1201, 1862
- international, 14, 344, 651, 787, 1021, 1031, 1621, 2053
- interpretation of results, 726, 728, 1156, 1450, 1610, 1960
- large scale, 1013, 1469, 1887
- mail, 5, 21, 22, 76, 123, 127, 187, 203, 240, 249, 271, 273, 280, 296, 330, 333, 337, 396, 403, 422, 439, 442, 484, 537, 538, 564, 583, 597, 624, 632, 633, 648, 649, 667, 669, 670, 671, 672, 682, 684, 689, 718, 719, 720, 723, 725, 734, 738, 739, 740, 742, 744, 787, 792, 815, 818, 829, 852, 863, 865, 897, 930, 938, 949, 950, 952, 958, 983, 986, 987, 1000, 1008, 1037, 1076, 1099, 1120, 1128, 1159, 1162, 1163, 1203, 1205, 1207, 1213, 1235, 1262, 1273, 1274, 1281, 1314, 1347, 1357, 1358, 1359, 1391, 1401, 1435, 1473, 1493, 1494, 1503, 1509, 1528, 1553, 1582, 1586, 1588, 1612, 1637, 1639, 1659, 1664, 1665, 1666, 1669, 1673, 1679, 1692, 1749, 1763, 1769, 1770, 1775, 1792, 1812, 1813, 1816, 1824, 1831, 1865, 1866, 1871, 1912, 1926, 1948, 1978, 1979, 2019, 2027, 2029, 2030, 2041, 2058, 2158
- mathematical model of error in, 901, 1468, 1941
- media, 27, 29, 158, 282, 283

method, 12, 132, 133, 142,
 197, 264, 333, 413, 443,
 636, 911, 1026, 1053,
 1087, 1091, 1137, 1246,
 1247, 1471, 1949, 1960,
 1981, 1987, 2032, 2051,
 2062, 2122, 2133
prediction, 1192
presentation of results, 1387,
 2121
public opinion, 14, 344, 645,
 910, 940, 1031, 1164,
 1554, 1621, 1626, 2038
readership, 6, 23, 127, 155,
 159, 161, 294, 425, 476,
 908, 965, 1011, 1058,
 1096, 1100, 1273, 1295,
 1476, 1787, 1865, 1968,
 2155
road traffic, 1368
sample, 533, 568, 623, 729,
 905, 1348, 1462, 1469,
 1627, 1959, 2004
secondary analysis of data
 from, 1158, 1676, 2160
self-survey, 404, 912, 1191,
 1777
social, 122, 265, 654, 780,
 811, 816, 992, 1053, 1321,
 1323, 1326, 1360, 1794,
 1868, 2045, 2122
sociometric, 1897, 1898
standards for conducting, 548,
 1223, 1368, 1907
telephone, 22, 240, 592, 986,
 1003, 1067, 1127, 1335,
 1555, 1906, 1986
total error measurement, 84,
 298, 903, 1308
tourist, 1575
wartime, 265, 492, 547, 1013,
 1164, 1224
See also: ETHICS
'SURVEY-BY-RADIO'
TECHNIQUE, 2126
'SURVEY-BY-TELEVISION'
TECHNIQUE
 in public opinion research,
 1877

SURVEY METHOD
 and research design, 1087,
 1471
 comparison with other
 methods of data collection,
 132, 133, 142, 197, 636,
 1981
 history of, 636, 1053
 in industrial market research,
 333, 1041
 in morale measurement, 911,
 1091, 2051
 in organisational research, 443,
 1949
 in sexual behaviour research,
 272, 413, 433, 1026, 1137,
 1960, 2032
 in sociological research,
 636, 1249, 1471, 1562,
 2062
 limitations of, 264, 636, 2133
 research methodology, 12,
 766, 1026, 1246, 1247,
 2062
 validity, 264, 1087, 2122,
 2133

SYSTEMATIC SPACE
SAMPLING, 900, 1344

TABULATION
 manual, 46, 1548, 1578
 mechanical, 46, 199, 1001,
 1548
 of sociometric data, 199
 pre-planning questionnaire for,
 46, 1174, 2145
 tabulation schedule recorder,
 1995

TABULATOR
 use in data processing, 647,
 700, 1094
 use in Guttman scaling, 1852

TAMMETER
 used in television audience
 research, 618, 1999, 2048

TANDEM INTERVIEW, 1132,
 1133

TANIMETER *See* TAMMETER

TAPE-RECORDING, of interview
  acceptability, 157, 306, 640
  advantages, 305
  and error, 161, 640, 2148
  as check on quality of
    interviewing, 482, 640, 853,
    1552, 2148
  compared with written
    recording, 482, 640
  cost, 305, 640
  effect on accuracy of recording
    of responses, 161, 1552
  effect on accuracy of
    respondent's responses, 157,
    161, 305
  ethics, 204
  for speech interaction
    measurement, 2096
  in field research, 305, 306, 640
  in readership surveys, 161
  of telephone interview, 821
  technical aspects of recording,
    204, 306, 640
  transcribing, 305, 306

TASTE-TESTING
  and response sets, 1757
  discrimination testing, 834,
    839, 1747
  expectation effects, 844
  experimental design, 843, 1954
  monadic tests, 427, 833
  order effects, 192
  paired comparisons, 427, 684,
    833, 834, 1678
  panels, 611, 1615, 1747,
    1776
  preference testing, 91, 192,
    684, 711, 833, 834, 843,
    844, 1583, 1678, 1747,
    1757, 1954
  ranking methods, 590
  reliability of taster's
    judgement, 684, 844, 849,
    850, 1678
  sensitivity of taster's
    judgement, 844, 849, 850,
    1678
  triad comparisons procedure,
    839, 843, 849, 850, 1678

TELEPHONE
  advance call in mail survey,
    1866, 2027
  directory as sampling frame,
    22, 465, 1906
  in audience research, 200, 373,
    469, 591, 1007, 1077,
    1422, 1667
  in industrial market research,
    21, 22, 333
  interview, 21, 22, 60, 200,
    240, 331, 333, 373, 463,
    469, 592, 821, 972, 986,
    1003, 1077, 1126, 1202,
    1335, 1422, 1499, 1513,
    1555, 1667, 1748, 1937,
    1986
  surveys, 22, 240, 592, 986,
    1003, 1067, 1127, 1335,
    1555, 1906, 1986
  use in reducing survey costs,
    1937
  used to interview scattered
    samples, 592, 1937
  used to make appointment
    with respondent, 653, 1768,
    1937
  used to screen rare
    populations, 1937

TELEPHONE, in audience
research
  combination telephone
    coincidental and diary
    method, 469
  telephone call method, 200,
    373, 1007, 1077
  telephone coincidental
    method, 1077, 1422, 1667

TELEPHONE INTERVIEW
  advantages, 240, 1335, 1555,
    1748, 1937
  comparison with other data
    collection methods, 331,
    986, 1202, 1513
  comparison with other
    methods of consumer
    purchase measurement, 60
  cost of, 1335, 1937

in audience research, 200, 373, 469, 1422
in industrial marketing research, 21, 22, 333
in longitudinal studies, 463
in public opinion polling, 821
in radio audience research, 1667
in readership research, 331
limitations, 240, 1126, 1667, 1748, 1937
of scattered samples, 592, 1937
principles for conducting, 240, 1003, 1986
questionnaire design for, 240
responses to questions in, 1202, 1513, 1748
tape-recording of, 821
validity, 1202

TELEPHONE SURVEYS
control of interviewer performance, 592, 1003, 1335
in industrial market research, 22
respondent selection within household, 1986
sample bias, 1067, 1127
sample design, 591, 1335, 1906
versus mail surveys, 22, 240, 986

TELEVISION AUDIENCE RESEARCH TECHNIQUES
aided recall, 613, 615, 617, 618, 1436, 1511, 1699
bias related to 456, 469, 937
button-pressing methods, 1253, 1254, 1814
comparison of various techniques, 617, 618
diaries, 456, 459, 469, 617, 618, 733, 1065, 1580, 1999, 2000
error related to, 469, 618
exposure-probability index, 1199
factor analysis, 1709
for audience reaction measurement, 822, 1253, 1254, 1814, 1819
for audience size measurement, 31, 373, 469, 613, 617, 618, 733, 797, 1422, 1580, 1699, 1814, 1819, 1999
for measuring TV commerical audiences, 937, 1511
for measuring TV sets in use, 626, 1580, 1999
for measuring TV viewing frequency, 31, 310, 456, 459, 1049, 1999
for programme effects measurement, 143, 144, 152, 154, 164, 637, 1543, 1982
panels, 310, 456, 459, 617, 618, 733, 937, 1065, 1818, 1819, 1877, 1999
programme classification, 881
recording meters, 617, 618, 733, 937, 1999, 2047, 2048
TAM, 618, 1999
telephone call method, 373, 469, 937
telephone coincidental method, 1422
used by BBC, 1818, 1819
validation of, 2046

THEATRE AUDIENCE RESEARCH TECHNIQUES
for rating theatrical performances, 1221

THERAPEUTIC INTERVIEW, 979, 1383

THURSTONE SCALING
comparison with Likert scaling, 603, 1243
comparison with method of reciprocal averages, 1002
comparison with self-rating scales, 1655, 1656
descriptive review of, 448, 573, 1056, 1140, 2009, 2010, 2049, 2050

effect of judge's own opinions, 685, 981, 982, 1103, 1585, 1620, 1755
instructions to judges, 2094
method of successive intervals, 1056, 1103, 1631, 1827
neutral responses, 602
of paired comparisons data, 2142
rational origins, 1973
reliability, 365, 980
scoring methods, 1244, 1700
self-reference items, 1755
use in question design, 1421
validity, 365, 685, 981, 982, 1331, 1332, 1415

TIME TESTS, 1061

TRANSCRIBING
checking, 305
cost of, 306
errors in, 305
of tape-recorded interview, 305, 306
transcribing procedures, 305

TRIAD COMPARISONS PROCEDURE
bias in, 843
used in product testing, 522, 843, 849, 850, 1678

TRUE EXPERIMENTAL RESEARCH DESIGNS
multiple X groups, 341
post-test only control group design, 98, 341
pretest-post-test control group design, 98, 341
Solomon four-group design, 98, 341, 356
sources of invalidity in, 98, 341
two-control group, 356

UNAIDED RECALL
and order effects, 1950
comparison with aided recall, 1319, 1602, 1604, 1870
in advertising research, 1355, 1870
in audience research, 200, 373, 1077, 1319, 1950
in readership research, 1319

UNDER-CLAIMING *See* UNDER-REPORTING

UNDER-REPORTING
error due to, 113, 159, 351, 353, 377, 413, 415, 677, 875, 909, 1142, 1143, 1367, 1404, 1405, 1480, 1648
of delinquent behaviour, 415
of illness, 354, 1204, 1377, 1481
of income, 875
of product purchases, 1269
under-claiming by respondent, 113, 155, 159, 351, 352, 353, 354, 377, 413, 415, 677, 875, 909, 1142, 1204, 1269, 1273, 1367, 1377, 1404, 1480, 1481, 1648

UNSTANDARDISED INTERVIEW *See* UNSTRUCTURED INTERVIEW

UNSTRUCTURED INTERVIEW
analysis of interview material, 2140
comparison with structured interview, 1305, 1491, 2035
functions of, 1728
unstructured depth interview, 1535
use in qualitative research, 1728

VALIDATION
in readership research, 476
of advertising research techniques, 88
of financial survey data, 868
of new research techniques, 88
of sample design, 45
of television audience research techniques, 2046

VALIDITY
concurrent, 88
construct, 88, 342, 495

methods of securing, 868, 2078
of attitude research techniques,
  316, 384, 455, 701, 873,
  1022, 1027, 1079, 1141,
  1184, 1331, 1332, 1351,
  1529, 2009, 2010
of attitude scaling techniques,
  16, 118, 286, 324, 365,
  416, 515, 685, 687, 866,
  870, 873, 981, 982, 1060,
  1079, 1141, 1331, 1332,
  1384, 1415, 1742, 1753,
  2065, 2078, 2169
of certain research designs, 341
of closed questions, 1756, 1797
of data from informants, 340,
  524, 1101, 1420, 1947,
  1983, 1984, 2016, 2043,
  2171
of depth interview, 790, 1215,
  1260
of 'don't know' responses, 1690
of forced-choice scaling
  techniques, 82, 1644, 1985,
  2169
of Likert technique, 118,
  1079, 1243
of 'lost-letter' technique, 1427,
  2089
of mail-ballot polling, 185,
  327, 1919
of mail survey method, 632,
  633, 1076, 1205, 1213,
  1314, 1553, 1769, 1871,
  1912, 1978
of memory dependent
  questions, 701, 830
of motivation research
  techniques, 279
of open questions, 1558, 1797
of panel method, 619, 937,
  977, 1212, 1216, 1509,
  1514, 2130
of participant observation
  technique, 1159, 1490,
  2017, 2171
of personal interview method,
  92, 281, 632, 633, 1101,
  1231, 1249, 1305, 1382,
  1514, 1547, 1944

of polling questions, 236, 453,
  990, 991, 1083
of preference testing
  techniques, 1079
of projective questions, 1876
of projective techniques, 566,
  1351, 1595, 1671, 1685,
  1733, 1734, 1872, 1873,
  1876, 2162
of public opinion research
  techniques, 229, 234, 236,
  247, 327, 329, 421, 486,
  489, 491, 562, 688, 691,
  783, 828, 925, 940, 1082,
  1083, 1087, 1088, 1089,
  1090, 1247, 1259, 1331,
  1332, 1465, 1642, 1651,
  1715, 2089, 2115
of rating scales, 33, 1498,
  1805, 1929, 2137
of responses in health surveys,
  113, 377, 435
of responses in mail surveys,
  632, 633, 1314, 1509,
  1769
of responses in personal
  interviews, 33, 92, 113,
  234, 351, 421, 453, 554,
  632, 633, 976, 1101, 1202,
  1232, 1377, 1420, 1509,
  1514, 1547, 2060, 2115
of responses in self-completion
  questionnaires, 33, 351, 415,
  879, 1163, 1929
of responses in telephone
  interviews, 1202
of self-completion
  questionnaire method, 7,
  351, 415, 971, 1163, 1230,
  1840, 1929
of social science experiments,
  341, 889
of the survey method, 264,
  1087, 2122, 2133
predictive, 4, 247, 324, 329,
  365, 491, 562, 691, 1038,
  1070, 1082, 1089, 1547,
  2137
techniques for increasing,
  1377, 1687

tests of, 342, 415, 495, 691,
701, 830, 1259, 1420,
1498, 1687, 2078

VIEWER PANELS *See* **PANELS**

VALUE ANALYSIS, 2085

VISUAL AIDS, 353, 1808

VISUAL ANALYSIS, 1512

VOLUNTEER BIAS
and birth order of volunteers,
284, 367, 557, 1695, 2026,
2036
and group testing, 145, 150,
156, 367, 505, 978, 1693
and psychological
characteristics of volunteers,
139, 140, 1974
and psychological experiments,
140, 367, 557, 1229, 1654,
1693, 2026, 2036
and sociological characteristics
of volunteers, 139
control of, 145, 150
in studies of sexual behaviour,
188, 1389, 1815, 1960,
2032
sample bias, 145, 188, 290,
367, 505, 557, 1026, 1389,
1654, 1974, 2026, 2032,
2033

VOLUNTEERS
bias due to, 139, 140, 145,
150, 156, 188, 284, 290,
367, 505, 557, 978, 1026,

bias due to (*contd.*)
1229, 1389, 1654, 1693,
1695, 1815, 1960, 1974,
2026, 2032, 2033, 2036
birth order of, 284, 367, 557,
1695, 2026, 2036
comparison with
non-volunteers, 150, 156,
1689, 1695
intelligence of, 505, 1695, 1990
1990
motivation of, 67, 217, 290,
1695
personality differences from
non-volunteers, 140, 978,
1176, 1386, 1389, 1654,
1689, 1695, 1815, 1974,
1990

WEIGHTING
by card-duplication, 1698
effect on precision, 1019, 2172
for matching purposes, 27
for non-response, 422, 501,
508, 586, 612, 1123, 1201,
1587, 1592, 1593, 1823
to correct for sample bias,
1019, 1524, 1698

ZERO-POINT
and attitude change
measurement, 346, 873
and attitude intensity
measurement, 872, 873
effect of choice of social
object, 970
effect of scaling technique, 970
effect of stimulus context, 970

LIST OF BOOKS

A selection of texts, consisting of major contributions to research into the methodology and techniques of market and social research.

ADLER, Max K. 1965. *Lectures in market research*. Edited by Jacqueline Marrian. London: Crosby Lockwood, 1965 (1969 reprint). xi, 120 pp.

ADLER, Max K. 1965. *Modern market research: a guide for business executives*. London: Crosby Lockwood, 1965. 176 pp.

ANDERSON, Harold H. *and* ANDERSON, Gladys L., *eds*. 1951. *An introduction to projective techniques*.... New York: Prentice-Hall, 1951. xxiv, 720 pp.

AWAD, Elias M. 1970. *Automatic data processing: principles and procedures*. 2nd ed. Englewood Cliffs, New Jersey: Prentice-Hall 1970. xiv, 495 pp.

BACKSTROM, Charles Herbert *and* HURSH, Gerald D. 1963. *Survey research*. Evanston, Illinois: Northwestern University Press, 1963. xxiii, 192 pp.

BELL, John Elderkin. 1948. *Projective techniques: a dynamic approach to the study of the personality*. New York, London: Longmans Green, 1948 (1951 reprint). xvi, 533 pp.

BELSON, William A. 1962. *Studies in readership*. London: Business Publications, 1962. vi, 266 pp.

BELSON, William A. 1967. *The impact of television: methods and findings in program research*. London: Crosby Lockwood, 1967. x, 400 pp.

BERELSON, Bernard *and* JANOWITZ, Morris 1953. *Reader in public opinion and communication*. New York: Glencoe Free Press, 1953. xi, 611 pp.

BEVERIDGE, W. E. 1968. *Problem solving interviews*. London: Allen and Unwin, 1968. 123 pp.

BLALOCK, Hubert M., *Jr*. 1961. *Causal inferences in nonexperimental research*. Chapel Hill: University of North Carolina Press, 1961 (1964 reprint). xiii, 200 pp.

BLALOCK, Hubert M., *Jr. and* BLALOCK, Ann B., *eds.* 1968. *Methodology in social research.* New York, London: McGraw-Hill, 1968. 493 pp.

BLALOCK, Hubert M. *Jr., ed.* 1972. *Causal models in the social sciences.* London: Macmillan, 1972. xi, 515 pp.

BRITT, Steuart Henderson. 1966. *Consumer behavior and the behavioral sciences: theories and applications.* New York, London: Wiley, 1966. xxxii, 592 pp.

CAMPBELL, Donald Thomas *and* STANLEY, Julian Cecil. 1966. *Experimental and quasi-experimental designs for research.* Chicago: Rand McNally, 1968. ix, 84 pp.

CATTELL, R. B. 1952. *Factor analysis.* . . . New York: Harper, 1952. xiii, 462 pp.

CHAPIN, Francis Stuart. 1947. *Experimental designs in sociological research.* New York: Harper, 1947. x, 206 pp.

COCHRAN, William G. 1967. *Sampling techniques.* 2nd ed. New York: Wiley, 1967. xvii, 413 pp.

CONWAY, Freda. 1967. *Sampling: an introduction for social scientists.* London: Allen and Unwin, 1967. 160 pp.

COOLEY, William W. *and* LOHNES, Paul R. 1965. *Multivariate procedures for the behavioral sciences.* New York: Wiley, 1965. x, 211 pp.

CRISP, Richard D. 1957. *Marketing research.* New York, London: McGraw-Hill, 1957. xii, 798 pp.

DALENIUS, Tore. 1957. *Sampling in Sweden: contributions to the methods and theories of sample survey practice.* Stockholm: Almqvist and Wiksell, 1957. viii, 247 pp.

DELENS, A. H. R. 1964. *Principles of market research.* London: Crosby Lockwood, 1964. 254 pp.

DEMING, W. Edwards. 1960. *Sample design in business research.* New York, London: Wiley, 1960. xx, 517 pp.

DEXTER, Lewis Anthony. 1970. *Elite and specialized interviewing.* Evanston: Northwestern University Press, 1970. xiv, 205 pp.

EDWARDS, Allen L. 1957. *Techniques of attitude scale construction.* New York: Appleton-Century-Crofts, 1957. xiii, 256 pp.

ERDOS, Paul L. 1970. *Professional mail surveys.* New York, London: McGraw-Hill, 1970. xi, 289 pp.

FENLASON, Anne F. 1962. *Essentials in interviewing.* ... Rev. ed. by Grace Beals Ferguson and Arthur C. Abrahamson. New York, London: Harper and Row, 1962. xvi, 372 pp.

FESTINGER, Leon *and* KATZ, Daniel, *eds.* 1966. *Research methods in the behavioral sciences.* New York, London: Holt, Rinehart and Winston, 1966, xi, 660 pp.

FISHBEIN, Martin, *ed.* 1967. *Readings in attitude theory and measurement.* New York: Wiley, 1967. 499 pp.

FISHER, *Sir* Robert Aylmer. 1960. *The design of experiments.* 7th ed. Edinburgh: Oliver and Boyd, 1960. xv, 248 pp.

GALTON, Johan. 1967. *Theory and methods of social research.* Oslo: Universitetsforlaget; London: Allen and Unwin, 1967. 534 pp.

GARRETT, Annette. 1942. *Interviewing: its principles and methods.* New York: Family Service Association, 1942 (1968 reprint). 123 pp.

GLOCK, Charles Y., *ed.* 1967. *Survey research in the social sciences.* New York: Russell Sage, 1967. xxi, 543 pp.

GOODE, William J. *and* HATT, Paul K. 1952. *Methods in social research.* New York, London: McGraw-Hill, 1952. vii, 386 pp.

GOULD, Julius *and* KOLB, William L., *eds.* *A dictionary of the social sciences.* London: Tavistock, 1964. xvi, 761 pp.

GREEN, Paul E. *and* CARMONE, Frank J. 1970. *Multidimensional scaling and related techniques in marketing analysis.* Boston, Massachusetts: Allyn and Bacon, 1970. ix, 203 pp.

GREEN, Paul E. *and* TULL, Donald S. 1970. *Research for marketing decisions.* 2nd ed. Englewood Cliffs, New Jersey: Prentice-Hall, 1970. xii, 644 pp.

GUILFORD, J. P. 1954. *Psychometric methods.* 2nd ed. New York, London: McGraw-Hill, 1954. ix, 597 pp.

HANSEN, Morris H., HURWITZ, William N. *and* MADOW, William G. 1953. *Sample survey methods and theory.* New York, London: Wiley, 1953 (1966 reprint). 2v. (xxii, 638, xiii, 332 pp.)

HARMAN, Harry H. 1967. *Modern factor analysis.* 2nd ed. Chicago, London: University of Chicago Press, 1967. xx, 474 pp.

HENRY, Harry. 1958. *Motivation research: its practice and uses for advertising, marketing, and other business purposes.* London: Crosby Lockwood, 1958. 220 pp.

HILL, Joseph E. *and* KERBER, August. 1967. *Models, methods and analytical procedures in education research.* Detroit: Wayne State University Press, 1967. xii, 550 pp.

HIRSCHI, Travis *and* SELVIN, Hanan. 1967. *Delinquency research: an appraisal of analytic methods.* New York: Free Press; London: Collier-Macmillan, 1967. xiv, 280 pp.

HOPE, Keith. 1968. *Methods of multivariate analysis.* London: University of London Press, 1968. 288 pp.

HYMAN, Herbert H. *et al.* 1954. *Interviewing in social research.* Chicago, London: University of Chicago Press, 1954 (1965 reprint). xvi, 415 pp.

HYMAN, Herbert. 1966. *Survey design and analysis: principles, cases and procedures.* New York: Free Press; London: Collier-Macmillan, 1966. xxiii, 424 pp.

KAHN, Robert L. *and* CANNELL, Charles F. 1957. *The dynamics of interviewing: theory, technique and cases.* New York, London: Wiley, 1957 (1967 reprint). x, 368 pp.

KISH, Leslie. 1965. *Survey sampling.* New York: Wiley, 1965. xvi, 643 pp.

LAZARSFELD, Paul F. *and* ROSENBERG, Morris. 1955. *The language of social research. . . .* New York: Free Press; London: Collier-Macmillan, 1955 (1967 reprint). xiii, 590 pp.

LEONHARD, Dietz. 1967. *The human equation in marketing research.* New York: American Management Association, 1967. 176 pp.

LERNER, Daniel *and* LASSWELL, Harold D., eds. 1951. *The policy sciences.* Stanford, California: Stanford Unversity Press, 1951 (1965 reprint). xiv, 344 pp.

LUCAS, Darrell Blaine *and* BRITT, Steuart Henderson. 1950. *Advertising psychology and research.* New York, London: McGraw-Hill, 1950. xi, 765 pp.

LUCK, David J., WALES, Hugh G. *and* TAYLOR, Donald A. 1970. *Marketing research.* 3rd ed. Englewood Cliffs, New Jersey: Prentice-Hall, 1970. ix, 645 pp.

MADGE, John. 1953. *The tools of social science.* London: Longmans, 1953 (1967 reprint). x, 308 pp.

MAXWELL, A. E. 1961. *Analysing qualitative data.* London: Methuen, 1961 (1967 reprint). 163 pp.

MILLER, Delbert C. 1970. *Handbook of research design and social measurement.* 2nd ed. New York: David McKay, 1970. xiii, 432 pp.

MOSER, C. A. *and* KALTON, G. 1971. *Survey methods in social investigation.* London: Heinemann, 1971. xvii, 549 pp.

OPPENHEIM, A. N. 1966. *Questionnaire design and attitude measurement.* London: Heinemann, 1966. ix, 298 pp.

OSGOOD, Charles E., SUCI, George J. *and* TANNENBAUM, Percy H. 1957. *The measurement of meaning.* Urbana, Illinois, London: University of Illinois Press, 1957 (1967 reprint). 346 pp.

PALDA, Kristian S. 1964. *The measurement of cumulative advertising effects.* Englewood Cliffs, New Jersey: Prentice-Hall, 1964. xiv, 101 pp.

PARTEN, Mildred B. 1950. *Surveys, polls and samples: practical procedures.* New York, London: Harper and Row; Weatherhill: Tokyo, 1950 (1965 reprint). xii, 624 pp.

PAYNE, Stanley L. 1951. *The art of asking questions.* Princeton, New Jersey: Princeton University Press, 1951 (1965 reprint). xiv, 249 pp.

PHILLIPS, Bernard S. 1966. *Social research: strategy and tactics.* New York: Macmillan; London: Collier-Macmillan, 1966. xii, 336 pp.

RICHARDSON, Stephen A., DOHRENWEND, Barbara Snell *and* KLEIN, David. 1965. *Interviewing: its forms and functions.* New York, London: Basic Books, 1965. viii, 380 pp.

ROBINSON, John P., RUSK, Jerrold G. *and* HEAD, Kendra B. 1968. *Measures of political attitudes.* Ann Arbor, Michigan: University of Michigan, Survey Research Center, 1968 (1969 reprint). viii, 702 pp.

ROBINSON, John P. *and* SHAVER, Phillip R. 1969. *Measures of social psychological attitudes.* Ann Arbor, Michigan: Univeristy of Michigan, Survey Research Center, 1969 (1970 reprint). v, 662 pp.

ROSENBERG, Morris. 1968. *The logic of survey analysis.* New York, London: Basic Books, 1968. xvi, 283 pp.

ROSENTHAL, Robert. 1966. *Experimenter effects in behavioural research.* New York: Appleton-Century-Crofts, 1966. xiii, 464 pp.

RUMMEL, J. Francis *and* BALLAINE, Wesley C. 1963. *Research methodology in business.* New York, London: Harper and Row, 1963. xvi, 359 pp.

SCHYBERGER, Bo W:son. 1965. *Methods of readership research.* Lund: University of Lund, Department of Business Administration, 1965, v, 266 pp.

SEIBERT, Joseph *and* WILLS, Gordon., *eds.* 1970. *Marketing research: selected readings.* Harmondsworth, Middlesex: Penguin Books, 1970. 392 pp.

SELLTIZ, Claire, *et al.* 1965. *Research methods in social relations.* London: Methuen, 1965 (1967 reprint). xvi, 622 pp.

SHAW, Marvin E. *and* WRIGHT, Jack M. 1967. *Scales for the measurement of attitudes.* New York, London: McGraw-Hill, 1967. xxii, 604 pp.

SIEGEL, Sidney. 1956. *Nonparametric statistics for the behavioral sciences.* New York, London: McGraw-Hill; Tokyo: Kogakusha Company, 1956. xvii, 312 pp.

SIMON, Julian L. 1969. *Basic research methods in social science: the art of empirical investigation.* New York: Random House, 1969. xiv, 525 pp.

SMITH, Joan Macfarlane. 1972. *Interviewing in market and social research.* London: Routledge and Kegan Paul, 1972. 184 pp.

SNIDER, James G. *and* OSGOOD, Charles E., *eds.* 1969. *Semantic differential technique: a sourcebook.* Chicago: Aldine, 1969. xiii, 681 pp.

SONQUIST, John A. 1970. *Multivariate model building: the validation of a search strategy.* Ann Arbor, Michigan: University of Michigan, Survey Research Center, 1970. xiii, 244 pp.

STACEY, Margaret. 1969. *Methods of social research.* London: Pergamon Press, 1969. x, 173 pp.

STACEY, Margaret, *ed.* 1969. *Comparability in social research.* London: Heinemann for the British Sociological Association and the SSRC, 1969. xvii, 134 pp.

STACEY, Nicholas A. H. *and* WILSON, Aubrey. 1963. *Industrial marketing research: management and technique.* London: Hutchison, 1963. 284 pp.

STEPHAN, Frederick F. *and* McCARTHY, Philip J. 1958. *Sampling opinions: an analysis of survey procedure.* New York: Wiley; London: Chapman and Hall, 1958. xxi, 451 pp.

STRAUS, Murray A. *and* NELSON, Joel I. 1968. *Sociological analysis: an empirical approach through replication.* New York, London: Harper and Row, 1968. ix, 355 pp.

STRAUS, Murray A. 1969. *Family measurement techniques: abstracts of published instruments 1935-1965.* Minneapolis, Minnesota: University of Minnesota, 1969. 316 pp.

SUDMAN, Seymour. 1967.   *Reducing the cost of surveys.* Chicago: Aldine, 1967. xv, 246 pp.

THURSTONE, L. L. 1959.   *The measurement of values.* Chicago: University of Chicago Press, 1959. viii, 322 pp.

TORGERSON, Warren S. 1958.   *Theory and methods of scaling.* New York, London: Wiley, 1958 (1967 reprint). xiii, 460 pp.

TRYON, Robert C. *and* BAILEY, Daniel E. 1970.   *Cluster analysis.* New York, London: McGraw-Hill, 1970. xiv, 347 pp.

UNITED NATIONS. Statistical Office. 1964.   *Handbook of household surveys: a practical guide for inquiries on levels of living.* New York: United Nations, 1964. iii, 172 pp. (Studies in methods, series F, no. 10).

VARMA, M. 1965.   *An introduction to educational and psychological research.* London: Asia Publishing House, 1965. xi, 208 pp.

WAKEFORD, John. 1968.   *The strategy of social inquiry....* London: Macmillan, 1968. 272 pp.

WEBB, Eugene J., *et al.* 1966.   *Unobtrusive measures: nonreactive research in the social sciences.* Chicago: Rand McNally, 1966. viii, 225 pp.

WELFORD, A. T., *et al.*, eds. 1962.   *Society: problems and methods of study.* London: Routledge and Kegan Paul, 1962. vi, 586 pp.

WITTS, L. J., ed. 1964.   *Medical surveys and clinical trials....* London: Oxford University Press, 1964. xi, 367 pp.

YATES, Frank. 1965.   *Sampling methods for censuses and surveys.* 3rd ed. London: Griffin, 1965. xvi, 440 pp.

YATES, Frank. 1970.   *Experimental design....* London: Griffin, 1970. xi, 296 pp.

YOUNG, Pauline V. 1966.   *Scientific social surveys and research....* Englewood Cliffs, New Jersey: Prentice-Hall, 1966. vii, 576 pp.

ZARKOVICH, S. S. 1965.   *Sampling methods and censuses.* Rome: FAO, 1965. 213 pp.

LIST OF PERIODICALS REFERRED TO IN THE BIBLIOGRAPHY

Readers requiring photocopies of articles from the periodicals listed below may obtain them through their local library. Many of these periodicals are also available on loan through the regional and national inter-library loan systems.

Admap.
Advancement of Science.
Agricultural Economics Research.
American Journal of Hygiene.
American Journal of Psychology.
American Journal of Sociology.
American Psychologist.
American Sociological Review.
American Statistical Association. *Proceedings of the Social Statistics Section.*
American Statistician. (Superseded American Statistical Association Bulletin).
Applied Anthropology. *See* Human Organization.
Applied Psychology Monographs. (Incorporated in Psychological Monographs).
Applied Statistics.
Archives of Psychology. (After 1945: incorporated in Psychological Monographs).
Behavioral Science.
Biometrics.
British Journal of Marketing. *See* European Journal of Marketing.
British Journal of Psychology.
British Journal of Social and Clinical Psychology.
Bulletin of the American Statistical Association. (Superseded by American Statistician).
Bulletin of the British Psychological Society.
Bulletin of the International Statistical Institute.

Business Horizons.
Business Review.
Commentary. *See* Journal of the Market Research Society.
Demography.
Dissertation Abstracts.
Educational and Psychological Measurement.
ESOMAR Journal.
European Journal of Marketing. Vols. 1-5, 1967-1971 as British Journal of Marketing.
European Marketing Research Review.
Human Factor. *See* Occupational Psychology.
Human Organization. Vols. 1-7, 1942-1948 as Applied Anthropology.
Human Relations.
IPA Forum.
Industrial Medicine and Surgery.
International Journal of Opinion and Attitude Research.
Journal for Social Research.
Journal of Abnormal and Social Psychology. *See* Journal of Abnormal Psychology.
Journal of Abnormal Psychology. Vols. 16-69, 1921-1964 as Journal of Abnormal and Social Psychology. *See also* Journal of Personality and Social Psychology.
Journal of Advertising Research.
Journal of Applied Psychology.
Journal of Applied Social Psychology.
Journal of Applied Sociology. *See* Sociology and Social Research.
Journal of Clinical Psychology.
Journal of Consulting Psychology. *See* Journal of Consulting and Clinical Psychology.
Journal of Consulting and Clinical Psychology. Vols. 1-37, 1937-1967 as Journal of Consulting Psychology.
Journal of Educational Psychology.
Journal of Educational Research.
Journal of Educational Sociology.
Journal of Experimental Psychology.
Journal of Experimental Social Psychology.
Journal of General Psychology.

Journal of Genetic Psychology. Vols. 1-31, 1891-1924 as Psychological Seminary; vols. 32-83, 1925-1953 as Pedagogical Seminary and Journal of Genetic Psychology.

Journal of Marketing.

Journal of Marketing Research.

Journal of Personality. Vols. 1-13, 1932-1945 as Character and Personality.

Journal of Personality and Social Psychology. (Supersedes in part Journal of Abnormal and Social Psychology).

Journal of Personnel Research.

Journal of Psychology.

Journal of Social Issues.

Journal of Social Psychology.

Journal of the American Statistical Association.

Journal of the Market Research Society. Vols. 1-9, 1959-1969 as Commentary.

Journal of the Royal Statistical Society.

Journalism Quarterly.

Marketing Communications. Vols. 1-294, 1888-1967 as Printer's Ink.

Metra.

Mind.

Multivariate Behavioural Research.

Nature.

Occupational Psychology. Vols. 1-5, 1922-1931 as National Institute of Industrial Psychology. *Journal*; vols. 6-11, 1932-1937 as Human Factor.

Pedagogical Seminary. *See* Journal of Genetic Psychology.

Polls.

Population Studies.

Printer's Ink. *See* Marketing Communications.

Proceedings of the American Philosophical Association.

Psychiatry.

Psychological Bulletin.

Psychological Monographs. Vols. 1-12, no. 51, 1896-1910 as Psychological Review. Monograph supplements.

Psychological Record.

Psychological Review.

Psychological Review. Monograph supplements. *See* Psychological Monographs.

Psychometrika.

Public Opinion Quarterly.

Quarterly Journal of Experimental Psychology.

Review of the International Statistical Institute.

Sankhya.

School and Society.

Scientific Business.

Social Forces.

Social Service. *See* Social Service Quarterly.

Social Service Quarterly. Vols. 21-28, 1947-1955 as Social Service; vols. 10-20, 1929-1939 as Social Service Review; vols. 1-9, 1920-1928 as Social Service Bulletin.

Sociological Review.

Sociology and Social Research. Vols. 1-5, 1916-1921 as Studies in Sociology; vols. 6-11, 1921-1927 as Journal of Applied Sociology.

Sociology of Education. Vols. 1-36, 1927-1962 as Journal of Educational Sociology.

Sociometry.

Southwestern Social Science Quarterly.

The Incorporated Statistician. *See* The Statistician.

The Statistician. Vols. 1-11, 1950-1961 as The Incorporated Statistician.

References have also been drawn from the following series:

Advertising Research Foundation Annual Conference. *Conference Papers.*

European Society for Opinion and Marketing Research. *Congress papers.*

Market Research Society Annual Conference. *Conference papers.*

National Center for Health Statistics. *Vital and Health Statistics.*

Office of Population Censuses and Surveys. Social Survey Division. *Methodological series.*

The Marcel Dassault Awards.

The Thomson Medals and Awards for Media Research.